The
Humiliation
of Sinners

The Humiliation of Sinners

Public Penance in
Thirteenth-Century France

Mary C. Mansfield

Cornell University Press

ITHACA AND LONDON

First published in 1995 by Cornell University Press
First printing, Cornell paperbacks, 2005

Library of Congress Cataloging-in-Publication Data

Mansfield, Mary C., 1960–1989.
   The humiliation of sinners : public penance in thirteenth-century
France / Mary C. Mansfield.
      p.   cm.
   Revision of the author's thesis (doctoral), University of
California, Berkeley, 1989, originally presented under the title:
The public humiliation of sinners.
   Includes bibliographical references and index.
   ISBN 0-8014-2939-0 (cloth: alk. paper)
   ISBN 0-8014-8994-6 (pbk.: alk. paper)

   1. Penance—History—France.   2. France—Church
history—987–1515.   3. Catholic Church—Discipline—History.
I. Title.
BX2263.F8M36   1994
265'.6'094409022—dc20   94-27815

Printed in the United States of America

Cornell University Press strives to use environmentally responsible suppliers
and materials to the fullest extent possible in the publishing of its books.
Such materials include vegetable-based, low-VOC inks and acid-free papers
that are recycled, totally chlorine-free, or partly composed of nonwood fibers.
For further information, visit our website at www.cornellpress.cornell.edu.

Cloth printing   10 9 8 7 6 5 4 3 2 1
Paperback printing   10 9 8 7 6 5 4 3 2 1

Contents

Foreword

The author of this book died in an automobile accident in France on August 31, 1989. She had completed her doctoral dissertation in medieval history at the University of California, Berkeley, the preceding April, and she had made some changes in Chapters 1, 2, and 3 during the summer of 1989. It is that revised work, reviewed by her advisers at Berkeley and lightly edited by her father, which is printed here under a new title.

"The humiliation of sinners" in public penance refers to the public aspect of what goes on in private. It calls into question any simple demarcation of public from private, of crime from sin, as well as the notion that public and private are necessarily in tension with each other. Mary Mansfield addresses these modern certitudes historically, attending to the debates of historians. Her work is the craft of a professional historian. But the main question, as she shows in the extent of her own discussions and observations, is as broad as any human question, reaching into philosophy, theology, sociology, anthropology, and political science.

The historical inquiry takes place against the background of the twelfth-century "penitential revolution" that came to a climax in the new requirement, imposed by the Fourth Lateran Council in 1215, and still in force today, that every Christian (*omnis utriusque*) confess once a year during Lent. The penitential revolution was a turn to protecting and nurturing the individual Christian soul's relationship with God, to the primacy of contrition in that soul over every relation with other human beings, to the creation of a new secret life of the soul, known only to God and confessor —altogether a new privacy. That revolution of "interiority" is often said, by medievalists, to have first set in motion a tendency toward the individualism characteristic of modern times, which is reflected in our vague but significant expression, "the private sphere." Some historians of the Renaissance, however, contesting the honor, and wishing to postpone the onset of modern individualism to their own period, have insisted on the communal quality of late medieval religion as opposed to Protestant piety or Renaissance self-aggrandizement.

Entering the debate, and distributing justice if not penance to all parties, Mary Mansfield has produced a work that focuses on a specific and workable question among unwieldy generalities. But this focus is designed to reveal the import of her book. Her technical accomplishment in historical research should not be allowed to obscure its ambition. Her work demonstrates the survival of public forms of penance despite the penitential revolution, and this in Northern France, the very center of the revolution.

The existence of public penance at this time may come as a surprise to many historians. The author proves its continuance with an exceedingly painstaking and wide-ranging survey of theological treatises, confessors' manuals, episcopal registers, provincial statutes, chronicles, city statutes, and of pontificals, ordinals, and other orders of liturgy almost entirely in manuscript form. Not content with the distinctions of the Paris theologians announcing the new priority of individual contrition in private, she turns to the practices of the church in all their variety which were to apply those distinctions; and she finds the results of the revolution to be in great part unintended. In application, the theology did not produce genuine interior piety, to say nothing of modern individualism (neither of which is easy to define), so much as a routinized, legalized confession based on the two courts (*fora*): the confessional court of the conscience, technically interior but nonetheless legal in practice, and the external, public courts of the church.

That Scholastic distinction, in a sense forced upon theologians and canonists alike, failed to take adequate account of the phenomenon of shame that makes every distinction between public and private difficult and tenuous. Public penance survived by finding its place in neither of the two courts but in a convenient no-man's-land between external excommunication and interior contrition. That region is also an inconvenient middle for the two parties of historians, neither "interior" as the medievalists have maintained nor "communal" as the Renaissance historians have said. As against the former, private confession, which was done until the sixteenth century without benefit of confessional, was far less interior in actual practice than the twelfth-century theologians would have liked (see Chapters 2 and 3). Though confession was now individual and auricular, no longer out loud nor done through heads of households acting as representatives, it still required submission, reconciliation, restitution, and reparation, and thus emphasized sins against neighbors that might endanger the peace of a city or parish.

As against the arguments of the Renaissance historians, the author gives reason for doubting that the politics of public penance was genuinely communal. Although penitential processions and other collective penances attempted to create the impression of a Christian city united through alternation of rejoicing and expiation, the rites of penance, when examined for political import, reveal that such shows of unity were usually efforts both to mask rivalry and to express triumph over a rival (see Chapters 5, 8, and 9). Nor would one wish to deny the reality of the penitential revolution as a consequence of describing it more precisely and more fully, and with attention to the counterpoint of public penance. After that revolution, the Christian community, if it can be spoken of as one, became a new community, with a different communal character not captured by the abstraction "communalism."

Chapters 6 and 7 on liturgy, based on Mary Mansfield's analysis of more than seventy-five manuscripts, constitute the centerpiece of her research, in which she is able to convey a wonderful and an almost palpable sense of the materials. She shows that the Northern French liturgists, despite their notorious antiquarianism, experimented wide-ly in an attempt to give new meaning through small changes in an-cient rites. Yet, although the liturgists tried many variants of peniten-tial rites, some very specific and interesting trends emerge. In the course of the thirteenth century, the practice slowly spread of giving ashes not only to penitents but to everyone on Ash Wednesday. One incidental result was the development of Mardi Gras (see Chapter 5), but another, more important consequence was the transformation of public penance. Before 1150, it had been a communal rite teaching a lesson to all that the individual's salvation depended on the commu-nity and the community's sanctity, on the expiation of a few. After that time, public penance became an exemplary show of less seriousness, or a collective absolution in the Lenten rites, both of which effected a certain separation of political from divine justice. That such separa-tion was not fully possible, or fully desired, is revealed by the use of public penance by bishops, and even secular powers (see Chapter 8), to intervene in tricky cases fit neither for public justice nor private confession. The problem remained: Christian penance cannot be per-fectly private, because of the need to see sinners humiliated; yet it cannot be merely communal, because of the individual's private relationship with God.

This book is published as the author left it, but not, of course, as she would have published it. Its merits do not need our praise. We cannot say what improvements would have occurred to her in reflecting on it. We do know that she had wished to rewrite Chapters 6 and 7 so as to make them less technical in appearance. In addition, just before her death she had returned to the French manuscript collections to see whether the genealogy established in Chapter 7 for rites of public penance in north-central French pontificals could be extended to the pontificals themselves as a documentary class. She certainly would have brought the bibliography and footnotes up to date. We have not checked her manuscript transcriptions.

The acknowledgments are the author's. We would like to add the names of Bruce Venarde for help in translation and Sharon R. Krause for preparation of the manuscript.

Mary C. Mansfield was born in Cambridge, Massachusetts, on January 2, 1960. She grew up in Lexington, Massachusetts, graduating from Lexington High School in 1977. She then attended Cornell University, where she was a member of Telluride House, receiving a B.A. *summa cum laude* in history in 1981. Next, she went on a Marshall scholarship to St. John's College, Oxford, and took an M. Phil. degree in 1983 with a thesis titled "Concepts of Sin and Purity in Alan of Lille's Polemical and Pastoral Works." She received a Ph.D. in history in May 1989 at the University of California, Berkeley.

In the same disastrous crash died Mary's mother, Margaret B. Mansfield, and her husband, Eric Wefald, to whom she would have dedicated this book. She would also have wanted to salute her surviving brothers, Edward and William. Her teachers knew her as a brilliant student and a young friend of extraordinary promise. To her father, she was, and is, his pride and joy.

GERARD E. CASPARY
HARVEY C. MANSFIELD

Acknowledgments

I thank the Marshall Aid Commemoration Commission, the Regents of the University of California, and the Charlotte W. Newcombe Foundation for the financial support that sustained, respectively, my first work on penance, the manuscript research, and the writing of my dissertation. The research would not have been possible without the very generous help of librarians at the Bibliothèque Nationale, the British Library, and numerous municipal libraries in France. Most important was the assistance of the Institut de Recherche et d'Histoire des Textes, where I consulted numerous microfilms of liturgical manuscripts in French provincial libraries. I am especially grateful to Guy Lanoe of the Institut for directing me to a microfiche copy of an otherwise unavailable manuscript in a private collection. Finally, my work has gained much from the encouragement and suggestions of teachers at Oxford and Berkeley, including Karl Leyser, Alison Peden, Thomas N. Bisson, Gene Brucker, and Danuta Shanzer. I am above all indebted to my dissertation supervisor, Gerard E. Caspary, whose extremely careful reading and constant advice improved the final result immeasurably.

M. C. M.

Abbreviations

HF: *Recueil des historiens des Gaules et de la France*. Paris, 1738–1905.

Mansi: J. D. Mansi. *Sacrorum conciliorum noua et amplissima collectio*. Venice, 1759–1798, repr. Paris, 1903–1927. Cited by volume and column.

PGD: *Le pontifical de Guillaume Durand*. Ed. Michel Andrieu. *Le pontifical romain au Moyen-Age*, 3. Studi e Testi, 88. Vatican City, 1940.

PL: J. P. Migne, ed., *Patrologiae cursus completus: Series latina*. Paris, 1844–1902. Cited by volume and column.

Pontal I: Odette Pontal, ed. *Les statuts synodaux français du XIIIe siècle*, 1. Collection des documents inédits sur l'histoire de France, 9. Paris, 1971.

Pontal II: Odette Pontal, ed. *Les statuts synodaux français du XIIIe siècle*, 2. Collection des documents inédits sur l'histoire de France, 9, Paris, 1983.

Powicke and Cheney: F. M. Powicke and C. R. Cheney, eds. *Councils and Synods with Other Documents Relating to the English Church*, 2 (A.D. 1205–1313). Oxford, 1964.

PRC: *Le pontifical de la curie romaine au XIIIe siècle*. Ed. Michel Andrieu. *Le pontifical romain au Moyen-Age*, 2. Studi e Testi, 87. Vatican City, 1939.

PRG: Cyrille Vogel, with Reinhard Elze, eds. *Le pontifical romano-germanique du dixieme siècle*, Studi e Testi, 226, 227, 269. Vatican City, 1963–1972.

PRS: *Le pontifical romain du XIIe siècle*. Ed. Michel Andrieu. *Le pontifical romain au Moyen-Age*, 1. Studi e Testi, 86. Vatican City, 1938.

Varin: Pierre Varin, ed. *Archives administratives de la ville de Reims*. Collection de documents inédits sur l'histoire de France. Paris, 1839. Cited by volume and page.

The
Humiliation
of Sinners

CHAPTER ONE

Penance and Privacy

In 1184, the bishop of Auxerre placed the town under an interdict because of a dispute with Count Pierre de Courtenay of Nevers. The interdict was a lengthy one, and some years into it, a distraught mother of Auxerre brought her dead child to the count and insisted on a Christian burial, trying to shame him with her predicament. The count shamed the bishop instead. He had his men force a burial inside the bishop's very bedchamber. When the bishop and count made peace in 1204 and the interdict was lifted, the count had to undergo an extraordinary penance. On Palm Sunday, 1204, he appeared in sackcloth and ashes before a great crowd of nobles, prelates, and people; entered the bishop's bedchamber; dug up the now decayed body with his own hands; and carried it to the cemetery for reburial.[1] The bishop repaid humiliation with humiliation.

This was a particularly memorable spectacle, but public penances of all sorts continued to be a familiar sight in thirteenth-century France. Such public humiliations were not inflicted on great men only. Imposed by bishops and priests, on great nobles and poor peasants, for shocking crimes and for minor brawls, these public processions and pilgrimages survived the reforms of the Fourth Lateran Council in 1215. Indeed, long after the thirteenth century, public humiliation remained a favorite punishment for both secular and religious of-

---

1. Robert d'Auxerre, *Chronologia*, HF 18:269. Cf. the similar penance imposed by the bishop of Chartres in the early thirteenth century on certain noblemen who hanged a cleric, and even a like "penance" set by Philip Augustus for a knight who hanged a *conversus*: Ralph of Coggeshall, *Chronicon Anglicanum*, ed. J. Stevenson, Rolls Series (London, 1875), pp. 199–201. For the imposition of penances by secular authorities, see Chapter 8. And after the servants of the earl of Leicester lured a thief out of his sanctuary, Bishop Hugh of Lincoln made them dig up the thief's body and carry it around all the neighboring churches; then they were flogged by the canons of Lincoln cathedral; cited by James B. Given, *Society and Homicide in Thirteenth-Century England* (Stanford, Calif., 1977), pp. 197–198.

fenses, and the expression *faire amende honorable*, once reserved for the performance of just such spectacles, has become a general term for suffering humiliation, "eating crow." Historians have often neglected these public penances in their accounts of the evolution of penance or of punishment in general in the thirteenth century. My book examines a phenomenon sometimes supposed not to exist.

The reason for the neglect is that historians have long distinguished between early and later medieval forms of penance. In their view, the early medieval rite took two main forms, the dramatic public humiliation of the sinner, and the "tariffed" private penances of the local penitentials, which assigned heavy penalties of fasting, alms, or money redemptions for each crime according to fixed tables: the "tariffs." That second, private form of penance then began to evolve, and it supposedly came to replace the public rite. The twelfth century saw the arrival of a new emphasis by academic theologians on private confession and the necessity of contrition. Those early Scholastic theologians did not invent private confession, and the Fourth Lateran in 1215 was not the first council to demand at least annual confession; but by the end of the twelfth century, the theory had changed enough that the old tariff books seemed irrelevant, and a new genre, the *summa confessorum*, was born. The new genre sought to advise the confessor how to elicit the penitent's secret sins and heartfelt tears. As for the first type of penance, the ancient public humiliation of sinners, the penance once forced on Theodosius and Henry II of England (in 1172, for the murder of Thomas Becket), many historians have assumed that it just withered away.[2]

The history of public penance is critical to a familiar but still significant debate about the timing and causes of the rise of ethical and religious individualism in the West, a privatization of religious conduct that seems virtually unparalleled in history. Many medievalists have seen a growing emphasis on the emotional state of the individual penitent as one manifestation of an increasing awareness of the individual in twelfth-century thought. Whether they describe the phenomenon as "the discovery of the individual" or the "renewed commitment to the examination of the inner life" or "the responsibility of the individual" in politics, some have asserted that the twelfth and perhaps the thirteenth centuries were the stage for that profound shift in Western culture once loosely attributed to the Renaissance or

---

2. See, for example, Bernhard Poschmann, *Penance and the Anointing of the Sick*, trans. F. Courtney (London, 1964), pp. 131–138, 149–164; and Cyrille Vogel, *Le pécheur et la pénitence au Moyen Age* (Paris, 1969), pp. 27–36. For further details, see the review of the literature below.

the Reformation.[3] They have focused on evidence drawn from the intellectual elite, and they have tried to identify a mental transformation in twelfth-century sources such as letter collections, autobiographies, and confessors' manuals—altogether a "twelfth-century renaissance" to challenge the Italian quattrocento.[4] Other medievalists have reached deeper into sources such as liturgy, hagiography, literature, and necrologies, and they have in the meantime shifted the focus from the twelfth century exclusively. Several scholars have argued for the pre-Renaissance beginnings of individualist attitudes to death, for example, whether expressed in private masses or in endowed chantries or in beliefs about the next world.[5] Their timetables vary, but like the partisans of the twelfth-century Renaissance, these medievalists have argued that the birth of modern individualism belongs in some way to the medieval period. And while they have ranged beyond intellectual history in the narrow sense, very few have attempted integrated analyses of changes in both religious practice and intellectual life; and fewer still have directly challenged the community studies of the early modern social historians.

Most historians of early modern society and religion have denied the periodization of the medievalists. John Bossy, for instance, has commented that one medievalist's description of the shift to individual penance might more aptly be applied to the sixteenth century than

3. For the first phrase, see Colin Morris, *The Discovery of the Individual, 1050–1200* (New York, 1972), esp. pp. 3–10, 140–160. For the second, see John Benton, "Consciousness of Self and Perceptions of Individuality," in *Renaissance and Renewal in the Twelfth Century*, ed. R. L. Benson and G. Constable (Cambridge, Mass., 1977), pp. 263–295. Benton, p. 264, explicitly rejects Morris's formulation but agrees that the twelfth century does witness an increased emphasis on intention and the individual soul. See also Benton's "Individualism and Conformity in Medieval Western Europe," in *Individualism and Conformity in Classical Islam*, ed. Amin Banani and Speros Vryonis, Jr. (Wiesbaden, 1977), pp. 145–158. For the third, see Walter Ullmann, *The Individual and Society in the Middle Ages* (Baltimore, Md., 1966), esp. p. 65 and pp. 110–123, who argues that feudal practice and humanistic thought came to reverse the submersion of the individual in medieval political theology; he dates the most important shift fifty to one hundred years later than Benton and Morris. Two other medievalists have argued that while the twelfth century saw a new stress on the interior life, it was balanced by a renewed interest in forms of community: Brian Tierney, review of Morris's *Discovery of the Individual, Journal of Ecclesiastical History* 24 (1980): 295–296; and Caroline Walker Bynum, "Did the Twelfth Century Discover the Individual?" in *Jesus as Mother: Studies in the Spirituality of the High Middle Ages* (Berkeley, Calif., 1982), pp. 85–109.

4. Charles Homer Haskins's *The Renaissance of the Twelfth Century* (Cambridge, Mass., 1927) is the seminal book. A fiftieth-anniversary conference of medievalists offered refinements but did not fundamentally challenge the concept: Benson and Constable, eds., *Renaissance and Renewal in the Twelfth Century*.

5. Cyrille Vogel, "Une mutation cultuelle inexpliquée: Le passage de l'eucharistie communautaire à la messe privée," *Revue des sciences religieuses* 54 (1980): 231–250; Joel T. Rosenthal, *The Purchase of Paradise: Gift Giving and the Aristocracy, 1307–1485* (London, 1972), p. 17; A. J. Gurevic, "Au Moyen Age: Conscience individuelle et image de l'au-delà," *Annales: Economies, sociétés, civilisations* 37 (1982): 255–275, a critique of Philippe Ariès, *The Hour of Our Death*, trans. H. Weaver (New York, 1981; first published 1977).

to the twelfth.[6] Other writers have described large kin-groups in the sixteenth and seventeenth centuries as quasicommunities and have argued that affective individualism makes an appearance only after the decline of such families.[7] In general, early modernists have considered the rumors of a medieval death for communalism exaggerated. Even before Burckhardt's day they dated the origins of modern individualism to the Renaissance or later, and all the contemporary activity in the field has simply confirmed this fundamental judgment. Ironically, the shift in emphasis in early modern studies from political institutions and intellectual achievements to popular culture and local groups has sharpened the conviction that individualism arrived late, indeed much later than the Italian Renaissance. We return to the early modernists in the concluding chapter, which discusses the implications of the transformation of public penance for the debate about religion in the early modern period.

The long-standing controversy over the rise of individualism has not lost relevance today even as many Westerners assume that religious beliefs are inevitably a matter of the secret conscience. Modern Western Christianity itself still bears the mark of its conception in a time and place in which religion was an affair of state and the safety and the salvation of whole communities was believed to depend on the preservation of the right relation with the divine. Indeed, without abandoning the modern principle of the freedom of religion, some Christians have recently voiced an increasing disquiet over the individualism—or even pietism—of much contemporary religion. "Community" is in fashion again. It is worth asking now whether our longing for community in religion and secular life represents something substantial in human life or is nothing more than foolish nostalgia.[8] We may begin by reconsidering the roots of the great shift away from community and in particular the relationship between the loss of community in religion and the incipient institutions of modernity in the later Middle Ages, such as urbanism and the centralized state, from which no amount of nostalgia for community can free us.

6. John Bossy, "The Social History of Confession in the Age of the Reformation," *Transactions of the Royal Historical Society*, 5th ser., 25 (1975): 22.

7. See Edward Shorter, *The Making of the Modern Family* (New York, 1975), esp. pp. 3, 55; and Lawrence Stone, *The Family, Sex, and Marriage in England, 1500–1800*, abridged ed. (New York, 1979), pp. 69–89. For critiques of the thesis about individualism and the family, see Barbara Hanawalt, *The Ties That Bound: Peasant Families in Medieval England* (Oxford, 1986), pp. 9, 257–266; and more radically, Alan Macfarlane, *The Origins of English Individualism: The Family, Property, and Social Transition* (Oxford, 1978).

8. Instructive here is Alan Macfarlane's comment that the "belief in such 'communities' is one of the most powerful myths in industrial society," in his "History, Anthropology, and the Study of Communities," *Social History*, no. 5 (May, 1977): 632.

By looking at the survivals of the old public penances after the advent of Scholasticism, I hope to contribute to the debate from a new point of view. Public penance is both a neglected aspect of thirteenth-century religious life and a crucial one. For religious individualism privacy of the conscience is perhaps the most critical test, where deliberate, public humiliation of sinners is perhaps the most powerful means of instilling conformity in a community. Public penances simultaneously promised salvation in the next world and public order in this. Indeed, as we shall see, public humiliations included not only strictly religious penances but also sanctions invoked by both secular and ecclesiastical authorities to suppress crime. So the evolution of penance is a fitting place to start an investigation of the origins of religious individualism. And finally, through public penance we can learn something of assumptions about privacy and public life among the laity, not just about the theories of the theologians, who dominate most discussions of twelfth-century individualism. In short, here is a new window on an old unsolved problem.

The Historiography of Penance

A necessary first step for such a study of thirteenth-century public penance, however, is the reconsideration of how the historiographical tradition has come to neglect it as moribund. In the sixteenth century, Protestants and Roman Catholics alike claimed the moral high ground of unimpeachable antiquity for their views of penance, but neither side actually investigated the evidence for penance in the Middle Ages. For Protestant sects, it was enough to observe that Roman Catholic penance was not biblical; for Catholics, the admission of an evolution rather than an unbroken tradition was an awkward one. The historical study of the sacrament of penance began appropriately in the seventeenth century with the monumental effort of a Huguenot turned Oratorian, Jean Morin (1591–1659). As with John Henry Newman in the nineteenth century, it was precisely the convert to the Roman church who initiated frank historical investigation in a reaction against sheer biblicism. After a Calvinist education at La Rochelle and Leiden, Morin converted to Roman Catholicism and joined the Congregation of the Oratory in 1618. He dedicated his life to biblical criticism and historical scholarship with the aim of converting other Protestants and Jews. An independent spirit in an age of time-servers, Morin sidestepped Richelieu's efforts to enlist him as a propagandist, and found time instead to complete a massive history of penance from the beginning of the church to around 1300, relying heavily on the liturgical manuscripts of the royal library.[9] The unfortunate lack of a systematic identification of his sources comparable to Aimé-Georges Martimort's updating of Edmond Martène's *De antiquis ecclesiae ritibus libri*[10] makes Morin's work difficult to use today, and many sources now available were closed to Morin; yet his insights remain striking. Morin was deeply sympathetic to the ancient public penances, which he recognized, from his study of the liturgy, survived well beyond 1215. His lukewarm attitude to auricular confession and his suspicion of Port Royal's rigorism led to controversy and the neglect of his work until after his death.[11] Yet the *Commentarius historicus* remained for centuries the most fair-minded and the most scholarly treatment of penance.[12]

Unfortunately, Henry Charles Lea's thorough and thoroughly tendentious *History of Auricular Confession* has been more influential on the direction of modern scholarship.[13] Lea's book both polarized subsequent debate and focused attention on private penance to the neglect of other issues. Lea presented auricular confession as a novelty foisted on the church by Innocent III and fellow theologians and canonists, who were intent on using it to control the laity. The most important Roman Catholic historian of penance in the first half of the twentieth century, Bernhard Poschmann, took up Lea's challenge, arguing that the modern system of private penance was essentially in place by the late eleventh century, even if theological thinking lagged behind. Poschmann's considerable scholarship concentrated on the ancient and early medieval period, for he was confident that the evo-

9. Jean Morin, *Commentarius historicus de disciplina in administratione sacramenti poenitentiae tredecim primis seculis in ecclesia occidentali, et hucusque in orientali observata, in decem libros distinctus* (Paris, 1651). For Morin's life, see Michaud, *Biographie universelle* (Paris, 1854–), 29: 327–329.

10. Aimé-Georges Martimort, *La documentation liturgique de Dom Edmond Martène*, Studi e Testi, 279 (Vatican City, 1978), catalogs the manuscripts edited in Edmond Martène, *De antiquis ecclesiae ritibus libri* (Antwerp, 1736–1738, repr. Hildesheim, 1967).

11. Morin's chief opponent on penance during his lifetime was the Jesuit Jacques Sirmond (1559–1651), who published a pamphlet in response to Morin, *Historia poenitentiae publicae* (Paris, 1651) at the age of 92. This work dealt only with the early Middle Ages. In the tradition of Roman Catholic polemics, Sirmond minimized the importance of public penance and claimed that early medieval absolutions were not simply declaratory. For Sirmond's life, see Michaud, *Biographie universelle*, 39:415–416.

12. Martène's *De antiquis ecclesiae ritibus libri* printed a great number of important liturgical sources on penance, and in his commentary, he noted that public penance survived longer in certain French towns than at Rome (IV. xvii, vol. III, col. 161); but his work was not intended to be a history of penance as such.

13. Henry Charles Lea, *A History of Auricular Confession and Indulgences in the Latin Church* (Philadelphia, 1896, repr. New York, 1968).

lution of penance was essentially complete by 1100.[14] He had little to say about the supposedly anomalous and obsolete public penance.

While traces of this confessional debate survive, more recently a balance has been struck on the issue.[15] Cyrille Vogel and other Catholic historians have largely accepted that private sacramental confession, while not a radical innovation sprung by the ecclesiastical hierarchy on an unwitting laity, did take new life from the twelfth-century theology of personal intention.[16] Vogel's work has set off extensive investigations into the "contritionism" of late-twelfth-century thought on the eve of the Fourth Lateran Council. But a subtler appreciation of early Scholastic theology and of the origins of private penance has not advanced our knowledge of how penance in all its varieties actually worked in practice before and after 1215. The Fourth Lateran's requirement of annual private penance, moreover, is still seen as the end of the road, rather than one stage in a complex evolution. To that extent, Lea's agenda remains influential.

Vogel's effort to outline the ancestry of the forms of penance belongs to this tradition, and it has gone unchallenged in recent historiography. In a chart summarizing his conclusions, Vogel suggests that from the Carolingian period to the twelfth century there were two types of penance ("bipartite penance"): a public ritual for serious public sins and tariffed penances for serious secret sins. Tariffed penances were listed in the penitential books, often along with money redemptions for each level of fasting; Vogel takes them to be essentially private. But from the thirteenth century on, penance became "tripartite." Scholastic theologians after 1200, he notes, usually enu-

14. Poschmann, *Penance and the Anointing of the Sick*, p. 156; his more detailed efforts focused on the pre-Carolingian period: *Paenitentia secunda: Die kirchliche Busse im ältesten Christentum bis Cyprian und Origenes*, Theophaneia, 1 (Bonn, 1940), and *Die abendländische Kirchenbusse im Ausgang des christlichen Altertums*, Münchener Studien zur historischen Theologie, 7 (Munich, 1928). Cf. the similar views of E. Amann, "Pénitence–sacrement, I–II," in *Dictionnaire de théologie catholique* (Paris, 1933), 12a, cols. 904–906; and even recently, Pierre Adnès, "Pénitence," in *Dictionnaire de spiritualité* (Paris, 1984), 12:1, col. 970.

15. According to Alexander Murray, "Confession as a Historical Source in the Thirteenth Century," in *The Writing of History in the Middle Ages: Essays Presented to Richard William Southern*, ed. R. H. C. Davis and J. M. Wallace-Hadrill (Oxford, 1981), p. 279, this is still the central debate about penance. I believe he exaggerates; few historians would now agree with Poschmann and Oscar D. Watkins, *A History of Penance* (London, 1920), whom Murray cites, that lay private sacramental penance was very common at least two hundred years before the Fourth Lateran. To that extent, Lea and the Protestant theologians have won. But really the debate has shifted to an investigation of the twelfth-century developments.

16. Cf. Vogel, *Le pécheur et la pénitence*, p. 31; Jean-Charles Payen, "La pénitence dans le contexte culturel des XIIe et XIIIe siècles: Des doctrines contritionnistes aux pénitentiels vernaculaires," *Revue des sciences philosophiques et théologiques* 61 (1977): 399–428; and Pierre-Marie Gy, "Les bases de la pénitence moderne," *La Maison-Dieu* 117 (1974): 63–85.

merated three types of penance. In Vogel's interpretation, the theologians' "public solemn penance" was the heir of public penance; private sacramental penance was the heir of the tariffs; and alongside these two, a new form arrived, nonsolemn public penance, which he identifies with involuntary penitential pilgrimage.[17] Vogel recognizes that such penitential pilgrimages were not in fact an invention of the thirteenth century, but he nonetheless treats "tripartite penance" as the outcome of the Fourth Lateran Council.[18] Yet according to Vogel, both solemn and nonsolemn public penances atrophy after 1200. Taking flight at dusk like the owl of Minerva, the theologians develop a description of three types of penance just as two of those types disappear forever. Their "tripartite penance" is really the modern system of private sacramental confession, since the first two elements soon became insignificant. Once again, we have reached the end of the road by 1215. Lea, Poschmann, and Vogel could agree on one thing: private sacramental penance was the wave of the future, and public penance was doomed to become the mere shell of ancient penance.[19] Morin's suggestions about the liturgy were forgotten.

A consensus on definitions and sources inspires the conclusion on which historians of medieval penance from Lea to Vogel agree. They share both a reliance on mostly theological evidence and an acceptance of the Scholastic definition of penance as their model. While such fidelity to medieval concepts promises a certain authenticity, it carries a danger, too: The historians of medieval theology end up reading pre-Scholastic penance through Scholastic categories. Since the medieval categories were themselves by no means stable, the historian who uses them risks making an unconscious choice to favor one period's view over another's, and worse, to impose that model on the evidence of an earlier age. Much discussion of the history of moral and sacramental theology has been unconsciously teleological, resulting in a search for ancestors of modern species and the neglect of

17. Vogel, *Le pécheur et la pénitence*, p. 35.

18. Elsewhere, Vogel acknowledges that penitential pilgrimages and more private satisfactions were imposed in tariffed penance long before the thirteenth century: Vogel, "Le pèlerinage pénitentiel," in *Pellegrinaggi e culto dei santi in Europa fino alla crociata*, Convegni del Centro di studi sulla spiritualità medievale, 4 (Todi, 1963), p. 43.

19. Lea, *A History of Auricular Confession*, 1:48–49; Poschmann, *Penance and the Anointing of the Sick*, p. 154; Vogel, *Le pécheur et la pénitence*, pp. 27–36. Cf. Gustav Adolf Benrath, "Busse V," in *Theologische Realenzyklopädie* (Berlin, 1981), 7:452–473; and Josef Andreas Jungmann, "Bussriten," and Karl Rahner, "Buss-sakrament," in *Lexikon für Theologie und Kirche* (Freiburg, 1958), 2:823–826 and 826–838, who note respectively the independence of the Gallican liturgy and the continued emphasis on solemn penance in canon law to 1200 at least, but who offer no view on the survival of the solemn rite.

medieval species that seem to have had no progeny. The Scholastic model of penance, moreover, often assumes like the Scholastic theologians themselves that clerical culture influenced the laity but never the reverse. So, solemn penance after 1200 or collective penances like Rogation procession in any period are ignored or treated as folkloric curiosities, irrelevant to the main evolutionary line visible in the theology. The preoccupation of medievalists with the theology of penance has led to the surprising neglect of ecclesiastical sources other than theology, such as the liturgy, local synodal statutes, and episcopal registers.

By contrast, many recent historians of early modern religion have refused to endorse the definitions of the Scholastic theologians and have studied penance not as an isolated sacrament but as part of a system. From the perspective of the Protestant Reformation, sacramental confession, indulgences, relics, pilgrimages, and private masses all appear as different manifestations of the same late medieval religious fever, and the reformers viewed them all with similar suspicion. Historians of the sixteenth century, like many of the reformers they study, have preferred to treat the various rituals of medieval religion as different aspects of a single impulse.[20] As a result, late medieval Christianity becomes a backdrop for the dramatic changes of the Protestant and Catholic Reformations. Several French works concerned with the origins of "de-Christianization" and secularization have treated medieval Christianity from the longest of perspectives as a more than thousand-year phase in European history that decisively ended between 1600 and 1800.[21] To be sure, not all early modernists have adopted a foreshortened view of medieval religious history or have regarded late medieval religion as unambiguously communal; for example, Thomas Tentler has argued that private

20. Two of the best of such discussions are those of A. N. Galpern, *The Religions of the People in Sixteenth-Century Champagne* (Cambridge, Mass., 1976); and John Bossy, *Christianity in the West, 1400–1700* (Oxford, 1985).

21. See especially Jean Delumeau, *Le catholicisme entre Luther et Voltaire* (Paris, 1971); and Michel Vovelle, *Piété baroque et déchristianisation en Provence au XVIIIe siècle* (Paris, 1973). Similar in this respect is Michel Foucault's *Discipline and Punish: The Birth of the Prison*, trans. A. Sheridan (New York, 1977). His description of the new disciplinary punishment in the eighteenth century sounds very like medievalists' account of late-twelfth-century confession or early modernists' treatment of post-Reformation penance. "Now quite a different question of truth is inscribed in the course of the penal judgement. . . . It is no longer simply: 'What law punishes this offense?' But: 'What would be the most appropriate measures to take? How do we see the future development of the offender? . . .' A whole order of assessing, diagnostic, prognostic, normative judgements concerning the criminal have become lodged in the framework of penal judgement" (p. 19). Later (pp. 226–227), Foucault recognizes the problem but insists that the shift he has outlined is more significant than earlier ones.

confession before Luther was indeed designed to teach penitents to feel individual guilt.[22] In general, however, the early modernists' interest in disparate phenomena and long-term changes helps correct the medievalists' overemphasis on Scholastic theology, even though it sometimes obscures changes within the medieval period, changes not as sudden and dramatic in their consequences as those of the Reformation, but perhaps just as significant. As we shall find, what looks like communal religion on the eve of the Reformation is different from the communal religion of northern France on the eve of the Fourth Lateran Council.

These early modernists' occasional use of recent sociology and anthropology has sometimes confirmed their tendency to see disparate religious phenomena as part of a unified and even relatively stable system. Sociologists since Ferdinand Tönnies have used the concept of community, *Gemeinschaft*, as both tool of analysis and unit of investigation in the "community studies" that form the staple of empirical scholarship in the field.[23] And much social anthropology influential in recent historiography has emphasized the coordinated functioning of seemingly incongruous rites and beliefs in a given society. The view has been ingrained since Emile Durkheim, who expressed it most explicitly.[24] Many of those who have disowned his search for the primitive essence of religion have remained influenced by his teaching that disparate religious rites do not function independently but rather combine to promote social unity. Victor Turner, for example, has chosen the term *communitas* to describe the experience of pilgrims and other participants in sacred rites.[25] In a different direction, René Girard has argued that "if religious man worships violence it is only insofar as the worship of violence is supposed to bring peace."[26] One

22. Thomas N. Tentler, *Sin and Confession on the Eve of the Reformation* (Princeton, N.J., 1977), pp. 161–162, criticizes Bossy directly. Some historians of late medieval religion have dated the most important shift to individualism to the period following the Black Death. See, especially, Jacques Chiffoleau, *La comptabilité de l'au-delà: Les hommes, la mort, et la religion dans la région d'Avignon à la fin du Moyen Age (vers 1320–vers 1480)*, Collection de l'Ecole française de Rome, 47 (Rome, 1980).

23. Ferdinand Tönnies, *Community and Society (Gemeinschaft und Gesellschaft)*, trans. Charles P. Loomis (East Lansing, Mich., 1957; first published 1887); see also Alan Macfarlane, "History, Anthropology, and the Study of Communities," pp. 631–652.

24. Emile Durkheim, *The Elementary Forms of the Religious Life*, trans. J. W. Swain (New York, 1915).

25. Victor W. Turner, *The Ritual Process* (Chicago, 1969), pp. 128–129, 154; Victor W. Turner and Edith Turner, *Image and Pilgrimage in Christian Culture* (New York, 1978), p. 32.

26. René Girard with J.-M. Oughourlian and G. Lefort, *Things Hidden since the Foundation of the World*, trans. S. Bann and M. Metteer (Stanford, Calif., 1987), p. 32; cf. Girard, *La violence et le sacré* (Paris, 1972).

need not endorse a naive functionalism to believe that social peace is a dream, perhaps the perennial dream, expressed in religious ritual.

Applied to medieval penitential rites, the anthropological perspective implies that the purpose of the Rogation procession is not essentially the protection of the crops, nor the purpose of solemn penance essentially the disciplining of misbehaving individuals or even the assurance of an individual's eternal salvation. There may be many idols for social anthropology, but there is only one God: society. The belief that religious ritual is fundamentally about the resolution of social conflict has shaped many historians' use of that discipline. It is easy to see the appeal of this model in comparison with the attempts of some early anthropologists to reduce religious ritual to magic, that is, to the material benefits the participants sought or were assumed to seek. As a result, however, the focus of many anthropologists and subsequently many historians has been, if not precisely Durkheim's search for origins, at least the search for the supposedly primitive, the folkloric rather than the refined. The highest level of generalization is presumed to represent the most fundamental and so also the oldest stratum of religion. As we have seen, some historians of medieval penance have emphasized theological change to the exclusion of actual practice. Historians influenced by anthropology have sometimes erred in the other direction by seeking a layer of unspoiled folkloric religion and neglecting other evidence.

The danger in the social interpretation of religious ritual lies in its potential to obscure variety and change. If every ritual really teaches social cohesion and the supremacy of the community, it is hard to explain why rituals change so dramatically, except when the community disintegrates for unrelated, exogenous reasons. "Community" is itself a term applied perhaps too loosely, without sufficient attention to problems of definition. Similarly abused in modern histories are "private" and "public," not least because medieval writers themselves applied the terms without defining them. In a stimulating approach to the problem, Georges Duby has begun to sketch the history of these words in the introduction to an anthropologically informed treatment of private life in the Middle Ages. Many medieval writers applied the term *publicus* to sovereign or regalian power, and *privatus* to the household, the *familia*.[27] The *familia* should not conjure up images of cozy domesticity; this is the household of servants and armed retainers,

27. Georges Duby, "Ouverture: Pouvoir privé, pouvoir public," in *Histoire de la vie privée*, ed. P. Ariès and G. Duby, vol. 2, *De l'Europe féodale à la Renaissance* (Paris, 1985), pp. 19–23.

long immune from royal interference. We shall find, however, that this politico-legal definition was not the only definition of privacy current at our starting point in 1200, and its future would be limited by increasing royal power. Even on the political level, this definition of privacy hardly suffices. What of the vast range of powers between the king and the lord or *paterfamilias*? What of duties to neighbors, to customers and employees, to the commune, or to the church? A study of public and private sin and penance is a good place to begin.

In regard to penance, the medieval use of the terms "public" and "private" was as ill-defined as it was insistent. This is a distinction that runs through thirteenth-century theology and canon law, but is never sufficiently examined or explained. We need to know what thirteenth-century people considered public and private in practice and in theory. This is a story of the difference between public and private life, but it is even more a story of a collective self-deception about the difference between public and private life. We need to imitate the traditional medievalist's close scrutiny of the exact language and preoccupations of the evidence if we wish to understand the evolution of privacy and publicity.

I refer constantly to the terminology of penance in theology and canon law, but I also attempt to remedy the too-narrow focus of histories of medieval penance by looking at sources and types of penance that they neglect. Liturgy as well as theology, processions as well as sacramental confession, will receive due attention. Chapter 2, on theology, begins the investigation, because the theologians' common assumptions and common inconsistencies reveal the lingering desire to see bad men humiliated hidden behind the pat slogans for private penance. This chapter examines several systems of classification that the theologians applied to penance, including interior and exterior penance; duties to God, neighbor, and the church; and the judicial and penitential *fora*, as well as the "tripartite penance" mentioned above. In the end, these schemes failed to describe the reality the theologians knew, and they failed especially to account for public penance. But they may suggest to us hidden doubts about private penance and the inevitable disappointments of the "contritionist" teachings of the manuals. Chapter 3 considers the practical implementation of Canon 21 of the Fourth Lateran Council and the procedures of private penance developed by the canonists and particularly by French bishops in their synodal statutes. These statutes suggest what the bishops conceived as the central goals of Canon 21, and they reveal a surprising tolerance for the exposure and humiliation of even secret sinners. Chapter 4 outlines the procedure of all types of public penances, relying again on synodal statutes, but turning as well to episcopal and monastic registers and narrative evidence where available. Chapters 5, 6, and 7 examine liturgical evidence. Chapter 5 covers communal rites of penances and what we may call the "ritual logic" behind expiation and celebration in the cycles of the year, the expectations, that is, of the public for public penance. Chapters 6 and 7 treat in turn the evolution of the Roman and the French liturgy of penance, based on a study of over seventy-five liturgical manuscripts. These chapters trace a rapid development from the scapegoating of early medieval penance to an exemplary punishment that taught a lesson to the audience but did not promise communal salvation through the humiliation of the few. Chapter 8 considers public penance in its urban setting, including its use in peacemaking and enforcing public order. A study of primarily narrative sources reveals why religious and even secular authorities long continued to see public penance as a desirable alternative to more conventional penalties. Indeed, Flemish cities routinely imposed one form of public penance, the involuntary pilgrimage, in the fourteenth and fifteenth centuries. Finally, Chapter 9 returns to the larger question of the demise of communal religion and sets forth the implications of my conclusions for the debate about individualism between medievalists and early modernists.

Temporal and Spatial Limits

The spatial and temporal limits of this study require some comment, for the very notion of a regional history of a sacrament in principle common to all of Catholic Christianity may surprise some readers. We find a great deal of regional variation, however, in the practice and even in the theory of the public version of penance. In particular, a Rome-centered perspective is wholly inadequate for a rite that even contemporary theologians, canonists, and bishops noticed was evolving differently in different parts of Western Europe. The practice of public penance in northern French cities, moreover, depended on a number of peculiar local conditions, such as ill-defined public authority, multiple conflicts over jurisdiction, and rich merchants threatened by accusations of usury. These local and regional peculiarities are essential to understanding both public penance and the concepts of public and private spheres. The relative paucity of sources rules out a detailed local investigation; my study ranges over the whole of northern France and over a whole century.

In addition, I have, where convenient, made forays into other regions and periods for comparison. "Northern France," in any case a vague phrase, I define for practical purposes as the ecclesiastical provinces of Tours, Rouen, Sens, and Reims—a definition that includes Cambrai, French-speaking but part of the Empire in the thirteenth century, and areas of Netherlandish-speaking Flanders then under Capetian suzerainty within the province of Reims. Most of the surviving liturgical evidence comes from the provinces of Sens and Reims, from the towns, that is, of Flanders, Picardy, Artois, Champagne, and the Ile-de-France. Less survives from Normandy, although other types of sources partially compensate for this gap. Virtually no evidence on penitential practices survives from Brittany, and so the far west will receive little attention.

The heartland of northern France is the focus of my study. In the thirteenth century, this area boasted the richest cities north of the Alps; these *bonnes villes* owed allegiance and paid taxes to the richest king in Europe. Indeed, Paris may well have been the largest city in western Europe in 1300.[28] And Paris was precisely the center of the new university theology of penance, a theology that spread the gospel of inner contrition and secret confession in the twelfth and thirteenth centuries. If any bishops should have had a whiff of the new teaching, it should have been those in northern France. Intellectually as well as politically and economically, northeastern France was at the center. It cannot be dismissed as a stagnant backwater.

As for temporal limits, the thirteenth century is not a vague phrase, but it is perhaps an arbitrary one. I use it very loosely for the years from the appearance of the new *summae confessorum* around 1200 until the popular revolts and the beginning of the Hundred Years War in the early fourteenth century, conflicts that marked the end of a period of relative political and economic stability in the region. In short, I examine the century or so after the Fourth Lateran to see what happened to the old public rite in the towns of northern France; where appropriate it will range outside these limits. For instance, because liturgical change is inevitably glacial, all the available and relevant liturgical books datable between 1150 and 1350 are brought into service.

The Sources

Sources for the study of medieval religious practice are often scarce and difficult to interpret. Once we push the study of penance beyond

---

28. Cf. Bronislaw Geremek, "Paris la plus grande ville de l'Occident médiéval?" *Acta Poloniae Historica* 18 (1968): 18–37, and below, Chapter 8.

the identification of theologians' points of view, the use of evidence becomes a major concern. Although detailed comments on the problems of particular types of sources are offered later as the occasion arises, here it suffices to note what strategies are available. The theology and canon law of penance and especially their vulgarization in the confessors' manuals and summary abridgments are an obvious starting point. I have already remarked the danger of accepting Scholastic definitions and opinions as normative. But these works do reveal something of their authors' shared assumptions and shared doubts, if not always in ways that their authors intended. The dialogue between the theories of an intellectual elite and the religious impulses of the uneducated is a major theme of this study. As we have seen, most historians have preferred to concentrate on one side of this dialogue to the exclusion of the other. Read carefully, however, even the most academic of thirteenth-century theology suggests doubts about privacy and publicity lurking behind the smooth facade of the sacramental system. The theologians and canonists responded to the same hopes and fears as did the bishops and the bishops' flocks. If the intellectuals did not always reform contemporary practice to their satisfaction, it was not because of popular indifference to public humiliation or to the privacy of the conscience.

From theology and academic canon law we may turn to the actual enactments of diocesan synods. Recent cataloging and editing have made the extensive surviving statutes readily accessible.[29] Unfortunately, episcopal registers and visitation records have rarely survived, though their collation likewise became more regular after 1200. The single major exception, Eudes Rigaud's *Regestrum visitationum*, is invaluable.[30] Here we can see exactly how a northern French archbishop—a theologian himself—imposed public penance on laymen and clerics in his diocese. Sometimes his decisions confirm the theory expressed in diocesan law and Scholastic theology; sometimes they surprise.

Liturgical commentaries and liturgical books proper, particularly pontificals and ordinals, are an extremely important source for the evolution of public penance; they alone allow us to examine the transformation of ritual in some detail. Liturgical sources pose several problems. They are generally conservative, and although they are less studied works than academic theology, they are still the products of educated clerics. Nevertheless, with proper caution they may reward

29. André Artonne, Louis Guizard, and Odette Pontal, *Répertoire des statuts synodaux des diocèses de l'ancienne France du XIIIe à la fin du XVIIIe siècle*, 2d ed., Documents, études, et répertoires publiés par l'Institut de recherche et d'histoire des textes, 8 (Paris, 1969); and Pontal I.

30. Eudes Rigaud, *Regestrum visitationum*, ed. T. Bonnin (Rouen, 1852).

the historian. Rites of public penance changed more rapidly than any other in the pontificals, and so we need not fear that the evidence represents a fossil from an earlier era. And clerical and Latin though they are, liturgical books at least prescribe the actual rituals that northern French laymen joined and watched. They are "how-to" books of the most immediate sort, designed not to convince the priest or bishop of the value of their recommendations, like the confessors' manuals, but simply to lead him step-by-step through the process. Liturgical commentators like Jean Beleth and Guillaume Durand fill in gaps in the surviving sources and indicate interpretations of symbols and rites, interpretations that reflect academic concerns but are nonetheless telling.[31]

Narratives—histories, chronicles, and memoirs—are the final major source for public penances. Often they merely mention incidents of public penance without elaboration. In a couple of instances, they provide more complete information on the circumstances surrounding the case. Such evidence survives, for example, for a series of early-thirteenth-century riots in Reims and the public penitential processions that followed, and this evidence permits a more extensive analysis of the way public penance worked in the political life of a city. Other sources are only intermittently useful. Collections of *exempla* for use in sermons, for instance, emphasized the promotion of regular private confession, and can offer revealing evidence of anxieties about public exposure, but they are disappointingly silent about public penance itself. Public penance needed no preaching campaigns; as a rule, it was not voluntary. Scattered references to public penance also appear in cartularies as conditions for settlements of disputes, but the occurrences are so sporadic that it is impractical to attempt a systematic search. In general, however, public penance is so common in thirteenth-century sources that its recent neglect is all the more surprising.

In medieval Latin, one word, *penitentia*, could mean both the sinner's saving contrition and the satisfactory penalty imposed by the priest. English since the Reformation has distinguished between "doing penance" and "being penitent," but one word, *penitere*, covered both senses in Latin. Sometimes medieval writers applied the word *penitentia* to the whole process, sometimes to part of the process, but never argumentatively to exclude one aspect or the other. The purpose of

---

31. Jean Beleth, *Summa de ecclesiasticis officiis*, ed. H. Douteil, Corpus Christianorum Continuatio Medievalis, 41–41A (Turnholt, 1976); Guillaume Durand, *Rationale divinorum officiorum* (Venice, 1577).

penance was first and most obviously the reconciliation with God th; promised eternal salvation, but it was also the reconciliation with th institutional church through the authority of its sacraments and it, priests. Public penance, even more than private penance, shared in the double nature of the sacrament. It was normally only half voluntary, as much a punishment imposed as a sacrifice assumed, as much a lesson to the populace as redemption for the individual, as much reconciliation with church and neighbor as reconciliation with God. Perhaps that is why public penance was so compelling to those who watched it and why it so intriguing to those who now read about it. Public penance acts out a utopian dream: It declares the hope that God's justice can be visible on earth.

CHAPTER TWO

The Failure of a Theology of Private Penance

In 1215, the Fourth Lateran Council required all Christians to confess once a year during Lent. Even before that, a number of Parisian theologians prepared a new sort of manual to train parish priests to administer confession and to satisfy their own intellectual quest for a more consistent theology of penance. The new *summae confessorum*, as they are generally known,[1] took many forms, from simple treatises a few folios long on contrition and confession, to the massive *summae* of theology and canon law, far too complex to train parish priests and intended rather to train those who trained them. Pierre Michaud-Quantin has counted over seven hundred such works of all types written between 1200 and 1500.[2] These works refined, applied, and, above all, popularized the new theology of the twelfth-century schools. Not surprisingly, the first wave of manuals in the late twelfth and early thirteenth centuries was overwhelmingly French in origin; they were composed chiefly by Parisian teachers and by Englishmen who had crossed the Channel to study and perhaps teach or adminis-

---

1. Rather anachronistically, since as Pierre Michaud-Quantin and Leonard Boyle have observed, John of Freiburg was apparently the first to apply the title to his own work, ca. 1298: Michaud-Quantin, "Les méthodes de la pastorale du XIIIe au XVe siècle," in *Methoden in Wissenschaft und Kunst des Mittelalters*, Miscellanea mediaevalia, 7 (Berlin, 1970), pp. 76–91, and Boyle, "The *Summa confessorum* of John of Freiburg and the Popularization of the Moral Teaching of St. Thomas and Some of his Contemporaries," in *St. Thomas Aquinas, 1274–1974: Commemorative Studies* (Toronto, 1974), 2:248n.

2. Michaud-Quantin, "Les méthodes de la pastorale du XIIIe au XVe siècle," pp. 83–84. Michaud-Quantin's *Sommes de casuistique et manuels de confession au Moyen Age (XII–XVI siècles)*, Analecta mediaevalia Namurcensia, 3 (Louvain, 1962), is the best general guide to the genre. Leonard Boyle's, "*Summae confessorum*," in *Les genres littéraires dans les sources théologiques et philosophiques médiévales* (Louvain, 1982), pp. 227–237, is perhaps an overly fine analysis of the different subspecies of penitential *summae*. Johannes Dietterle's "Die Summae confessorum," *Zeitschrift für Kirchengeschichte* 24 (1903): 353–374, 520–548; 25 (1904): 248–272; 26 (1905): 59–81, 350–364; 27 (1906): 166–188, 296–310, 431–442; 28 (1907): 401–431, remains useful as a guide to penitential *summae* with a canonical slant.

ter penance themselves.[3] With these books, a parish priest, theologian, or bishop might learn how the greatest theologians of the day and not a few second-raters anatomized the species of penance, the powers of the priest, and the sacred economy of reconciliation. Amid the hubbub of theological disputes over *casus*, the historian may detect certain recurring phrases, fashionable assumptions, and nagging questions that provide a clue to the theologians' hopes and doubts.

Every late-twelfth- and early-thirteenth-century author sprinkled his penitential manual with multifarious lists to organize and classify every aspect of his subject.[4] We find three parts of penance, four senses of binding and four of loosing, fourteen species of avarice, three advantages of contrition, and so forth. Whether they were largely devotional tracts aimed at encouraging a change of heart and teaching how to instill it in others or massive juridical compendia, the manuals tried to classify and enumerate every topic in their grasp. Partly, of course, the popularizers were making their lessons digestible and memorable. But the passion for classification perhaps indicates as well a lingering doubt about the adequacy of the theological solutions. There are many too many distinctions. Dozens of variations revolve around a few central themes, recurrent ambiguities that each generation, and even each writer, tried to resolve in a slightly different way. Some of the most successful general schemes in moral theology have become familiar, and their evolution has received a great deal of scholarly attention. The distinctions between the judicial and penitential *fora*, and the related theology of the keys, are two such whose invention and articulation have inspired sustained investigation, and not unreasonably, for they reveal the Scholastic teachings on the rights and duties of clerics from deacon to pope as well as the place of penance in an increasingly bureaucratized church.

In this chapter, however, I speak in detail of three less familiar

---

3. See Jean Longère, "Quelques *summa de poenitentia* à la fin du XIIe et au début du XIIIe siècle," in *La piété populaire au Moyen Age*, Actes du 99e Congrès national des sociétés savantes, Besançon, 1974, Philologie et histoire jusqu'à 1610, 1 (Paris, 1977), p. 50, for the Parisian links of most of the early *summae*.

4. Cf. Michaud-Quantin, "Textes pénitentiels languedociens au XIIIe siècle," *Le credo, la morale, et l'inquisition*, Cahiers de Fanjeaux, 6 (Toulouse, 1971), p. 163; Payen, "La pénitence dans le contexte culturel des XIIe et XIIIe siècles," p. 415, attributes the phenomenon to a thirteenth-century reaction to late-twelfth-century emotionalism, but really all the manuals are full of such schemes, and emotionalism and mnemonic schemes were by no means incompatible. See, for example, the jurist Paul of Hungary's old-fashioned and emotional *rationes penitentie* (1220), packed with numerical divisions, in *Bibliotheca casinensis seu Codicum manuscriptorum* (Montecassino, 1878–1880), vol. 4, Florilegium casinense, pp. 191–215. On the attribution of this work, see P. Mandonnet, "La 'Summa de Poenitentia Magistri Pauli presbyteri S. Nicolai' (Magister Paulus de Hungaria O.P. 1220–1221)," in *Aus der Geisteswelt des Mittelalters: Studien und Texte; Martin Grabmann zur Vollendung des 60. Lebensjahres*, Beiträge zur Geschichte der Philosophie und Theologie des Mittelalters, suppl. 3 (1935), pp. 525–544.

distinctions associated with penance: "tripartite" penance; exterior and interior penance; and obligations to God, church, and neighbor. Although popular in the twelfth and thirteenth centuries, these distinctions were unquestionably less successful than the more familiar ones. Scholastic theologians never constructed wholly satisfactory definitions of their terms, and their attempts never achieved the status of the more familiar distinctions, which survived the medieval period. It is the failure of these distinctions that makes them so revealing, however. I look through them and behind them for some deeper ambivalences that helped make them necessary, ambivalences that might be summed up in different, unstated, pairs: private shame and public humiliation; free absolution and costly restitution; the silent heart and the cacophony of instruction. That analysis sheds new light on the more familiar Scholastic definitions, especially the two *fora*, restitution, and public and private duties. In the end, we shall come to understand the limitations of the theologians'—and perhaps our own—simple distinctions between public and private spheres.

Sources

Of the dozens of confessors' manuals, I examine primarily those composed in the Parisian schools and northern France, with only limited attention to works from other regions. Even my coverage of Parisian material will not be exhaustive, if only because no comprehensive catalog exists. In addition, treatments of penance in most of the important academic *summae* of canon law and theology from the thirteenth century require attention; in any case, it is often difficult to draw a line between the more complex manuals and general treatments of the sacraments. Chronologically, this study focuses chiefly on the first wave of popularizations, which were produced between 1180 and 1230. These writers prepared the ground for the Fourth Lateran Council's Canon 21, and, after 1215, they spread its message. They tinkered with the late-twelfth-century theology that they had learned in the schools or in some cases had themselves developed. Their works are closest to the spirit of early Scholastic theology, and depend most completely on the innovations of Peter Abelard and the school of Gilbert of Poitiers. As we shall see, the way these writers adapted that theology to the teaching of penance long determined the future direction of investigation and classification. Production of innovative handbooks on penance slowed after Ramón de Peñafort's *Summa de poenitentia* in 1235, although shorter, generally anonymous, treatises continued to be composed, and the early tracts continued to be re-copied virtually unabated through 1300 or so. We look to these later works and to the thirteenth-century canonical and theological *summae* to continue the story through the century. The end of the century is a fitting stopping point. Around 1300, John of Freiburg and other popularizers of Thomas Aquinas, Bonaventure, and Hostiensis signal the onset of a new wave of major treatments of penance.[5] The canonico-theological encyclopedias that resulted endured to the Council of Trent and beyond, but this second wave does not occupy us as much as the first. The composition and influence of these works lie outside the chronological limits of this study, and, in any case, these late medieval *summae* tend to follow the paths set out by earlier writers.

"Tripartite Penance"

By 1200, there were three types of penance: private penance, non-solemn public penance, and solemn public penance. This is affirmed by many thirteenth-century manuals, and so concurs the greatest modern historian of penance, Cyrille Vogel.[6] According to this scheme, in the solemn version, the bishop, not a mere priest, would ritually expel and later reconcile the penitents; this solemn rite was only to be applied to laymen, and even then only for the most notorious and heinous crimes. Nonsolemn public penance, by contrast, could be imposed by priests, on clerics as well as laymen, and it was generally less ritually formal than the solemn variety. Its classic form was the penitential pilgrimage. Private penance, finally, was the secret confession to a priest followed by satisfaction imposed and absolution (not necessarily in that order), that is, the familiar rite made compulsory by the Fourth Lateran. How was this classification originally conceived, and was its arrival around 1200 the result of the appearance of a new type of penance, or simply a new formulation of an unchanged reality?

For an answer, we must return momentarily to the late eleventh century, when Lanfranc wrote a treatise on the secret of confession. In it he recognizes two sorts of penance, and neither one corresponds precisely to any of the eventual three types nor to Vogel's "bipartite penance" comprising tariffed and public forms.[7] He teaches his read-

5. Boyle, "The *Summa confessorum* of John of Freiburg," pp. 245–246.
6. Vogel, *Le pécheur et la pénitence*, pp. 34–35.
7. Vogel, *Le pécheur et la pénitence*, pp. 33–36.

ers, probably monks or other clerics, to confess their *secret* sins to deacons or priests, as they choose. But *public* sins must be confessed to priests. "In this we know that we must confess secret things to an ecclesiastic of any order, but open ones are proper only for priests, through whom the Church both looses and binds things which it knows publicly."[8] The point of the treatise is to proselytize for frequent confession without fear of disclosure, and so secret sins and secret confession take pride of place, both in Lanfranc's treatise and in similar pre-Scholastic works.[9] Public penance, by contrast, is simply the familiar reality, which Lanfranc need only note in passing. It is clearly not voluntary; confession of public sins obviously does not reveal anything that man or God did not know; instead, it implies submission to the discipline of the church. Only penance for public sins requires the intervention of the priest (not necessarily a bishop), and so it is in this sense more fully "sacramental" than the voluntary but salutary private confession, though we must beware of using this term before the development of a theory of the sacraments in the twelfth century. Lanfranc encourages his clerical readers to confess secret sins privately, and in this he hardly departs from the monastic tradition of confession among the brothers.

We note that "tariffed" penance, in Vogel's scheme the supposed ancestor of sacramental private penance, does not appear as a separate type of penance at all. Lanfranc doubtless knew of tariffed penance and the penitentials, but probably he considered them partly subsumed under the category of public penance—for many of the canons explicitly applied to public crimes and virtually all implied public satisfaction—and partly under the category of private penance, informal though it remained. On the eve of a new academic theology, Lanfranc and his contemporaries were teaching a language of tears and contrition, but they did not contemplate the abandonment of public penance, or indeed, any serious reorganization of the

8. Lanfranc, *Libellus de celanda confessione*, PL 150:629: "In hoc cognoscimus quia de occultis omni ecclesiastico ordini confiteri debemus; de apertis vero solis convenit sacerdotibus, per quos Ecclesia, quae publice novit, et solvit et ligat."

9. See, for example, the pseudo-Augustinian *De vera et falsa confessione*, PL 40:1113–1130. For its dating to the beginning of the twelfth century, see Ludwig Hödl, *Die Geschichte der scholastischen Literatur und der Theologie der Schlüsselgewalt*, Beiträge zur Geschichte der Philosophie und Theologie des Mittelalters, 38.4 (Münster, 1960), pp. 158–163. For the preoccupation with confession and inner contrition in Lanfranc, Peter Damian, pseudo-Augustine, and other contemporary writers, see Roberto Rusconi, "*Ordinate confiteri*: La confessione dei peccati nelle 'summae de casibus' e nei manuali per i confessori (meta XII–inizio XIV secolo)," in *L'aveu: Antiquité et Moyen-Age*, Collection de l'Ecole française de Rome, 88 (Rome, 1986), p. 299; and Nicole Bériou, "La confession dans les écrits théologiques et pastoreaux du XIIIe siècle: Médication de l'âme ou demande judiciaire," in *L'aveu*, pp. 263n, 265.

system. We find in Lanfranc and his contemporaries a notable lack of interest in the classification of types of penance and in the status of the tariffs in the penitential books. The penitential books themselves had not explained whether their tariffs belonged to private or public penance,[10] and Lanfranc and his contemporaries did not bother to clarify the point. Of course, Lanfranc's belief that he was only repeating unchanged the teachings of the early church was mistaken, and penitential practices did shift even between the Carolingian period and 1100. Yet, his unstated conviction that there was no evolution of "types of penances" contrasts not only with the historical awareness of a modern critic but with the precise classifications of later theologians. We should not understand Lanfranc's emphasis on contrition and confession, then, as an effort to edge aside public penance with private. The neat, modern term "bipartite penance" is a fiction.[11]

Even when the classifying tendencies of early Scholastic theology were well underway in the midtwelfth century, theologians hesitated to develop a classification of penance. Like Lanfranc, the pseudo-Peter of Blois, writing verses on penance around 1150, simply promoted a heightened emotionalism alongside his version of the familiar Carolingian tag: "If there be public harm, let the penalty be public; if even a heinous thing may remain hidden, let the penalty be too."[12] This is the most common sort of work on penance composed in the twelfth century, nine parts exhortation to one part traditional dogma. But even the most original theologians of the twelfth century, those who first differentiated the *culpa*, or "guilt," and *poena*, or "penalty," incurred in sin, or who explored the nature of the sacraments in general, did not seek to explain the implications of these distinctions for the system of penance any more than had that versifier. Hugh of

10. Gianfranco Garancini, "Persona, peccato, penitenza: Studi sulla disciplina penitenziale nell'Alto Medio Evo," *Rivista di storia del diritto italiano* 47 (1974): 44, argues that the tariffed penances might better be called "personal" than "private." They might in fact involve public satisfactions, but they always emphasized the personal relationship between the individual sinner and the priest. For the opposing view that the tariffs helped spread private penance, see, besides Vogel, T. P. Oakley, "Some Neglected Aspects in the History of Penance," *Catholic Historical Review* 24 (1938): 306.

11. For the difficulties of applying "bipartite penance" to early medieval realities, see H. Platelle, "Pratiques pénitentielles et mentalités religieuses au Moyen Age: La pénitence des parricides et l'esprit de l'ordalie," *Mélanges de science religieuse* 40 (1983): 134, where he tries to identify the exile of parricides as private, tariffed penance as opposed to solemn public penance, though no penance was more spectacularly public. Peter of Poitiers would later say that parricides receive solemn penance, *Summa de confessione* (= *Compilatio praesens*), ed. J. Longère, Corpus Christianorum Continuatio Mediaevalis, 51 (Turnholt, 1980), pp. 80–81. The labels are at best abstract and misleading.

12. ps-Peter of Blois, *De poenitentia*, PL 207:1156: "Publica sit poena, fuerit a publica noxa./ Si lateat licet enormis, lateat quoque poena." See Michaud-Quantin, *Sommes de casuistique et manuels de confession*, p. 19, on the date and authorship of these verses.

Saint Victor and Abelard showed little interest in anatomizing types of penance, and they did not even mention the "solemn" variety. Discussions of the varieties of penance as such first make an appearance when theologians became aware of the conflict of canons about the application or iterability of penance. Peter Lombard explained the circumstances that required "solemn" penance, which he said was for "more serious sins"—not necessarily more public—in order to account for some patristic prohibitions against repeating penance.[13] He neither described solemn penance in any detail nor defined other varieties of penance. Instead, his main interests lay in pinpointing the moment of grace and forgiveness and in measuring the role of the priest, the penitent, and God. In effect, this theology of contrition applied to all kinds of penance, and Peter did not use it to differentiate among them. Gratian and several of the early decretists began to differentiate between what they called either "solemn" or "public" penance and "private" penance; no distinction was drawn between solemn and nonsolemn public penance.[14] For the most part, however, theologians and canonists puzzled over the metaphysical consequences of confession, and popularizers kept to praises of contrition and a minimum of schematic innovation.

"Tripartite penance"[15] first makes an appearance in two works of the 1160s, in the *Sententiae de sacramentis*, probably composed by Peter Comestor, and in an anonymous commentary on Gratian's *Decretum*. Writing around 1165–1166, Peter mentions three types of penance, "quedam sollempnis . . . quedam publica, quedam privata." Solemn penance, he says, involves ejection from the church and a regime of fasts; public penance like private penance may be repeated.[16] He does

13. Peter Lombard, *Sententiae in IV libris distinctae*, Spicilegium Bonaventurianum, 4–5 (Grottaferrata, 1971–1981), IV D.14 c.4, vol. II, pp. 321–322. Peter further notes that the prohibition of the repetition of solemn penance is not observed in some churches: "in quibusdam ecclesiis non servatur." See below, Chapter 4.

14. Gratian, *Decretum*, ed. E. Friedberg (Leipzig, 1871), D.50 c.61 and D.50 c.64, col. 200–201; Terence P. McLaughlin, ed., *The Summa Parisiensis on the Decretum Gratiani* (ca. 1160), (Toronto, 1952), D.50 c.26 q.6, pp. 233–234; Rufinus of Bologna (d. ca. 1192), *Summa decretorum*, ed. H. Singer (Paderborn, 1902, repr. Aalen, 1963), D.50 c.1, pp. 114–115 and D.50 c.58, p. 130. Rufinus complains that monastic confinement does not seem to fit either private or *publica*, that is, *sollemnis, penitentia*. And cf. Bernard of Pavia (d. 1213), *Summa decretalium*, ed. E. A. D. Laspeyres (Regensburg, 1860, repr. Graz, 1956), V.33.2, p. 270, who still uses the bipartite distinction in his commentary on 1 Comp.

15. The adjective is a misnomer, since the scheme classifies three types or rites of penance, not three parts of penance, as with the familiar trio of contrition, confession, and satisfaction. But it has become the standard shorthand for solemn, nonsolemn public, and private. See Vogel, *Le pécheur et la pénitence*, pp. 31–36.

16. Raymond M. Martin, ed., *Pierre le Mangeur: De sacramentis*, appendix to Henri Weisweiler, *Maître Simon et son groupe: De sacramentis*, Spicilegium sacrum Lovaniense, 17 (Louvain, 1937), 73*–74*; for the attribution and dating, see Martin's introduction, pp. xvi*–xxviii*. Peter's description of public penance is discussed at greater length in Chapter 4.

not define nonsolemn public penance or explain what circumstances require it; he simply mentions it while explaining the iterability of all but solemn penance. The anonymous author of the commentary on Gratian, headed *Elegantius in iure divino*, writing around 1169 in the Rhineland, was influenced by Parisian teaching,[17] and perhaps by Peter. He describes penance as occult or manifest, and if manifest, either solemn or nonsolemn.[18] Again, the author only mentions nonsolemn public penance as a way of accounting for discrepancies in Gratian's treatment of solemn penance. It is the version that may be imposed on priests.

A distinction between solemn and nonsolemn public penance had thus twice proved useful in sorting out contradictory authorities, but nothing much came of it during the next three decades, as theologians remained preoccupied with the necessity of confession, the priest's power of absolution, and definitions of vice and virtue. Around 1200, Alan of Lille, the first Parisian master to write a practical confessors' manual incorporating the theological sophistication of the school of Gilbert of Poitiers, began to describe three different varieties of penance, but his treatment was uncharacteristically muddled. Only with considerable effort can we discern the outline of a tripartite penance. Alan does mention "solemn penance" from time to time, inter alia, in his discussion of the satisfactions required for a variety of sins.[19] A formal classification of penance appears late in the text, however, where Alan tries to distinguish between solemn and private in secular and in ecclesiastical penalties.[20] His attempt to consider secular "penances" and spiritual expiation in parallel, abortive though it inevitably was, is a sign of how undeveloped was any distinction between disciplinary and expiatory rites, and between a judicial or ecclesiastical forum and the interior forum. We shall see later how this was typical of the early thirteenth century. At any rate, Alan turns hastily from secular to church penances. "Some ecclesiastical penances are solemn,

17. For the influence of Parisian teaching on Rhenish canonists of the mid– to late twelfth century, see Stephan Kuttner, "Réflexions sur les Brocards des Glossateurs," in *Mélanges Joseph de Ghellinck* (Gembloux, 1951), 2:783–785.

18. Gerard Fransen, with Stephan Kuttner, eds., *Summa "Elegantius in iure diuino" seu Coloniensis*, Monumenta Iuris Canonici, ser. A, Corpus Glossatorum, 1 (New York, 1969), II.109–114, vol. I, pp. 94–96.

19. Alan of Lille, *Liber poenitentialis*, ed. Jean Longère, Analecta mediaevalia Namurcensia, 17–18 (Louvain, 1965), II.51, vol. 2, p. 73; II.75, vol. 2, p. 87; III.20, vol. 2, p. 138; III.23, vol. 2, p. 140. For the identification of this long recension as Alan's own and the dating, see P. Michaud-Quantin, "Le 'Liber penitentialis' d'Alain de Lille: Le témoignage des manuscrits belges et français," *Cîteaux* 10 (1959): 93–106; J. Longère, "Alain de Lille, Liber poenitentialis: Les traditions moyennes et courtes," *Archives d'histoire doctrinale et littéraire du Moyen Age* 40 (1965): 169–242; and Longère's introduction to the edition, vol. 1, pp. 133–160.

20. Alan of Lille, *Liber poenitentialis*, III.6, vol. 2, p. 130.

others private. Solemn is that imposed for major or notorious crimes, or for those to which someone has confessed, or for those of which someone has been convicted: this is usually called *carena*. As it concerns major crimes, so it pertains to the higher prelates of the Church to impose it."[21] The first thing to note here is Alan's identification of solemn penance and the *carena*. The latter term was derived from *quadragesima*, the forty-day fast that was the most important feature of the multiyear penances in the tariffed penitentials. A murderer, for example, would have had to complete three *quadragesimae* of fasting each year for seven years, or pay a sufficient redemption. The term *carena* came to be applied vaguely to the whole process, and Alan, who considers such serious tariffed penances as the equivalent of solemn public penance, applies it to the solemn rite. Usage of the term remained very loose, but throughout the thirteenth century it always referred in some way to public penance. The important point is that a word that originally designated the seven-year tariffed penance eventually signified public penance.[22] For by the *carena* even secret crimes may be exposed. Nothing could demonstrate more clearly the inadequacy of historical schemes explaining private penance as the sole heir of the tariffs, and solemn penance as the heir of the ancient Christian public penance.

In this passage, Alan recognizes but two types of penance, "solemn" and private; but in the next chapter he subdivides public penance itself into two varieties. "Certain public penance for major and public sins is to be imposed on clerics, but not on those like laymen, that is, who are not in the choir with the other psalm-singers, or at the common table with the others who eat."[23] Alan's version still falls short of the classic formulation cited by Vogel in several key ways. Public penance of either type should be imposed, Alan says, for major and/or (*vel*) public sins. And further, the nonsolemn public penance in Alan's

---

21. Alan of Lille, *Liber poenitentialis*, III.7, vol. 2, pp. 130–131: "Ecclesiasticarum poenitentiarum alia solemnis, alia privata. Solemnis est, quae pro majoribus criminibus, vel notoriis, vel pro his criminibus quae quis confessus est, vel de quibus quisque convictus est, infligitur, quae carena solet appellari; et sicut de majoribus criminibus est, ita ad majores Ecclesiae praelatos pertinet hanc infligere."

22. According to Jungmann, *carena* meant only nonsolemn public penance, in opposition to solemn penance: "Carena," in *Lexikon für Theologie und Kirche* (Freiburg, 1958), 2, col. 940; *Die lateinischen Bussriten in ihrer geschichtlichen Entwicklung*, Forschungen zur Geschichte des innerkirchlichen Lebens, 3–4 (Innsbruck, 1932), pp. 68–69. The error of his view is clear enough from this passage of Alan's, and from Du Cange's article on *carena* that Jungmann himself cites: *Glossarium Mediae et Infimae Latinitatis*, new ed. (1883–1887), 2:167. Note, too, that Bernard of Pavia (d. 1213), *Summa decretalium*, V.33.2, p. 270, called *carena* a form of solemn penance, in distinction to the two other forms, pilgrimage and monastic confinement.

23. Alan of Lille, *Liber poenitentialis*, III.9, vol. 2, p. 131: "Quaedam tamen publica poenitentia clericis pro majoribus et publicis peccatis infligenda est, sed non talis qualis laicis, scilicet ut non sint in choro cum aliis psallentibus, nec ad mensam cum prandentibus."

description was exclusively for clerics, indeed exclusively for monks or canons; Alan does not mention penitential pilgrimage for laymen, which in the classic formulation was the most often mentioned type of "nonsolemn public penance"; nor does he describe any nonsolemn public penances for less notorious public crimes committed by laymen.

The muddle, the hesitation, the deviations from the classic form are unsurprising. Alan began with the canons in the old penitentials like Burchard's, applied the new theology, and ended up with an inconsistent mix of old and new. The old canons whose cataloging represents the major task of Alan's book seemed to refer sometimes to public, sometimes to private sins. Some satisfactions to be imposed, such as the *poenitentia septennis* (seven-year penance), certainly required the solemn rite.[24] Thus, Alan could not identify the tariffs he found with either public or private penance. They were simply the well-known standards of punishment in a world that did not care much to distinguish the two. "Solemn penance" was by contrast the new formulation, and Alan's definition remained a little shaky. The way that the tariffs and old penitential books applied indiscriminately to public and private penance doubtless encouraged a fuzziness about the application of the new solemn penance. A Carolingian tag much repeated by later theologians insisted that public penance was to be imposed for public sins. Indeed, as one much-loved definition ran, public penance was to be applied to crimes that moved the whole church or whole city, as Regino of Prüm wrote in the ninth century, a "public and notorious [crime] . . . which disturbed the whole Church."[25] But a distinction between major crimes and public crimes was in practice not so easy to draw, and Alan and other twelfth-century theologians did not expend much effort on the issue.[26] Most major sins were likely to be public, and vice versa. Alan's treatment is the

24. Alan of Lille, *Liber poenitentialis*, II.75, vol. 2, p. 87.
25. Regino of Prüm, *Libri duo de synodalibus causis et disciplinis ecclesiasticis*, ed. F. G. A. Wasserschleben (Leipzig, 1840, repr. Graz, 1964), pp. 135–136: "publicum et vulgatum . . . quod universam Ecclesiam commoverit." Cf. Burchard of Worms, *Decretorum libri viginti*, XIX.40, PL 140:988. The tag seems to have come from fourth-century canons of a council of Carthage; Gratian cited the tag in its original form, which henceforward became standard in theology and canon law: "talis paenitentia non imponatur, nisi pro crimine publico, vel vulgarissimo, quod totam commoverit urbem," *Decretum*, ed. E. Friedberg, Corpus Iuris Canonici, 1 (Leipzig, 1871), C.26 q.6 c.14, col. 1041. The city replaces the church as representative of the wider community. See Paul Anciaux, *La théologie du sacrement de pénitence au XIIe siècle* (Louvain, 1949), pp. 150n–152n, for examples of its use in the twelfth century.
26. Anciaux, *La théologie du sacrement de pénitence*, pp. 150–153, argues that penitential discipline was softening as theologians gradually accepted the imposition of solemn public penance only in very serious cases, not for all public sins. But there is really no such evolution; the later theologians he cites were all just paraphrasing the ancient canon copied in Regino and the *Decretum*.

first clue that the conception of solemn penance as a separate type is really an invention of the late twelfth century.

In spite of the hesitance of the early definitions, "tripartite penance" caught on quickly among other writers of confessors' manuals, and eventually it became a commonplace in thirteenth-century canonical theological *summae*.[27] Just before 1215, Robert Courson did not mention tripartite penance, but he was one of the last to omit it.[28] Between 1208 and 1216, Robert of Flamborough, Peter of Poitiers, and Thomas of Chobham, all three writing in Paris, began to develop the distinction beyond Alan's adumbration. Still awkward is the discussion of Peter of Poitiers, who composed his *summa* while a canon of Saint Victor in Paris, perhaps in 1216 or 1217. Peter provides quite a different definition of public nonsolemn penance from Alan's.

It does not seem that one making penance for secret sins should, unwilling, be strictly confined to a certain kind of satisfaction; he can atone or otherwise make amends. It is otherwise for open sins, as we see in solemn penance, also called *carena*, which is usually imposed for more heinous sins, like parricide. . . . This penance has a certain form and statutes. Similarly, both lesser homicides and other public penitents have some certain form, as when on Ash Wednesday they are expelled from the church with a certain form. Correspondingly they are received on Maundy Thursday with a certain form. And this penance is called public, not solemn. Also, in many cases, entry to a church is forbidden to many in penance for a time.[29]

27. The best review of the use of the tripartite classification in the thirteenth century remains that of Jean Morin, *Commentarius historicus*, V.25, pp. 319–321, but Morin, unaware of Alan's *Liber poenitentialis* or the twelfth-century canonists, believes that Peter of Poitiers was the first to use the scheme.

28. V. L. Kennedy, "Robert Courson on Penance," *Mediaeval Studies* 7 (1945): 290–336.

29. Peter of Poitiers, *Summa de confessione*, pp. 80–81: "Non videtur quod pro peccatis occultis debeat paenitens aliquis artari praecise ad aliquid genus satisfactionis nolens, sed redimere potest vel aliter compensare. Secus est, in manifestis, sicut est videre in sollemni paenitentia, quae et carena dicitur, quae iniungi solet pro peccatis enormioribus, ut pro parricidio. . . . Haec enim paenitentia certam habet formam et statuta. Similiter et minores homicidae et alii publice paenitentes quamdam habent certam formam; ut in die cineris eiecti de ecclesia cum certa forma. Cum certa forma aeque in die cenae recipiuntur. Et haec paenitentia dicitur publica non sollemnis. In multis quoque casibus multis ad tempus ingressus ecclesiae in paenitentia prohibetur." A. Teetaert, "Le 'Liber poenitentialis' de Pierre de Poitiers," in *Aus der Geisteswelt des Mittelalters: Studien und Texte; Martin Grabmann zur Vollendung des 60. Lebensjahres*, Beiträge zur Geschichte der Philosophie und Theologie des Mittelalters, suppl. 3 (1935), pp. 328–329, has dated it to the eve of the Fourth Lateran Council, 1210–1215. C. R. Cheney has placed it after the council, arguing that its citations of the "second Lateran" refer to what we call the fourth: "The Numbering of the Lateran Councils of 1179 and 1215," in *Medieval Texts and Studies* (Oxford, 1973), pp. 203–208. Peter's *summa* is, in any case, an awkward attempt, probably not composed much later than 1216, since a spate of better organized and more comprehensive *summae* were released soon after the council.

Peter explains confidently that secret penance is for secret sins, pu⎸⎸
for public; but who imposes the *carena*, again meaning solemn ⎸
ance, and on whom, lay or cleric? The definition is hardly com⎸
And while this solemn penance has perhaps such a "certain f⎸ ⎸"
that he does not describe it for his readers, the other public penai⎸⎸e,
though it has "quamdam . . . certam formam," does need some elaboration. It is nothing like Alan's punishment for choir monks, but
rather, oddly enough, very similar to the rite of solemn penance as we
must assume Peter knew it. In fact, there is no apparent difference at
all between Peter's solemn and nonsolemn public penance, except that
the latter should be applied for somewhat less heinous crimes. One
suspects that public nonsolemn penance is not a rite itself, but a "none
of the above," much like the informal penitential exclusion Peter
mentions at the end of this passage. The survival of that exclusion, a
little less complete than excommunication, is a sign of the continued
lack of distinction between the judicial and interior *fora*. In sum,
Peter's treatment of solemn penance is perhaps a little more confident
than Alan's, though still imprecise; his system of classification does
not encompass the full variety of public rites of penance he knows to
be practiced.

Two near contemporaries of Peter, Robert of Flamborough and
Thomas of Chobham, finally outlined the distinction in what became
its classic form. Here is Robert's formulation, composed just before
the Fourth Lateran:

> Some penance is solemn, some public, some private. Solemn is that
> which is done on Ash Wednesday, when the penitents are expelled
> from the church, with solemnity, in ashes and sackcloth. This also is
> public, because it is done publicly. Public and nonsolemn is that
> which is done before the church without the above-mentioned so-
> lemnity, like pilgrimage. Private is that which is done daily and
> privately before a priest. No one except a bishop or someone acting
> on his authority imposes solemn penance. . . . A simple priest may
> enjoin public penance, as well as private, and at any time.[30]

30. Robert of Flamborough, *Liber poenitentialis*, ed. J. J. Francis Firth, Pontifical Institute
of Mediaeval Studies, Studies and Texts, 18 (Toronto, 1971), V.236, p. 205: "Poenitentia alia
sollemnis, alia publica, alia privata. Sollemnis est quae fit in capite jejunii, quando cum
sollemnitate in cinere et cilicio ejiciuntur ab ecclesia poenitentes. Haec etiam est publica, quia
publice fit. Publica et non sollemnis est quae fit in facie ecclesiae sine supradicta sollemnitate,
ut peregrinatio. Privata est illa quae cotidie fit privatim coram sacerdote. Sollemnem poenitentiam non iniungit aliquis nisi episcopus vel aliquis ejus auctoritate. . . . Publicam poenitentiam, sicut et privatam, simplex iniungit sacerdos et quolibet tempore." This redaction was
probably prepared 1208–1213, according to Firth. Cf. Thomas of Chobham, *Summa confessorum*, ed. F. Broomfield, Analecta mediaevalia Namurcensia, 25 (Louvain, 1968), pp. 13–14.
Thomas seems to have been the first to put this classification at the beginning of his work, in a
comprehensive explanation of the species of penance.

Robert goes on to explain that solemn penance is not to be imposed on a cleric, and that the layman who incurs it may never repeat it, nor marry, nor return to secular business—though, he admits, the latter two restrictions are not very frequently enforced.[31] Robert wants the now carefully defined solemn penance to inherit the rigor of ancient penance in the books, but he freely concedes that the modern practice often departs from that bookish severity. Other theologians defended the new ways explicitly.

Thirteenth-century canonical and theological *summae* mostly reiterated the now tripartite formulation in its standard form.[32] Hostiensis noted that the distinction between solemn and nonsolemn penance was not well-drawn, but he was one of the few to worry aloud.[33] Many of the anonymous writers of short tracts on penance merely ignored the tripartite classification. Of course, after the first theological popularizations of the early decades of the thirteenth century, the tract writers settled down to emotional exhortations to confession or cursory summaries of puzzles of jurisdiction, restitution, and the keys. The limited aims of these works perhaps precluded any extended interest in outlining the types of penance.[34] The few manuals that do approach the subject take a different tack from the classic tripartite penance, and they tell us as much about the perceived classifications of penance and how they corresponded to reality as do the better known *summae* of Alexander of Hales or Aquinas, which simply endorsed the formula.

An anonymous tract surviving in two early thirteenth-century

31. Robert of Flamborough, *Liber poenitentialis*, V.237–9, pp. 205–207.

32. Ramón de Peñafort, *Summa de poenitentia et matrimonio* (Rome, 1603; repr. Farnborough, 1967), III.34, pp. 440–442; Albert the Great, *Commentarii in IV sententiarum*, ed. S. C. A. Borgnet, *Opera omnia* (Paris, 1894), vol. 29, IV. D.14 a.28, pp. 432–433; Goffredus Tranensis, *Summa super titulis decretorum* (Lyon, 1519; repr. Aalen, 1968), V.38, pp. 476–477; Thomas Aquinas, *Commentum in quatuor libros sententiarum magistri Petri Lombardi*, *Opera omnia* (Parma, 1858, repr. New York, 1948), IV D.14 q.1 a.5.2, vol. 7:2, pp. 694–695; Innocent V (Pierre de Tarentaise), *In IV libros sententiarum commentaria* (Toulouse, 1649–1652), IV D.14 q.1 a.7.2, vol. 4, p. 153; John of Freiburg, *Summa confessorum* (Augsburg, 1476), III.34.8; John of Erfurt, *Die Summa confessorum*, ed. N. Brieskorn (Frankfurt, 1980) I.1.2, vol. II:1, p. 49. See also Eudes de Cheriton, BN latin 2593, f. 7v; and Joseph Goering, "The *Summa de penitentia* of Magister Serlo," *Mediaeval Studies* 38 (1976): 8.

33. Hostiensis, *Summa aurea* (Venice, 1578, repr. Turin, 1963), V.56.55, cols. 1825–1826, remarks that some *improprie* use "solemn" and "public" interchangeably, or call monastic confinement "solemn" penance (e.g., Bernard of Pavia). Cf. Tancredus Bononiensis (d. 1234/6) on 2 Comp. 5.17.1 (=X.5.38.7), Bibl. Vat., Vat. lat. 1377, f. 95v, for a similar comment. In the passage cited and in his *In I–VI Decretalium libros commentaria* (Venice, 1581; repr. Turin, 1965), V. de poen. et rem. 7, f. 100, Hostiensis himself argues idiosyncratically that nonsolemn public penance cannot be imposed on priests "quia idem iudicium est de publica et solenni."

34. Typical are two versions of a tract edited by P. Michaud-Quantin, "Deux formulaires pour la confession du milieu du XIIIe siècle," *Recherches de théologie ancienne et médiévale* 31 (1964): 43–62, which expatiated on the perfect confession and the seven deadly sins.

northern French manuscripts describes an undifferentiated public penance comparable to that of Lanfranc's time. "Let us suppose, therefore, one who has committed homicide and confesses publicly. The priest imposes on him penance which is thus apportioned: In the first days let him perform the *carina*. . . . Penance completed, let him return home. . . . At the end of the year, let him be introduced into the church."[35] The sinner goes on to do six more years of penance. The author adds that he has "found" public penances (in the books he consulted, doubtless) that arranged the seven years of penance differently or specified only forty days.[36] He does not identify the *carina* or *carena* with solemn penance, as did Alan of Lille and Peter of Poitiers, but he considers it part of a public penance that can be imposed by any priest. The vagueness of the usage is further indication that the distinction between solemn and nonsolemn public penance is unclear. The author also describes what must be private confession, although, like Lanfranc, he does not explicitly propose a two-part system.[37] One passage on confession suggests a familiarity with a universal or nearly universal Lenten confession characteristic of a later date, possibly even after the Fourth Lateran. The priest, the author explains, should make sure the married man confesses first, and only then his wife.[38]

The longevity of the old canons and their multiyear penances despite the new theological distinctions has sometimes surprised historians, but the evidence that they survived through the thirteenth century is overwhelming. Robert de Sorbon might complain in the middle of the thirteenth century about the ignorance of priests who still thought every mortal sin required a seven-year penance in accordance with the books,[39] but the old tariffs were copied and recopied

35. Michaud-Quantin, "Un manuel de confession archaïque dans le manuscrit Avranches 136," *Sacris Erudiri* 17 (1966): 27–28: "Ponatur ergo aliquis, qui fecit homicidium et confitetur publice. Huic sacerdos poenitentiam iniungit, quae ita dividitur: Primus diebus faciet carinam. . . . Perfecta poenitentia, poterit redire in domum suam. . . . Completo anni circulo, in ecclesiam introducatur." The surviving copies are in Avranches BM 136 and BN latin 13582.

36. Michaud-Quantin, "Un manuel de confession archaïque," p. 28.

37. This and other "archaisms" in the text have led its editor to suppose that it must have been written no later than 1165 or so, but as Michaud-Quantin admits, there is no real *terminus ad quem* before the copying of the manuscripts themselves after 1200. In any case, at least two scribes thought the tract worth copying a full half-century after Michaud-Quantin's postulated date of composition. Michaud-Quantin, "Un manuel de confession archaïque," pp. 6, 53–54.

38. Michaud-Quantin, "Un manuel de confession archaïque," p. 54. The author cites the *Decretum*—Burchard's, not Gratian's—as his authority for confession at the beginning of Lent, but his subsequent words suggest that he considers lay confession at Lent to be in fact normal practice—an assumption very rare before 1200.

39. Robert de Sorbon, *De tribus dietis*, ed. F. Chambon, Collection de textes pour servir à l'étude et à l'enseignement de l'histoire (Paris, 1902), pp. 50–51.

in spite of these and similar objections. Bartholomew of Exeter, Alan of Lille, Robert of Flamborough, and Thomas of Chobham all quoted the canons, and their works survive in numerous manuscripts copied throughout the century.[40] In addition to the thirteenth-century text just cited, other minor mid-thirteenth-century tracts also continued to use the tariffs. An English "Master Serlo" writing after 1234 first repeated accurately and in full the new tripartite formula, which he probably knew from Ramón de Peñafort. But he quoted with approval the old canons stipulating that uxoricides, parricides, and so forth must enter a monastery or at least do public penance, canons that never distinguished secret from public crimes. Serlo did not bother to update them.[41] A very short tract copied in a manuscript near the end of the thirteenth century was perhaps more "archaic" than either of these, providing its readers with old tariffs, including punishments for pagan rites but not for usury, and distinguishing public from private penance only in the most general terms.[42] The author does not mention "solemn" penance. We need not see the survival of the canons as mindless antiquarianism on the part of provincial masters. A decretal of Gregory IX revived a twelve-year penance from the Carolingian council of Mainz, and toward the end of the thirteenth century, Hostiensis and John of Freiburg enjoined priests to know the old canons. Secret penances for secret sins are indeed "arbitrary," that is, at the priest's discretion, they said, but the canons do apply in public cases.[43] In short, scribes kept copying the canons because they were still useful, especially for the application of public penance.

Meanwhile, a surprising number of theologians continued to refer to solemn penance as in some way more truly "sacramental" than any other form. We have noted Lanfranc's belief that private penance did not require a priest; a half-century later, Peter Lombard added that

40. Cf. Longère, "Quelques *summa de poenitentia*, pp. 51–53, on the manuscript history and use of penitential canons in these works. The space devoted to the canons diminished in Robert's and Thomas's works. See Adrian Morey, ed., *Bartholomew of Exeter: Bishop and Canonist* (Cambridge, 1937), pp. 164–166, on the recopying of Bartholomew's penitential in the thirteenth century.

41. Joseph Goering, "The *Summa de penitentia* of Magister Serlo," *Mediaeval Studies* 38 (1976): 17.

42. BN n.a.l. 352, f. 27v. See A. Teetaert, "Quelques 'summae de paenitentia' anonymes dans la Bibliothèque nationale de Paris," in *Miscellanea Giovanni Mercati*, Studi et Testi, 122, 2: 337–339. For other examples of survival, see T. P. Oakley, "The Penitentials as Sources for Medieval History," *Speculum* 15 (1940): 211.

43. X.5.38.2, E. Friedberg, ed., *Decretalium collectiones*, Corpus Iuris Canonici, 2 (Leipzig, 1879), col. 884; Hostiensis, *Summa aurea*, 5.56.60, cols. 1837–1838; John of Freiburg, *Summa confessorum*, III.34.125. John of Erfurt, *Summa confessorum*, I.1.1 vol. 2:1, p. 35, says that priests should know the canons, but only as a way of understanding the differences between sins.

the reason solemn penance alone could not be repeated was *pro reverentia sacramenti*, a formulation repeated in the middle of the thirteenth century by Albert the Great and Pierre de Tarentaise, among others.[44] Robert of Flamborough asserted flatly that private penance was no sacrament, "nullum est sacramentum."[45] The *Glossa ordinaria* on Gratian's *Decretum* and several other mid-thirteenth-century writers were also explicit, offering the view that solemn penance may not be repeated because it is sacramental, "quia sacramentalis est."[46] These theologians did not elaborate their reasons for believing public penance more sacramental; it was something they simply assumed.

Such throwbacks to an earlier system of classification show more than the inconsistencies of theologians in the throes of adjustment. The tripartite system gained popularity quickly among the sophisticated schoolmen of Paris preparing compendia of penance and theology more because it explained contradictions in their sources than because it corresponded to the practices evolving before their eyes. As Jean Morin pointed out three hundred years ago, the distinction between solemn penance and nonsolemn public penance conveniently explained away old canons that contradicted each other over the rites and their applicability in different cases.[47] If one canon told the priest to impose public penance and another reserved it to the bishop, later theologians might reason that the canons were dealing with two separate rites. The same distinction also helped out where current practice contradicted the canons. The classification of penances evolved by a process of progressive pigeonholing. Private penance was defined first, then solemn penance, then, at last, nonsolemn public penance. Lanfranc, interested in private confession, briefly mentioned another kind of penance in an aside. Public penance was

---

44. Peter Lombard, *Sententiae*, IV D.14 c.4, p. 321; Albert the Great, *Commentarii in IV sententiarum*, IV D.4 a.27C, p. 451; Pierre de Tarentaise, *In IV libros sententiarum*, IV D.14 q.1 a.7.2, vol. 4, p. 153.

45. Robert of Flamborough, *Liber poenitentialis*, II.48, p. 84.

46. Rufinus of Bologna (d. 1192), *Summa decretorum*, C.33 q.3 D.2, p. 502; Johannes Teutonicus, *Decretum Gratiani nouissime post ceteras omnes impressiones unacumque glossis Joannis Teutonici et Bartholomei Brixiensis* (Venice, 1528), D.50 c.62, f. 83v; cf. a similar tack in Stephen of Tournai (d. 1203), *Die Summa über das Decretum Gratiani*, ed. J. F. von Schulte (Giessen, 1891, repr. Aalen, 1965), D.50 C.63, pp. 75–76. The idea even reappears in a tract surviving in fourteenth- and fifteenth-century MSS: BN latin 15162, f. 100v; see Teetaert, "Quelques 'Summae de paenitentia,'" pp. 330–333. In the late 1140s or 1150s, a master Simon stated flatly that only solemn penance should be called sacramental: Weisweiler, ed., *Maître Simon et son groupe*, p. 22. Contrary to Weisweiler's opinion, p. clii, that this view is rare even in the twelfth century, see Anciaux, *La théologie du sacrement de pénitence*, pp. 152–153, 365–366, for more examples. On the idea's relative decline after 1200, see A. Vanneste, "La théologie de la pénitence chez quelques maîtres parisiens de la première moitié du XIIIe siècle," *Ephemerides theologicae Lovanienses* 28 (1952): 31–32.

47. Morin, *Commentarius historicus*, V.25, pp. 322–323.

the other variety, and Lanfranc did not waste time describing it. Theologians like Alan then started to define solemn public penance in order to organize the varied cases they found in the books they consulted. The *carena* must be solemn, Alan reckoned, while tariffs for sins of thought must belong to private penance. Nonsolemn public penance long remained a "none of the above" category, as indeed all public penance had been in the twelfth century. Eventually Robert of Flamborough tried to define it, and by the middle of the century, Albert the Great discussed its varieties in some detail.[48]

But not *all* thirteenth-century writers papered over inconsistencies with such consummate skill, and the failures are occasionally telling. Public penance remained resistant to dissection. Priests still excluded parishioners from church, bishops still sent town rowdies on penitential pilgrimages, and it was often hard to say whether these were public or solemn penances, or even excommunications. This is not to argue that the changes in terminology meant little or that they reflect nothing more than an increasing preoccupation with classification and the reconciliation of authorities. For there were real changes in the practice of penance over the twelfth and thirteenth centuries, including an increase in the number of lay confessions. But the evolution in practice does not correspond at all to the evolution in theory. Clearly, we must start the analysis by freeing ourselves from the overly schematic views of some Scholastic theologians and recognize instead the real ambivalences behind their efforts.

Interior and Exterior Penance

Another distinction, even more awkward and confused, but just as widespread in early Scholastic theology, is the distinction between "interior" and "exterior" penance. While the distinction as such has been little discussed, the early Scholastic emphasis on interiority and its implications of moral individualism have rightly received a great deal of attention. To be sure, even early writers of penitentials, such as Burchard and Theodore of Canterbury, considered true contrition essential to true forgiveness.[49] But only twelfth-century theologians

48. Albert the Great, *Commentarii in IV sententiarum*, IV D.4 a.28, vol. 29, pp. 452–453. Albert distinguished public nonsolemn penance done by priests from public nonsolemn penance imposed by simple priests and often requiring a pilgrimage.

49. Pierre J. Payer, "The Humanism of the Penitentials and the Continuity of the Penitential Tradition," *Mediaeval Studies* 46 (1984): 340–354, argues that historians have underestimated the interest of the older *libri penitentiales* in contrition and the flexibility of satisfac-

developed a new theory of sin, guilt, and redemption, one that trie'
to identify the separate effects of contrition, confession, and satisfac
tion. Following Peter Abelard's strict identification of sin with intei
tion,[50] theologians came to distinguish the sinner's *culpa* (guilt) d(
serving damnation and the *poena* (penalty due).[51] Eventually th(
argued that purgatorial suffering might take care of temporal pen;
ties so long as true contrition inspired by grace earned forgiveness {
the *culpa*.[52] The guilt, not the temporal penalty, was the block t(
eternal salvation, and its cure, contrition or confession (depending on
the theologian), came to receive more attention than the satisfactions
that remitted the *poena*. So the new casuistical genre of confessors'
manuals taught techniques for teasing out confessions and for using
the information garnered in them to adapt the penance to the circumstances of the sin.[53] Private penance meant above all private *confession.*

Perhaps the most striking evidence of the new theology was the
growing devotional literature directed at laymen. Sermon *exempla* and
vernacular romances alike tried to teach the saving grace of tearful
confession.[54] Secrecy was the reassuring promise of the preachers and
storytellers. You could tell your confessor anything. He was your
friend, your comforter, your therapist (*medicus*). He would reveal
none of it. In fact, by the mid–thirteenth century, he was often a

---

tions, and that they have therefore exaggerated the difference between the earlier books and
the later confessors' manuals. But the real issue is not the recognition of contrition or the lack
of it, but the role theologians of each age allotted to satisfaction, or rather, the invention of a
clear distinction between the consequences of satisfaction and those of contrition. See Poschmann, *Penance and the Anointing of the Sick*, p. 141.

50. Abelard, *Ethics*, ed. and trans. D. Luscombe (Oxford, 1971), pp. 42–44, 54–56.

51. See Poschmann, *Penance and the Anointing of the Sick*, pp. 157–162; and Vogel, "Le
péché et la pénitence," in *Pastorale du péché*, ed. P. Delhaye et al., Bibliothèque de théologie,
série 2, Théologie Morale, 8 (Paris, 1961), p. 228, for summaries of the theological developments.

52. Abelard, *Ethics*, p. 88; Alan of Lille, *Liber poenitentialis* IV.44, p. 153, and *Summa
"Quoniam homines,"* ed. P. Glorieux, *Archives d'histoire doctrinale et littéraire du Moyen Age* 20
(1953): 356; A. Landgraf, *Dogmengeschichte der Frühscholastik* (Regensburg, 1952–1955), vol.
IV.2, pp. 161–171.

53. Michaud-Quantin's "A propos des premières Summae confessorum: Théologie et
droit canonique," *Recherches de théologie ancienne et médiévale* 26 (1959): 279–291, is the best
summary of the effect of the new theology on the genre.

54. For the *exempla* literature, see Jacques Berlioz, "'Quand dire c'est faire dire': *Exempla*
et confession chez Etienne de Bourbon," in *Faire croire: Modalités de la diffusion et de la réception
des messages religieux du XIIe au XVe siècle*, Collection de l'Ecole française de Rome, 51 (Rome,
1981), p. 332; Berlioz and Colette Ribancourt, "Images de la confession dans la prédication
au début du XIVe siècle: L'exemple de l'*Alphabetum Narrationum* d'Arnold de Liège," in
Pratiques de la confession, ed. Groupe de la Bussière (Paris, 1983), pp. 101–110; and Nicole
Bériou, "Autour de Latran IV (1215): La naissance de la confession moderne et sa diffusion,"
in *Pratiques de la confession*, p. 85. For the romances, see Payen, "La pénitence dans le contexte
culturel," pp. 402–403, 410–413.

mendicant friar from outside the parish. Often in vernacular stories, the confessor was a hermit, even more removed than any friar from the compromises and gossiping of the neighborhood.[55] Sinners must have yearned for privacy. Saints, like good friends, never told tales. Etienne de Bourbon told and retold the ancient story of a sinner tormented by his conscience but unable to bring himself to confess the crime. The man writes the sin on a piece of paper and, weeping, places it in the hands of the statue of a saint. Eventually someone comes and tries to read the paper, but finds it to be blank, erased by the forgiving saint.[56] In another oft-repeated story, a ship is battered by a storm, and one of the passengers, conscious that he is the Jonah endangering the lives of all, declares his crime aloud. The sea calms, and all on board miraculously forget his confession.[57] Confession redeems immediately. This lucky sinner does not follow Jonah into the belly of the whale. We note as well the longing for secrecy in a world that must have afforded very little of it. Doubtless, few trusted that their confessed sins would escape the round of gossip. Without the help of miracles, however, the Christian had no choice but to display the trust that was a form of friendship or *amicitia*. Sharing your secrets with someone is a great sign of love, explained one tract on penance. Confession would make God a secret friend.[58]

The private life protected here was not the world of the *familia* nor that of the neighborhood or the marketplace, as we today might define the private sphere. This is a definition of privacy quite different from that discussed by Georges Duby: Instead of the privacy of the household, we have the privacy of the soul. Early Scholastic theologians and their popularizers were so concerned to protect this inter-

---

55. In a late-thirteenth-century Franciscan collection of *exempla*, a husband suggests to his embarrassed wife that she confess to "one of the brothers who come each day and then leave." J. T. Welter, *Le speculum laicorum*, Thesaurus exemplorum, fasc. 5 (Paris, 1914), p. 30; Payen, "La pénitence dans le contexte culturel," p. 411.

56. A. Lecoy de la Marche, *Anecdotes historiques, légendes et apologues tirés du recueil inédit d'Etienne de Bourbon*, Société de l'histoire de France, publication 58 (Paris, 1877), III.4, pp. 155–156; T. F. Crane, ed., *The Exempla or Illustrative Stories from the Sermones Vulgares of Jacques de Vitry* (London, 1890; repr. New York, 1971), pp. 100, 121; Jean Gobi, *Scala celi* (Ulm, 1480), f. 43v; cf. Berlioz, "'Quand dire c'est faire dire,'" p. 332.

57. Lecoy de la Marche, *Anecdotes historiques,*, III.4, p. 160; Crane, *The Exempla or Illustrative Stories*, pp. 126–127; Caesarius of Heisterbach, *Dialogus miraculorum*, ed. J. Strange (Cologne, 1851), I.21, pp. 136–137; Gobi, *Scala celi*, f. 46r; cf. Berlioz and Ribancourt, "Images de la confession," p. 104.

58. BN latin 16435, f. 25v. Cf. Thomas Aquinas, *Summa theologiae*, III q.84 a.5 ad 2, "Requirit enim caritas quod homo doleat de offensa in amicum commissa, et quod amico homo reconciliari studeat," following the reading suggested by Pierre-Marie Gy, "Les définitions de la confession après le quatrième concile du Latran," in *L'aveu: Antiquité et Moyen-Age*, Collection de l'Ecole française de Rome, 88 (Rome, 1986), p. 294. Cf. also Robert Mannyng's *Handlyng Synne*, ed. Idelle Sullens, Medieval and Renaissance Texts and Studies, 14 (Binghamton, N.Y., 1983), p. 270, ll. 10859–60: "Penaunce pyneth thy flessh the fende/ And pleseth god and makth hym frende."

nal, secret world because they lumped together *all* external obligations and actions—to the family, to neighbors, to the church, and to
the king—into what they called "exterior" sin and penance. Thus,
the theological manifestation of the longing for privacy is the distinction that many theologians drew between interior and exterior penance. That classification had already been familiar to mid-twelfth-
century theologians and canonists.[59] Around 1200, it was the one that
many writers found most comprehensive and most satisfying. Alan of
Lille, for example, describes interior and exterior penance not as two
parts or varieties of the same thing but as two different ways of using
the same word. "Sometimes penance means the heart's contrition,
when someone bewails his crimes, not wanting to repeat those already
committed. . . . Or penance means the satisfaction accompanying
penance, which means penance [*poenitentia*] as in 'penalty binding
man' [*poena tenens hominem*]. This one is called exterior, the aforementioned interior."[60] Before we can distinguish different rites of penance used in different cases, Alan suggests, we must first establish
what we are talking about. Interior penance is not exactly private
penance, but rather the secret change in the sinner's heart. Exterior
penance is something a sinner is bound to do, "as the penalty binding
the man." The priest might assign a satisfaction to be done in private,
or the sinner might incur the penalty automatically, as in excommunication *latae sententiae*. Of course, satisfaction is related to contrition: "Satisfactions peculiar to the church are called penances because
they frequently proceed from interior penance."[61] But they are not
the same. The three types of ecclesiastical penance—solemn, nonsolemn public, and private—are *all* penances in the exterior sense.
They are all satisfactions imposed in one way or another by the
church. Behind them rests something more mysterious and sacred,
the conversion of the heart.

Peter Cantor uses "exterior penance" similarly, but without explic-

59. Hugh of Saint Victor, *De sacramentis Christianae fidei*, II, D.14 c.2, PL 176:554–555;
Peter Lombard, *Sententiae*, IV D.14 c.2.2, p. 316; IV D.17 c.1.13, p. 346; IV, D.20 c.2.2, p. 374.
Cf. also Peter Comestor's distinction between interior and exterior satisfaction, that is, contrition vs. confession and good works, *Tractatus de sacramentis*, p. 66*; Guy d'Orchelles' distinction between interior and exterior confession, that is, contrition and actual confession, *De
sacramento paenitentiae* (1215–1220), ed. D. and O. van den Eynde, Franciscan Institute Publications, Text series, 4 (St. Bonaventure, N.Y., 1953), p. 104; and Huguccio's distinction
between interior and exterior confession and satisfaction, cited by Anciaux, *La Théologie du
sacrement de la pénitence*, p. 444.

60. Alan of Lille, *Liber poenitentialis*, III.4, vol. II, p. 129: "Poenitentia aliquando cordis
contritio dicitur, quando quis deflet delicta, nolens amplius iterare commissa. . . . Vel poenitentia dicitur etiam satisfactio poenitentiam comitans; quae dicitur poenitentia quasi poena
tenens hominem. Haec dicitur exterior, praedicta vero interior."

61. Alan of Lille, *Liber poenitentialis*, III.6, vol. II, p. 130: "Satisfactiones vero ecclesiastice
proprie dicuntur poenitentiae, quia ex interiori poenitentia frequenter solent procedere."

itly dividing an interior from an exterior sense. He explains that a man may not undertake the care of souls or the religious life while bound by "exterior penance." "For how may someone who is in any way bound to make satisfaction penitentially presume to undertake the burden of pastoral care, or voluntarily take any vow?"[62] Exterior penance is essentially involuntary. It may be private or the talk of the town, but, like a lien on a house, it blocks any new undertaking of merit. We may recall Peter's distinction between private and solemn binding,[63] which is closer to Alan's interior and exterior senses than it is to tripartite penance. Private binding is voluntary; solemn binding is the decision of the priest and canons. Peter's *ligatio privata* is not quite the same as Alan's *penitentia interior*, for it embraces voluntary works, such as fasts and prayers, and even abstention from communion. But the solemn ligation is the same as Alan's exterior penance. Like Alan, Peter wants to set off the moral world of the individual from the interfering hand of any other human being.

Other writers preferred Alan's vocabulary. Pierre de Roissy, an early-thirteenth-century theologian who was strongly influenced by Robert Courson, again defined "exterior" penance as imposed works of satisfaction, such as fasts, vigils, prayers, and alms.[64] And two anonymous thirteenth-century tracts linked the distinction among exterior and interior penance to a distinction between the parts of penance, that is, contrition and satisfaction. In one: "Some penance is interior, some exterior. The interior is contrition . . . exterior penance also consists in two things: confession and satisfaction."[65] This usage subtly began to shift the meaning of the distinction away from Alan's intentions. For Alan, as we have seen, interior and exterior penance were not necessarily two stages in the same process, but two senses of the same word. For minor sins, one could have interior penance, that is, be contrite, without ever proceeding to confession and satisfaction. These anonymous authors, by contrast, were thinking of the actual procedure of private sacramental penance. They found it increasingly difficult to conceive of an interior world wholly beyond the priest's interference.

---

62. Peter Cantor, *Summa de sacramentis et animae consiliis*, 2, ed. J.-A. Duganquier, Analecta mediaevalia Namurcensia, 7 (Louvain, 1957), I.105, p. 164: "Quomodo enim presumet aliquis honus cure pastoralis suscipere vel aliquid voluntarie vovere, quod subitum erat, qui omnimodo tenetur ut penitentie satisfaciat?"

63. Peter Cantor, *Summa de sacramentis*, IV.141, p. 330; cf. Appendix II.6, p. 437.

64. BN n.a.l. 232, f. 111r.

65. BN latin 13582, f. 71v-72r: "Penitencia alia interior alia exterior. Interior est contricio . . . penitencia exterior, in duobus consistit, scilicet in confessione, et satisfactione." Very similar is BN latin 3238F, f. 86r.

In the same line of evolution away from Alan's definitions, Robert of Courson chose to speak not of exterior and interior penance but of the *forum penitentiale* of the church militant and the eternal election of God, "in which, without any preceding merits, the Lord through an infusion of grace . . . and internal contrition remits all sins of the penitent and afterward the priest in his *forum* has his own means of remitting the same sins."[66]

Robert posits another, still more secret, scene of judgment behind the penitential forum. Later in the thirteenth century, theologians and canonists would *contrast* the interior, penitential forum with the exterior, judicial forum. Yet Robert's explicit definition here of the relations between the sinner and God as a court, along the lines of the court of the priest, is significant for that future contrast. He took *penitentia interior* into the realm of judgment. Like the anonymous thirteenth-century authors cited above, Robert recognized a single process; first God grants contrition, then the priest remits the same sin.

A tract probably datable to the beginning of the fourteenth century went still further when it distinguished the interior penance necessary according to natural law, which is, it said, confession to God, from the exterior or sacramental penance necessary "from which God is made man," that is, the penance done through the intercession of the ministers of the keys.[67] Exterior penance is not simply satisfaction or even confession but the sacrament as a whole. Like Robert and unlike Alan or Peter, this writer makes interior penance legally obligatory, a debt owed the divine court. Unlike Robert, he also distinguishes interior penance from exterior historically. Interior penance belongs to natural law and presumably to Old Testament law; exterior penance derives from the law of the New Testament. We may note in passing that, paradoxically, the incarnation has the effect of imposing new obligations where none existed before. Typical of mid-thirteenth-century and fourteenth-century writers, this author resists Robert's circumscription of the power of the keys.

Thus, theologians from 1215 on tended to drift away from the early emphasis on an inward, purely voluntary contrition. Interior penance became instead a preliminary stage, first either in the history of man

66. BN latin 3258, f. 29v–30r: "in quo dominus sine omnibus meritis precedentibus per infusionem gratie . . . et contritionis interne remittit omnia peccata penitentis et postmodum sacerdos in suo foro habet suum modum remittendi eadem peccata."

67. "ex quo deus factus est homo"; BN latin 15162, f. 100r. This is a fifteenth-century MS; there are two fourteenth-century copies in Bibl. Maz. 924 and 986. The tract refers to Boniface VIII, f. 190v, but discusses solemn and other public penances at length, clear evidence of the continuing vitality of the early thirteenth-century ways of thought.

or in the story of each sinner's reconciliation. Such a retreat from early paeans to a pure contrition becomes more comprehensible when we remember its by-products. It could and did create impossible psychological pressures. Everyone had always expected the penitent to be contrite and to fear for his or her salvation; now theologians expected laymen and women to calculate that contrition precisely. Robert Courson demanded that those who had previously confessed and done works of penance "without charity" repeat the confession and satisfaction with contrition. And he posed his clerical readers a tougher question: Suppose one of your parishioners is not sure whether he is in charity, and asks you whether he may receive the host on the feast day? "This is very difficult to resolve. Nevertheless it seems to us that this should be said without prejudice: The priest ought not order anyone at the aforementioned juncture that he partake of the Eucharist. Rather he ought to leave him to his own conscience and his own judgment, and say to him that he shall consider whether in his conscience he senses celestial savor and gladness."[68] Robert adds that clerics should tell the parishioner that if he does feel his heart hardened, it would be dangerous indeed to receive communion. For a writer who could think so practically about day-to-day problems such as usury and indulgence hawkers, this is a boldly unrealistic answer.

Peter Cantor, like Robert an apt critic of contemporary society, springs another kind of psychological trap. Peter asks whether the living can do more help to a soul in purgatory with greater suffrages like prayers and fasts than with lesser. Yes, Peter answers, not only do greater exterior afflictions, fasts, or alms help more, but the more the charity, the faster the soul escapes from purgatory. But there is a catch: "Yet everyone should attend to this for greater merit: Whatever is done should be done out of charity. For if the increase of prayer or sacrifices comes from natural affection, by which someone is moved toward one individual more than the rest, it will not make an increase in merit."[69] Like Robert, Peter demands a minute calculus of emotions. The more the son fears for the father because he is his father, the less all those suffrages will do any good. These writers expect an impossible level of soul-searching by laymen. It is the price of the

68. Kennedy, "Robert Courson on Penance," 299: "Hoc soluere difficillimum est; tamen nobis sine preiudicio uidetur hic dicendum quod sacerdos non debet iniungere alicui in predicto articulo constituto ut accedat ad eucharistiam; immo debet eum sue relinquere conscientie et proprie arbitrio et ei dicere ut attendat utrum in conscientia sentiat illum celestem saporem et iocunditatem."

69. Peter Cantor, Summa de sacramentis, I.109, p. 184: "Hoc tamen ad meritum maius attendat quilibet, quod ex caritate fiat quicquid fit. Nam si ex naturali affectione, qua quis mouetur plus erga unum quam erga reliquum, prouenit illud crementum uel suffragiorum uel crutiatuum, non faciet crementum in merito."

emphasis on intention. Later theologians told laymen to forget the vagaries of their emotions and obey the law.[70]

God, Neighbor, and Church

We can trace a similar evolution away from the claims of the heart in another system of classification intended to balance them with the claims of society, with the need to show sin atoned for and crime punished. The schema appears sometimes as a pair, sometimes as a trio: our duties to God and to neighbor, or our duties to God, to neighbor, and to the church. Remarkably, the first theologians who used it did not suggest any correspondence between offenses against the church and those sins scandalizing the whole church that required public penance, or even a correspondence between offenses against neighbor and either public or private sins. This scheme developed quite independently, but its evolution nevertheless reflected some of the same doubts about privatizing penance that we have seen in "tripartite penance." Following the development of this popular classification helps us probe further the reasons for the failure of a theology of private penance and also helps us understand the need for a new theology of the keys and the two *fora*.

Around 1170, Peter of Poitiers, a master of theology in Paris and future chancellor of Notre-Dame, and not to be confused with the canon of Saint Victor of the same name who wrote a confessors' manual, applied the three-part classification with great clarity but little specificity. "When someone sins against his neighbor in mortal sin, he offends three persons: God, the church, and neighbor. . . . Therefore if he wishes to make satisfaction to God, he should be deeply contrite and do penance for his sin. . . . Then he shall make satisfaction to the church by confessing his sin and doing temporal penance. Finally he shall make satisfaction to the neighbor he sinned against."[71] One satisfies one's neighbor, Peter continues, by asking his

---

70. See Michaud-Quantin, "La conscience individuelle et ses droits chez les moralistes de la fin du Moyen-Age," in *Universalismus und Partikularismus im Mittelalter*, Miscellanea mediaevalia, 5 (Berlin, 1968), pp. 50–55. Theologians and canonists alike agreed with Gratian (C.28 q.1 c.14 p.5) that "omne quod contra conscientiam fit, edificat ad gehennam," but emphasized the unreliability of the untutored conscience, and the necessity of relying on the decisions of the church and one's pastor in particular. Cf. also Roberto Rusconi, "De la prédication à la confession: Transmission et contrôle de modèles de comportement au XIIIe siècle," in *Faire croire: Modalités de la diffusion et de la réception des messages religieux du XIIe au XVe siècle*, Collection de l'Ecole française de Rome, 51 (Rome, 1981), pp. 81–82.

71. Peter of Poitiers, *Sententiarum libri quinque*, III.16, PL 211:1077: "quando aliquis peccat in proximum suum mortali peccato, tres personas offendit, Deum, Ecclesiam, prox-

forgiveness. The appeal of the scheme lay in its ability to explain the different stages of penance. Why need a sinner go to confession, perform satisfactory acts, and make peace when his contrition alone, according to early Scholastic thought, had ensured reconciliation with God? Here was the answer. Peter does not distinguish much between types of sins and the type of reconciliation they require because he has focused his attention solely on sins against neighbors. What is clear is that reconciliation with God is presacramental.

Around twenty-five years later, Alan of Lille applied the classificatory scheme, now reduced to sins against God and sins against neighbor, not like Peter of Poitiers to differentiate stages of penance but instead to differentiate types of sins, precisely the point that Peter failed to address.[72] Alan was trying to explain why penances are imposed for exterior sins like theft rather than interior ones like avarice. To a thinker trained in Abelard's teaching, after all, sin is culpable because it represents the heart's contempt of God. Theft is wrong because it is an act of avarice. Alan's response appeals to our duties to other people.

On this it must be said that in exterior sins, we sin against God and neighbor: against God, because we act contrary to divine precept, against neighbor, by bad example. Guilt [reatus] against God is indeed remitted through interior contrition with respect to the guilt, that is, so far as it concerns the debt of eternal punishment and thus is remitted with respect to God. But because he has sinned against his neighbor, there remains penance to be imposed on him. But by interior sins we do not sin except against God because in this type of sin, we do not set an example of sinning for a neighbor.[73]

imum. . . . Si ergo Deo velit satisfacere, oportet ut graviter conteratur et poeniteat de peccato suo. . . . Deinde oportet ut satisfaciat Ecclesiae confitendo peccatum et poenitentiam temporalem agendo. Demum oportet ut satisfaciat proximo in quem peccavit." For the author and date of this work, see Philip S. Moore, *The Works of Peter of Poitiers, Master in Theology and Chancellor of Paris (1193–1205)*, Publications in Mediaeval Studies, 1 (Notre Dame, Ind., 1936), pp. 21, 27–48.

72. Hödl, *Die Geschichte der scholastischen Literatur und der Theologie der Schlüsselgewalt*, p. 238, argues that Alan's scheme found favor among other theologians once the third term, sins against the church, was added. But Peter of Poitiers had already established the three-part version, and, in any case, the scheme was very significantly modified in thirteenth-century theology, as we shall see.

73. Alan of Lille, *Liber poenitentialis*, III.3, vol. II, pp. 128–129: "Ad hoc dicendum est quod in exterioribus peccatis, peccamus in Deum et proximum. Contra Deum, quia agimus contra divinum praeceptum; contra proximum per pravum exemplum. Per contritionem vero interiorem remittitur reatus in Deum, quoad reatum, id est quantum ad debitum poenae aeternae et sic remissum est quoad Deum. Sed quia peccavit contra proximum, restat poenitentia ei infligenda. Peccatis vero interioribus non peccamus nisi in Deum, quia per hujus modi peccatum, non proponimus proximo exemplum peccandi."

In his response, Alan welds together two separate ideas. Fir⸱ argues that there are two different kinds of sins: interior and ex⸱ Exterior sins are those in which we sin against our neighbor as ⸱ against God. Our neighbor suffers by our bad example; so, ⸱ Alan, there are no "victimless crimes." Here we have a problem rior sins are not necessarily public. The point of the *quaesti⸱* explain the punishment of theft, homicide, and so forth, not to ⸱, ⸱;⸱ guish notorious theft from secret theft. So how does the neighbor suffer from the bad example of a secret crime? Surely there are some external acts that neither injure another human being directly nor are known to anyone. It was difficult to cover every type of sin using this scheme of classification.[74]

Alan then returns to Peter of Poitiers's idea that God and man both demand requital for the wrong done to them, but in different ways. A sin will, by definition, offend God; it may also offend man as well. To disobey the supreme being in the least degree incurs the supreme penalty, *debitum poenae aeternae*, that is, the *reatus*. Injuries against human beings, on the other hand, require only a temporal payment, the one that the penitent makes by completing the round of satisfactions (restitution, fasting, alms, or whatever) imposed by the human priest. The priest who assigns penance for a sin confessed to him actually collects a fine on behalf of the church militant, or indeed on behalf of the "neighbor," but not on God's behalf. The rite of private penance itself remains for Alan chiefly a social institution. Beyond and behind it still lay interior penance and the secret life of the heart of an individual man. To recapitulate, we have interior penance (in Alan's sense) to pay God for the *reatus* or eternal penalty of interior sins, and interior and exterior penance to pay God and neighbor respectively for the eternal and temporal penalty of exterior sins.

Several writers more or less contemporary with Alan worked with one or the other elements of his synthesis, but they did not combine them into a comprehensive theology of sin, guilt, and punishment, as he had attempted. Some were interested in the classification of sins. Peter Cantor, for instance, used an older three-part classification, sins against God, ourselves, and our neighbors, to organize the bulk of his

---

74. One southern French synodal statute did bring in a fourth category, sins against self, in an attempt to account for all types of sins. All sins offended God; some, like obstinacy, offended the church; some, like rapine, offended one's neighbor; some, like fornication, offended one's self as well: Mansi 24:981–995 (Rodez, 1289). See R. Foreville, "Les statuts synodaux et le renouveau pastoral du XIIIe siècle dans le Midi de la France," in *Le credo, la morale, et l'inquisition*, Cahiers de Fanjeaux, 6 (Toulouse, 1971), pp. 145–146. But the difference between sins against God and sins against the church remained unclear.

summa on penance;[75] an anonymous late twelfth-century writer imitated Peter's scheme on a smaller scale.[76] This might help take care of those victimless crimes that did not set a bad example, but Alan doubtless avoided it because it was inconsistent with the interior and exterior sins and penances. Some theologians, on the other hand, used only the second element in Alan's synthesis, the concepts of *reatus* or eternal penalty, and the temporal penalty. Near the end of the twelfth century, for example, Senatus, the prior of Worcester, defended remissions of imposed penance because that penance was only a human institution. "In these cases bishops do not remit the guilt or the penalty with which we are held liable to God, although they may waive any which man imposes. For the penalty is twofold: God inspires the first through remorse, and the priest imposes the second—in alms, vigils, fasts in sackcloth and ashes—for a certain number of years or days which are called penitential and which, when they are relaxed, are said to remit penance on penitential days."[77] The terminology is slightly different from Alan's, but the concept is very similar. We are bound to God in both guilt (*culpa*) and eternal penalty (*poena*). We are bound to man by a temporal *poena* set by the priest. What a man imposes, a man may forgive. Senatus's and Alan's formulation limits the priest's power of the keys and, in Senatus's case, defends indulgences by circumscribing their effect. At the beginning

75. Peter Cantor, *Summa de sacramentis*, 2:220–278. John Baldwin claims that, around 1200, Peter, among others, linked a division between sins against God and sins against the church to another more fundamental division, that between interior and exterior penance; he argues that this theology eventually led to the division of two *fora*: *Masters, Princes, and Merchants: The Social Views of Peter the Chanter and His Circle* (Princeton, N.J., 1970), 1: 51. I have not found such a synthesis in Peter, and indeed it is not quite accurate for Alan either. It is important to recognize the difference between the early distinction of interior and exterior penance and a later distinction between the two *fora* or rites of penance.

76. Michaud-Quantin, "Un manuel de confession archaïque," 19. A twelfth-century English writer used the same trio—God, self, and neighbor—to classify the types of tears of penitence we owe to each ("lacrime compunctionis nobis ipsis . . . lacrimas compassionis debemus proximis; lacrimas deuotionis deo"): A. Wilmart, "Un opuscule sur la confession composé par Guy de Southwick vers la fin du XIIe siècle," *Recherches de théologie ancienne et médiévale* 7 (1935): 342. Here the distinction is not applied to any theological argument, but it shows the idea of divided duties in circulation well before Alan applied it.

77. P. Delhaye, "Deux textes de Senatus de Worcester sur la pénitence," *Recherches de théologie ancienne et médiévale* 19 (1952): 206–207: "pontifices in casibus istis nec culpam remittunt nec penam qua tenemur obnoxii Deo, quamquam illam relaxent quam imponit homo. Est quippe duplex pena: primam inspirat Deus per compunctionem, secundam infligit sacerdos in elemosinis, uigiliis, ieiuniis in cinere et cilicio, sub certo annorum numero vel dierum qui penitentiales dicuntur, quos, cum relaxant, penitentiam in dies penitentiales remittere dicuntur." What are the *dies penitentiales*? Perhaps Lent, or more generally the period that the sinner spends in the status of penitent; these might be identical. In Senatus's traditional view of the sacrament, the sinner would normally spend a certain number of days or years as a recognized penitent before being absolved and returned to the full status of communicant Christian.

of the thirteenth century, however, only Alan had drawn this kind of discussion of the keys into classifications of species of sins and penance.[78] In a sense, Alan had linked the fortunes of his classification to his teaching on the keys.

Pierre de Roissy's treatment of the problem, written shortly before 1215, is so similar to Alan's that we must suspect Alan's influence, though for the most part Pierre used Robert of Flamborough's *summa* as his model.[79] Pierre does not distinguish two types of sins, only two offenses in the same sin. "When a man sins, he does wrong against God and neighbor: against God because he acts contrary to divine precept, against neighbor through bad example."[80] Otherwise his analysis is identical to Alan's, and certainly represents no improvement. The sinner's repentence remits the *reatus* or *debitum poene eterne* with regard to God. The priest imposes a greater or lesser satisfaction for the debt to neighbor.

Thomas of Chobham was the next writer to offer a synthesis, and the results are superficially similar to Alan's. It looks like the only change is to restore the trio in Peter of Poitiers's version, speaking of offenses against God, our neighbor, and the church. Sometimes, he explains, we sin against the first, sometimes the first and second, sometimes against all three. "When only God is offended by a sin, satisfaction is owed to God alone; when a neighbor is harmed as well, satisfaction is owed to the neighbor. Each of these can be done in private. But when the whole Church is offended, then satisfaction must be made through either public or solemn penance."[81] It seems at first that Thomas has simply improved on Peter's and Alan's formulations by differentiating clearly between the different types of offenses. Though Thomas does not discuss explicitly *how* we sin against God, neighbor, or church, his version suggests that he distinguishes sins setting a bad example, those against the church, which are to be paid for publicly, from those injuring a neighbor, which are to be paid

---

78. Delhaye, "Deux textes de Senatus de Worcester," p. 212, suggests that Senatus in his treatment of *culpa* and *poena* distinguished interior and exterior sins and penances, but this is an extrapolation.

79. For the relation between Pierre and Robert and the dating of both, see Stephan Kuttner, "Pierre de Roissy and Robert of Flamborough," *Traditio* 2 (1944): 493, 498; and F. Firth, "More about Robert of Flamborough's Penitential," *Traditio* 17 (1961): 532.

80. BN n.a.l. 232, f. 109r: "Cum homo peccat, delinquit contra deum, et contra proximum, contra deum quia agit contra diuinum preceptum, contra proximum, per prauum exemplum."

81. Thomas of Chobham, *Summa confessorum*, p. 13: "Quando autem offenditur deus tantum per peccatum, debet satisfieri soli deo. Quando autem leditur proximus, debet satisfieri proximo, et utrumque istorum potest fieri in priuato. Quando autem offenditur tota ecclesia, tunc satisfaciendum est vel per publicam penitentiam vel per sollemnem."

for privately. The problem cases, those which are neither public nor injure anyone, are presumably sins against God. For Thomas removes any link between sins against God and interior sins and penance; indeed, he avoids any discussion of interior and exterior worlds entirely.

This change is subtle but significant. What had been a classification of senses of the word penance now became a classification of rites of penance. For Alan, the crucial task had been to divide the interior life of sinful intentions and mental conversion from the external world of acts and punishments, whether public or private, ecclesiastical or secular. That external world was inevitably a social world, and so, to a mind steeped in Abelardian moral theology, inevitably insignificant. The threefold distinction, by contrast, obviously weakened the force of the contrast between divine and human obligations. At the same time as it threatened the primacy of the secret life of the soul, Thomas's version also altered Alan's concept of duties to neighbor. Alan made no distinction between an external life among neighbors and the public life visible to the whole church or city. The only private world that mattered was that of the individual soul's communion with God. He drew no connections between the various obligations of family, friendship, church, or politics. And Peter of Poitiers had even described offenses against a neighbor as one step *more public* than offenses against the church. But for Thomas and others who cared deeply about setting private sacramental penance apart from public rites, a different line had to be drawn between private and public moral life. Duties to neighbor became part of a new private morality. Public life, where crimes had to be paid for publicly, might be called the city or it might be called the church. That is why solemn public penance was imposed for crimes that offended "the whole city" or the church; sometimes the two might be practically identical. Life with family and neighbors was another matter. This smaller world had important responsibilities, too, but they were not responsibilities to a community, secular or divine. Thomas was not the first to use a three-part distinction among duties to God, neighbor, and the church, but he was the first to carve out within that distinction a sphere of private morality, a sphere guarded by the sanctions of private penance. This is a change worth keeping in mind when we examine the changing boundaries of private and public life in contemporary northern French cities.

In one important respect, Thomas clung to the idea of a secret life of the soul. Sins against God alone remained unrecoverable by any human penal institution, whether private or public, ecclesiastical or secular. Private sacramental penance was for offenses against one's neighbor.[82] A couple of anonymous mid-thirteenth-century writers took the last step. The priest might now collect God's own debts. In doing so, the priest should impose penances, explains one author, that are the contrary of the penitent's sin. If the sinner offended in giving others a bad example, he must give a good example by doing public penance. Private penance, too, must correspond to the nature of the offense. "Because the sinner has offended God, let one impose prayer; because he has offended his neighbor, let him impose contributions to the church and other works of mercy; because he has sinned against his own body with illicit pleasure, let him impose fasts and those which pertain to pain of the flesh."[83] Here we return to the earlier trio of God, neighbor, and self, but the old-fashioned air is only superficial. Duties to church or city have already been dealt with as public sins that incur public penance. The author prefers to focus on the first two-thirds of Thomas's trio, and he expands it again to three. But unlike Thomas, he does not fence off duties to God from private penance. The priest now imposes the prayers that Thomas— and certainly Alan—would have expected the penitent to impose on himself. Private sacramental penance has swallowed up the still more private world of the soul.

A quick look at more famous thirteenth-century theologians will show how the new way of looking at duties to God, neighbor, and church had taken hold. In a telling formulation, Alexander of Hales distinguished the supremely sacramental reconciliation to God from the reconciliation to the church. "It is one thing to speak of penance as satisfaction to the Church, another to speak of it as sacrament." We must confess interior as well as exterior sins because penance was a sacrament reconciling Christians to God as well as the means of recon-

---

82. We may note the early-thirteenth-century hesitance of William of Middleton, *Quaestiones de sacramentis*, ed. C. Piana and G. Gal, Bibliotheca Franciscana Scholastica medii aevi, 22–23 (Quaracchi, 1961), VI p.3 q.15, pp. 1052–1053: "duplex est poenitentia: quaedam quae solummodo consistit in contritio, quaedam quae consistit in contritione, confessione et satisfactione; et utraque est sacramentum; sed primo modo sumpta non est sacramentum Ecclesiae, sed secundo modo." This rather old-fashioned writer considers reconciliation with God both sacramental and nonsacramental.

83. BN latin 14891, f. 298r-v: "Quia peccator deum offendit iniungat ei orationes, quia proximum offendit iniungat ei ecclesias, et alia misericordie opera, quia in corpus proprium peccauit per illicitam delectationem iniungat ei ieiunia et ea que ad carnis afflictionem pertinent." BN latin 14927, f. 176v, has a very similar passage. BN latin 14927 tract is much shorter, only two folios long, f. 175–176, but is evidently not a simple extract from the longer BN latin 14891. Possibly its compiler ran together short excerpts from BN latin 14891 and other manuscripts. (Teetaert, "Quelques 'summae de paenitentiae,'" pp. 320–321, 329–330, lists them as separate treatises and does not notice their relationship.) The *ecclesias* that the priest was directed to impose were contributions to the building of churches, a common means of paying satisfaction and earning indulgences.

ciling Christians to the church.[84] When Bonaventure discussed the obligation to restore ill-gotten gains, he carefully distinguished a duty to God fulfilled in sacramental satisfaction from a duty to neighbor fulfilled extrasacramentally by restitution.[85] We have come full circle. Where previously the sacrament settled debts to neighbor and the church, now it settles debts to God and the church. Of course, contrition was still an essential element in reconciliation with God; the uncontrite sinner who performed sacramental penance might be apparently reconciled with the church, but he certainly did not receive remission of his sins. If the sacrament proceeded properly, however, it made peace between the sinner and God.

The shift in the meaning of the classification had taken place quickly. Alan had hardly built it up from elements commonplace in late-twelfth-century theology when Thomas of Chobham set it on a radically different course. After Peter of Roissy, Alan's version never reappeared. Its quick demise clearly was linked to the failure of its circumscribed theology of the keys. As is well known, most theologians until 1215 or so taught that the priest only imposed satisfaction for the temporal penalty (*poena*) due sin. From the 1170s, a newly defined purgatory was understood to inflict temporal punishments on sinners who in contrition on earth had already satisfied the eternal penalty. Some theologians described the priest's task as substituting suffering here and now for suffering in purgatory, just as those inventing purgatory had described its function as substituting suffering there for suffering here. One temporal penalty might be exchanged for another.[86] The early theology of the keys supposed still that hu-

84. Alexander of Hales, *Glossa in quatuor libros sententiarum Petri Lombardi*, Bibliotheca Franciscana Scholastica medii aevi, 15 (Quaracchi, 1957), IV D.16.1, p. 253: "Aliter est enim loqui de paenitentia ut est satisfactivum Ecclesiae et aliter ut est sacramentum." See José Luis Larrabe," Teologia de la penitencia y de la confesión segùn S. Buenaventura," *Estudios Franciscanos* 77 (1976): 194. Alexander's *Quaestiones disputatae "antequam esset frater"*, Q.56 d.3 m.2, vol. II, pp. 1086–1087, eventually comes to a similar conclusion. Though he notes that "Deo autem fit reconciliatio per contritionem, Ecclesiae per confessionem," he argues that every mortal sin offends the church as well as God, and therefore he notes, "necessaria est confessio non tantum peccatorum exteriorum, sed etiam interiorum," contradicting Alan directly.

85. Bonaventure, *Commentaria in quatuor libros sententiarum magistri Petri Lombardi*, *Opera omnia* (Quaracchi, 1889), IV D.15 p.2 a.2 1.4, pp. 374–375. Bonaventure admits that restitution may be considered part of satisfaction in the general sense, "pars satisfactionis communiter . . . sumtae." Bossy, "The Social History of Confession," pp. 25–26, has taken this to mean that laymen commonly mistook restitution for penance. But Bonaventure probably only meant that there are narrower and wider senses of the word, and if he had any misconceptions in mind, they were likely those of earlier Scholastic theologians like Peter Cantor. Actually, Peter's discussion of the excommunicant who wants absolution and offers restitution but not repentance, *Summa de sacramentis*, IV.148, pp. 360–361, is much better evidence for Bossy's contention.

86. See Lea, *A History of Auricular Confession*, 1: 140–141; Payen, "La pénitence dans le contexte culturel," p. 407; and Phillipe Delhaye, "Deux textes de Senatus de Worcester,"

man relations in every sphere were regulated by a calculus of debts and satisfactions. Pain paid for pain. Early Scholastic theologians like Alan of Lille who introduced interiority into their discussions of penance had not intended to link that internal world of remorse and contrition to the external routine of offense and satisfactory repayment. Early Scholastic theology considered interior contrition still more private than private sacramental penance. By contrast, the revised thirteenth-century theology of the keys and the revised calculus of duties to God and neighbor drew interior and exterior duties alike under the wing of private sacramental penance and the personal confessor. That redefined penance could now reach to offenses against God himself. Peter Cantor's and Robert of Flamborough's encouragement of individual lay soul-searching was impossible to sustain. Duty to God, once a personal and truly secret and individual matter, now became subject to the same sacramental system as public morality. The sacramentalization of private morality did not destroy theologians' belief in the necessity of true contrition—nothing could—but it did reveal a deep ambivalence about secrecy and public exposure. Behind all the praise of contrition lurks a longing for public humiliation.

The Two Fora and Theological Ambivalence

By the 1230s and 1240s, theologians and canonists articulated in concert with the new theology of the keys a new distinction between the penitential and judicial *fora*.[87] This distinction, now well known to historians of medieval theology, is not to be confused with the older distinction between interior and exterior penance so popular until around 1215 or so. The old "interior penance" had been the secret, unsacramental, saving contrition that brought peace with God. The new penitential or interior forum as it developed in the thirteenth century referred instead to private sacramental penance, which in

---

p. 224, among others for the priest's power of remission; See Michaud-Quantin, *Sommes de casuistique et manuels de confession*, pp. 19–20; and J. Le Goff, *La naissance du Purgatoire* (Paris, 1981), pp. 388–395, for the application of that power to purgatory.

87. Hödl, *Die Geschichte der scholastischen Literatur und der Theologie der Schlüsselgewalt*, p. 373, argues that Guillaume d'Auxerre's *Summa aurea* (1215–1229) marks the end of early Scholastic theology with its clear separation of the power of excommunication from the power of the keys in penance; cf. also A. Vanneste, "La théologie de la pénitence chez quelques maîtres parisiens," p. 49; François Russo, "Pénitence et excommunication: Etude historique sur les rapports entre la théologie et le droit canon dans le domaine pénitentiel du IXe au XIIIe siècle," *Recherches de science religieuse* 33 (1946): 450; and Elisabeth Vodola, *Excommunication in the Middle Ages* (Berkeley, Calif., 1986), pp. 42–43.

Thomas of Chobham's terms reestablished peace with God and neighbor. The exterior or judicial forum dealt with offenses against the church. The new distinction between the *fora* was not a refinement of the old distinction between interior and exterior penance,[88] since both *fora* were really heirs of exterior penance in the old sense. Like Thomas of Chobham's new trio and like the theology of the keys, the distinction between *fora* marked a real departure from earlier thinking.

So much for a summary of the change; we may now look at the reasons for it. Robert of Courson's treatise shows the system in transition on the eve of the Fourth Lateran. Several times he refers to the "penitential forum," especially in his treatment of problems of restitution.[89] He does not use the term "judicial forum," and he seems to prefer "penitential forum" to describe the rights of the priest in assigning restitution precisely because there the obligations of the sinner were more clear-cut. Restitution, as we shall shortly see, was not flexible or "arbitrary," unlike the satisfaction imposed by a priest. It was an absolute debt due before any satisfaction, any penance, private or public, might be allowed. No wonder Robert found the legal analogy suggested by the word "forum" apt for penance. He contrasts the penitential forum not with the judicial forum but explicitly with a still higher scene of judgment in heaven, the divine election by which God infuses the grace of contrition without any preceding merit of the sinner.[90] Robert recognizes by implication a threefold system: an interior penance, a penitential forum, and exterior law. Very quickly other writers would push aside interior penance and focus on the two laws. Increasingly, theologians as well as canonists treated penance as a species of law.[91]

The exterior forum came to be defined as the sphere of excommunication, the interior as that of penance. It was a distinction that left public penance in a kind of limbo. Alexander of Hales suggested that public penance belonged to both the penitential and judicial *fora*, but this solution never became accepted.[92] Thomas Aquinas found

88. This is contrary to suggestions by Baldwin, *Masters, Princes, and Merchants*, 1: 51–52; and Charles Munier, "Discipline pénitentielle et droit pénal ecclésial: Alliances et différenciation," *Concilium* 107 (1975): 25–26.

89. Kennedy, "Robert Courson on Penance," p. 334.

90. BN latin 3258, f. 29v.

91. For a full account of the increasingly juridical literature of penance, see Michaud-Quantin, *Sommes de casuistique et manuels de confession*, pp. 23–24, 34–36, 42–43; see also his "A propos des premières Summae confessorum," pp. 300–305; also Joseph Goering, "The *Summa* of Master Serlo and Thirteenth-Century Penitential Literature," *Mediaeval Studies* 40 (1978): 305–307.

92. Alexander of Hales, *Quaestiones disputatae "antequam esset frater"*, Q.56 d.3 m.2, vol. II, p. 1087.

himself hard put to explain the existence of a public penance, since penance was the "occult forum."[93] The distinction between the two *fora* did clarify the status of private sacramental penance, the sphere of our duties to neighbor, but it left the duties to the church rather unclear. What was the difference between excommunication and public penance? Several thirteenth-century writers found it difficult to explain. At the beginning of the century, Peter Cantor wondered why parish priests had the right to suspend parishioners from entrance to the church—then a common practice—when they did not have the right to excommunicate. And if a bishop could delegate his power of excommunication to a subordinate—also very common—could such a delegate subdeacon, or even a layman, impose penances as well? Peter was probably thinking of cases reserved to the bishop, but "it is difficult to know."[94] Senatus of Worcester worried about the same problem: How can a bishop delegate jurisdiction over public sins? The practice seemed to conflict with the teaching on the keys applicable to private sins and private penance.[95] Writers discussing the keys came to lump together public penance and excommunication.[96] In a typical formulation, an anonymous author remarked that one could impose excommunication to force a recalcitrant wrongdoer to undergo solemn penance.[97]

In practice and in theory the line between excommunication and public penance remained obscure; at times it may have been difficult to distinguish excommunication from penance. In theory, public penances should be voluntary, but even theologians were willing to stretch this requirement. Scholastic theologians and canonists eventually used the epicycles of orders and jurisdiction to help clarify the rights to impose private and public penance and excommunication,[98] but the sheer complexity of their responses indicates the difficulties they faced. Like "tripartite penance," the two *fora* and the trio of "God, neighbor, and the church" were inadequate solutions concealing a confused theology.

93. Thomas Aquinas, *Commentum in quatuor libros sententiarum*, IV D.14 q.1 a.5, vol. 7:2, pp. 694–695. Thomas asks how solemn penance is possible if penance is the occult forum; he responds that solemn penance "quantum ad injunctionem exigit forum occultum . . . sed executio non exigit forum occultum; et hoc non est inconveniens." Cf. Bernard of Pavia (d. 1213), *Summa decretalium*, V.33, p. 269: penances are imposed by "occulto iudicio."

94. "Difficile est intelligere"; Peter Cantor, *Summa de sacramentis*, vol. IV.141–142, pp. 334–337.

95. Delhaye, "Deux textes de Senatus de Worcester," p. 218.

96. See, e.g., Pierre of Roissy, BN n.a.l. 232, f. 115r.

97. BN latin 15162, f. 100v. This is a fifteenth-century MS, but the text also exists in fourteenth-century copies.

98. The concepts of orders and jurisdiction actually predated the full definition of the two *fora*; mid-thirteenth-century theologians applied them to the new problems the *fora* raised. See Russo, "Pénitence et excommunication," pp. 447–453.

Historians like Henry Charles Lea have long seen the thirteenth-century reaction against the emotionalism of twelfth-century theology of penance as the triumph of legalism and sacerdotalism over individualism. To the contrary, it was the very success of the theologians writing around 1200 that killed the "contritionism" they promoted. Alan of Lille and other teachers of the new moral theology only wanted to spread the gospel of private confession, and the Fourth Lateran Council was the victory of the reformers. But as the canon required confession of all, confession became routine. The tears of twelfth-century confessions give way to a legal formality.[99] Many later writers tried just as hard to arouse a sense of contrition in listeners and readers. The *exempla* promoting confession survived unabated into the thirteenth century and show that the longing for a private, informal sphere survived, too. By midcentury, however, the literature of penance had split into distinct genres. A whole series of tear-jerking devotional works for laymen flourished; the sophisticated canonical tracts that explained the sacrament to confessors and theologians developed separately. As we have seen, the theologians who around 1200 combined exhortation with sacramental subtleties were quite willing to wring laymen's souls with doubts of conscience. The new preachers of conscience omitted the doubts and taught the simplest possible faith for a mass market. Alan could hardly have considered himself betrayed when he was popularized.

If the longing for a secret repentance survived, so did another longing for the exposure and humiliation of sinners. The trio of God, neighbor, and church is a reminder of the need to balance spiritual obligations to God with earthly obligations to everyone else. Should someone forget earthly rights and wrongs, theologians and priests could remind him in a hurry. The continued demand for earthly satisfaction explains the strange afterlife of the canons supposedly made redundant by the new theology. We may recall that alongside the little catalogs of canonical puzzles, alongside the minor paeans to contrition, some copyists kept returning to old favorites among the *libri penitentiales*, or at least to modern summaries. Burchard's terrifying sentences never quite went out of style, at least in excerpt, at least in the manuscripts. Besides the customary medieval respect for ancient texts, a major reason for the canons' continued circulation must have been the spectacular humiliation they promised for evil men.

Confession itself was the scene of the theologians'—and also the lay Christians'—ambivalence about privacy. Many obviously dreamed of

99. See Payen, "La pénitence dans le contexte culturel," pp. 424–427, for a discussion of a parallel change in the vernacular literature of confession.

unburdening their souls in secrecy and freedom, and, as we have seen, sermon stories nurtured that dream. But theologians also expected confession to shame and humiliate. That was, after all, its purpose. God already knew what the penitent would say, and if the confession was private, the priest could not reveal what he had learned "as God, not man."[100] In theory, no one acquired any new information. But the sinner would be embarrassed, and that was part of the punishment.[101] Etienne de Bourbon, the same who offered confessing sinners the promise of miraculous secrecy, was happy to use shame to draw them to confession. A priest he knew in the diocese of Reims, ran one *exemplum*, knew that a woman was a secret sinner, but she would not confess. He rang the church bells and told the gathered villagers that since he had no relic of a woman completely free of sin, he planned to enclose her in a silver reliquary. Shamed by his goading, she confessed.[102] If theologians did sometimes try to protect the secrecy of confession and shield the world of the soul, it was because they understood the power of shame to control the will. Many were happy to bend the dicta that confession should be spontaneous and that tears of shame and fear were no true contrition.

One question pursued by several thirteenth-century theologians shows a conscious effort to define public and private sins more precisely for the sake of public shaming. The alternatives of public humiliation and eternal secrecy were so stark that theologians attempted to explain what sins deserved each outcome. The occasion for doing so came in reconciling Gospel instructions on penance with reality. In Matthew 18:15–17, Jesus says that if a brother sins against you, you should first correct him privately; if that fails, bring two or three witnesses to him; if that fails, "tell it to the church." Some said that

100. Thomas Aquinas, *Commentum in quatuor libros sententiarum*, IV D.21 q.3 a.1 qc.3, vol. 7:2, p. 859; cf. Guido de Baysio, *Ennarationes super Decreto, autore pise Rosarium appellari maluit* (henceforth cited as *Rosarium*) (Lyon, 1549), C.33 q.3 d.6 c.2, f. 37v, and the fourteenth-century text in BN latin 15162, f. 116v. The phrase also appears in a synodal statute of Coutances, Mansi 25:33 (1300, c. 15). But Duns Scotus disagreed, *Quaestiones in quartum librum sententiarum, Opera omnia*, 16–21, D.21 q.2, pp. 731–733: Since the priest obviously absolved in his own person, not God's, he heard confessions in his own person, though he remained bound to keep the secret.

101. A commonplace in twelfth- and thirteenth-century theology; see, for example, Peter Cantor, *Verbum abbreviatum*, c.143, PL 205:342: "ipsa oris confessio, maxima est pars satisfactionis." Thomas of Chobham, *Summa confessorum*, I.2, pp. 8–9; Albert the Great, *Commentarii in IV sententiarum*, IV D.16 a.24, vol. 29, p. 594. Albert denied that the shame of confession was properly speaking a part of satisfaction; he did not deny it helped punish the sinner.

102. Lecoy de la Marche, *Anecdotes historiques de Bourbon*, III.4, pp. 162–163; cf. Berlioz, "'Quand dire c'est faire dire,'" p. 301. Some *exempla* suggest that shame (*pudor*) can be sinful as an obstacle to confession. See, for example, a thirteenth-century French story in J. T. Welter, ed., *La tabula exemplorum secundum ordinem alphabeti*, Thesaurus exemplorum, fasc. 3 (Paris and Toulouse, 1926), p. 61. The skillful confessor will know how to use shame to his advantage.

only prelates could apply this procedure, referred to as "fraternal correction";[103] others said it applied to all Christians, or all except monks, but only under certain circumstances. Guillaume d'Auxerre said it applied to both public and secret sins. If a "few" know of the crime, then fraternal correction is straightforward. And if you are the only one to know, and the sin is iterable, like adultery, you may properly tell "good men," who might then catch the offender in the act; if the sin is not iterable, then you may still tell others to help correct this brother, so long as you avoid malice or indiscretion. Indiscretion is defined as "making manifest a crime" without proof.[104] Clearly Guillaume thought a sin or a reproval remained in some sense not exposed if only a "few" knew of it. And if the sinner did not hasten to confession at the first warning, the threat of at least limited exposure was a perfectly legitimate weapon.

Albert the Great and Richard of Middleton believed that only secret sins might be so treated, while notorious sins and, Richard adds, sins that endangered the public, might naturally be denounced at once in public. But if there were no witnesses besides you, and the offender denied it, they felt that there was no way to move to the second stage, and nothing to do but pray for the sinner's conversion.[105] As Thomas Aquinas put it, Jesus was talking about sin "not entirely public nor entirely secret," known to "some" but not many. Thomas added that after warning the sinner, one should first tell a prelate, then bring in witnesses, then tell the church.[106] The prelate is best placed to convert the sinner, after all; but it was a procedure that many sinners would have considered tattling. Fraternal correction was never a practical institution, but it remains interesting because it tested the theologians' belief in keeping secrets. Guillaume d'Auxerre allowed leeway to expose secret sins that might be repeated; Richard of Middleton permitted exposure to protect the public good. In the end, there was very little that one might not talk about, at least among a few trusted men. Only sins hidden to all but the sinner and God were truly exempt, and that of course excluded virtually all sins with a victim, and especially those with more than one victim. The attempt to define public and

103. Guillaume d'Auxerre, *Summa aurea*, ed. J. Ribaillier, Spicilegium Bonaventurianum, 16–19 (Grottaferrata, 1980–1986), III tr.53 c.1, vol. 18B, p.1036, cites this view but disagrees.

104. Guillaume d'Auxerre, *Summa aurea*, III tr.53 c.2, pp. 1040–1041.

105. Albert the Great, *Commentarii in IV sententiarum*, IV D.19 a.21, vol. 29, pp. 826–828; and Richard of Middleton, *Super quatuor libros sententiarum Petri Lombardi quaestiones* (Brixen, 1591; repr. Frankfurt-am-Main, 1963), IV D.19 a.3 q.1, pp. 316–317.

106. Thomas Aquinas, *Commentum in quatuor libros sententiarum*, IV D.19 q.2 a.3 qc.2 ad 1–4, vol. VII:B, p. 835: "non . . . omnino publicum nec omnino occultum."

private spheres unambiguously never quite worked, and the theologians all appealed to a vague middle ground where sins might be discussed if not shouted from the rooftops.

Paying Moral Debts

There were other breaches in the fortress of privacy. Thirteenth-century theologians also balanced an emphasis on intention with the demand for complete restitution for offenses committed. This was not quite a new idea. Everyone had long accepted that stolen money must be repaid, and that, in general, restitution was a precondition for penance, public or private. Canon 22 of the Second Lateran Council in 1139 condemned as false the penance of a sinner who did not make satisfaction to the one offended.[107] Restitution would often be the most painful part of penance. Louis IX said that the devil tempted usurers and robbers to give money to God rather than restore their ill-gotten gains; even the speaking of the word *rendre* is hard because the *r*'s are like rasps in the throat.[108] The pious at least might take the obligation of restitution quite seriously, but it was certainly enough to scare off many of the less pious.[109] With little appreciation for such weakness, Scholastic theologians made restitution an obsession. It was part of the sinner's duty to repay offenses against neighbor or the Church, whether considered as part of the sacrament or as something extrasacramental but no less obligatory. They worried about the limits of restitution. Obviously a usurer had to restore the interest paid and a thief had to restore the money stolen, but what about those whose incompetence, negligence, or silence caused some loss? Peter Cantor, typical of early Scholastic theologians, expected the highest standards. Judges, counselors, teachers, and lawyers who err out of mere ignorance are bound to make up the loss to the victim. Peter admits that a court would not enforce such strictness, because only fraud was actionable there. God's standard was higher, however, because He made it the duty of judges and advisers to know their business.[110]

Thirteenth-century theologians shared Peter's stringent expecta-

---

107. *Conciliorum oecumenicorum decreta*, 3d ed., ed. J. Alberigo et al. (Bologna, 1973), p. 202.

108. Jean de Joinville, *Histoire de Saint Louis*, ed. N. de Wailly (Paris, 1868), p. 11.

109. So said Humbert of Romans in a sermon, cited in A. Murray, "Religion among the Poor in Thirteenth-Century France: The Testimony of Humbert de Romans," *Traditio* 30 (1974): 305–306.

110. Peter Cantor, *Summa de sacramentis*, II.122, p. 246.

tions, although they typically argued that restitution was not, properly speaking, part of satisfaction but only a prerequisite for penance. As Albert the Great put it, one could be reconciled to one's neighbor through restitution without being reconciled to God through true contrition and penance.[111] Some theologians asked how restitution could be required for usury but not for homicide, for instance, and like Peter they attempted to explain in detail which sinners owed repayment.[112] The question of restitution afforded the opportunity to discuss knotty questions of ethics. Duns Scotus considered a particularly interesting problem: What about making restitution for a damaged reputation? And what if one had damaged a neighbor's reputation by accusing him of a crime that he had in fact committed? Scotus decided that it was indeed a sin to make a true accusation if the crime were secret, that is, if fewer than three witnessed it. Such a witness to a "secret" crime might still avoid sinful defamation if he carefully stated that he was just reporting what he had heard, but even this was risky. On the other hand, a man who lied in denying a secret crime and thereby defamed his accuser could keep his crime secret and not restore his accuser's good name.[113] These questions of restitution, and the discussion of fraternal correction, display a deep concern about protecting spheres of privacy and publicity.

The enormous attention paid to restitution is related to the growing awareness of usury in the thirteenth century. Theologians considered usurers thieves and usury a subtle form of theft that required a subtle analysis of repayment. But perhaps it was just as much the growing interest in restitution that focused attention on usury. Thomas of Chobham had pointed the way toward the creation of a sphere of morality distinct from both the inner world of the soul and civic responsibilities, the sphere of the neighborhood, of relations

---

111. Albert the Great, *Commentarii in IV sententiarum*, IV D.15 a.45, vol. 29, pp. 534–535. See also Guillaume d'Auvergne, *De sacramento poenitentiae*, in *Opera omnia* (Paris, 1674, repr. Frankfurt-am-Main, 1963), c.20, vol. I, p. 505; Guillaume d'Auxerre, *Summa aurea*, IV tr.11 c.6 q.1, vol. 18B, pp. 286–288; Alexander of Hales, *Glossa in quatuor libros sententiarum*, IV D.15, pp. 249–251; Bonaventure, *Commentaria in quartum libros sententiarum*, IV D.15 p.2 a.2 q.4, pp. 375–376; Pierre de Tarentaise, *In IV libros sententiarum*, IV D.15 q.2 a.3, p. 165; Richard of Middleton, *Super quatuor libros sententiarum*, IV D.15 a.5 q.1, p. 217; Duns Scotus, *Quaestiones in quartum librum sententiarum*, D.15 q.2, vol. 18, p. 255. Thomas Aquinas, however, argues that true reconciliation to one's neighbor involves both more and less than restitution: Reconciliation requires humility, not just physical repayment, and an impoverished penitent may be reconciled without actually paying. See his *Commentum in quatuor libros sententiarum*, IV D.15 q.1 a.5 qc.1–2, vol. VII:2, pp. 713–715.

112. See, for example, Guillaume d'Auvergne, *De sacramento poenitentiae*, c.20, vol. I, p. 505; Richard of Middleton, *Super quatuor libros sententiarum*, IV D.15 a.5 q.2–6, pp. 218–224; and Duns Scotus, *Quaestiones in quartum librum sententiarum*, D.15 q.3, vol. 18, pp. 357–367.

113. Duns Scotus, *Quaestiones in quartum librum sententiarum*, D.15 q.4, vol. 18, pp. 391–406.

with other individuals.[114] The discussion of fraternal correction also suggested this middle ground. We might now call it "private life," but it is not to be confused with the truly private world of the individual soul. Restitution defined one's duties in the middle private sphere.[115] In principle, it was an obligation owed by one individual to another, and great pains must be taken to find and repay the actual victims. It was not enough to repay the community, much less the state. This is why Louis IX sought papal dispensation to give money to the poor in lieu of restitution to those abused by royal officers. Thirteenth-century theologians would carefully differentiate restitution from satisfaction to God or from reconciliation to the church. One could make a private peace with individuals without making peace with God or the community. And if theologians sometimes mitigated satisfactions imposed by the priest, they always held the line on restitution. No purgatory could expiate unrestored goods. No vicarious suffrages or alms could compensate for what the sinner himself did not do. This sphere of morality was sanctioned by divine law, but it made its demands on every individual here and now on earth.

At this point, it is worth pausing to reflect on the idea of penance as paying off a debt. Phrases borrowed from accounting still pervade our language of morals so much that it is easy to pass over the metaphor without thought. We still expect wrongdoers to "pay their debt to society" and the good to act "to their credit." It is a tricky matter for the theologian to explain why Christians "bought at a price"—that of Christ's redemption—still need, themselves, to pay for their sins. Medieval writers taught that baptism alone was free, but thereafter forgiveness of the temporal penalty due must be paid for by suffering. They taught that after Christ's incarnation, satisfaction for sins must share in and imitate Christ's satisfaction.[116] In the end, solutions like these only restated the problem. Saying that sin incurred a debt that had to be repaid was more than a metaphor. When Bonaventure called the *poena* from sin a *pretium* (price), he not only meant that God had to be repaid but that the currency of repayment was liquid: Another Christian could pay instead.[117] Theologians used such phrases with none of the conscious sense of paradox that they applied to the *admirabile commercium* (wonderful exchange) of Christ's incarna-

114. Thomas of Chobham, *Summa confessorum*, p. 13.
115. I differ here from John Bossy, *Christianity in the West*, p. 47, who has interpreted the theological and popular interest in restitution in the later Middle Ages as evidence of a continuing belief that penance above all made peace with the community, because sin "was a state of offense inhering in communities rather than in individuals."
116. See, e.g., Thomas Aquinas, *Summa contra gentiles*, in *Opera omnia* (Leonine ed., Rome, 1930), IV.72, vol.15, p. 225; cf. J. A. Spitzig, *Sacramental Penance in the Twelfth and Thirteenth Centuries* (Washington, D.C., 1947), pp. 58, 141.
117. Bonaventure, *Commentaria in quatuor libros sententiarum*, IV D.20 p.2 a.1 q.1, p.531.

tion and passion.[118] Penance paid a debt neither by analogy nor in paradox; the exchange was literal and exact. Yet what could be more puzzling and paradoxical than the notion that evil done might be recalled by payments in units of a moral currency, indeed the notion that this currency, like money, was an abstract measure of value that could be exchanged? How could blasphemy against heaven be repaired by the profanity of currency?

The idea that offenses against God or man required repayment in a "moral currency" could hardly have been more deep-rooted and permanent.[119] The most extravagant praise of the power of contrition never touched it. No one doubted that after contrition a penalty remained to be expiated, and that need for repayment was doubtless a constant counterbalance to promises of secrecy. God and man had to be bought off. The offended had to see the offender make good, and this meant in some sense the humiliation of the sinner before God and his minister in private confession for offenses against God, and before the human neighbor when restitution was required. The shame of confession and the bitterness of restitution deterred sinners from the sweetness of sharing secrets with a friend.

Scholastic theology undoubtedly failed to provide an adequate model of existing varieties of penance; it particularly failed to define public penances and differentiate them adequately from excommunication. We have found that "tripartite penance" never made any sense as a description of contemporary or historic practice; it was simply an artificial construct developed piecemeal to explain contradictory authorities. "Solemn public penance" and "nonsolemn public penance" were labels newly minted in late-twelfth-century thought for what most still considered the only truly sacramental form of the rite. The inadequacy of their definitions is not a sign of the disappearance of the phenomena. Rather, private confession was the chief aim and moral intentions the chief interest of the writers whose popularizations around 1200 set the tone and themes for several generations of manuals and treatises. Alan of Lille and all his imitators undoubtedly cared more about measuring and refining contrition and charity than about rites of solemn penance. But even as a theology of private penance, the teaching in the *summae* and manuals had

---

118. Cf. Martin Herz, *Sacrum Commercium: Eine begriffsgeschichtliche Studie zur Theologie der römischen Liturgiesprache*, Münchener Theologische Studien, 2.15 (Munich, 1958); and Suzanne Poque, "Christus Mercator," *Recherches de science religieuse* 48 (1960): 564–577.

119. See Bossy, *Christianity in the West*, p. 4, for this principle; the phrase "moral currency" is his. See also P. Legendre, "*De confessis*: Remarques sur le statut de la parole dans la première scolastique," in *L'aveu. Antiquité et Moyen-Age*, p. 403, for penance and the economy of exchange.

limited success. The effort to define an "interior penance" of ⋅   ul
independent of any sacramental interference quickly faded.   a-
bly, routine confession failed to bring universal contrition; th   i-
lus of charity dried up the emotions it was meant to n⋅   :.
Thirteenth-century theologians shied away from dreams of int   y
and settled for the world of private morality. Restitution and ⋅ ⋅ ⋅ ⋅ ⋅ e
private sacramental confession were the ways an individual might pay
debts to others and to God. This not-so-happy medium did not quite
put to rest lingering dreams of a truly secret world of the soul or, more
strikingly, of the public humiliation of enemies. Later thirteenth-
century theologians attempted again and again to define the boundaries of private and public duties, but they never found a way to resolve
their ambivalence about privacy. In Chapter 3, I show how this ambivalence shaped the interpretation of *Omnis utriusque* and the implementation of private penance.

CHAPTER THREE

The Publicity of Private Penance

In Chapter 2, I exposed a gap between the explicit views of many Scholastic theologians and the assumptions behind them. Here, I turn from the theology of the great masters and the second-rate compilers to another theology, implied and unstated, of council decrees and routine judgments. Perhaps it is paradoxical to speak of a theology or theory in the practice itself. Yet bishops, priests, and even laymen practiced penance not instinctively but in accordance with some general principles, no less powerful because they were left unstated. Their theorizing differed not in kind but in degree from that of the university masters, whose careful schemes and lists concealed, as we have seen, profound ambivalences about penance. In this chapter and in Chapter 4, I examine these unexpressed principles and the actual practice of penance, beginning here with the interpretation of Canon 21 of the Fourth Lateran Council and the procedure of private penance, and turning later to the application of public and solemn penance.

The Sources

It is a demanding task to establish what thirteenth-century sinners did to atone for their sins, as evidence of procedure and practice is elusive. We can be reasonably certain, for instance, that a note in Archbishop Eudes Rigaud's register about his ejection of the penitents from the Cathedral of Rouen on Ash Wednesday, February 17, 1248, means that he in fact expelled the penitents.[1] We can conclude

---

1. Eudes Rigaud, *Regestrum visitationum*, p. 31.

that solemn penance continued to be practiced in mid-thirteenth-century Rouen, although we cannot tell how many penitents submitted to it. Unfortunately, Eudes's register is one of very few of its kind to survive from northern France, and other narrative sources provide only incidental information on penance. The rule making of bishops in local synodal statutes thus becomes an invaluable, though problematic source. Northern French synodal statutes help complete our picture of thirteenth-century realities and reformers' intentions alike. Sometimes we may refer to English and southern French statutes for comparison, since they derive from the same tradition of legislation, but they depart from the northern French in interesting ways.

Synodal statutes present the same difficulties to historians as any other laws. Repeated prohibitions in the canons may be signs of an intractable problem, or of its successful suppression, or sometimes even of the antiquarian tastes of the bishops who directed the synod. So while some of the evidence reviewed in these chapters, such as the occasional chronicle or memoir, for instance, needs little explanation, this crucial source for the varieties of penances and the impact of the new theology and the Fourth Lateran Council requires more attention. This is especially true because synodal statutes were themselves artifacts of the great reform of ecclesiastical discipline that also inspired the Fourth Lateran itself.[2]

Few diocesan statutes compiled before 1200 survive from northern France; fewer still from pre–Fourth Lateran England, and none at all from southern France. Twelfth-century synods relied on the oral transmission of rules from bishop to priest to parishioners or very brief circulating *precepta communia*,[3] procedures entirely inadequate for the ambitious pastoral programs of the reformers around 1200. The early surviving French and English diocesan statutes, such as those of Eudes de Sully for Paris and those of Stephen Langton for Canterbury, were not only drawn up shortly before the great ecu-

2. The slow ongoing project of cataloging and eventually editing all the French synodal canons, which has borne fruit in the *Répertoire des statuts synodaux des diocèses de l'ancienne France du XIIIe à la fin du XVIIIe siècle* and in Pontal's edition *Les statuts synodaux français du XIIIe siècle*, vols. 1–2, has made the task of comparing French canons immeasurably simpler. But many of the texts are still available only scattered in sometimes unreliable editions or even manuscripts; the dating of many synods is uncertain. With so much reissuing of canons, as we will see below, many collections are simply republications of earlier material made around 1300 or so.

3. C. R. Cheney, "Statute-making in the English Church in the Thirteenth Century," in *Mediaeval Texts and Studies* (Oxford, 1973), pp. 141–142; Joseph Avril, "Les 'Precepta synodalia' de Roger de Cambrai," *Bulletin of Medieval Canon Law*, n.s. 2 (1972): 7. See B. Jacqueline, "Les synodes du diocèse de Coutances avant le Concile de Trente," *Revue historique de droit français et étranger*, 4th ser., 29 (1951): 142, for another probable example of such summary *precepta*, dating from 1185–1199.

menical council, probably just before 1200 for Eudes's, 1213–1214 for Langton's, but most likely as part of the same program of reform.[4] When Innocent III, a competent theologian himself, sent out summons for the ecumenical council, he asked his archbishops and bishops to inquire into necessary reforms. The early-thirteenth-century canons in England and France were probably in some sense preliminary drafts for the Lateran's decrees. Provincial councils in the twelfth century had concentrated on the reform of clerical morals; now Parisian bishops and Paris-trained Schoolmen like Langton, Robert Courson, Richard Poore, and Thomas of Chobham turned their attention to lay discipline as well. Some politically minded bishops like Hubert Walter joined the early movement for teaching lay discipline through the statutes.[5] For the most part, however, the impulse came from theologians and their friends in the episcopacy. A small circle of intellectuals trained in Paris pursued the study of the sacraments and the reform of the church. These practical theologians and their heirs, so well described by John Baldwin,[6] debated the new theory of the sacraments, wrote the ground-breaking confessors' manuals, and inscribed their hopes in the synodal statutes.

After 1215, the early Parisian canons of Eudes de Sully would become the prototype for a whole family of western French statutes, and they influenced synodal activity elsewhere in France, in England, and even as far afield as Portugal for the rest of the century and beyond.[7] The later diocesan synods came slowly to adopt as their own some of the language of the Lateran Council, including by midcentury Canon 21, *Omnis utriusque*; but the original model was Eudes de Sully's, and

4. C. R. Cheney, *English Synodalia of the Thirteenth Century* (Oxford, 1941), pp. 34–38, and "The Earliest English Diocesan Statutes," *English Historical Review* 75 (1960): 13–14; Raymonde Foreville, *Latran I, II, III, et Latran IV* (Paris, 1965), p. 315. Older than Eudes's statutes are those of Roger de Wawrin, bishop of Cambrai (1181–1191), but these are very short notes dealing primarily with clerical morals; see Avril, "Les 'Precepta synodalia,'" pp. 7–15. For the relation between the reform movement and early Italian synodal statutes, see M. Maccarrone, "'Cura animarum' e 'parochialis sacerdos' nella costituzione del IV concilio lateranense (1215). Applicazioni in Italia nel sec. XIII," in *Pievi e parrocchie in Italia nel basso medioevo*, Atti del VI Convegno di Storia della chiesa in Italia, Florence, 1981, Italia Sacra, 35–36 (Rome, 1984), 1: 81–195.

5. Cheney, "Statute-making in the English Church in the Thirteenth Century," p. 142; Pontal, *Les statuts synodaux*, pp. 44–46.

6. Baldwin, *Masters, Princes, and Merchants*.

7. Pontal, "Les plus anciens statuts synodaux d'Angers et leur expansion dans les diocèses de l'ouest de la France," *Revue d'histoire de l'église de France* 46 (1960): 54–59. Cf. also on the diffusion of these French statutes: Raymonde Foreville, "La réception des conciles généraux dans l'Eglise et la province de Rouen au XIIIe siècle," in *Droit privé et institutions régionales: Etudes historiques offertes à Jean Yver* (Paris, 1976), pp. 245–246n; Joseph Avril, *Le gouvernement des évêques et la vie religieuse dans le diocèse d'Angers (1148–1240)* (Paris, 1984), pp. 588–589; and Isais da Rosa Pereira, "Les statuts synodaux d'Eudes de Sully au Portugal," *L'année canonique* 15 (1971): 459–480.

the original inspiration, the Parisian masters'. Statutes based on that model proliferated after 1215.[8] English synodal statutes were similarly mosaics of earlier efforts. C. R. Cheney has identified several families each dependent on a common source.[9] English canons are occasionally significantly different from French ones, but there is no consistent regional pattern of variation among French dioceses.

The family resemblance reflects a common procedure of enactment, as well as deliberate copying. French diocesan synods were brief, generally lasting only a day or two, too short for much innovation. The bishop usually had no intention of actually consulting the priests in attendance about the composition of the canons, anyway; in general, he relied on a secretary to frame his ideas. By 1200, diocesan synods rarely acted as tribunals for clerical discipline, which was left to the bishop's official or, occasionally, to the provincial council. Nor were these synods in any sense legislative bodies with the task of constructing new laws to right new wrongs; they served to publicize rules already established, to inform the bishop about local problems, and, every now and then, to give solemn approval to minor adjustments of older principles.[10] The relative monotony, of course, does not render the collections useless as evidence. The definitions they pronounced and the concerns they evoked were deeply rooted, and there is some slight, but consistent, chronological evolution.

Synods and their canons were not the only manifestations of this thirteenth-century episcopal effort in reform and discipline; visitations of local clergy, regular and secular, were another. Unfortunately, few episcopal registers and visitation records have survived for northern France, and, except for Eudes Rigaud's, most provide little insight into the customs governing penance.[11] The scarcity of alternative sources makes Eudes Rigaud's passionately detailed record all the more valuable, particularly for the analysis of public penance in

---

8. A few exceptional synods departed from the pattern at the very end of the thirteenth century; see Olga Dobiache-Rojdestvensky, *La vie paroissiale en France au XIIIe siècle d'après les actes épiscopaux* (Paris, 1911), p. 59.

9. Cheney, "Statute-making in the English Church in the Thirteenth Century," pp. 142–148.

10. Dobiache-Rojdestvensky, *La vie paroissiale*, pp. 53–55; Cheney, *English Synodalia*, pp. 19, 44–50; Pontal, *Les statuts synodaux*, pp. 26–27; and Pontal I, pp. lvii–lxiii.

11. On the unusual dimensions of Eudes's register, which included more personal detail, records of sermons delivered, and so forth, see C. R. Cheney, *Episcopal Visitation of Monasteries in the Thirteenth Century* (Manchester, 1931), p. 9. Besides Eudes's, there is a useful fourteenth-century monastic register: M. G. Dupont, "Le registre de l'officialité de Cerisy, 1314–1457," *Mémoires de la société des antiquaires de Normandie* 30 (1880): 271–662. Another register survives only in fragments, with little relevance to penance: Léopold Delisle, "Visites pastorales de maître Henri de Vezelai, archidiacre d'Hiémois en 1267 et 1268," *Bibliothèque de l'Ecole des chartes* 54 (1893): 457–467.

Chapter 4. Even more than Eudes de Sully at the beginning of the century, Eudes Rigaud was familiar with contemporary theology. No mean theologian himself, before his election to the archbishopric of Rouen, he wrote a commentary on Peter Lombard's *Sentences* and collaborated on a commentary on the Rule of Saint Francis.[12] His register, like Eudes de Sully's canons, reveals the practical decision making of a bishop thoroughly familiar with more academic schemes of classification.

Bishops used the synods not just to lay down rules but to train the clergy and indirectly to improve lay participation in the sacraments of the parish church. The statute making of the thirteenth century coincided with the definition of territorial parishes, each with a *proprius sacerdos* through whom the theologians and bishops could reach the laity.[13] It was not enough merely to tell laymen to confess annually during Lent. English statutes, for instance, often provided priests with confessors' guides of half a dozen folios included right in the text.[14] Some English bishops commissioned more extensive confessors' manuals or were patrons of their authors.[15] Robert of Flamborough dedicated his *Liber penitentialis* to Richard Poore, the bishop of Salisbury and former companion of Langton at Paris; Thomas of Chobham was the subdean of Salisbury cathedral during Poore's pontificate.[16] By contrast, most French canons only laid down broad principles about confession and satisfactions, telling priests that they

12. For Eudes's life, see E. Amann, "Eudes Rigaud," in *Dictionnaire de théologie catholique* (Paris, 1937), 13b, cols. 2703–2705; and Williel R. Thomson, *Friars in the Cathedral: The First Franciscan Bishops, 1226–1261* (Toronto, 1975), pp. 77-91. Cf. L. Oliger, ed., *Expositio quattuor magistrorum super regulam fratrum Minorum* (Rome, 1950). The first three books of the *Sentences* commentary attributed to Eudes are authentic, K. F. Lynch, "The Alleged Fourth Book of Odo Rigaud on the Sentences and Related Documents," *Franciscan Studies* 9 (1949): 87–145.

13. H. Platelle, "La paroisse et son curé jusqu'à la fin du XIIIe siècle. Orientations de la recherche actuelle," in *L'encadrement religieux des fidèles au Moyen-Age et jusqu'au Concile de Trente*, Actes du 109e Congrès national des Sociétés savantes, Dijon, 1984, Section d'histoire médiévale et de philologie, 1 (Paris, 1985), pp. 11, 21–22; cf. Maccarrone, "'Cura animarum,'" pp. 85, 92, 111.

14. Cheney, *English Synodalia*, pp. 41–43. For examples, see Powicke and Cheney, pp. 220–226 (Coventry, 1224–1237, tract issued by Alexander of Stavensby); pp. 305, 321 (Worcester, 1240, reference to a lost tract prepared for clergy attending the synod); and pp. 1060–1077 (Exeter, 1287, manual of Peter Quinel).

15. E. J. Arnould, *Le manuel des péchés: Etude de la littérature religieuse anglo-normande (XIIIe siècle)* (Paris, 1940), p. 27; D. W. Robertson, "The *Manuel des Péchés* and an English Episcopal Decree," *Modern Language Notes* 60 (1945): 440–444; Cheney, "Some Aspects of Diocesan Legislation," p. 190.

16. Cheney, "Some Aspects of Diocesan Legislation," p. 187, and "Statute-Making in the English Church," p. 144, both in C. R. Cheney, *Medieval Text and Studies* (Oxford, 1973). Cf. Michaud-Quantin, *Sommes de casuistique*, p. 30, on a guide to confession attributed to Robert Grosseteste, translated later in the century into French, H. Urtel, ed., "Eine altfranzösische Beichte," *Zeitschrift für romanische Philologie* 33 (1909): 571–575.

should consider the circumstances of a sin, for example.[17] They did, however, often insist, like the English statutes, that every priest own a "manual" (*manualis*) for administering baptism, extreme unction, and so forth, and sometimes also an ordinal of the cathedral's use.[18] Thus, confessors' handbooks, visitation registers, synodal statutes, and even the liturgical guides for priests all grew more common after 1215, and all were part of a single effort to train the clergy in order to reach the laity in the parish, individually and as a whole. Penance, even private sacramental penance, was a central means of this discipline and of the constitution of the community of the parish.

Although synods and visitation records emerge from the same milieu that produced the theology and handbooks examined in Chapter 2, they represented a far less systematic and less conscious application of general assumptions about penance than the most cursory handbook or sermons. The authors of the statutes completely ignored the tidy systems of tripartite penance or the two *fora* that they had learned in Paris. And some thirteenth-century synods—like some contemporary confessors' handbooks—neglected to dispose of the old tariffs that the new theology might theoretically have rendered obsolete.[19] The imposition and interpretation of the rule of annual

17. Michaud-Quantin, *Sommes de casuistique*, p. 31; Baldwin, *Masters, Princes, and Merchants*, 1: 54–55. Eudes de Sully recommended that the clergy own compilations of penitential canons along with liturgical handbooks: Pontal I, p. 70 (Paris, ca. 1200, c. 50); Avril, *Le gouvernement des évêques*, p. 602, shows the influence of Alan of Lille and Robert of Flamborough's works on the briefly stated principles of the canons. But later in the century, some southern French synodal statutes included quasi manuals similar to those in many English statutes: e.g. Bibl. Vat. lat. 9868, f. 183r–185v (Carcassonne, 1270).

18. The "manual" is now generally called a "ritual." See Chapters 5 and 6 for descriptions of rituals, ordinals, and related liturgical books. For examples of the requirement: Pontal I, p. 70 (Paris, ca. 1200, c. 49); A. Gosse, *Histoire de l'abbaye et de l'ancienne congrégation des chanoines réguliers d'Arrouaise* (Lille, 1786), p. 582 (Arras, thirteenth century, c. 5); Mansi, 23:377 (Rouen, 1235, c. 28). For the requirement to possess a manual and an ordinal, see Edmond Martène and Ursin Durand, *Veterum scriptorum et monumentorum historicum, dogmaticorum, moraliorum, amplissima collectio* (Paris, 1733), vol. VIII, col. 1544 (Soissons, thirteenth century, c. 57). William Maskell, *Monumentae Ritualia Ecclesiae Anglicanae* (London, 1846–1847), vol. I, pp. clxxxviii–cxciii, has printed some thirteenth-century English parish inventories showing that most parishes actually possessed manuals as well as a variety of missals and psalters.

19. Eudes de Sully cited the old tariffs: Pontal I, p. 70 (c. 50); the western French synodal statutes included transcriptions from older penitential collections, such as Burchard's penitential, cited through more contemporary works, such as manuals of Alan of Lille and Robert of Flamborough. As Avril, *Le gouvernement des évêques*, p. 710, points out, the preservation of the tariffs occasionally led to inconsistencies, such as the citation of the old canonical penalty for a woman sinning with her confessor alongside the contemporary rule that this case is reserved to the bishop and his penitentiary for judgment. See also Guillaume Le Maire's citation of draconian ancient canons to threaten clerical fornicators (Angers, 1312, c.1): Henri Arnauld, *Statuts du diocèse d'Angers depuis environ l'an 1240 jusqu'en l'an 1679* (Angers, 1680), pp. 103–104. See above, Chapter 2, on the survival of the old tariffs in the confessors' manuals themselves.

confession, however, is the most constructive lesson about the theology of the statutes that evolved alongside the explicit theology of the intellectuals.

The Interpretation of Omnis utriusque

Occasional theologians and church councils before the thirteenth century had recommended annual or even triannual confession for laymen, but only the decree of the ecumenical council at the Lateran in 1215–1216 attempted to make annual confession truly universal. The words of Canon 21, known from its opening words as *Omnis utriusque*, would seem to speak for themselves.

> Every one of the faithful of both sexes after reaching the age of discretion should at least once a year faithfully confess alone [*solus*] all his sins to his own priest, and should attempt to fulfill the penance [*penitentia*] imposed with all his strength, receiving the sacrament of the Eucharist reverently at least at Easter, unless perhaps by the advice of his own priest for some reasonable cause he should abstain from receiving it for a time. Otherwise let him be kept from entering the church during his lifetime and on his death let him be denied Christian burial.[20]

The canon also requires frequent publication of the decree and prudence and discretion on the part of the confessor. Two remarks on the text itself are in order. The use of *penitentia* to mean the penalty of satisfaction assigned, rather than the whole process, still less the confession, is notable because it indicates how far the satisfaction remained, at the beginning of the thirteenth century, the essential ingredient in penance.[21] As priests came to impose less arduous satisfactions later in the century, the confession and absolution alone were increasingly seen as *penitentia*.

Most interesting is the word *solus*, a usage without parallel in con-

---

20. *Conciliorum oecumenicorum decreta*, p. 245: "Omnis utriusque sexus fidelis postquam ad annos discretionis pervenerit, omnia sua solus peccata saltem semel in anno fideliter confiteatur proprio sacerdoti; et injunctam sibi poenitentiam pro viribus studeat adimplere, suscipiens reverenter ad minus in Pascha Eucharistiae sacramentum; nisi forte de proprii sacerdotis consilio ob aliquam rationabilem causam, ad tempus ab ejus perceptione duxerit abstinendum; alioquin et vivens ab ingressu ecclesiae arceatur, et moriens Christiana careat sepultura."

21. Bériou, "Autour de Latran IV (1215)," pp. 75–76, remarks on the usage, but does not explain it.

temporary theology and canon law.[22] The ordinary term to describe private penance is, of course, *penitentia privata*. I suspect that the authors of the canon, while intending the penance to be private, had a slightly different emphasis in mind. Before the Fourth Lateran, some parishes knew a kind of general confession in which several parishioners confessed together a common list of sins. Caesarius of Heisterbach tells the story of a priest some years earlier who gathered six or eight parishioners at a time and asked them to repeat after him an omnibus confession of sins read out to them; then he would impose the same penance on all. One old man, accustomed to this procedure, was baffled when a new priest demanded that he confess his sins before giving him the viaticum. "Do me the confession," the man said, meaning that the priest should read him the words for him to repeat. The priest insisted on a personal confession, so at last the man answered, "I confess I have sinned in adulteries, thefts, rapine, homicides, perjuries . . ." "Did you really do all that?" "Oh no, sir, none of it." The man died without being persuaded to confess his own sins.[23] The Fourth Lateran Council meant to exclude such confessions by several people at a time, just like a synod of Bordeaux in 1234 that expressly outlawed priests from receiving two parishioners at a time in confession.[24] *Omnis utriusque* stipulated that each Christian had to appear alone, *solus*. The word refers to the loneliness rather than the secrecy of the confrontation. French interpretations of the text were consistent with this emphasis.

The interpretation of the canon in northern French dioceses depended, first, on its publication. *Omnis utriusque* required its own frequent publication in churches, lest anyone make ignorance an ex-

22. Unfortunately, canonists had little to say. Hostiensis, *In I–VI Decretalium*, V. De poen. et rem., 12, merely says that *solus* means "solus peccator soli presbitero debet . . . confiteri," which restates rather than explains the usage. Roberto Rusconi, "I francescani e la confessione nel secolo XIII," in *Francescanesimo e vita religiosa dei laici nel '200*, Atti dell'VIII Convegno internazionale, Assisi, 1980 (Assisi, 1981), p. 253, has explained *solus* as indicating private confession, but without saying why the odd word was used. One set of statutes omits the word in its rendition of Canon 21: François Pommeraye, *Sanctae Rotomagensis Ecclesiae concilia ac synodalia decreta* (Rouen, 1677), p. 239 (Rouen, first half of thirteenth century), but it is hard to tell whether this was intentional.

23. Caesarius of Heisterbach, *Dialogus miraculorum*, XLV, vol. I, p. 64.

24. Pontal II, p. 48 (Bordeaux, 1234, c. 8); see J. Longère, "La prédication et l'instruction des fidèles selon les conciles et les statuts synodaux depuis l'Antiquité tardive jusqu'au XIIIe siècle," in *L'encadrement religieux*, pp. 406–407. A number of southern French statutes also specifically forbade deacons to hear confessions, even of the sick or the young. These suggest that many in the south continued to make their confessions to deacons, believing such private confessions were somehow less sacramental and could be done informally: Pontal II, p. 194 (Sisteron, 1225–1235, c. 28); Mansi 23:1194 (Clermont, 1268, c. 7); Mansi 24:383–384 (Poitiers, 1280, c. 5). We may recall that Lanfranc specifically agreed that deacons could hear confessions: *Libellus de celanda confessione*, PL 150:629.

cuse.[25] But for a long time northern French bishops neglected to incorporate it in their own statutes. They did generally require annual confession, but they preferred other texts to the language of Canon 21. Many borrowed Eudes de Sully's pre-Lateran statute on the subject. At the very end of the twelfth century, Eudes's synod at Paris had told priests to enjoin on their parishioners frequent confession, especially at the beginning of Lent,[26] and this vague rule found its way into many French synodal books by the early 1220s.[27] A somewhat stronger injunction, though still less exacting than *Omnis utriusque*, appeared in the Parisian statutes of Guillaume de Seignelay (1219–1224), and continued to be reissued for nearly a century by various synods.[28] Only after considerable delay, and then not in all dioceses, did bishops start to cite *Omnis utriusque* itself.[29]

In short, it is difficult to say just when in the century the Lateran's rule was affirmed by all the northern French diocesan synods because so many records of the earlier local canons survive only in collections from the end of the century. The evolution of the statutes of Cambrai and of Paris, at least, seems to suggest that *Omnis utriusque* became part of the local canonical tradition only after midcentury. There is no question here of an attempt to flout the decisions of an ecumenical council. Instead, the precise wording preferred by the northern French versions reveals what substitute the bishops saw as sufficient, that is, what they considered to be the gist of a law of annual confession. They interpreted it primarily as a means not of placing responsibility on the individual conscience but of ensuring public honor for the sacraments in every town and country parish.

This interpretation of the rule of confession was especially characteristic of northern France, although it had some influence across the Channel. In England, bishops were similarly slow to cite *Omnis utriusque* in their statutes, and some continued to repeat Eudes de Sully's vague wording on annual confession for some decades after 1215.[30]

25. *Conciliorum oecumenicorum decreta*, p. 245.

26. Pontal I, p. 64 (Paris, ca. 1200, c. 36).

27. BN latin 11067, f. 4v (Noyon, thirteenth century); Gosse, *Histoire de l'abbaye . . . d'Arrouaise*, p. 583 (Arras, thirteenth century, c. 7).

28. Pontal I, p. 100 (c. 8); for its diffusion, see below, where its content is also discussed.

29. Pontal I, p. 190 (Synodal of the West, c. 75); BN latin 15172, f. 146r (Lisieux, before 1321); Martène and Durand, *Veterum scriptorum*, vol. VIII, col. 1543 (Soissons, thirteenth century, c. 45); P. C. Boeren, "Les plus anciens statuts du diocèse de Cambrai (XIIIe siècle)", *Revue de droit canonique* (Strasbourg), 3 (1953): 381 (Cambrai, after 1260, tit. VII).

30. See Marion Gibbs and Jane Lang, *Bishops and Reform, 1215–1276* (London, 1934), pp. 101–130, esp. p. 123, for the slow spread of the influence of the Fourth Lateran in England. For statutes with the vague version of the rule of annual confession, see Powicke and Cheney, p. 188 (unknown diocese, 1225–1230, c. 44), p. 454 (Chichester, 1245–1252, c. 16), p. 638 (London, 1245–1259, c. 24).

But the English dioceses did not take up Guillaume de Seignelay's version, nor did they develop any interpretations of their own. In the Midi, on the other hand, where bishops began to issue synodal statutes rather later than in the north, close paraphrases and precise quotations of *Omnis utriusque* nevertheless appear in the earliest statutes, only ten to fifteen years after the Fourth Lateran Council.[31] Alternative versions of the rule of confession were very rare. Only one French diocese south of the Loire echoed Guillaume de Seignelay's version instead of the Fourth Lateran's, and its statutes repeated *Omnis utriusque* for good measure.[32] Southern French statutes and liturgy imitated Roman models much more closely than their northern French counterparts; the influence of Roman custom in the Midi long predates the arrival of the papal court in Avignon.

The northern French interpretation, therefore, is worthy of further attention here. Eudes de Sully's statutes from around 1200, the first set to require something like annual confession, instructed the priest to recommend frequent confession and to insist that all his parishioners at the beginning of Lent "come generally" to confession.[33] The term *generaliter* would seem to mean more or less everyone, but this canon is much vaguer than *Omnis utriusque* on the point, and, unlike the Lateran's version, it does not comment on who is to be the confessor, nor does it impose any punishment on those who do not confess. Eudes's canon also differs from the Lateran's version in that its primary purpose was to teach laymen that frequent confession was a good thing, not to link Lenten confession to a required Easter communion. So at the beginning of the century, Eudes de Sully was spreading the ideas of contemporary masters by encouraging more frequent confession. He was not yet setting up a mechanism in the parish to see that everyone obeyed, and certainly he was not making this confession a sine qua non for salvation.[34] Experiencing wide diffusion between 1200 and the 1220s, this statute aimed at education rather than canonical enforcement. In this it parallels the early confessors' manuals, which praised contrition and interior penance, but did not yet define an interior *forum* along the lines of exterior ecclesiastical jurisdiction.

31. Pontal II, p. 22 (Albi, 1230, c. 40); Pontal II, pp. 192 and 214 (Sisteron, 1225–1235, c. 26 and 64); Mansi 32:300 (Autun, 1286, c. 77); Bibl. Vat. lat. 1065 f. 32ra (Poitiers, 1259–1271); and Bibl. Vat. lat. 9868, f. 182v (Carcassonne 1270).

32. Mansi 23:1193 (Clermont, 1268, c. 7); these statutes in general show many similarities with those of Guillaume de Seignelay and the synodal of the West.

33. Pontal I, p. 64: "Frequenter presbyteri moneant ad confessionem, et precipue ab initio quadragesime instanter precipiant venire generaliter ad confessionem."

34. By the end of the century, by contrast, the bishop of Coutances was instructing priests to tell parishioners precisely this. Mansi 25:38 (Coutances, 1300, c. 25).

By the 1220s, Guillaume de Seignelay's statutes for Paris made the rule more precise and included provisions for enforcement. Priests were to admonish all parishioners "that everyone, at least heads of households [*patresfamilias et matres*], should go to confession before Palm Sunday, and those who may be negligent in this would, as penalty, not be admitted to confession until after the octave of Easter, and until that time they will fast from meat just as in Lent."[35] This statute had a surprisingly wide distribution. It was reissued in Parisian statutes, probably between 1228 and 1248, in a slightly different version in early-thirteenth-century statutes of Cambrai, again in statutes of Rouen in 1245, and even in early fourteenth-century statutes of Rouen and Bayeux.[36] Although the synods clearly intended this canon to fulfill the function of *Omnis utriusque*, several key differences remain. Guillaume does not attempt to link confession and communion, and indeed, the French canons contain no requirement of annual *communion* until around midcentury; most expressly adopt the language of the Lateran Council.[37] The punishment for disobedience, furthermore, is an extension of the Lenten fast, perhaps difficult to enforce on the indifferent parishioner, but at least in theory a way of marking the offender in the town or village still more dramatically than simple exclusion from communion or a report to the archdeacon, the immediate effects under the Lateran's Canon 21. The guilty would still be eating fish when everyone else was busy celebrating

35. Pontal I, pp. 100–101 (c. 8): "quod omnes, saltem patresfamilias et matres, ad confessionem veniant ante Pascha Floridum; et qui in hoc negligentes fuerint, in penam, usque post octavas Pasche, ad confessionem non admittantur sed usque ad illud tempus a carnibus jejunabunt sicut in quadragesima."

36. Mansi, 23:767 (Paris, prob. 1228–1248, c. 8); Pommeraye, *Sanctae Rotomagensis Ecclesiae concilia*, p. 256 (Rouen, 1245); Guillaume Bessin, *Concilia Rotomagensis provinciae* (Rouen, 1717), vol. II, p. 241 (Bayeux, beginning of the fourteenth century, c. 33), and vol. II, p. 85 (Rouen, 1311, c. 19); Boeren, "Les plus anciens statuts du diocèse de Cambrai (XIIIe siècle)," p. 137 (Cambrai, first half thirteenth century). The statute of Bayeux does not mention *matres*, only *patresfamilias*. For this statute's diffusion, see J. Avril, "Remarques sur un aspect de la vie religieuse paroissiale: La pratique de la confession et de la communion du Xe au XIVe siècle," in *L'encadrement religieux*, pp. 353–354.

37. Louis Braeckmans, *Confession et communion au Moyen Age et au Concile de Trente* (Gembloux, 1971), has investigated the gradual establishment of the view among theologians and canonists that communion should always be preceded by confession, and that the purpose of the Fourth Lateran's canon 21 was to ensure this confession. But he starts from the assumption that annual communion was an already recognized requirement, and asks when confession came to be seen as a complementary necessity; similar is Gy's approach, "Les bases de la pénitence moderne," pp. 73–74, though he argues against Braeckmans that the link between the two is very old; cf. also on this J. Avril, "Remarques sur un aspect de la vie religieuse," pp. 346–350, who perhaps takes the canons on the subject too seriously as evidence of actual practice. Their assumption of long-standing annual communion is a natural one, since several early medieval councils had attempted to require it. But in the thirteenth century, at least northern French synods put a great deal of emphasis on confession and relatively little on communion.

Easter and speculating what sins the confession-shy must have committed.[38]

Most striking of all is the decision to concentrate enforcement on the *patresfamilias et matres*, that is, heads of households. Unmarried men and women, servants, apprentices, and the unemployed, together a very substantial part of the population of town and country, might escape participation in the sacrament. Doubtless the bishop hoped that *patresfamilias* would help set an example for their *familia*, that is, for the servants as well as the children. If the priest could induce at least the most conspicuous and responsible members of the community to obedience, then perhaps some of the servants could be tempted to imitate the good behavior of those whose favor and whose bread they desired. If a good example did not persuade them, then at least the law of the church would be visibly upheld by the pillars of the community. Even later in the century, when for the most part synods used the exact text of *Omnis utriusque* to state the requirement of annual confession, bishops and reformers evidently continued to expect more of the heads of households. In the south, Humbert de Romans complained in his sermons that too many servants never attended church at all; but, significantly, he placed the greatest blame on their masters, who, he said, too often set an example of godlessness for their male employees and sometimes actually prohibited their female servants from taking the time to attend.[39] In 1314, in fact, the statutes of Orléans tried to make the heads actually responsible for the participation of the rest of the household. "Let them also admonish the heads of households [*patresfamilias et matresfamilias*] in the same way that they send their households to confession within the aforesaid time limit."[40] The tradition in the canons that those married and with

---

38. It is possible that the rule was enforced. In Artois, the last day of Eastertide used to be known as "Pâques à Maniers" (i.e., *meuniers*), apparently because millers proverbially were so sinful that they only confessed after Lent was over: M. A. Demont, "Le blé dans les traditions populaires artésiennes," *Revue de folklore français et de folklore colonial* 6 (1935): 49. But this is a late tradition, and impossible to document for the medieval period.

39. Cited in Murray, "Religion among the Poor in Thirteenth-Century France," p. 302. See Bibl. Vat. lat. 9868, f. 233r-v (Carcassonne, 1278–1280), for a southern French statute that exempts servants from the requirement to sit through until the end of the mass on Sundays. The notion that heads of households owed a greater participation in the sacraments than unattached young men was extremely durable; see, for example, George Eliot's *Silas Marner*, chapter 10, on English village life during the Napoleonic Wars: "The inhabitants of Raveloe were not severely regular in their church-going, and perhaps there was hardly a person in the parish who would not have held that to go to church every Sunday in the calendar would have shown a greedy desire to stand well with Heaven. . . . At the same time, it was understood to be requisite for all who were not household servants, or young men, to take the sacrament at one of the great festivals."

40. Alfonse del Bene, *Codex statutorum synodalium dioecesis aurelianensis* (Orléans, 1674), pp. 129–130: "Moneantur etiam Patresfamilias et Matresfamilias similiter quod mittant suas familias ad confessionem infra terminum praenotatum."

children or servants had a greater responsibility than those on the economic and social fringes of the community, shows that the bishops had something different in mind from the abstract praises of contrition in much contemporary theology. If it was impossible to arouse penitential shame and tears in every layman—as these canons assume—then at least the reformers might forge a visible Christian community out of the parish, a community based on the conspicuous participation of all important residents in certain central sacraments and feasts. Private penance, secret though the sins confessed in it may have remained, was and was supposed to be a public affirmation of faith and obedience.

The theologians and canonists themselves did not in fact concur in any simple interpretation of *Omnis utriusque*, particularly in the question of who were bound to confess. No writer argued that young servants were actually exempt, but in the first half of the century, some theologians and canonists held that the law obligated to annual confession only those conscious of having committed mortal sin. As we saw in Chapter 2, just before 1215 Robert Courson had suggested that a parishioner unsure of whether he was in a state of charity at Easter should be told to consult his own conscience. "Indeed he [the priest] ought to leave it to his [the parishioner's] conscience and own judgment and to say to him that he should await whether he feels in his conscience that celestial odor and joy."[41] Pierre-Marie Gy has shown that some theologians held a similar view even after 1215.[42] Johannes Teutonicus, and, more emphatically, Albert the Great said that the rule of confession did not bind those not in mortal sin. Thomas Aquinas and Pierre de Tarentaise, wary of such latitude, suggested that those not in mortal sin should approach the parish priest to tell him this, but need not actually confess. On the other hand, Alexander of Hales, Bonaventure, Richard of Middleton, and Guillaume de Rennes held that *Omnis utriusque* bound all to confess without exception, which came to be the standard view.[43] All had

---

41. Kennedy, "Robert Courson on Penance," pp. 297–299: "immo debet eum sue relinquere conscientie et proprie arbitrio et ei dicere ut attendat utrum in conscientia sentiat illum celestem saporem et iocunditatem."

42. Gy, "Les bases de la pénitence moderne," pp. 77–78, and "Les définitions de la confession après le quatrième concile du Latran," in *L'aveu: Antiquité et Moyen-Age*, p. 287.

43. Johannes Teutonicus, in A. Garcia y Garcia, *Constitutiones Concilii quarti Lateranensis una cum Commentariis glossatorum*, Monumenta Iuris Canonici, ser. A, Corpus Glossatorum, 2 (Rome, 1981), p. 208 (cf. Bibl. Vat. lat. 1377, f. 310r); Albert the Great, *Commentarii in IV sententiarum*, IV D.17 a.64, vol. 29, p. 758, and *De sacramentis*, Q.2 a.12, in *Opera omnia*, vol. 26, p. 105; Thomas Aquinas, *Commentum in quatuor libros sententiarum*, IV D.17 q.3 a.1 qc ad 3; Pierre de Tarentaise, *In IV libros sententiarum*, IV D.17 q.1 a.4, pp. 192–193; Alexander of Hales, *Quaestiones disputatae*, Q.56 d.3 m.3, pp. 1088–1089; Bonaventure, *Commentaria in*

agreed that a central purpose of the confession required by *Omnis utriusque* was preparation for the annual Easter communion, which was also required;[44] and thus one could conceivably argue that those not in mortal sin could safely partake without prior confession. But the latitude of conscience allowed by early Scholastic theologians quickly disappeared. Thomas and especially the Franciscans hesitated to allow the naive parishioner to consult his own conscience. Better that he should go to confession and let the priest decide whether his sins are mortal. Better, too, that the priest know his parishioner to be free of mortal sins and not simply avoiding him out of shame or indifference. A priest ignorant of the consciences of his flock could hardly guide his parish to all the moral and sacramental improvements that the synods now demanded. By the late thirteenth century, many French synodal canons routinely required the priest to present to diocesan officials a list of those who had failed to confess.[45]

The early Dominicans' latitude to lay parishioners was probably no more accepted in contemporary France than Robert Courson's conscience-consulting layman. Synods both early and late breathe not a word about excluding those guilty of only venial sin. In fact, as we have seen, when they drew a distinction between masters and servants not found in the theology, they excused many from confession and communion who doubtless were guilty of mortal sin, while binding others who were not. Still, the theological debate on the purpose and application of *Omnis utriusque* has some lessons for our investigation. Theologians on both sides regarded it as a critical purpose of the canon on confession that laymen of the parish should unite in an annual communion and that a single priest should be familiar with the consciences of each of his parishioners and so know the weaknesses of the parish as a whole. The public demonstration of unity in participation was as important as the individual benefits of participation alone.

The twelfth century had seen a large-scale redefinition of parishes

---

quatuor libros sententiarum, IV D.17 p.1 a.2 q.1, pp. 442–443; Richard of Middleton, *Super quatuor libros sententiarum*, IV D.17 a.2 q.4, pp. 249–250; Guillaume de Rennes, commentary on Ramón de Peñafort, *Summa de poenitentia*, 3.34.20, p. 454. Oddly, most canonists seem to have neglected this important issue.

44. Gy, "Les bases de la pénitence moderne," pp. 77–78; Braeckmans, *Confession et communion au moyen âge*, esp. pp. 42–50.

45. Pontal II, p. 132 (Rouen, first half of the thirteenth century); Gosse, *Histoire de l'abbaye . . . d'Arrouaise*, p. 604 (Arras, 1291); T. Gousset, ed., *Les actes de la province ecclésiastique de Reims* (Reims, 1842–1844), 2: 447 (Cambrai, ca. 1300–1310); Martène and Durand, *Thesaurus novus anecdotorum* (Paris, 1717), vol. IV, col. 1108 (Tréguier, 1334, c. 74). For examples from southern synods, see Bibl. Vat. lat. 9868, f. 183r (Carcassonne, 1270); and Mansi 24:995 (Cahors, Rodez, Tulle, pre-1318, c. 15).

and the building of churches to accomodate an expanded population and higher expectations for lay piety. Thirteenth-century bishops and theologians used synodal stautes to put some life into the new administrative districts.[46] Many statutes gave the parish priest new duties in ensuring at least an outward respect for the sacraments in addition to, and in connection with, the requirement of annual confession and communion. The statutes of Arras, for example, instructed the pastor to tell his parishioners to attend church frequently; to hear the office at least on Sundays and feast days; to observe the feasts, fasts, and vigils of the diocese; to learn and to say the Lord's Prayer, Creed, and Ave Maria; and to take the vows of marriage only with deliberation and counsel, that is, not secretly. Like absence from confession and communion, nonobservance of feasts and fasts was now to be penalized by denunciation in church.[47] Disobedience or mere neglect would be punished by public humiliation, a weapon doubtless much more effective against the conspicuous *patresfamilias* of town or village than against unattached day laborers or servants. The canon even tried to set up a mechanism for a parish-by-parish investigation of disobedience.

> Priests should meet three times a year in every deanery in an appropriate place so that they may hear preaching, the synodal statutes may be read, and diligent inquiries may be made concerning the behavior of the priests and the state of the parish and the parishioners, whether any there are suspected of heresy or usury or contempt of the Eucharist (if one has not received it at least once a year), or suspected of sacrilege, secret marriage, and suchlike. And these things are to be corrected if possible, or reported to the bishop.[48]

The bishop and his archdeacons expected the parish priest to watch and report everything that went on among his lay flock; the bishop and his archdeacons would watch the priests.

The mention of heresy as one particularly dangerous sin for the parish priest to detect and report raises the question of the link be-

---

46. See Foreville, "Les statuts synodaux et le renouveau pastoral," p. 120.
47. Gosse, *Histoire de l'abbaye . . . d'Arrouaise*, p. 587 (Arras, thirteenth century, c. 11).
48. Gosse, *Histoire de l'abbaye . . . d'Arrouaise*, p. 588 (Arras, thirteenth century, c. 11): "Ter in anno in quolibet decanatu ad locum congruum conveniant Sacerdotes ut ibi audiant predicationem, et statuta Synodi legantur, et de vita Sacerdotum et statu Parochie et Parochianorum diligenter inquiratur; si ibidem sunt aliqui suspecti de heresi, vel usura, vel contemptu Eucaristie, si non recipiatur saltem ad minus semel in anno, sacrilegio, furtivis nuptiis, et hujusmodi; et hec emendentur, si fieri potest, vel Episcopo nuncientur." See also Foreville, "Les statuts synodaux et le renouveau pastoral," p. 124.

tween the enforcement of *Omnis utriusque* and the enforcement of orthodoxy. The issue is an important one not only because of Henry Charles Lea's contention that Innocent III instituted Canon 21 as a measure against heresy,[49] but also because it bears on the use of *Omnis utriusque* as a means to build a Christian community. First, disobedience to the canon might itself be taken as heresy. At the end of the twelfth century, Peter Cantor assumed that if an excommunicant who has confessed and been reconciled outside the parish is refused Easter communion when he returns to his village, his neighbors would take him to be a Cathar.[50] The assumption suggests that parishioners attending Easter mass watched their coparishioners carefully; anyone barred must be guilty of heresy. Peter does not say whether contemporary Frenchmen thought heresy the most likely cause of excommunication, or rather indifference to excommunication the mark of the heretic. Some late canons, adopting the latter assumption, demanded that excommunicants who neglected to seek reconciliation with the church should be denounced "as suspected of heresy."[51] Neither Peter nor the statutes made the leap of reasoning that anyone who neglected communion or confession was actually a heretic, but the canons did try to brand flagrant and obstinate offenders of these and other church laws as heretics, perhaps as Cathars. They did not share our distinction between disobedience and disbelief.

It is less clear whether, as Lea suggests, priests used confession as a primary means of ferreting out and punishing heretics. Some canonists and theologians disputed whether a confessor hearing an admission of heresy could break the seal and use this knowledge. Ramón de Peñafort seemed to think that the priest should warn the bishop in general terms; at any rate, he held, the priest is not quite bound to keep quiet, because one who admits to holding heretical beliefs, rather than recanting them, cannot make true penance. But Alexander of Hales, Bonaventure, and most other subsequent theologians held instead that the seal is unbreakable, since, as some put it, anything the

49. "It is not uncharitable to assume that [Canon 21's] object was ecclesiastical aggrandizement and increased facilities for the detection of heresy," Lea, *A History of Auricular Confession*, 1: 242. Actually, one Roman Catholic writer has agreed that the exposing of heretics was a key aim of Canon 21, even if he has not endorsed Lea's formulation: Gabriel Le Bras, *Institutions ecclésiastiques de la Chrétienté médiévale, Histoire de l'Eglise*, 12 (Paris, 1959), p. 134. More reliable, however, is Pierre-Marie Gy's discussion of this view: "Le précepte de la confession annuelle (Latran IV, c. 21) et la détection des hérétiques: S. Bonaventure et S. Thomas contre S. Raymond de Peñafort," *Revue des sciences philosophiques et théologiques* 58 (1974): 444–450.
50. Peter Cantor, *Summa de sacramentis*, IV q.148, p. 359.
51. Mansi 25:54–55 (Coutances, 1294): "tamquam suspecti de heresi"; Gousset, *Les actes . . . de Reims*, vol. II, p. 473 (Compiègne, 1301, c. 6).

priest hears in confession he knows only as God, not man. Priests, some said, might warn the bishop in a vague way that heresy was around, and no more.[52] Two northern French synods included heresy in the list of sins whose absolution was reserved to the bishop; this would expose the heretic in a quasi-public way, although no more than many other sinners.[53] In the Midi, where heresy was so much more of a threat, several bishops also made heresy a reserved sin, but they also allowed more privacy for those who had committed reserved sins in secret, which would have greatly diminished the utility of confession to expose heretics.[54] In general, there is little evidence that southern French bishops any more than their northern colleagues saw annual confession as a major weapon against heresy; the Inquisition and not synodal statutes or annual confession played this role.[55]

Certainly heretics as a rule received spectacularly public penances in the thirteenth century, but such heretics were generally discovered through an inquisition after denunciation, rather than through private confession.[56] On occasion, bishops might lay down more explicit rules against heresy in their statutes, prohibiting, for example, that laymen should dispute the Catholic faith among themselves in public

52. For the idea that the priest hears as God, not man, see above, Chapter 2. For the warnings of heresy, see Léon Honoré, Le secret de la confession (Bruges, 1924), p. 55; and Gy, "Le précepte de la confession annuelle (Latran IV, c. 21) et la détection des hérétiques," pp. 446–448. See Ramón de Peñafort, Summa de poenitentia, 3.34.60, pp. 490–491; Bonaventure, Commentaria in quatuor libros sententiarum, IV D.21 p.2 a.2 q.1, pp. 566–567; Pierre de Tarentaise, In IV libros sententiarum commentaria, IV D.21 q.4 a.1, pp. 241–242; Thomas Aquinas, Commentum in quatuor libros sententiarum IV D.21 q.3 a.1 qc. 1, pp. 858–859; Richard of Middleton, Super quatuor libros sententiarum IV D.21, a.4, q.2, pp. 340–342; Guido de Baysio, Rosarium, C.33 q.3 D.6 c.2, f. 371v.

53. Boeren, "Les plus anciens statuts du diocèse de Cambrai, p. 135 (Cambrai, 1287–1288, c. 3). BN latin 11067, f. 10v (Noyon, thirteenth century). See below on reserved cases in general.

54. Pontal II, pp. 318–320 (Nîmes, Arles, Béziers, etc., 1252, c. 63–65); and Bibl. Vat. lat. 9868, f. 185v (Carcassonne, 1270). These statutes make heresy a reserved sin but exempt all those who have committed reserved sins in secret from the need to be presented to the bishop. See below on reserved sins in general.

55. Foreville, "Les statuts synodaux et le renouveau pastoral," pp. 127–136. Cathar heretics and perhaps a very few Waldensians were known in mid-thirteenth-century Burgundy, Champagne, and Flanders; the inquisitor Robert Le Bougre, for instance, burned twenty alleged heretics, including three echévins, in Cambrai in 1236, and three years later another 183 in Mont-Aimé, in rural Champagne. See Charles Homer Haskins, Studies in Mediaeval Culture (Oxford, 1929), pp. 193–195. Yves Dossat, "L'hérésie en Champagne aux XIIe et XIIIe siècles," reprinted in his Eglise et hérésie en France au XIIIe siècle, (London, 1982), pp. 57–73. But many contemporaries thought that Robert's campaigns were largely unnecessary, and the synods devoted little space to the problem of heresy.

56. See Lea, A History of Auricular Confession, 2: 87, for examples. A. Cazenave, "Aveu et contrition: Manuels de confesseurs et interrogatoires d'Inquisition en Languedoc et en Catalogne," in La piété populaire au Moyen Age, Actes du 99e Congrès national des sociétés savantes, Besançon, 1974, Philologie et histoire jusqu'à 1610, 1 (Paris, 1977), pp. 333–349, argues for the existence d'une affinité between the confessional and the inquisition in southern France. But the similarity in their use of self-accusation does not mean that the two procedures were confused or combined.

or in private.[57] But this had nothing to do with *Omnis utriusque*. In England, where heresy was not a practical problem, one statute did tell confessors to report heretics to the bishop in order to suppress new heresies in the region.[58] Other English canons are quite silent on this point, however, and it is likely that this one reflected an individual bishop's desire for comprehesiveness rather than a well-planned campaign. In conclusion, then, there is little evidence that Innocent III or French and English prelates consistently fashioned *Omnis utriusque* into a weapon against heresy. The safest conclusion is that theologians and bishops alike thought that the purpose of *Omnis utriusque* was the obvious one of increased lay confession and communion for their own sake. They thought of confession and communion as the visible signs of parish participation in the wider church, alongside church marriage and observance of feasts and fasts. In short, bishops nearly everywhere believed sensibly enough that the battle for orthodox allegiance had to be won before any attempt should be made to deepen lay devotion or to build visible communities by joining in the sacraments.

Our discussion of the purpose of annual confession in the view of the theologians and the bishops has so far taken no account of the actual extent of its observance. Studies for the later Middle Ages, such as Jacques Toussaert's research into Flemish religiosity, suggest that Lenten confession and Easter communion were far from universal after the Black Death.[59] No comparable statistical study can confirm our suspicions that participation was just as spotty in thirteenth-century France. Nicole Bériou has plausibly suggested that the practice of annual confession probably did increase over the course of the century after starting from a low base. This may be more as a result of lay social pressures, including the influence of confraternities, than from priestly injunctions[60]—although, as we have seen, the priests deliberately used social pressure to coerce their parishioners. As late

57. Bibl. Vat. lat. 9868, f. 273v (Carcassonne, ca. 1300; against public disputations only), and f. 305v (Carcassonne, 1309; against public and private disputations).

58. Powicke and Cheney, p. 371 (Salisbury, 1238–1244, c. 14). Why should the diocese of Salisbury, hardly noted for heresy in the thirteenth century, be the only one among English or northern French dioceses to invoke the church's right to expose heretics?

59. Jacques Toussaert, *Le sentiment religieux en Flandre à la fin du Moyen-Age* (Paris, 1963), pp. 109, 124–129.

60. Bériou, "Autour de Latran IV (1215)," pp. 89–90. A. Murray, citing Humbert de Romans's complaints, doubts that there was much compliance, "Piety and Impiety in Thirteenth-Century Italy," in *Popular Belief and Practice*, ed. G. J. Cuming and D. Baker, Studies in Church History, 8 (Cambridge, 1972), pp. 92–93; similar is the view of Paul Adam, *La vie paroissiale en France au XIVe siècle* (Paris, 1964). But J. Avril, "Remarques sur un aspect de la vie religieuse paroissiale," pp. 354–358, is rather more optimistic about compliance; he points to occasional synods that enjoined more than annual confession. Evidence about actual practice is very hard to come by.

as 1295, Bishop Guillaume Le Maire of Angers complained that he found some (*nonnullos*) who abstained from confession and communion over a series of years.[61] But even a guess at the percentage of participants around 1300 is quite impossible, and we cannot tell whether abstainers held back out of sheer indifference, shame, or hostility to others in the parish.[62]

We do know that many preferred to confess to friars, in part to escape the embarrassment of confession to a fellow villager, and some succeeded in evading the parish priest even in Lent.[63] Neglect of Lenten confession together with confession to the friars probably weakened efforts to use annual confession and communion to build the parish. And the long list of rules for sacraments and observances that each parish priest was supposed to enforce would likely strain their knowledge and patience, especially in the light of the frequency of bad behavior among the parish clergy themselves, at least as evident in Eudes Rigaud's register. It is hard to imagine such unprepossessing clergymen pursuing half the duties that the synods so seriously imposed on them. The synods themselves inevitably took account of the limits of lay devotion and clerical leadership by admitting that *Omnis utriusque* would not really be enforced on everyone, and more generally by requiring a standard of participation far below that demanded later by the Council of Trent. The bishops tried to improve parishioners' observance, not perfect it.

Private Penance in Practice

If the interpretation of *Omnis utriusque* added a deliberately public dimension to private penance, the practical operation of penance unintentionally magnified that public dimension. Every stage of private penance, from confession to satisfaction, might threaten the privacy of the penitent. We may follow the penitent's path step by step.

---

61. Arnauld, *Statuts du diocèse d'Angers*, p. 87 (Angers, 1295, c. 1). A synod of Tréguier in 1334 complained that many neglected confession for ten years or more: Martène and Durand, *Thesaurus novus anecdotorum*, vol. IV, col. 1108 (c. 74).

62. Bossy, *Christianity in the West*, p. 47, has suggested that in the later Middle Ages, the chief reason for failure to confess, besides concubinage, was that the parishioner was in a state of hostility with his neighbor and had no intention of making peace; there is no real evidence for this.

63. Murray, "Confession as a Historical Source in the Thirteenth Century," p. 285. See Welter, *Le Speculum laicorum*, p. 30, cited in Chapter 2: a husband recommends confession to a traveling friar. Payen argues implausibly that the new emphasis on lay confession at all times of the year eroded the traditional communalism of penance: "La pénitence dans le contexte culturel," p. 426. Non-Lenten confession outside of a confraternal context was likely a rarity.

To begin with, until Carlo Borromeo invented the confessional,
Lenten confession was a surprisingly open affair.[64] The seal of confession, of course, applied only to the content, not to the fact of
confession. The priest was supposed to report all those who had not
appeared to him or had leave to confess to another. Sermons preaching penance usually preceded Lenten confession; collective communion generally followed. Most parishioners could see for themselves
who appeared when, and they drew their own conclusions.[65]

The circumstances, therefore, did nothing to conceal the fact of
confession, and they had very little to protect its content. French
synods almost without exception insisted that confession be held in a
conspicuous place. "Let priests choose a very public [communiorem]
place in the church for hearing confessions, so that they may be seen
in public [communiter] by all; and let no one receive confessions in
hidden places or outside the church except in great necessity or in
case of sickness."[66] Whether the canons called for an "eminent place"
or an "open" or a "public" place within the small parish church, they
must have made privacy extremely difficult. English canons almost
always phrased the demand slightly differently, making explicit the
link between publicity and the prevention of scandal with women
penitents. "However, confessions of women should be heard in an
exposed place in sight of people, but not in their hearing."[67] And,
"Let women confess in open and without a curtain, so that they may

64. See Bossy, "The Social History of Confession," pp. 24–29.
65. Lester K. Little, "Les techniques de la confession et la confession comme technique,"
in Faire croire, pp. 89–90. As we have seen above, in a later period sinful millers were proverbially slow to confess. Peter Cantor approves of parish priests rebuking non-confessing laymen in everyone's presence: Summa de sacramentis, III q.137, p. 321. Still, the growing universality of confession may have provided some measure of anonymity.
66. Pontal I, p. 62 (Paris, ca. 1200, c. 27): "Ad audiendum confessiones, communiorem
locum in ecclesia sibi eligant sacerdotes, ut communiter ab omnibus videri possint: et in locis
abditis aut extra ecclesiam nullus recipiat confessiones, nisi in magna necessitate vel infirmi-
tate." A great many synodal statutes repeat the canon nearly word for word, e.g.: Pontal I,
p. 192 (Synodal of the West, c. 192); Pontal II, p. 152 (Le Mans, 1240–1247, c. 9); Mansi
23:387 (Rouen, 1235, c. 83), 25:38 (Coutances, ca. 1300, c. 34), 25:75 (Bayeux, ca. 1300,
c. 81), 23:737 (Le Mans, 1247); BN latin 11067, f. 4r (Noyon, thirteenth century); Gosse,
Histoire de l'abbaye . . . d'Arrouaise, p. 538 (Arras, thirteenth century); Gousset, Les actes . . . de
Reims, vol. II, p. 444 (Cambrai, 1300–1310); BN latin 15172, f. 146v (Lisieux, before 1321).
See Nicole Lemaître, "Confession privée et confession publique dans les paroisses du XVIe
siècle," Revue d'histoire de l'Eglise de France 69, no. 183 (1983), p. 193, on the survival of the rule
in sixteenth-century statutes.
67. Powicke and Cheney, p. 32 (Canterbury, 1213–1214, c. 42), and p. 594 (Wells, 1258?,
c. 6): "Confessiones autem mulierum audiantur in propatulo quantum ad visum hominum,
non quantum ad auditum." A couple of English statutes use the French wording, but apply
the rule particularly to women: Powicke and Cheney, p. 144 (unknown diocese; 1222–1225, c.
27), and p. 637 (London, 1245–1259, c. 19). One calls for the presence of a third person at
confessions of women, with the observer to stay out of earshot: p. 370 (Salisbury, 1238–1244,
c. 12).

be seen but not heard."[68] The English statutes suggest that at least some dioceses there must have used a veil routinely to protect the privacy of male penitents; it seems to have been unknown in France. Among southern French synods, some follow the northern French pattern on this topic, some the English, emphasizing the need for openness with women.[69] But not even this latter type of statute actually restricts the rule to female penitents. If we can discern a purpose in the northern French version, it seems to be the general principle of the openness of the sacraments, in line with the prohibitions on secret marriage or nocturnal meetings and dances at the cemetery. Significantly, the northern French statutes place the greatest stress on the prohibition of confession at night or outside of church, rather than on the prevention of scandal with female penitents. Whatever the idea behind the rule, overhearing confessions must have been an occasional possibility. Meanwhile, within confraternities and within especially religious communities, leaders stringently enforced the rules of periodic confession by checking with the appropriate confessor—although they did not necessarily find out what the brother or sister had said.[70]

Under certain circumstances, the secrecy of confession might be even less well-guarded. Angry lay victims or misbehaving priests might pose threats to the seal. Laymen might think the seal worse than unnecessary when it conflicted with a demand for justice and blood vengeance. Exemplary tales from all through the Middle Ages reveal the problem. In one story, a priest is killed for protecting the secrecy of a peasant who had killed a rich man.[71] The theologian Peter Cantor wonders whether a confessor ought to reveal knowledge of conspiracy against a prince; he concludes that the priest should intimate the danger in general terms.[72] Most stories tell of priests risking injury to protect the seal; doubtless, priestly tattling was not as edifying—or as comforting—a story for a preacher's lay audience. A

68. Powicke and Cheney, p. 992 (Exeter, 1287, c. 5): "Mulieres in aperto et extra velum confiteantur, non ut audiri valeant sed videri"; and see also p. 454 (Chichester, 1245–1252, c. 16). The London council cited above also refers to the veil.

69. For rules of the northern French type: Bibl. Vat. reg. lat. 1065, f. 32ra (Poitiers, 1259–1271); Mansi 32:293 (Autun, 1286, c. 28), 24:986 (Cahors, Rodez, Tulle, before 1318, c. 14). For an emphasis on confessions of women ("et precipue si fuerint mulieres"): Pontal II, p. 288 (Nîmes, Arles, Béziers, etc., 1252, c. 25); Bibl. Vat. lat. 9868, f. 183r (Carcassonne, 1270). See Dobiache-Rojdestvensky, La vie paroissiale, p. 63, for a review of this rule in southern French synods.

70. Little, "Les techniques de la confession," p. 90.

71. Robert de Sorbon, De tribus dietis, pp. 43–44. The story is repeated by Peter of Luxembourg, ca. 1380: cf. Hervé Martin, "Confession et contrôle social à la fin du Moyen Age," in Pratiques de la confession, p. 120.

72. Peter Cantor, Summa de sacramentis, III q.136, pp. 316–320.

number of *exempla*, however, appeal to their fears as well as to their hopes. In one standard tale, a priest threatens to reveal a woman's sins if she does not sleep with him. A miracle intervenes to protect her anonymity.[73] In another story, a woman confesses that she has killed her son-in-law. The priest reveals it to the victim's kin, who have her condemned to be burnt. Miraculously, the flames do not touch her. They strike her with a lance, but she still takes three days to die.[74] One could imagine more satisfactory miracles, and in any case, not every sinner could have expected divine intervention at all. Early after 1215, Peter of Poitiers accepted the indiscretion of one's parish priest as a legitimate excuse for choosing to confess to another.[75] While some parishioners preferred to confess to passing friars rather than to their pastor, secular priests struck back by raising fears about friars' discretion, too. Occasional midcentury statutes forbade jealous parish priests from accusing Franciscan and Dominican confessors of breaking the seal.[76] Meanwhile, theologians and synodal statutes warned against priests' letting parishioners guess at someone's sins by dropping hints in sermons. A priest might give too many specific examples in preaching against usury, for example.[77] We cannot tell how many priests misbehaved, but probably the greatest danger to secrecy was not a priest's outright revelation of culprit to victim, but the ordinary and untraceable gossip based on half-heard whispers and a little speculative deduction. Simply losing face before the village priest himself could be unbearable even without the explicit threat of further revelation. In one sermon *exemplum*, a woman tells her husband that she consented in the murder of her mother. Her husband tells her to confess to the priest, but she replied, "How could I reveal such a crime to someone I see everyday?" She could not even raise the courage to tell a passing friar, and she strangled herself in despair.[78]

The nature of the subsequent stages of private penance made further speculative deduction possible. Secret confession was only the first step; the priest then had to determine whether any of the sins fell under the categories reserved to the bishop or pope, and if not,

73. Gobi, *Scala celi,* f. 46r-v. Other stories have laymen or devils dressing as priests to hear confessions, f. 44r, 48v.

74. From an exemplum of Arnold of Liège (late thirteenth century), cited in Jacques Berlioz, "Les ordalies dans les *exempla* de la confession (XIIIe-XIVe siècles)," *L'aveu,* pp. 330–331.

75. Peter of Poitiers, *Summa de confessione,* pp. 79–80.

76. Dobiache-Rojdestvensky, *La vie paroissiale,* pp. 126–127; Pontal II, p. 155 (Le Mans 1240–1247); Mansi 24:380 (Saintes, 1280, c. 15).

77. Peter Cantor, *Summa de sacramentis,* III q.137, pp. 320–321; but Peter says the priest may go right ahead so long as the usurers are already notorious.

78. Welter, *Le speculum laicorum,* p. 30.

whether any restitution had to be made to the victim. Only then would the priest assign satisfaction to be performed, and this, too, was a source of parish suspicion and gossip. We may look at these stages in order. Most synodal statutes included a standard list of cases reserved to the bishop and pope, in practice most often heard by their special officers for penance, the penitentiaries (*penitentiarii*). According to the statutes of Paris from the beginning of the century, the priest was required to send to his superiors anyone who confessed to homicide, sacrilege, homosexual acts, incest, the rape of virgins, assault against parents, broken vows, and "suchlike"; the pope alone had jurisdiction in cases of assault on clerics, arson, and simony.[79] Many dioceses also specified adultery and abortion among cases reserved to the bishop. With few other revisions and clarifications, these lists remained the rule.[80] Southern French synods as a rule provided long and specific lists of the sins that required absolution by the bishop or his representative, and many made a point of including heresy among the sins named.[81] English synods occasionally provided similar lists, or at least referred to the principle of reserved cases without further specifics.[82] Oddly, at Cambrai and Soissons, but apparently nowhere else, thirteenth-century statutes required the priest to send to the bishop all who had confessed to theft, a demand that doubtless must have greatly swelled the numbers of penitents traveling to the cathedral city for absolution.[83] By the end of the century, the bishop of Cambrai at least had struck it off the list.[84]

The reservation of certain cases to the bishop and pope clearly

---

79. Pontal I, p. 62 (c. 29 and 30).

80. See, e.g., Mansi, 23:382 (Rouen, 1235, c. 62), and 23:744 (Le Mans, 1247); BN latin 11067, f. 4v (Noyon, thirteenth century); Gosse, *Histoire de l'abbaye . . . d'Arrouaise*, p. 538 (Arras, thirteenth century, c. 8); Gousset, *Les actes . . . de Reims*, pp. 444–445 (Cambrai, 1300–1310); BN latin 15172, f. 151r (Lisieux, before 1321). Martène and Durand, *Thesaurus novus anecdotorum* (Paris, 1717) vol. IV, col. 1099 (Tréguier, 1334, c. 9).

81. Pontal II, pp. 196–198 (Sisteron, 1225–1235, c. 32); Pontal II, p. 24 (Albi, 1230, c. 42); Pontal II, p. 52 (Bordeaux, 1234, c. 12); Pontal II, p. 318 (Nîmes, Arles, Béziers, etc., 1252, c. 63); Mansi 23:1199 (Clermont, 1268, c. 7); Bibl. Vat. lat. 1065, f. 32ra (Poitiers, 1259–1271); Bibl. Vat. lat. 9868, f. 185v (Carcassonne, 1270); Mansi 24:380 (Saintes, 1280, c. 14), 32:293 (Autun, 1286, c. 30), and 24:984–985 (Cahors, Rodez, Tulle, pre-1318, c. 14). Some of these statutes included sexual relations with Jews and Saracens among reserved sins.

82. Powicke and Cheney, p. 133 (Winchester, 1224, c. 49; mentions only perjury); p. 638 (London, 1245–1259, c. 21, a complete list); p. 900 (Lambeth, 1281, c. 7; mentions only voluntary homicide); p. 1084 (Chichester, 1289, c. 11; refers only to "enormia . . . delicta" in general).

83. Boeren, "Les plus anciens statuts du diocèse de Cambrai," 3:136 (first half of the thirteenth century) and 4:135 (1287–1288). The list of the reserved cases given at the end of the latter statutes does not quite correspond to the sins mentioned as reserved in the text, and does not include theft (4:155). Martène and Durand, *Veterum scriptorum*, vol. VIII, col. 1542 (Soissons, thirteenth century).

84. Gousset, *Les actes . . . de Reims*, II, pp. 444–445 (Cambrai, 1300–1310).

threatened the seal of confession. Not surprisingly, the practice originated in the theology of public penance and excommunication.[85] In
the twelfth century, for instance, we find Senatus, the prior of Worcester from 1189 to 1196, stipulating that every penitent owing solemn
penance, even for a secret sin, must go to the bishop for absolution.
"Therefore, where solemn penance is required, a simple priest does
not release the penitent, not even if the offense is secret, because in
certain cases, I hear that not even an abbot may absolve someone
subject to him—which is worth noting."[86] Senatus recognizes that the
principle he enunciates may sound extraordinary. Even a monk may
have to answer to an authority above his abbot, and even for something discovered only in secret confession. Of course, here Senatus is
saying that reserved cases are the same as those that require solemn
penance. Later, the concept of reserving certain secret and certain
public sins will survive; but the bishop will no longer necessarily impose public *solemn* penance for reserved secret sins. The desire to
reserve certain *sins* to the bishop's jurisdiction was unquestionably the
result of reserving certain *rituals* of penance (that is, solemn penance
and excommunication) to the bishop.[87] When the theologians no
longer allowed public penances for any secret sins, the bishops rather
inconsistently kept control of the absolution of these sins. In fact, the
reservation of certain sins to bishop and pope amounted to a quasi-
public penance.

Any requirement to send penitents to the bishop obviously risked
exposing them to the speculation and gossip of their neighbors.[88]
The northern French manuals and statutes explicitly recognized the
danger, but they insisted nonetheless that even secret reserved sins
must be referred to superiors. Like Senatus, the bishops noticed that
reservation of cases was an anomaly. Outside northern France, occasional statutes made provision for recalcitrant sinners. In England, a
statute of Winchester tried to make secret perjurers who revealed
their sin in confession go to the bishop for absolution, but it frankly
admitted the difficulty of enforcement. "All those who have perjured

85. S. L. Pérez López, "El sacramento de la penitencia en las costituciones sinodales de
Galicia (1215–1563) y su contexto histórico," *Estudios Mindonienses* 2 (1986): 90, denies any
connection between the reservation of sins and public penance, which he asserts disappeared,
but his own evidence contradicts this conclusion.

86. Delhaye, "Deux textes de Senatus de Worcester sur la pénitence," p. 220: "Ubi ergo
solempnis exigitur penitentia, minor sacerdos confitentem non soluit, nec etiam si occultum
fuerit delictum, quod in certis casibus exaudio in quibus nec etiam abbas sibi subiectum
absoluere potest, quod est notabile."

87. J. Avril, *Le gouvernement des évêques*, 2:715.

88. A. Murray, "Confession as a Historical Source," p. 283; Lea, *A History of Auricular
Confession*, 1:438.

themselves with false testimony in inquests and assizes or elsewhere should be sent to us for absolution, even if it is hidden, if they can be induced to do this in any way. But if the perjury is hidden and they cannot be induced to come to our penitentiary, let penance be imposed on them, lest they die in this sin."[89] Clearly, it was going to be hard to coax such a sinner to make the trek to the cathedral and possibly expose his guilt to his enemies and the king's justices. In the south of France, bishops in a number of statutes reluctantly conceded that those who had *secretly* committed reserved sins and stubbornly refused to go to the cathedral city could have their penances set by simple priests, but only with proper consultation of the bishop's representatives about the case, "if this could be done conveniently."[90] Northern French synods, more favorable to the exposure of sinners, never went this far. One synod at Cambrai tried to limit the reservation in cases of adultery only to protect a modicum of secrecy. All men who confessed to adultery must go to the bishop or his penitentiary, but only those women who were notorious for their adultery were required to go.[91] Adultery was a particularly sensitive problem. Husbands might guess that their wives had committed adultery if they saw them dispatched to the cathedral city, and, as we shall see, the satisfactions imposed in such cases might be as much a clue as the reservation. Other French statutes did not imitate this arrangement, however. Both French and English canons routinely told parish priests to consult with discretion learned clerics or their superiors if they were not sure about what absolution a given sin required.[92] The consultation must have taken some tact. Doubtless many observant laymen could have drawn their own conclusions from the actions of the confessor and penitent after a confession.

After the priest determined that a confessing penitent had not committed any reserved sins, but before he could impose any satisfac-

---

89. Powicke and Cheney, p. 133 (Winchester, 1224, c. 49): "Omnes qui recognitionibus et assisis vel alibi falso testimonio periuri sunt ad nos mittantur absolvendi, licet etiam sit occultum, si ad hoc aliquo modo induci possunt. Si vero occultum fuerit periurium et induci non possint ut ad penitentiarium nostrum accedant, iniungatur eis penitentia ne in ipso peccato moriantur."

90. Pontal II, p. 320 (Nîmes, Arles, Béziers, etc., 1252, c. 64); Bibl. Vat. lat. 9868, f. 185 (Carcassonne, 1270).

91. Boeren, "Les plus anciens statuts du diocèse de Cambrai," 4:135 (Cambrai, 1287–1288, c. 3): "adulteria mulierum que sunt notoria et manifesta quantum ad mulieres." For the development of the office of *penitentiarius*, see below, Chapter 4.

92. E.g., Martène and Durand, *Veterum scriptorum*, vol. VIII, col. 1542 (Soissons, thirteenth century, c. 38); Gosse, *Histoire de l'abbaye . . . d'Arrouaise*, p. 583 (Arras, thirteenth century, c. 7); BN latin 11067, f. 4v (Noyon, thirteenth century); Boeren, "Les plus anciens statuts du diocèse de Cambria," 3:136 (Cambrai, first half of the thirteenth century). Powicke and Cheney, p. 74, (Salisbury, 1217–1219, c. 42), p. 994 (Exeter, 1287, c. 5).

tion, he had to ensure the payment of restitution to the victims. As we saw in Chapter 2, theologians argued that the offenses committed by sinners against their God, their neighbors, and their church required different types of recompense. For Peter Cantor and some other late-twelfth-century theologians, restitution was the payment to neighbor or the church; satisfaction and contrition, the payment to God. For Bonaventure and other midcentury theologians, restitution had become in theory an extrasacramental payment, but no less obligatory. More significantly, all agreed that sins like usury, theft, and fraud required a very literal satisfaction to the actual victims. Rape, too, might require a payment to the family or to the husband of the woman. And almost all the statutes, agreeing with the theologians, insisted on the absolute necessity of restitution, and especially warned against the solicitation of alms or masses before this debt was paid.[93] Priests were advised to question different classes of men very carefully about certain likely crimes requiring restitution. Merchants were liable to fraud and usury,[94] knights liable to stealing from their serfs.[95]

Here was a regular source of public gossip.[96] Some canons explicitly tried to protect the anonymity of the penitent by letting him make restitution through an intermediary wherever possible,[97] but the duty of repayment was absolute, the privacy of the penitent only desirable. In general, either the mediator or the culprit himself had to secure the assurance of the victim that the repayment was satisfactory. The victims were literally the dying penitent's "creditors," and the church would see them repaid before the heirs could collect.[98] The only

93. See, for example, Pontal, I, p. 64 (Paris, ca. 1200, c. 34), and p. 212 (Synodal of the West, c. 107); Mansi 23:393–394 (Rouen, 1235, c. 111–113), and 25:42–43, cols. 42–43 (Coutances, 1300, c. 44); BN latin 11067, f. 28r-v (Noyon, 1319); Boeren, "Les plus anciens statuts du diocèse de Cambrai," 3:136–137 (Cambrai, first half of the thirteenth century); Martène and Durand, *Thesaurus novus anecdotorum*, vol. IV, col. 1100 (Tréguier, 1334, c. 21). Oddly, in one synod, restitution is apparently titled a counsel, not a precept: Martène and Durand, *Veterum scriptorum*, vol. VIII, col. 1543 (Soissons, thirteenth century, c. 42). This may be a mistake of medieval or modern editors. English synods similarly require restitution before alms or satisfaction, e.g., Powicke and Cheney, p. 74 (Salisbury, 1217–1219, c. 44). For southern synods requiring restitution, see Pontal II, pp. 308–312 (Nîmes, Arles, Béziers, etc., 1252, c. 48–53); Mansi 24:993 (Cahors, Rodez, Tulle, pre-1318, c. 15); Bibl. Vat. lat. 9868, f. 185r (Carcassonne, 1270).

94. Mansi 23:393–394 (Rouen, 1235, c. 113).

95. Powicke and Cheney, p. 221 (Coventry, 1224–1237, from Alexander of Stavensby's tract on confession and penance).

96. See Bossy, *Christianity in the West*, pp. 47–48, on the problem of reconciling restitution with privacy.

97. E.g., Pontal I, p. 214 (Synodal of the West, c. 108); Mansi 23:393 (Rouen, 1235, c. 111), and 25:42 (Coutances, 1300, c. 44).

98. BN latin 11067, f. 28r-v (Noyon, 1319).

legitimate excuses for not paying were the failure to find the victim or his heirs or the indigence of the penitent. In the first case, the penitent might instead pay the amount due the victim to the poor or to the church. In the second, the statutes actually encouraged the impoverished penitent to approach his victim and ask for the forgiveness of the debt, a tactic that most bishops recognized was unrealistic. "But if the injury is serious and the offender cannot pay, he ought to seek forgiveness in person, that is, from the victim, if he dares; otherwise, let him do this through the mediation of some good man, without any names given; and he should make satisfaction with fasts and prayers and corporal discipline [i.e., flagellation]."[99] It might be dangerous for the culprit to appear before his victim or his victim's heirs. Robert Courson suggested that the penitent first approach his victim and offer as much as he could afford, and then depart on crusade.[100] This may have been a prudent way out. The threat of punishment by secular authorities, to say nothing of vengeance from the victim's family, made the situation perilous. However much the theologians approved of royal sanctions against excommunicants, they excluded any cooperation of the church in exposing criminals to secular law.[101]

The obligation of restitution could force wealthy usurers to confront poor borrowers, oppressive knights to face their serfs, pilfering servants to own up to their masters. Restitution in the villages exposed all the hostility of peasants or servants against their lords; restitution in the cities humiliated the most prominent bankers. We should recall that the church defined as usury many common means of raising capital. A merchant who made a successful investment might find his priest in Lent demanding that he return profit and capital together to a fellow merchant who was a "victim" in the eyes of the church. Repayment by a lone thief to an unsuspecting victim would surely have been the exception. Normally, the victim or borrower would likely have suspected the culprit already, and there may well have been long-standing enmity between the two, whether or not they were social equals. In the northern French cities, a single bourgeois often lorded over the neighborhood where he lived—sometimes even called his "fief"—as landowner, patron, employer, and, especially,

99. Mansi 23:393 (Rouen, 1235, c. 111); Pontal I, p. 214 (Synodal of the West, c. 108): "Si vero grave sit damnum, et laesor non possit solvere, debet petere personaliter veniam, scilicet a damnificato, si audeat; alioquin hoc faciat aliquo bono viro mediante, nemine nominato; et ipse satisfaciat jejuniis et orationibus, et corporalibus disciplinis."

100. Kennedy, "Robert Courson on Penance," p. 334. How the penitent could then afford the crusade is unclear.

101. N. M. Haring, "Peter Cantor's View on Ecclesiastical Excommunication and Its Practical Consequences," *Mediaeval Studies* 11 (1949): 109.

moneylender.[102] Under such circumstances, anonymity in restitution must have been nearly impossible in even the largest towns.

The victim owed restitution had the right to insist on the excommunication of a penitent refusing to make restitution if the penitent could not prove his penury; this was the origin of some excommunications, which dragged the issue out of secrecy to the exterior forum. According to Peter Cantor, some say that the priest should send the penitent to the bishop or the archdeacon, who will examine whether he can pay. A penitent who refuses to go must be conditionally excommunicated. The priest tells him: You are excommunicated if you are lying about your ability to repay. Others held that the penitent must be brought to face his victim directly. Yet the victim might be hostile: "But what if he is so exasperated that he wants to attack him immediately?" Better, Peter suggests, simply to excommunicate the recalcitrant sinner unconditionally.[103] A second problem follows. What should the priest do if after a dying penitent agrees to make restitution, the priest hurries off to secure the victim's agreement, but when he returns to the deathbed, the penitent is dead, the heirs refuse to keep the bargain, and the unpaid victim now insists on excommunication of the dead culprit? Peter could not solve the question to his own satisfaction.[104] In these examples, the parish priest must intervene between enemies who want to keep up the quarrel and somehow stay at peace with the church. Restitution and excommunication had become weapons in a very public war of wills.

The ideal in restitution was the establishment of a genuine peace between thief or usurer and his victims. The culprit should secure his victim's forgiveness "not with armed entreaties but with devout supplications," Robert Courson specified.[105] The payment should be offered and accepted graciously. The powerful and rich tried to make only token payments to intimidated victims; thus the executors of the ruthless Douaisien Jehan Boinebroke settled at cut-rate the claims of the employees and clients whom Jehan had cheated during his lifetime.[106] That the executors and Jehan's victims both assumed the existence of a religious duty to return illegitimate profits shows the

---

102. Raymond Cazelles, "Le Parisien au temps de Saint Louis," in *Septième centenaire de la mort de Saint Louis*, Actes des Colloques de Royaumont et de Paris, 1970 (Paris, 1976), p. 102.

103. Peter Cantor, *Summa de sacramentis*, Appendix II, q.10, p. 444: "Sed quid si ipse adeo est exacerbatus ut statim uelit in eum irruere?"

104. Peter Cantor, *Summa de sacramentis*, Appendix II, q.10, p. 445.

105. Kennedy, "Robert Courson on Penance," p. 334: "non per preces armatas sed deuotas supplicationes."

106. Georges Espinas, *Les origines du capitalisme*, Vol. 1, *Sire Jehan Boinebroke* (Lille, 1933), pp. 13–43.

strength of the ideal of restitution. And theologians warned that half-measures would not suffice. Ideally, in fact, the thief would seek forgiveness in person whether or not he could repay the sum owed. The synods hoped that none would come to communion with any rancor in their hearts.[107] But bishops and theologians recognized that restitution was an ambiguous means of peacemaking, one that often ended in the humiliation of one party rather than the mutual understanding of both. A certain amount of recrimination, even vengeance, was inevitable. A Christian, after all, could legitimately pursue collection of those debts incurred against him. Two theologians said that it was permissible for an ordinary layman to show signs of rancor to another Christian who had injured him, by snubbing a greeting or by refusing to exchange the peace in church.[108] Most important here, restitution opened the secret world of sin and confession to public observation. At times it may have patched up neighbor's quarrels and reconciled the poor to the rich. At other times, it surely aroused old grievances and forged a weapon for the enemies of a contrite sinner seeking salvation.

If the penitent managed to make a secret confession, and he was not caught by the reservation of certain cases or by the responsibility of restitution, one final duty might still expose him. For at least in the early thirteenth century, virtually every sinner guilty of mortal sin had to perform some sort of satisfaction imposed by the priest to pay off the temporal penalty (*pena*) owed after absolution had removed the eternal guilt (*culpa*). The saying of prayers and psalms, now so familiar a duty after confession, was then quite rare for laymen.[109] Inherited from the old lists of tariffed penances, most satisfactions for laymen had been conceived in an age when privacy took second place to humiliation. Lengthy fasts, a favorite penalty, could hardly be hidden in a small neighborhood or village, much less within a family. Astute laymen might deduce the crime from the punishment.[110] One sermon *exemplum* sought to reassure nervous penitents that God would not allow their penances to reveal their crimes while reminding

107. E.g., BN latin 11067, f. 10v (Noyon, thirteenth century).

108. Peter of Poitiers, *Summa de sacramentis*, V.16, PL 211:1077; Pierre de Tarentaise, *Questiones super quartum sententiarum*, BN latin 14899, f. 24v. This was the counsel for the *imperfectus*. According to the chancellor of Notre-Dame, it was not permissible actually to hate or feel rancor, but only to show the signs of rancor, *signa rancoris*. How this would be possible, he does not say.

109. See Martin, "Confession et contrôle social à la fin du Moyen Age," p. 131, for the survival of the rigorist penalties; see Baldwin, *Masters, Princes and Merchants*, 2:96n163, for the imposition of prayers as satisfaction on students at the end of the twelfth century.

110. Murray, "Confession as a Historical Source in the Thirteenth Century," p. 283.

us of lay fears that their confessions would be exposed by malicious priests. A wife who had poisoned her stepson, so the story went, confessed her sin and received from her priest a penance of long fasts and the wearing of an iron girdle. The priest spilled the whole story to her husband, who refused to believe him. So the priest told the husband to stay home one day and spy on her completing the penance. But though his wife fasted and beat herself until the blood flowed, by a miracle the husband saw nothing but a splendid feast and her skin as fresh as ever.[111] A convenient miracle would save more than embarrassment, no doubt; a husband convinced that his wife had killed his son might take vengeance on the spot. The increasing "arbitrariness" of penances, the leeway that the priest might take in assigning satisfaction, might have made guessing a little more complicated; yet, paradoxically, the gradual decline of harsh satisfactions over the century would have allowed neighbors to infer that the imposition of a tough penalty indicated a particularly nasty sin.[112]

Theologians and bishops took various measures to protect penitents, measures that invariably depended on the good will and discretion of the parish priest. Manuals with an English or Norman connection and English synodal statutes consistently warned priests not to reveal one spouse's adultery to the other through the imposition of satisfaction, though without explaining how this was to be done.[113] One southern French synod took a similar tack.[114] Evidently, the characteristically delicate southern French and English bishops and theologians understood that the exposure would likely embitter the marriage and indeed frighten adulterers away from confessing in the first place. French manuals and canons that dealt with the problem seemed to worry less specifically about husbands and wives and instead held out the possibility of commuting a conspicuous fast into some less obvious means of satisfaction for any kind of sin. They apparently wanted to prevent the social embarrassment of having to fast as a guest or a host, but not the exposure before one's intimate family.[115] As in the act of confession itself, we find the English guard-

---

111. Gobi, *Scala celi*, f. 45r-v.

112. Lea, *A History of Auricular Confession*, 1:442.

113. Michaud-Quantin, "Un manuel de confession archaïque," p. 54; Eudes de Cheriton, *Tractatus de paenitentia*, BN latin 2593, f. 7r; Powicke and Cheney, p. 71 (Salisbury, 1217–1219, c. 34), pp. 144–145 (unknown diocese, 1222–1225?, c. 29), p. 188 (unknown diocese, 1225–1230?, c. 43), p. 370 (Salisbury, 1238, c. 11), p. 455 (Chichester, 1245–1252, c. 18), p. 594 (Wells, 1258?, c. 6), p. 639 (London, 1245–1259, c. 27), and p. 992 (Exeter, 1287, c. 5).

114. Bibl. Vat. lat. 9868, f. 185r (Carcassonne, 1270).

115. Pontal I, p. 222 (Synodal of the West, c. 120); Peter of Poitiers, *Summa de confessione*, pp. 55–56.

ing the privacy of penitents more strenuously than did the French; they drew the circle of protection more closely around the individual. The French bishops were concerned for a man's reputation among his neighbors, but not so much for his standing among intimates.

Neither English nor French statutes invariably sought to preserve reputation. If a man or woman had robbed or cheated, or if they had committed a reserved sin, the canons almost welcomed the exposure and humiliation that followed. Yet, in certain cases, they did offer a little protection from the gaze of the public. Those who had committed sexual sins such as fornication or sometimes adultery were less likely to be forced into view than those who had robbed or cheated, whether surreptitiously or publicly. So the rules did not put into practice the long-standing tag of the theologians that public sins should be punished publicly and secret sins secretly. Rather, in practice, the rules allowed sins considered as offenses against society, whether or not they were public, to be exposed, whereas sins considered inherently more private received a larger measure of protection, whether or not they were actually committed in secret. The statutes reflected an unspoken distinction between social and individual sins, a distinction that in practice might outweigh the official distinction between public and private sins and penance.

In sum, the very bishops most familiar with the new theology and most consciously trying to implement it actually spread a "private" Lenten confession and penance that often exposed parishioners' secrets and humiliated them before their neighbors. The publicity of the new private penance could hardly be called accidental, for its chief causes, such as the duty of restitution and the reservation of cases, were cornerstones of the canons of penance. The implied theology of the synodal statutes contrasts sharply with the endless praises of contrition and privacy in much contemporary theology—but not so sharply with the quiet assumptions expressed in the theological classifications, the schemes exposed Chapter 2. Both were torn between contradictory longings for humiliation of offenders and the security of secrecy. Secrecy usually yielded to openness when justice was at stake.

The old "interior penance" of twelfth-century theologians had been a secret and unsacramental matter; it was an issue between a sinner and God, with no mediator. Thirteenth-century theologians came to define a private sacramental penance that regulated relations with both God and neighbor through the priest. Bishops, too, interpreted *Omnis utriusque* in the light of duties to neighbor as well as to God. They wanted sturdy *patresfamilias* who set a good example to the parish. They wanted merchants to repay to their customers every sou fradulently gained. They even permitted exposure of sinners whose secret crimes by their very nature touched others in the parish. These were the lessons they read in *Omnis utriusque*, even as they read there the value of tearful contrition and secret confession. In the bishops' restricted interpretation, the new requirement of private sacramental confession became less revolutionary, less a challenge to public penance, than it might seem at first glance. Their hesitance in its implementation helps explain the survival of the traditional public penance, our next subject.

CHAPTER FOUR

The Varieties of Public Penance

The Fourth Lateran Council and the promotion of annual confession that ensued did little to dampen enthusiasm for traditional public penances. As we have seen, by 1215, theologians had made considerable progress in defining and distinguishing types of penance. Just after the Council, Thomas of Chobham described tripartite penance in what became its classic form: private penance, solemn public penance, and nonsolemn public penance. And as we have seen, too, this progressive redefining is deceptive. Solemn and nonsolemn public penance alike were artificial intellectual constructs invented less to describe contemporary practice than to satisfy a desire for neatness and consistency. They helped explain why patristic theology, Carolingian councils, and eleventh-century tariffed penitentials gave conflicting opinions on whether penance could be repeated or who might undergo what rite. Thomas and other Scholastic writers could attribute varying opinions to different types of penance and so save the appearances. As we turn to the practice of penance as it is described in diocesan synodal statutes, episcopal registers, and related sources, we must expect the varieties to diverge from the neat classifications of the theology. Nevertheless, for the sake of simplicity, I borrow those classifications to organize the exposition, and I treat first solemn, Lenten penance and then all nonsolemn public penances. This review of the procedures of public penances will show the inadequacy of the labels. The tidy schemes hid a more confusing and obscure reality.

The Survival of Solemn Penance

Measuring the survival of solemn public penance requires a working definition to apply to the sources. I take as "solemn penance" rites that required the penitent to be expelled from the church on Ash Wednesday and readmitted Maundy Thursday.[1] This is a conservative standard that does not take account of ambiguous cases. On many occasions of public penance, the sources simply do not make clear whether the penitent was expelled and readmitted in the solemn rite, demonstrating the survival of solemn penance. As the discussion moves from the demonstration of survival to the analysis of procedure, however, I consider the problems of distinguishing between solemn and nonsolemn rites.

Thirteenth-century theologians paid little attention to the details of public solemn penance. Contemporary French synodal statutes likewise mentioned the term "solemn penance" only occasionally. Around 1200, Eudes de Sully's statutes for Paris mention that the priest should take care that parishioners doing solemn penance go to the cathedral church on Ash Wednesday to be expelled and on Maundy Thursday to be received by the bishop.[2] Statutes from Cambrai throughout the century explain that solemn penance is to be imposed for any notorious crime that disturbs the whole town, "quod totam villam commovit,"[3] a phrase, we may recall, that had become a commonplace of theology and canon law. Instructions for the diocese of Rouen in 1245 and again in 1311 echoed Eudes de Sully's instruction to send solemn penitents to appear at the cathedral on Ash Wednesday and Maundy Thursday.[4] These texts are simply reminders of the routine to be followed. We cannot conclude much about the frequency of solemn penance from their presence, nor indeed about the alleged disappearance of solemn penance from the absence of such reminders in many collections of statutes. The bishops may simply have regarded such penance as sufficiently well known and unproblematic; private confession was the novelty.

French statutes, then, refer to solemn penance, but they provide no indication of a change in the frequency of its application. English statutes also witness the survival of the solemn rite; a few suggest, though, that in some places solemn penance was not imposed as often as the synods might prefer. An early-thirteenth-century synod in

---

1. The sole appearance of the word "sollemnis" in the text is unfortunately not a foolproof guide, since "sollemnis" could sometimes be as vague a word as "solemn" today. Thus I rely here primarily on references to the Lenten expulsion or reconciliation or to a context which clearly indicates the Lenten rite.

2. Pontal I, p. 101 (Paris, ca. 1200, c. 9); reaffirmed in Guillaume d'Auvergne's statutes, Mansi 22:767 (Paris, 1228–1248, c. 9).

3. Boeren, "Les plus anciens statuts du diocèse de Cambrai," 3:139 (Cambrai, first half of the thirteenth century, c. 3), and 4:136 (Cambrai, 1287–1288, c. 3); Gousset, *Les actes . . . de Reims*, vol. II, p. 446 (Cambrai, 1300–1310).

4. Pommeraye, *Sanctae Rotomagensis Ecclesiae concilia*, p. 256 (precepts for rural deans, Rouen, 1245); and Bessin, *Concilia Rotomagensis provinciae*, II, p. 85 (Rouen, 1311, c. 18).

Winchester warned priests to send public penitents to the bishop's penitentiary; a little later, a provincial decree of Canterbury demanded public solemn penance for women convicted of sexual relations with a priest. At midcentury the statutes of Winchester insisted that laymen guilty of crimes requiring corporal or solemn penance must not be allowed to pay a fee instead, unless the sinner's social standing made the penance improper (*propter persone honestatem*), or unless another satisfaction would prompt greater penitence.[5] The rule may indicate that some priests were allowing solemn penitents to escape the rigor of the law. Less ambiguous is a statute issued by the Council of Lambeth in 1281. It explicitly tried to revive what it referred to as the obsolescent practice of solemn penance.

> Further, although according to the sacred canons more serious sins, such as incest and the like, are to be punished with solemn penance, as these very notorious sins disturb the whole city with their scandal, by neglect penance of this sort seems to have almost fallen into oblivion, and consequently audacious and horrifying crimes and outrages of this sort seem to have increased. We therefore direct that this sort of solemn penance henceforth be imposed according to the canonical sanctions.[6]

The council recommends some old-time religion as an antidote to the crime wave. Here at last is a medieval witness of declining use of solemn public penance, at least in the province of Canterbury. Perhaps other English statutes had mentioned solemn penance because the bishops feared that it was dying out in their dioceses, too. The occasional warnings against too frequent commutations of solemn penance may possibly signify an effort to restore a decreasing rigor.

Nevertheless, not all the English evidence suggests that the solemn rite had fallen "almost into oblivion" on the island. In the very year following the Council of Lambeth, an entry in the register of Bishop

5. Powicke and Cheney II, p. 133 (Winchester, 1224, c. 46; this may, however, refer to nonsolemn public penance); pp. 154–155 (Canterbury, 1225); p. 409 (Winchester, 1247?, c.44). See also p. 235 (Exeter, 1225–1237, c. 28, public penitents to go to the penitentiary); p. 370 (Salisbury, 1238–1244, c. 10, same); p. 616 (Wells, 1258, c. 58, solemn penance not to be commuted); p. 721 (Winchester, 1262–1265, c. 96, solemn or public penance only to be commuted in special circumstances); and pp. 1028–1029 (Exeter, 1287, solemn penance not to be commuted).

6. Powicke and Cheney II, pp. 899–900 (Lambeth, 1281, c.7): "Preterea cum iuxta sacros canones peccata graviora, ut incestus et similia, que vulgatissima suo scandalo totam commovent civitatem, sint solempni penitentia castiganda, quorumdam tamen negligentia id agente, huiusmodi penitentia videtur quasi in oblivionem tradita, et crevisse per consequens audacia huiusmodi horrenda facinora et flagitia perpetrandi; quocirca precipimus ut huiusmodi penitentia solempnis de cetero imponatur secundum canonicas sanctiones."

Quinel of Exeter reported the penalty incurred by one Jane Baschet, convicted of adultery. "Jane should stand outside the church at Bedeford on Sundays and feast days during the whole of Lent, until the Thursday before Easter, and then come to Exeter to be reconciled, as is the custom."[7] It was still the custom in 1282 to reconcile public penitents at the cathedral. A statute from the synod of Exeter in 1287 confirms that the solemn rite was then customary in the diocese. Concerned that his penitentiary was being overburdened by the large number of public penitents coming on Ash Wednesday to the cathedral, the bishop provided for the appointing of several assistants; in another canon the same year, he further forbade commutation of solemn penance, "which is sacramental" (que sacramentalis est), echoing the canonists' description of solemn penance as the only sacramental version.[8]

The synodal statutes of southern France, on the other hand, suggest that public penance was far less important in that region than in England or north of the Loire. In only one case do diocesan statutes unambiguously require parish priests to send solemn penitents to the cathedral on Ash Wednesday, in a canon patterned after the northern French model.[9] Indeed, it is the imitation of the northern statutes in the midcentury statutes of Clermont that may explain this exception. In addition, a late-thirteenth-century synod of Limoges provides that public penitents and excommunicants should not be admitted to communion on Easter, but that they may receive blessed bread just as on other Sundays.[10] And finally, several statutes remind parish priests to be sure to send those who had publicly committed reserved sins to the bishop for their penance; any relaxation of the rules of reserved cases applied only to secret crimes.[11] Nothing is said, however, about whether the penance at the cathedral was to be public. This scant

7. Cited in William Maskell, Monumenta Ritualia Ecclesiae Anglicanae (London, 1846–1847), vol. I, p. ccxciv: "Johanna stet singulis dominicis et festivis extra ecclesiam Bideford per totam quadragesimam, usque ad diem Jovis proximam ante Pascha, et tunc veniet et apud Exon. reconciliandam, ut est moris."

8. Powicke and Cheney, p. 994 (Exeter, 1287, c. 5), and pp. 1028–1029 (c. 31). See Chapter 2 above on the phrase, "quia (or que) sacramentalis est."

9. Mansi 23:1193 (Clermont, 1268, c. 7). The synod further stipulates, Mansi 23:1199, that priests who hear of notorious sins generating scandal should, if they cannot correct the matter, report the case to the archpriest, and the archpriest to the archdeacon, and the archdeacon to the bishop; the statute does not state what sort of penance is to follow. This canon, too, follows closely the northern French model; cf. Pontal II, p. 155 (Le Mans, 1240–1247, c. 36).

10. A. Lecler, "Anciens statuts du diocèse de Limoges," Bulletin de la société archéologique et historique du Limousin 40, no. 1 (1892): 148 (Limoges, 1275–1294).

11. Pontal II, p. 320 (Nîmes, Arles, Béziers, Uzès, 1252, c. 65); and Bibl. Vat. lat. 9868, f. 274v (Carcassonne, ca. 1300).

harvest of statutes relating to public penance suggests that all versions of the rite were far less common in the Midi than in northern France, and that southern French bishops, unlike some of their English colleagues, were not interested in reviving it.

The practice of solemn penance varied from region to region, and only a comparative study of statutes and other evidence throughout western Europe could paint a complete picture.[12] If the Lambeth council recognized a falloff, other English and especially northern French dioceses did not. Some historians of penance have recognized the inconsistency of the record.[13] A few medieval writers, too, saw that solemn penance was something of a regional observance. In the 1320s, for instance, Durand de Saint Pourçain wrote that "today many churches do not engage in solemn penances,"[14] implying that at least some churches did know the custom as late as the fourteenth century. The evidence shows that the development of even so universal an institution as penance diverged dramatically in different regions between 1150 and 1350 or so, and that theologians and canonists acknowledged the divergence without embarrassment. The attempt to regularize canon law never implied an effort to eliminate all local variation. As we shall see in Chapter 7, which treats the liturgy, inclusion of the rite in manuscript pontificals similarly varied from one area to another. Roman usage abandoned solemn penance early, but the rite survived in some north Italian dioceses through the twelfth century. In northern France and in the Rhineland it thrived throughout the thirteenth century and beyond. In the south of France, by contrast, the statutes imply a relatively early demise, a conclusion that is supported by liturgical evidence as well. In England, practice apparently varied by diocese.[15] Historians might be tempted to regard Roman practice as normative, but it does not help the inquiry to label one direction backward and another an emerging trend. Only further

---

12. I have not systematically studied statutes other than the French and English, but it is interesting to note the survival of public penance in fifteenth- and sixteenth-century Galician canons: Pérez López, "El sacramento de la penitencia en las costituciones sinodales de Galicia (1215–1563)," pp. 113–115. Chapter 7 briefly discusses the liturgical evidence for public penance in some regions closer to northern France.

13. See, e.g., Lea, *A History of Auricular Confession,* 2:79–80; C. Vogel, "Les rites de la pénitence publique aux Xe et XIe siècles," in *Mélanges René Crozet,* ed. Pierre Gallais and Yves-Jean Riou (Poitiers, 1966), 1:141.

14. Durand de Saint Pourçain, *In Petri Lombardi Sententias Theologicas Commentariorum libri IIII* (Venice, 1571, repr. Ridgewood, N.J., 1964), IIII, D. xiv, q. 4, f. 329r: "plures Ecclesiae hodie de solemnibus poenitentiis non se intromittunt." A little earlier, Hostiensis, clearly most familiar with Italian practice, referred to public penance as rarely practiced, though without mentioning regional differences: *Summa aurea,* I de off. archipres. 3, col. 271.

15. See Vogel, "Les rites de la pénitence publique," pp. 141, 148, for the abandonment of solemn public penance in Rome; for its survival elsewhere, see below, Chapter 7.

investigation of different areas of western Europe will allow us to map the life of solemn and nonsolemn public penance in every region.

The abundance of evidence for solemn penance in northern France indicates not intermittent survivals but routine use. In mid-century Rouen, Eudes Rigaud noted repeatedly his ejection of penitents on Ash Wednesday and their reception on Maundy Thursday.[16] Evidence from liturgical books is a little more open to challenge, because sometimes scribes with respect for the old ways and prayers copied rites, such as royal coronations, not actually practiced in that city. But no taste for the antiquarian can explain why some fifty scribes of northern French pontificals tinkered with more than forty different versions of public penance from 1150 to 1350, nor why so many in the same period troubled to make marginal additions or changes to the rites already copied.[17] Surely the constant innovation and adjustment in the Lenten rites meant that these were no museum pieces. Cathedral ordinals, mere handy outlines of annual rites and practices, and so less liable to the antiquarian respect for the sacred words of traditional prayers, similarly described solemn public penance. And a customal of the cathedral of Bayeux from 1270 mentioned it among the duties of the archdeacon.[18] Such ordinals and collections of customs omitted the defunct or unpracticed rites, such as that of royal coronation, that the pontificals might include.

The few writers of liturgical commentaries who knew something of northern French practice confirm this picture. John Beleth, writing most likely in Paris before 1165, described the expulsion and readmission of penitents as central events of Ash Wednesday and Maundy Thursday.[19] Around 1195, Praepositinus of Cremona, another chancellor of Notre-Dame at Paris, described solemn penance.[20] Another

16. Eudes Rigaud, *Regestrum visitationum, passim.* On four of nine Ash Wednesdays spent at Rouen, Eudes explicitly mentions the ejection of the penitents. For the other five, he mentions preaching and celebrating the office for the day, but not the rite itself. On seven of sixteen Maundy Thursdays at Rouen, he provides no information about the rites or mentions only the consecration of chrism. On six more, he mentions absolutions or "customary rites," as well. For the final three, he explicitly mentions the introduction of the penitents, too. In years where the Ash Wednesday entry does not mention the ejection of penitents, the Maundy Thursday entry is more likely to mention their reception; so there is no evolution away from the rite.

17. The liturgical evidence on Ash Wednesday and Maundy Thursday rites is discussed in detail in Chapters 6 and 7.

18. Raoul Langevin, *Consuetudines et statuta ecclesie Baiocensis,* ed. Ulysse Chevalier, *Ordinaire et coutumier de l'Eglise cathédrale de Bayeux (XIIIe s.),* Bibliothèque liturgique, 8 (Paris, 1902), pp. 306, 387.

19. John Beleth, *Summa de ecclesiasticis officiis,* c. 89, p. 159, and c. 95, p. 167.

20. Praepositinus of Cremona, *Tractatus de officiis,* ed. James A. Corbett, Publications in Mediaeval Studies, 21 (Notre Dame, Ind., 1969), I.265, p. 68, and I.171, p. 100.

Lombard who taught for a time in Paris in the 1170s, Sicard of Cremona, included it in his *Mitrale*, composed around 1200.[21] Guy d'Orchelles, who taught in Paris around 1217–1233, was likewise familiar with solemn penance.[22] Guillaume Durand the Elder, bishop of Mende and long resident in Rome, can provide only ambiguous evidence for affairs north of the Loire, but at the end of the century, he included solemn penance in the *Rationale*, and he gave it a more elaborate form in his pontifical than it had possessed in the twelfth- and thirteenth-century Roman liturgy.[23] And finally, conspicuous public penances during Lent and other periods were frequently imposed on offenders in the northern French and Flemish cities throughout the thirteenth century. Indeed, public pilgrimages, a version of the public penances, were a common civil penalty in Flanders and the Rhineland through the end of Middle Ages. Precisely that region closest to the new Parisian theology of secret contrition and private confession remained a heartland of the old ritual of humiliation.

The Procedure of Solemn Penance

Once the mere survival of solemn penance in northern France has been established, we may turn to an investigation of the procedure bishops followed. Here the problem of definition becomes more acute. According to the textbook definition, solemn penance could be imposed only once and only on laymen; it was a prerogative of the bishop; and he expelled the penitents on Ash Wednesday and received them Maundy Thursday. These rules were violated. Abbots and priests could sometimes expel penitents; and in some places solemn penance was repeated. The textbook definition is not to be taken too seriously. Although I focus in this section on the procedure associated with the Lenten expulsion and reconciliation, evidence about other public penances is relevant. Later, I show how non-Lenten public penances confirm many of the conclusions suggested here.

21. Sicard of Cremona, *Mitrale seu de officiis ecclesiasticis summa*, VI.4, and VI.12, PL 213:255, 302.

22. Guy d'Orchelles, "The 'Summa de Officiis Ecclesiae' of Guy d'Orchelles," ed. V. L. Kennedy, *Mediaeval Studies* 1 (1939): 24, 48, 51; see also Guy's *Tractatus de Sacramentis*, ed. D. van den Eynde and O. van den Eynde, Franciscan Institute Publications, Text series, 4 (St. Bonaventure, N.Y., 1953), p. 106.

23. Guillaume Durand, *Rationale divinorum officiorum*, VI.28, f. 197v, and VI.73, f. 220v; PGD III.1, pp. 552–557, and III.2, pp. 559–569. The twelfth-century Roman pontifical repeats the Romano-Germanic Pontifical's extensive Maundy Thursday reconciliation, but omits the Ash Wednesday expulsion; the thirteenth-century version barely mentions the reconciliation among the day's activities. It is unlikely that the rite was much used in either case. See PRS XXVIII, pp. 209–210; and PRC XLII, p. 455. See Chapter 6 for a discussion of these rites.

The procedure of solemn penance itself is obscure at every
unlike the routine of private penance, which, we may recall, ↑
familiar and well-documented course from confession, through
sible restitution, absolution, and completion of satisfaction. Wh₂
tiated the imposition of solemn penance? Obviously, someone ⋮   ⸱
have committed a crime serious enough to provoke outrage in thᵢ   ₁v
or village. The parish priest was to take notice and send the offeⁿₐₑᵣ ⸱
to the bishop, the archdeacon, or, most often, the penitentiary for
further examination and the solemn rite, just as the French and English statutes insisted. Or perhaps the bishop himself could be the first
to take notice of the offense. One may wonder how a man or woman
who scandalized a community managed to escape punishment by the
king's men, or even the bishop's men, when the bishop was the local
secular lord. The answer, as we shall see more fully in Chapter 5, is
that secular justice did punish most ordinary criminals, who would
never undergo public penance at all. The religious rite was instead
imposed most often on a few categories of offenders. Some had committed sins ordinarily not justiciable in secular courts, such as priestly
concubinage and violence against clerics and church property, or
crimes that were ordinarily punished by both secular and ecclesiastical
courts, such as adultery, usury, and blasphemy.[24] On many occasions,
negotiated settlements, which often included a version of public penance, kept secular sins like rioting and violent assault out of the secular courts. As we shall see, a bishop might intervene in a dispute
between families and assign humiliating penances to satisfy the victims; or urban riots might be punished with penance instead of hangings.

At any rate, the procedure was at best only semivoluntary. The
bishops did not use direct force to impose solemn penance, or indeed
to impose any penance. But they could threaten action in the ecclesiastical courts and excommunication, and the recalcitrant excommunicant risked secular penalties such as confiscation and even outla-
wry. Public penance from at least the Carolingian period was an
unsolicited punishment required to absolve certain specified sins.[25]
Around 1200, the canonist Huguccio explicitly sanctioned the common practice of excommunicating the public sinner who refused pub-

24. On occasion, such moral offenses as blasphemy, adultery, and usury might be the
subject of secular punishment. Cf. Guillaume de Nangis, *Gesta Sancti Ludovici*, HF 18:394,
398. Such crimes were conceived as fundamentally spiritual matters, in whose enforcement
the secular authority was, however, supposed to contribute. See Philippe de Beaumanoir,
Coutumes de Beauvaisis, ed. A. Salmon, Collection de textes pour servir à l'étude et à l'enseignement de l'histoire (Paris, 1899–1900), XI.337–338, vol. I, p. 164.

25. Michel Rubellin, "Vision de la société chrétienne à travers la confession et la pénitence au IXe siècle," in *Pratiques de la confession*, p. 59.

lic penance in order to force him to submit to the rite. He added that secret sinners who wanted to do public penance could do so; but such volunteers must have been rare.[26] Clearly, many public penitents endured their humiliation to escape a worse fate. Few, if any, penitents volunteered to undergo the public and solemn rite. All the stories show formal public penance, solemn or not, to be the result of capitulation or plea bargaining. Of course, informal voluntary public penances did exist, although they are not part of this story. Self-flagellation and fasting were popular means of expiating guilt, first among monks, later among laymen, too. Here the Christian could tailor the measure of his own suffering and humiliation. With the formal public penance in question, someone with ecclesiastical jurisdiction decided the penalty. Solemn public penance was for criminals, not saints.

Who judged the penitent? Generally, as we have seen, the bishop or his representative, the penitentiary [penitentiarius]. Although bishops had probably long delegated the imposition of penances and many other affairs, the existence of one or more diocesan penitentiaries, who were charged with the exclusive task of exercising all specifically episcopal rights in penance (reserved cases and public penances[27]), was probably a recent phenomenon. Twelfth- and early-thirteenth-century theologians were still trying to puzzle out the status of all these representatives. Senatus of Worcester and eventually Peter Cantor wondered how the bishop could delegate authority in public penances to mere subdeacons, for instance. It seemed to make nonsense of the reservation of private confession and absolution to priests.[28] Yet, the practice spread regardless of theological hesitations. The Fourth Lateran Council encouraged the creation of an episcopal civil service when it called for assistants to the bishops for hearing confessions and imposing penances as well as for preaching,[29] and penitentiaries appear in most diocesan statutes of northern France and England by 1250 or so.[30]

26. Huguccio, Summa decretorum, Admont Stiftsbibliothek. 7, on D.50 c. 63, f. 74va.

27. Occasionally the penitentiaries also heard the confessions of clergy of the diocese and imposed penances on them. See, e.g., Mansi 23:386 (Rouen, 1235, c. 81).

28. Delhaye, "Deux textes de Senatus de Worcester," p. 218; Peter Cantor, Summa de sacramentis, IV.141–142, pp. 334–337. Cf. Hostiensis, who is still uncertain about episcopal representatives imposing solemn penance: Summa aurea, V.56.55, col. 1825.

29. Fourth Lateran Council, c. 10, Conciliorum oecumenicorum decreta, pp. 239–240; but contrary to Boeren's view, "Les plus anciens statuts du diocèse de Cambrai," 3:30n, the council did not inaugurate the appointment of diocesan penitentiaries.

30. Cf. Pontal I, p. 174 (Synodal of the West, c. 59); Martène and Durand, Veterum scriptorum, VIII, col. 1536 (Soissons, thirteenth century, c. 2); Mansi 23:386 (Rouen, 1235, c. 81); Powicke and Cheney pp. 133–134 (Winchester, 1224, c. 42, 46, and 49), pp. 188–189

In theory, these experts on penance practiced outside the operation of the ecclesiastical courts that were developing at the same time. The courts grew up between 1150 and 1250 as an increasingly formal tribunal for cases that fell into the bishop's spiritual jurisdiction, as distinct from his secular court. The spiritual jurisdiction embraced what came to be called the external forum, that is, excommunication, but also benefices, wills, tithes, debts, marriage, and slander.[31] The bishop or his official (*officialis*) presided. In theory, then, both solemn and nonsolemn public penance belonged to the internal forum and fell outside the court's jurisdiction. Unlike that jurisdiction, too, the bishop's cognizance in public penance was in principle unlimited, an important advantage for the bishop in an age when so many crosscutting rights of ecclesiastical institutions restrained his freedom to administer justice. In principle, no monastic institutions were exempt from the bishop's ancient right to expel and receive sinners.[32]

In practice, however, the administration of public penances and the administration of ecclesiastical justice went hand in hand. The bishop's official, for instance, might threaten or actually impose excommunication pursuant to a case in the ecclesiastical court; to relieve himself of the penalty, the excommunicant might be required to perform solemn or nonsolemn public penance and so go before the penitentiary. Or, the bishop and his penitentiary might intervene in a case that had not yet run its course and settle it by imposing some form of public penance. Some of the public penances that appear in Eudes Rigaud's register resulted from just such an informal settlement.[33] Finally, the bishop might sidestep the court procedure entirely by investigating sins and imposing public penance in his own person or through a delegate outside the rank of episcopal officials.[34] In most of these cases, we cannot tell whether solemn or nonsolemn penance was imposed. In any case, however bureaucratic the ecclesiastical court procedure became in the thirteenth century, the bishop and his appointees never lost sight of the goal of reconciling men and

---

(unknown diocese, 1225–1230, c. 52), p. 235 (Exeter, 1224–1237, c. 28 and 30), p. 370 (Salisbury, 1238–1244, c. 10). The appearance of the office may possibly be dated to midcentury in Cambrai, where statutes from a synod between 1238 and 1244 omitted any reference to penitentiaries, but synods from 1260 on specified the delegate's duties. So argues Boeren, "Les plus anciens statuts du diocèse de Cambrai," 30, 3:378 (Cambrai, 1260, c. 1), and 4:155–156 (Cambrai, 1287/88, c. 17). Of course, the omission may just be an oversight.

31. Colin Morris, "A Consistory Court in the Middle Ages," *Journal of Ecclesiastical History* 14 (1963): 151–152, 157–159.

32. See Avril, *Le gouvernement des évêques*, p. 197n.

33. Pierre Andrieu-Guitrancourt, *L'archevêque Eudes Rigaud et la vie de l'église au XIIIe siècle* (Paris, 1938), p. 314.

34. Andrieu-Guitrancourt, *L'archevêque Eudes Rigaud*, p. 315.

women to God and the church through settlement and penance.[35] Public penances fell into a gray area between the external and internal fora, but they were no less useful for that. Bishops found their flexibility convenient. When we deal with nonsolemn public penance, we shall see how the overlap with excommunication and even secular penalties made it a preferred means of settlement.

Normally, then, solemn public penance was an episcopal function, although the precise procedure varied. Occasionally, abbots might exercise jurisdiction, especially in England, where they often held episcopal rights. Around 1300, the abbot of Evesham, for instance, presided over the solemn rite in Lent.[36] The First Lateran Council in 1123 and again the Fourth Lateran Council in 1215 complained about what they saw as monastic usurpations of episcopal authority in imposing public (solemn?) penance, and they tried to put an end to the practice.[37] Some French monastic liturgical books continued to include rites of solemn penance, though these seem to diminish after 1215. Monasteries that practiced solemn penance were generally great houses in sizable cities without a bishop. At least in northern France, when a bishop was readily available, he and his penitentiary enjoyed a monopoly.[38]

Somewhat different from the question of judgment was the question of the actual conduct of the liturgy. In principle, theologians and canonists agreed, the actual ceremonial imposition of solemn penance was strictly an episcopal function. But considerations of convenience made stand-ins necessary, and there seem to have been increasingly explicit provisions for them. Around 1200, the canonist Huguccio explained that another priest could, if necessary, take the bishop's place at the ejection and reconciliation.[39] Eudes Rigaud's register indicates that this peripatetic bishop spent nine of twenty-one Ash

35. Morris, "A Consistory Court," p. 158.

36. Henry Austin Wilson, ed., *Officium Ecclesiasticum Abbatum secundum usum Eveshamensis Monasterii*, Henry Bradshaw Society, 6 (London, 1893), cols. 60–67, 71–80.

37. First Lateran Council, c. 16, and Fourth Lateran Council, c. 60, *Conciliorum oecumenicorum decreta*, pp. 193, 262. After 1250, Hostiensis was still objecting to abbots imposing solemn penance, except where "super hoc sit privilegiatus," or for other good cause: *Summa aurea*, V.56.55, col. 1825.

38. Wilson, *Officium . . . secundum usum Eveshamensis Monasterii*, p. 196, is mistaken when he suggests that French abbeys never had this prerogative. See Chapter 6 for a full review of solemn penance in monastic service books. Guillaume de Rennes, commenting on Ramón de Peñafort, *Summa de poenitentia*, 3.34.6, p. 441, asks whether Dominicans and Franciscans may impose solemn penance; he decides that they cannot unless they have a special mandate or where it is the custom. These penances, he says, are reserved to the penitentiaries.

39. Huguccio, *Summa decretorum*, Admont Stiftsbibliothek 7, on D.50 c.63, f. 74rb. See also the *Summa Bambergensis*, Bamberg, Staatsbibliothek Can. 42., on D.50 c.63, f. 39rb, which reports that one may make an exception to the rule limiting solemn penance to bishops "in necessitate."

Wednesdays and sixteen of twenty-one Maundy Thursdays at Rouen, rates that show he was making a special effort to be at his cathedral for these feasts. Normally, only business with the king in Paris kept him away. It is likely that when he was present, he personally conducted both ejection and reception. He frequently mentions both, and when there is no explicit reference, he often speaks of the "customary" rites or office, which probably covers solemn penance.[40] It is not clear what happened when he was absent from Rouen. Some thirteenth- and fourteenth-century pontificals and ordinals mention the possibility of a temporary substitute for the bishop; so perhaps Huguccio's recommendations were taken to heart.[41]

Once dispatched to the cathedral, did the penitent confess? The crime, after all, was already public, indeed a scandal to the city. The penitent probably was expected to confess anyway, both to acknowledge his or her guilt and to receive absolution for other, possibly secret sins.[42] The Exeter statute mentions confession to the bishop's penitentiary. In the liturgy, the tenth-century Romano-Germanic Pontifical had provided an extended public form to the confession of public penitents on Ash Wednesday.[43] This was not included in twelfth-century and later French and English pontificals, but some mentioned an inquiry into the penitents' sins and way of life before the expulsion on Ash Wednesday: "archpriests of parishes and priests of penances, who must diligently investigate their behavior [*conversationem*]."[44] Was this an open inquiry, even an investigation into their reputation? Perhaps there was some sort of secret confession before or after an open avowal of guilt for the public crime; the evidence is not clear.

In any case, the next step would be the rite of expulsion on Ash

40. Eudes Rigaud, *Regestrum visitationum*. Business at Paris accounts for eight of the absences on Ash Wednesday: p. 205 (1254); p. 240 (1255); p. 332 (1258); p. 359 (1259); p. 421 (1261); p. 454 (1262—he was just outside of Paris); p. 509 (1264); and p. 596 (1267). On three occasions, he was perhaps close enough to have returned to Rouen but did not: p. 270 (Ash Wednesday, 1256); p. 272 (Maundy Thursday, 1256); and p. 334 (Maundy Thursday, 1258).

41. See, e.g. Cambrai BM 223 (pontifical of Cambrai, first half thirteenth century), f. 157r-v; Abbeville BM 8 (pontifical of Amiens, beginning or first half fourteenth century), f. 1r and 9v; Auxerre BM 53 (pontifical of Auxerre, first half fourteenth century), f. 62r; BN latin 1301 (ordinal of Coutances, fourteenth century), f. 126v–127r.

42. Morin, *Commentarius historicus*, p. 440.

43. PRG XCIX.50–53, pp. 16–17. Vogel interprets this passage as a separate rite of private confession for all Christians, but there is no evidence for this view. See Chapter 6. This preliminary confession of solemn penitents even in the early pontifical casts doubt on M. Rubellin's argument ("Vision de la société chrétienne," p. 60) that the punitive nature of public penance put religious confession out of the question.

44. E.g., BN latin 934 (Sens, second half or end twelfth century), f. 63v–68v. This rite is printed by Martène, *De antiquis ecclesiae ritibus libri*, I.6.7.16, vol. I, cols. 815–818, but with a crucial and telling misprint of *conscientias* for *conversationem*.

Wednesday; its liturgy is examined in Chapter 5. Then followed Lent and presumably some sort of satisfaction by the penitent. What did he or she do? The question is surprisingly difficult to answer. Before the twelfth century, before, that is, theologians or canonists defined "solemn" and "nonsolemn" public penance, it seems that penitents might often have spent Lent confined in some sort of prison or in the dependencies of some church or convent. They may have continued to attend the offices at the cathedral during Lent in a porch set aside for their use; blessings of the penitents were sometimes read at the Lenten Monday, Wednesday and Friday offices. The Gelasian sacramentaries prescribed enclosure of the penitents until Maundy Thursday, and some of the old penitentials maintain this tradition. In the tenth century, the Romano-Germanic Pontifical and Regino of Prüm referred to priests appointed to supervise the conduct of penitents during Lent, perhaps in some sort of enclosure.[45]

But by the mid–twelfth century, Lenten incarceration was rare or unknown in northern France. Around 1160, Peter Comestor described two different customs, the second of which he identified as Italian; the first is likely the French practice familiar to him.

> Solemn [penance] is that which is done in front of everyone and before the church, when one is sent into exile for seven years, seeking their bread on foot from door to door. . . . Or as is done in Italy, when someone stays in front of the doors of the church or in the porch through Lent in the manner of beggars and is fasting in hairshirt and ashes on bread and water for three days a week, and he gives the remainder of his food to the dogs, to show the horror of his crime. Afterwards, he is brought out by the priest on the great day of the Last Supper [Maundy Thursday] in front of everyone, and he is introduced into the church.[46]

Peter expounds here two different procedures, one presumably French, the second explicitly Italian. The first, the seven-year exile,

45. Josef Andreas Jungmann, *Die lateinischen Bussriten*, pp. 64–67, 70; Vogel, "Les rites de la pénitence publique," pp. 141–142, and his "Pénitence et excommunication dans l'Eglise ancienne et durant le haut Moyen Age," *Concilium* 107 (1975): 17; G. G. Meersseman, "I penitenti nei secoli XI e XII" in *I laici nella "Societas christiana" dei secoli XI e XII*, Atti della terza Settimana internazionale di Studio, Passo della Mendola, 1965 (Milan, 1968), p. 344.

46. Peter Comestor, *Tractatus de sacramentis*, ed. Raymond M. Martin, as an appendix to Henri Weisweiler, *Maître Simon et son groupe: De sacramentis*, p. 73*: "Sollempnis [penitentia] est que fit coram omnibus et in facie Ecclesie, quando scilicet quis mittitur in exilium per vii annos, pedibus querens panem hostiatim. . . . Vel sicut fit in Italia, quando quis pre foribus ecclesie vel in porticu ecclesie manet per quadragesimam in modico tugurio et est in cinere et cilicio ieiunans in pane et aqua tribus diebus in ebdomada, et residuum cibi sui dat canibus ad horrorem sceleris sui denotandum. Postea verum a sacerdote magna die cene extrahitur inde coram omnibus et in ecclesiam introducitur."

recalls the multiyear public punishment described in certain eleventh-century penitentials and long recopied in the new manuals. An anonymous tract of the later twelfth century, for instance, described this procedure, with the important difference that the penitent should be partially reconciled before the whole seven years were out. During Lent, the priest was to see that the penitent stayed in a "safe place"; after a year, the penitent would be reintroduced to the church; but only after seven years would the penance be complete.[47] And at the end of the century, Alan of Lille included Burchard's penalty for voluntary homicide: a continuous forty days on bread and water (the *carena*), then seven years of frequent fasting as specified. After the first year, the penitent would be reintroduced into the church. Alan suggested that the rigor of such statutes should be moderated by the confessor.[48] Soon, the seven years began to give way to a gentler discipline, at least among canonists. Commenting on Ramón de Peñafort, Guillaume de Rennes referred to satisfactions of one to three years in public penance, and John of Freiburg was still citing this standard around 1300. The penitent would be introduced into the church every Maundy Thursday.[49] Peter's remarks about non-Italian customs thus conform reasonably well to contemporary reports, especially those from north of the Alps. By the thirteenth century, northern customs evidently still took the same general form, but the punishment was shorter and milder.

Peter's account shows that at least some Italian dioceses outside Rome imposed solemn penance. At least in Peter's account, the Italians seem to have relied more on the short, sharp shock. The penitent evidently stayed where he was, under some sort of supervision. He may well have lived in the confines of a monastery: Peter's description sounds very like the customary public (nonsolemn) penance in many religious orders, especially in the statutes for new orders of laymen such as the Templars, *penitenti*, and brothers and sisters serving urban hospices.[50] Offending members were not expelled from and readmit-

---

47. Michaud-Quantin, "Un manuel de confession archaïque," pp. 27–28. Cf. Rufinus of Bologna, *Summa decretorum*, D.50 c.64, p. 132, who specified that the penitent should be publicly reconciled every Maundy Thursday until he completes his satisfaction; he noted that Burchard expected no reconciliation at all until the satisfaction was complete, but says this new rule abrogates Burchard's.

48. Alan of Lille, *Liber poenitentialis*, II.14, vol. II, pp. 55–57.

49. Guillaume de Rennes, gloss on Ramón de Peñafort, *Summa de poenitentia*, 3.34.6, pp. 440–441; John of Freiburg, *Summa confessorum*, 3.34.8. It is hard to tell whether John is accurate about contemporary practice.

50. Cf. M. Barber, *The Trial of the Templars* (Cambridge, 1978), p. 149 (late-thirteenth-century penances among Templars); P. Louvet, *Histoire et antiquitez du Pais de Beauvaisis* (Beauvais, 1631), pp. 532–535 (rule of *religieux* and *religieuses* of the Hôtel Dieu of Saint-Jean, Beauvais, 1246); Servus Gieben, "I Penitenti di San Francesco nei Paesi Bassi (secoli XIII-XIV)," in *Il movimento francescano della Penitenza nella società medioevale*, ed. Mariano D'Alatri,

ted into the church, but they were often forced to stand publicly before other members in sackcloth and ashes, and the leftovers from their plates were cast to the dogs, as Peter describes. Significantly, Peter's account is also consistent with the early-thirteenth-century Sienese *Ordo officiorum*, which speaks of incarceration during Lent.[51] Once again, we may wonder whether the custom Peter describes belongs in any real sense to solemn, as distinct from nonsolemn, public penance. Nevertheless, his information about the difference between Italian and transalpine customs is plausible. Public penance of all sorts seems to have been much rarer in Italy than in northern France, and it may have been reserved there for truly extraordinary criminals, who required more supervision.

As we have already seen, thirteenth-century *summae confessorum* suggest that the northern practice of solemn penance may have evolved somewhat after Peter Comestor wrote, as the full seven-year *carena* grew more rare. Those French statutes calling for the priest to be sure to send solemn penitents to the cathedral on Ash Wednesday and again on Maundy Thursday similarly imply that the penitent would normally leave the parish at the beginning of Lent for the expulsion, but would return to his or her parish in the meantime for the satisfaction. It is harder to find confirming evidence in specific cases. Eudes Rigaud unfortunately fails to identify those penitents he expelled on Ash Wednesdays; nor does he say anything about their satisfactions. His register and other sources do say quite a bit about public penitents who may or may not have undergone the solemn rite; common satisfactions were long or short pilgrimages or humiliating processions to various neighboring churches in sackcloth and ashes.[52] These may well have been customary for solemn penitents.

In England, the statutes were almost as vague. An early council of Winchester, echoed by a synod of Chichester, warned priests to make sure that public solemn penitents completed their penances, that is, satisfactions, or else they should be sent to the penitentiary to be expelled once again.[53] The language implies that the satisfaction was

---

Atti del 3° Convegno di Studi francescani (Rome, 1980), p. 74 (regulations of the beghards of Middelburg, 1331). The statutes of Italian *penitenti* generally required exposure of misbehaving brothers or sisters within the community, then exclusion from the company of the rest and public correction, but they do not specify the type of correction: G. G. Meersseman, "Premier auctarium au dossier de l'ordre de la Pénitence au XIIIe siècle: Le Manuel des Pénitents de Brescia," *Revue d'histoire ecclesiastique* 62 (1967): 47, and his *Dossier de l'Ordre de la Pénitence au XIIIe siècle*, Spicilegium Friburgense, 7 (Fribourg, 1961), pp. 90, 137, 153.

51. Jungmann, *Die lateinischen Bussriten*, p. 67; Vogel, "Les rites de la pénitence publique," p. 142.

52. See below for details.

53. Powicke and Cheney, p. 133 (Winchester, 1224, c. 46); p. 455 (Chichester, 1245–1252, c. 19).

to be done in the parish, as in contemporary France. A midcentury statute, again from Winchester, gives some hint of the satisfaction that might be performed there. "If, however, a layman is convicted of or has confessed any crime for which a corporal or solemn penalty [*pena corporalis vel sollempnis*] should be inflicted on him by law, on no account may the aforesaid penalty be redeemed with money."[54] The wording "Corporalis vel sollempnis" may imply the two were considered interchangeable in this diocese, because such penances entailed some sort of public beating. The statute insists that in public cases the penitent must personally suffer the corporal punishment. In private cases still covered by the tariffs of the *libri penitentiales*, it had long been the custom to allow redemptions for fasts and corporal punishments. The synodal statutes of London mention corporal and financial penalties in public cases. "And we direct that if any man or woman should correct his or her manifest sin either with a fine or with a corporal penalty, that his or her correction should be made public."[55] It seems that corporal punishments were quite common in England for solemn and other public penances. Thirteenth-century French records never mention such a custom in connection with specifically "solemn" penance, although many public penitents were flogged or pilloried, and Eudes's solemn penitents may have met the same fate.

Over the centuries, then, several types of satisfaction seem to have been tried, including imprisonment, corporal punishment, and humiliating processions or rituals. Of these, imprisonment disappeared from the record in France from the twelfth century on. In principle, it is perhaps the most secular form, essentially a punishment rather than a satisfaction. It kept offenders out of further trouble, and it permitted the closest supervision of any penalty imposed with it. It had been part of penance when bishops used penance to participate in law enforcement and when Carolingian kings made penitential discipline the subject of capitularies. Although imprisonment survived as a secular punishment, it died out as a means of penance. Later bishops preferred satisfactions more obviously distinct from the secular application of main force. Flogging might also seem to us to be punishment rather than satisfaction, but at least it had a long tradition of use in voluntary monastic piety. When it was used on public penitents, it normally was inflicted during a humiliating procession. French bishops in the thirteenth century preferred to inflict

54. Powicke and Cheney, p. 409 (Winchester, 1247?, c. 44): "Si quis autem laicus de aliquo crimine convictus fuerit aut confessus propter quod pena corporalis vel sollempnis ei de iure debeat infligi, nulla ratione liceat ei penam predictam redimere per peccuniam."

55. Powicke and Cheney, p. 632 (London, 1245–1259, c. 6): "Et precipimus quod si aliquis vel aliqua debeat corrigere suum manifestum peccatum vel per penam pecuniariam vel per penam corporalem, quod eius correctio publicetur."

humiliation through expulsion from the church, processions, and pilgrimages. These were the most symbolic of the possible penalties and the furthest from secular practice. Bishops recognized that solemn penitents submitted to the rite only under threat of something worse, but they selected the satisfactions most similar to purely voluntary displays of penitence. Solemn penance was half voluntary expiation, half involuntary punishment. Solemn penitents were criminals, but they acted the part of saints.

In any case, the penitent completed his satisfaction and received absolution from the bishop, if not necessarily in that order.[56] But he never quite returned to his former status. Ancient and early medieval procedure had required some sinners to live as penitents in a monastery or at least celibate and uninvolved in secular business until death. By the thirteenth century, only one rule survived as an echo of this practice.[57] Most theologians and canonists agreed that solemn public penitents were not supposed to repeat the rite, because this rule would encourage respect for the sacrament (*pro reverentia sacramenti*), and it would instill fear of sinning.[58] Noniterability had been part of a system that required lifelong penance, and it was difficult to explain when the system faded away. Now that penitents no longer found themselves immured in monasteries for life, they might well have a second chance to scandalize town or country with their crimes. Presumably, repeat offenders could be made to undergo a nonsolemn public penance.

It is hard to tell how much noniterability was the rule for solemn, Lenten penance in the thirteenth century. Already in the mid–twelfth century, Peter Lombard remarked that in some churches (*in quibusdam ecclesiis*) solemn penance could indeed be repeated, and the section *de penitentia* included in Gratian's *Decretum* stated that such penance could be repeated "apud quosdam," a formulation that would seem to mean "according to some authorities," rather than "in some churches."[59] Otto of Lucca referred to the noniterability of solemn penance as an old custom that still survived in some places. "And formerly that penance was not repeated, and in some churches this is

---

56. See Chapters 6 and 7 on the timing and form of absolutions.

57. Meersseman, "I penitenti nei secoli XI e XII," pp. 330–331, traces the decline of the prohibition of marriage for public penitents; it had disappeared by the middle of the twelfth century.

58. Cf. Anciaux, *La théologie du sacrement de pénitence*, pp. 150–154, and the *Tractatus de septem sacramentis ecclesie*, in H. Weisweiler, ed., *Maître Simon et son groupe*, pp. 89–90. See above, Chapter 2, for the view that solemn penance alone is sacramental.

59. Peter Lombard, *Sententiae*, IV D. 14 c.4, vol. II, pp. 321–322; Gratian, *Decretum* C.33 q.3 d.3 c.21, col. 1215.

still kept out of reverence for the sacrament."[60] Around the same time, Peter Comestor borrowed the Lombard's opinion without attribution, then added his own obscure explanation, "because in some churches there is no solemn penance of this kind."[61] Peter Comestor either meant that churches not practicing solemn penance did not bother about its iterability, or, more likely, that some churches did practice solemn penance, but not in this particular way. Around the same time, the canonist Rolandus stated that solemn penance was not repeatable according to the custom of the Gallican churches.[62] Meanwhile, several twelfth-century canonists agreed with Gratian that solemn penance could be iterable; one decretist from Cologne noted that solemn penance was customarily repeated in Germany.[63] But most such comments are too vague to permit us to trace a complete map of regional practice, and the question seems to have been neglected after 1200 or so. Did the French bishops allow repeated solemn penance in the thirteenth century? If we believe Rolandus, probably not. Perhaps the tradition of noniterability retained its vitality in regions where the rite of solemn penance was itself most vital.

The procedure of solemn penance is obscure in large part because of the limitations of the evidence. Too many notices of solemn penance offer no detail at all on the penitents, on the crimes they committed, on the actions that brought them to the bishop's attention, or on what happened to them besides the ritual expulsion and readmission. To some extent, however, the procedure appears confusing because it was confusing. The bishops who imposed solemn penance inherited rules, such as noniterability, that had grown up in a different time,

60. Otto of Lucca, *Summa sententiarum*, VI.72, PL 176:150: "Et olim illa poenitentia non iterabatur et adhuc quidem in quibusdam ecclesiis hoc servatur pro reverentia sacramenti." See Anciaux, *La théologie du sacrement de pénitence*, p. 150n.

61. Peter Comestor, *De sacramentis*, in Weisweiler, *Maître Simon et son groupe*, pp. 74*–75*: "quia in quibusdam ecclesiis non habetur huiusmodi penitentia sollempnis."

62. Rolandus, in *Die Sentenzen Rolands*, ed. A. M. Gietl (Freiburg, 1891; repr. Amsterdam, 1969), p. 240. See Anciaux, *La théologie du sacrement de pénitence*, p. 151. For the rejection of the identification of the canonist Rolandus as the future Alexander III, see J. T. Noonan, "Who Was Rolandus," in *Law, Church, and Society. Essays in Honor of Stephan Kuttner*, ed. K. Pennington and R. Somerville (Philadelphia, 1977), pp. 21–48.

63. Cf. McLaughlin, *The Summa Parisiensis on the Decretum Gratiani*, D.50 c.60, p. 47, which seems to suggest that the Milanese held to noniterability; Rufinus of Bologna, *Summa decretorum*, C.33 q.3, p. 502; Fransen, with Kuttner, *Summa "Elegantius in iure diuino" seu Coloniensis*, III.113, vol. I, pp. 94–95: "Germania nostra lege ista non constringitur quia canon comprovincialis est." Two other canonists simply state that solemn penance could be repeated in some churches, without specifying which: *Summa "Tractaturus Magister,"* BN latin 15994, f. 17ra; Huguccio, *Summa decretorum*, Admont Stiftsbibliothek 7, f. 74rb, and 496rb. However, Johannes Teutonicus's gloss, which became standard, did not mention the possibility of repeating solemn penance, "quia est sacramentum": *Decretum Gratiani . . . unacumque glossis*, D.50 c.62, f. 83r-v.

and now seemed anomalous. Above all, the developing definition of the exterior forum on the theoretical level and of the ecclesiastical courts on the practical level made the role and procedure of solemn penance obscure. Its routine remained quasi-judicial. The initial public outcry and denunciation to the bishop was followed by an inquiry and, if deemed necessary, a formal satisfaction as punishment. The penitent did not volunteer his participation. It was demanded of him, with some threat of further sanctions if he did not cooperate. Yet the process did not take place inside the new ecclesiastical courts; indeed, the bishops may have used it consciously to bypass the courts. Anomaly and inconsistency did not kill off solemn penance, which remained a useful alternative all the same.

Instances of Public Penance

While explicitly "solemn" penance is often an elusive quarry, public penances of the nonsolemn or simply unspecified variety abound in the statutes and narratives of northern French history. Eudes Rigaud mentions over a dozen cases of public penance in the two decades covered by his register, in addition to the solemn expulsions on Ash Wednesday and numerous absolutions from excommunication where the promised satisfaction is not recorded. In Scholastic theology, "nonsolemn public penance" arrived late as an afterthought to cover all the cases that did not fall into the categories of private or solemn penance. In practice, a wide variety of public penances flourished throughout the twelfth and thirteenth centuries.

A few examples of the many public penances to appear in Eudes's register and other sources give some impression of the differing circumstances that led to its imposition and the procedures that then followed. We may recall here the story of the count of Nevers, forced to dig up the decaying corpse of the child he had ordered buried in the bishop's chamber during an interdict.[64] This was a common enough punishment for nobles who had offended the sanctuary of a church or the sanctity of a cleric's person. The bishop of Chartres, for instance, required several noblemen who had summarily hanged a cleric to return to the tomb and disinter the corpse with their bare hands and nails, then take the body and rebury it in a cemetery with honor.[65] Similar stories are told of Bishop Hugh of Lincoln's punish-

---

64. Robert d'Auxerre, *Chronologia*, HF 18:269.
65. Ralph of Coggeshall, *Chronicon Anglicanum*, pp. 200–201. The incident is not dated, but follows upon a similar case from the reign of Philip Augustus.

ment of several sanctuary-breakers, and Philip Augustus's punishment of a castellan who had hanged a *conversus*.[66]

These were particularly dramatic and memorable instances, recorded for posterity by chroniclers. Severer than most, they were not
isolated cases of public penance. On several occasions, Eudes Rigaud
similarly punished laymen who had harmed his property or infringed
upon his authority by imposing public penances.[67] Sometimes he
made pilgrimages part of the settlement to a dispute to which he was
not party, but only arbiter. In one case, Eudes was settling a feud
started by a murder. Both sides apparently agreed to accept his decision, and so he listened to their stories and rendered judgment. "January 26. At the same [*Aliermont*]. Today we submitted the following
judgment, in the litigation which had been long standing between
William of Sauqueville and Thomas, a miller, both citizens of Dieppe,
anent the death of William's brother, for both had chosen us as arbitrator in every respect."[68] The judgment follows in French. Thomas
the miller, accused of killing William's brother, must make pilgrimages to Santiago de Compostela and to Saint-Gilles-du-Gard in
Provence and pay for two thousand masses and the expenses of four
crusaders for the benefit of the victim's soul. It was an expensive
penalty, even for a miller and bourgeois of Dieppe, but the crime was
a serious one. The punishment took exactly the same form as many
public penances. The oddest feature is what Eudes wanted Thomas to
do before leaving. For the satisfaction of the other party—"for the
honor of the other party and to appease their hearts"—Thomas was
to present sixty good men, twenty priests, twenty knights, and twenty
in holy orders either in William's house or in the church of Saint
James in Dieppe, to swear to Thomas's innocence. "That he did not,

66. For Hugh of Lincoln, see Given, *Society and Homicide in Thirteenth-Century England*,
pp. 197–193; for Philip's imposition of public penance at Preuilly-sur-Claise (Indre-et-Loire),
see Ralph of Coggeshall, *Chronicon Anglicanum*, pp. 199–200. See also the case of late-
thirteenth-century sanctuary-breakers in Lille forced to make a penitential procession and
bury the corpse of the man they killed: H. Platelle in L. Trenard, ed., *Histoire de Lille* (Lille,
n.d.), pp. 345–346.

67. Cf. Eudes Rigaud, *Regestrum visitationum*, pp. 23–24 (January 21, 1248), p. 55 (December 11, 1249), p. 579 (May 23, 1267).

68. Eudes Rigaud, *Regestrum visitationum*, p. 507: "VII. Kl. Februarii (Jan. 26, 1264)
Apud Alacrem Montem. Ipsa die ibidem, protulimus dictum nostrum super contentione que
diu fuerat et erat inter Guillelmum de Sauquevilla, et Thomam, molendinarium, burgenses
Deppe, super morte fratris dicti Guillelmi, qui quidem in nos alto et basso compromiserant
super contentione predicta, sub forma et verbis sequentibus, in gallico." The translation is
that of S. M. Brown and J. F. O'Sullivan, trans., *The Register of Eudes of Rouen* (New York,
1964), p. 577. See also Eudes's *Regestrum visitationum*, p. 166 (September 4, 1253), for the
accusation by the dean of Meulan against two squires (*armigeri*) of Us for horse theft. They all
agreed to accept Eudes's decision; the register does not mention any testimony or oaths, but
Eudes sentenced the squires to a public penance.

out of malice or intrigue or hatred for the dead man, do that which led to his death, and that what had happened was not and had never been any burden to him; and we personally are of the opinion that they can fittingly and properly take this oath."[69] Eudes says he believes these compurgators could swear truthfully (*bien et loiaument*) that Thomas had not compassed the death of William's brother. Far be it from an archbishop to encourage men to perjure themselves. But if Thomas had been innocent, and the death accidental or the fault of another, why the heavy penalty? Theologically speaking, this cannot be penance. A just God does not require satisfaction from the innocent. But the punishment took the same form as the average public penance, and doubtless few laymen or even clerics could have reckoned the difference. To the untheological eye, Eudes had simply and sensibly used penance to restore the peace.

Clerics were also liable. Eudes's visitations were often the occasion for airing dirty linen, and that might mean public penance. On November 6, 1259, Eudes visited the nuns at Bondeville, and finding that the prioress had given the nuns the seal of the convent without his knowledge, he sentenced her to the discipline (*quod disciplinam unam acciperet*) in chapter in the presence of the convent.[70] On December 11, 1263, he visited the chapter of Saint Mellon. Luke the vicar escaped judicial proceedings to deprive him of his benefice on grounds of incontinence when he agreed to exchange his benefice for another, presumably of lesser value. But on the same day, Luke the deacon, likewise defamed of incontinence, got off lightly when he confessed his guilt and asked for penance. Eudes told him to say the Psalter five times before the Feast of the Purification (February 2, six weeks away) and to make the short pilgrimage to Mont-Saint-Michel.[71] This was not the private confession whose seal cannot be broken but the public acknowledgment of public sinning, followed by public penance.

Bishops also applied public penance in cases that had already formally come before their ecclesiastical courts. Guillaume Le Maire, bishop of Angers between 1291 and 1317, generally reveals far less about disciplinary actions in his journal than Eudes had in his register, but one case shows the routine in his courts. On May 30, 1291,

---

69. "pour lonneur di lautre partie et pour appaisement de leur cuers"; "que il ne par malice ne par appensement, ne par hainne quil eust au mort ne fist cele chose de quo cele mort vint, ne puis que ce auint ne fu que ne li pesast et poise encore, et nous meesmes cuidons quil bien et loiaument puissent faire ce serement." The translation is that of Brown and O'Sullivan, *The Register of Eudes of Rouen*, p. 578.

70. Eudes Rigaud, *Regestrum visitationum*, p. 348.

71. Eudes Rigaud, *Regestrum visitationum*, p. 477.

one Colin the forester, of the parish of Saint-Pierre-de-Precigny, promised before Guillaume to break off his incestuous relationship with Catherine, the second cousin of his dead wife, and to pay one hundred sous if he went back to her. As punishment, Guillaume required Colin to appear on Pentecost in his parish church to receive the customary pilgrim's purse and staff from the priest; the priest was to tell everyone gathered on the feast day why Colin had received the penalty. Then Colin should walk barefoot to Mont-Saint-Michel. And finally, he should pay fifteen sous for the repair of the parish bells before Michaelmas. Catherine, on the other hand, had not appeared in court, and Bishop Guillaume excommunicated her for contumacy.[72] Here public penance had been integrated into the routine of the exterior forum. The threat of excommunication that hung over every sinner who faced public penance had become explicit.

Similarly, in the early fourteenth century, the official of Cerisy-le-Forêt, a monastery in the diocese of Bayeux that enjoyed episcopal rights of jurisdiction, regularly turned to public penances as convenient punishments for minor offenses. Sinners too poor to pay the fine for fornication underwent public penances. One such woman who bore a bastard child was appointed to go in the public procession on Palm Sunday bareheaded, barefoot, in her tunic, "so that other women should abstain from such a crime." The official sent gossiping women or quarreling spouses to the pillory. And one Germaine la Rosée, after confessing to practicing sortilege and healing with spells, was assigned to do a public penance, again unspecified, "because her sin was public."[73] Here, public penances were everyday punishments for everyday offenses; they were imposed like fines as the outcome of a court's decision.

Synodal statutes provide further evidence of the way the rite was applied. Just after the Fourth Lateran, the Council of Salisbury warned that concubines of priests were liable to public penance for their public sins. A decree for the province of Canterbury declared that such a concubine should be punished with public penance, just like an adulterer, and if she was already married, she should receive double the penalty for adultery.[74] At midcentury, the statutes of Lon-

---

72. Guillaume le Maire, *Liber Guillelmi Majoris*, ed. C. Port, Collection de documents inédits sur l'histoire de France, Mélanges historiques, 2 (Paris, 1877), pp. 244–245.

73. Dupont, "Le registre de l'officialité de Cerisy, 1314–1457," pp. 271–662. For public penances in lieu of fines, see p. 289 (1314), p. 294 (1314), pp. 381–382 (1330), and probably p. 374 (1326), a barefoot procession in tunic imposed on a woman for fornication, but with no mention of poverty. For the pillory: p. 312 (1315), p. 373 (1325), and p. 400 (1335). For Germaine la Rosée: p. 297 (1314).

74. Powicke and Cheney, p. 62 (Salisbury, 1217–1219, c. 9); pp. 154–155 (Canterbury, 1225). The guilty priest would be suspended and receive an unspecified severe penance.

don demanded rectors, vicars, and chaplains to inquire whether any parishioner was defamed among good men for adultery, incontinence, any sin "against nature," usury, sorcery, perjury, or false witness. As we have seen, according to these statutes, the penalty for such manifest crimes, whether it is a fine or a corporal punishment, "must be made public."[75] Around 1262, the statutes of Winchester reminded that clerics convicted of or confessing to those crimes that for laymen required solemn or public penance would be suspended, sent to the penitentiary, and given letters specifying the satisfaction required so that the appropriate priest could supervise it.[76]

Most of these examples come from English statutes. French statutes only occasionally refer to the requirement of public penance for certain crimes. This is probably an accident of phrasing. They very frequently insist that those who openly commit certain crimes, especially usury, prostitution, and sacrilege, should be publicly denounced in the parish church, reported to the bishop, and, some statutes add, excommunicated if they refuse to amend their ways.[77] As we can see from Eudes's register, the only way out of excommunication in these circumstances was public penance. French synods concentrated on the first part of the process, the threat or actual imposition of excommunication, since many manifest sinners might never agree to submit to the penance that would release them.

The Procedure of Nonsolemn Public Penances

These statutes and the actual examples suffice to demonstrate the variety of sins punished by public penance and the inventiveness of the satisfactions imposed. Public penance could embarrass a political enemy, settle a feud, humiliate a rich banker, or discipline a poor deacon. Bishops might send a sinner on a pilgrimage, make him march around local churches in hairshirt and ashes, instruct his priest to publicize his crimes, or even force him to dig up and rebury a child's body. Still, certain general rules governed the procedure of public penance. As with private and solemn penance, we may follow the process from start to finish. In many respects, public penance

75. Powicke and Cheney, p. 632 (London, 1245–1259, c. 6).
76. Powicke and Cheney, p. 721 (Winchester, 1262–1265, c. 96).
77. BN latin 11067, f. 21v–22r (Noyon, 1304); Pontal II, p. 155 (Le Mans, 1240–1247, c. 36); Gosse, *Histoire de l'abbaye . . . d'Arrouaise*, p. 588 (Arras, thirteenth century, c. XI); Gousset, *Les actes . . . de Reims*, II, p. 441 (Cambrai, 1300–1310), and II, p. 358 (council of Saint Quentin for province of Reims, 1231); Martène and Durand, *Veterum scriptorum*, VII, col. 1279 (Orléans, before 1314), VII, cols. 1353–1356 (Cambrai, 1334), and VIII, col. 1550 (Soissons, 1334, c. 2); del Bene, *Codex statutorum . . . aurelianensis*, p. 223 (Orléans, ca. 1324).

worked like solemn penance, and, in fact, the abundant eviden⸱ ⸱⸱r
its procedure may sometimes complete the picture from the li⸱⸱⸱ ⸱d
sources for the solemn rite.

First, in principle, nonsolemn public penance, unlike the solemn
rite and excommunication, could be imposed by any priest.[78] Most of
the examples of such rites that survive in narrative sources for northern France, however, show a bishop or a court with episcopal jurisdiction imposing the sentence. The French statutes do grant priests the
right, and indeed, the obligation, to exclude notorious usurers and
other sinners from the sacraments until they make amends and do
penance; the very grant of that right, however, implies that the synod
controls such excommunications. Theologians and canonists agreed
that priests could impose some public penances. Thomas Aquinas, for
instance, defined nonsolemn public penance as that which any parish
priest can publicly impose, "in facie ecclesie."[79] Thomas and the other
theologians who described the nonsolemn rite in this way clearly suggest that they believed village priests routinely imposed such penances on their parishioners. Some writers even noted that simple
priests occasionally excommunicated their parishioners on their own
authority. Peter Cantor, for example, attempted to reconcile this observance with the theory that excommunication was an episcopal
function.[80] Presumably, priests excluding parishioners from the sacraments were also imposing public penance; the distinction may not
have been clear. In the same vein, we find priests imposing pilgrimages on their parishioners, evidently as part of public penance as
well as in ostensibly secret confessions.[81] Quite likely, priests used

78. A synodal statute of Lisbon, 1233–1247, reserves public sins to the bishop: "Item in
peccatis public et notoriis non potest iniungi penitentia nisi solum per episcopum vel eius
vicarium," cited in da Rosa Pereira, "Les statuts synodaux d'Eudes de Sully au Portugal,"
p. 472. However, this exceptional statute may be referring only to exceptionally notorious
crimes, which normally ended in the imposition of solemn penance by the bishop.

79. Thomas Aquinas, *Commentum in quatuor libros sententiarum*, IV D.14 q.1 a.5, p. 695;
closely dependent on him or on Thomas's source are the anonymous tract in BN latin 15162,
f. 101r, and Eudes de Cheriton, *Tractatus de paenitentia*, BN latin 2593, 7v. Eudes uses the
accusative, "in faciem ecclesie." In Ferrara, the cathedral chapter in 1135 claimed a monopoly
on the right to impose public penances as well as to baptize in the city or its suburb: Mauro
Ronzani, "Aspetti e problemi delle pievi e delle parrochie cittadine nell'Italia centro-
settentrionale," in *Pievi e parrochie in Italia nel basso medioevo (sec. XIII–XV)*, Atti del VI Convegno di Storia della chiesa in Italia, Florence, 1981, Italia Sacra, 35–36 (Rome, 1984), p. 330.
They clearly based their claim on the theory that *pievi* within the city should be wholly
dependent on the chapter, like mere chaplaincies, not on any notion that such penances (or
baptisms) were always an episcopal function.

80. Peter Cantor, *Summa de sacramentis*, IV.142, pp. 335–336: "Vnde uidetur quod possit
[sacerdos] suspendere parrochianum suum ab introitu ecclesie precepto sui superioris, quo-
tiens apparet inobediens per contumatiam."

81. A canon published by Boeren, "Les plus anciens statuts du diocèse de Cambrai," 3:
378 (Cambrai, 1260), seems to refer to public pilgrimages to the cathedral. More common are
references to pilgrimages imposed in supposedly secret confession; see above, Chapter 3.

both expulsion and minor pilgrimages against misbehaving parishioners in very simple cases that have escaped the notice of narrative sources. Ordinary thirteenth-century Frenchmen probably saw processions, pilgrimages, and excommunications imposed by both bishops and priests; only the theologians and canonists tried to distinguish different rites according to whether priest or bishop presided.

While, in theory, solemn penance punished laymen who had scandalized the entire town, other public penances were supposed to punish clerics guilty of any public sins, in addition to those laymen guilty of manifest but not scandalous sins, a distinction that was obviously difficult to draw. Public penance for public sins, secret for secret sins, ran the cliché in theology and canon law; occasional diocesan statutes reminded priests to obey this dictum.[82] This principle of different procedures for public and secret sins was so ingrained that Eudes and other bishops considered these sins to be virtually different species. Publicity and secrecy were not understood in the way they are now, however. We generally consider the publicity or privacy of a crime to be a matter of pure happenstance rather than as related to the nature of the crime. Medieval legal thought ran a different course, whether the subject was religious expiation or secular punishment. English common law, to cite a familiar example, distinguished murder, which then referred only to secret homicide, from ordinary homicide. English and Continental law alike distinguished the secret crime that required inquiry or jury from the manifest offense that could be, and should be, punished on the spot. In the *Roman de Renart*, Bruyant the bull insists that Ysengrin should not be required to make a legal complaint about Renart's seduction of Ysengrin's wife.

> How can Ysengrin make a complaint
> About something that is so open
> And well known and unconcealed?[83]

Self-evident crimes demanded instant revenge or punishment—in this case, Bruyant suggests, immediate castration. The belief that publicity was something intrinsic to a crime, however, meant that sometimes victims called crimes public because they were public by nature, rather than public in the particular instance. Thus, in Chapter 3 we

82. E.g., Mansi 23:743 (Le Mans, 1247). And the official of Cerisy invoked it to explain his judgment in two cases: Dupont, "Le registre de l'officialité de Cerisy, 1314–1457," 297 (1314), and p. 382 (1330).

83. Jean Dufournet and Andrée Meline, eds., *Le roman de Renart* (Paris, 1985), Branche I, ll. 88–90, p. 46: "Comment doit Ysengrin plaider/ De chose qui si est aperte/ Et conneüe et descoverte?"

found that certain types of sins were considered more public th.... others and therefore received less protection from exposure in the procedures of private penance. What bishops considered a "public sin" and so liable to public penance depended as much on the type of sin as on the circumstances of its commission. So a Flemish lord Asego who confessed around 1170 to the public offense of distributing false coin at his wedding was thus punished as a public sinner, though only his secret confession seems to have revealed the crime.[84]

This is the context for the distinction between manifest and secret crimes in the penitential system. Some of the crimes that incurred public penance were indeed perfectly self-evident. They required no inquiry or confession. So it is with the count of Nevers's misbehavior during the interdict. In most cases, however, a sin or series of sins came to light only as a matter of ill repute that had to be considered further. In spite of Bruyant's blunt demand for punishment, this was the case with Renart and Hersant's adultery. This was often the case with human adultery, prostitution, and usury. According to canon law, such cases fell into a middle category, somewhere between the fully public and the fully private. Ill fame was indeed weaker proof than what was truly notorious or manifest, that is, self-evident to everyone. Further proof had to follow such ill fame, unlike the notoriety that convicted without any need for legal procedure, just as the *Roman de Renart* explained.[85] The careful distinction between degrees of evidence reflected the same concern about shades of publicity and privacy that we found in some thirteenth-century theologians. Notoriety indicated absolute publicity, the kind of citywide scandal that was traditionally the basis of solemn public penance. Ill fame represented something less, a crime that should be brought into the public sphere but was not already evident to all. And in the end, canonists drew the most crucial line between public and private differently than we might. Accepting rumor as the basis for further procedure allowed far more sins to be considered public than we would normally define that way. A crime might be public without the explicit testimony of a

---

84. The Abbot of Mariengaarde assigned him a pilgrimage to the Holy Land and considered imposing a still more humiliating local penance: *Vita Fretherici*, in Aem. W. Wybrands, ed., *Gesta abbatum orti sancte Marie* (Leeuwarden, 1879), pp. 34–37; cited in Jan van Herwaarden, *Opgelegde bedevaarten* (Assen, Amsterdam, 1978), p. 453n.

85. See Francesco Migliorino, *Fama e infamia: Problemi della società medievale nel pensiero giuridico nei secoli XII e XIII* (Catania, 1985), pp. 45–58, for *fama* in the canonists. In brief, notoriety indicated the highest standard of obviousness, self-evident in the fact itself; what was manifest was slightly less obvious, though known by certain knowledge or authorities; while ill-fame was based only on suspicion or uncertain authority, but nonetheless normally required further investigation and/or canonical purgation. Cf. Ramón de Peñafort, *Summa de poenitentia*, 3.31.4, pp. 365–366.

single witness. All that was necessary was the bad opinion of respect-
able neighbors.

The technical term in the statutes and registers was *infamia*.[86] A
priest might be *infamatus* or *diffamatus* for keeping a concubine, a
merchant for collecting on usurious loans. Public *infamia* was therefore a common first step in the process toward public penance. When
Eudes Rigaud visited local churches, his first task was to sniff out
infamia against clerics.[87] Once the evil rumor swept the streets, the
statutes demanded public denunciation in the churches, and excommunication in the end if no penance was done.[88] In accordance with
the canonists, a council of Noyon distinguished between usurers and
concubines self-evidently guilty ("those whom the evidence of the
deed detects") and those *diffamatos*. The first, bound by excommunication, were to be denounced in their parishes; the second were
to be warned three times and then denied ecclesiastical burial.[89] On
the other hand, if there was no *infamia* or open scandal, there were no
grounds for further ecclesiastical investigation. The defenders of the
Templars argued that the commission of inquisition could not legally
proceed since the Templars were not first defamed of heresy.[90]

One principle is clear. *Infamia* alone was enough to spark further
inquiry or even force the defamed to clear himself with an oath. As we
would put it, *infamia* could make a man or woman guilty unless

---

86. Migliorino, *Fama e infamia*, pp. 79–90, 183–186; Peter Landau, *Die Entstehung des
kanonischen Infamiebegriffs von Gratian bis zur Glossa Ordinaria*, Forschungen zur kirchlichen
Rechtsgeschichte und zum Kirchenrecht, 5 (Cologne, 1966), esp. pp. 1–11. The canonists
distinguished *infamia ipso iure*, or legal disability deriving from certain conditions, from this
infamia facti, or serious rumor. Several argued that *infamia facti* only required canonical
purgation if the ill-fame came from good men, not from enemies.

87. Andrieu-Guitrancourt, *L'archevêque Eudes Rigaud*, p. 299: Eudes found eighty-six
clerics *infamati* in 1250 alone. For the procedure of monastic and other visitation, see Cheney,
Episcopal Visitation of Monasteries in the Thirteenth Century, pp. 78–79; and Noël Coulet, *Les
visites pastorales*, Typologie des sources du Moyen Age occidental, 23 (Turnholt, 1977), pp. 30–
32.

88. Powicke and Cheney, p. 632 (London, 1245–1259, c. 5–6); Martène and Durand,
Veterum scriptorum, VII, col. 1357 (Cambrai, 1334), VII, col. 1279 (Orléans, before 1314),
VIII, col. 1547 (Soissons, thirteenth century, c. 92), and VIII, col. 1550 (Soissons, 1334, c. 2);
Gosse, *Histoire de l'abbaye . . . d'Arrouaise*, p. 588 (Arras, thirteenth century); Gousset, *Les
actes . . . de Reims*, II, p. 358 (council of Saint Quentin for province of Reims, 1231, c. 2). The
same idea of the legal consequences of persistent rumor made a showing in the rules for
religious houses. Brothers of the Hôtel Dieu of Saint-Jean, Beauvais, who were the subject of
fraternal clamorings were to be punished in chapter: P. Louvet, *Histoire . . . de Beauvaisis*,
p. 532; from the rule dated 1246.

89. BN latin 11067, f. 21v–22r (Noyon, 1304): "quos facti evidentia detegit." An early-
fourteenth-century council of Cambrai, however, lumped together usurers known "aut per
facti evidentiam . . . uel alterius notorie et manifeste vobis." Both received three warnings
before excommunication (Martène and Durand, *Veterum scriptorum*, VII, col. 1354).

90. Barber, *The Trial of the Templars*, p. 141. The same point is made more generally in the
statutes of Exeter, 1287: Powicke and Cheney, p. 1029 (c. 32). See Vodola, *Excommunication in
the Middle Ages*, p. 34, on defamation as a prerequisite for *inquisitio*.

proven innocent.[91] Similarly, in French secular procedure, spread suspicion, *fama*, was grounds enough to arrest the accus͏   l investigate his guilt.[92] The credence that both penitential and s͏   ır law gave to rumor is understandable in a world in which nei͏   ɔrs likely knew a great deal of each other's affairs, and particul͏ar s͏ıns, such as adultery and usury, would likely have been the talk of every city street. Sometimes, what friends and enemies thought was true mattered more than what was really true. That is why Eudes Rigaud sent Thomas the miller on pilgrimage even though he was unimpressed by the testimony against him. The theologians themselves had observed that public sinners offended the church chiefly by setting a bad example. According to the bishop's own practical theology, a bad reputation among one's neighbor's was proof enough of the bad example a sinner had set, and he therefore deserved punishment.

Once a sinner's notoriety was established, the synods often prescribed effective excommunication.The statutes covered an increasing number of defamed crimes, from usury, arson, and homicide to violation of churches and cemeteries and infringement of ecclesiastical liberties.[93] Procedure varied. Sometimes the statute explicitly used the term excommunication; quite often it simply told the priest to refuse the sacraments to the offender. A council of Soissons recommended a series of private, and then public, warnings in imitation of the Gospel's teaching (Matt. 18:15–18). "If anyone is suspected of usury by the public report of the area, let him be confronted by his priest, first in secret, secondly with witnesses, and finally directly and publicly in the church, so that he should desist from usury."[94] If the usurer still refused to make amends, he was to be refused the sacraments. Procedure varied, but such shaming of "rumored" sinners was commonplace. Some statutes required public warnings before excommunication; some required no warning at all.[95] In 1231, the council

91. Andrieu-Guitrancourt, *L'archevêque Eudes Rigaud*, p. 299, intent on defending the rural clergy, argues that they were often defamed out of boredom and envy, and that they were only rarely guilty. Whatever the motives for the accusation, however, Eudes took the rumors seriously and demanded compurgation or confession.

92. Roger Grand, "Justice criminelle, procédure et peines dans les villes aux XIIIe et XIVe siècles," *Bibliothèque de l'Ecole des chartes* 52 (1941): 58.

93. Dobiache-Rojdestavensky, *La vie paroissiale en France*, p. 105.

94. Martène and Durand, *Veterum scriptorum*, VIII, col. 1547 (Soissons, thirteenth century, c. 92): "si quis per publicam famam loci suspectus fuerit de usura, conveniatur a sacerdote suo, primo in secreto, secundo additis testibus, tertio indilate publice in ecclesia, ut ab usura desistat." For the theologians' discussion of "fraternal correction," see above, Chapter 2. This is one of the few cases of such a procedure in lay discipline.

95. Three warnings: BN latin 11067, f. 21v (Noyon, 1304); Martène and Durand, *Veterum scriptorum*, VII, col. 1279 (Orléans, before 1314, c. 55). No warning: Gousset, *Les actes . . . de Reims*, II, pp. 441 (Cambrai, 1300–1310); Mansi 23:744 (Le Mans, 1247); BN latin

of Saint-Quentin for the province of Reims provided for the case of
the usurer by reputation whom nobody dared accuse in person. The
statute allowed the usurer to make a "canonical purgation," that is,
compurgation, which required the accused to assemble a certain number of men of good repute to swear to his innocence. If the reputed
usurer failed, he was to be punished.[96]

Beyond this varied advice, the statutes are silent. Eudes Rigaud's
register complements their evidence on procedure. Eudes spent
much of his time disciplining clerics *infamati* for various misdeeds,
particularly for lapses from celibacy. Once the *infamia* reached his
ears, Eudes confronted the reputed wrongdoer, either privately, or
more likely in the presence of Eudes's secretary, who recorded for the
register what happened. Often the sinning cleric confessed, but, as we
have seen, this was no private sacramental confession; it was a formal
avowal of guilt with judicial consequences. When the cleric denied the
story, and there was no compelling evidence from witnesses, the bishop would allow him to try to find compurgators to attest to his innocence.[97] Eudes often set a date for the oath, but many failed to produce the requisite number, usually seven, on time. After all, how
many priests of unblemished repute would a rural deacon know, and
how many could he persuade to take his side in front of the skeptical
archbishop? If Eudes declared the compurgation failed, an inconti-
nent priest might be called to appear at a later date before the archbishop and his official, then and there to lose his benefice and perhaps also receive some public penance.[98] Clerics in minor orders,
priests not in possession of a parish church, and some first-time of-

---

11067, f. 22r (Noyon, 1304); Martène and Durand, *Veterum scriptorum*, VII, 1357 (Cambrai,
1334); Gosse *Histoire de l'abbaye . . . d'Arrouaise*, p. 591 (Arras, thirteenth century, c. 15).

96. Gousset, *Les actes . . . de Reims*, II, p. 358.

97. Andrieu-Guitrancourt, *L'archevêque Eudes Rigaud*, pp. 306, 310–311. Cf., for example, Eudes, *Regestrum visitationum*, p. 358 (February 3, 1259), and p. 363 (March 15, 1259);
and Dupont, "Le registre de l'officialité de Cerisy," p. 320 (1316), for a homicide that resulted
in a particularly thorough, but inconclusive, investigation, then compurgation. For the canon
law of compurgation, see especially Ramón de Peñafort, *Summa de poenitentia*, 3.31.1–6,
pp. 324–368; although this seems like an old-fashioned form of proof, it remained standard
throughout the thirteenth century.

98. See, for example, Eudes's report on the repeated failure of the *infamatus* Richard, the
priest of Calleville, to assemble compurgators to clear himself of incontinence; Eudes required him to appear before him or his official two weeks later to hear Eudes's verdict; under
this pressure, Richard resigned his benefice: *Regestrum visitationum*, pp. 363–364 (March 15
and April 29, 1259). Eudes's editor Bonnin printed as an appendix to the register, pp. 649–
674, the written oaths from defamed priests who were unable to clear themselves by compurgation, stating that they will be resigning their benefices for so long as Eudes demands it,
without further appeal. These were originally part of the *Regestrum visitationum* itself.

fenders usually got off more lightly. Quite often, Eudes simply assigned an immediate public penance in lieu of further punishment.[99]

Laymen, too, might be defamed and called to account. On January 22, 1264, Geoffroy de Cuverville, a knight defamed of adultery, appeared before Eudes and was found guilty by means unspecified. The French statutes permitted laymen to establish their innocence with lay compurgators. This procedure appears once in the register of Cerisy, but Eudes did not favor it.[100] In any case, Eudes made Geoffroy take an oath before witnesses that under forfeiture of twenty *livres tournois* he would not relapse with the same woman and he would make a pilgrimage to Saint-Gilles-du-Gard in Provence before mid-August.[101]

More commonly, laymen came before bishops not on account of defaming rumors but because they had already been excommunicated, often for violence against priests or church property. In January 1248, Eudes recorded a sentence against Gautier Charue, who had been excommunicated for leading the commune of Gamaches in an attack on an archepiscopal manor in which one man was killed. In order to be absolved, Gautier would pay damages and publicly display his penance at ten different churches and cathedrals, along with eleven other prominent men of the commune.[102] In another case, the layman apparently had not yet been excommunicated, but he expected to incur the sentence, and he hastened to accept public penance from Eudes to stave it off. Guillaume de Dabeuf had contracted a clandestine marriage against the precise orders of Eudes's official, and he agreed to submit to corporal punishment ("quamcumque penam corporalem") and a fine. Eudes sent him on pilgrimages to Rome, Bari, and Saint-Gilles-du-Gard; he did not record whether Guillaume also had to undergo some more explicitly corporal punishment, such as flogging.[103] Some excommunicants escaped such elaborate humiliation. In December 1249, Eudes agreed to absolve Guillaume l'Orcher, who had been excommunicated for preventing Eudes's nominee

99. See, for example, the case of the priest at Saint-Martin, defamed of incontinence; after confessing, he apparently received only a warning (*Regestrum visitationum*, p. 47, July 16, 1249); or the case of the defamed chaplain Simon, who confessed to incontinence and received straight away a warning and a "suitable penance" from Eudes (pp. 470–471, October 1, 1263); or the case of Luke the deacon, cited above (p. 477, December 11, 1263); Luke agreed to resign his benefice if he was ever defamed again and could not purge himself.

100. Dupont, "Le registre de l'officialité de Cerisy," p. 340 (1320): A layman defamed of fornication is warned, then excommunicated; he admits the rumor (*confitetur famam*) to six suitable men, and promises to purge himself.

101. Eudes Rigaud, *Regestrum visitationum*, pp. 506–507.

102. Eudes Rigaud, *Regestrum visitationum*, pp. 23–24.

103. Eudes Rigaud, *Regestrum visitationum*, pp. 544–545 (May 12, 1266).

to a benefice from occupying his church. Guillaume took an oath before a great number of knights and clerics to make amends to Eudes and the nominee.[104] These are cases of threats or disrespect of episcopal authority; actually striking a cleric was a sin that incurred automatic excommunication; it could be absolved only by the pope or his representative. Both Eudes, acting as the papal representative, and the papal curia itself used public penances—barefoot processions from church to church, beatings, and the like—as satisfaction in these cases.[105]

In all these cases, it is difficult to distinguish what belongs to the external forum and the bishop's court from the internal forum of sacramental penance. Once again, we see that the vague procedure of public penance made it a convenient middle ground between the two starkly defined legal alternatives. Eudes Rigaud had an official for the external forum and doubtless a penitentiary to supervise the administration of the internal forum, but the register so often shows the archbishop himself, fully competent in both *fora*, intervening without channeling the case into one of these alternatives. Sometimes, as we have seen, external judicial proceedings had already begun when Eudes intervened before the case went any further, absolved the now contrite sinner, and assigned a public satisfaction. Occasionally, he made the absolution conditional on the performance of the satisfaction.[106] At other times, Eudes prevented the case from coming before his court at all by opting for the informality of public penance. In either case, the archbishop did not explicitly distinguish between absolutions for excommunication in the external forum from absolutions for mortal sin in the internal forum; his register records an absolution, nothing more. At Cerisy, there was in fact no internal forum at issue. Technically, the monastery's official only had jurisdiction in the external forum. His register generally did not refer to absolution; these were punishments, and the guilty "made amends."[107]

104. Eudes Rigaud, *Regestrum visitationum*, p. 55. See also the cases of Raoul d'Aulages, excommunicated for nonpayment of the clerical heath tax, and of Julien Sarrazins and Bartholomew Chevalier, engaged in some sort of conflict with the priest at Saint-Pierre-de-Neufchâtel, p. 38 (May 15, 1249).

105. Eudes Rigaud, *Regestrum visitationum*, pp. 362–363 (March 12, 1259); see John of Freiburg, *Summa confessorum*, 3.34.12, for a discussion of curial practice. Unlike Eudes, John says that only the severest violence, "homicide and suchlike," should require public satisfaction.

106. Andrieu-Guitrancourt, *L'archevêque Eudes Rigaud*, p. 318.

107. The register says the guilty "gagiavit emendam" or "voluit facere emendam": Dupont, "Le registre de l'officialité de Cerisy," p. 291 (1314), and p. 297 (1314). In one case where a Jean Jaquet had struck a cleric, he was required to submit to the official ("gagiavit nobis emendam"), and then had to promise to go to the penitentiary of Bayeux to be absolved

But the public penances that the official imposed looked exactly like the penances Eudes set outside of any court procedure, and he justified them by borrowing the theologian's *dictum* about sacramental penance: public penance for public sins.

This conflation of the internal and external *fora* coincided with the procedure assumed by the synodal statutes. There, the bishops demanded that notorious usurers, for instance, be warned and then punished with exclusion from the sacraments, a sort of de facto excommunication that needed no episcopal decision or proceeding in the bishop's ecclesiastical court. As excommunication or the threat of excommunication hung over the sinner, the bishop could intervene if he chose, assign a satisfaction, and give absolution. This was Eudes's procedure, and that of other bishops of his day.[108] The flexibility of public penance made it an attractive way of regulating the diocese, especially since bishop could impose public penance over any inhabitant of his diocese, even those exempt from his ecclesiastical jurisdiction. How convenient for a case to slip unnoticed from the external to the internal forum, where the bishop's authority was unchallenged. When we looked at the procedure of *private* penance, we found private cases slipping into the realm of semipublic exposure. Here, we find fully public lawsuits slipping into the less formal, less absolute, and readily available realm of public penance.

The confusion, both theoretical and practical, between excommunication and public penance was thus of great utility for bishops. A specific case of this confusion was excommunication *latae sententiae*, that which fell automatically on anyone who committed openly or secretly one of a number of listed crimes, chiefly heresy, disobedience to the decisions of the Holy See, violence against a cleric, simony, clerical concubinage, and lay investiture.[109] The fact of automatic excommunication is familiar enough that I need only recall it here. Some crimes had been punishable by automatic excommunication since the Carolingian period, but with the intense study of canon law and the increasing distinction between *fora*, an anomaly came to be recognized. Canonists and some theologians questioned how it was

---

("quod faceret se absolvi a penitenciario ecclesie baiocensi"): p. 505 (1377). Striking a cleric was a case reserved to the pope, his penitentiary, or bishops as his representative. Cerisy had no authority to stand in for the bishop's rights in the internal forum.

108. See Avril, *Le gouvernement des évêques*, pp. 197–198, for twelfth-century Angers, for example.

109. Peter Huizing, "The Earliest Development of Excommunication Latae Sententiae by Gratian and the Earliest Decretists," *Studia Gratiana* 3 (1955): 279–309.

possible to cut someone off secretly from the body of the church.[110] They worried about what a Christian should do if he happens upon someone he alone knows to have been automatically excommunicated. Should the good Christian shun the excommunicant, thereby exposing the secret crime to all the world? There were several solutions in a study so careful.[111] Similar to excommunications *latae sententiae* were the increasingly common general sentences of excommunication, those of the unknown culprit for a named crime, such as absconding with a book belonging to the bishop's friend.[112] What would happen if such an excommunicated culprit should appear before a priest and confess to the secret crime? In theory, even secret excommunicants were excluded from sacramental penance until they publicly came forward, but, in practice, it was difficult to prevent the guilty one from salving his conscience by confession and absolution from an unsuspecting priest.[113] Like any other excommunication, general and *latae sententiae* excommunications might be lifted only on condition of performance of a public penance set by the bishop. Such excommunications inevitably confused the internal and external *fora*. The important point here is that excommunication *latae sententiae* was not unusual in its confusion of internal and external *fora*. It was just a special case, unusually well-documented by the canonists, of the much more general phenomenon of hauling secret sinners into the light of day.

Satisfactory Punishments in Public Penances

Once the public sinner had submitted, he or she generally had to complete a specified public satisfaction. Evidence about satisfactions for nonsolemn penances is much more abundant than that for solemn penances. By definition, of course, public penance had to be in some

110. N. M. Häring, "Peter Cantor's View on Ecclesiastical Excommunication and Its Practical Consequences," *Mediaeval Studies* 11 (1949): 110; G. May, "Bann," In *Theologische Realenzyklopädie*, 5:174; Huizing, "The Earliest Development of Excommunication Latae Sententiae," pp. 277–320; Vodola, *Excommunication in the Middle Ages*, pp. 28–31.

111. Vodola, *Excommunication in the Middle Ages*, pp. 48–53; Häring, "Peter Cantor's View on Ecclesiastical Excommunication," pp. 100–101.

112. Huizing, "The Earliest Development of Excommunication Latae Sententiae," pp. 310, 315–316; Adam, *La vie paroissiale en France au XIVe siècle*, p. 99; Rosalind Hill, "Public Penance: Some Problems of a Thirteenth-Century Bishop," *History* ser. 2, 36 (1951): 214–215, and "The Theory and Practice of Excommunication in Medieval England," *History* 42 (1957): 9.

113. Vodola, *Excommunication in the Middle Ages*, pp. 56–57. In the fourteenth century, certain confessors were finally empowered to absolve excommunicants *latae sententiae* without further ado.

respect a public matter, if not in the rite of expulsion and readmission, then in the punishment. So it is not surprising to find that pilgrimages and processions with or without public beatings were preferred in serious cases. As we have seen, bishops often chose pilgrimages for fornicating clerics and lay troublemakers. Favorite destinations from northern France were Mont-Saint-Michel for minor sins, Saint-Gilles-du-Gard and Rome for major ones. Such pilgrims were supposed to go barefoot, keep a fast except on Sundays and feasts, and spend but one night in town; some had to wear a cross sewn on their tunic.[114] Anyone could recognize their status from their dress, but at least the embarrassment occurred far from home. Late in the century, some theologians criticized penitential pilgrimages as a temptation to misbehavior, and Bishop Oliver Sutton of Lincoln (1280–1299) never imposed pilgrimages other than crusades, perhaps in concurrence with this view.[115] But the French bishops clearly endorsed this measure of punishment. If pilgrims sometimes misbehaved, at least they had to leave behind the town and the enmities they had sown.

Several thirteenth-century theologians in defining a tripartite penance had described pilgrimage as the main form of nonsolemn public penance, even as a characteristic that set it apart from the solemn rite.[116] This is surely an exaggeration, since the public satisfaction imposed took many forms, but it is an understandable one. Penitential pilgrimage had its origins in the exile required for certain sins in *libri penitentiales*; from the ninth century onward, bishops and church courts preferred to set a definite goal for the journey.[117] During the late twelfth century and the early thirteenth century, when theologians were rereading the old books of tariffs and trying to classify what they found according to the tripartite system, it was easy to identify all the *carenae* and seven-year penances with the solemn rite and all the pilgrimages with the nonsolemn rite. This intellectual

---

114. Ludovic de Valon, "Les pèlerinages expiatoires et judiciaires de la Belgique à Roc-Amadour au Moyen Age," *Bulletin trimestriel de la Société des études littéraires, scientifiques, et artistiques du Lot* 58 (1937): 33.

115. Vogel, "Le pèlerinage pénitentiel," p. 50; Hill, "Public Penance: Some Problems of a Thirteenth-Century Bishop," pp. 217–218.

116. See above, Chapter 2, on definitions of nonsolemn penance and, e.g., Robert of Flamborough, *Liber poenitentialis*, V.236, p. 205; Thomas Aquinas, *Summa theologiae*, Suppl. q. 28, a.3; Eudes of Cheriton, *Tractatus de paenitentia*, BN latin 2593, f. 8r; BN latin 15162, f. 101r. Vogel, "Le pèlerinage pénitentiel," p. 43, goes beyond the medieval evidence when he suggests that nonsolemn public penance and penitential pilgrimage simply were identical.

117. Vogel, "Le pèlerinage pénitentiel," pp. 57–59; de Valon, "Les pèlerinages expiatoires et judiciaires de la Belgique aux sanctuaires de la Provence au Moyen-Age," *Provincia: Revue trimestrielle d'histoire et d'archéologie provençales* 15 (1935): 31–32; Pierre-André Sigal, *Les marcheurs de Dieu: Pèlerinages et pèlerins au Moyen Age* (Paris, 1974), pp. 17–19.

exercise did not describe the practice. Not only pilgrimages but many other types of satisfactions came to be imposed in all public penances.

Bishops were evidently reluctant to shame clergymen too much in front of their parishioners, but laymen often had to make some sort of public satisfaction nearer home. Although some bishops and abbots were conscious of the dangers of undermining the authority of a prominent layman by humiliation, if the crime was sufficiently shocking or directly flouted ecclesiastical authority, even men of standing might not escape.[118] We may recall the count of Nevers who had to dig up and rebury a putrefying body. More common were processions at local churches. In 1208, the monks of Pontron (diocese of Angers) accused the lord Guillaume de Cargouët of mistreating one of their number while he wrangled with them over a piece of land; when he lost his trial before the feudal court, he lost the land and had to make amends besides by going to the abbey in his shirt, with a cord around his neck, to be beaten in the presence of the abbot and the monks.[119] In 1253, at Juziers in Normandy, in 1253, Eudes Rigaud adjudicated an argument between the dean of Meulan and a couple of squires. He sentenced the laymen to appear at the churches of Us and Notre-Dame-de-Pontoise barefoot, wearing only their shirts, and carrying rods (*virgas*).[120]

Sometimes the scale was grander. In the case of the attack on the Eudes's manor at Aliermont in 1248, Gautier Charue and eleven other prominent members of the commune had to make Sunday processions to the cathedrals of Rouen, Evreux, Lisieux, Beauvais, Amiens, and Dreux, three times to the church of Aliermont, and once each to the churches of Saint-Aubin and Saint-Vaast, and Gamaches. Eudes wanted it to be an instructive spectacle. "You shall walk with barefoot in shirt and breeches, heads uncovered; you [Gautier] shall walk barefoot in linen drawers and haircloth shirt, bareheaded. Each of you shall carry a wand in his hand and shall receive discipline from priests at the end of the processions, the crime for which you suffer such

---

118. Cf. the case cited above in which the Abbot of Mariengaarde ca. 1170 imposed a pilgrimage to the Holy Land on a certain Asego, who had confessed giving false money to the poor on his wedding day, in preference to a local public penance: "Maluit eciam taliter penitere eum, quam per publicam satisfactionem notum fieri crimen eius: cuius occasione possent multa mala pullulare." *Vita Fretherici*, in Wybrands, ed., *Gesta abbatum orti sancte Marie*, pp. 34–37.

119. Cited by Avril, *Le gouvernement des évêques*, pp. 421-422. Twice Avril (pp. 189, 197–198) refers to public penance as only "theoretically in use"; but his own examples of its imposition in specific cases and its liturgical survival suggest that its application was anything but theoretical in this area.

120. Eudes Rigaud, *Regestrum visitationum*, p. 166 (September 4, 1253).

things made public at each procession."[121] No attempt was made t(
see that those actually guilty in the attack should be the ones to suffe
the point was to shame and discredit the important men of Gamacl
in front of their neighbors and, indeed, throughout the provii
They likely considered it a more wrenching penalty than the finan
amends they also made. Very important men could be humiliated (
way if, like the count of Nevers, they had offended sufficiently imp.
tant enemies. Directly challenging a bishop or the canons who represented a town's ecclesiastical aristocracy would risk a humiliation calculated to undermine the offender's political authority. In 1276, the
canons of Saint-Pierre at Lille, seeing a cleric who had taken sanctuary killed by the *bailli* and the seigneur de Cysoing, appealed to the
papal legate, who required the guilty first to cross town barefoot,
bareheaded, and in their shirts to take the victim's corpse to reburial
in the cloister. But that was not all; every year thereafter the seigneur
de Cysoing and his successors had to follow an annual procession at
Lille in scarlet to perpetuate the memory of this crime and its punishment. His heirs were still fulfilling the penance at the end of the
sixteenth century.[122] A much milder processional penance imposed
by Bishop Oliver Sutton in Lincoln aroused complaints that the penalty threatened the dignity of men whose position required the respect
of their neighbors.[123] But shaming was the chief aim of such penances, and they remained a common form of punishment for laymen
at least in England and northern France.

The penances preferred by bishops—processional humiliations
and pilgrimages—were similar to those imposed in connection with
the Lenten rite. Incarceration seems to have been unknown. Corporal
punishment—chiefly beatings—were always public, as befits public
penance. The goal seems to have been to publicize the sin as widely as
possible. If the sinner was not yet a scandal to the city, he certainly
would be once he completed one of Eudes's schemes. These punishments were both like and unlike those imposed in the secular courts.
Spectacular in the performance, their effects were impermanent, unlike many secular punishments. The mutilations and hangings famil-

121. Eudes Rigaud, *Regestrum visitationum*, p. 24 (January 21, 1248): "Videlicet, quod ipsi,
nudi pedibus, in camisia et in braccis, discoopertis capitibus, tu autem [Gautier], nudis pedibus, cum femoralibus lineis et camisia de sacco, discooperto capite, incedatis; singuli vestrum
virgas in manibus tenentes, disciplinas, in fine processionum, a sacerdotibus recepturi, reatu,
pro quo talia sustinetis, in singulis processionibus, publicato."
122. Platelle in L. Trenard, ed. *Histoire de Lille*, pp. 345–346.
123. Hill, "Public Penance: Some Problems of a Thirteenth-Century Bishop," pp. 221–
223.

iar to secular courts were unknown in public penances. Unknown, too, was permanent banishment. And, unlike mere secular punishments, spiritual public penances reconciled the sinner with God and the church. However harsh they seemed, public penances mimed the voluntary discipline of the monastic ascetic.

But the satisfactions imposed in public penances were also like secular penalties. Ecclesiastical courts did not have a monopoly on the deliberate use of social embarrassment as a penalty. Secular courts sometimes used it alone or in conjunction with other punishments for minor crimes like trivial thefts or for adultery.[124] Occasionally, the secular authority might itself impose something very like an ecclesiastical public penance; so, Philip Augustus ordered a knight publicly to dig up and rebury the *conversus* he had hanged.[125] Eventually, from around 1300, the *échevins* of northern France and Flanders would send those guilty of serious violence on long pilgrimages.[126] The immediate secular authority, of course, may have been the bishop himself in his capacity as secular lord of all or part of the city, and so it is not surprising that there was some blurring between secular and religious penalties. In certain important cases, such as the punishment of the riots in Reims, the bishop in both capacities cooperated with the king in assessing the penalty. And when the bishop acted as arbitrator of a violent quarrel or attack, like Eudes Rigaud in the case of Thomas the miller, the line between spiritual reconciliation and secular settlement would have been further blurred. In other words, these public penances of dramatic humiliation were sometimes convenient alternatives to more conventional secular punishments. In Chapter 8, I discuss more fully what circumstances made public penance seem the better choice. Briefly, the bishops and secular authorities alike resorted to humiliating public and solemn penances when other legal forms of punishment were inappropriate, usually because the offenders only came to justice after negotiation. Humiliating penances became a kind of extralegal settlement. Thirteenth-century public penance fell into a gray area between the ecclesiastical interior forum and exterior forum; it also fell into a gray area between ecclesiastical justice and secular justice.

---

124. Grand, "Justice criminelle, procédure et peines dans les villes au XIIIe et XIVe siècles," pp. 95–99; his examples come from thirteenth-century Auvergne and Burgundy.
125. Ralph of Coggeshall, *Chronicon Anglicanum*, pp. 199–200. The incident is not dated but simply noted at the end of Philip's reign.
126. Herwaarden, *Opgelegde bedevaarten*; and see below, Chapter 8.

Conclusion

Peter Huizing has written of excommunication *latae sententiae* that it "was the restoration of the primitive penal discipline" of the church in a new guise.[127] The history of public penances suggests that the spirit of that discipline had hardly been extinguished, in spite of centuries of "tariffed" penances and paeans to contrition. Bishops still pursued public sinners with humiliation, and even private sinners risked embarrassing exposure. Indeed, the very distinction between public and private sins, a distinction ubiquitous in medieval tracts and essential to modern attempts to classify penances, was tendentious. Everything about penance apparently depended on whether the sin was private or public. The careful efforts to distinguish degrees of publicity and privacy reflected a desire to balance the claims of the city with those of the heart. Theologians and bishops alike hoped to reconcile contradictory urges to humiliate and to shield the sinner by defining in great detail which sinners should meet which response. In principle, the private sin was to be guarded even unto death; the public sin was to be made the talk of the diocese or even of all Christendom. Such a matter was too crucial to be left to chance. Some sins had to be declared in public in effect, whether they were so in fact. Some sins "offended the church" whether or not they were committed before witnesses.

Yet this static picture of a longing to expose and humiliate the sinner does not tell the whole truth. Public penance survived without interruption, but it changed. As we have already seen, the satisfactions bishops preferred to impose shifted from supervised imprisonments and multiyear fastings to brief, but occasionally spectacular, processions. A complete account of the changes and the reasons behind them awaits an analysis of the rituals of penance themselves and of the expectations of all the participants: clergy, penitents, and people.

127. Huizing, "The Earliest Development of Excommunication Latae Sententiae," p. 319.

CHAPTER FIVE

Collective Expiation, Collective Rejoicing

Only a small minority of thirteenth-century Frenchmen would ever have submitted personally to the rigors of the public penances described in Chapter 4. Rare indeed was the layman whose crimes had so scandalized his neighbors as to attract the attention of the archbishop of Rouen. The great majority, however, must have witnessed the rite at some point; the surviving evidence suggests that some form of public penance took place at least once a year in the towns, most often on Sundays and feast days, when peasants from the surrounding villages would likely be present. Outside the towns themselves, the spectacle must have been less frequent, though hardly unknown; parish priests barred parishioners from the door of the church or sent them on pilgrimages to distant shrines or just to the mother cathedral. To witness public penance was to participate in it. The parishioners or strangers who watched the bishop expel the penitents from the cathedral were as essential to the ceremony as the bishop or penitents themselves. Publicity was impossible without a public.

An understanding of the meaning of penance for that public is crucial to the examination of the liturgy of public penance in subsequent chapters. The evolution of the relation between the individual penitents who submitted to the rite and the onlookers for whose benefit the rite was played out is the central theme of this account of the development of public penance between the twelfth and the fourteenth centuries. In this chapter, therefore, I discuss the audience and their expectations about penance. I survey the seasonal penances of the ecclesiastical year from Advent to Pentecost and the pilgrimage season, omitting for the moment discussion of Ash Wednesday and Maundy Thursday, whose rites of individual solemn penance, eventually extended in analogy to all worshipers, I examine in Chapters 6 and 7.

Theologians' Penance and Popular Penance

Those who watched others do penance had to do penance themselves; if it was impossible to live without sin, it was also impossible not to owe a debt to God. Thirteenth-century Frenchmen often paid that debt in secret or semisecret confession and satisfaction; but they also joined in collective public displays of penance. The men and women who gathered in the cathedral every Ash Wednesday came as much for their own rite of penance as for the spectacle of another's expulsion. Lent had long been the season of penance for all Christians, not just for those guilty of terrible crimes; Maundy Thursday was the day for general absolutions as well as for the reception of individuals. Peasants and townsmen who knew implicitly that the days of late April and May were the proper season for personal penitential pilgrimages knew also that these were the perilous weeks when the Major Litany and Rogations atoned for the sins of the community and warded off danger to the crops and war.

Twelfth- and thirteenth-century theologians, however, neglected popular and communal forms of penance in their treatment of the sacrament or, indeed, of redemption in general. Episcopal benedictions, the blessing of water, and the Lord's Prayer made the briefest of appearances in some *quaestiones* on the forgiveness of venial sins, as did general confession.[1] Participation in all these familiar public rites redeemed the inevitable venial sins of Christians who had duly confessed and accepted sacramental penance for their mortal transgressions. Some thirteenth-century theologians did discuss briefly the so-called sacramentals such as blessings of water, foods, crops, houses, and so forth. These blessings were useful against the predations of demons (*insidia demonis*), who rage in the natural world since

---

1. For the redemption of venial sins through benedictions, sacramentals, fasts, and alms, see Peter Lombard, *Sententiae*, IV D.16 c.6, vol. II, pp. 341–342; Alexander of Hales, *Glossa in quator libros sententiarum*, IV D.16 c.16–17, pp. 264–265; Richard of Middleton, *Super quatuor libros sententiarum*, IV D.16 a.5 q.1, pp. 234–235; Ramón de Peñafort, *Summa de poenitentia*, 3.34.58, pp. 488–489; Johannes Teutonicus, *Glossa ordinaria*, D50.c64, *Decretum Gratiani . . . unacumque glossis*, f. 83v; Hostiensis, *In I–VI Decretalium*, V. De poen. et rem. c.12, f. 101a; John of Freiburg, *Summa confessorum*, 3.34.156. When they spoke of general confession, the theologians and canonists meant the routine weekly confession; for the Lenten general confession, see below, Chapter 7.

the Fall, and some, such as holy water, could help remit venial sin.[2] Other sacramentals, such as the blessings of vestments, chalices, and churches, simply helped perfect and consecrate things necessary for the cult; they did not sanctify human beings.[3] Entirely absent from these discussions were the more colorful observations of Rogations and the Major Litany.

Even the limited role permitted the rites by twelfth-century theologians came to be further circumscribed. Thirteenth-century writers defined "sacramentals" precisely in contrast to the sacraments that offered true redemption. The sacramentals worked *ex opere operante*, not *ex opere operato*; unlike sacraments, they signified something hidden, but they did not effect that which they signified.[4] Benedictions were only medicinal to the degree that they excited the warmth of love that truly remits venial sin.[5] Other popular rites eventually suffered a similar fate. Late in the century, for instance, Richard of Middleton carefully distinguished what he called sacramental general confession, by which he meant the individual penitent's general statement of guilt in secret confession to the priest, from what he called nonsacramental general confession, the collective, liturgical declaration in the publicity of the church. Only the former remits venial sin *ex vi sacramenti*; the latter does not itself remit sin, but helps men and women experience redemptive contrition.[6] In short, collective liturgical rites played only a small role in early Scholastic theology, and they became insignificant in later writings.

The theologians' neglect, however, must not be construed as sheer ignorance or contempt. After all, sacramentals and especially collective penitential processions figured largely in commentaries on the liturgy, which were often composed by theologians. Liturgical sources together with the commentaries offer an opportunity to see where popular and clerical assumptions correspond. Although laymen could not understand the Latin of the liturgy, they could make sense of the Rogations' circumambulations of the city, or the barefoot marches, or Palm Sunday's blessings of boxwood and flowers. The

---

2. Adolph Franz, *Die kirchlichen Benediktionen im Mittelalter* (Freiburg, 1909), vol. I, pp. 8–35; vol. II, pp. 26n, 147, cites the most important treatments.

3. Franz, *Die kirchlichen Benediktionen*, p. 11.

4. Cf. Franz, *Die kirchlichen Benediktionen*, p. 10.

5. Richard of Middleton, *Super quatuor libros sententiarum*, IV D.16 a.5 q.1 ad 2, p. 235, and IV D.21 a.3 q.1, pp. 338–339.

6. Richard of Middleton, *Super quatuor libros sententiarum*, IV D.21 a.3 q.1, pp. 338–339. We may recall here Caesarius of Heisterbach's story about the old man who tried to confess by rote a whole catalog of sins to his priest because he mistook the old general confession said publicly in his village church for the specific confession that alone was now considered sacramental and earned absolution: *Dialogus miraculorum*, XLV, vol. 1, p. 64.

theological silence does not reflect clerical dismay at popular enthusiasms, as one might think. Nor did the theologians exclude the possibility—and indeed the necessity—of mutual aid against the effects of sin. In fact, scholastic theology developed a whole calculus of the exchange of merits. To pay for the debts incurred by sin, every Christian could call on the treasury of merits of the whole church and on the individual efforts of his friends. The failure to address communal penances, therefore, represents neither a contempt for popular religion nor an exclusive individualism. The theologians explicitly manipulated a logic of exchange in order to account for the compensatory aid that one Christian might bestow on another and that the church bestowed on all. The liturgists and the rites they analyzed, on the other hand, silently embodied another sort of logic, a ritual logic, that complemented rather than rivaled theological analysis. Where a Bonaventure posed and answered a question about the possibility of one Christian doing penance for another,[7] the liturgists posed and answered other questions that the theologians neglected: What was the meaning of the Rogation dragon? In what sense did the Palm Sunday procession imitate Christ's passion?[8] Where theology sought to explain how God's eternal plan, Christ's suffering, the church's sacraments, and individual merit combined to win personal salvation, the liturgy expressed unspoken definitions of sacred and profane and so also the mirroring of the eternal order in this world of material objects.

Even a brief look at the liturgical calendar will make apparent the paradoxical nature of ritual penance as a cure for sin. We might expect clear-cut periods of remorse and rejoicing, but the reality is different. This survey of the calendar makes use of a variety of sources, but especially twelfth- and thirteenth-century liturgical commentaries and the processionals and ordinals of cathedrals and other major churches. Liturgists such as Jean Beleth, Sicard of Cremona, and Guillaume Durand outlined contemporary practice and interpreted its symbolism. If their typological interpretations sometimes strike us as strained, they are nonetheless a clue to the rhythms of sacrifice and victory that lie behind the liturgy. Ordinals provided brief synopses of the rites for every feast; they became more common in the thirteenth century under the influence of synodal statutes that required parish churches to possess a copy of the cathedral's use.[9]

7. Bonaventure, *Commentaria in quatuor libros sententiarum*, IV D.20 p.2 a.1 q.1, "Utrum unus pro alio possit satisfacere," vol. IV, pp. 529–530.
8. E.g. Sicard of Cremona, *Mitrale*, VII.6, PL 213:368, and VI.10, PL. 213:293.
9. See H. R. Philippeau, "A propos du Coutumier de Norwich," *Scriptorium* 3 (1949):

Processionals, rare before 1200, collected antiphons and sometimes prayers to be used in processions like Palm Sunday and Rogations.[10]

Advent to Septuagesima

The church year began with Advent, in liturgical theory a penitential season of preparation before Christ's birth. In fact, by the thirteenth century, Advent had generally lost for laity and clergy alike what limited penitential significance it had previously possessed. Advent did remain one of the three *quadragesimae*, or forty-day fasts, that monks and most solemn public penitents observed. Before the twelfth century, Advent also had been an obligatory fast for all clerics, and the observance subsisted in the Roman church and some regions into the early thirteenth century, but it died away without an official effort at revival.[11] It was never a popular fast. Saint Louis's biographers make much of the king's observance of Lenten austerity during the season, when he subsisted *en pures viandes de quaresmes*, including complete abstinence from fruit and fish on Fridays in Advent. Here was clear evidence of sanctity.[12]

The liturgists called the season the *tempus revocationis*, because it represented God's recalling humanity away from sin.[13] (They reckoned four main *tempora* in the year: the *tempus deviationis* from Septuagesima to Easter; the *tempus reconciliationis* from Easter to the octave of Pentecost; the *tempus peregrinationis* from the octave of Pentecost to Advent; and the *tempus revocationis*. The awkward period from Christmas to Septuagesima belonged in part to a *tempus regressionis*, in

---

295–302, for a typology of ordinals, and Pierre-Marie Gy, "L'ordinaire de Mende, une oeuvre inédite de Guillaume Durand l'ancien," in *Liturgie et musique (XIe–XIVe s.)*, Cahiers de Fanjeaux, 17 (Toulouse, 1982), pp. 242–243, for the influence of the statutes.

10. H. Leclercq in the *Dictionnaire d'archéologie chrétienne et de liturgie* (Paris, 1942), vol. 14:2, col. 1896, incorrectly states that processionals did not exist before the end of the Middle Ages. See Pierre-Marie Gy, "Collectaire, rituel, processionnal," *Revue des sciences philosophiques et théologiques* 44 (1960): 467–468; and Terence Bailey, *The Processions of Sarum and the Western Church*, Pontifical Institute of Mediaeval Studies, Studies and Texts, 21 (Toronto, 1971), pp. 3–4, 79–80.

11. Grégoire Lozinski, *La bataille de Caresme et de Charnage*, Bibliothèque de l'Ecole des Hautes Etudes, Sciences historiques et philosophiques, fasc. 262 (Paris, 1933), p. 42.

12. *Vie de Saint Louis par le confesseur de la reine Marguerite*, HF 20:107; Geoffroy de Beaulieu, *Vita sancti Ludovici*, HF 20:10–11; Guillaume de Nangis, *Gesta sancti Ludovici*, HF 20:404; *Chronicon anonymi Cadomensis*, HF 22:22; *Beati Ludovici vita e veteri lectionario*, HF 23:161; *Beati Ludovici vita*, HF 23:169.

13. Jean Beleth, *Summa de ecclesiasticis officiis*, c. 55, pp. 99–100; Guy d'Orchelles, "The 'Summa de Officiis Ecclesiae' of Guy d'Orchelles," p. 35; Guillaume Durand, *Rationale divinorum officiorum*, VI.1, f. 165v.

part to the *tempus peregrinationis*.[14]) Christmas, the feast that was Advent's culmination, signified, like Easter, redemption from sin.[15] Although this penitential theme for Advent was expressed in the black or violet vestments that were standard for days of penance, it was not marked by the processions, the veiling of ornaments, the denuding of altars, and the liturgical austerity that marked Lent.[16]

The contrast between penitential premise and liturgical reality was striking enough that Guillaume Durand offered an explanation. Why were alleluias sung in Advent but not in Lent? Durand explained that there are two types of fast, that of grief, *meroris*, and that of exultation, *exultationis*. The Lenten fast is wholly one of grief, and so songs of joy are omitted; Advent is partly a fast of joy for the first coming of Christ, partly of grief, for the Second Coming.[17] The whole explanation is strained. As Guillaume later explains, even Lent has its own moments of joyous liturgy, and it is not so clear why the Second Coming should be a time of mourning for the saved in the same way as Lent. The point is that Durand recognized the inconsistency. Advent was a pallid season of preparation in comparison to the vivid sufferings of Lent in the popular imagination. Lent rather than Advent had early and permanently become the focal point of Christian penance. Advent's failure to become a second Lent obviously has something to do with the early preeminence of Easter and the late development of Christmas. Advent's tepid popularity probably also has to do with the psychology of penance, however. Penance is a mimetic sacrifice, and Easter is the feast of sacrifice. Christmas is too unambiguously joyful to be a fitting climax for penance. Indeed, the cycle of raucous popular and clerical celebrations between Christmas and Epiphany not only completely overshadowed the weeks of Advent but was apparently far more important than the Carnival days of misrule, at least until the thirteenth century.

Another puzzling case of an occasion penitential in principle but not in ecclesiastical or popular practice was Candlemas, the feast on

14. See for example Beleth's discussion, *Summa de ecclesiasticis officiis*, c. 56, pp. 101–103; the other *tempora* will be treated below when the occasions arise.

15. Guillaume Durand, *Rationale divinorum officiorum*, calls the feast of the Circumcision a week after Christmas "octava resurrectionis a culpa et a poena," VI.15, f. 183v.

16. For colors, see K. A. Heinrich Kellner, *Heortology: A History of the Christian Festivals from Their Origin to the Present Day*, trans. from second German ed. (London, 1980), pp. 429–430; Polycarp Radó, *Enchiridion Liturgicum* (Rome, 1961), vol. 2, pp. 1445–1446. In Lent, church ornaments were hidden or covered, the crosses veiled, alleluias suspended, and bells rung only simply or occasionally; see Beleth, *Summa de ecclesiasticis officiis*, cc. 85–86, pp. 154–156.

17. Guillaume Durand, *Rationale divinorum officiorum*, VI.2, f. 168r-v.

February 2 commemorating the presentation of Jesus in the Temple and, eventually, the Purification of the Virgin. Candlemas processions in the west certainly possessed all the trappings of penitential supplication, including the black vestments and a barefoot march with candles. Medieval and modern liturgists have generally traced its origin to the Roman pagan Amburvalia and Lupercalia, both occasions of purification and expiation.[18] Despite the procession's mournful symbolism, the liturgy for Candlemas, the prayers and antiphons, all remained resolutely unpenitential.[19] They commemorated the presentation in the Temple without so much as a sideways glance at expiation. So, too, the commentators devoted their attention to the themes of Mary's humility and the fulfillment of the Old Law. The early-thirteenth-century liturgist Sicard of Cremona suggested an analogy between the observance of the Law and Gospel in the Presentation forty days after Christ's birth and the forty days of penance that prepared Christians for presentation in heaven. Other writers avoided even this hint of our purification from sin in the feast of Mary's Purification.[20] The liturgy suggests that the people and the clergy participated in the candlelit procession. But on the popular level, the feast was a minor one, without the elaborate folkloric heirs in northern France that would mark the religious occasion that truly stirred the imagination.[21]

Septuagesima to Palm Sunday

The winter cycle of Advent, Christmas, Epiphany, and associated feasts, therefore, contributed little to communal rites of penance; it is

18. The story of the Roman connection dates at least to Bede's *De temporum ratione* XII, PL 90:351–352, and has been popular ever since (cf. Beleth, *Summa de ecclesiasticis officiis*, c. 81, p. 149); but it may just reflect Bede's taste for the baptism of pagan sanctuaries and rites. For a review of the procession itself, see Bailey, *The Processions of Sarum and the Western Church*, p. 94; but Bailey ignores the gulf between the trappings of penance and the overall celebratory effect. As we shall see, candles could be an ambiguous symbol; they appear in celebrations as well as supplications, doubtless because of their expense.

19. PRG XCIX.13–28, vol. II, pp. 5–10; in a short prayer, XCIX.14, vol. II, p. 6, there is the briefest invocation of Mary's intercession for the forgiveness of sins. The other prayers speak of light dispelling darkness and the joy of Simeon. Very similar is PRS XXVII, pp. 206–209; the rite is omitted in PRC and PGD. The English and northern French pontificals I have checked often depart from the order or prayers of PRG, but never from the well-worn themes. In fact, the later pontificals never even reflect the shift in the emphasis of the feast on the theological level from the Presentation to the Purification of the Virgin.

20. Sicard of Cremona, *Mitrale*, V.11, PL 213:242–244; Guy d'Orchelles, "The 'Summa de Officiis Ecclesiae' of Guy d'Orchelles," pp. 42–43; Guillaume Durand, *Rationale divinorum officiorum*, VII.7, f. 287v–288r.

21. See Arnold van Gennep, *Le folklore de la Flandre et du Hainaut français* (Paris, 1935), 1: 313–316. Typical popular rites include the blessing of candles to be burned later during sickness, storms, and so forth, and occasional processions accompanying the clergy.

within the two cycles of Easter and Pentecost that we must direct our search in this and the following chapters. The Easter cycle, considered in the widest sense, ran a full ten weeks from Septuagesima Sunday to the octave of Easter itself. Although some aspects of the medieval celebrations of the cycle remain irritatingly obscure, here at last the complexity of the relationship between penance and rejoicing, between sacrifice and redemption, becomes clear. The apparently simple movement from the expiation of Lent to the fulfillment of Easter is deceptive.

First, the agricultural connections to the cycle were unclear. Since medieval Europeans reckoned spring and summer as beginning about a month earlier than the modern equivalents,[22] the Lenten fast and Easter celebration do not represent winter and spring in the agricultural calendar, but the beginning and end of spring. Any notion, then, that Easter marked the renewal of vegetation with the coming thaw, or indeed, any major break in the agricultural rhythm of the villager bespeaks a modern rather than a medieval sensibility. Spring itself was Lenten; Lent was springlike. We cannot look for a simple correspondence between the rhythms of agriculture and a shift from gloomy expiation to cheerful redemption.[23]

Second, the beginning of the Lenten cycle was indefinite. In theory, according to Guy d'Orchelles and Guillaume Durand, monks began their Lenten fasting at Septuagesima (or to be exact, the Monday after), other clerics at Quinquagesima, and laymen and women at Quadregesima, the first Sunday of Lent.[24] It is doubtful how far such a rule was observed in thirteenth-century France. Jean Beleth and Thomas of Chobham specified Ash Wednesday as the beginning for laymen and Quinquagesima Monday, two days earlier, for clerics;

22. See Julio Caro-Baroja, Le carnaval, trans. S. Sesé-Léger (Paris, 1979; first published Madrid, 1965), pp. 163–164; and George C. Homans, English Villagers of the Thirteenth Century (Cambridge, Mass., 1941), p. 354. Cf. also medieval English and German use of "lenten" and "lenz" for spring; the modern words only appeared in the sixteenth century. Of course, by 1250, the date according to the Julian calendar then in use would have anticipated the true astronomical date by about eight days; but this is not enough to account for the month or longer gap between medieval and modern reckoning.

23. The link between the ecclesiastical calendar and the urban cycle of work has never been much discussed. J. Heers notes that the midafternoon bells of nones or vespers were often the signal during Lent for the end of work for workers in the towns of northern France and Flanders: Le travail au Moyen Age (Paris, 1965), p. 82. The workers' "Lent" often ran much longer than the ecclesiastical variety, in places right through the summer. In principle, these bells were rung to call Christians to the vesper service that clerics hoped they would attend daily during Lent; then everyone could break their fast, eating, of course, the permitted Lenten foods. In practice, it seems, everyone ran home at the first sound of nones and ate; cf. the complaints to that effect by a late thirteenth-century writer in BN n.a.l 352, f. 34r.

24. Guy d'Orchelles, "The 'Summa de Officiis Ecclesiae' of Guy d'Orchelles," p. 46; Guillaume Durand, Rationale divinorum officiorum, VI.24, f. 190v.

they made no mention of monks.[25] When Bishop Nicolas Gellant of Angers addressed the issue in a synodal statute in 1274, however, he enjoined the clergy to begin their fast on Quinquaquesima, but he implied clearly that getting everyone to start from Quadragesima Monday (not even Ash Wednesday) was struggle enough.[26] Under these circumstances, priests probably began their fasts at various times, and their parishioners followed suit on Ash Wednesday, the following Sunday (or really the next Monday), or still later. As for Lenten confession, some councils before the Fourth Lateran stipulated that it should take place either on or before Ash Wednesday, but *Omnis utriusque* and its northern French interpretations only required confession before Easter.[27] The English term "Shrove Tuesday" implies that the laity made their confessions on the day before Ash Wednesday, but the usage only appears in the fifteenth century.[28] Thus, in the thirteenth century, the focus on Ash Wednesday as the start of Lent may have been blurred. As we shall see, however, during the thirteenth century the Ash Wednesday liturgy acquired a new communal rite—the imposition of ashes on parishioners—alongside the old rite of the expulsion of public penitents.

It is perhaps this fluidity in the beginning of Lent that makes Carnival so difficult to trace in popular religion before the later Middle Ages. After all, without a near-universal consensus that the fast began on Ash Wednesday, a bacchic Mardi Gras made little sense. Evidence for Carnival before the late Middle Ages is surprisingly scarce. Twelfth- and even thirteenth-century liturgical commentators did not mention it, though they discussed and criticized all manner of popular dancing and drinking associated with other religious seasons.

By the thirteenth century, Carnival makes an appearance in literature in a series of "battles of Carnival and Lent," of which Juan Ruiz's

25. Jean Beleth, *Summa de ecclesiasticis officiis*, c. 77–78, pp. 143–144; Thomas of Chobham, *Summa confessorum*, VI.3.3, p. 282.

26. H. Arnauld, *Statuts du diocèse d'Angers*, pp. 67–68: "per septem hebdomades ante sanctum Pascha omnes, et maxime omnes clerici ab esu carnium abstinere debeant; sed quia sicut discreta debet esse vita clericorum a laicorum conversatione, ita et jejunio debet fieri discretio inter eos; monemus et exhortamur in Domino omnes Presbyteros nostrae Diocesis, ut post diem Dominicam ante Cineres usque ad Pascha carnibus non utantur." Van Gennep describes Carnevalesque satires practiced in central and southern French villages on Ash Wednesday itself, with the onset of Lent itself to follow the next day; in England and Milan this seems to have been the rule: *Manuel de folklore français contemporain* (Paris, 1947), vol. I:3, pp. 1049–1059. But Van Gennep's French parodies may be quite recent.

27. Jungmann, *Die lateinischen Bussriten*, pp. 173–174, discusses this problem, but is perhaps too confident of the universality of a rule of pre–Ash Wednesday confession than his evidence allows; and he does not consider the effect of *Omnis utriusque*.

28. *Oxford English Dictionary*, s.v. Shrove-tide: "the absence of evidence for this group of words until the 15th c. is remarkable." Contrast Jungmann, *Die lateinischen Bussriten*, p. 174n, who assumes that the phrase and practice existed continuously since the Anglo-Saxon period.

fourteenth-century treatment is perhaps the most famous. Of the four thirteenth-century examples, one came from Picardy or Normandy, and three from northern Italy.[29] Presumably the literary treatment depended on a thriving popular tradition by midcentury at least. One cannot assume, however, that the familiar modern folkloric rite dates back still further to an indefinite time immemorial, much less to a pagan cultural substratum surviving beneath a veneer of Christianity.[30] On the contrary, pre-thirteenth-century mentions of popular rites of misrule refer not to Carnival but to the feasts of the twelve days of Christmas.[31] The surviving evidence suggests that sometime between 1150 and 1250, the penance of Advent gradually became less important, and the celebrations of Carnival and the penance of Ash Wednesday more so.[32] The winter celebrations do seem to have survived into the early modern period, when they were extirpated by zealous bishops and Protestants.

John Bossy has attempted to explain why from 1500 or so Carnival developed in certain regions, chiefly Italy, Iberia, and most of France and Germany, but not in others, chiefly northwestern France, the British Isles, most of the Netherlands, northern Germany, and Scandinavia. He suggests that the regions where Carnival failed to take hold were those where, in the early Middle Ages, the private penitential tariffs were first invented and spread; Carnival developed where the traditional public penance of the Roman rites "had been left in the air by the further progress of privacy after 1215."[33] It is hard to see

29. Lozinski, *La bataille de caresme et de charnage*, pp. 40–43, argues that the anonymous French literary battle surviving in five thirteenth and fourteenth-century MSS can only be dated to the thirteenth century without further precision; for the other literary "battles," see P. Camporesi, *La maschera di Bertoldo: G. C. Croce e la letteratura carnevalesca* (Turin, 1976), pp. 16n, 48n; and Martine Grinberg and Sam Kinser, "Les combats de carnaval et de carême: Trajets d'une métaphore," *Annales: Economies. sociétés, civilisations* 38 (1983): 65–98. For the absence of early medieval evidence for Carnival, see also Bossy, *Christianity in the West*, p. 42.

30. Heers, *Fêtes des fous et carnavals* (Paris, 1983), pp. 31–43, and 297–298, recognizes that Carnival, like the winter feasts, did not originate in pagan or even a secular culture. But he retains an unambiguous distinction between the profane and sacred: though clerics participate, and though the feasts are timed to the ecclesiastical calendar, dancing and mocking authority are profane breeches of sacred solemnity. He fails to see the complementary character of satire and authority, of the profane and the sacred.

31. All of Camporesi's pre-1250 examples of *letteratura carnevalesca* refer to the winter feasts: *La maschera de Bertoldo*, pp. 67–68, 247–248.

32. Heers, *Fêtes des fous et carnavals*, pp. 223–224, 300, recognizes that Carnival is a later development than the winter cycle, but he does not hazard to say when Carnival first appeared or began to replace the Feasts of Fools, beyond noting that the process began before the sixteenth century.

33. Bossy, *Christianity in the West*, pp. 44–45; Caro-Baroja, *Le carnaval*, pp. 30–33, 211, scrupulously avoids any attempt to explain the origins of the feast. Oddly, the Feast of Fools seems to present quite a different geographical pattern, corresponding neither to Carnival regions nor to non-Carnival regions. According to Heers, *Fêtes des fous et carnavals*, p. 177, it was chiefly popular in northern France, Germany, and England.

how the follies of Carnival could compensate for the absence of the old public penance; nor why the public rites disappeared at all if they were so regretted by the populace that lost them; nor why Carnival should flourish in northern France, where public penance survived, and in Italy, where the public rites fast disappeared. Yet Bossy's intuition that the development of Carnival is related to the evolution of rites of penance remains attractive. The first hints of Carnival around 1250 coincide with the establishment of Ash Wednesday as a significant rite of penance for the whole community, not just for the public penitents alone; clearly Carnival depends on a dramatic Ash Wednesday. An examination of the regional pattern would require further investigation of the medieval origins of Carnival and a fuller survey of penance in the various regions. At this stage, therefore, any conclusions are necessarily speculative. But if Frenchmen north of the Loire did celebrate Carnival in the thirteenth century—and the evidence suggests that they did by 1250 or so—then it probably looked something like the still familiar tragicomic rites of misrule.[34] Carnival, after all, could never take its eye off Lent; it could parody Lenten sobriety but could not make time stand still. Violence unleashed only for the moment was violence tamed. There remained a consistent penitential logic to the cycle.

Lent, on the other hand, could not take its eye off Easter. Liturgists called the entire season from Septuagesima to the octave of Easter the *tempus deuiationis*, the season of straying; Guillaume Durand added that it was the "judicial season of captivity." In Lent, Durand suggested, the church militant simultaneously reenacts both the Fall of Man, whose story was told in the chapters of Genesis read during those weeks, and the Babylonian captivity. The ten weeks of the season represent the Decalogue.[35] The church regresses, as it were, to the predicament of Israel before Jesus, in captivity to the Babylonians, in captivity to the law, and in captivity to sin. But Lent does not quite replicate the predicament of Israel without Christ; limited to but two months of the year, restricted by the resurrection that would soon arrive, Lent tames and redeems the servitude of the Law just as Carni-

---

34. If the liturgists ignored Carnival, they did describe popular Rogation processions that sound rather like modern Carnival animal dances described by Caro-Baroja, *Le carnaval*, pp. 183–192, 259–268; in both cases, villagers dressed as animals (a dragon at Rogations, often bulls in the Spanish Carnival) danced triumphantly for a time, only to be overcome and "killed." The liturgists saw the death of the dragon as the defeat of the devil, but it is clear that northern French dragons were just as ambivalent figures as the Carnival bulls, which were cheered when they danced, and cheered when they died.

35. Jean Beleth, *Summa de ecclesiasticis officiis*, c. 55, p. 99; Guy d'Orchelles, "The 'Summa de Officiis Ecclesiae' of Guy d'Orchelles," p. 35; Guillaume Durand, *Rationale divinorum officiorum*, VI.24, f.190r–191r.

val tames violence. The promise of Easter means that Lent represents the life of each individual Christian; every true penitent can trust that his suffering will be rewarded by blessedness, or at least "the certain expectation of purgatory."[36]

No more a season of unambiguous sorrow than Carnival was a time of unambiguous joy, Lent's seven weeks are broken by three major interruptions to the gloom. In northern France, the first Sunday of Lent, Quadragesima, was called Brandons, meaning torches, or Béhourdis, in reference to customary tournaments. Eudes Rigaud treated Brandons as an important feast, and he made special note of his sermons on this occasion at Rouen.[37] For Eudes, of course, it marked, along with Ash Wednesday, the beginning of the Lenten season, and he doubtless preached on penance and the fast. His listeners' minds may well have wandered to the banquets customary on the day, or to the nighttime running of torches and candles to cleanse the fields and orchards of evil influences, or to the jousting with behours, or wooden lances.[38] Four weeks later followed Laetare Sunday, or Dimanche des Fontaines, in mid-Lent, which was associated in some areas of France and elsewhere with a festive procession to bless the wells and springs, analogous to the purification of the fields on Brandons.[39] Even the liturgists remarked on the extraordinary jollity of the day, known by its introit, "Rejoice Jerusalem." They explained, first, that everyone needed a break, in Durand's phrase, "quoddam recreationis solatium." The day also represented the return from exile in Babylon, the seventh age of the world, not merely the expectation of future beatitude but the contemplation of actual beatitude here and now, in Durand's phrase again, "quasi praesentis contemplatio."[40]

36. Guillaume Durand, Rationale divinorum officiorum, VI.24, f. 191r.

37. Eudes Rigaud, Regestrum visitationum, pp. 220, 298, 395, 538, 571, 618. The itinerant archbishop was clearly more likely to spend the day at Rouen on Brandons than on an ordinary Sunday, though the beginning of Lent was a busy time with frequent parlements in Paris.

38. See Margit Sahlin, Etude sur la carole médiévale (Uppsala, 1940), p. 158; Roger Lecotté and Georges Marguet, La Fête du "Bois-Hourdy" ou "de la Folie" à Chambly (Oise), Publication de la Fédération folklorique d' Ile de France, fasc. 3 (Persan, 1947); and Jacques Heers, Fêtes, jeux, et joutes dans les sociétés d'occident à la fin du Moyen Age (Montreal and Paris, 1971), pp. 53–55. Exceptionally, such local burnings and runnings of torches called "Bois Hourdy" in northern France took place on other feasts instead of Brandons, such as Saint Christopher's Day (July 25) or the Assumption (August 15); see Lecotté and Marguet, La Fête du "Bois-Hourdy," pp. 6–8. In addition, John the Baptist's Nativity at Midsummer was typically celebrated with torches and bonfires: see Jean Beleth, Summa de ecclesiasticis officiis, c. 137, p. 267.

39. O. B. Hardison, Christian Rite and Christian Drama in the Middle Ages (Baltimore, Md., 1965), p. 105; for the rite in Lorraine, see Sahlin, Etude sur la carole médiévale, p. 173. The evidence on the medieval celebration of the feast does not permit any exact mapping of the spread of the blessings of wells.

40. Jean Beleth, Summa de ecclesiasticis officiis, c. 93, p. 165; Guillaume Durand, Rationale divinorum officiorum, VI.53, f. 206v–207r.

In the end, the liturgists' analyses of the elaborate system of representation in the season of Lent taught lessons strikingly similar to the message implied in the popular rites. The effort of some historians—and some medieval liturgists—to trace the popular celebrations of Carnival, Brandons, or Rogations to vague pagan and crypto-pagan beginnings[41] is misguided, not because such independent influences are wholly implausible but because they are irrelevant to an explanation of the survival and evolution of both official and unofficial rites. It is unhelpful to treat Brandons and Carnival, for instance, as mere survivals of a distant past, because evidence for them is scant indeed before the thirteenth century, but also because we must explain why they did survive.[42] Here the liturgists help confirm by their interpretation of the Lenten cycle as a whole what we may already suspect about elements of the cycle. The torches and tourneys of Brandons spread from the thirteenth century onward because they expressed the assumptions that fire purifies, that suffering redeems, and that fellowship sanctifies. Jean Beleth and Guillaume Durand endorsed these assumptions, too, when they explained how a time of captivity hid a foretaste of freedom.[43]

Palm Sunday Processions

The climax of Lenten celebrations, to use a paradoxical but appropriate phrase, arrived with Palm Sunday, the third and final break in the Lenten gloom. In northern French towns, as almost everywhere in Europe, this was the occasion for a procession in imitation of Christ's entry into Jerusalem. A procession of cathedral clergy typically left the city proper early in the morning and made its way to a hill, a cross, or an abbey a couple of miles distant; the bishop stood outside and exorcised, blessed, and distributed the "palms" (in northern Europe, often flowers, laurel, and boxwood, and in southern Europe, often olive branches), and preached to the gathered people. Then all en-

41. See, for example, Heers, *Fêtes, jeux, et joutes*, pp. 53–54; Sahlin, *Etude sur la carole médiévale*, pp. 158, 173; and Lecotté and Marguet, *La fête du "Bois-Hourdy,"* p. 3.

42. See Caro-Baroja, *Le carnaval*, p. 306.

43. The existence and extent of an independent quasi-pagan folkloric culture has been the subject of much recent debate. Schmitt, among others, has revived the view that genuine popular religion owed little to clerical guidance: "'Religion populaire' et culture folklorique," pp. 941–953. John Van Engen, "The Christian Middle Ages as an Historiographical Problem," *American Historical Review* 91 (1986): 519–552, rightly stresses the fusion of the two cultures, but unfortunately, p. 550, still mistakenly identifies the folkloric with the magical, and so takes benedictions and exorcisms, for instance, as a quasi-pagan element, rather than as the genuine expression of popular Christian belief.

tered the city gates and proceeded to the cathedral itself.[44] The clergy in procession often carried a representation of Christ either as a cross now unveiled for the first time in six weeks; or as the consecrated host, in Norman and some English rites; or as the gospel book, as in one rite reproduced in the tenth-century Romano-Germanic Pontifical; or as a wooden figure on a wooden ass with wheels, as often in the Rhineland.[45] Townspeople represented the people of Jerusalem. The liturgy coordinated the actions of the participants with the words of the Gospel. As they walked, the clergy on behalf of the gathered people repeated the antiphons *Pueri Hebreorum tollentes ramos, Occurrunt turbe,* and *Cum approprinquasset Jhesus Ierosolimis,* antiphons that told the Gospel story that was being reenacted before them.[46] Often when the procession reached the walls of the city, or the cathedral, to mark the entry itself, the choir boys were sent ahead to climb to the tower and sing the *Gloria laus* and *Benedictus qui venit* responsively with the clergy below.[47]

Everyone in the Palm Sunday celebrations acted a part: the clergy played the disciples, the townspeople played the crowd, the cross or consecrated host was Jesus himself. The ritual imitation remained as stable and unchanging throughout the central Middle Ages as it was elaborate. The exorcisms and benedictions of "palms" that were often the centerpiece of the rite were remarkably consistent in theme and tone. Many northern French versions survive, but all were based on

44. See, for example, Ulysse Chevalier, ed., *Ordinaires de l'Eglise cathédrale de Laon (XIIe et XIIIe siècles),* Bibliothèque liturgique, 6 (Paris, 1897), pp. 104–105, from a manuscript ordinal belonging to the beginning of the thirteenth century. In some English churches, the bishop blessed the palms before leaving the cathedral, and the path of the procession was much shorter: see J. B. L. Tolhurst, ed., *The Customary of the Cathedral Priory Church of Norwich,* Henry Bradshaw Society, 82 (London, 1948), pp. 76–77, from a manuscript ordinal of ca. 1260; exceptionally, too, this was an afternoon procession. Northern French Palm Sunday processions were invariably elaborate.

45. Kellner, *Heortology,* p. 69; Edmund Bishop, *Liturgica historica* (Oxford, 1918), pp. 276–300; John Walter Tyrer, *Historical Survey of Holy Week,* Alcuin Club Collections, 29 (Oxford, 1932), pp. 56–57; Bailey, *The Processions of Sarum and the Western Church,* pp. 72–74, 116–117. For the *corps saint* procession in Rouen, see the *Ordinale canonicorum regularium S. Laudi Rotomagensis,* PL 147:167–168; for the gospel book, "quod intelligitur Christus," see PRG XCIX.195, vol. II, p. 51.

46. See Chevalier, ed. *Ordinaire et coutumier de l'Eglise cathédrale de Bayeux (XIIIe siècle),* Bibliothèque liturgique, 8 (Paris, 1902), p. 119: "Cantore incipiente ant. *Occurrunt turbe,* et utroque choro eam pariter concinente, concurrunt hinc inde universi [ad] Crucem adorandam, mittentes seu proicientes ramos et flores circa eam"; and PRG XCIX.185, vol. II, p. 47: "Respondent scola ex parte populi antiphonam: *Occurrunt turbae.*"

47. The twelfth-century PRS has this rite: XXIX.17, pp. 213–214. Among French pontificals, see among many others Chevalier, ed., *Ordinaire et coutumier . . . de Bayeux,* p. 120; and Chevalier, ed., *Sacramentaire et martyrologe de l'abbaye de Saint-Rémy: Martyrologe, calendrier, ordinaires, et prosaire de la métropole de Reims (VIIIe-XIIIe siècles),* Bibliothèque liturgique, 7 (Paris, 1900), p. 120.

the blessings in the Romano-Germanic pontifical.[48] These recalled the olive branch delivered to Noah as a sign of peace, the anointing of David (Jerusalem's king before Christ), and Christ's own triumphal entry; and they called on God to redeem his people in the Second Coming. As Christ was the new David, so the townspeople were the new Israel. The distribution of palms that followed made possible the exact imitation of the crowds who greeted Jesus.

The theme of prayers and ritual alike was the confident plea for redemption of the whole people as one, not the expiation of individual sins. Indeed, the liturgy of Palm Sunday hardly made reference to the self-inflicted griefs of Lent or to the system of penance that measured merits against sins and calculated the balance for each Christian. Unlike the Rogation Days' chants, for instance, the supplications here were limited to the briefest chant of *Kyrie eleison*. Instead of sin or suffering, the triumphant liturgy proclaimed Christ the king and promised the palm of victory to loyal Christians. As the prayers traced the history of God's faithfulness from Noah through prophets and kings to Jesus, symbolized by the olive, the palm, and the oil of anointing,[49] an Old Testament piety infused the rite itself. The Christian people advanced on an historical path to redemption precisely through its perfect annual imitation of the triumphant welcome long ago. Not incidentally, the rite stamped the Christian church as the true Israel, as opposed to the false heirs who still lived alongside Christians in every French town and increasingly in the thirteenth century attracted fear and suspicion.[50] Palm Sunday could be the

48. PRG XCIX.162–206, vol. II, pp. 40–54; particularly popular in northern French pontificals were prayers XCIX.170, 171, 176, 177, 181 (= PRS XXIX.10). In general, the French pontificals abbreviated the PRG's extremely lengthy *ordo* and jumbled the order of the prayers, but hardly ever really innovated. They even clung to some of the blessings that made extensive reference to olive branches, appropriate to Rome but not north of the Loire. Some features and prayers of the twelfth-century PRS, not in the PRG, notably the station at the walls of the city, appear in French pontificals. But as the French liturgy also routinely includes prayers from the PRG not in the PRS, it seems unlikely that the PRS was the normal *fons proximus*. In general, the French liturgy for all rites was based on versions of the PRG and of antecedents of the PRG. The later Roman pontificals, the PRC and the PGD, do not include Palm Sunday rites.

49. See especially PRG XCIX.170, and 177, vol. II, pp. 43–45; the first speaks of the flood and Noah, the second retraces history from Noah to Jacob, to Christ the new David, and finally to the Second Coming "cum palmis victoriae."

50. Cf. the attacks of the Pastoureaux on Jews in 1251, Guillaume de Nangis, *Gesta Sancti Ludovici*, HF 20:382–383; accusations of Jewish plots on Christian children, e.g., Thomas de Cantimpré, *Miraculorum et exemplorum memorabilium sui temporis libri duo* (= *Bonum universale de apibus*) (Douai, 1605), II.29.23, pp. 305–306; and the panic in 1321 about a supposed conspiracy of lepers and Jews to poison all the wells in France, in the Continuation of Guillaume de Nangis's *Chronicon* HF 20:628–629, and the *Chronique anonyme*, HF 21:152. Perennial fears about secret enemies poisoning wells help explain the popularity of rites of purification of the water sources on Brandons, Holy Saturday, and Saint John the Baptist's Day.

occasion for excluding false Christians as well, when the bishop announced excommunications at the sermon under the cross.[51] It was an appropriate day for public penance,[52] not only because the humiliated unfortunate would make quite a spectacle for the big crowds but because as a feast of unity it was a fitting time to restore those who had fallen from the people of God.

The Palm Sunday show brought together other older ecclesiastical institutions in town under the ritual control of the cathedral canons and the bishop, pastor of the new Israel. The procession typically started from the cathedral in the *cité*, and then went out through the city gates toward the *bourg*, a suburb two or three miles distant, usually dominated by an old house of regular canons or Benedictine monks who were often rivals of the cathedral canons in prestige and authority. A delicate diplomacy emerges from the bare outlines in the ordinals. At Chartres, the bishop, the cathedral canons, the black monks of Saint-Jean-en-Vallée, and other clergy processed out of the *cité* down to the *basse ville* below, to the church of Saint-Cheron, where they were joined by its regular canons; there the cathedral canons distributed "palms" and the prior of Saint-Cheron gave out boxwood. On they all went to a large cross on the hill opposite the *cité*, where the bishop preached to the people. On the return, the procession stopped at Saint Bartholomew's, close by the old walls of the *cité*.[53] Each of these institutions had its role and its rights preserved. At Sens, the cathedral canons marched out to the Benedictine abbey of Saint-Pierre-le-Vif, several miles to the east of the *cité*, where they were formally received by the monks. There the archbishop, or if he was away, the abbot or prior, blessed the "palms" and distributed them to the gathered people; then canons and monks returned together to the cathedral, stopping briefly just outside the walls, at the square in front of Saint Mary's. Meanwhile, the monks of Saint-Remi, a smaller abbey outside the walls of the *cité*, made their own procession to Saint-Symphorien, a nearby abbey, and did not participate in the larger celebration.[54] A clear hierarchy of prestige is established from the cathedral canons on down. Only the greatest of monasteries or canon-

51. BN latin 1794 (ordinal of Saint-Jean-en-Vallée, Chartres, twelfth-thirteenth century), f. 91v.

52. Dupont, "Le registre de l'officialité de Cerisy," pp. 381–382 (1330).

53. Yves Delaporte, *L'ordinaire chartrain du XIIIe siècle*, Mémoires de la Société archéologique d'Eure-et-Loir, 18–19 (Chartres, 1952–1953) pp. 103–104; BN latin 1794 (ordinal of Saint-Jean-en-Vallée, Chartres), fol. 91r-v. Delaporte notes, p. 33, that the thirteenth-century cathedral ordinal remained in use, with some alterations, through the sixteenth century.

54. Sens BM 7 (processional of the cathedral of Sens, thirteenth century) f. 50r–64v; Sens BM 23 (ordinal of Saint-Pierre-le-Vif, Sens, end of the thirteenth century), pp. 64–65; Sens BM 20 (Ritual of Saint-Remi, Sens, fourteenth century), pp. 53–70.

ries joined the cathedral in the central popular festival; ancient usage codified in written ordinals determined the rights of each. Newer foundations, including Dominican and Franciscan houses, were shut out of these celebrations.

In these towns, relations seem to have been amicable enough, and the dignity of ancient rivals was respected. Elsewhere, the processions at times reflected the bad blood between different institutions. At Reims, where relations between cathedral canons and the black monks of Saint-Remi were particularly strained during the thirteenth century, the cathedral canons along with the nuns of nearby Saint-Pierre-lès-Dames marched out toward the Bourg Saint-Remi, but stopped at the parish church and Benedictine priory of Saint-Maurice, just short of entering the ban of Saint-Remi itself. There the archbishop preached to the people, and then the procession turned back toward the *cité*, evidently without being received by the monks of Saint-Remi. Just before they reentered the walls of the *cité*, the procession paused to sing antiphons at Saint-Denis below the towers of the wall.[55] South of the Loire in Limoges, the monks of Saint-Martial claimed the ancestral right to process to the Place Saint-Paul and then join the cathedral canons in a general procession to Saint-Martin. In 1263, the canons denied their rival monks this dignity, and for six or seven years Palm Sunday was the occasion for an unseemly shoving match in the Place, until at last the monks paid the canons thirty-five pounds to confirm their rights.[56] Unlike the Rogation processions in which the clergy of nearly every old foundation took part, and which made a station at nearly all the older churches, the main Palm Sunday procession typically only involved a few of the greatest and oldest churches, and it defined their relations with a careful weighing of dignity. The Palm Sunday liturgy taught the supremacy of the bishop, pastor of the new Israel.

Liturgical commentators came to reflect on the intentions behind the dramatic reenactment of Christ's entry into Jerusalem in the Palm Sunday rites. Their interpretations confirm our deductions so far. Jean Beleth emphasized both the literal imitation of the historical events and the moral significance of the laurel and boxwood often distributed in northern France; the branches are symbols of the vir-

---

55. Chevalier, *Sacramentaire . . . de Reims*, pp. 277–278.
56. *Major Chronicon Lemovicense*, HF 21:774: "fuit contentio inter canonicos civitatis et conventum Sancti Martialis, quia canonici dicebant ipsos monachos Sancti Martialis primo debere recedere de platea Sancti Pauli." I take this to mean that the canons wanted the monks to leave the Place Saint-Paul in a lesser procession on their own, rather than join the main procession. Either the canons expected the monks to process in advance to the monastery of Saint-Martin, where the flowers would be blessed, and receive the canons there, in a position of lesser dignity, or they wanted the monks kept out of the main celebrations altogether.

tues we bring Christ.[57] Near the end of the twelfth century, Prae-positinus of Cremona simply explained that the rite was supposed to recall the procession of the "pueri Hebreorum."[58] Soon after, Sicard of Cremona contrasted the mimetic Palm Sunday procession with the symbolic weekly Sunday processions that canons or monks would make within and around their cathedral or abbey. "For this is the proclaiming of the Passion; those are indeed significant and remind-ing of the Lord's resurrection, as of the ascension."[59] The Palm Sun-day rite plainly recounts the story of the passion; Sunday processions signify the resurrection. At the end of the century, Guillaume Durand echoed this view, but he returned at the same time to Beleth's empha-sis on the moral ascesis implicit in the reenactment.[60] Once again, we find that the cyclical imitation of historical suffering every year was bound to the redemptive victory granted the whole Christian people.

The ordinary mass transcends history; the eucharist is Christ's heavenly body, not his historical body.[61] The Palm Sunday procession, by contrast, precisely imitates the suffering of the historical Christ. It was a fitting climax for the Lenten period of penance that demanded every Christian's actual imitation of Christ's sacrifice. The mass is a transcendent, abstract, and costless sacrifice; the heavenly victory is implicit from the start. Lent, Palm Sunday, and Maundy Thursday[62] take each Christian through the historical path of suffering to the historical expectation of redemption. Like every satisfaction imposed by a priest, the cycle was a reminder that while Christ's sacrifice bought every Christian's soul, every Christian sinner had to buy it again in imitative atonement for his sins. What made the imitation bearable was that Christians endured it in unity: the unity of fasting, of Brandons, of Laetare Sunday, of Palm Sunday, and of Maundy Thursday, Good Friday, and Easter itself.

The Litanies and Pentecost

I leave the central rites of Ash Wednesday and Maundy Thursday to a more thorough review in later chapters and pass directly here to

57. Jean Beleth, *Summa de ecclesiasticis officiis*, c. 94, p. 166; cf. Honorius Augustodunen-sis, *Speculum Ecclesiae*, Dominica in Palmis, PL 172:920.

58. Praepositinus of Cremona, *Tractatus de officiis*, I.160, p. 95.

59. Sicard of Cremona, *Mitrale*, VI.10, PL 213:293: "Haec enim est praeconium pas-sionis, illae vero significativae sunt et rememorativae Dominicae resurrectionis, vel ascen-sionis."

60. Guillaume Durand, *Rationale divinorum officiorum*, VI.67, ff. 214r–215r.

61. Cf. Thomas Aquinas, *Summa theologiae* 3 q.76 a.5–6, vol. XII, pp. 185–187.

62. For the festive as well as penitential aspects of Maundy Thursday, see below, Chap-ters 6 and 7, and Tyrer, *Historical Survey of Holy Week*, p. 71.

post-Easter penances. The cycle of Pentecost that followed at the end of the medieval spring and the beginning of summer was a focus for communal penitential activity only second to the Lenten period. Unlike Lent, it was not marked by any clear dramatic procession from beginning to end; in fact, since two of its major celebrations, Rogations (the Minor Litany) and Pentecost were movable, and the third, the Major Litany, was fixed on Saint Mark the Evangelist's Day, April 25, the order would inevitably vary from year to year. Elaborate notations in ordinals tried to sort out what would happen if April 25 fell on a Sunday, within the octave of Easter, or on another important feast. The ordinals establish that although the Litany happened to coincide with Saint Mark's Day, the supplications and the commemoration of the saint were quite distinct. If the liturgy had to be rejuggled because April 25 fell on some major feast, the Major Litany and Saint Mark's would be moved independently.[63] According to the liturgists, both Rogations and the Major Litany had been instituted as penitential supplications to God and his saints for protection in a season given to crop-destroying thunderstorms and wars.[64] In northern France, the rites of the Major Litany, evidently so-called in contrast to the ordinary Sunday processions,[65] consisted in a paler, abbreviated version of the three-day Rogations supplications. The liturgical books sometimes simply directed the reader to adapt part of the Rogations ceremonies.[66] It will therefore concern us less here. In both the Major and Minor Litanies, however, we may trace a studied ambivalence, the same alternation between suffering and the triumph of the community that we found in the Lenten cycle.

63. See, for example, Chevalier, *Ordinaires de l'Eglise cathédrale de Laon*, pp. 267–268 (early thirteenth century). See also the later-thirteenth-century ordinal of Reims, where the Major Litany is treated in the Temporale alongside Rogations and Saint Mark's Day separately in the Sanctorale: Chevalier, *Sacramentaire . . . de Reims*, pp. 141–143, 181. A statute of Rouen from 1245 instructing parish priests to ask their dean how to sort out fasts and processions, especially around Saint Mark's Day, suggests that confusion was not unknown: Bessin, *Concilia Rotomagensis provinciae*, vol. II, p. 79.

64. Jean Beleth, *Summa de ecclesiasticis officiis*, c. 123, p. 236; Guy d'Orchelles, "The 'Summa de officiis ecclesiae' of Guy d'Orchelles," p. 57; Sicard of Cremona, *Mitrale*, VII.6, PL 213:368; Guillaume Durand, *Rationale divinorum officiorum*, VI.102, f. 259r.

65. The medieval liturgists offer various stories of its origin in the turning aside of a flood or pestilence by a procession led by Gregory the Great: Jean Beleth, *Summa de ecclesiasticis officiis*, c. 122, p. 233; Guy d'Orchelles, "The 'Summa de officiis ecclesiae' of Guy d'Orchelles," p. 56; Sicard of Cremona, *Mitrale*, VII.6, PL 213:367. For its explanation as a Christian adaptation of the Roman *Robigalia*, a procession for the protection of the fields and fruit (from *robigo*, blight), see Kellner, *Heortology*, pp. 189–191; and Walter Howard Frere, *Studies in Early Roman Liturgy*, Vol. 1, *The Kalendar* (London, 1930), pp. 98–99.

66. See, for example, Rouen BM (A 551), f. 71v (processional of Rouen, thirteenth century), J.-B.-N. Blin, ed. *Ordinal de l'abbaye de Saint-Pierre-sur-Dive* (Paris, 1887), p. 101 (Norman, 1275); see also Jean Beleth, who emphasizes Rogations and mentions the Major Litany only in passing, *Summa de ecclesiasticis officiis*, c. 129–133, pp. 196–199.

The three-day Rogation processions on the Monday, Tuesday, and Wednesday before Ascension Day were much more important in northern France, perhaps because as movable feasts linked to the timing of Easter, they could not be eliminated from the calendar when they chanced to coincide with an important feast, as might happen to the Major Litany. These communal processions, older still than the Major Litany, originated in fifth-century Vienne and were brought to Rome under Leo III (795–816), when the Roman liturgy underwent heavy Frankish influence.[67] The supplicatory prayers that accompanied the processions through the city seem to be a later addition, of the ninth or tenth century; the prayers themselves came to be known as litanies after the word for the processions.[68] Although for the most part the litanies asked for expiation for sins, many of the antiphons actually struck a more joyful note. Like the Palm Sunday antiphons, these spoke of the rejoicing of the church as the new Israel.[69] The liturgy fused the expiation of the sins of the community with the celebration of community, a theme notable in the method of procession as well. Ordinals and ceremonials detail the routes to be taken on each day. In thirteenth-century rites, nearly all the clergy from the older establishments in and around the city would participate in a single procession, visiting over the three days most of the older churches, and pausing to chant litanies invoking the saint to whom the church had been dedicated. Each group of clergy carried the relics of their foundations. The city's entire population, men, women, and children, were expected to join the procession,[70] walking barefoot and in somber penitential attire, just like the clergy. At least in principle, this was a penance of the community united.[71] Unlike the Palm Sunday ritual, the liturgy of Rogations in theory made a

67. Kellner, *Heortology*, pp. 190–193; John Dowden, *The Church Year and Kalendar* (Cambridge, 1910), pp. 86–87.

68. Ernst Kantorowicz, *Laudes Regiae* (Berkeley, Calif., 1958), p. 13; Bishop, *Liturgica historica*, p. 149.

69. Bailey, *The Processions of Sarum and the Western Church*, pp. 130–131. Bailey cites for example the antiphon "Platee Ierusalem gaudebunt et omnes vici eius canticum letitie dicant," often sung on the Major Litany and Rogation Days. And since both litanies fell within the Easter season, alleluias were added at the end of the antiphons.

70. Two late-thirteenth-century statutes of Angers complained that because of the neglect of parish priests and chaplains, some processions—one statute specifically mentioned Rogations and the Major Litany—were not being properly performed at all in places. He instructed priests to tell their parishioners to show up, or at least to send one person per family: Arnauld, *Statuts du diocèse d'Angers*, pp. 73, 93 (Angers, 1281, c.2, and 1299, c.1). And an anonymous tract of the same period amid other complaints of neglect of rites of penance specifies that the Major Litany should be observed by dressing in poor clothes, the sprinkling of ashes, and so forth. But these are the only hints of neglect in the villages, and at any rate the processions were clearly performed in the cathedral cities.

71. Bossy, *Christianity in the West*, p. 73.

place for everyone, all in due order of dignity.[72] With the extremely rapid growth of the northern French towns in the twelfth and thirteenth centuries, however, the processions that had previously visited every church and marked the boundaries failed to include the new suburbs. In Chapter 8, on penance in the cities, I discuss the religious geography of town and suburb in greater detail; for the moment, we may observe at least the attempt to make a complete circuit of the city's holy places.[73]

More significant here than the litanies themselves was the march of the dragon that accompanied them in many French and Flemish cities. As described in Jean Beleth's twelfth-century *Summa*, on the Monday and Tuesday of Rogations, a dragon holding its tail high (*cum longe cauda et inflata*) was carried in the very front of the procession, preceding even the cross and banners. On Wednesday, the dragon followed the cross with its tail down. The liturgists agreed in interpreting the dragon as the devil, the prince of the world who rages against humanity, but who is conquered by Christ in the end.[74] Modern historians have sometimes looked for a pagan, folkloric origin of the rite. As it survived and even spread to other cities into the sixteenth century and beyond, the dragon was not an unambiguously maleficent figure. Townsmen frequently gave it familiar names and fed it by throwing coins or small pastries into its gaping mouth, apparently regarding the dragon as a symbol of the city.[75]

Whatever its origin, the dragon carried in procession from the twelfth century onward seems to have been an ambivalent figure, both a festive symbol that lightened an otherwise dour procession and a figure of fun when on the third day it succumbed to the cross and to the city's bishop-saint. Whether anybody besides the liturgical commentators accepted the explanation that the dragon was the devil is unclear, but there is no evidence of a conflict between clerical and

72. For the ordering of Rogation litanies, see Jean Beleth, *Summa de ecclesiasticis officiis*, c. 123, p. 235.

73. See Noël Coulet, "Processions, espace urbain, communauté civique," in *Liturgie et musique*, pp. 391–392, for a discussion of the "sacralization of urban space" in the Midi.

74. Jean Beleth, *Summa de ecclesiasticis officiis*, c. 123, p. 236; cf. Praepositinus of Cremona, *Tractatus de officiis*, II.133, p. 198; and Sicard of Cremona, *Mitrale*, VII.6, PL 213:368–369. In England, sometimes banners painted with lions or dragons filled a similar function: Bailey, *The Processions of Sarum and the Western Church*, p. 25.

75. Philippe Gabet, "Les dragons processionnels sont-ils ou non bénéfiques?" *Bulletin de la Société de mythologie française* 92 (1974): 16–46; Germaine Maillet, *Religion et traditions populaires aux XIIe et XIIIe siècles*, Travaux du Comité du folklore champenois, 7 (Châlons-sur-Marne, 1978), pp. 55–56. Cf. also the Tarasque, a monster with a long tail carried from Ascension to Pentecost Monday at Tarascon, near Arles, and then tamed by Sainte-Marthe on her feast day, July 29; it has been interpreted as representative of the community: Louis Dumont, *La tarasque* (Paris, 1951), pp. 92–97, 228.

popular views. The lighthearted popular treatment of the dragon simply recalls the traditional theological lesson of the devil's foolish impotence before Christ. And the clerical acceptance of the practice strongly suggests that theologians who saw the rite considered it not pagan idolatry but an innocent drama that taught the ultimate defeat of threats to human life and perhaps encouraged a little local patriotism around the city's saint. The choice of joyful antiphons suggests an effort by the clergy themselves to stress confident unity alongside the expiation of the sins of all.[76] There is no clearer example of the deliberate ambiguity of rites and symbols that characterized communal penances.

Pentecost as such had no particularly penitential connotation in theology, yet it has some interest for us here. The descent of the Holy Spirit and the origin of the church might be dramatized on the day itself—by the release of doves in the cathedral, for instance. The spiritual unity that was Pentecost's promise could have a penitential edge in semiofficial rites; as we shall see, it was a favorite season for individual and communal pilgrimages. But first, the popular celebration of that unity itself deserves a closer look. Secular rites included summer dances, knightings, tournaments, crown-wearings, and various other festivities.[77] In 1267, following tradition, Louis IX had his son Philip knighted in Paris at Pentecost, in the most impressive (*solemne*) feast anybody had ever seen, there or elsewhere. Silken bunting draped the streets, and rich and poor rushed to join the procession through Paris dressed in new colorful clothes for the occasion. And,

76. Some historians have tried to see in some or all Rogation processions a challenge by folkloric culture against the prevailing clerical interpretation. Gabet, "Les dragons processionnels sont-ils ou non bénéfiques?" unfortunately tries answer the question of his title with an unambiguous yes in most cases. Others have considered the general festiveness of Rogations processions as the popular rejection of clerically demanded penitential seriousness: see Sahlin, *Etude sur la carole médiévale*, p. 156; and Heers, *Fêtes, jeux, et joutes*, p. 53. More subtle is the analysis of Jacques Le Goff, "Ecclesiastical Culture and Folklore in the Middle Ages: Saint Marcellus of Paris and the Dragon," in *Time, Work, and Culture in the Middle Ages*, trans. A. Goldhammer (Chicago, 1980), pp. 159–188, where the dragon is treated as an emblem of both the bishop's triumph, itself a point of local pride, and a less religious civic allegiance as well; the popular and clerical views were distinct, but not necessarily antagonistic. Similar is the interpretation of the Tarascon dragon by Dumont, *La tarasque*, pp. 220–229, though he stresses more the priority of a popular, non-Christian significance.

77. Sahlin, *Etude sur la carole médiévale*, pp. 161–162, 167; Jean-Claude Schmitt, "'Jeunes' et danse des chevaux de bois. Le folklore méridional dans la littérature des 'exempla' (XIIIe-XIVe siècles)," in *La religion populaire en Languedoc du XIIIe siècle à la moitié du XIVe siècle*, Cahiers de Fanjeaux, 11 (Toulouse, 1976), pp. 140–148; *Chronique anonyme intitulée anciennes chroniques de Flandres*, HF 22:399. The *Chronicon comitum Flandrensium* reports that Philip Augustus ordered tournaments at Paris on May 1, 1200: J.-J. de Smet, ed., *Corpus chronicorum Flandriae* (Brussels, 1837–1841), 1:132. Cf. also the *Chronicon Leodiense*, HF:18:632. In 1215 in Liège, a Master Olivier abolished the great tournament set for the first week in June and established a day of preaching, probably for the crusade, in its place.

an anonymous Parisian chronicler informs us, everyone carried great candles in celebration ("habentes quilibet coram se cereum grossum ardentem")[78]—an indication of the possible festive adaptation of a typically penitential symbol.

It seems, too, that the initiatory tournaments and knightings common in this season were linked to the Pentecostal feast of souls celebrated on Pentecost or shortly thereafter. In one southern French example, an adolescent mock jousting took place at night in a cemetery, an appropriate setting for the symbolic death and rebirth of initiation.[79] Pentecost, after all, celebrated the unity of the church in all its members, living and dead. The celebration of community or initiation into the community inevitably meant a remembrance of the dead, both in the feast of souls and in the pre-Pentecost supplications to the very special dead, the saints still immanent in relics. Celebration was never far from expiation.

At the same time, expiatory pilgrimages and processions of the season borrowed the more cheerful trappings of Pentecost dances. In some Rhineland towns, the week of Pentecost was the occasion for processions to churches. The clergy sang litanies to the saints, while laymen and women of the surrounding region danced through the town to the church; they even danced three times around the altar.[80] These dancing pilgrimages simply elaborated a rite common all over northern Europe. And Pentecost week was often the occasion for the annual pilgrimage of country parishioners to their mother cathedral, a journey that the bishops and their synods attempted to encourage by linking it to promises of indulgences and by advising confessors to substitute such a pilgrimage for other penitential satisfactions.[81] Such

78. Cf. a thirteenth-century Parisian chronicle printed by Léopold Delisle, "Notes sur quelques manuscrits du Musée britannique," *Mémoires de la Société de l'histoire de Paris et de l'Ile de France* 4 (1877): 188; and Guillaume de Nangis, *Gesta Sancti Ludovici* HF 20:428; the sheer expense of large candles rendered them an appropriate token of both sacrificial expiation and conspicuous consumption. Cf. also Philip Augustus's knighting of his son at Compiègne, Pentecost 1209, Alberic of Trois Fontaines, *Chronicon*, HF 18:775; and Philip the Fair's knighting of his three sons in Paris, Pentecost 1313, in the Continuation of Guillaume de Nangis's *Chronicon*, HF 20:607, the *Chronique anonyme intitulée anciennes chroniques de Flandres*, HF 22:399, and the *Chronicon comitum Flandrensium*, in de Smet, ed., *Corpus chronicorum Flandriae*, 1:176–177.

79. Schmitt, "'Jeunes' et danse des chevaux de bois," pp. 140–148. The rite involving nonnoble youths dancing with wooden horses and mock-woundings in a cemetery appears in thirteenth- and fourteenth-century *exempla*.

80. Sahlin, *Etude sur la carole médiévale*, pp. 162–163; such processions were known in Echternach (Luxembourg), Trier, Cologne, Aachen, Brussels, and some cities further east.

81. Cf. Pontal I, p. 88 (Paris, ca. 1200, c. 101); Boeren, "Les plus anciens statuts," 4:136–137 (Cambrai, 1287/8); Martène and Durand, *Thesaurus novus anecdotorum*, IV, col. 955 (Nantes, 1520); and Thomas of Chobham, *Summa confessorum* VI.3.3, pp. 276–277. Such pilgrimages to the cathedral also took place on the feast day of the patron saint. Similarly, the second Sunday after Pentecost was the occasion for the great procession to Notre-Dame-de-

pilgrimages might be individual commutations of penances or the occasion for a whole village to visit the city. The relics of the cathedral, which had just the week before been removed to grace the Rogation processions around the city, were now during the Monday, Tuesday, and Wednesday after Pentecost exposed to the gaze of the faithful of the whole diocese who made the trip.[82] The advantage to the bishop and his chapter was obvious enough; the pilgrimage popularized devotion to their saint and funneled donations from the countryside for his cathedral.[83] And while it encouraged diocesan loyalty, the pilgrimage by parish fostered local parish loyalties—so much so that at times rival parishes meeting in town came to blows.[84] For the individual parishioner, the promise was that of any penitential pilgrimage: remission of sins and indulgences. In short, the three days after Pentecost reproduced for the diocese as a whole the same choreographed fusion of local loyalties and expiation of sins that the Rogation Days before Pentecost provided for the city.

Pentecost and the weeks that followed were the favorite season for embarking on individual pilgrimages of any sort, including crusades, voluntary expeditions, and the penal pilgrimages imposed by the Flemish cities.[85] It was a suitable time in part, to be sure, because in late May and June the roads would at last be dry enough for a long journey. But the season also seemed a particularly appropriate one for fulfilling vows, seeking the saints' aid on the eve of a longer expedition, or approaching relics for healing of body or mind. Thus did Jean de Joinville trek barelegged and on foot to the relics of Saint-Urbain and Blécourt before leaving for the crusade in 1248.[86] The

---

la-Treille at Lille, instituted in 1270: H. Platelle in Louis Trenard, ed. *Histoire de Lille*, I, p. 359.

82. Avril, *Le gouvernement des évêques*, p. 749.

83. A charter from Orléans in 1175 attested to the linkage between the Pentecost pilgrimage and parishional "gifts" to the cathedral: "Cum igitur in nostra diocesi est secundum universalem fere consuetudinem gallicane ecclesie temporibus nostris statutum, videlicet quod circumpositi parrochiani episcopali et matrici ecclesie annis singulis in festo Pentecostes munus impendant"; cited by Avril, *Le gouvernement des évêques*, p. 749n.

84. Homans, *English Villagers of the Thirteenth Century*, pp. 372–373; and Given, *Society and Homicide*, p. 163. Cf. Victor Turner, *Dramas, Fields, and Metaphors: Symbolic Action in Human Society* (Ithaca, N.Y., 1974), p. 212: "Pilgrimages are, in a way, both instruments and indicators of a sort of mystical regionalism as well as of a mystical nationalism." In the same vein, Alphonse Dupront, "La religion populaire dans l'histoire de l'Europe occidentale," *Revue d'histoire de l'église de France* 64 (1978): 196–197, describes the Pentecost Monday pilgrimages as a popular catharsis.

85. Cf. St. Louis's preparations for the crusade in May 1248, including a barefoot pilgrimage to Saint-Denis, and the processions that accompanied his departure: William Chester Jordan, *Louis IX and the Challenge of the Crusade* (Princeton, N.J., 1979), p. 109; Bernard Gui, *Chronicon regum francorum*, HF 21:696; Pierre Coral et al., *Majus Chronicon Lemovicense*, HF 21:766.

86. Jean de Joinville, *Histoire de Saint Louis*, 27, p. 52.

liturgists called the long weeks between the octave of Pentecost and Advent the *tempus peregrinationis*, the time of conflict and battle, *luctus et pugne*.[87] The season, they explained, hearkened back to the strivings of the church between the descent of the Holy Spirit at Pentecost and the Second Coming and of each individual Christian until his death, taught figuratively in the readings from Kings, Maccabees, and Job assigned to these weeks. Summer crusades brought the figure to life. It was the season for suffering on the road to triumph. On this, literary allegory and popular practice agreed.

Collective Expiation in Crisis

With the pilgrimages of Pentecost, the major penitential rites of the year were over; celebrations in mid and late summer were more emphatically celebratory than penitential.[88] Analogous, however, to the cyclical rites of penance played out every year were the collective litanies and processions performed in times of crisis. Several northern French ordinals and processionals explicitly provided for processions in time of drought, storms, war, and so forth, tuning the vaguer antiphons of Rogations to the precise demands of the occasion.[89] Such collective expiations in times of crisis continued to dot the pages of thirteenth-century chronicles. Occasions range from the threat to the crusader states to the illness of Count Robert d'Artois to mere local floods and droughts that lasted a few weeks.[90] One chronicler of the miracles of Sainte Geneviève boasted that her relics led the supplicatory procession safely across the flooding Seine on the Petit-Pont just as the ark of the Covenant led the people of Israel dry-shod through the waters Jordan.[91] Like Palm Sunday and Rogations cele-

87. Jean Beleth, *Summa de ecclesiasticis officiis*, c. 55, pp. 99–100; Guy d'Orchelles, "The 'Summa de Officiis Ecclesiae' of Guy d'Orchelles," p. 35; Guillaume Durand, *Rationale divinorum officiorum* VI.115, f. 269r.

88. Saint John the Baptist's Day was, however, the occasion for the purification of fields and wells with torches, as on Brandons: cf. Jean Beleth, *Summa de ecclesiasticis officiis*, c. 137, p. 267; and Guillaume Durand, *Rationale divinorum officiorum*, VII.14, f. 291v–292r. These rites of purification inevitably had a penitential or expiatory aspect.

89. See, e.g. BN latin 8898, f. 184r–190v (ritual-processional of Soissons, second half of the twelfth century); and Rouen BM 222 (A 551), f. 81r–90v (processional of Rouen, thirteenth century).

90. *Chronicon Leodiense*, HF 18:630; *Fragmentum de miraculis Sanctae Genovefae*, HF 23:137–138; Pierre Desportes, *Reims et les rémois aux XIIIe et XIVe siècles* (Paris, 1979), p. 108: When Christian supplicatory processions failed to end a mid-twelfth-century drought around Reims, the Jewish community proposed to make their own procession; the cathedral's *scholasticus* Alberic refused the challenge.

91. Fragment on the miracles of Saint-Geneviève, HF 18:797.

brations, these expiatory processions experienced the confidence of Old Testament triumphs as well as the humility of suffering sinners.

A parish priest could figure out how to make up his own rites in a crisis.[92] Joinville writes that once when adverse winds were keeping the crusaders' ships off Cyprus, the dean of Maurupt provided a solution. Whenever his parish suffered from bad weather, he said, he needed only make three processions around the area on three successive Saturdays to put a quick end to it. No doubt patience helped, too. The crusaders followed his prescription precisely, making processions around the two masts of the ship; sure enough, by the third Saturday, they reached port.[93] Penance might be appropriate, too, just before a decision, in a potential rather than actual crisis. We find monks and canons saying penitential psalms and the litany before electing an abbot or a bishop, for example.[94] And penitential psalms and litanies had long been associated generally with new beginnings, such as the eve of a bishop's consecration or even the coronation of a king.[95] Supplicatory litanies were introduced into coronations in the ninth century, to be sung alongside the triumphant litany of the *laudes*.[96] The rite combined chants of humility with chants of jubilation.

Conclusion

Our survey of rites has confirmed that popular and elite assumptions about collective expiation coincide. Of course, these attitudes were not wholly identical. Bishops and theologians preferred litanies to tournaments and daytime processions from church to church to nocturnal dances in cemeteries. Theologians and church councils had very early vented their spleen over what they saw as shameful antics

92. In a late-thirteenth-century council, Bishop Nicolas Gellant of Angers forbade anyone other than the bishop to impose public processions, and enjoined parish priests to prohibit the observance of such local-initiative processions: Arnauld, *Statuts du diocèse d'Angers*, p. 63 (Angers, 1271). This was not a general prohibition of penitential processions, contrary to the view of Avril, *Le gouvernement des évêques*, p. 715n. Ten years later the same bishop complained of insufficient attendance at the traditional processions, and insisted that at least one member of each family be made to attend: Arnauld, *Statuts du diocèse d'Angers*, pp. 73–74 (Angers, 1281). And at the end of the century, Bishop Guillaume Le Maire reminded parish priests of their duty to lead processions for the Major and Minor Litanies and other occasions: Arnauld, *Statuts du diocèse d'Angers*, p. 93 (Angers, 1299). So the issue was invention of new processions and the neglect of old. No other council complains about such improvisations, however.

93. Joinville, *Histoire de Saint Louis*, 28, pp. 54–55.

94. Jocelin of Brakelond, *The Chronicle of Jocelin of Brakelond*, ed. and trans. H. E. Butler (London, 1949), p. 11; and Guillaume le Maire, *Livre de Guillaume le Maire*, p. 208.

95. Guillaume le Maire, *Livre de Guillaume le Maire*, p. 245.

96. Kantorowicz, *Laudes Regiae*, pp. 14, 90–91.

but what modern historians have recognized as feasting with the dead.[97] It was the fear of misunderstanding that had induced the church to eliminate the early Christian penitential vigil on the eve of major feasts.[98] For the most part, however, the medieval clergy was content to divert the taste for feasts and dancing to sober daytime litanies or even real dances conducted under clerical supervision. Only in the sixteenth century did bishops make much of an attempt to extirpate clerical dances or even the parodic Feast of Fools.[99] In the earlier period, they condemned the circumstances, not the dances. The medieval preacher had considered illegitimate dances the work of the devil, not mere worldly entertainment. It was the sixteenth-century point of view, by contrast, that dances and feasting were irreverent celebrations that rendered them profane as such, and that required that they be driven from sacred places. Profanity, identified with paganism, was now the threat. Where Bede and Jean Beleth had been proud to boast of the conversion of pagan feasts to Christian purposes, sixteenth-century reformers thought that a pagan or pseudopagan ancestry might damn the offspring.[100]

For the most part, the liturgy bridged the gap between literate sophistication and deep-seated popular patterns of thought. The profound suspicion of popular rites evinced by Protestant and Catholic reformers alike in later years must not be read back into the thirteenth century. Medieval theologians neglected collective rites of penance, but they did not condemn them. They did not challenge the unstated axioms that sin and its expiation could be collective as well as individual, that material suffering could be turned aside by supplica-

97. E. K. Chambers, *The Mediaeval Stage* (Oxford, 1903), pp. 161–162; L. Gougaud, "La danse dans les églises," *Revue d'histoire ecclésiastique* 15 (1914): 12–13, lists councils that condemned such dancing from the sixth to the seventeenth century; cf. Sahlin, *Etude sur la carole médiévale*, pp. 140–141, 185. For an interpretation of these dances, see Schmitt, "'Jeunes' et danse des chevaux de bois," p. 150.

98. Gabriele Winkler, "L'aspect pénitentiel dans les Offices du soir en Orient et en Occident," in *Liturgie et rémission des péchés*, Bibliotheca "Ephemerides Liturgicae," Subsidia, 3 (Rome, 1975), pp. 291–293. Some thirteenth-century commentators who explained the church's conversion of vigils into fasts continued to regard nocturnal dancing as a problem in their own day: Thomas of Chobham, *Summa confessorum* VI.3.1, p. 268; and Guillaume Durand, *Rationale divinorum officiorum*, VI.7, f. 174v. Here at least was a popular rite of truly *longue durée*.

99. Heers, *Fêtes des fous et carnavals*, pp. 189–190; Henri Villetard, "La danse ecclésiastique à la Métropole de Sens," *Bulletin de la Société archéologique de Sens* 26 (1911): 120–121.

100. Sahlin, *Etude sur la carole médiévale*, p. 144, cites a thirteenth-century Parisian sermon that contrasts the processions of God ("in qua portantur cerei flores et crux et vexilla") and the processions of the devil ("scilicet choreas . . . cum cantilenis et floribus rosarum et violarum in capellis capitis et in manibus"). But later complaints are more comprehensive and make paganism or profanity the culprit. Heers, *Fêtes des fous et carnavals*, p. 181, cites a condemnation of the Feast of Fools by the University of Paris in 1444: It is a pagan survival, they say, which leads to the contempt of God and the episcopal office.

tion and expiation, and that the celebration of unity in tandem with collective self-abasement could restore the parish or city to its former status as the people of God.

We can draw several conclusions about these axioms, conclusions that suggest lines of inquiry for the rites of solemn penance I discuss in Chapters 6 and 7. Most surprising perhaps is the frequent difficulty of distinguishing penitential from nonpenitential rites. The Lenten Brandons and Palm Sunday, for instance, were more obviously self-assertive celebrations; but they promised expiation as well. Rogation processions were most obviously intended to expiate the sins that threatened to bring divine retribution on the crops; but they taught town unity as well. Penitent Christians in sackcloth and ashes sang happy tunes about the triumph of their friends, the saints.[101] The admission of collective guilt constituted the Christian city as the people of God. Clerical liturgy and popular ritual alike enlisted the sacred drama of guilt and redemption in the service of political unity and, on Palm Sunday, of ecclesiastical hierarchy. The sacred and the profane were complementary, a fact to be remembered when we consider the northern French and Flemish adaptation of individual public penance as a secular punishment for secular crimes.

In fact, we may outline a spectrum of expiatory rites, from the transcendent and costless sacrifice of the eucharist, to the imitation of the historical Christ's sacrifice in the Palm Sunday liturgy, to the truly costly personal expiation of the public penitent. All these rites have in common the complementarity of expiation and celebration and the linkage between purification from sins and the constitution of a community. They differ in the degree to which they make literal that expiation in a particular moment or person. As we shall see, the early rites of public penance made scapegoats of certain individuals. Paradoxically, perhaps, it was precisely such traditional individual public penances that were the most communal of the rites of expiation, more so even than the Palm Sunday or Rogation processions. Collective processions preached unity by joining at one moment the individual prayers of many people. By teaching the purification of all through the sacrifice of a one or a few, however, public penances compelled a vivid recognition of mutual dependence.

The analysis here has unveiled a Christian ritual logic that was common through much of western Europe, through much of the

101. Modern observers expecting a consistent tone are often irritated. See, for example, Karl Young's complaint that the use of the joyful *Quis est iste rex gloriae* in English reenactments of the deposition in the sepulchre is inept, *The Drama of the Medieval Church* (Oxford, 1933), 1:172.

Middle Ages. In the following chapters on the rites of public penance themselves, I consider what was particular to northern France and to the thirteenth century, a local dialect, as it were, of the Christian language of ritual. Here we have emphasized the continuity of rites through the medieval period. Rogation processions, for example, were not an invention of the high Middle Ages, nor did they succumb to changes in the theology or canon law of penance in the thirteenth century, or indeed in the sixteenth century. Such remarkable continuity surpasses mere survival. Nevertheless, the evidence hints at some slow change. Between 1150 and 1250 or so, as we have seen, the focus for feasts of misrule began to shift from the days after Christmas to the days before Lent, from the Feast of Fools to Carnival. Northern France in the early thirteenth century saw two more marked changes in ritual and liturgy. The first change was in the relation between public penitent and the public community in the rites of Ash Wednesday and Maundy Thursday. The second was the evolution of ecclesiastical drama independent of the liturgy. Demonstrating a connection between these changes is my task in Chapters 6 and 7.

CHAPTER SIX

The Liturgy of Penance
and the Roman Tradition

Liturgical books and especially pontificals are the most important evidence for the evolution of public penance in the period before and after the Fourth Lateran Council. Instead of scattered references as in the canons of diocesan synods or in chronicles, we find in the northern French liturgy a relatively complete series of rites of public penance from the mid–twelfth century to the mid–thirteenth century. The northern French tradition cannot be understood, however, without further consideration of the nature of liturgical evidence, the peculiarities of pontificals, and the evolution of the Roman liturgy, which both strongly influenced rites north of the Alps and, after the medieval period, became authoritative throughout the Roman Catholic church. The preliminaries are the subject of this chapter; and in Chapter 7, I review the evidence of the northern French pontificals themselves.

Few of the rubrics and fewer still of the prayers in northern French rites do not derive ultimately from one of the pontificals loosely grouped in the Roman tradition, especially the Gelasian sacramentaries and the Romano-Germanic pontifical. The "Roman tradition," to be sure, was itself based largely on sources north of the Alps as well as on the pre-Carolingian liturgy of the Rome. Indeed, several trends emerge common to Roman and French rites, though the timing and results differ. First, we find a change in the significance of the expulsion of the penitents, manifested in the provision of absolutions even as they are expelled from the church on Ash Wednesday. Second, the pontificals begin to introduce collective penitential rites for the whole Christian faithful during Lent. And finally, in tandem with this second change, we may detect a shift in the relation between the penitents and their audience. But before we consider the origins and fate of the Roman rites of public penance, we must first look at the use of liturgy as evidence for public penance on either side of the Alps.

Liturgical Sources and Public Penance

Several difficulties have contributed to the relative neglect of liturgical evidence in spite of its seeming appeal to historians now routinely trained by anthropological method to keep an eye out for ritual in premodern societies. Christian liturgy, like all ritual guarded by a literate elite, has always been resistant to change, a circumstance that has rendered suspect any contextual explanation of what change does occur. If the tenth-century Romano-Germanic pontifical, for example, includes a particular prayer in the rite of penance, the conventional explanation will be that the prayer appears in its source. If this were the only level on which analysis may be pursued, it would be impossible to situate the Romano-Germanic pontifical in its tenth-century religious or cultural context. And in fact, liturgical studies have concentrated on genealogies of manuscript exemplars and derivative copies rather than theological or social changes that may have dictated a new liturgy.[1]

Undoubtedly some rites hardly altered over many centuries. The canon of the mass, to take the most obvious example, remained stable because of its central importance from ancient times. Generally, as one moves outward from the canon first to the rest of the liturgy of the mass, then to the daily office, and finally to occasional rites like penance, one finds at each step more tolerance for alteration. Lacking an explicit form established in early texts, and practiced too infrequently for the clergy to know them by heart, rites on the outer circles, as it were, have always undergone more variation in time and place. A few occasional rites petrified, paradoxically, from sheer disuse. Rites for the royal coronation, for instance, find their way into most every French pontifical of the thirteenth century, though only the archbishop of Reims ever had call to use one. Few of these pontificals' compilers bothered to keep up with the latest fashion in coronation; many simply reproduced the old tenth-century rite in the Romano-Germanic pontifical.[2] In a yet more striking example

1. Cf. Edmund Bishop, *Liturgica historica*, p. 298, "In fact, it is very difficult and very unsafe to attempt strict historical deductions from liturgical formulae, new or old." Vogel and Jungmann to some extent represent exceptions, although they too hesitate to draw conclusions from the post-1200 evolution of penitential rites.

2. As one would expect, pre-1204 Norman pontificals were loyal to the English rite that appears in the tenth-century "Pontifical of Edgar"; even a fourteenth-century pontifical of

of blind traditionalism, a twelfth-century pontifical of Chartres prescribes for the mass on the octave of Christmas a station at "s. An-
astasiam."[3] There was no such church in Chartres; the scribe simply
copied information for a procession at Rome without thinking.

Were this slavish copying characteristic of the rites of penance, any
attempt to trace the development of an implicit theology in the liturgy
alongside the explicit theology of the treatises would be futile. Luckily
this is not the case. Rather than two or three standard versions, we
find among northern French pontificals virtually as many versions of
solemn penance as pontificals. Not that the preparers composed original prayers or offered unprecedented scripts for the rite, but in
almost every case they rearranged prayers and roles as if dissatis-
fied with the text they had before them. This proliferation is quite extraordinary; no other episcopal rite shows anything like this variety.
The rites for the anointing and penance of the sick that appeared in
many pontificals, but which could be performed by priests as well as
bishops, show a similar variety; at least into the mid–fourteenth century, public or semiprivate penance refused to settle into any pattern
sanctioned by tradition. Public penance took one form in early
fourteenth-century Auxerre, a slightly different form thirty miles
away at Sens, and an entirely different shape at Rouen. More significant, however, was chronological variation, which is the main emphasis of Chapter 7. We can follow the evolution of northern French rites
from the early twelfth century to the late thirteenth century and
beyond. And in several pontificals, scribes altered the rites for penance in the margin or added new pages.[4] The variety strongly suggests both that the rite was not moribund and that an historical interpretation is possible. If, as Christine Mohrmann has aptly suggested,

---

Rouen still has it. Most pontificals of Sens and Auxerre long preferred the PRG rite, though
one cannot be sure why. Almost all other French pontificals, even those from eastern France,
instead preferred the Anglo-Frankish rite; many recopied it long after it became obsolete
around 1220. The new thirteenth-century French rite that replaced it appears in a couple of
mid-thirteenth-century pontificals from dioceses near Reims, Châlons-sur-Marne, and
Meaux, and also in a mid-fourteenth-century Sens manuscript (no pontifical of Reims survives for the relevant period). In short, after reviewing all pontificals with a coronation rite
(excluding pre-1204 Norman examples), one finds that over half give a version never used by
the French kings or were obsolete when copied.

3. BN latin 945, f. 92r (pontifical of Chartres, second half or end of the twelfth century).
The procession appears in the middle of a partial missal copied into the pontifical.

4. Besançon BM 138 (Beauvais, second half or end of the thirteenth century, with late-
fourteenth- or fifteenth-century additions); Arras BM 469 (Saint-Vaast, Arras, second half or
end of the thirteenth century, with fourteenth century additions); Reims BM 343 (Reims,
beginning thirteenth century, with a roughly contemporary rite of solemn penance in a
completely different hand on a separate quire); Orléans BM 144 (Chartres, beginning thirteenth century, with various thirteenth-century alterations).

Christian liturgical compositions are mosaics of stock stylistic formulas inherited from the past,[5] the rearrangement of the *tesserae* was not necessarily arbitrary or accidental. The selection of texts and their arrangement constantly changed.

A related if less serious difficulty presented by liturgical sources rests in their extended life span. Even where a given rite had not petrified into a centuries-old formula, the prayers as practiced could rarely have represented the latest views on the subject. There would inevitably have been a lag between the new fashion and its incorporation into a new book. Pontificals in particular were very expensive books, each composed invariably in a large ornamental hand that consumed at least a couple of hundred folios; after 1250 or so, they often included rich miniatures as well. No one would have wanted to discard such a book without good cause, though occasionally the very luxury of the pontifical must have induced some rich bishops to commission one to celebrate their elections.

In general, northern French pontificals between 1150 and 1350 probably had an average life span of fifty years or so. That is, where a good series of pontificals for a given see survives, new versions appear at very roughly fifty-year intervals.[6] A number of pontificals were updated by scribes in the margins, and these alterations are particularly useful in showing recent developments. Obviously, where only one pontifical survives for a city, no such determination is possible. It may be that my method slightly overestimates the rapidity of replacement by focusing on richer sees, where more pontificals would have been composed and so preserved. In any case, the analysis that follows

5. Christine Mohrmann, *Liturgical Latin: Its Origins and Character* (London, 1959), p. 24.
6. We can establish the average life span of a pontifical from dioceses where we know that more than one pontifical was composed between 1150 and 1350. The following list includes pontificals destroyed after the Middle Ages but whose description survives, pontificals in restoration and unconsulted, and mutilated copies; it excludes sees with only one surviving pontifical. The dates are generally Leroquais's. In some cases there are two pontificals of the same approximate date; even in these, the rites of penances in the two manuscripts usually differ.

Amiens: middle of the thirteenth century; first half of the fourteenth century.
Arras: second half of the thirteenth century (two MSS); end of the thirteenth century.
Cambrai: beginning of the thirteenth century; first half of the thirteenth century.
Châlons-sur-Marne: second half of the thirteenth century (two MSS).
Chartres: second half or end of the twelfth century; beginning of the thirteenth century; middle of the thirteenth century.
Paris: twelfth century; first half of the thirteenth century; second half of the thirteenth century.
Reims: second half or end of the twelfth century; beginning of the thirteenth century.
Sens: Second half or end of the twelfth century; end of the twelfth century; beginning of the thirteenth century; first half of the fourteenth century (two MSS); middle of the fourteenth century.
Troyes: second half of the twelfth century; thirteenth century.

in Chapter 7, based on the pontificals and, where possible, confirmed by ordinals and other texts, generally reveals a pattern of slow change.[7] The rich survival and precise dating of treatises and confessors' manuals made possible fine distinctions between theology before and after the Fourth Lateran Council in 1215; such precision in fixing moments of transition and sources of influence is not possible with liturgical sources.

Liturgical books were nearly always compiled anonymously— Guillaume Durand's pontifical is a notable exception—and the anonymity of authorship leaves us wondering whose expectations about penance are expressed. Are these compositions of some theological sophistication or are they more naive? Often, no doubt, the author or at least supervisor of the project would have been the *cantor* or dean of the cathedral, a figure who was occasionally a fine theologian like Peter Cantor but more often a cleric of more modest intellectual achievements. An early-thirteenth-century *De ordine officium* of Laon is ascribed to a dean named Adam who decided to reconstruct and reform the cathedral service there after a destructive raid by Enguerrand III de Coucy.[8] A twelfth-century pontifical of Mainz actually pictures its compiler or scribe (*scriptor*), identified only as the monk Frederick, handing the book to Archbishop Christian I (1167–1181).[9]

Unfortunately, nothing else is known about Adam or Frederick, but one may imagine that the authors were typically conscientious cathedral clergy or monks of better than average education. Compiler rather than scribe would seem the best description, as a rule, for the writers did seem to feel free to tinker with the rites of penance in their exemplars. Did the bishop complain that the solemn penance in the book was unsatisfactory, and ask for a new version? Did a canon schooled at Paris point out that theology called for an absolution on Ash Wednesday itself? Or did the impetus for change come from the man who put pen to parchment? We can evaluate the sophistication of the author only from the product. Although it is tempting to assume that they were produced by provincial minds for bishops most interested in decorative miniatures, we may be faced with a phenomenon

7. Ordinals, which typically contained brief outlines of a cathedral's rites in a crabbed hand full of abbreviations, had much longer life spans than the more luxurious pontificals. Doubtless this was because they had no value as presentation pieces, and the schematized arrangement made restructuring the specifics unnecessary. The Ash Wednesday rite, for example, might just tell the bishop to expel the penitents without further detail. And, as with the antiphonals and processionals that similarly were used over long periods, much of the ordinals' contents, such as the antiphons and responses for the office, changed very little over the centuries.

8. U. Chevalier, *Ordinaires de l'église cathédrale de Laon*, pp. xviii–xxiii.

9. BN latin 946, f. 127v.

like Eudes Rigaud's register, the work of real theologians who put aside their theories when necessary. At times, in fact, the liturgical books actually anticipated theological changes.

Alongside problems of authorship we must consider problems of the relation of the audience to the text. Surely the bishop and the cathedral clergy who said the prayers would have grasped not only the meaning of the Latin, but something of the biblical echoes and the symbolism behind the gestures. More complex is the issue of lay comprehension of the liturgy. Certainly by the thirteenth century, northern French and especially Flemish laymen would not normally have understood the prayers, hymns, and lessons that were still ordinarily composed and said in Latin. Already in the twelfth century, liturgical commentators were discussing ways to overcome the barrier of ignorance; Jean Beleth suggested that the celebrant should expound the Lord's Prayer and Creed in the vernacular.[10] Presumably, however, any layman could have followed most of the rite of penance or at least have recognized a benediction or absolution. When the bishop called "Venite, venite" to the penitents on Maundy Thursday and gestured them to come in the church, the meaning would have been apparent to all. So one need not fear that the liturgy represented an effort in academic calisthenics. In the end, we may even postulate an historians' *lex orandi* parallel to that of the theologians: Only in prayers and gestures lies the test of an intellectual theory's strength and appeal outside itself. To discover, for example, whether the new theology of the keys that demanded the declarative absolution, *Ego te absolvo*, ever escaped the precincts of the Parisian schools,[11] we must reckon with the evidence of the contemporary liturgy.

Among the liturgical books, cathedral ordinals occasionally provide brief outlines of rites of public penance, but they never give full prayers and rubrics. Rituals, that is, handbooks of rites for priests, rarely include anything of relevance, not even rites of nonsolemn public penance, which by common agreement simple priests could legitimately perform.[12] Pontificals are the best source for public pen-

---

10. Jean Beleth, *Summa de ecclesiasticis officiis*, c. 116, p. 218; cf. Enrico Cattaneo, "La partecipazione dei laici alla liturgia," in *I laici nella "Societas christiana" dei secoli XI e XII*, pp. 406–417, for a discussion of this problem and the development of vernacular devotional aids. Cattaneo points to the self-evident drama of major feasts and seasons, especially Lent, as important educators of laymen.

11. Thomas Aquinas, *De forma absolutionis paenitentiae sacramentalis ad Magistrum Ordinis*, in *Opera omnia* (Leonine edition, Rome, 1968), vol. XL:B-C, p. C40, admits that the "Ego te absolvo" formula was hardly ever used even a mere thirty years before his treatise; but we will see in Chapter 7 how even Thomas's estimation of the new form's popularity is exaggerated.

12. Until the thirteenth century in France and Germany, most rituals were monastic; after 1215, when synodal statutes began to demand that priests keep a *manuale* (i.e., a ritual), parish

ance because they spell out rites in detail, complete with rubrics a⟨ ⟩ the full texts of prayers (*orationes*), and sometimes with a jot of exp⟨ ⟩ atory commentary.[13] In principle, pontificals collected the prei ⟨ ⟩ tive rites of bishops, and so naturally included solemn penance. I h₊ t compilation had evolved slowly both in Rome and north of the Alps between the ninth century and the twelfth century as a practical combination of all noneucharistic *ordines* and the relevant prayers from the sacramentaries, thus enabling the bishop to consult a single book for these rites. Meanwhile, eucharistic liturgy became the purview of the new missal.[14] Typically, then, the new pontificals were limited to the thorough coverage of a few occasional episcopal rites, chiefly solemn penance, ordinations, the consecration and reconciliation of churches, episcopal benedictions for important feast days, and blessings of ecclesiastical ornaments and household items.

In fact, pontificals occasionally strayed from this model. Some French pontificals omitted a few rites or included a partial missal. Many imitated the Roman pontificals by including rites for anointing and absolution of the sick that a simple priest would normally have performed. And some pontificals had in fact been prepared for abbots, either for an abbot with some episcopal prerogatives or as a compendium of monastic rituals, omitting inappropriate rites like confirmation and the consecration of churches.[15] Yet, these so-called abbatial pontificals often do include rites of solemn penance, either because the scribe slavishly copied an episcopal exemplar, or more often, I believe, because the abbot did in fact expel and receive penitents. Of the twelve northern French and Flemish pontificals prepared for monasteries between 1150 and 1350, three apparently do not contain rites of public penance.[16] In two further pontificals from

---

rituals grew more common. Cf. Gy, "Collectaire, rituel, processional," pp. 455–460. The content remained similar; like monastic rituals, parish rituals usually provided deathbed penitential rites but no rites of public penance. See below for why nonsolemn public penance rarely appears in liturgical books.

13. Cf. Troyes, Trésor de la cathédrale 4, f. 143r-v (Pontifical of Troyes, second half of the twelfth century); I have not been able to identify the source.

14. For this evolution see V. Leroquais, *Les pontificaux manuscrits des bibliothèques publiques de France* (Paris, 1937), 1:xv–xxiii; and C. Vogel, *Introduction aux sources de l'histoire du culte chrétien au Moyen Age*, Biblioteca degli "Studi medievali," 1 (Spoleto, 1966?), pp. 182–183. The first use of the term *pontificale* appears at the turn of the thirteenth and fourteenth centuries in a Roman manuscript.

15. Gy, "Collectaire, rituel, processional," pp. 465–466; cf. Leroquais, *Les pontificaux manuscrits*, 1:ix.

16. BL Add. 38,645 (Saint-Sauveur, Anchin, near Arras, 12th c.) and Sens BM 13 (unknown monastery, diocese of Rouen, early fourteenth century) are unambiguous. For Sens BM 13, see René-Jean Hesbert, "Les manuscrits liturgiques de l'église de Rouen," *Bulletin philologique et historique (jusqu'à 1715)* (1955–1956), p. 481. BN n.a.l. 2358 (Saint-Corneille,

Arras, critical lacunas prevent a firm decision, but a surviving ordinal suggests that there were no lay penitents.[17] One monastic pontifical of Corbie has an *ordo ad reconciliandos penitentes*, but no unambiguous expulsion and reception.[18] In the six remaining cases, there are clear rites of expulsion and reconciliation. These last six pontificals were prepared for major monasteries whose abbots might well be expected to have enjoyed the episcopal prerogative in this matter: Sint Pieters, Ghent; Saint-Bertin, in Saint-Omer, ter Doest near Bruges; Saint-Amand-en-Pevèle (diocese of Tournai); Saint-Martin, Tournai; and probably Mont-Saint-Michel, near Avranches. Not coincidentally, these were mostly very important abbeys, and in the first three cases, they were located in population centers without an episcopal see.[19] In addition, one quasi ordinal and one pontifical from southern French abbeys apparently possessed rites of public penance, and one English pontifical certainly did.[20] A pontifical would normally only be pre-

Compiègne, thirteenth century), f. 47r–48r, has an *absolutio in cena domini*, with prayers borrowed from the PRG's solemn penance, but it is apparently intended to be said over monks or lay visitors, not actual lay public penitents. For this manuscript, see Gy, "Collectaire, rituel, processional," pp. 465–466.

17. The mutilated pontificals are from Saint-Vaast, Arras: Arras BM 702 (end of the thirteenth century and beginning of the fourteenth century), and Arras BM 469 (second half or end of the thirteenth century). Cf. L. Brou, ed., *The Monastic Ordinale of St. Vedast's Abbey, Arras*, Henry Bradshaw Society, 86–87 (Bedford, 1957); the Ash Wednesday and Maundy Thursday rites in this early-fourteenth-century text (pp. 148–149, 156–157) include no expulsion or reception of penitents.

18. Amiens BM 195 (Corbie, beginning or first half of the thirteenth century), f. 54r–63v; it may be a monastic adaptation of the rite. It is not clear whether actual lay penitents were expelled and reconciled.

19. The six cases with rites of solemn penance are: Brussels BR 1505–1506 (Sint Pieters, Ghent, twelfth century); Saint-Omer BM 98 (probably Saint-Bertin, twelfth century); Bruges BM 318 (probably ter Doest, thirteenth century); BN latin 953 (Saint-Amand, diocese of Tournai, twelfth century); Brussels BR II. 1013 (Saint Martin, Tournai, early thirteenth century); and BN latin 14832 (Mont-Saint-Michel or Avranches, first half or middle of the twelfth century). (For the origin of BN latin 14832, see Leroquais, *Les pontificaux manuscrits*, 2:192–193, who calls it a pontifical of Avranches; and Fernand Combaluzier, "Un pontifical de Mont-Saint-Michel," in *Millénaire monastique du Mont-Saint-Michel* (Paris, 1966–1971), 1:397–398, who calls it monastic.) Of these six, the pontificals of Saint-Amand, Saint-Martin, and Saint-Bertin actually refer to the *episcopus* presiding over solemn penance; this may reflect slavish copying or simply the recognition that when an abbot presided it was in virtue of his episcopal rights. The pontifical of Ghent provides a non-Lenten rite of public penance as well as an adaptation of the Lenten rite. See below, Chapter 7.

20. BN latin 1341, (a monastic ordinal with extensive additions, diocese of Limoges, end of the twelfth or beginning of the thirteenth century), f. 26r-v, includes an order *de reconciliatione penitentium* on Maundy Thursday; but besides citing certain ancient *auctoritates*, stressing the imposition of hands, it gives little further information. It may not represent an actual rite in use at the abbey. BN latin 944 (pontifical, etc., probably Saint-Gérard, Aurillac, twelfth century), f. 113r–114r, has an *absolutio super penitentes* separate from Wednesday and Thursday rites. It includes a number of *orationes* and deprecative absolutions, but no *Venite* or reintroduction into the church. Since the prayers include plural references to penitents, it seems to be a rite for solemn or nonsolemn public penance, not individual penance. H. A. Wilson has printed a monastic pontifical of Evesham (diocese of Westminster) from around

pared for an important abbot who claimed some episcopal rights. Ordinals and rituals were more common, and often were prepared for monasteries and canons without such claims; out of more than ten such from northern France from the twelfth century through the fourteenth century, only two provide even an ambiguous *absolutio super penitentes* that likely refers to lay public penitents.[21] Finally, it is worth noting that most of the French and Flemish abbatial pontificals, and all of the ones with solemn penance, were composed before 1250. It may be that the First and Fourth Lateran Council's canons against abbatial imposition of public penance were slowly affecting practice.[22]

Missing from nearly all of these sources, however, is a description of the liturgy of most nonsolemn public penances, the non-Lenten expulsion of penitents and humiliations, to be performed outside the church under the charge of a bishop or simple priest.[23] Pontificals do include prayers for the blessing of a pilgrim's staff or satchel, blessings that would have been integrated into some types of nonsolemn public penance. But as a rule neither pontificals nor priestly rituals provide any liturgy for public penances not tied to Ash Wednesday and Maundy Thursday. Yet we know from chronicles and Eudes's register that

1300 that explicitly refers to the abbot expelling and reconciling penitents: *Officium Ecclesiasticum Abbatum secundum usum Eveshamensis Monasterii*. Finally, we may note that a tenth-century pontifical of Saint Germans, Cornwall, also provides an elaborate rite *ad reconciliandos poenitentes* on Maundy Thursday, with a bishop presiding: Martène, *De antiquis ecclesiae ritibus libri*, I.6.7.2, vol. I, cols. 768–774.

21. The two with the *absolutio super penitentes* are both from Sens: Sens BM 24 (ritual of Saint-Pierre-le-Vif, Sens, thirteenth century), pp. 72–75; Sens BM 20 (ritual of Saint-Remi, Sens, fourteenth century), pp. 95–98. The rituals and ordinals that do not contain rites of public penance are:

    Sens BM 23 (ordinal of Saint-Pierre-le-Vif, Sens, end of the thirteenth or beginning of the fourteenth century).
    BN latin 9970 (ordinal of Saint-Trinité, Fontainebleau, thirteenth century).
    BN latin 1236 (ordinal of unidentified abbey, thirteenth century).
    Paris, Bibl. Mazarine 526, and BN latin 976 (Ordinals of Saint-Denis, thirteenth century).
    J.-B.-N. Blin, *Ordinal de l'abbaye de Saint-Pierre-sur-Dive* (diocese of Séez, 1275).
    BN latin 18042, 18043, 18044, and 18045 (rituals and ordinals of Saint-Corneille, Compiègne, thirteenth century).
    Ordinarium Canonicorum Regularium S. Laudi Rotomagensis, PL 147:157–192 (ordinal, Saint-Lô, Rouen, thirteenth to fourteenth century).
    Brou, *The Monastic Ordinale of St. Vedast's Abbey*, Arras.

22. *Conciliorum oecumenicorum decreta*, p. 193 (c. 16), and p. 262 (c. 60). See above, Chapter 4.

23. One exception seems to be the non-Lenten "absolution of penitents" to be performed by a priest in front of the church, in Brussels BR 1505–1506, f. 27r-v, a pontifical of Sint Pieters, Ghent. It includes three prayers borrowed from the PRG's Thursday rite, but no true absolution. The priest touches the penitents with his staff (*baculo*), and brings them into the church.

such penances were quite common. Since it is not conceivable that the rite disappeared from the surviving kinds of books or that some other sort containing it did not survive, we must conclude that a liturgy of nonsolemn penance as such simply did not exist. As we saw in Chapter 4, flexibility and informality characterized the non-Lenten humiliations that the bishops imposed on offenders. The nonsolemn rite was virtually by definition a nonliturgical ritual, concocted for the occasion by the bishop, priest, or other authority who had imposed it. Some offenders might have had to tramp from church to church holding candles; others might have been sent on a series of pilgrimages; others would have dug up a body with their bare hands. There was no written rite to cover all these possibilities. Certain Ash Wednesday and Maundy Thursday injunctions, prayers, and absolutions would have been appropriate for the start or conclusion of the processions; but if bishops and priests borrowed portions of the solemn rite, they do not tell us. In sum, almost all of the liturgical evidence addresses the Lenten rite, whereas much of the nonliturgical evidence touches on the nonsolemn versions. The disparity is unfortunate, but inevitable.

The Early Roman Liturgy of Penance

The Roman tradition has determined most historians' view of the evolution of penance. The supposed demise of solemn public penance is most evident, after all, in the succession of Roman curial pontificals from the tenth to the thirteenth century, and moreover, the Roman tradition is the only one to have been extensively studied. The pioneering but sporadic editions of non-Roman texts by Jean Morin and Edmond Martène have found few successors, and even the material they provide has not been sufficiently analyzed.[24] Thus, the predominantly Roman interpretative surveys of Josef Jungmann and Cyrille Vogel, plus Vogel's and Michel Andrieu's editions of Roman texts, remain the inevitable starting point for any further analysis, whether of Roman or French texts.[25]

---

24. The evidence printed in Morin's *Commentarius historicus de disciplina* remains difficult to use because his manuscript sources have not been systematically identified, as have Martène's by Martimort, *La documentation liturgique de Dom Edmond Martène*. Martimort's labors and Victor Leroquais's magnificent catalogs, particularly *Les pontificaux manuscrits*, have made study of the non-Roman liturgy of penance possible; but the most important modern interpreter of the French evidence on the liturgy of penance remains Josef Andreas Jungmann's *Die lateinischen Bussriten*; but even this thorough and acute analysis of penitential liturgies is essentially concerned with the Roman tradition.

25. Of Vogel's many articles, two of the most important are "Les rites de la pénitence

Our story begins in earnest with the tenth-century Romano-Germanic pontifical, but some background on the early medieval rite is in order. Public penance in some form was practiced in the Christian west from at least the middle of the third century. The early Christian liturgy is less clear. From at least the early fifth century at Rome, Maundy Thursday was the occasion for the public reconciliation of penitents.[26] The liturgy of the beginning of penance was not established until at least the seventh century, however. Ash Wednesday developed much later than Maundy Thursday. Public penance implied the exclusion of the sinner from the church in a quasi excommunication, but there seems to have been no Wednesday ceremony of dismissal as such.[27]

The first full rite for an Ash Wednesday beginning of public penance followed by a reconciliation on Maundy Thursday appears in the so-called Gelasian sacramentary, an eighth-century manuscript (Vat. Reg. lat. 316) based probably on seventh-century sources.[28] A slightly different form appears in the later eighth-century Frankish Gelasian sacramentaries.[29] Still different versions appear in Benedict of Aniane's early-ninth-century supplement to the Gregorian sacramentary and various ninth-century revised manuscripts of the Gregorian or Gregorian-Gelasian hybrids. The version of the Gregorian sacramentary sent to Charlemagne (the "Hadrianum") had not possessed a rite of public penance, and since the later Gregorian texts that do have it are evidently dependent on the Gelasian, we shall take the Gelasian versions as our starting point.[30] They make it clear that this rite was

publique aux Xe et XIe siècles," 1:137–144, and "Les rituels de la pénitence tarifée," in *Liturgia opera divina e umana: Studi sulla riforma liturgica offerti a S. E. Mons. Annibale Bugnini in occasione del suo 70 compleanno*, ed. P. Jounel et al., Bibliotheca "Ephemerides Liturgicae," Subsidia 26 (Rome, 1983), pp. 419–427.

26. Vogel, "Les rites de la pénitence publique," p. 143; Bailey, *The Processions of Sarum and the Western Church*, pp. 109–110. The Mozarabic rite made Good Friday the day for reconciliation: Gy, "Histoire liturgique du Sacrement de Pénitence," *La Maison-Dieu* 56 (1958): 12.

27. Jungmann, *Die lateinischen Bussriten*, p. 44; Vogel, "Les rites de la pénitence publique," pp. 139–140.

28. L. C. Mohlberg with L. Eizenhöfer and P. Siffrin, eds., *Liber sacramentorum Romanae Aeclesiae ordinis anni circuli*, Rerum ecclesiasticarum documenta, ser. maior, fontes, 4 (Rome, 1960), XV–XVI and XXXVIII, pp. 17–18, 55–57. For the dating of the Gelasian sacramentaries, see A. Chavasse, *Le sacramentaire gélasien*, Bibliothèque de théologie, série 4, Histoire de la théologie, 1 (Paris-Tournai, 1958), pp. 141–155, where he identifies part of the Wednesday rite and the whole of the Thursday rite as additions to adapt the putative original Gelasian for the use of the Roman presbyteral *tituli*.

29. C. Mohlberg, *Das fränkische Sacramentarium Gelasianum*, 3d ed., Liturgiegeschichtliche Quellen und Forschungen, 1–2 (Münster, 1971), 48 and 92, pp. 37–38, and 68–73. See also on the Gelasian rites of public penance Vogel, "Le péché et la pénitence," pp. 226–227, and "Les rites de la pénitence publique," pp. 138–139.

30. Jean Deshusses, *Le sacramentaire Grégorien*, Spicilegium Friburgense, 16, 24, 28 (Fribourg, 1971–1982), 1:451–453 (Supplementum Anianense); 1:694 (additions to "corrected" MS of the Hadrianum, Maundy Thursday only); 3:113–118 (various "corrected" MSS of the

reserved for sinners guilty of scandalous crimes; a separate rite had developed in conjunction with the "tariffs" of private penance.

Many of the elements of the rite of solemn penance familiar to a thirteenth-century Frenchman are already present here. The chief among the Gelasian's innovations were the establishment of a liturgy of penance separate from the celebration of the mass, the choice of Ash Wednesday as the date for the beginning of public penance, the composition of new prayers, and the rite of reconciliation.[31] Its administration was generally reserved to the bishop, who would sprinkle the penitents with water and ashes and clothe them in the *cilicium* or hairshirt that would be the mark of the penitents' status in their years of separation and expiation. Penitents were then to be confined until Maundy Thursday while they performed their satisfaction, probably in a monastery, but there was not yet a dramatic ceremony of expulsion.[32] Either at the end of that Lent, or a few years later, but in any case on Maundy Thursday, the bishop would reconcile the penitents. The penitent would leave his place of penitence and prostrate himself outside the cathedral. The deacon presented them to the bishop: "Now, venerable bishop, is the accepted time, the day of propitiation" (cf. 2 Cor. 6:2); the bishop or a priest would then warn the penitents against relapses and say a series of prayers of pardon.[33] As we found in Chapter 4, this would not in itself mean the end of their fasting or exclusion from the sacraments and kiss of peace. The sinner had to continue with his fasting until the fifth or seventh year, each year returning Maundy Thursday for this partial reconciliation. The Frankish Gelasian added a separate rite for the eventual readmission of the penitents to communion.[34] Many of the prayers in the Gelasian sacramentary were carried into the Roman *ordines*, into the Romano-Germanic Pontifical, and into local French and English pontificals of

---

Hadrianum and of Benedict of Aniane's Gregorian). For the ascription of the supplement to Benedict of Aniane rather than Alcuin, see 1:64–67, and 3:66–75. Public penance also does not appear in the Paduense, a ninth-century text representing a different branch of the Gregorian than the Hadrianum. For a hybrid Gelasian-Gregorian sacramentary with a rite of public penance based on the Frankish Gelasian rite, see the late-eighth-century *Liber sacramentorum Gellonensis*, Corpus Christianorum Continuatio Mediaevalis, 159 (Turnholt, 1981), pp. 33–34, 76–78.

31. Jungmann, *Die lateinischen Bussriten*, p. 51.

32. Cf. Jungmann, *Die lateinischen Bussriten*, p. 45; Vogel, "Les rites de la pénitence publique," p. 139. The Gelasian sacramentaries do envisage at least the possibility of a simple priest officiating on Maundy Thursday: "Post haec admonetur ab episcopo sive ab alio sacerdote," etc: *Liber sacramentorum*, XXXVIII, p. 57.

33. *Liber sacramentorum*, XXXVIII, pp. 56–57; and Mohlberg, *Das fränkische Sacramentarium*, 92, pp. 69–70: "Adest, o venerabilis pontifex, tempus acceptum, dies propitiationis" See Jungmann, *Die lateinischen Bussriten*, pp. 76–77.

34. Mohlberg, *Das fränkische Sacramentarium*, 93, pp. 71–73.

the High Middle Ages. In fact, many French pontificals preserved features of the Gelasian and Frankish Gelasian rites that the tenth-century Romano-Germanic pontifical had eliminated.[35] Thus, the general arrangement and many of the specific prayers of solemn penance date at least to the middle of the eighth century.

Although the Romano-Frankish Gelasian sacramentaries eventually crossed the Alps and reached Rome during the Ottonian *renovatio* of the tenth century,[36] northern Europe, and particularly Germany, remained the region of greatest liturgical vitality for the sacrament of penance. In his *De synodalibus causis*, a collection of conciliar canons, Regino of Prüm (d. 915) included a description of the rite, which he incorrectly attributed to a pre-Carolingian Council of Agde in Languedoc. This was in fact the solemn penance for public sinners that Germans practiced at the beginning of the tenth century. Burchard of Worms copied the supposed canon into his *Decretum*, Gratian followed suit, and many French pontificals incorporated much of it as a rubric for the Ash Wednesday service.

At the beginning of Lent all penitents who undertake or who have undertaken public penance shall show themselves to the bishop of the city before the doors of the church, dressed in sackcloth, barefoot, faces cast down to the ground, by their very dress and expression proclaiming themselves to be guilty. Here the deans ought to be present, that is the archpriest of the parishes, along with witnesses, that is the priests of the penitents, and they shall conscientiously examine their conduct; he [the bishop] shall enjoin penance, according to the measure of the guilt in the fixed degrees. Afterwards he shall lead them into the church and, prostrate on the ground and in tears, he along with all the clergy shall chant the seven penitential psalms for their absolution. Then rising from prayer, as the canons dictate, he shall lay hands on them, sprinkle holy water over them,

---

35. Cf. for example, the shorter version of the prayer *Deus humani generis* in the Gelasian sacramentaries (*Liber sacramentorum*, p. 57; and Mohlberg, *Das fränkische Sacramentarium*, pp. 70–71), and most French pontificals; the PRG has a much longer version. Similarly, certain French pontificals preserve the conflated prayers and presentation, *Adest, o venerabilis*, that exists in the Gelasian (*Liber sacramentorum*, p. 56; and Mohlberg, *Das fränkische Sacramentarium*, pp. 69–70) but was separated in PRG XCIX.225C–227C into an exchange between the archdeacon and bishop. See Chapter 7 for details.

36. The oldest surviving rite of solemn penance composed at Rome is Andrieu's Ordo L, a version of the tenth-century PRG XCIX, first appearing in early-eleventh-century manuscripts coincident with the arrival in Rome of the PRG itself: M. Andrieu, *Les ordines romani du Haut Moyen Age*, Vol. 5, *Ordo L*, Spicilegium sacrum Lovaniense, Etudes et documents, 29 (Louvain, 1961), c.18, pp. 108–127, and c.25, pp. 193–207; Cyrille Vogel with Reinhard Elze, *Le pontifical romano-germanique du dixième siècle*, Studi e Testi, 226, 227, 269, vol. III, p. 37.

first place ashes, then cover their heads with sackcloth, and with groans and great sighs he shall declare that just as Adam was expelled from paradise, so too they are banished from the church for their sins. After these actions he shall order the ministers to drive them outside the doors. The clergy shall follow them with the responsory "In the sweat of thy face thou shall eat bread," etc. (Gen. 3:19) so that seeing the holy church disturbed and made to tremble at their sins, they shall not value penance little. At the sacred Lord's Supper [i.e., Maundy Thursday] they shall again present themselves at the entrance of the church.[37]

The careful use of the present and perfect tenses in the first sentence ("omnes . . . qui . . . suscipiunt aut susceperunt") reveals that Regino expects penitents who have already undertaken the multiyear expiations—what are later described as the *carena*—to appear every year alongside the new public penitents on Ash Wednesday, and presumably on Maundy Thursday, too. Regino expects the rural dean or archpriest to investigate the conduct (*conversationem*) of the penitents.[38] This suggests some sort of extended confession as well as the consultation of the parish priest, a procedure that appears both in the Romano-Germanic pontifical and in later versions. We note that the bishop offers prayers on Ash Wednesday for their "absolution." He does not pronounce a final absolution in the technical sense; the sinner is freed neither from the guilt (*culpa*) incurred by his offense nor from the need to complete his satisfaction. Both the Gelasian and

---

37. Regino of Prüm, *Libri duo de synodalibus causis et disciplinis ecclesiasticis*, pp. 136–137; also in PL 132:245–246: "In capite Quadragesimae omnes poenitentes qui publicam suscipiunt aut susceperunt poenitentiam, ante fores ecclesiae se repraesentent episcopo civitatis, sacco induti, nudis pedibus, vultibus in terram prostratis, reos se esse ipso habitu et vultu proclamantes; ubi adesse debent decani, id est archipresbyteri parochiarum, cum testibus, id est presbyteri poenitentium, qui eorum conversationem diligenter inspicere debent; et secundum modum culpae poenitentiam per praefixos gradus injungat. Post haec in ecclesiam eos introducat, et cum omni clero septem poenitentiae psalmos in terram prostatus cum lacrymis pro eorum absolutione decantet. Tum consurgens ab oratione, juxta id quod canones jubent, manus eis imponat, aquam benedictam super eos spargat, cinerem prius mittat, dein cilicio capita eorum cooperiat, et cum gemitu ac crebris suspiriis denuntiet quod sicut Adam projectus est de paradiso, ita et ipsi ab Ecclesia ob peccata ejiciantur. Post haec jubeat ministros ut eos extra januas expellant. Clerus vero prosequatur eos cum responsorio: *In sudore vultus tui vesceris pane tuo,* etc. (Genesis 3), ut videntes sanctam Ecclesiam ob facinora sua tremefactam et commotam, non parvipendant poenitentiam. In sacra autem Domini coena rursus ecclesiae liminibus se praesentent." Cf. Burchard of Worms, *Decretorum libri viginti,* XIX.26, PL 140:984; and Gratian, *Decretum,* D.50 c.64, col. 201.

38. In a revealing error, Martène printed "conscientias" for "conversationem" in his edition of a French pontifical that copied Regino's description: *De antiquis ecclesiae ritibus libri* I.6.7.16, vol. I, col. 816 (=BN latin 934, Pontifical of Sens, second half or end twelfth century). The seventeenth-century scholar assumed that the confessor would be interested in the state of the sinner's soul, not his outward behavior and reputation.

Romano-Germanic pontificals' Ash Wednesday services provide not even deprecative absolutions but simply prayers on behalf of the penitent. Faithful to the ancient liturgy of penance, Regino has the bishop who receives the penitents lay his hands upon them ("manus eis imponat"). But he breaks new ground when he prescribes the dramatic expulsion at the end of the service, echoing Adam's expulsion from Paradise. In later versions of the rite, even those dependent on Regino, the traditional imposition of hands disappears. Dramatic logic demanded that the Ash Wednesday service teach in gestures the separation and eventual expulsion of the penitent; only during the reconciliation of the Maundy Thursday rite would the bishop actually touch the penitent sinner.

The Romano-Germanic pontifical, first composed in Mainz between 950 and 961/63,[39] represents, with some alterations, the liturgical expression of the model described in Regino's text. This was a collective work, prepared under the direction of Archbishop William of Mainz, Otto I's archchancellor; the lost prototype came from the scriptorium of Saint Alban of Mainz. The compilers obviously drew on the Gelasian sacramentaries and on Regino himself.[40] They seem to have introduced two major changes of their own. First, they eliminated the episcopal laying-on of hands in the Ash Wednesday ceremony; and second, they added a dramatic gesture of reinclusion on Maundy Thursday. The bishop called for the penitents to come back in ("Venite, venite, venite"), and then he drew them with linked hands into the church.[41] Otherwise, the committee's work was one of compilation and organization. Their effort was so successful that the Romano-Germanic pontifical became the most influential non-eucharistic liturgical work in western Europe.[42]

So influential was its treatment of penance that a closer look is indispensable for understanding both the Roman and French traditions. While the Maundy Thursday reconciliation is relatively straightforward, it is difficult at times to follow the intentions of the compilers in the Ash Wednesday rite. It starts without any reference to a bishop, and, in fact, the first steps seem to take place outside the church. As it appears in the manuscripts, the *ordo* begins with the

39. For the manuscripts and dating of the PRG, see Vogel, *Le pontifical romano-germanique*, III, pp. 6–28, and "Le pontifical romano-germanique du Xe siècle: Nature, date, et importance du document," *Cahiers de civilisation médiévale* 6 (1963): 29–42.

40. Vogel, *Le pontifical romano-germanique*, III, pp. 11, 51, and "Le pontifical romano-germanique," pp. 38.

41. See the Appendix for a comparison of the PRG's *Venite* and northern French versions.

42. Vogel, "Le pontifical romano-germanique," p. 28, and "Les rites de la pénitence publique," pp. 143, 144.

deacon telling the gathered people that all Christians are to come on this day to true confession and true penance ("ad veram confessionem veramque penitentiam festinantius accedant"), and then to return on Maundy Thursday for reconciliation.[43] If a penitent's proposed journey or occupation or simple stupidity ("aut ita forte hebes est") makes this impossible, the priest should enjoin an annual penance and reconcile him at once. For the others, the priest is directed to say a prayer and then question each about his or her vices and assign an appropriate penance in proportion to his or her sins and sex, age, and condition. Evidently, the priest questioned each individually ("Deinde iubeat eum sacerdos sedere contra se"), but there is no indication about privacy. Then the priest was supposed to question the penitent about his or her belief in the articles of faith: "Credis in Deum patrem et filium et spiritum sanctum?"

At this point, the manuscripts include an extended *Confessio penitentis*, in fact a confession of all kinds of sins, just like the general confessions that were long part of the Lenten liturgy in much of northern Europe and that Caesarius of Heisterbach decried as no substitute for an individual confession of particular sins.[44] The priest pronounces a prayer for the penitent's forgiveness: "Misereatur tui omnipotens Deus et dimittat tibi omnia peccata tua." The priest should then inform the penitent of his or her penance and say the seven penitential psalms, the Lord's Prayer, and a lengthy list of short *preces*. Then follow eight *orationes* for mercy; if "time and place are suitable," the priest and penitents should enter the church and say yet more psalms and *preces*. So far, there has been not one word of a bishop, of a cathedral, or of scandalous sins. Is this public penance? Or is it a rite of private penance for Ash Wednesday? The question is a difficult one.

And then, without further rubrics or explanation, we meet another prayer labeled just like the others, "Sequitur oratio. Deus cuius indulgentia cuncti indigent, memento famuli tui N." ("The prayer follows. God, whose indulgence all crave together, remember your servant."), followed by a *Missa post confessionem*. Then comes the imposition of ashes on the head of the penitent ("super caput penitentis"), the giving of the hairshirt, and the expulsion from the church. We may note in passing that here only the sinners ritually expelled received ashes. A final section gives the blessing of the ashes, presumably to be com-

---

43. See PRG XCIX.44–80, vol. II, pp. 14–23, for the whole Wednesday *ordo*. The only substantial discussion of the rite is to be found in Vogel, *Le pécheur et la pénitence*, pp. 208–213, but as will be seen, I disagree with his conclusions.

44. Caesarius of Heisterbach, *Dialogus miraculorum*, Dist. III, c. xlv, vol. I, p. 64. See above, Chapter 3.

pleted that day before the rest of the rite. Vogel has argued that the
prayer *Deus cuius indulgentia* (XCIX.66) marks the beginning of an
entirely new *ordo*, a rite of public penance distinct from the rite of
private penance that has gone before.[45] After all, the first sections
that we have reviewed seem to instruct a priest to hear confessions
from everybody (*omnes Christiani*) individually, and the rite resembles
other liturgies for individual penance that survive in the books of
penitential tariffs. The interrogation about the creed, for example, is
a standard feature in these texts, including the Romano-Germanic
pontifical's own rite of private penance.[46] There is no textual evidence for Vogel's decision to break the *ordo* into two parts, no recension that shows two *ordines* instead of one. Not a single scribe who
copied this popular text over several centuries inserted an appropriate rubric to warn his readers, *incipit ordo*. On the contrary, the rubric
for the mass for Vogel's second order calls it the *Missa post confessionem*,
referring directly to the confession that Vogel would separate from
it. And the twelfth-century Roman pontifical that succeeded the
Romano-Germanic pontifical begins its Ash Wednesday rite neither
with the confession and creed nor with the *oratio* XCIX.66 that Vogel
cites as the real beginning of the rite of public penance. It starts, as we
shall see, with a benediction of ashes, and it entirely omits both confession and expulsion of penitents.[47] And the French, German, and
English pontificals that owed the structure of their rites of solemn
penance to the Romano-Germanic version borrowed freely from
prayers on either side of Vogel's divide.[48]

Vogel's interpretation is appealing but untenable. Somehow we are
faced with what the compilers considered a whole. Rather than a rite
of private penance followed by a rite of solemn public penance, we
have a single rite of confession and expulsion. Probably the *omnes
Christiani* at the beginning of the rite is not to be taken too seriously.
There is no indication in contemporary canons or in the writings of
such theologians as Regino or Burchard that all Christians were expected to show up on Ash Wednesday, still less appear for reconciliation on Maundy Thursday. The Romano-Germanic rite, furthermore, describes the participant with the noun *penitentem*,[49] a word

---

45. Vogel, *Le pécheur et la pénitence*, p. 213.
46. Cf. Regino of Prüm, *Libri duo de synodalibus causis et disciplinis ecclesiasticis*, I.304, p. 141;
Burchard, *Decretum*, XIX.4, PL 140:950; PRG CXXXVI.5, vol. II, p. 235; and Vogel, "Les
rituels de la pénitence tarifée," p. 425.
47. PRS XXVII, pp. 209–210.
48. Particular favorites included PRG XCIX.57–64, 72, 74–76.
49. PRG XCIX.44, p. 14: "Denique cum sacerdos susceperit penitentem, si laicus est
dimisso baculo, quisquis vero ille est sive laicus sive clericus seu monachus suppliciter inclinet
se ante sacerdotem."

normally reserved for someone belonging to the *ordo* of penitents, that is, an officially recognized penitent and not an ordinary contrite Christian. The confession before the church that follows is not surprising, since confession and the assignment of a satisfaction to be completed normally preceded any penance. And it corresponds closely to Regino's instructions.[50] What of the creed? Perhaps the Rhenish compilers knew of its use in the tariff books of penance and thought it an appropriate addition. The *orationes* that follow seem to be appropriate for the serious sinner, not for the mass of Christians who would be showing up were this some sort of omnibus parish confession day.[51] In short, the rite in its entirety may be interpreted as a public penance, along the lines of Regino's outline thirty years earlier.

To understand the Rhenish rite, we may usefully compare it with several near contemporary but independent French and British rites published by Edmond Martène. Like the Romano-Germanic pontifical, these generally fleshed out the sketchy rite of the Gelasian sacramentaries with elaborate instructions. A tenth-century Cornish pontifical begins with a long rubric that seems to describe the penance that every Christian must come to perform, "Quotiescumque Christiani ad poenitentiam accedunt, jejunia damus" ("However often Christians assent to penitence, we give fasts"), and it explicitly refers to the redemptions of so many shillings for weeks of fasting known to us from the penitential tariffs. But then it continues directly with the Ash Wednesday prayers of the Gelasian Sacramentary, labeled "Ratio ad dandam penitentiam" ("The manner of giving penitence"), and an instruction to expel the sinners guilty of serious crimes. The Maundy Thursday reconciliation with its absolutions follows, without the Romano-Germanic pontifical's characteristic Maundy Thursday *Venite*.[52] In short, as in the Rhenish rite, it moves seamlessly from the penance of the many to the stricter penance of the few. Public pen-

---

50. Note how Regino similarly indicates that the examination of the penitents takes place outside the church; it would have been an inevitably public business: *Libri duo de synodalibus causis et disciplinis ecclesiasticis*, pp. 136–137.

51. At least so thought later liturgists, who consistently used them for solemn penitents. Their use of the singular (e.g. "Praeveniat hunc famulum tuum, quaesumus, domine, misericordia tua") is compatible with either interpretation.

52. Martène, *De antiquis ecclesiae ritibus libri*, I.6.7.2, vol. I, cols. 768–774; Martimort has identified this as Rouen BM A 27, a tenth-century pontifical of Saint Germans, Cornwall. Though it does not yet borrow the PRG's *Venite* (see below), it does have several important prayers in the form in which they appear in the PRG rather than the Gelasian. It may be based on an intermediate stage between the two. Somewhat similar is a more or less contemporary rite from Fleury, edited by Martène, I.6.7.5, vol. I, cols. 785–789, according to Martimort, from Florence, Bibl. Med. Laur. Libri 82. It describes tariffed penance (with the tariffs actually included) but adds that in very grave cases—*causas criminales*—certain collects are to be said *super caput*, referring, perhaps, to an imposition of hands. Again, some sort of public penance is described as an option to replace more ordinary penance.

ance is not a separate *ordo* but a simple variation on the single rite of penance.[53]

To take another example, a late-ninth-century rite from Saint-Gatien, Tours, is labeled *Ordo privatae seu annualis poenitentiae*; and it begins with a prologue similar in wording to the Romano-Germanic pontifical. Although it seems to be a monastic manuscript, this is a rite for lay penance. Priests are to warn that those who by custom confess to them ("eos qui sibi confiteri solent") should appear on Ash Wednesday for the assignment of a penance to be observed during Lent. Then follows the interrogatory creed and confession and a large selection of prayers, including ones from both sides of Vogel's divide in the Romano-Germanic pontifical. The rubric mentions the necessity of reconciliation, but no such rite is included; there is not even an expulsion.[54] Yet this is not quite private penance in the narrow sense. It is bound, like public penance, to the cycle of Lent, and it has adopted the prayers of the Gelasian public penance. Finally, Martène has published a slightly later manuscript also from Saint-Gatien, Tours, probably intended mainly for the monks themselves. After the interrogatory creed, it includes a general confession of all possible sins exactly like the one in the Romano-Germanic pontifical. There is again no expulsion, since this is for monks, but the rite then borrows the prayers and imposition of hands from the Gelasian sacramentaries.[55]

These rites help us to understand the evolution of the liturgy between the Gelasian sacramentaries and the Romano-Germanic pontifical. In fact, textual similarities suggest that several such rites were sources or based on sources for the compilers in the Rhineland. The key to understanding all of them is to remember that private and public Lenten rites were not as clearly differentiated in the tenth century as they would later come to be. Instead of two separate *ordines*, we find a single combined rite in each of these ninth- and tenth-century pontificals and sacramentaries.[56] Some of these, like the

---

53. Cf. also Jungmann, *Die lateinischen Bussriten*, pp. 267–269, on several early Carolingian rites of penance, in which confessing penitents are assigned highly public or less public penances depending on circumstances.

54. Martène, *De antiquis ecclesiae ritibus libri*, I.6.7.4, vol. I, cols. 782–784. Martimort has identified the sources as BN n.a.l. 1589, from Tours near the end of the ninth century, and Tours BM 184, from ninth-century Tours.

55. Martène, *De antiquis ecclesiae ritibus libri*, I.6.7.3, vol. I, cols. 774–781. Is it for monks? Although it is labeled *Ordo qualiter confiteri debet homo reatum suum*, the confession begins with sins "against the holy rule," and especially refers to sins of impurity while saying mass, etc. Martimort identifies its source as BN latin 9430, from early-tenth-century Tours.

56. They do sometimes have a separate rite for deathbed penance: cf. PRG CXLIV–CXLV, vol. II, pp. 270–277. And the PRG also has a non-Lenten rite of private, tariff-type penance, CXXXVI, vol. II, pp. 234–245.

Lenten rite in the Romano-Germanic pontifical, come to a clear climax with the expulsion of public penitents; others treat public penance as a variation from penance for less serious crimes; still others are mainly adapted for the ordinary penitent, but borrow much of the ritual of public penance. I suspect that the compilers of the Romano-Germanic pontifical hoped that everyone would show up for an Ash Wednesday confession; they certainly hoped that everyone would watch the public penance. But they quickly focused the rite on the serious sinners. It may not even have been entirely predetermined before Ash Wednesday who would do public penance, as in later centuries. Many sinners would show up; all would be assigned satisfactions, and those who were guilty of scandalous crimes would be publicly expelled. The same canons concerning years of fasting applied whether or not the penance was public.[57] In the end, the liturgy confirms our conclusions about the pre-Scholastic theology of penance. "Solemn public penance" is the paradoxical invention of the twelfth-century program of teaching universal contrition and universal private confession. The tenth-century compilers of the Romano-Germanic pontifical thought nothing odd about filling out Regino's outline with bits and pieces from late Carolingian rites for ordinary penitents, including a creed and a confession. It is only a post-Scholastic way of thinking that places tariffs and the expulsion of penitents into two entirely separate categories.

Fortunately, Maundy Thursday observances are more straightforward.[58] Whatever the Ash Wednesday rite may have said about all Christians showing up for reconciliation at the end of Lent, it is forgotten a few folios later. This is the reconciliation of recognized penitents—the word public is still not used—who have been doing their penance in some appointed place. They must present themselves at the cathedral, where the archdeacon will petition the bishop on their behalf, "Adest, o venerabilis pontifex, tempus acceptum" (cf. 2 Cor. 6:2). The bishop responds that he too is a sinner, "Iniquitates meas ego cognosco." And after the archdeacon once more petitions the bishop for the penitents, the bishop calls them to come in, "Venite." This was the compilers' most significant piece of composition, a revised, more dramatic version of the old imposition of hands. Each time he calls, the penitents kneel, then rise, then come forward a bit. The penitents are passed by hand (manuatim) from their priests to the archdeacon, then from the archdeacon to the bishop. At last introduced into the church, the bishop pronounces a number of prayers

57. Cf. Morin, Commentarius historicus, VII.21, pp. 491–492.
58. PRG XCIX.224–251, pp. 58–67.

for forgiveness. Several deprecative absolutions follow, labeled in a
as "plural," in case there is more than one penitent, and "sin   ."
for just one. The rite closes with an aspersion of specially l d
water, thurification, and a warning to the penitents not to ret   o
their sins.[59] This elegant formulation, with its dramatically r-
lined introduction of the penitents into the church, withstood r
experimentation much more than the more awkward and conl 5
Ash Wednesday rites.

Yet the rite must be understood as a whole, expulsion and reconciliation as two acts in the same drama. As we saw, the expulsion on
Ash Wednesday hardly made clear a separation between the public
penitent and Christians who come to contrition at Lent. Still more
oddly, the confession proposed in the rite listed every crime imagin-
able. It was as if on Ash Wednesday all sins ever committed by anyone
would be openly declared, repented, and expiated. Perhaps that is
precisely the meaning. The individuality of the public penitent is lost,
and he is a representative for the whole church. Only a few sinners
may actually be expelled, but their expulsion from the church is a
type of everyman's, of *omnes Christiani*, of Adam's expulsion from
Paradise. In the Maundy Thursday drama of reconciliation that follows, the exchange between the archdeacon speaking for the penitents and the bishop speaking for the church reiterates the common
experience of all. "Peccavi, impie egi" ("I have sinned; I have acted
impiously"), begins the archdeacon. "Averte faciem tuam a peccatis
meis" ("Turn your face from my sins"), replies the bishop (XCIX:225–
226). Two sides confront each other. First bishop and archdeacon play
the parts of church and sinner, then new *dramatis personae* appear as
two deacons speak for bishop and penitent. The bishop (and his deacon), representing the church, freely confesses his own sin and offers
forgiveness, but at the same time is a stern master, making the penitents stop and kneel three times on the way to reconciliation.

The Christian faithful as such take no direct part in these Ash
Wednesday and Maundy Thursday rites. They have no lines to say, no
town processions to join. Their nonparticipation here stands in contrast with their important role in the other rites of collective expiation
discussed in Chapter 5 and, for that matter, with their role in the
contemporary Mozarabic liturgy for Good Friday, in which the whole

---

59. PRG XCIX.251, vol. II, p. 67. The blessing for the water used appears separately, PRG
CVI, vol. II, p. 154. Like other contemporary exorcisms of water, it prays for the dispersion
of unclean spirits, "ut . . . omnis spiritus inmundus locum illic ulterius non habeat." I have
not found such a blessing or use of water in any other French or Roman rite of public
penance.

people joined the public penitents and the clergy in a cry of *indulgentia* (pardon) for the penitents and for the church alike.[60] Nevertheless, the Roman rite of solemn penance was not merely disciplinary,[61] nor was the role of the audience as insignificant as it may at first seem. Most obviously, the prayers of gathered Christians aid the efforts of the individual sinners. At the same time, the community as a whole benefits. A notion of the purification of the whole through the expulsion of the sinning few is clearly at work here.[62] Like the Mozarabic Good Friday rite, the Ash Wednesday and Maundy Thursday rites in the early Roman tradition were the popular climaxes of Lent. There were as yet no ashes for all on Wednesday or indulgences for all on Thursday to hold their attention. Lent exacted sacrifice from all and promised expiation for all, but the Roman rite focused liturgical attention on a representative few, the scapegoat penitents and the shepherd bishop, himself a sinner, too.

Public penitents were only symbolic scapegoats in a play, and their expulsion from Christian society only ritual and temporary. The dramatic expulsion and reintroduction of penitents was the most important feature of the Western ritual of public penance, underlined but not invented by the Romano-Germanic pontifical. The expulsion clearly denoted the quasi excommunication of the sinner, whose crimes had already threatened his initiation into the body of Christ.[63] Serious sins inevitably and invisibly expel the sinner from the true church into the unsanctified world from which he had come. The ritual expulsion, while visibly mirroring the sinner's fall and the Fall of Adam, simultaneously reversed the sinner's self-expulsion. The sinner now penitent ritually left the church not to return to the profane world from which he came, but to occupy instead a special sacred status, analogous to that of monks or the clergy. Neither inside nor outside the church, the profaned penitent paradoxically borrowed the tokens of sanctity. The *ordo* of penitents were bound by many of the same restrictions as monks, such as celibacy and the prohibition of military service; their regimes of fasting only extended monastic and clerical rules. Unlike the tonsured clergy, however, penitents were

---

60. Marius Férotin, *Le liber ordinum en usage dans l'église wisigothique et mozarabe d'Espagne du cinquième au onzième siècle*, Monumenta Ecclesiae Liturgica, 5 (Paris, 1904), I.84, pp. 193–204, esp. p. 202; Gy, "Histoire liturgique du Sacrement de pénitence," p. 12.

61. Cf. Wolfgang Lentzen-Deis, *Busse als Bekenntnisvollzug*, Freiburger Theologische Studien, 86 (Freiburg, 1969), pp. 24–25.

62. Cf. Michel Rubellin, "Vision de la société chrétienne à travers la confession et la pénitence au IXe siècle," in *Pratiques de la confession*, p. 63.

63. Cf. Arnold van Gennep, *The Rites of Passage*, trans. M. B. Vizedom and G. L. Caffee (Chicago, 1960; first published 1908), pp. 94n, 96, 168n.

forbidden to shave. Hair was an ambiguous sign; both tonsure and unshorn hair and beards were commonly taken as signs of special holiness.[64] The pattern is the same one discussed in chapter 5; like the Christian people as a whole at Rogations, the public penitents proclaimed their sinfulness and adopted, if in a muted form, the signs of holiness and promised salvation. As with the Carnival that looked forward to Lent, and the Lent that looked forward to Easter, the penitents' suffering was only temporary and limited, their ritual expulsion a real reconciliation. For the populace who watched, the expulsion of sinners promised divine judgment on earth; for the sinners themselves, it promised forgiveness. Even here, even among the sinners who had shocked the conscience of the city, expiation and suffering concealed rejoicing.

Twelfth- and Thirteenth-Century Roman Pontificals

The Romano-Germanic pontifical immediately found a wide audience, especially north of the Alps. It survives in a great number of copies from Rhineland dioceses, as one would expect. Most important for our interests, it was the basis for all northern French pontificals in the twelfth century.[65] But the Roman liturgy itself followed a different path. The *Pontificale Romanum Saeculi XII* was based on the Roman copies of the Rhenish model, but we find ourselves in a new world. Its compilers omitted virtually the entire Ash Wednesday rite, except for the benediction and imposition of ashes at Saint Anastasia.[66] In a marked departure from the Romano-Germanic pontifical, the pope or priest now evidently distributed ashes to everyone, male and female: "Interim ponit romanus pontifex vel sacerdos cineres super capita virorum ac mulierum."[67] This was to be a crucial change; the distribution of ashes to all reveals the diminishing significance of the rite of expulsion for a few. Whereas in the tenth-century rite the Christian community as a whole benefited from the public penance of individuals, here, a new rite was provided for each lay Christian, and

64. Cf. a remark in the *Chroniques de Saint Denis* about the leader of the Pastoureaux: "Et vint devant eus atout une grant barbe, aussi comme se il fust homme de penitance," HF 21:115.
65. Vogel, "Le pontifical romano-germanique," p. 42; cf. his introduction to the PRG, pp. 44–55.
66. PRS XXVIII, pp. 209–210. Unlike the PRG, the PRS really is a papal rite, adapted thoroughly to the needs of the curia.
67. PRC XXVII.5, p. 209.

this distribution of ashes, not public penance, became the main focus of the day for laymen. The arrival of the distribution to the whole faithful is surprisingly hard to date, especially, in the French pontificals. As for Roman practice, in a council at Benevento in 1091, Pope Urban II had decreed that all Christians should receive ashes at the beginning of Lent; until then it had been reserved for penitents, the clergy, and those voluntary penitents, monks.[68] At least in Rome this usage quickly caught hold, since it appears in the twelfth-century rite. After the ashes followed a prayer for Christians as they entered upon their fast, then a long procession through the city accompanied by antiphons and litanies, which led to a mass at Saint Sabina on the Aventine. This looks very like the modern rite, devoid of scapegoats and drama. Whether the northern import of the expulsion of penitents had ever grown roots in the Roman liturgy is doubtful.[69]

Maundy Thursday is a puzzling matter, however. Three distinct *ordines* survive, of which the first two, XXX A and XXX B, are copied sequentially in a recension surviving in Rhenish manuscripts; the third, XXX C, exists in a second, thoroughly Roman recension.[70] Briefly, XXX A reproduces the rite of the Romano-Germanic pontifical, including the benediction of oils and the reception of penitents.[71] XXX B is a shortened version of the benediction of oils alone, with some alterations. This represents a more conservative adaptation of the tradition. The more fully Roman version XXX C made more substantial changes. It includes the benediction of oils in some detail, but only a short note that on this day penitents are to be relieved with forgiveness, and that they should present themselves at the church "at

---

68. Martène, *De antiquis ecclesiae ritibus libri*, IV.17, vol. III, col. 160. R. Rusconi, "De la prédication à la confession," p. 68, has stated that the new practice spread throughout Europe in the eleventh century, but he offers no proof.

69. Gy, "Histoire liturgique du Sacrement de Pénitence," p. 16, thinks that neither expulsion nor reception was ever really practiced in Rome, though both appear in Roman copies of the PRG, and the latter in copies of the PRS (see below). In the absence of corroborating evidence, it is impossible to say for sure. For the rapid demise of public penance at Rome, see also Jungmann, *Die lateinischen Bussriten*, pp. 68–69.

70. PRS XXXA–XXXC, pp. 214–234. The second recension exists in a seventeenth-century copy of a pontifical from the crusader states, which probably received its liturgy from the papal legate. The first recension is in a manuscript most likely from Mainz.

71. Actually, the portion of the PRG copied in XXX A is really two *ordines*, not one. The first *ordo* (XXX A.1–26, pp. 214–219, cf. PRG XCIX.222–251, vol. 2, pp. 59–67) instructs the priests to prepare for the consecration of oils; has the bells rung at terce, so that all will come to the church "where the chrism will be consecrated"; then describes the reconciliation of penitents. The second *ordo* (XXX A.27–62, pp. 219–226, cf. PRG XCIX.252, vol. 2, p. 67) has the bells rung for mass and the other hours, then instructs the priests to receive the "bishop" in procession at terce, then proceeds to the consecration of the oils. This awkward division of the day's labors is in the PRG as well. Evidently, the reconciliation of the penitents was to take place just after terce (roughly 9:00 A.M.), to be followed by the consecration of the oils.

terce or sext."[72] It seems likely that the compilers of the XXX C recension respected the authority of their source, but had little use for the reception of penitents and schemed at least to demote it, if not to expunge it altogether. In effect, one version of the pontifical (XXX A and B) tried copying the Thursday *ordo* with it and immediately providing another *ordo* without it, and the other (XXX C) gave it three sentences and moved on. Well before 1215, solemn penance was fading at Rome; it did not take an annual requirement of private penance to make the public rite obsolete there.

The twelfth-century Roman pontifical was not an official production of the curia, but a reworking of the tenth-century source in the light of local tastes, just like contemporary French pontificals compiled for each diocese. There were a number of versions, and none of them experienced a very wide diffusion. The first official papal production, the Pontifical of the Roman Curia, quickly gained ground against them.[73] Its first recension dates probably from Innocent III's pontificate, that is, right under the shadow of *Omnis utriusque*; a later longer version was compiled around midcentury.[74] In general, the compilers paid little attention to solemn penance. All the manuscripts of the early version and almost all of the others do not possess any sort of rite for Ash Wednesday, and so we cannot tell whether all the people received ashes. Curiously, a few manuscripts of the later recension revive part of the old instructions for Ash Wednesday solemn penance from Regino of Prüm, under the rubric "Ordo penitentium: In capite quadragesime omnes penitentes, qui publicam susceperunt penitentiam, ante fores ecclesie se representant episcopo." The compilers abbreviate Regino's text, instructing the bishop to introduce the penitents into the church, put ashes on their heads, and expel them from church. They add a new detail: the ejected penitents carry lighted candles as they walk out of the church. And finally, the rite adds, again following Regino, on Maundy Thursday the penitents are

---

72. PRS XXX C, pp. 228–234: "Hac die etiam poenitentibus per indulgentiam subvenitur. . . . Hora tertia vel sexta sonetur compana, ut veniant omnes ad ecclesiam, in qua debet chrisma consecrari. Tunc egrediantur poenitentes de loco in quo poenitentiam suo, ut gremio ecclesiae praesentatur a pontifice, qui sedere debet prae foribus ecclesiae. Et praesentet eos cum antiphonis et orationibus." And that is all it says about penitents. The compiler may have been confused by the PRG's ambiguity over times (see note 71 above), or may not have cared much where to place a rite that seemed insignificant.

73. Vogel, "Le pontifical romano-germanique," pp. 46–47.

74. Vogel, *Introduction aux sources*, pp. 206–207; PRC, introduction of Andrieu, pp. 229–309. There was also a mixed recension, whose manuscripts were based on the short version, but which added certain features found in the longer, more complete version. Surprisingly, both the early and the mixed versions continued to be copied even after the compilation of the new one.

to be reintroduced to the church.[75] As a whole, it is but a sketch of the ritual elaborated in Regino and made familiar by Gratian.[76] Significantly, the presiding prelate is called *episcopus*, though this is a curial pontifical, adapted throughout to the needs of papal ceremony at Rome. It may well be that the rite in this later version of the pontifical is an antiquarian effort, based primarily on canonical sources, not on either of the older pontificals in use at Rome.

Manuscripts of all recensions copy the Maundy Thursday rite XXX C from the twelfth-century Roman pontifical, a rite that first mentions that the penitents are to be forgiven (*per indulgentiam subvenitur*), and later very briefly notes that they should appear after terce or sext for reconciliation.[77] One change is significant for the future. The rite adds that after sext, the pope should go to the palace, and standing high above, should preach a sermon to the people. Then, according to the mid-thirteenth-century recension, "The sentences are read out and then, after confession by the cardinal deacon and absolution by the pope, indulgence is given to the people."[78] In other words, sentences of excommunication should be pronounced, and the cardinal deacon should lead the people in some kind of general confession, or at least say it on their behalf. Then the pope pronounces absolution and an indulgence.[79] This popular rite in effect filled the vacuum left by the decline of solemn penance and provided a fitting coda to Lenten self-sacrifice. Instead of the scapegoating of the solemn penitent, we find the united participation of the whole Christian people, just as in Ash Wednesday the ashes are now distributed to all, not merely to the sinning few. The French evolution was different. North

75. PRC Appendix III, pp. 578–579.

76. Regino of Prüm, *Libri duo de synodalibus causis et disciplinis ecclesiasticis*, pp. 136–137; Gratian, *Decretum*, D.50 c.64, col. 201.

77. PRC XLII.1–3, p. 455. Most of the manuscripts note that the antiphons and *orationes* to be used in the reconciliation may be found later in the book, in the "Ordo ad reconciliandum penitentem" (= PRC XLVII, pp. 484–486). This is a rite for absolution in private, probably used most often at the sinner's deathbed, since it appears in the PRC just before the "Ordo ad visitandum infirmum," and a rite of extreme unction. The *orationes* it provides are similar to those of the PRG's rites for penance of the sick, and have nothing in common with the traditional prayers of solemn penance. They ask for the restoration of health and do not refer to any separation from the church. The compilers clearly borrowed these prayers for Maundy Thursday because they had no idea what their source (the PRS) meant when it called for prayers here.

78. PRC XLII.4, p. 456: "recitantur sentencie et, facta confessione per dyaconum cardinalem et absolutione per papam, datur populo indulgentia." It also appears in a couple of the manuscripts of the early recension.

79. I have translated *indulgentia* as indulgence here, where it is clearly used in the new, technical sense. When the solemn penitents are said above, PRC XLII.1, to be "per indulgentiam subvenitur," the compilers have borrowed the vague language of the twelfth-century pontificals, and mean simply "forgiveness."

of the Loire, solemn penance would survive intact through the thirteenth century and beyond. Eventually, in late medieval France, from the end of the fourteenth century to the Counter-Reformation, liturgical general confession became attached to Lent and especially to Maundy Thursday, and the episcopal absolution and the indulgence that followed became the main attraction of the day for the people who attended, without, however, ever entirely supplanting the rite of public penance. But in Rome, public penance died young, and the collective penitential rites simply took over. When Pope Clement V moved to Avignon in 1309, he brought the curial pontifical with him, and so its influence spread to southern France, formerly home to a native tradition based on the Romano-Germanic pontifical.[80]

The last of the medieval pontificals of the Roman tradition was the work of a single individual, Guillaume Durand, and unlike its predecessor composed by a committee, it was not commissioned by any pope. As his *Rationale* shows, Durand commanded a profound knowledge of earlier liturgists, and his pontifical, completed by 1296, was equally the result of considerable scholarship. Faced with so many alternatives from the sources before him—the Romano-Germanic pontifical, the twelfth- and thirteenth-century curial pontificals, and even Spanish books—Durand tried to include as much as possible.[81] Thus, his rite of solemn penance was the most complete version intended for Roman use since the tenth century. Under careful examination, however, one finds that Durand's superficial traditionalism conceals the abandonment of the old scapegoating rite. On Ash Wednesday, the penitents appear to be "solemnly expelled" around the third hour (about 9:00 A.M.); it is significantly the first time that the rite is called "solemn." As in theology, so in liturgy, the term's appearance indicates a conscious effort to distinguish among types of penance. The names of the penitents are written down, and their satisfactions are assigned by the bishop's penitentiary. Meanwhile, the

---

80. For the transmission of the PRG, see Vogel, "Le pontifical romano-germanique," p. 52; for the southern French tradition, see below, Chapter 7.

81. On the date and sources of the PGD, see Ludwig Fischer, "Der 'Ordinarius Papae' und der 'Pontificalis Ordinis Liber' des Wilhelm Duranti des Älteren," *Römische Quartalschrift* 18 (1930): 15–21. Fischer hypothesizes a "Stadt-Römische Sammlung" as PGD's source for some of the Holy Week liturgy and benedictions—but not the Ash Wednesday rite, which evidently did not appear in this source. As R. Cabie points out, "Le pontifical de Guillaume Durand l'ancien et les livres liturgiques languedociens," *Liturgie et musique (IXe–XIVe siècles)*, Cahiers de Fanjeaux, 17 (Toulouse, 1982), pp. 229, 235, we know very little about PGD's sources beyond the well-known Roman pontificals; he has traced one of his Ash Wednesday prayers (PGD III. I. 7, p. 553) to a pontifical of Braga. It may be that some of PGD's novel arrangements, if not the prayers, are Durand's own invention; see Vogel, *Introduction aux sources*, p. 210.

bishop blesses the ashes. Then each archpriest in turn calls by name the penitents of his archpresbytery (roughly equivalent to the northern rural deaneries); they come into the church holding burning candles and prostrate themselves on the ground, taking care, no doubt, not to set fire to anything.[82] The archpriest or bishop places ashes on each, and then follow various antiphons, psalms, litanies, short *preces*, and *orationes* said "pro illorum absolutione." No actual absolution follows; instead the penitents are expelled, still holding their candles, with a warning to spend Lent in fasts, prayers, pilgrimages, alms, and other good works. And, "these things accomplished, the bishop should prepare himself for mass around the ninth hour," at which time, it seems, the whole clergy and people receive ashes from the hands of a priest.[83] As a whole, this rite was not one of Guillaume Durand's more successful compositions. Besides the awkwardness with the candles, he evidently expected people to appear to watch the expulsion early in the morning, then wait around or leave and return to the cathedral four or five hours later. By separating the rites, he made it unlikely that much of an audience would appear for the expulsion. In spite of his antiquarian efforts, the rite of solemn penance remained as marginalized as in the late Roman pontificals.

On Maundy Thursday, in a reversal of the ordinary pattern, Durand set the reconciliation of penitents *after* an early morning *mandatum*, the washing of the feet of the poor.[84] He prefaced the rite with traditional but obsolete descriptions of penance from Popes Innocent I and Vigilius, texts that also appear in his *Rationale*.[85] Durand then noted that some churches have a mass said at an altar near the doors of the church, where the penitents are standing ready, and he provided the texts as an option.[86] After the mass, priests hear the confes-

---

82. Cf. the long recension of the PRC, Appendix III.1, p. 578, where penitents leave with burning candles. Durand supplied his rubric to explain how the penitents got them, but his solution is extremely awkward. Some French pontificals more sensibly have the penitents leave with extinguished candles or lamps, symbolic of their expulsion from the church: cf. BN latin 962, f. 199r (Sens, middle or second half of the fourteenth century); and Besançon BM 138, illustration on f. 117r (Beauvais, second half or end of the thirteenth century). It is typical of the weakening of the expulsion in the late Roman texts that they have the penitents leave like baptized Christians with candles lit, not like excommunicants, with candles extinguished.

83. PGD III.1, pp. 552–557.

84. PGD III.2.1–7, pp. 557–559.

85. Guillaume Durand, *Rationale divinorum officiorum*, VI.73, f. 220v; they appear as well in a southern French monastic ordinal: BN latin 1341, f. 26r-v (diocese of Limoges, end of twelfth or beginning of thirteenth century). Innocent stated that penitents, whether they have committed very serious or minor crimes should appear Maundy Thursday for reconciliation; the text predates private penance. Vigilius referred to the imposition of hands, not used in penance since the Carolingians.

86. PGD III.2.8, pp. 559–560. It is just possible that the note, "Sane in quibusdam ecclesiis," applies to more than just that mass that follows immediately, and that Durand is describing all or much of the reconciliation as a local option.

sions of the penitents and question those who observed their penances; they must note down the penitents' names, the terms of their satisfactions, and the particulars of their cases.[87] As the noon hour approaches, the bishop then should discuss with the priests whether the penitents are worthy to be reconciled. Evidently Durand was unhappy with the vagueness of the early texts, which assumed that every one should receive at least this reconciliation. The mechanism he provided implicitly compared public penance to the external forum: these were *causae*, the investigation an *inquisitio*. Such language would be unthinkable in the early rites, and is unknown even in contemporary texts from northern France.

The reconciliation proper followed. A note late in the rite reminds us that the people were supposed to attend, but Durand omits any mention of gathering them with bells.[88] The rite was similar in general outline to the rite of the Romano-Germanic pontifical, with the presentation to the bishop followed by the *Venite*, the actual introduction into the cathedral, and *orationes*. The absolution remained in the traditional deprecative form.[89] In places, the Thursday rite was even more elaborate than its tenth-century source, and Durand could not resist a somewhat complicated choreography with candles.[90] A typically late-thirteenth-century addition was the optional indulgence for the penitents at the end; unlike the contemporary curial pontificals, Durand's version says nothing about popular indulgences.[91] Significant, too, was a change hidden in the selection of *orationes* and in the details of the introduction of the penitents. We may recall the confession that the Romano-Germanic pontifical had the bishop utter in response to the archdeacon's presentation of the penitents, "Iniquitates meas ego cognosco, et delictum meum contra me est semper."[92] Guillaume Durand transfers these words to a much later section, breaks them into versicles and responses, and assigns them not to the bishop, but to the archpriest and the choir, evidently representing the

87. PGD III.2.9, p. 560: "Et notata fideliter habeant nomina et annos penitentie, ac delicta et circumstantias singulorum, ut sic, cum hora requisitionis advenerit, quid de singulis pontificalis censeat auctoritas clarescat et universorum causas et liberius et expeditius decenere possit."
88. PGD III.2.32, p. 565: "et clerus et populus ad terram prosternuntur."
89. PGD III.2.11–41, pp. 560–568. For the late survival of deprecatory absolutions, see Gy, "Les définitions de la confession aprés le quatrième concile du Latran," in *L'aveu: Antiquité et Moyen-Age*, Collection de l'Ecole française de Rome, 88 (Rome, 1986), pp. 288–290.
90. PGD III.2.12–18, pp. 560–561. The penitents hold unlit candles when they arrive at the door; two subdeacons come toward them with candles lit, say an antiphon, extinguish their candles, and return to the altar. Then the eldest deacon approaches them again with a lit candle and lights theirs before returning to the altar. Then the penitents are presented to the bishop, "Adest, o venerabilis," as in the PRG. We never hear what the penitents do with the lit candles when they come into the church and prostrate themselves at the foot of the bishop.
91. PGD III.2.42, p. 569.
92. PRG XCIX.226C, vol. I, p. 60.

penitents themselves, or more generally all Christians.[93] The penitents are no longer passed to the altar, as it were, from the hands of the priests to the archdeacon, and from the archdeacon to the bishop; instead they present themselves directly to the bishop, who receives each in his hands.[94]

Durand's version has diffused the energy of the original. No longer does the bishop declare his own sin before reconciling the sinners before him; no longer does he represent the Christian people as sinners and saved. The bishop still receives the penitents, but the new gesture is tepid. The penitents present themselves to the bishop just as excommunicants in the external forum would; the gradual reintroduction symbolized in the tenth-century rite is obscured. The rite as a whole is more appropriate for the correction of a few misbehaving sinners than for the ritual cleansing of the community.

This peculiar rite spread to southern France with Guillaume Durand's pontifical, where it rivaled the popularity of the thirteenth-century curial version under the papacy at Avignon. When Guillaume Durand's pontifical became the basis for the first printed pontifical in 1485, itself the source of modern Roman pontificals, Durand's version of solemn penance came to be reprinted, if not practiced, into the twentieth century.[95] Such indisputable antiquarianism has perhaps inclined historians to think that all rites of solemn penance in post-twelfth-century texts are suspect. The sequence in France, however, was nothing like that in Rome. Whereas in pontificals based on the Roman tradition, solemn penance had obviously withered only to be revived later as a curiosity by Guillaume Durand, in the north, the rite evolved but survived. North of the Loire, the new collective penitential rites for the ordinary faithful supplemented rather than supplanted the old individual public penance. North of the Loire, the liturgists rewrote the old ritual instead of embalming it.

---

93. PGD III.2. 27, p. 564.

94. PGD III.2.27, p. 564: "pontifex accipit unum ex illis per manum, omnibus aliis se similiter ad manus tenentibus."

95. Marc Dykmans, *Le pontifical romain révisé au XVe siècle*, Studi e Testi, 311 (Vatican City, 1985), pp. 149–157; Gy, "Histoire liturgique du sacrement de pénitence," p. 16; Vogel, "Le pontifical romano-germanique," pp. 48, 54, and "Les rites de la pénitence publique," p. 144.

CHAPTER SEVEN

The Transformation of Public Penance in Northern French Pontificals, ca. 1150–1350

The story of public penance at Rome is one of limited initial acceptance followed by rapid disappearance. By contrast, only a cursory glance at northern French pontificals through the fourteenth century suffices to establish the survival of the rite in that region. The review here will not be cursory, however, because there is a more important lesson to be learned from this vast wealth of material. Public penance indeed survived, but a rapid transformation took place in its ritual, a transformation indicative of a new role for the public penitents and a new role for the public.

This review proceeds in fifty-year sections, primarily because often that is all the precision that may be applied to the dating of the manuscripts. There are thirty-eight such pontificals datable between 1150 and 1350 that unambiguously contain rites of public penance. In addition, fifteen ordinals and processionals mention public penitents. Among the pontificals, there are only four pairs of identical rites, plus two more pairs where a corrector has altered a rite previously identical to that in an earlier pontifical.[1] These liturgical manuscripts are the only real evidence for the evolution of penitential ritual; even the liturgical commentaries are usually too vague to be of much use.[2] While the sheer variety of rites renders impossible a full

---

1. The pairs of duplicate rites are: BN latin 953 and Brussels BR II.1013; BN latin 945 and Rouen 370; Châlons-sur-Marne BM 45 and Reims BM 344; and BL Egerton 931 and BN latin 962. In addition, Orléans BM 144 has the same rite as BN latin 945, and Abbeville BM 8 the same as Amiens BM 196, but correcting hands soon after their composition altered the rites.

2. The early liturgical commentators mostly mention the expulsion and reconciliation without attempting any description: Jean Beleth, *Summa de ecclesiasticis officiis*, c. 89 and 95, pp. 159 and 167; Sicard of Cremona, *Mitrale*, VI.4 and VI.12, PL 213:255, 302; Praepositinus of Cremona, *Tractatus de officiis*, I.170, p. 99. Beleth also mentions confessions in church followed by *iudicia*; this would have been the confessions of public penitents and other serious sinners, perhaps like that described in the PRG. For Guillaume Durand and Gilbert de Tournai, see below.

genealogy of pontificals or rites, it is useful to discuss briefly each of these rites of penance and, where possible, to compare each rite to earlier and later ones of the same family or diocese.

Amidst all this variety, two key themes quickly emerge, themes first suggested in my account of Roman rites but most striking here. First, the nature and placement of absolutions in the rite changes rapidly. The new theology of the keys would imply the need for absolution even before the completion of satisfaction; but we will see that liturgical developments did not always follow the lead of the theology. Second, and less obviously, the later pontificals indicate new roles for public penitents and their audience. This change manifested itself in a variety of ways, including both new rituals for the public as a whole and alterations in the ritual for the penitents. This second change allows us to consider the relation between the collective penances described in Chapter 5 and individual public penance.

Northern French Pontificals, ca. 1150–ca. 1200

Northern French pontificals of the tenth and eleventh century are very rare, and in any case, they are discussed only insofar as they set the stage for later developments.[3] Virtually all northern French pontificals from the twelfth century onward borrowed the framework of the rite of public penance from the Romano-Germanic pontifical, modified by continuing Gelasian influence in the text of the prayers. Northern French rites up to the tenth century or so had been faithful to Gelasian simplicity or had combined the Gelasian's prayers with a few more instructions about confession.[4] We may conclude that the Rhenish pontifical's rite of public penance probably arrived in France in the eleventh century, and it first had an impact on eastern dioceses: Reims and Châlons-sur-Marne. Two pontificals of Reims from the tenth and the eleventh centuries illustrate the change: The first has a rite based on the Gelasian, and the second provides a rite based on the Romano-Germanic pontifical alongside what is presumably the old rite, effaced by a corrector. Furthermore, an eleventh-century pon-

---

3. Leroquais, *Les pontificaux manuscrits*, vol. I, pp. xxv lists four, including two eleventh-century pontificals of Nevers and Châlons-sur-Marne, and tenth- and eleventh-century pontificals of Reims; Martène had access to a few more. Before the twelfth century, sacramentaries sometimes included the rite of public penance.

4. See the rites cited above in comparison with the PRG; like the PRG, they typically move seamlessly from confession to public penance, although they generally omit the expulsion.

tifical of Châlons-sur-Marne gives the new and old together.[5] Outside eastern France, a couple of Norman rites remained loyal to the old Gelasian rite,[6] but an eleventh-century rite of Beauvais already shows the new version based on the Romano-Germanic pontifical.[7] All pre-twelfth-century French rites of whatever genealogy retained certain features characteristic of the early medieval treatment of public penance: There was no absolution for the penitents on Wednesday, and there was no provision of ashes or absolutions for the whole people alongside the penitents. We shall keep an eye on these benchmarks as we turn to the late-twelfth-century rites, based primarily on the Romano-Germanic pontifical.

Although these late-twelfth-century pontificals owe so much to one source, there is too much variety to develop a simple family tree of penitential rites in the way that we can trace a genealogy of Roman pontificals from the tenth century on. Thirteen pontificals approximately datable to 1150–1200 survive from northern French dioceses. (A couple of these can only be dated to the twelfth century, without further specification.) Liturgists all over northern France by now relied on the tenth-century rite from the Rhineland; they and their successors generally ignored all later Roman pontificals. At times, the French liturgists still reached back behind the tenth-century rite to the prayers and sequence of rites found in the Gelasian sacramentaries. Some northern French pontificals, for instance, even omitted the Maundy Thursday *Venite* that was perhaps the most important contribution of the Romano-Germanic compilers or cited prayers in the forms in which they appear in the Gelasian. The most striking observation we can draw from the study of these pontificals is not their fidelity to eighth- or tenth-century sources but their experimentation with entirely new forms, experimentation begun even before the impact of the new moral theology and the Fourth Lateran Council.

5. The tenth-century MS of Reims, Reims BM 340, has been printed by Martène, *De antiquis ecclesiae ritibus libri*, I.6.7.9, vol. I, col. 797. I have not examined the other two MSS, Reims BM 341, and Troyes BM 2262, but have relied on Leroquais's descriptions, which are adequate for this purpose: *Les pontificaux manuscrits*, vol. II, pp. 277, 389–390.

6. See, for example, two eleventh-century Norman rites in one manuscript, both published by Martène, *De antiquis ecclesiae ritibus libri*, I.6.7.1, vol. I, cols. 766–768, and I.6.7.7, vol. I, cols. 791–792: The first is an Ash Wednesday and Maundy Thursday combination much like the Gelasian rite; the second, part of a more extensive Maundy Thursday service that still omits any of the characteristic features of the PRG. Cf. also a tenth-century pontifical of Reims, Martène, *De antiquis ecclesiae ritibus libri*, I.6.7.9, vol. I, col. 797. A little out of our territory, a late-eleventh-century pontifical of Saint-Pierre-de-Vierzon, the so-called "pontifical of Poitiers," provided an extremely elaborate Thursday service referring to Roman usage that nonetheless avoided any of the innovations of the PRG: Martène, *De antiquis ecclesiae ritibus libri*, IV.22, vol. III, cols. 284–303.

7. This pontifical is discussed below: Martène, *De antiquis ecclesiae ritibus libri*, I.6.7.8, vol. I, cols. 793–797.

To understand these innovations, we must look in some detail at the pontificals. Of thirteen pontificals composed between 1150 and 1200, five full and possibly one partial pontifical belong to a related group of manuscripts first prepared for dioceses in northeast France and around Paris, a group that I call for convenience' sake the north-central family.[8] Two of the complete twelfth-century pontificals in this family were prepared for the archbishop of Sens, one for the bishop of Troyes, and one for the bishop of Chartres. The partial pontifical comes from Reims; a late-twelfth- or early-thirteenth-century ordinal of the cathedral of Reims helps us fill in its gaps.[9] In addition, one monastic pontifical is also a family member, with Maundy Thursday rites clearly cousin to those from Sens and Chartres, but with no Ash Wednesday rites; I discuss it separately, along with other monastic rites.

We may digress here briefly on the ramifications of the north-central family, by far the most important group of rites of penance in this region. To help date its origins, we may turn to two rites of the tenth and eleventh centuries printed by Edmond Martène, one not belonging to the family, the second an early member. In the first, a tenth-century pontifical of Reims, there is no trace of the Romano-Germanic pontifical, no presentation of the penitents to the bishop, no *Venite*, no hand-to-hand reintroduction. There is only a series of prayers for the penitents.[10] In the second, from an eleventh-century pontifical of Beauvais, evidence of Rhenish influence is everywhere. Ash Wednesday begins with a long rubric from Regino, almost identical to the passage quoted in Chapter 6. The Maundy Thursday rite includes the *Venite*, presentation, and reintroduction, in that order, a reversal of the Romano-Germanic pontifical's order; I consider the implications of reversing the order later.[11] Aside from reordering the reconciliation of penitents in this way, this pontifical departed from Rhineland models in favoring certain prayers that appear in the tenth-century rite from Reims, and in the Gelasian sacramentaries. The north-central family of rites was thus invented at the moment of

8. Jungmann first identified the existence of such a family, *Die lateinischen Bussriten*, pp. 98–100, though without the use of manuscript sources, he was not aware of its extent and branchings, and he did not recognize the pre-twelfth-century origins of this family.

9. Reims BM 342 (Reims, second half or the end of the twelfth century) probably belongs to this group; nothing remains of its rites of solemn penance except for the benediction of ashes, fol. 66v–67r. The ordinal has been printed by Chevalier, *Sacramentaire . . . de Reims*, pp. 261–305, with the Ash Wednesday and Maundy Thursday rites on pp. 274–275, 279–280.

10. Martène, *De antiquis ecclesiae ritibus libri*, I.6.7.9, vol. I, col. 797.

11. Martène, *De antiquis ecclesiae ritibus libri*, I.6.7.8, vol. I, cols. 793–797.

fusion of the new Rhenish influence with the older Gelasian tradition; although one of its earliest exemplars is from Beauvais, it may have originated in eastern France, perhaps in Reims or Châlons-sur-Marne. We shall find that while some later pontificals not belonging to the north-central family also show Rhenish and Gelasian influence, members of the north-central family arrange these elements in characteristic and fairly consistent ways. And only members of the north-central family borrow from Regino. Thus, we may hypothesize an eleventh-century ancestral rite (or rites) combining these three influences (see the chart) that is the source for all the later branches. (The rite of Beauvais printed by Martène is probably not the ancestral rite, since a pontifical of Sens combines the three influences but is evidently independent of influence from the rite of Beauvais.)

The family survives in a number of clearly distinguishable branches, most consistently evident in variations of Maundy Thursday rites. I have chiefly used the Thursday rites to set out the different branches of the family, and a chart and a table are included here to diagram their probable relationships. Ash Wednesday rites are less helpful to establish the relationship between different branches. In twelfth-century pontificals of this family, they either are missing, as in the monastic pontificals in what I shall call the Tournai-Laon branch, or they feature a long rubric followed by a number of prayers, in all the other branches, as will be described shortly. But after 1200, this Ash Wednesday rite suffered radical transformations in the majority of pontificals of this family, and thus it is useless for distinguishing between branches. It is important to understand that the chart of the family does not pretend to identify a stemma of manuscripts or sections of manuscripts. There are far too many gaps and contaminations to offer any such conclusions. Almost all liturgists assembling rites of public penance consulted at least two other rites for the task, not necessarily belonging to the same family or branch. So the chart simply suggests relations between the branches or groups of manuscripts, and notes one example from each branch. The names of the branches are inevitably arbitrary and do not imply that the diocese named consistently had pontificals of that branch. For example, the chart indicates that the Sens branch, in fact represented by only one pontifical of that diocese, has no close relatives among the other north-central rites, while the branches of Tournai-Laon and Châlons-sur-Marne are closely related. Several of these branches, moreover, are only represented by thirteenth-century manuscripts, and so are discussed in later sections of this chapter. Setting out the different

CHART OF THE BRANCHES OF THE NORTH-CENTRAL FAMILY OF RITES

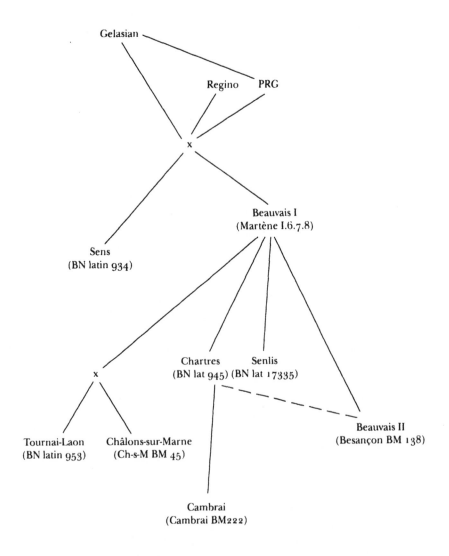

Note: The manuscripts cited are those I have taken as normative for each branch. This should not be interpreted as a putative stemma of these manuscripts; it is only a diagram to clarify probable relationships among the various groups of rites within the north-central family. See the text for further details.

Each branch is defined here by a few key features of its Maundy Thursday, or in two instances, Ash Wednesday rites, and the manuscripts of each branch are listed.

BEAUVAIS I
Martène I.6.7.8
two-part *absolutio* and *reconciliatio;* repeated *Venite.*

SENS
BN latin 934
no *Sedente* opening rite, no presentation

CHARTRES
BN latin 945
Sens BM 9
Troyes, Trésor de la cathédrale, 4
Orléans BM 144
Reims BM 342
Reims BM 343
Rouen BM 370
run-together presentation (PRG XCIX.225C–227C); repeated *Venite*

SENLIS
BN latin 17335
IRHT Coll. priv. 25
run-together presentation (PRG XCIX.225C–227C)

TOURNAI-LAON
BN latin 953
Brussels BR II.1013
Laon BM 224
Bibl. Ste-Geneviève 148
repeated *Venite;* omits Ash Wednesday rite

CHÂLONS-SUR-MARNE
Châlons-sur-Marne BM 45
Reims BM 344
repeated *Venite;* keeps Ash Wednesday rite

CAMBRAI
Cambrai BM 222
Cambrai BM 223
run-together presentation (PRG XCIX.225C–227C); repeated *Venite;* PRG XCIX.245 in long Rhenish rather than short Gelasian form

BEAUVAIS II
Besançon BM 138
two-part *absolutio* and *reconciliatio;* run-together presentation (PRG XCIX.225C–227C); PRG XCIX.245 in long Rhenish rather than short Gelasian form; repeated *Venite*

branches should make clear what is new in rites and what is simply part of the family inheritance.

With this background in mind, we may now look in some detail at the five late-twelfth-century examples of this family. One of these is printed by Martène, from BN latin 934, a pontifical of Sens, datable to the second half or the end of the twelfth century; it is the only surviving representative of what I have called the Sens branch.[12] Like the eleventh-century pontifical of Beauvais just cited, it is heavily influenced by both Regino and the Romano-Germanic pontifical as well as the Gelasian sacramentaries. Both Beauvais I, represented in this eleventh-century rite of Beauvais, and Sens (BN latin 934) depart considerably from the Romano-Germanic pontifical; Sens shared Beauvais I's Ash Wednesday rite, but its Maundy Thursday rite was significantly different. We may compare systematically the two in order to show how they represent two different branches of the family.

To begin with Wednesday, the eleventh-century Beauvais pontifical has Regino's description of the entire ritual process of public penance, including his strictures on Thursday, which are copied out in full as the prologue of the Ash Wednesday rite, "Ordo quomodo poenitentes in quadragesima episcopo debent se presentare" ("Rite by which penitents should present themselves to the bishop in Lent"). It then attaches at the end of the Wednesday rite an "absolutio poenitentium in capite jejunii" ("absolution of penitents on Ash Wednesday"), with prayers, but not absolutions, culled from both the Wednesday and the Thursday rites in the Romano-Germanic pontifical. The Sens rite was very similar (see Appendix). This two-part rite was in fact an awkward collage of an explanatory rubric from one source and prayers from another rather than a unified composition. But while its origins may have lain in antiquarian collecting, the future of this collage was to be more significant. Faced with the clumsy combination of rubric and prayers, later liturgists tried to make sense out of it, and the ways they adapted it indicate changing ideas about absolutions. For the moment, however, it is enough to note the feature in passing as a marker for this family.

For Maundy Thursday, this pontifical of Beauvais, but not the Sens rite or the other members of the north-central family, imitated the two-part Wednesday rite in another oddly bifurcated collage. Beau-

---

12 Martène, *De antiquis ecclesiae ritibus libri*, I.6.7.16, vol. I, cols. 816–818; BN latin 934, f. 63v–68v. Oaths to archbishops Pierre de Corbeil (1200–1222) and Gautier Cornut (1222–1241) added on the first three folios suggest that this pontifical was used at least into the 1220s. BN latin 934 seems to be closer than Sens BM 9 to the older model of the eastern French family, but I cannot say for sure whether it is the older pontifical.

vais I first provided something called an "Absolutio poenitentium in
Coena Domini" ("Absolution of penitents on Maundy Thursday"),
again a series of prayers, not absolutions, and then attached the so-
called *reconciliatio* of penitents proper, with the Romano-Germanic
Venite and then the presentation to the bishop, reversing the normal
order. BN latin 934 shares a similar Ash Wednesday rite with Beauvais I, but its Maundy Thursday rite was different. On Ash Wednesday, it retained the two-part division, with the so-called *absolutio poenitentium*, while on Thursday it omitted the first part of the rite, the
absolutio, and, as we shall shortly see, it both split and shortened the
Venite, omitting the presentation entirely.

The two-part Ash Wednesday rite possessed by both Beauvais I and
BN latin 934 was a distinguishing feature of eleventh- and twelfth-
century manuscripts of the whole north-central family. Among these
north-central rites, only the monastic pontificals lack it. Five twelfth-
century members of this family have it; but none of them have the
two-part rite for Thursday that appears in Beauvais I. On Ash Wednesday, all five provide Regino's summary description, and then the
seven penitential psalms and a series of *preces* and six *orationes*, which
they borrow from the Romano-Germanic pontifical's Wednesday and
Thursday rites.[13] They probably were intended to be said before the
imposition of ashes, where according to Regino's instructions, "cum
omni clero septem poenitentiae psalmos in terram prostratus cum
lacrymis pro eorum absolutione decantet" ("prostrate on the ground
and in tears, he along with all the clergy shall chant the seven penitential psalms for their absolution"). In addition, five members of the
north-central family have a separate "benediction of ashes," copied
alongside benedictions of such objects as palms, wells, and bread.[14]

A key feature of many pontificals in this family is their use of the
term *absolutio* in the two-part Wednesday service. What is an absolution? According to the compilers of the Romano-Germanic pontifical,
it was a prayer that used some form of the word *absolvere* or *absolutio*
and that invoked the power of the keys. This is what they labeled
absolutiones. These absolutions could be deprecative, using a phrase
such as "ipse te absolvat per ministerium nostrum," ("may He absolve
you through our ministry") or first-person plural indicative, "absolvimus vos" ("we absolve you"); in either case, they appear only on
Thursday.[15] Unlike the "Ego te absolvo" ("I absolve you") of the thir-

---

13. The *orationes* (with some variants) are PRG XCIX.57, 67, 237, 59, 60, 61. PRG
XCIX.57, 67, 59 also appear on Thursday as PRG XCIX.231, 236, 232.
14. BN latin 934, f. 128r-v; Sens BM 9, f. 41r; BN latin 945, f. 177v–178r; Troyes,
Trésor de la Cathédrale, 4, f. 157r-v; Reims BM 342, f. 66v–67r.
15. PRG XCIX.249; and XCIX.247, vol. II, pp. 65–66.

teenth century, these phrases characteristically appear not at the beginning but only after words recounting Christ's promise of powers of forgiveness to Peter. In the Romano-Germanic pontifical, other, more general, prayers for the penitents' forgiveness that appear in both Ash Wednesday and Maundy Thursday services were not labeled *absolutiones*. Early French usage was looser, however. We have just noted that eleventh- and twelfth-century rites of the north-central family referred to just such vague prayers of forgiveness as an *absolutio*, usually in Wednesday services, but sometimes even on Thursday. There was as yet little sense that the validity of the rite depended on the presence of an absolution in the narrow sense, much less on any particular formula.[16] The compilers of the Romano-Germanic pontifical evidently believed that an absolution in the narrower sense should properly complete the ceremony of penance, but even they put less emphasis on the words of absolution than on the actions of satisfaction and the gestures of reconciliation.

It marks a significant change when French rites first apply the label for Ash Wednesday prayers and then, as we shall see, use the absolutions themselves before the completion of satisfaction. Both the labeling and the substance are significant. The use of the label alone suggests the new idea that the penitents should be released or "absolved" before they complete their satisfaction; additionally, the use of the absolutions shows a new concern with the precise authority for that release. For the sake of clarity, I continue to refer to absolutions in the narrow sense of the Roman tradition as "true absolutions," to distinguish them from other prayers of forgiveness.[17] Eventually, French pontificals adopted the Roman usage and reserved *absolutio* for specific indicative or deprecative absolutions.

We may now return to the evolution of the Thursday rite in this family, which is a little more complex. As we have noted, most of the other twelfth-century members of the north-central family feature the characteristic two-part Ash Wednesday rite. While their Thursday rites are not doubled, they are nevertheless significantly closer to the Beauvais I text than to BN latin 934. (See chart.) They imitate only part of the Thursday collage of Beauvais I, that is, but they imitate it quite closely. BN latin 934 has a simpler, but independent, Thursday rite. We may identify a branch of Chartres, comprising Sens BM 9

16. See Poschmann, *Penance and the Anointing of the Sick*, p. 148.

17. Jungmann, *Die lateinischen Bussriten*, pp. 202–205, 241, has distinguished "sacramental" and "nonsacramental absolutions," roughly corresponding to my distinction between real absolutions and those in name only. But as Jungmann admits, it is difficult to speak of "sacramental absolutions" before Scholastic theologians defined either sacraments or absolutions. Instead, it is important to recognize the importance of the label alone.

and pontificals of Troyes and of Chartres. This branch represents a revision of the Beauvais I rite, or at least of something more like Beauvais I than like BN latin 934. Sens BM 9 first follows the two-part doubled Ash Wednesday rite, then retains the Thursday rite of Beauvais I, but without the long introductory *absolutio*.[18] Another characteristic feature in this and other rites of the Chartres branch is a long presentation of the penitents to the bishop that follows the Gelasian text of this section in running together rubrics and text, as opposed to the treatment in PRG XCIX.225C–227C, where the presentation is broken up to make a dialogue between the archdeacon and the bishop.[19] (See Appendix.) A contemporary pontifical of Chartres, BN latin 945, has a rite very similar, if more elaborate, and I have named this branch after it.[20] The late-twelfth-century pontifical of Troyes has the same Ash Wednesday rite, but it adds a very long explanatory rubric for Maundy Thursday; the Thursday rite is similar to that in Sens BM 9 and the pontifical of Chartres.[21]

The pontifical from Reims, another late-twelfth-century rite of the north-central family, is too mutilated for full identification. The near contemporary ordinal of Reims is typically sketchy, but it mentions the Wednesday ejection. On Thursday, it noted, the archbishop should proceed from parish to parish saying absolutions over the gathered people; then he should absolve the people gathered in his cathedral. In midafternoon—later than in most cities—the bishop reconciles the penitents with a text that seems to place Reims in the Chartres branch of this family.[22] What we know about Reims is thus at

---

18. Sens BM 9, f. 9r–13v; it also omits the Ash Wednesday sermon, just like the pontifical of Beauvais, but unlike BN latin 934.

19. Cf. the Gelasian *Liber sacramentorum*, XXXVIII, pp. 56–57; Mohlberg, *Das fränkische Sacramentarium Gelasianum*, 92, pp. 69–70. In the Gelasian rites, what would become rubrics in the PRG are simply treated as part of the text, though the effect is a little awkward, and perhaps the Gelasian compilers never really intended a run-on presentation but expected the speakers to sort out rubrics and speeches for themselves. It is even more awkward in the north-central texts, which change the first part of the discourse addressing the bishop on behalf of the penitents into first person plural from the first person singular of the Gelasian and PRG, then without a break abruptly shift back into the first person singular.

20. BN latin 945, f. 126v–134r. See Appendix II.

21. Troyes, Trésor de la Cathédrale, 4, f. 141v–148v. The Ash Wednesday rite contains thirteenth-century marginal corrections to be discussed below. The Maundy Thursday begins with a very long rubric that seems to be culled from a theologian or liturgist, but I have not identified the source. The rest of the rite is close to the version of the Romano-Germanic Pontifical's prayers that appears in BN latin 945, the late twelfth-century pontifical of Chartres.

22. Chevalier, *Le sacramentaire . . . de Reims*, pp. 274–275, 279–280. According to this ordinal, the reconciliation begins with the penitents approaching the bishop sitting in front of the church; then the archdeacon presents the penitents, *Adest, o venerabilis*; and then, it reads, "the remainder follows in order." In texts of the Beauvais and Chartres branches, the first part of the *Venite* comes between the approach of the penitents and the *Adest*. Either the Reims

least consistent with this conclusion. Once again, virtually all members of the north-central family have the characteristic doubled Wednesday rite, but we may identify here two different versions of the Thursday rite, with the Chartres branch of the family more dependent on the Romano-Germanic pontifical and the Sens branch less so.

This analysis suggests several conclusions. The Wednesday rite, with its combination of Regino's descriptive rubric and a number of prayers labeled as an "absolution," is the most striking and consistent feature. We cannot explain it as simple fidelity to the model of the eleventh-century Beauvais manuscript, since it is not exactly identical in every text, and the compilers felt no compunction about altering other features. Instead, they must have found it attractive for two reasons. First, these prayers were necessary to fill in what Regino's outline alone did not provide. And second, from the late eleventh century on, the liturgy was moving to include an early absolution for the penitents on Ash Wednesday, in addition to the final reconciliation by the bishop on Maundy Thursday; while the penitents still would return for something called a *reconciliatio* at the end of Lent, their restoration to grace would no longer depend on this gesture. By contrast, when Regino had said that on Wednesday the bishop, with the clergy, "pro eorum absolutione decantet" ("shall chant for their absolution"), he did not even mean a deprecative absolution; they simply prayed for the eventual forgiveness of the sinners. This Chartres branch of the north-central family represents an intermediate form between Regino and the eventual adoption of immediate absolutions.[23] There is now something labeled an "absolution" on Wednesday, although these are really just prayers borrowed in part from the Thursday service. By contrast, the Thursday rite is labeled a "reconciliation," as if the absolution has already been completed. We will soon see that several other twelfth-century pontificals moved toward providing a Wednesday absolution. Such a development even before Scholastic theology had fully worked out the justification in the power of the keys for immediate absolution before the completion of the required satisfaction suggests that the theology may have been responding to the liturgy as much as the other way around.

The Thursday rite throughout this important family was moving in

---

text is more faithful to the PRG, or, more likely, it is just another sketchy ordinal. On the parish absolutions, see below.

23. Jungmann, *Die lateinischen Bussriten*, p. 218, speaks of the northern French rites as a bridge to the new type of indicative absolutions. Since such absolutions hardly ever appear even in very late rites of public penance, this conclusion is unwarranted, but Jungmann correctly observes the transition from an emphasis on the reconciliation to an emphasis on the absolution, pp. 252, 276–277.

the same direction. We have already noted that the rite in BN latin 934 had borrowed the *Venite*, but in a subdued form. In fact, the Romano-Germanic pontifical had first placed the presentation of the penitents to the bishop, *Adest, o venerabilis*, then the *Venite*, said once, twice, then three times, and the actual reintroduction of the penitents into the church. BN latin 934 has the penitents immediately introduced into the church (*Primo in ecclesiam introducantur*), as the bishop says *Venite* just once; then follow various prayers, another whole series of invitations, *Venite*, and then the penitents are passed from the archdeacon to the bishop. Where the Romano-Germanic pontifical had logically presented the penitents outside the church and made their gradual reintroduction the climax, these French pontificals treated the penitents as already virtually introduced. The *Venite* was just an added touch. What I have called the Chartres branch of this family, actually including pontificals from Chartres, Sens, and Troyes, reproduced the prayers of the Romano-Germanic pontifical more faithfully, but they, too, placed the *Venite* and introduction as the very first step; only then followed the presentation to the bishop. This reversal, as we shall see, is too common in French pontificals to be ascribed to mere confusion about the proper order. By the twelfth century, they are already starting to assume that the expelled penitents can be brought right into the church without further ado, an assumption based in turn on the belief that the penitents had always remained members of the church. Like the evolution toward early absolution, the reversal of the *Venite* and the presentation points to a transformation of the basis of the early medieval rite. Once a quasi excommunication, public penance increasingly imitated the gentler embrace of the private rite.

One final feature of these manuscripts is worthy of note. In each pontifical, the Wednesday rite follows Regino in mentioning the aspersion of ashes on the heads of the penitents alone; there is no evidence that the ordinary faithful received ashes, too. All of them place a benediction of ashes in a separate section of the manuscript, alongside other benedictions of objects that were distributed more generally: of bread, houses, wells, and palm fronds. It may be that the compilers had begun to think of the blessing of the ashes as distinct from the rest of the rite of expulsion. Later pontificals would set it apart precisely because the rite with the ashes by then belonged to everyone, not just a few. The arrangement here may be a harbinger of that new practice.

Other families of pontificals were less close-knit but still identifiable. One such was the Anglo-Norman group, including a mid-twelfth-century pontifical of Rouen and a pontifical of Avranches or Mont-Saint-Michel dating from the first half or middle of the twelfth century.[24] On the other side of the channel, it is represented by a later twelfth-century pontifical, from Canterbury or one of its suffragan dioceses, itself closely related to the Avranches/Mont-Saint-Michel text.[25] In general, their penitential rites mix features from the Romano-Germanic pontifical and Anglo-Saxon texts, the latter based ultimately on the same Gallican Gelasian sacramentaries that gave rise to the French tradition. This testifies to an evolution parallel to that in the north-central French texts.

The Ash Wednesday rite of Avranches/Mont-Saint-Michel and Canterbury, called the *ordo ad dandam penitentiam*, shows some similarities to contemporary monastic rites, as we shall see. After the penitent's confession follow the penitential psalms and a series of *preces* and *orationes*, both text and order borrowed from the Romano-Germanic pontifical. Then appears something different, labeled in the Avranches/Mont-Saint-Michel text *absolutio super eundem*. First follows a plural indicative absolution, "Absoluimus te uice beati petri apostolorum principis" ("We absolve you in the place of Saint Peter, prince of the apostles"), then a deprecative absolution, "Omnipotens deus . . . ipse te benedicat et custodiat semper, detque tibi remissionem omnium peccatorum tuorum et uitam eternam" ("May omnipotent God himself bless you and keep you always, and may he grant you remission of all your sins and eternal life").[26] Only then are

24. BN n.a.l. 306, f. 37v–46r, 50v–59r; BN latin 14832, f. 145v–148v, 150v–155v. This latter pontifical has been identified by Leroquais as probably of Avranches: *Les pontificaux manuscrits*, vol. II, pp. 192–193. Fernand Combaluzier, "Un pontifical de Mont-Saint-Michel," pp. 383–384, 397–398, argues that virtually all of it was composed for the nearby monastery, since it contains various pieces at the end relevant specifically to Mont-Saint-Michel. Although it is clearly a truly episcopal pontifical, he argues that the monks could have kept it around for edification or episcopal visitations. This solution remains awkward, since it is hard to see why they would have wanted to commission it in the first place; no other French monastery commissioned such a thoroughly episcopal book. Besides, the litanies do not mention Saint Michael. The book may have been moved later to the abbey; eventually it ended up in the library of Saint-Victor in Paris.

25. Henry Austin, Wilson, ed., *The Pontifical of Magdalen College*, Henry Bradshaw Society, 39 (London, 1910), pp. 152–154, 156–159; very similar is the unpublished late-twelfth-century rite of Trinity College, Dublin, B.3.6, which I have not examined. Combaluzier has discussed the Magdalen College pontifical's close relationship with BN latin 14832. H. Chanteux, "Le manuscrit latin 14.832 de la Bibliothèque Nationale: Contribution à l'histoire du Pontifical Romano-Germanique," *Bulletin philologique et historique (jusqu'à 1715)* (1955–1956), pp. 485–498, has shown that both depended heavily on the so-called "Benedictional of Archbishop Robert," a pontifical brought from Winchester to Jumièges in the middle of the eleventh century, but both relied mostly on the PRG for guidance on public penance.

26. BN latin 14832, f. 146v–147r; Wilson, *The Pontifical of Magdalen College*, p. 153. See below on the evolution of absolutions. Generally, the deprecative absolution is the oldest form, the plural *absoluimus* the next oldest, and the indicative *ego te absolvo* the latest develop-

the ashes blessed and placed on the head of the penitent; finally, the bishop expels the penitents. There are apparently no ashes for anyone else. The Maundy Thursday rite in this and most other Anglo-Norman pontificals remains resolutely attached to the ordering and prayers of the Romano-Germanic pontifical; it begins with the presentation *Adest*, and proceeds with the *Venite*, introduction, and prayers as in its source.

The pontifical prepared for the archbishops of Rouen contains one of the most elaborate rites of solemn penance of any text, French or Roman. On the morning of Ash Wednesday, public penitents who had not yet been assigned a satisfaction were to receive one from their masters (*magistris suis*), a deliberately vague term presumably encompassing parish priests and episcopal penitentiaries. That afternoon, the bishop (there is no mention of the archbishop) would preach a sermon about Lenten duties to the gathered people and absolve them; this sermon and absolution were distinct from the rite of public penance for the few, with its own sermon and absolution, that then followed shortly after. Jean d'Avranches, archbishop of Rouen (1067–1079), mentioned in his *De officiis ecclesiasticis* an "absolution of the people" that is closely linked to public penance on both Ash Wednesday and Maundy Thursday. We cannot tell what sort of absolution he meant, but this was perhaps an early precursor of the twelfth-century rite that provided a sermon and absolution for the Christian faithful quite independent of individual public penance.[27] In this twelfth-century pontifical of Rouen, furthermore, the rite of public penance proper at first followed the general pattern of the Avranches/Mont-Saint-Michel and Canterbury pontificals, with the same plural indicative *absoluimus te*.[28] After the aspersion of ashes, the bishop was to call the penitents, up to that point hidden in various corners of the church, *quasi absconsi*: "Where are the fratricides, where are the in-

---

ment. The second "absolution" here seems to be borrowed from deathbed rites. It does not quite appeal to the power of binding and loosing, but it otherwise fits my definition of a "real" absolution.

27. Jean d'Avranches, *De officiis ecclesiasticis*, ed. R. Delamare (Paris, 1923), pp. 28, 30–31. Jean does not indicate that he is speaking specifically of Rouen, however, and his text is highly ambiguous. He refers on Ash Wednesday, p. 28, to the coming together of clergy and people before the altar: "clerus et populus ante altare, ab unoquoque confessione singulariter facta, et penitentia accepta, prosternantur, et sic ab episcopo vel a majore ecclesie sacerdote absolvantur"; then ashes were to be distributed. Penitents were to be ejected before the procession. These confessions made one-by-one could hardly be private under the circumstances. Could this be something like the seamless movement in the PRG from open standardized confession to public penance? Even so, the Wednesday absolution directly contradicts earlier procedure. Jean's directions for Maundy Thursday were similarly vague.

28. BN n.a.l. 306, f. 37v–40r. It omits the second absolution, and adds a number of other *orationes* from the PRG.

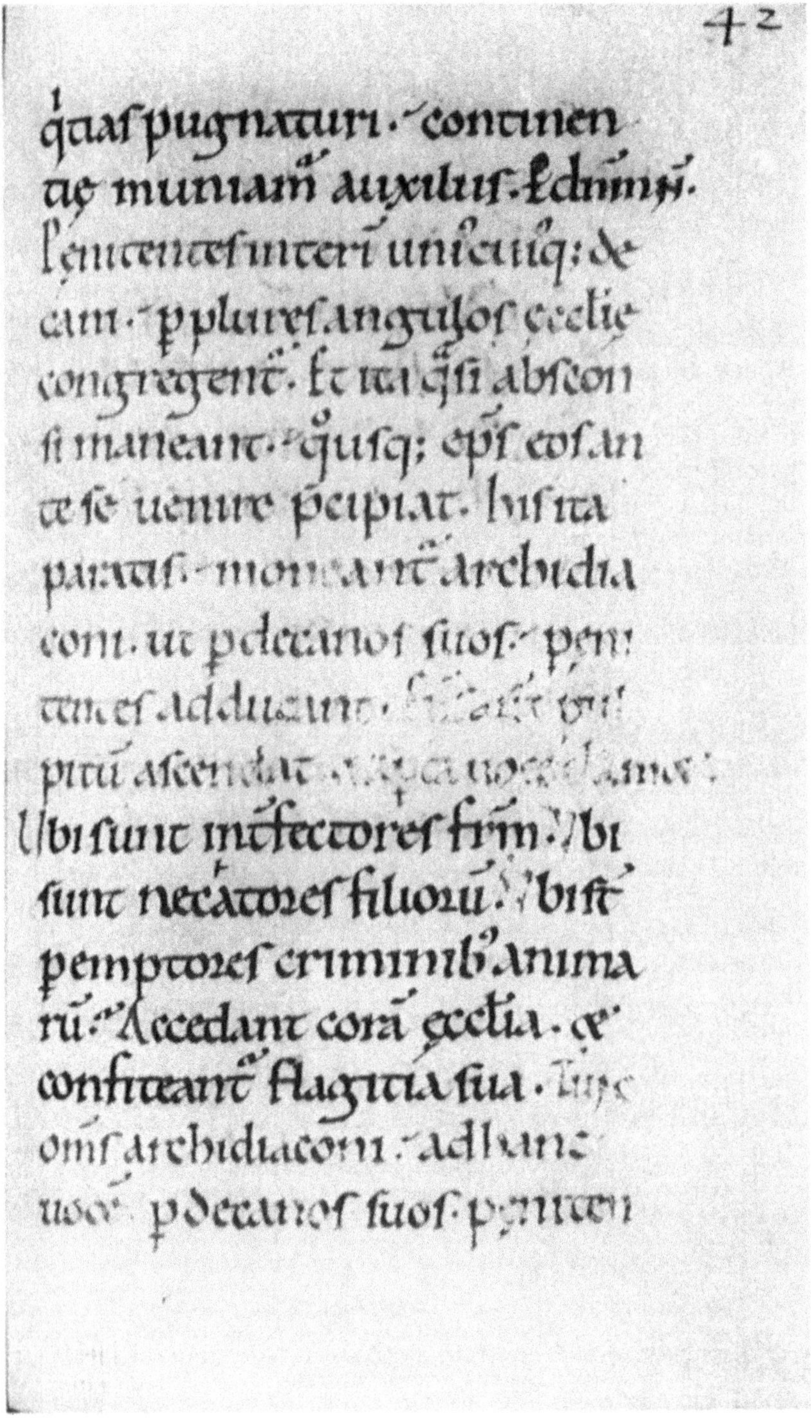

quas pugnaturi · continen
tie muniam auxiliis · Et dūmis·
sententes interi unicuiq: de
eam · p plures angulos ecclie
congregent · Et ita q̄ si abscon
si maneant · q̄usq; eps eos an
te se uenire pcipiat · bis ita
paratis · moneant archidia
coni · ut pdecanos suos · peni
tentes adducant · ... ō̄
pitū ascendat ... ...
Ubi sunt intfectores frm. Ibi
sunt necatores filiorū. Ibi st
pemptores criminibz anima
rū. Accedant corā ecclia · et
confiteant flagitia sua · ...
oms archidiaconi · adhanc
uocē pdecanos suos pniten

PLATE 1. Pontifical of Rouen, middle of the twelfth century. BN n.a.l. 306, f. 42r. Phot. Bibl. Nat. Paris

fanticides? . . . Let them come before the church and con⸢   their crimes."[29] The pontifical includes a second sermon to b⸢   ⸢ched explaining their expulsion: "It is fitting that . . . as the a⸥   says, your bodies be handed over to Satan that your spirits may ⸣   ⸣d in the day of the Lord."[30] We may contrast this arrangem⸢   ⸢ two distinct sermons for public and penitents with the older pr⸢   ⸢g of one sermon for both audiences integrating both themes.[31]   ⸥eni- tents are clothed in hairshirts and expelled in a procession that is accompanied by a series of antiphons. It is a curious mixture of the traditional dramatic scapegoating and the new separation of the Lenten rites for all Christians and the punishment of a few.

The Thursday rite was scarcely simpler. The penitents appeared at the doors of the cathedral around noon, and an archdeacon presented them to the bishop with a long speech similar, but not identical, to the familiar words of the Gelasian sacramentaries and the Romano-Germanic pontifical: "Adest tempus o uenerabilis pontifex votiuum afflictis" ("Now, o venerable bishop, is the time promised to the afflicted"). Only then followed the *Venite*, the introduction into the church, several prayers, and a true absolution. Then, as much later in Guillaume Durand's pontifical, the bishop asks the priests whether each penitent was worthy of "reconciliation," meaning perhaps the final completion of all satisfaction. Those worthy are greeted by the bishop with the kiss of peace and stand on the right; those not reconciled may only be received in church until the octave of Pentecost, and stand on the left. We may note that although Durand was to include a similar interrogation, he made no provision for unreconciled penitents; here, by contrast, the distinction still remains a real one, a sign that this rite presumes that at least some penitents will be performing multiyear penances.[32] The bishop pronounces more absolutions and prayers, and the reconciled penitents offer candles on the altar. This rite's intricate variations on relatively old-fashioned themes may re-

29. BN n.a.l. 306 f. 42r. "Ubi sunt interfectores fratrum. ubi sunt neccatores filiorum. ubi sunt peremptores criminibus animarum? Accedunt coram ecclesia. et confiteantur flagitia sua."

30. BN n.a.l. 306 42v. "Unde oportet uos ab eius communione pericere. et corpora uestra iuxta apostolum tradi sathane. ut salui sint spiritus in die domini." Cf. 1 Cor. 5:5. The sermon cites various ancient authorities, and reminds penitents to fast on bread and water according to the instructions of their priests and to abstain from riding horses, soldiering, bathing, shaving, and sexual intercourse.

31. Cf. PRG XCIX.44, vol. 2, p. 14 (Ash Wednesday); cf. also an eleventh-century pontifical of Evreux in Martène, *De antiquis ecclesiae ritibus libri*, I.6.7.7, vol. I, cols. 791–792, which refers to a single Thursday sermon to penitents and people together "sicut Ordo praecipit Romanus." It is interesting to note that the Rouen pontifical under discussion, BN n.a.l. 306, is entirely independent of this Norman predecessor.

32. PGD III.2.27, p. 564; BN n.a.l. 306, f. 58r-v.

flect the energies of an expert liturgist not unlike Guillaume Durand. But even the inventiveness of his work cannot obscure the general evolution of the Norman liturgy along lines quite different from those of the Roman tradition. The pontifical of Rouen is one of the earliest to mention an absolution of the people on Ash Wednesday that is clearly distinct from public penance. In the Romano-Germanic pontifical and in early northern French rites, we found that it is often difficult to draw a line between public penance and collective expiation; the few and the many are drawn together so that the many may pray.for the few and the few may show the many to be cleansed of sin. This feature of the rite of Rouen may go back even to the eleventh century; but only in the thirteenth century would most other dioceses borrow these separate absolutions and blessings for Ash Wednesday and Maundy Thursday.

The rite of public penance from Soissons shows no close kinship with those found in surviving contemporary pontificals, but is a witness to the same general evolution.[33] It provided the blessing of the ashes and a series of prayers, but there was no explicit expulsion; even the Thursday order *ad reconciliandos penitentes* is bare of rubrics; it gave a series of prayers, but no reintroduction or even genuine absolution.[34] Luckily, we know from another manuscript of Soissons, a near contemporary combination of processional, ritual, and pontifical, that this was only the barest sketch of the actual ritual.[35] This second manuscript, known as the "ceremonial of Bishop Nivelon," listed the same prayers, but filled in others, and it added full rubrics on the Wednesday ejection and Thursday reception. We know from marginal additions that this was the text used at Soissons well into the next century.[36] Its Ash Wednesday ritual was traditional, and it lacked an early absolution. Like the Rouennais rite, it began with a sermon to

33. BN latin 17334 (Soissons, adapted to usage of Saint-Corneille, Compiègne, second half or end of the twelfth century), f.65r–67v, 68v–70v.

34. Cf. the bare Ash Wednesday rites of BN latin 13315 (probably Trier, then Saint-Germain-des-Prés, twelfth century), f. 144v–145r, 149r–155r; Martène, *De antiquis ecclesiae ritibus libri*, IV.22, vol. III, col. 316–319, printed the Thursday rite. As one might expect from its origin, the Thursday rite was nearly identical to the PRG's. But the Wednesday rite included only several prayers for blessing the ashes, and no mention of an expulsion. Probably this was only the sketch of a fuller rite. According to Leroquais, *Les pontificaux manuscrits*, vol. II, p. 184, it was probably originally intended for Trier, then the name of the see was erased; it had arrived at Saint Germain-des-Prés by 1179. Leroquais notes its general similarity to a thirteenth-century pontifical of Reims, Rouen BM 370, but their rites of public penance are entirely different. See below.

35. BN latin 8898 (Soissons, ca. 1180), f. 40v–44r, and 52r–55v.

36. Cf. BN latin 8898, f. 55v; and besides, BN latin 17334 had by then made its way to Saint-Corneille, Compiègne, where the sketchiness of its rite of public penance would not be noticed.

the people, but this time, it concerned the public penance they were about to witness, not their own duties. On Thursday, once again, ¹ ⁺ *Venite* and introduction came first, before the presentation and oᵗʰᵉ ʳ prayers, as in rites of the north-central family.

Rounding out our collection of northern French pontificals from the second half of the twelfth century are four monastic pontificals. Of these, three have rites of public penance and so are relevant to this discussion, those of Sint Pieters, Ghent; Saint-Amand (diocese of Tournai); and Saint-Bertin, in Saint-Omer; the second of these belongs to the north-central family of rites.[37] The pontificals from Ghent and Saint-Amand lack full Wednesday rites; they give only benedictions of ashes. It may be that some monasteries had more call for the reconciliation, which in principle would be repeated every year in a multiyear penance, than for the original expulsion. For Thursday, the pontifical from Ghent provides a *reconciliatio penitentium*, a simple series of prayers, evidently intended to be adapted to be said both for the monks themselves and for lay penitents.[38] Quite separately it adds an "absolutio penitentium. hi autem iaceant ante fores aecclesie" ("absolution of penitents. They should lie before the doors of the church") with prayers borrowed from the Thursday rite for a priest to say over penitents. This is probably a non-Lenten reconciliation of public penitents, one of the very rare liturgical glimpses of non-Lenten, "nonsolemn" public penance.[39] These rites reflected a modest conversion of episcopal rites, stripped of the now customary dramatics. Closer to the original episcopal model were the rites from Saint-Omer and Tournai. Although their rites for Ash Wednesday differed both from each other and from other contemporary Wednesday rites, the Thursday rite in each is of a type already familiar to us. It began with the "bishop's" *Venite*, followed by the presentation *Adest*, and the final introduction, with another *Venite*.[40] This is the same pattern that appears in the family of north-central French pontificals. It is closer to the Beauvais I branch than to the BN latin 934 branch. I have identified these as belonging to a Tournai-Laon branch of rites

---

37. Brussels BR 1505–1506; BN latin 953; and Saint-Omer BM 98. The abbatial pontifical without a rite of public penance is BL Addit. 38,645, from Saint-Sauveur, Anchin, near Arras.

38. We may note the scribe's provision of first person plural and third person singular options, the former presumably for the monks, the latter for an outsider, e.g., "nostris (suis) meritis accusamur (atur)," Brussels BR 1505–1506, f. 23r.

39. Brussels BR 1505–1506, f. 27r–27v.

40. BN latin 953, f. 92v–96r; Saint-Omer BM 98, f. 80r–83r. The series of prayers is virtually identical in the two, but a close family resemblance is problematic, since the textual variants often do not match, and the Saint-Omer pontifical has a conventional Wednesday rite of ejection, unlike the Saint-Amand pontifical.

with a divided *Venite* as at Chartres, but no run-on presentation (PRG XCIX.225–227), and no Wednesday rite at all. The principle is the same as in the other rites of the family, however. The compilers presented the penitents as almost reconciled already, and indeed, in these Flemish abbatial pontificals, they included no true absolutions. In short, in spite of some modifications, the abbatial pontificals developed along similar lines as the rest, though independently from each other and from the episcopal pontificals.

This survey of late-twelfth-century pontificals has surely demonstrated the variety of their rites of public penance and the complexity of any analysis of them. Nevertheless, some general trends may be recognized. By 1150, northern French rites of public penance had already drifted away from the pattern of the Romano-Germanic pontifical. The early medieval Wednesday rites had smoothly yoked the initiation of Lent for the whole Christian people to the dramatic expulsion of the few; the twelfth-century French rites carefully segregated Lenten benedictions of the people from the sufferings of the few. Several hinted at an immediate Wednesday absolution of public penitents, similar to immediate absolutions in private penance. In the public rite, this shift inevitably began to diminish the significance of the Maundy Thursday reconciliation. Some pontificals signaled this change in the Thursday rite with an immediate introduction, before the *Adest* presentation. In addition to these changes, most pontificals discarded or severely cut back the old Romano-Germanic declarations of the bishop's own sinfulness before he called the penitents to approach.[41] One last change not yet remarked may be noted here as well. The Romano-Germanic pontifical's Wednesday's prayers referred to a single penitent, the Thursday prayers to plural penitents. Our northern French pontificals had begun by 1150 to change the singular noun and verb endings to plurals, and even more strikingly, to add above singular endings plural or plural feminine options; virtually all later northern French pontificals preserved these changes. The French compilers thus carefully tailored their rites to fit different possibilities. The penitents had become individuals, sometimes men, sometimes women, sometimes one, sometimes many, no longer faceless sinners expiating their crimes in front of and on behalf of others.

It is striking how many different pontificals took different roads to the same destination. The changes introduced by the northern French pontificals since the tenth century all led in the same direc-

---

41. Rites of the north-central family, for instance, either ran together PRG XCIX.225C–227C, transferring the bishop's confession of guilt (226C) to the archdeacon speaking on behalf of the penitents, or they simply dropped PRG 226C.

tion. The overall result was a paler ritual, drained of much of the color and drama of the early medieval scapegoating. Unlike the Roman pontificals, however, the French rites neither discarded public penance nor embalmed it. Northern French bishops continued to impose public penance frequently, but the salvation of the whole church declared by both early medieval penance and communal rites of penance in the High Middle Ages was already muted in these twelfth-century pontificals. The Romano-Germanic pontifical taught that sinners who had profaned the community if set apart in a special sacred status could redeem themselves and restore the purity of the church. In the later French pontificals, the bishops began to mete out punishment to the penitents in a drier ceremony stripped of much of the symbolism of sacred representative status. Visible here only in relatively subtle shifts of language and organization, these major changes will be fully apparent in thirteenth- and fourteenth-century texts. There, too, will be fully apparent the revolution in the relation between communal rites of penance and the individual expiation of public penitents.

Northern French Rites of the Early Thirteenth Century

In one sense, the first half of the thirteenth century saw a remarkable consolidation in the liturgical treatment of public penance. Of twelve northern French rites surviving in pontificals from this period,[42] no fewer than nine are members of the north-central family. I begin with an examination of the development of this group. But the reduction in variety is more apparent than real, since this family itself starts to branch out in a number of directions. In general, liturgists for this family continued to move toward immediate absolutions for the penitents on Ash Wednesday. Further, several of these pontificals attempted to correct the evident anomalies of the model or adjusted the rite to reflect a new understanding of the relation between ritual for the penitents and ritual for the public. The provision of ashes for the gathered people and general absolutions on Ash Wednesday and

42. There is also a pontifical of Le Mans, Le Mans BM 141, lacking the rite of public penance. And two pontificals of this period with the rite of public penance are recorded by Leroquais but were lost in World War II: Chartres BM 195 (Chartres) and Metz BM 1169 (Paris adapted the use of Sens). Leroquais's descriptions allow us to conclude that the first belonged to the north-central family, but nothing can be said about the branch; the rite of the second looks similar to Montpellier, Bibl. de la Faculté de médecine 399; see Leroquais, *Les pontificaux manuscrits*, vol. I, pp. 133–145, 223–231.

Maundy Thursday now begin to appear more widely. Such an addition of rites for the participation of the faithful sharpened the focus on Ash Wednesday as the start of Lent, just when *Omnis utriusque* was making Lent a more important season for the Christian people as well as the clergy. And, as we found in Chapter 5, the new focus on Ash Wednesday prepared the ground for Carnival, which was just coming into its own in the mid thirteenth century.

We may begin with a few of the most conservative rites. An early thirteenth-century pontifical of Reims preserved almost intact the Ash Wednesday and Maundy Thursday services of the Chartres branch of the family, exemplified by the late-twelfth-century pontifical of Chartres, BN latin 945. It was altered from that model only by certain textual variants in the prayers and a few late-thirteenth-century retouches.[43] Unfortunately, it cannot be compared to the mutilated late-twelfth-century pontifical of Reims, which had lost its Wednesday and Thursday rites.[44] Otherwise, very little has changed from the middle of the twelfth century. There is still a two-part Ash Wednesday rite, and still the *Venite* before the *Adesto* on Thursday.

A roughly contemporary rite, again from Reims, tried to reorder the awkward and confusing Ash Wednesday while leaving the Thursday rite from the Chartres branch intact.[45] This pontifical eliminated the first part of the two-part Wednesday rite, deleting the long rubric from Regino whose relation to the prayers had been unclear. It included the "Absolutio penitentium in capite ieiunii" ("Absolution of penitents on Ash Wednesday"), and it provided a standard deprecative absolution to match the content with the label. The compiler

43. Rouen BM 370 (A 34) (pontifical of Reims, first half or middle of the thirteenth century), f. 79v, 81v–89r; cf. BN latin 945 (pontifical of Chartres). A late-thirteenth-century hand added a few lines to the absolution at the end of Thursday, f. 87v, adding to the invocation of saints in it.

44. Reims BM 342. In addition to this and the two early-thirteenth-century Reims pontificals, Martène, *De antiquis ecclesiae ritibus libri*, I.6.7.14, vol. I, cols. 809–812, has printed a rite in a manuscript of Saint-Remi, Reims, unfortunately now lost, which he dated to around 1200. This is an episcopal rite completely unlike any of the others from Reims, or indeed elsewhere in northern France, and I wonder whether it was really written for Saint-Remi or for Reims at all. It begins with a number of prayers and absolutions borrowed largely from the PRG Thursday rite, but omitting any expulsion, ashes, or even reference to the day; then follows a Maundy Thursday reconciliation, with some prayers and absolutions from the PRG, some from unidentified sources. There is no presentation, *Venite*, or introduction into the church. Is this a rare rite of nonsolemn public penance? Martène's identifications are too unreliable to draw any conclusions.

45. Reims BM 343, f. 4r–8r. Leroquais dates this manuscript to the beginning of the century, earlier, that is, than Rouen BM 370. But the rites of public penance in Reims BM 343 are added by a different scribe on a separate quire from the rest of the MS, and may not be quite as old. Rouen BM 370 is an illuminated presentation piece, though full of scribal errors, while Reims BM 343 is a smaller, less handsome MS, perhaps intended more for use than for show.

evidently sensed the oddity of the rite as it stood and tried to make it unambiguous. Indeed, as we shall see shortly, a total of five early thirteenth-century rites of the north-central family abandoned the signature two-part Wednesday rite entirely and used the old mode for Maundy Thursday.

For the moment, however, we may turn to three more traditional members of the family, beginning with an early-thirteenth-century pontifical of Senlis or a neighboring diocese.[46] The Ash Wednesday rite followed the standard two-part outline of the twelfth-century, north-central family, but several new prayers were added in the second section. They were not true absolutions, but they were labeled *absolutio*. Also included were the words for the benediction of ashes that were missing in early versions of the family.[47] For the Thursday reconciliation, this pontifical began rather like the Chartres branch with a shortened *Venite* followed by the run-together Gelasian version of the introduction (in effect conflating PRG XCIX.225–227), but it closed with different deprecative absolutions, *Absolutionem et remissionem,* and it lacks the repetition of the *Venite* typical of the Chartres branch, and so is an example of what I call the Senlis branch (see chart and Appendix). Two early-thirteenth-century abbatial pontificals, from ter Doest and Saint-Martin, Tournai, were very similar to each other and to the twelfth-century pontifical of Saint-Amand-en-Pavèle (diocese of Tournai) examined earlier.[48] All three omitted the Ash Wednesday service and provided a Maundy Thursday reconciliation of penitents similar to the Chartres branch of the family.[49] They repeated the *Venite,* but they rectified the run-on presentation; as noted above, these manuscripts define what I call the Tournai-Laon branch. The particular versions of Saint-Martin and Saint-Amand

---

46. Paris, Institut de recherche et d'histoire des textes, Collection privée, 25, f. 88v–93r, 93v–98r. I am grateful to the Institut for access to this microfiche of a MS in a private collection.

47. The rather unusual choice and order of prayers on Ash Wednesday in Paris, IRHT Coll. priv. 25 is almost precisely identical with those of Montpellier, Bibl. de la Faculté de médecine 399 (Pontifical of Paris, beginning or first half of the thirteenth century), f. 101v–104v. But the textual variants are different, and more significantly, the whole outline of the two rites is quite distinct. The Parisian pontifical omits the long opening rubric and adds a sermon, true absolutions, and antiphons for the expulsion. Quite likely, both MSS depended on a common source for the sequence of prayers and fit them into two different frameworks.

48. Bruges, Stedelijke Openbare Bibliotheek 318 (pontifical of ter Doest, thirteenth century), f. 95v–99v; Brussels BR II. 1013 (pontifical of Saint-Martin, Tournai, thirteenth century), f. 112v–116v; cf. BN latin 953, f. 92v–96r. The minor textual variants of the pontifical of ter Doest are actually a little closer to those of BN latin 953 than are the variants of the pontifical of Saint-Martin.

49. The pontifical of ter Doest has something labeled as a benediction of ashes, but is in fact a benediction of incense: Bruges Stedelijke Openbare Bibliotheek 318, f. 132r-v.

were not adapted to the needs of an abbey, and their rubrics referred to a bishop. The author of the ter Doest pontifical, however, combined the reconciliation of public penitents with the typical abbatial rite of absolution of the monks in chapter. The Thursday service began with the *Venite* and presentation for public penitents; then followed the absolution *in capitulo*; it closed with the second half of the rite for public penitents. It seems that the absolution was intended for the penitents as well as for the monks; at least there was no alternative separate absolution for them later. Besides adapting the pontifical to monastic custom, this change effectively refocused the rite to some extent on the absolution, a shift that will be more marked in other contemporary pontificals. For the most part, the abbatial versions of public penance remained rather old-fashioned, as one might expect. The very imposition of public penance by abbots was dying out; monasteries were not a source of liturgical invention in this field.

So much for the relatively old-fashioned representatives of the north-central family. Other liturgists made more radical alterations in the model. An early-thirteenth-century pontifical of Chartres, evidently a member of the Chartres branch, followed its fifty-year-old predecessor in virtually every detail of its Ash Wednesday and Maundy Thursday rites. But several later scribes of the middle or second half of the thirteenth century conducted surgery on what they saw as the anomalous features of the liturgy.[50] Their hands eliminated the long rubric that begins the two-part Wednesday rite and added a benediction of the ashes, rubrics and antiphons for the expulsion, and a real absolution. The two-part rite as it stood had not explained what was to be said where; the revamped version made the sequence more straightforward. In addition, an ordinal, probably composed between 1225 and 1230, mentioned a sermon and absolution for the people before the expulsion of penitents, and the distribution of ashes to the laity afterwards, in effect adapting the rite for the laity as a whole, not just for the penitents.[51] For the rite of reconciliation, the pontifical's correctors again eliminated the opening rubric and indeed most of the rite, including the split presentation, the *Venite*, and several prayers; they added an absolution. The general effect was to dispose of the strange alternation of *Venite*, then run-on presentation,

50. Orléans BM 144 (121) (Pontifical of Chartres, beginning of the thirteenth century), f. 105v–111r. It is difficult to identify and date the various correcting hands with any precision. There seem to be three, all thirteenth century.

51. Yves Delaporte, ed., *L'ordinaire chartrain du XIIIe siècle, Mémoires de la Société archéologique d'Eure-et-Loir*, 18–19 (Chartres, 1952–1953), pp. 97–98. The ordinal, destroyed in 1944 but surviving in photographic reproduction, can be dated with certainty to 1204–1239, and probably to 1225–1230, pp. 22–23.

then prayers, then repetition of the presentation, then *Venite* that had characterized the old Chartres pontifical. It was a clumsy effort at simplification, since it left the manuscript an almost unreadable mess. The near-contemporary ordinal provides no information on public penance, but it added a sermon and absolution for the whole people.[52] Whatever the original intentions of the liturgists behind the ordinal and the corrections to the pontifical, more than mere simplification was the result. The new Wednesday rite spelled out the now more important benediction of ashes, and it included an absolution, in accordance with the new theology of penance. The pontifical's new rite of reconciliation gutted all the dramatic effects inherited from the Romano-Germanic pontifical and replaced them with simple prayers and a couple of absolutions. The bishop absolved the penitents as efficiently as possible and moved on to other business. That other business included absolutions for all laymen, and, at the beginning of Lent, the blessing of ashes for all. The bishop now addressed the penance of the whole people directly, not just through the penance of the public penitents. Like the rule of annual confession, the change tended to make the Lenten period a period of expiation for every member of the parish and every pilgrim to the cathedral.[53]

These were the effects of later corrections, perhaps even as late as the second half of the thirteenth century. We can see early-thirteenth-century revisions to the north-central model in several other pontificals. Two manuscripts of Cambrai, one from the beginning, the other from the first half of the thirteenth century, provide a convenient way to examine change in one diocese.[54] Both have Maundy Thursday rites similar to the pattern in the Chartres branch of the north-central family, but their Ash Wednesday rites are quite different. I have reckoned these pontificals as members of this family, but it is not certain

52. Delaporte, *L'ordinaire chartrain du XIIIe siècle*, p. 107. Delaporte asks in his introduction, p. 46, why the ordinal did not mention the reconciliation of public penitents, and he sensibly suggests that the ordinal was more concerned with the office of the choir and only tangentially with rites involving bishop and laity. He notes a cathedral record from 1700 stating that the north porch was (formerly?) the site for the reconciliation of the penitents by the penitentiary; and a liturgist in 1580 described a contemporary practice of absolving the reconciled penitents and people together on Thursday. These late reports do not correspond precisely to the rite outlined in thirteenth-century sources, but they at least confirm the survival of the rite.

53. Cf. the comments of Gy, "Histoire liturgique du Sacrement de Pénitence," p. 17, although he assumes the demise of the traditional public penance.

54. Cambrai BM 222 (pontifical of Cambrai, beginning of the thirteenth century), f. 114v–116r, 120r–140r; Cambrai BM 223 (pontifical of Cambrai, first half of the thirteenth century), f. 150r–155v, 156v–163v. Both have later-thirteenth-century marginal corrections, but Cambrai BM 223 has a few more, and was likely the MS used for this rite at Cambrai until 1300 or so.

whether a now-lost Cambrai manuscript followed the north-central pattern for both services, and then somehow the Wednesday rite and certain details of the Thursday rite were changed. At any rate, the first Cambrai pontifical incorporates several interesting features not found in most earlier manuscripts. It provided a separate, earlier benediction of ashes written for a bishop or priest and the benediction of ashes to be said by the bishop in the middle of the reconciliation of penitents. This certainly implies the imposition of ashes on the people as well as the penitents. The Maundy Thursday rite in general followed the model of the Chartres branch of the north-central family, but it added a long benediction of the penitents after their reconciliation, and then it provided an "absolutio alia super penitentes et super populum in cena domini" ("second absolution for the penitents and for the people on Maundy Thursday"). These differences are significant enough to allow us to consider this a separate "Cambrai branch," although it is most closely dependent on the Chartres branch. Several prayers followed the title *absolutio*, none of them true absolutions,[55] but at least the notion of providing absolutions for the people as well as for the penitents is both new and important. Like the provision of ashes for everyone, it heralds the new view of the relation between public penitents and audience.

The second pontifical from Cambrai extended this evolution when it altered the balance of the Ash Wednesday rite.[56] The service began with prayers and an absolution, evidently for the cathedral clergy or the public, since it precedes the handling of public penance. Only then does the bishop approach the penitents in the middle of the church, say a series of prayers, sprinkle ashes on their heads, and expel them. There is no general sermon about public penance; instead, the pontifical directs the bishop to explain to the *penitents* why they are being expelled. Then, the bishop blesses more ashes, which are distributed to "the rest": *capitibus ceterorum imponit*. The bishop and clergy proceed into the chapel and say a long general litany, including prayers for the king, peace, the whole Christian people, and penitents, followed by a related prayer for the forgiveness of sins. Clearly much of the rite is not intended for public penitents; but

55. Oddly, one of the prayers, *Deus humani generis*, appears in its shortened form at this point, Cambrai BM 222, f. 138r-v, although it appeared as well in its long form a few folios before in the reconciliation of the penitents, f. 129v–132r. The long form, = PRG XCIX.245, is much rarer in northern French pontificals than the short form, which is the version in the Gelasian sacramentaries. All the other north-central MSS use the short form. It looks like both these Cambrai MSS were corrected at some point against a MS of the PRG, not surprising in light of the ties between this diocese and the Empire.

56. Cambrai BM 223, f. 150r–155v.

which prayers here are for the clergy, and which are for the public? The litany in the chapel is surely for the clergy, and perhaps also the second benediction of ashes. The first absolution may well be for everybody. At any rate, the effect is to balance the public penance of individuals with the collective public penance represented in the saying of litanies for the whole people. The Maundy Thursday rite followed the outline of the earlier Cambrai manuscript. A later-thirteenth-century hand made considerable alterations to provide for the reconciliation of penitents in the absence of the bishop, and it corrected several of the prayers according to the Romano-Germanic pontifical.[57]

The last member of the north-central family from the early thirteenth century, a pontifical of Laon, is particularly interesting since it may be compared with an unusually detailed contemporary ordinal.[58] The two texts reveal that Laon goes even further in adapting Lenten rites of penance for the whole people as well as for the individual penitents. The pontifical and the ordinal, which survives in an early-thirteenth-century manuscript and was composed between 1178 and 1228,[59] detail a procedure for popular participation on Ash Wednesday roughly similar to that in Cambrai, though the rites themselves belong to different branches. The similarity comes from a similar evolution, not the dependence of one text on the other. Before the imposition of public penance, the canons proceed to the small church of Saint-Martin next to the cathedral and receive ashes there; then they return to the cathedral, say nones, and distribute ashes and hairshirts to the penitents, who are expelled.[60] Later, the pontifical provides a benediction of ashes separate from the main description of public penance.[61] On Maundy Thursday, the most striking innovation

57. Cambrai BM 223, 156v–163v. The thirteenth-century corrector(s) noted that prayers explicitly presenting the penitents to the bishop, such as *Adest o pontifex*, should be omitted in the bishop's absence. They also revised the presentation (= PRG XCIX.222–226) to reintroduce the breaks and rubrics that all the MSS of the Chartres and Senlis branch of the north-central family had lost.

58. Laon BM 224 (pontifical of Laon, beginning or first half of the thirteenth century), f. 184r–194v, 205r–v, 219r–v; and Chevalier, *Ordinaires de l'église cathédrale de Laon (XIIe et XIIIe s.)*, pp. 83–84, 108–110.

59. See Chevalier, *Ordinaires de l'église cathédrale de Laon*, pp. xii–xviii, for the dating.

60. The rite in Laon BM 224, f. 205r–v, is unusual because, like the instructions in the ordinal, it only outlines what was to be done without giving the text of prayers, and further, it appears *after* the reconciliation of the penitents. It seems to have been added to make the pontifical correspond to the ordinal; the pontifical's instructions are very similar but slightly more explicit.

61. Laon BM 224, f. 219r–v. This benediction appears to have been added in the thirteenth century by a hand different from that in the rest of the MS, and was only added to the table of contents after its original composition. Evidently, a corrector found it useful to include the benediction since the Ash Wednesday rite itself was a mere skeleton without flesh.

is the explicit provision for the bishop to say absolutions over clergy and people. The day starts with prime and an absolution of the canons. Then follow many prayers familiar from rites of public penance, but they precede not the reconciliation of penitents but another absolution of the canons. The bishop then proceeds in turn to four churches, including Saint-Jean in the *bourg* across the hill from the *cité*. After terce and sext, the bishop, now back at the cathedral, absolves the people of sin; mass and the reconciliation of public penance follow. This framework appears in the ordinal, and is repeated in later-thirteenth-century marginal additions to the pontifical. As for the rite of penance itself, it belongs to the Tournai-Laon branch of the north-central family, with minor differences from its monastic siblings. So, in the early thirteenth century, one popular absolution balanced the reconciliation of public penitents. Later in the thirteenth century, marginal corrections provided for absolutions of the people to be said in *each* of the four churches visited by the bishop as well as in the cathedral.[62] A fourteenth-century hand added a general litany to be said in each church; it included prayers for the king, the whole people, and for seasonable weather—but not specifically for public penitents.[63] Hardly any pontifical reveals more clearly the evolution of Lenten rites from 1200 to 1350. No longer does the expiation of a few scapegoats alone promise the salvation of the many. Collective expiation now supplements individual public penance.

The three remaining early-thirteenth-century pontificals do not belong to the north-central family, but their rites show a similar evolution. Some new features appear. A midcentury pontifical of Amiens, for instance, omits any *Venite* or presentation to the bishop; like the revamped rite of Chartres discussed above, it is a dull thing in comparison to the dramatic reconciliation step-by-step from priest to archdeacon to bishop found in the Romano-Germanic pontifical and most twelfth-century French pontificals.[64] At the end of the Maundy Thursday reconciliation of public penitents, the Amiens rite adds the *Confiteor*, perhaps a harbinger of the eventual fourteenth- and fifteenth-century practice of popular general confession on Maundy Thursday, which I discuss below. A pontifical from the abbey of Corbie similarly omits the presentation and *Venite,* and it turned to the Romano-Germanic pontifical for a particularly rare and obscure ab-

---

62. Laon BM 224, f. 188v.

63. Laon BM 224, f.189r–192v.

64. Amiens BM 196 (pontifical of Amiens, middle of the thirteenth century), 61v–63r. No Ash Wednesday rite survives in this partial pontifical; the rest of the Thursday rite is fairly conventional, a few short prayers followed by an unusual absolution and benediction.

solution for the penitents. This absolution was followed by another
one less precisely focused on penitents, a shorter "indulgen⋅ ⋅ ⋅ 'Indulgentiam et remissionem omnium peccatorum . . . tribu ⋅nd
the standard Maundy Thursday episcopal benediction.[65] ⅂ ⋅ter
two features almost always appear elsewhere as blessings he
whole people, not individual public penitents, and it is likely ⋅ ⋅ve
have here a double rite of absolution, first for the penitent few, ⋅⋅⋅en
for all Christians seeking a Thursday blessing as at Laon. Is this a ⋅⋅ue
indulgence in the technical sense, such as we find drawing Maundy
Thursday visitors to cathedrals and abbeys in late-thirteenth- and
fourteenth-century texts? The mere use of the word *indulgentiam* is
not proof. This may be still an absolution and general blessing without the particular promise of remission of time in purgatory. At any
rate, the provision of such a blessing for the people as a whole is a
novelty.

By contrast, a pontifical of Paris contains unusually elaborate rites
of public penance, but it again provides for a novel type of popular
participation.[66] On Ash Wednesday, the bishop begins with a series of
prayers presumably directed at the public penitents, then he says an
absolution and blessing over the people, "Deinde surgat episcopus
manuque extenta super populum dicat sequentem orationem absolutionis" ("Then the bishop shall rise and, with his hand extended over
the people, say the following prayer of absolution").[67] The pontifical
borrowed this absolution from the Romano-Germanic pontifical's
Maundy Thursday reconciliation of public penitents, and followed it
with the standard "Absolutionem et remissionem," and the blessing
and distribution of ashes, again evidently for the entire people. Interestingly, the pontifical then directs the bishop to repeat the twin absolutions just said, and then to expel the penitents. Presumably the
second absolution is directed at the penitents; we find here the beginnings of a doubling of the rite that will be completed in some other
thirteenth-century Wednesday services, notably that of Bayeux.[68] On

65. Amiens BM 195 (pontifical, lectionary, and collectionary of Corbie, beginning and
first half of the thirteenth century *and* end of the thirteenth century or beginning of the
fourteenth century), f. 54r–63v. There is also a benediction of ashes, f. 45v–46r. Both rites
appear in the early part of the MS. A later hand has enlarged on the final benediction of the
people on Thursday to refer to the *mandatum* and the analogy between washing feet and
washing away sins.

66. Montpellier, Bibl. de la Faculté de médecine 399 (pontifical of Paris, beginning or
first half of the thirteenth century), f. 101v–105v.

67. Montpellier, Bibl. de la Faculté de médecine 399, f. 103r.

68. Chevalier, *Ordinaire et coutumier de l'église cathédrale de Bayeux (XIIIe s.)*, pp. 102–103.
But at Bayeux, the first absolution and distribution of ashes was for the penitents, the second
for the cathedral clergy; evidently there was nothing for the people. See below.

Maundy Thursday, this Parisian pontifical, like the rite of Amiens and the revised rite of Chartres, eliminated both presentation and *Venite*, and with them all the drama.

Northern French Rites of the Late Thirteenth Century

Only five of the nine surviving pontificals from the second half of the thirteenth century contain rites of public penance. Two of the others came from the abbey of Saint-Vaast d'Arras,[69] and another was a pontifical of Paris that may have lost the relevant folios at some point.[70] The fourth and last without a clear rite of public penance was a pontifical of Cambrai, surviving only in a seventeenth-century copy by Jean Deslions, that provided a blessing of ashes, but no explicit expulsion or reception.[71] Since, as we have seen, the early-thirteenth-century pontifical of Cambrai had a rite of public penance with later-thirteenth-century marginal corrections, it may be that the bishop continued to use the earlier pontifical for this rite.[72] The relative dearth of late-thirteenth-century pontificals and rites of public penance is almost certainly accidental, and eight pontificals with public penance survive for the next fifty-year period. The survival of several mid- or late-thirteenth-century ordinals means that the scarcity of pontificals is no great obstacle to tracing the evolution of penance. Of the five pontifical rites we do have, three definitely belong to the

69. Arras BM 469 (pontifical of Saint-Vaast, Arras, second half or end of the thirteenth century); Arras BM 702 (pontifical of Saint-Vaast, Arras, end of the thirteenth century or beginning of the fourteenth century). The latter is so mutilated that it is hard to read, but evidently was very similar to the more complete Arras BM 469.

70. Paris, Bibl. de l'Arsenal 332. Leroquais, *Les pontificaux manuscrits*, vol. I, p. 272, notes the similarity of the rubrics of this MS to those of Montpellier, Bibl. de la Faculté de Médicine 399 and also to Metz BM 1169, an early-thirteenth-century pontifical of Paris, adapted to the use of Sens, unfortunately now lost. Both of these MSS contained rites of public penance, and it is safe to assume that Arsenal 332 originally did as well. And since fourteenth- and even sixteenth-century pontificals of Paris do contain the appropriate rites, we can be sure that public penance survived in the capital: cf. Sens BM 12 (pontifical of Paris, adapted to the use of Sens, first half of fourteenth century); and BN latin 956–957 (pontifical of Paris, sixteenth century).

71. Lyon BM 570, f. 255v. For this copy and Deslions (d. 1700), see M. Andrieu, "Le pontifical d'Apamée et autres textes liturgiques communiqués à dom Martène par Jean Deslions," *Revue Bénédictine* 48 (1936): 321–348.

72. Cambrai BM 223, f. 150r–155v, and 156r–163v. It is unclear why the new scribe should have copied some rites of the early-thirteenth-century book into the new MS but not others, nor why he should have changed the selection and content of the episcopal benedictions, normally one of the most consistent features from one pontifical to another: compare Lyon BM 570, f. 251v–252r, with Cambrai BM 223, f. 116v–117r. Without the original of the later pontifical, the mystery may never be resolved.

north-central family, including one from Noyon or Senlis, one from Beauvais, and one from Châlons-sur-Marne. The first belongs to the Senlis branch, the second is generally loyal to the tradition of the old eleventh-century Beauvais rite, and the last belongs to the Tournai-Laon branch of the family; no representatives of the other versions have survived. This may be due to chance or to the progressive evolution of the members of this family after 1200, which may obscure the traces of a branch in later pontificals. As a case in point, a pontifical of Meaux (discussed below) may be a shortened and revised rendering of a lost text related to one of the branches; but one cannot be sure of the relationship.[73]

The main trends in the liturgy of public penance after 1250 extend the changes that we have observed in earlier rites. Some Ash Wednesday rites direct the bishop to absolve the penitents at once, in advance of their satisfaction. Some pontificals minimize or omit the full Wednesday rite, providing only a benediction of ashes or possibly absolutions, and omitting the dramatic expulsion. It seems likely that some dioceses preferred to replace the full rite with a number of absolutions and blessings, for both penitents and everyone else. The provision of absolutions, distribution of ashes, and even indulgences for the general public became more explicit.[74] Two liturgists of the second half of the thirteenth century, Gilbert de Tournai and Guillaume Durand, confirm the trend to provide ashes for all, not just for penitents or clergy.[75] The public for public penance now busied themselves with their individual salvation and remission of purgatorial time, and while they still watched the humiliation of their fellows, the liturgy no longer taught them to think that the holiness or even the harmony of their community depended on that expiation of the few.

We may begin our review of the rites with a pontifical of Noyon or Senlis from the second half or the end of the thirteenth century that remained particularly loyal to the model exemplified in the first part

73. BN n.a.l. 1202 (pontifical of Meaux, middle or second half of the thirteenth century). See below.

74. On this trend, see Jungmann, *Die lateinischen Bussriten*, pp. 44, 102–104, 292. Jungmann, p. 104, sees indications even in the eleventh-century Beauvais I text (Martène, *De antiquis ecclesiae ritibus libri*, I.6.7.8) of such a provision for prayers specifically for the people in the two-part Maundy Thursday rite, but I found his argument inconclusive: The doubling there seems to come from a fusion of PRG and local traditions.

75. Guibert de Tournai, *Tractatus de officio episcopi et ecclesiae ceremoniis*, in *Maxima Bibliotheca Veterum Patrum* ed. M. de La Bigne, (Lyon, 1677), 25:415; Guillaume Durand, *Rationale divinorum officiorum*, f. 196v–197v. And in Durand's commentary, public penance has become just one event out of many on the day, not the focus, as it had been for Jean Beleth, for example; the de-emphasis is consistent with the rite he provides in his pontifical.

of the century in the pontifical of Senlis.[76] This liturgist of the Ile-de-France preserved the long descriptive rubric of Regino in the Ash Wednesday rite, though he sensibly split it up into different sections to show what prayers fit where in the rite. Its Maundy Thursday rite preserved the outline and prayers of the Chartres rite, including its Gelasian-based conflation of the three addresses separated in the Romano-Germanic pontifical (XCIX.225C–227C) into one long presentation without a rubric or break. Thus, the Noyon-Senlis pontifical still had the *Venite*, but only in its debased form, at the very beginning of the service. Where the Noyon-Senlis liturgist innovated was in the introduction of Maundy Thursday prayers and absolutions into the Ash Wednesday service. We may recall that the north-central family followed the long rubric with a rubric *absolutio penitentium*, but the prayers in this section were not "real" absolutions. The Noyon-Senlis liturgist corrected the anomaly by taking a large portion of the Thursday rite, including prayers and true absolutions, and copying it word-for-word into the Wednesday service.[77] These texts appeared on Thursday as well, along with prayers borrowed from the Wednesday rite, all with instructions to find the full text on Wednesday. The two days' rites were now nearly the same. There was no ambiguity about whether the penitents were fully absolved at the beginning of their ordeal; indeed, there was no distinct beginning and end, just a repeated series of prayers and absolutions. The clear entrance and exit that had defined early medieval public penance as a passage from one status to another had disappeared.

A contemporary pontifical of Meaux reveals a liturgist thinking along similar lines.[78] Oaths of fidelity to the bishops of Meaux show that this pontifical was in use from the 1270s to the 1350s at least.[79] Instead of separate rites, the contemporary table of contents prom-

76. BN latin 17335 (pontifical of Noyon or Senlis, second half or end of the thirteenth century), f. 122v–134v. Leroquais, *Les pontificaux manuscrits*, vol. II, p. 214, has pointed out that the oaths in the consecration of an abbot indicate Noyon, but the litanies indicate Senlis.

77. BN latin 17335, f. 123v–126v. The texts borrowed from the Thursday rite are *Adesto domine supplicationibus nostris et me qui etiam* (PRG XCIX.230); *Deus humani generis* (PRG XCIX.245, short Gelasian form); *Omnipotens deus qui beato petro apostolo suo* (=PRS XLIXB.20); *Dominus iesus christus qui dixit discipulis suis*; and *Absolutionem et remissionem*. See f. 133r–134v. Of the three absolutions at the end, only the very last is labeled as such. The first listed is striking, but nonetheless traditional, since it was specifically Christ, not God the Father, who promised the power of the keys to Peter. The absolution was itself borrowed from the visitation of the sick, which naturally tended to exchange prayers and absolutions with public penance.

78. BN n.a.l. 1202 (pontifical of Meaux, middle or second half of the thirteenth century).

79. Jean-Baptiste Molin, "Un pontifical de Meaux du XIIIe siècle," *Bulletin de la société d'histoire et de l'art du diocèse de Meaux* 6 (1955): 257–259.

ised a single "ordo ad reconciliandos penitentes in cena domini uel in capite ieiunii" ("rite for reconciliation of penitents on Maundy Thursday or Ash Wednesday"), which turns out to be a Maundy Thursday rite with instructions added to say the same absolution on Wednesday as well, "Eodem modo fit absolutio penitentium in capite ieiunii" ("Absolution of penitents is done in the same way on Ash Wednesday").[80] There was no reference anywhere to a benediction of ashes or expulsion. The use of one rite for both days and the use of a couple of distinctive absolutions in the Thursday rite itself make it look like a highly reworked and shortened version of the Senlis branch.[81] But it had none of signature features of this branch of the north-central family, such as the awkward conflated presentation (PRG XCIX.225C–227C), or the *Venite* before the presentation. Indeed, it had no presentation at all, but it set the *Venite* clumsily at the very end of the rite, after the absolution. Meaux was not far from Noyon or Senlis; perhaps the composers of the two pontificals together compared notes for public penance, if not for other rites.[82]

In any case, the two pontificals indicate how far beliefs about public penance had wandered from the early medieval pattern. In addition to the use of one rite for two, we may observe the priority given to the Thursday rite. Public penance now meant public reconciliation more than public expulsion. The casualness of the suggestion that one can use the Thursday prayers on Wednesday suggests that sometimes only one rite may have even been performed; it was not actually necessary to expel the penitents before reintroducing them. If absolution was all there was, once would do almost as well as twice. With the elimination of a clear beginning and ending, Lenten solemn public penance in this version had become increasingly indistinguishable from the nonsolemn type. It is not surprising, then, that a rubric at the beginning of this section of the Meaux manuscript implies that the reception of penitents is among the rites that may be performed by a simple priest.[83] We are reminded of the provision at Cambrai for the absence of the bishop. Public penance was not going away, but the old liturgical formality was being lost.

The pontifical of Châlons-sur-Marne possessed a rite of public penance closely related to the Tournai-Laon branch of the north-central family.[84] Unlike the abbatial pontificals and the pontifical of Laon,

80. BN n.a.l. 1202, f. 2v, 154v.
81. BN n.a.l. 1202, f. 154r-v.
82. Noyon-Senlis has not one but two old-fashioned coronation rites, the English and the French, BN latin 17335, f. 64; Meaux has the up-to-date French rite, BN n.a.l. 1202, f. 121r.
83. BN n.a.l. 1202, f. 145; see Molin, "Un pontifical de Meaux," p. 259.
84. Châlons-sur-Marne BM 45 (pontifical of Châlons-sur-Marne, second half or end of

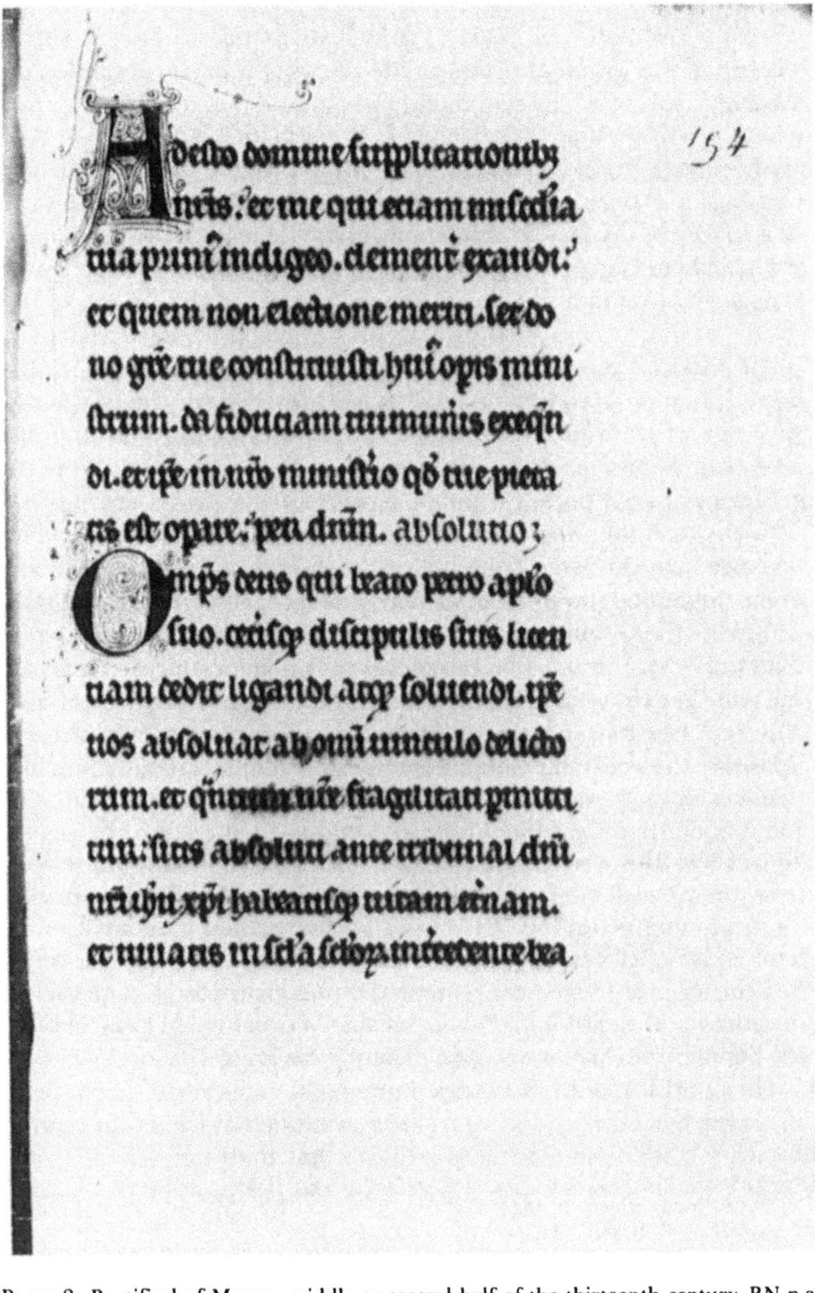

Adesto domine supplicationibus
nris. et me qui etiam misericordia pura indigeo. clementer exaudi.
et quem non electione meriti. sed do-
no gre tue constituisti huius operis mini-
strum. da fiduciam tui muneris exequen-
di. et ipse in nostro ministerio qod tue pietatis est opare. per dnm. absolutio ;
Omnips deus qui beato petro apostolo
suo. ceterisque discipulis suis licen-
tiam dedit ligandi atque soluendi. ipse
nos absoluat ab omni uinculo delicto-
rum. et quantum nostre fragilitati permit-
titur. sitis absoluti ante tribunal dni
nri ihu xpi habeatisque uitam eternam.
et uiuatis in secula seculorum incedente bea-

PLATE 2. Pontifical of Meaux, middle or second half of the thirteenth century. BN n.a.l. 1202, f. 154r. Phot. Bibl. Nat. Paris

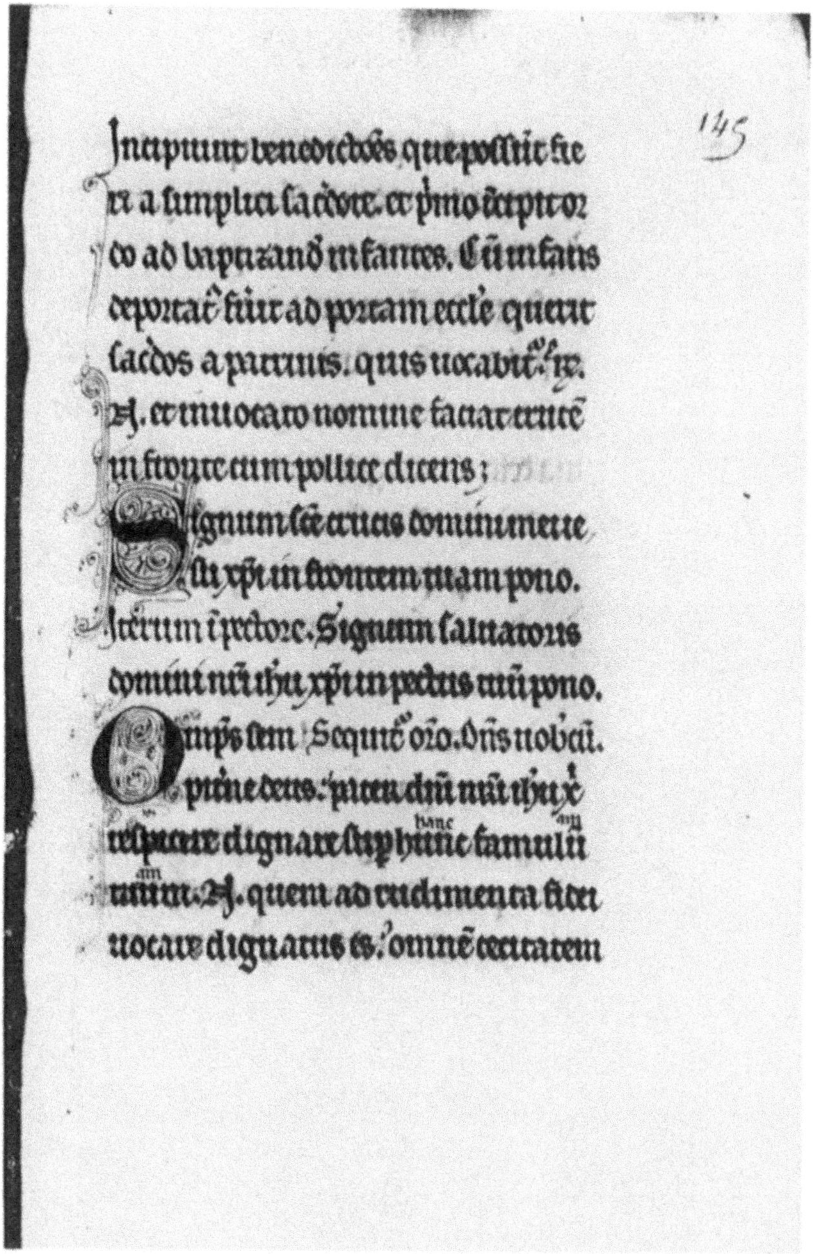

Incipiunt benedictões que possūt fie
ri a simplici sacdote. et pmo scriptor
co ad baptizand infantes. Cū infans
deportat. fuit ad portam eccle querit
sacdos a patrinis. quis vocabit. ꝗ.
ꝗ. et in illo eato nomine faciat crucē
in fronte cum pollice dicens ꞉
Signum sce crucis dominimette.
sui xp̄i in frontem tuam pono.
Iterum in pectore. Signum saluatous
domini nri ihu xp̄i in pectus tuū pono.
Oꝰmps sem. Sequitē oro. Dn̄s nobcū.
Oꝰ pr̄ine deus꞉ patrem dn̄i nr̄i ihu xp̄i
respicere dignare sup hanc famulū
tuū. ꝗ. quem ad rudimenta fidei
vocare dignatus es꞉ omnē cecitatem

PLATE 3. Pontifical of Meaux, middle or second half of the thirteenth century. BN n.a.l.
1202, f. 145r. Phot. Bibl. Nat. Paris

C·IIII

cordis ab eo expelle. dirumpe dñe la
queos sathane quib3 ñ ad colligaūt
Aperi ei domine ianuam pietatis tue
ut signo sapie tue imbutus omium
cupiditatū fetozib3 careat. et ad suauē
odorem preceptoz tuoz letus tibi i eccl'a
tua deseruiat. et pficiat de die in diem
ut idoneus efficiat accede ad gram bap
tismi tui pepta medicina. p eundem.

Preces ñras quesum' alia orano
dñe clement' exaudi. et hunc
electum tuū crucis dñice cui impressi
one eum signam' uirtute custodi. ut
magnitudinis glorie rudimenta ser
uans per custodiam mandatoz tuoz
ad regeneratois gñam puenire mere

2

however, it included full details on the Ash Wednesday expulsion, and not a mere benediction of ashes. In the Wednesday rite, appropriate rubrics added at various points took the place of the long opening rubric from Regino, and the order and choice of prayers differs from the putative model. But the structure remained comparatively traditional, with the omission of a distribution of ashes to all, or even of a genuine absolution for the penitents, though the rite as a whole is called an *absolutio*. The contemporary ordinal supplements our information. It demanded an absolution of the cathedral clergy, followed by what it calls an absolution of the people along with the penitents, though it specifies no text.[85] On Thursday, the pontifical and ordinal agreed that there was to be a collective absolution for the gathered faithful, as the pontifical put it, "communis absolutio omnium qui sunt in ecclesia" ("common absolution of all who are in the church"), followed at once by the reconciliation for the penitents, whom the bishop absolved as a group from the pulpit, "ibi faciat absolutionem communiter" ("there he should make absolution general").[86] The ordinal further provides early morning absolutions of the people by the bishop in the parish churches, as at Reims and Laon, and the absolution of the cathedral chapter, as in its Ash Wednesday rite.[87] Otherwise, the features of public penance are familiar, with the opening *Venite* followed by the presentation of the penitents, the reintroduction, and a series of prayers.

Like several early-thirteenth-century manuscripts that we have seen, a pontifical of Beauvais received extensive corrections after its composition. The rite in its first recension derives naturally enough from the Beauvais I branch of the north-central family.[88] It reproduced a long prayer of presentation found only in its eleventh-century predecessor from the diocese, and its structure was similar. But the Wednesday rite was rearranged, and the Thursday rite made more like the Chartres or Senlis branches to include, for instance, the

---

the thirteenth century), f. 80r–88r. These rites and indeed the whole pontifical are copied with very few changes into a pontifical of the same diocese from the beginning of the fourteenth century, Reims BM 344, especially f. 101r–110r. The earlier MS has a magnificent and delicate illuminated binding; the prompt preparation of a new copy of the pontifical was perhaps intended to preserve it from use.

85. BN latin 10579, f. 56r-v. The people and penitents convene, then the bishop absolves the people before the distribution of ashes: "facit absolutionem super populum. . . . Et episcopus imponit cineres super capita christianorum."

86. Châlons-sur-Marne BM 45, f. 83v, 86v.

87. BN latin 10579, f. 69r–70r. After the penitents are reintroduced and absolved, they offer candles at the altar, a gesture not mentioned in the pontifical.

88. Besançon BM 138 (Beauvais, second half or end of the thirteenth century), f. 117r–131v. There is also a fourteenth-century rite for Maundy Thursday, f. 115r–116v.

conflated presentation (PRG XCIX.225C–227C). On Wednesday, the liturgist has reversed the two parts of the old two-part, north-central rite; now, prayers precede the rubric from Regino. The first part is headed "absolutio penitentium in capite quadragesime super populum" ("absolution of penitents on Ash Wednesday for the people"), probably because the liturgist interpreted this part of the rite as a series of prayers for the whole people, independent of the expulsion of penitents that follows, with the heading "Incipit ordo quomodo penitentes qui publicani suscipiunt" ("Here begins the rite which public penitents perform"). A miniature on the side shows downcast, barefoot penitents in their shirts at the door of the church holding what look like extinguished candles.[89] Similarly, the original Maundy Thursday rite faithfully adopted the choice of prayers and structure of the Beauvais I version with modifications.[90] As in the Beauvais I rite, there were two parts to the Thursday rite, but again the liturgist in his rubric has interpreted the first part as a popular absolution (*super populum*) distinct from the reconciliation of the penitents that followed. The prayer that followed was the old eleventh-century one, and it referred to the clergy's responsibility to guide people to penance. In other words, this late-thirteenth-century adaptor made very few changes in the parts of the eleventh-century model he inherited, but perhaps unconsciously indicated a new understanding of how the parts were to work. Once again, a miniature illustrating public penance accompanied the rite. This one depicted the bishop extending his right hand to the hands of the penitents, again barefoot with bowed heads.[91]

So stood the rite at the time of its composition. One fourteenth-century hand eliminated the first section only of the Thursday service, and another added a new *absolutio super penitentes in die Cene* on separate folios. This new rite may be incomplete; it is certainly a dull business, simply the series of prayers favored by all the branches of the north-central family, minus rubrics, presentation, introduction, or even absolution.[92] It does not make much sense to eliminate a long prayer for popular absolution in the old rite and replace it with yet another absolution for the public penitents, a section not eliminated

89. Besançon BM 138, f. 117r–118v. The miniature is on f. 117r, at the beginning of the whole rite. Leroquais, *Les pontificaux manuscrits*, vol. I, pp. cxxxii–cxxxiv, warns that such illustrations cannot be taken too literally as exact descriptions of a ritual.
90. Besançon BM 138, f. 120r–123r.
91. Besançon BM 138, f. 120r. See Leroquais, *Les pontificaux manuscrits*, vol. III, plate XXXVII, for a reproduction.
92. Besançon BM 138, f. 115r–116v.

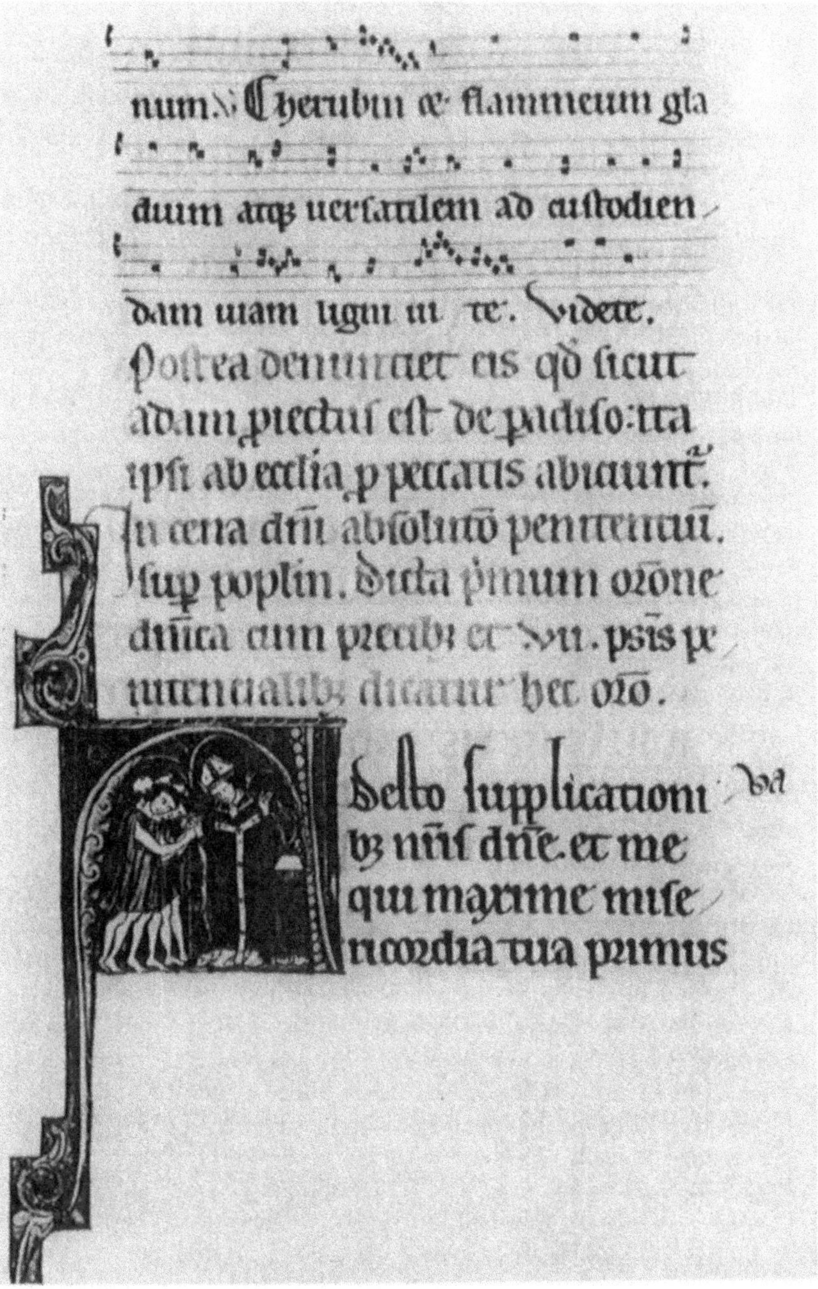

PLATE 5. "La réconciliation des pénitents le jeudi saint." Pontifical of Beauvais, second half or end of the thirteenth century. Besançon BM 138, f. 120r. Published in Victor Leroquais, *Les pontificaux manuscrits des bibliothèques publiques de France* (Paris, 1937), vol. 3, plate XXXVII.

by the corrector. Perhaps the label of the replacement is misleading, and this is really a series of prayers for the people. It is difficult to tell.

Fortunately, while the other pontificals and ordinals provide little evidence of evolution in the rite for the public penitents themselves, almost all unambiguously confirm the trend to invent separate absolutions for the public.[93] A mutilated pontifical of Arras, for instance, has several Maundy Thursday quasi absolutions for the people as a whole, beginning "Absolue quaesumus domine tuorum delicta populorum" ("Lord, we beseech you, absolve the sins of your people"), before the public penitents' *Venite*, entrance, and prayers; it has no Wednesday rite, though one may have been lost.[94] These are not true absolutions invoking the power of the keys, and it is difficult to say anything about their context since the folio that precedes them is missing. In one of these prayers, the "us" refers to the people as a whole, but in another, it refers specifically to the priests whose sins are to be forgiven, "Deus qui nos sacerdotes in populo tuo vocari voluisti" ("God, who wanted us to be called as priests for your people").[95] Possibly these were prayers said by the clergy generally *on behalf of* the people, not benedictions or absolutions *over* the Christian people actually gathered.

Ordinals varied in the degree of popular participation they envisioned. Dioceses around Paris and in Champagne seem to have provided for absolutions of the people faster than dioceses in Normandy or even Picardy; we have seen the precocious examples of Chartres, Laon, and Reims. At Sens, too, a thirteenth-century processional provided for ashes and now an indulgence for everybody at the beginning of Lent, plus a sermon and absolution for all on Maundy Thursday.[96] And an ordinal of Reims from the 1270s, departing here from the ordinal of the cathedral composed around 1200, directed that ashes be distributed to all on Ash Wednesday. The Maundy Thursday rite detailed multiple absolutions of the people, here following the instructions of the early Reims rite, imitated at Laon as well. In the morning, the archbishop walked from one parish to the next, saying absolutions in each. When he returned to the cathedral, he absolved the chapter, then he absolved the people gathered in the nave; the

---

93. A processional of Rouen mentions an Ash Wednesday absolution *in pulpito*, either for the people, or for the penitents, or both; its Thursday rite has been lost: Rouen BM 222, f. 8r.

94. Arras BM 405, f. 48r–50v.

95. Arras BM 405, f. 48r.

96. Sens BM 7, f. 31r–40r, f. 67r-v. The Wednesday expulsion of public penitents follows what seems to be a true indulgence for the people in the technical sense: "det indulgentiam populo." On Thursday, the introduction of penitents comes before the absolution for all. Cf. also a probable general absolution on Ash Wednesday noted in a contemporary ordinal of Sens, BN latin 1206, f. 51v.

reconciliation and absolution of the public penitents followed a few hours later.[97]

By contrast, an ordinal of Bayeux mirrored the rite of absolution for public penance with another absolution, this time specifically for the clergy.[98] First, the penitents on Ash Wednesday went to the door of the church, were absolved, and received ashes; after their expulsion, the bishop and hebdomadary priests returned to the altar in procession "as before," said the absolution "as before," and distributed ashes to the cathedral clergy "as before." In place of the expulsion, they made a short procession to a neighboring church. In this mid- to late-thirteenth-century ordinal, Maundy Thursday rites preserve the traditional presentation of the penitents, *Venite*, introduction, and absolution. An absolution of the canons follows "in the same way as above."[99] The customal of 1270, however, adds an absolution of the people.[100] An ordinal of Amiens from 1291 represented a compromise: It provided a general benediction for all on Ash Wednesday, but for Maundy Thursday, it mentioned only an absolution for the cathedral clergy.[101] The doubling of rites for penitents and clergy appears to be a half-way step to the doubling of rites for penitents and people.

Northern French Rites in the Early Fourteenth Century

After the beginning of the fourteenth century, innovation in the pontifical's treatment of public penance proceeded at a much slower

97. Chevalier, *Sacramentaire . . . de Reims*, pp. 113, 122–123; cf. pp. 274–275, 279–280 for the earlier rite.

98. Chevalier, *Ordinaire et coutumier de l'église cathédrale de Bayeux (XIII s.)*, pp. 102–103. This ordinal dates from the later thirteenth century. The customary of 1270 cites it; but it does include the feast of Saint Francis.

99. Chevalier, *Ordinaire et coutumier de l'église cathédrale de Bayeux (XIII s.)*, pp. 124–125; cf. pp. 306–307, where the same outline appears in the customary of 1270.

100. Raoul Langevin, *Consuetudines et statuta ecclesie baiocensis*, in Chevalier, *Ordinaire et coutumier de l'église cathédrale de Bayeux (XIII s.)*, p. 387: "et modo consueto eos (the public penitents) reconciliat Ecclesie, et facta absolutione super eos et super populum, fit sermo communis ad eos."

101. Durand, *Ordinaires de l'église Notre-Dame cathédrale d'Amiens par Raoul de Rouvroy (1291)*, Mémoires de la Société des antiquitaires de Picardie, Documents inédits concernant la province, 22 (Amiens and Paris, 1934), pp. 179–181, 222–226. Public penance is not mentioned here, but reconciled penitents are blessed on Maundy Thursday in an early-fourteenth-century pontifical of Amiens, Abbeville BM, 8 f. 8r–9v, as well as in the early-thirteenth-century pontifical, Amiens BM 196, f. 63r. It may be that the first part of the "absolutio" referred to in both MSS was directed at the people; the final benediction explicitly mentioned the penitents, however. The ordinal's report of Maundy Thursday celebrations likely omitted public penance because its treatment was too cursory.

pace. Two causes contributed to the decline of experimentation in the pontificals. First, in most dioceses a number of significant changes had already been installed in varying degrees: The prayers now referred to penitents with plural and feminine options; ashes and absolutions were now provided for the whole people; the bishop now absolved penitents at the start of their penance as well as at the end; and the symbolic drama of the reintroduction on Maundy Thursday faded as the penitents were treated as if they had never really been expelled. Liturgists in several dioceses prepared new pontificals after 1300 to reinforce these changes, but experimentation slowed in comparison to the previous century. Meanwhile, a subtle change was taking place in the organization and collation of liturgical books that inadvertently affected the pontificals' rites of penance. There had always been a certain amount of variation in the division of material between the diocesan ordinal and pontifical. Some dioceses had included public penance and public absolutions in both, some divided them between the two books. That variation increased after 1300, and the later pontificals, in particular, tended to be a little less comprehensive than the earlier ones. For example, they might relegate to the ordinal all the popular features of the Lenten liturgy. This shift may have occurred because pontificals from the fourteenth century onward were increasingly luxury items produced to celebrate the election of a particular bishop rather than to serve the diocese during several episcopates. This would explain a growing emphasis on the rites limited to the bishop and the exclusion of popular processions and absolutions involving the chapter. Thus, though a number of rites in the fourteenth-century pontificals look downright conservative, because they omit absolutions and sermons for the Christian faithful, a look at the ordinals often reveals that the retreat is illusory.

Of eleven pontificals surviving from the first half of the fourteenth century, three contain no rites of public penance; two of these three were very mutilated and missing other important *ordines*.[102] Of the eight remaining pontificals that do include public penance, three added little to thirteenth-century models. An early-fourteenth-century pontifical of Châlons-sur-Marne, for instance, simply copied out the already rather conventional rite of public penance in the late-

---

102. The three pontificals were all composed in the first half of the fourteenth century: Toulouse BM 119 (Lisieux); BN latin 972 (Arras); and Paris, Bibl. Mazarine 539 (Rouen). The Arras MS also lacks ordinations, and the Rouen MS lacks pontifical benedictions, among other things. There is also a very fragmentary pontifical of Guillaume de Thiéville, bishop of Coutances (1315–1347), BN latin 973, that in its present form lacks public penance and many other rites.

thirteenth-century pontifical of the diocese.[103] A pontifical of Auxerre cannot be compared to any others of the diocese, but it, too, outlined a rite of public penance like those typical of fifty years earlier. The liturgist stipulated true absolutions for the penitents and people together on Ash Wednesday, and apparently provided for the imposition of ashes on all the laity. The Thursday rite began with the *Venite*, moved to the introduction, and closed with the customary absolutions of the penitents.[104] Although an early-fourteenth-century pontifical of Senlis abandoned the model of earlier pontificals of Noyon-Senlis and of Senlis, it reverted to rites at least as traditional, including a Thursday service based on the Tournai-Laon branch of the north-central family.[105] In fact, this was the most old-fashioned of the three, omitting any mention of Ash Wednesday absolutions of the penitents or absolutions of the people on either day. These anonymous liturgists added nothing of substance to the inventions of their predecessors even where they continued to tinker with minor features of the rites.

Most interesting among the early- and mid-fourteenth-century rites are three pontificals composed for or adapted for use at Sens, plus one semi-ritual, semi-pontifical of Sens. The surfeit of manuscripts for the see is testimony to the wealth and prestige of the archbishops. Of the three true pontificals, two were deluxe presentation pieces prepared for the archbishops, and the third an elegant, if abridged, pontifical of Paris brought early to Sens and adapted to its use. This third manuscript, originating in Paris, is the earliest of the three. Many of its rites are drastically abridged, providing only brief summaries, as one might expect in an ordinal rather than a pontifical. For Ash Wednesday, the rubrics mention an absolution and imposition of ashes, then a sermon to the people, and the ejection of the penitents; it does not say whether the absolution is for people or penitents. The Thursday rite is even shorter, referring only to a "solemn absolution" before the consecration of oils.[106] A sixteenth-century pontifical of Paris will reassure us that public penance had

103. Reims BM 344, f. 101r–110r. Cf. Châlons-sur-Marne BM 45, f. 80r–88r.

104. Auxerre BM 53, f. 59r–60v (printed by Martène, *De antiquis ecclesiae ritibus libri*, IV.17.5, vol. 3, col. 146–147); f. 62r–63v. This rite is not related to the north-central family.

105. Paris, Bibl. Ste-Geneviève 148, f. 96v–104v. The Ash Wednesday rite does not seem to belong to any of the known families or branches, but is simply the straightforward set of prayers and blessings of ashes and hairshirts, without even an early absolution. The Maundy Thursday rite oddly begins with a rubric saying that public penance begins just after terce, but ends with an instruction to sound the bell for terce to summon everyone for the consecration of chrism. The latter rubric is borrowed without alteration from PRG XCIX.223, where it appears before the rite of public penance, indicating that the penitents are reconciled just after the bell, and just before the consecration of chrism.

106. Sens BM 12, f. 71r–72v.

not in fact disappeared in the capital.[107] The brevity of this fourteenth-century text probably indicates an experimental combination of liturgical genres; as we have seen, other liturgists were unsure how to divide rites between ordinal and pontifical.

The two pontificals originally prepared for the archbishop of Sens had the same rite of public penance, evidently the one copied from the other; fortunately, it was more explicit than the Parisian rite adapted for Sens. A coat of arms in the fifth leaf of what is probably the earlier of the two pontificals shows that the manuscript belonged to Archbishop Guillaume de Melun (1346–1378), the second fourteenth-century archbishop of that name. For determining priority, that represents a *terminus ante quem*, but it is no proof that the book was first prepared for him.[108] The oaths and litanies of the later manuscript, dated by Victor Leroquais to the middle or second half of the fourteenth century, prove that it was prepared for Sens, but its inclusion of the Parisian procession and benediction of Lendit and certain extra saints on the litanies suggest that it was used in Paris and Troyes as well, perhaps, Leroquais suggests, when the archbishop of Sens officiated in those cities.[109] We have noted that the two pontificals shared a common rite of public penance, separated only by minor variants. This was not the rite in either of the earlier manuscripts of Sens, and it is not recognizably a version of any branch of the north-central family.[110] But like the other fourteenth-century rites, it offered little new in substance. The penitents were formally absolved on Ash Wednesday; on Maundy Thursday, a rubric explained that each penitent should return with a candle and a *globus borreus*, that is, a sort of sphere filled with stuffing, whose significance is not clear.[111] A

107. BN latin 957, f. 81v–99v. See below for a discussion of this rite.

108. BL Egerton 931; see G. Leroy, "Note sur le pontifical de Guillaume II de Melun, archevêque de Sens (1346–1378)," *Bulletin historique et philologique* (1896): 557–562. I believe this is the earlier MS of the two, both because it seems to have been in existence at the earliest estimated time of composition of the other MS, and because the copyist of BN latin 962 sometimes abbreviated prayers given in full in BL Egerton 931.

109. BN latin 962. Leroquais, *Les pontificaux manuscrits*, vol. II, p. 81. Certainly the archbishop of Sens might celebrate certain rites in Paris; we found that Eudes Rigaud preached and said mass there often, although he was not the metropolitan. But would the archbishop of Sens preside at Lendit, a procession from Paris to Saint-Denis, regularly enough to make such a rite a useful addition to a pontifical? That seems less likely; but I cannot offer any alternative explanation. (This and other pontificals prepared for archbishops very commonly refer to the prelate as *pontifex* and/or *episcopus*; this is no indication of the actual officiant.) Nor can I explain why this second MS copied the long obsolete PRG version of the coronation *ordo*, f. 180v, not the contemporary French version in the first MS, BL Egerton 931, f. 183v.

110. BN latin 934 (pontifical of Sens, second half of the twelfth century); and Sens BM 9 (pontifical of Sens, second half or end of the twelfth century).

111. Du Cange, *Glossarium*, vol. I, p. 710: "globum borreum: tomento fartus, qui in die Cinerum poenitentibus dabatur, ab iisdem reportandus feria v in Coena Domini."

couple of prayers and absolutions followed; there was no presentation or *Venite*.[112] The framework of the rite differed little from early-thirteenth-century efforts. There was no mention of absolutions or ashes for the people here; instead, they were left to other books. That thirteenth-century processional of Sens still in use mentioned the distribution of ashes to all and an indulgence on Ash Wednesday.[113]

Finally, the fourth fourteenth-century manuscript of Sens, a ritual-pontifical, specified in very similar terms at least ashes and indulgences for all on Wednesday, and indulgences for all on Thursday, in addition to the expulsion and reconciliation of the penitents. This book also prescribed the new first-person indicative absolution, *Ego vos absolvo*, on Ash Wednesday, an early liturgical appearance of a formula long since established in the theology.[114] The apparent deference to tradition of the contemporary pontificals thus owes more to a new division of rites between the genres than to any genuine conservatism; the liturgists in these cases have simply limited the pontificals to public penance in the narrowest sense.

Each of the Sens pontificals complements the rite with an illustration, worthy of note because of their rarity, but not particularly enlightening about penance. In the first manuscript, alongside the middle of the Ash Wednesday service, a bishop (or archbishop) is shown with his right hand raised in benediction. With him stand clerics, identified by their tonsured heads; no laymen or women appear.[115] This may picture a benediction of penitents or of the people or the absolutions of the clergy long traditional on Ash Wednesday and Maundy Thursday alike. In the second, the miniature illustrates Maundy Thursday; a bishop standing *behind* barefoot male and female penitents ushers them into the door of the church. They are pictured holding candles, but no *globi*, and the rubric calls for the bishop to *face* the penitents at the door.[116] These are not accurate renderings of the specific rituals practiced at Sens, but iconic illustrations of a benediction or a reconciliation. Unfortunately, these un-

112. BL Egerton 931, f. 210v–218r; and BN latin 962, f. 196r–202r.

113. Sens BM 7, f. 31r–40r, 67r–68r. And a thirteenth-century ordinal of Sens referred to *orationes* over the people on Ash Wednesday, and absolutions evidently for the penitents and laity together on Maundy Thursday: BN latin 1206, f. 51v, 55v–56r.

114. Sens BM 27, pp. 307–345, 355–359. This text includes both priests and bishop's rites, while summarizing a little more than is normal in rituals and pontificals. The absolutions on Wednesday and Thursday may well be general absolutions, not limited to the public penitents. The *Ego vos absolvo* appears in the Wednesday rite, after the standard deprecatory absolutions.

115. BL Egerton 931, f. 211v.

116. BN latin 962, f. 200v; a reproduction of this miniature may be found in Leroquais, *Les pontificaux manuscrits*, vol. III, pl. lxxv.

helpful miniatures and the one in the pontifical of Beauvais are the only contemporary pictures of public penance that I have been able to examine.[117]

Two relevant pontificals of Amiens survive, one from the early part of the century, one probably a half-century younger at least and known to us only through a seventeenth-century copy; the later manuscript's rite of penance is a revised version of that in the earlier, itself a revision of the thirteenth-century rite for Amiens.[118] The second dates from the mid–fourteenth century at the earliest, since it includes the feast of *Corpus Christi*, which spread to northern France at about that time, and also the first-person singular indicative absolutions for private penance and excommunication, *Ego te absolvo*, again a late development in the northern French liturgy.[119] Now the early-fourteenth-century text shared with the thirteenth-century pontifical a Maundy Thursday service limited to an undramatic reconciliation of the penitents, plus, at the end of the rite, the *Confiteor* and absolution, perhaps to be said for the people. It added a benediction of ashes, but nothing else, for Ash Wednesday.[120] A somewhat later hand excised this final absolution, and the later-fourteenth-century pontifical reproduced the rite without it.[121] Would this indicate a reversion to the old limitation of Maundy Thursday services to the public penitents alone? More likely, the two pontificals do not tell the whole story. The ordinal of 1291 referred to a general absolution on Ash Wednesday missing in the pontificals;[122] these popular absolutions turn up only inconsistently in a variety of liturgical books.

Unfortunately, there are no western French pontificals with rites of public penance in the early fourteenth century, but three Norman and Angevin ordinals of the second half of the century may partially replace the missing evidence. Like the earlier Norman rites, the two ordinals here with rites of expulsion and reconciliation of penitents remained relatively loyal to the order in the Romano-Germanic Pontifical, adding only Wednesday absolutions for the penitents. These

117. Arras BM 13 (pontifical of Sens, mid to late fourteenth century), f. 92r, also portrays the absolution of public penitents, but this manuscript is in restoration.

118. Cf. Amiens BM 196 (pontifical of Amiens, mid–thirteenth century); Abbeville BM 8 (pontifical of Amiens, beginning or first half of the fourteenth century); Lyon BM 570, f. 178–218 (seventeenth-century copy by Jean Deslions of a pontifical of Amiens).

119. Lyon BM 570, f. 215v.

120. Amiens BM 196, f. 61v–63r; and Abbeville BM 8, f. 1r–10r, 120v–122r. The Abbeville MS also added a longer rubric, including what to do when the bishop was or was not present, f. 1r; cf. also the correcting hand, f. 9v.

121. Abbeville BM 8, f. 10r; and Lyon BM 570, f. 200v–202v. The later pontifical also added a prayer for the penitents not found in the earlier versions.

122. Durand, *Ordinaires de l'église Notre-Dame cathédrale d'Amiens*, p. 181.

were ordinals for the cathedrals of Coutances and Evreux. At Evreux, the text explicitly prescribed the distribution of ashes to all on Wednesday and absolutions for all on Thursday, while the more ambiguous ordinal of Coutances also probably intended the rites to be for the whole laity.[123] A third ordinal, prepared for parishes of the diocese of Tours, naturally omitted public penance as a primarily episcopal function, but it did prescribe an Ash Wednesday absolution and then ashes for the laity at the door of the church.[124] Although the Norman rites of public penance, like the English, would remain more conservative than those in northeastern France, these ordinals may reassure us that the provision of ashes and absolutions for the laity was well established everywhere north of the Loire.

The *Ego te absolvo* just mentioned is characteristic only of pontificals composed from 1350 or later. Those accustomed to the history of theology may find this a century too late: it was in the mid–thirteenth century that Thomas Aquinas asserted, albeit controversially, that the words *Ego te absolvo* are the necessary formula of absolution.[125] Thomas admitted that the first-person singular indicative formula was unknown hardly thirty years before he was writing; but he believed that this formula alone properly recognized the power of forgiveness bestowed in the ordained priest in sacramental penance, a view that came to be widely accepted.[126] Thomas made no mention of absolutions for public penitents, since his interest lay above all in the private rite. As a rule, liturgical books did not record the absolutions for private penance, but it seems that the new formula spread among confessors. Public penance was another matter. Its liturgy had a patina of age, and while the timing of absolutions was liable to adjustment, the formulas were relatively stable. A few Norman and English pontificals long preferred the first-person plural *absolvimus vos*, one of

---

123. R. Delamare, ed. *Ordo servicii de l'insigne cathédrale d'Evreux* (Paris, 1925), pp. 98–99, 130–133; BN latin 1301 (ordinal of Coutances, late fourteenth century), f. 105v–107v, 126v–128r. The rite of Coutances provided the traditional presentation, then the *Venite*, then reintroduction. The rite of Evreux mentioned only the *Venite* and reintroduction, but added that penitents who completed their penance should offer lit candles, and those who still had satisfaction left should offer extinguished candles, p. 133; cf. BN n.a.l. 306, f. 58v–59r, a twelfth-century pontifical of Rouen that had the finished penitents offer lit candles.

124. BN latin 1237, f. 14r. This is an abbreviated nonepiscopal ordinal; it lacks any rite of public penance and Thursday general absolutions.

125. Thomas Aquinas, *De forma absolutionis*, vol. XL:C, pp. 33–41. See Jungmann, *Die lateinischen Bussriten*, pp. 258–259.

126. Thomas Aquinas, *De forma absolutionis*, p. 40: "Addit etiam obiciendo quod vix triginta anni sunt quod omnes hac sola forma utebantur, 'Absolutionem et remissionem, etc.'"; for the acceptance of Thomas's view, see Gy, "Histoire liturgique du Sacrement de Pénitence," p. 18, and "Les définitions de la confession après le quatrième concile du Latran," pp. 290–295. There is a little evidence of the new formula's use in private penance in the late twelfth century: Vogel, "Les rituels de la pénitence tarifée," p. 425.

the options in the tenth-century Romano-Germanic pontifical. The plural softened the claim of the individual priest's or bishop's power of the keys and suggested that the church as a whole was absolving the penitent. Their preferred formula actually began with a reference to the penitents' condition and the grant of the keys, not with the stark *absolvimus* or *ego*, which softened the effect still further. Almost all northern French rites outside Normandy chose deprecative absolutions, sometimes borrowed from public penance in the Romano-Germanic pontifical, with or without slight adaptations; less often, they borrowed from rites of extreme unction. It is worth noting in passing that even these deathbed rites, conducted for one person in comparative privacy, never used the new indicative formula.[127]

The *Ego te absolvo* arrived very late and even then in a very few northern French pontifical rites for absolving excommunicants or penitents. Deprecative absolutions may have remained in use not only because of tradition but because the public rite naturally focused attention on the palpable humiliation and satisfaction of the penitent and not on the power of the bishop. Whatever the theology said, it looked like the penitent was earning his forgiveness, not receiving it from the priest. The solemnity of the rite, its liturgical demonstration, was its real guarantee of effectiveness. There may possibly have been an occasional private indicative absolution for a public penitent when he made his first confession, before any actual public rite, but this was not part of the liturgy. In his treatise, Thomas argued that the new formula should be the standard of sacramentality, but as we have seen, several contemporary authors of confessors' manuals still regarded public penance as somehow more sacramental than private. Indeed, Thomas himself continued to treat public penance as a sacramental form of penance. The *Ego te absolvo* probably never caught on in most rites from the thirteenth century through the sixteenth century because once the solemnity of public penance failed to guarantee its sacramentality, it was difficult to endow it with a new legitimacy borrowed awkwardly from the private rite. Solemn penance was either sacramental because it was solemn, or it was not sacramental at all. In any case, the liturgy of public penance did not follow the path prescribed by the theology.

In Chapter 6, on the Roman tradition of penance, I developed the

---

127. Such rites appear in the vast majority of pontificals and rituals that I have examined, and I have not found any use of the new formula. See also V. Fiala, "Die Sündenvergebung und das lateinische Stundengebet," in *Liturgie et rémission des péchés*, Bibliotheca "Ephemerides Liturgicae," Subsidia, 3 (Rome, 1975), pp. 97–98, 111, for the survival of the deprecative formula in the monastic liturgy.

argument that the early medieval rite of penance was not merely vaguely emotional, but it offered dramatic representation. In the Romano-Germanic pontifical, the bishop represented the people and admitted his own sin while expelling the penitents from participation in the body of the church. An archdeacon spoke *ex parte penitentium* ("for the penitents"), and he presented their appeal to the bishop for readmission to the church. It was of course a dramatic affair in the looser sense as well, a moment of heightened emotion framed by the gestures of prostration, dismissal, and eventual readmission hand-by-hand from the portal to the altar. Later rites of penance in northern France became considerably less dramatic in any sense. We have found pontificals switching the order of presentation and introduction or omitting the presentation altogether. The hand-to-hand reintroduction of penitents from priest to archdeacon to bishop dies out, while the Thursday liturgy increasingly treats the penitents as already reconciled.

It is perhaps more than simply an interesting coincidence that just when the liturgy of penance ceased to be dramatic in the twelfth and thirteenth centuries, ecclesiastical drama itself was beginning to develop an identity separate from that of the liturgy—especially in those regions, northern France, the Rhineland, and England, that still harbored public penance. The most important seasons for the new drama were festive occasions, such as the *Quem queritis* play at Easter, and the Christmas cycle of nativity and epiphany plays.[128] Penitential moments did not figure among the new plays, yet the coincidence is striking, and it is not so paradoxical as it may seem. While dramatic representation embedded in the liturgy itself faded, dramatic impersonation separate from the liturgy flourished. The difference between representation and impersonation before an audience marks the creation of a distance between the people and the ritual act.[129]

128. The origin of religious drama in the West has been much disputed. Chambers's pioneering study, *The Mediaeval Stage*, dated the first appearance of independent plays to the mid twelfth century and their evolution away from the liturgy to 1250–1350, particularly in Frankish lands, pp. 27–28, 69–96; but Chambers insists that the main impetus had to come from outside the church because of clerical hostility, p. 98, a view based on the untenable assumption of an antagonism between clerical and popular culture. Young, *The Drama of the Medieval Church*, argues that the true origin of medieval drama lay not in the liturgical representations but in tropes, 1:79–110, 178; he convincingly stresss the difference between liturgical representation and independent impersonation, but fails to see any evolutionary link between them. Hardison, *Christian Rite and Christian Drama in the Middle Ages*, esp. pp. 15–16, 41–43, tries to remedy these defects by tracing parallels between dramatic liturgy and the actual drama, but he assumes an unchanging "dramatic instinct" at work and so misses the real transformation that took place in the thirteeenth century.

129. Cf. the parallel evolution "from allegory to mimesis" and from rite to game to theater offered by Grinberg and Kinser, "Les combats de carnaval et de carême," p. 74, in their

The pattern suggests that a study of the origins of drama should focus on a change in the nature and purpose of the liturgy. A ritual of penance in which the audience were beneficiaries and also participants, at least by representation, gave way to a division of functions, in which the audience for public penance was just that, a passive group of spectators. The same faithful now actually participated in the benediction and distribution of ashes, but the rite and collective absolutions that followed were separated from the ritual for individual penitents. Simultaneously, the new Christmas and Easter liturgy separated and focused popular attention on a series of extraliturgical dramatic impersonations rather than, for example, the older Palm Sunday processions in which the whole town played the roles of the crowd at Jerusalem within the framework of the liturgy.

Later Developments and Other Regions

This survey of the rites of Lenten public penance has left us with a thriving but transformed institution. Yet the story does not end in 1350 in the midst of the Black Death and the Hundred Years War, nor was northern France the sole haven of public penance after 1200. For the sake of comparison, we may glance briefly first at the later liturgy of public penance from the fourteenth century through the seventeenth century, and then at the liturgy of adjacent regions: France south of the Loire, the Rhineland, and England. We may recall the analysis of the demise of public penance at Rome (see Chapter 6), a demise that many historians have taken to be the common fate of the rite. This brief comparative study will suggest that the truth is completely different. At least some pontificals in all these regions continued to reproduce some form of public penance as late as the fourteenth century, and, like the northern French rites, many continued to experiment with the framework of the rite in the twelfth and thirteenth centuries.

Victor Leroquais lists about thirty-seven northern French full or partial pontificals from the last half of the fourteenth through the end of the sixteenth century; at least eleven of these have rites of public penance, and approximately eighteen are so fragmentary that the absence should not surprise us. In addition, Leroquais lists one manuscript pontifical of Sens written in 1671 that contains a rite of

---

analysis of late medieval literary combats of Carnival and Lent; the apparently more "realistic" treatment of the later combats betokens a sharpened opposition between players (or author) and spectators.

public penance.[130] A few examples from such late rites of public penance may suggest how public penance evolved after 1350. A fifteenth-century pontifical of Rouen lacks any Ash Wednesday rite, but it prescribes the arrival of penitents at the west portal, followed by the presentation, the *Venite*, a sermon, and the benediction of penitents, treated as reconciled before their satisfaction.[131] A contemporary missal of Rouen printed by Martène supplies the Ash Wednesday rite; it begins with an absolution, perhaps for all the faithful, then follows with a traditional homily explaining their expulsion to the penitents, and then the actual expulsion.[132] A contemporary ordinal also printed by Martène confirms the pontifical's account of the Thursday afternoon reconciliation, but it adds an early morning general absolution for all.[133] All this is consistent enough with the rite established by the late-twelfth-century pontifical.[134] More strikingly old-fashioned still is a fifteenth-century pontifical of Angers that actually adapted and revised the text of the north-central family of rites, the only example I have found of this family in a western French pontifical.[135] The liturgist copied out Regino's rubric, now five centuries old, at the beginning of Ash Wednesday, in addition to the characteristic Thursday run-on presentation of the Chartres and Senlis branches of the family.

Lest one imagine that late northern French pontificals were content with antiquarian revivals for public penance, we observe a Parisian rite appearing in two late-fifteenth-century missals and in one early-sixteenth-century pontifical that prepared an elaborate and novel combination of public penance with popular absolutions and indulgences.[136] The Wednesday rite provided an absolution and benediction over the people; after the blessing, imposition of ashes, and sermon, it repeated the absolution and benediction. Perhaps the first was for the people, the second for the penitents. Or perhaps these were

---

130. Sens BM 11, in Leroquais, *Les pontificaux manuscrits*, vol. II, p. 335.

131. BN latin 969, f. 73v–74r.

132. Martène, *De antiquis ecclesiae ritibus libri*, IV.17.9, vol. 3, cols. 151–152; according to Martimort, this is Rouen BM A 11, a missal from around 1455.

133. Martène, *De antiquis ecclesiae ritibus libri*, IV.22.2, vol. II, cols. 237–238; Martimort identifies it as an ordinal of Rouen from the first half or middle of the fifteenth century.

134. Cf. BN n.a.l. 306, f. 37v–46r, 50v–59r.

135. BN latin 954, f. 54r–55v. The rubrics indicate that the actual prayers for Wednesday and Thursday appear in the missal; here at least a pontifical restricted its coverage to the bare framework of the rite. As we have noted, the division between genres was changing, and a full study of later rites of penance would require examination of missals as well as pontificals and ordinals.

136. Martène, *De antiquis ecclesiae ritibus libri*, IV.17.2, vol. 3, cols. 142–144, for the Ash Wednesday rite in the missals, according to Martimort, edited from BN latin 859–859A and BN latin 15280; BN latin 956–957 is the pontifical; there are significant differences between missals and the pontificals, especially in the rubrics.

both general absolutions, with the odd repetition as the residue of the thirteenth- and fourteenth-century combination of individual public penance with the penance of the faithful.[137] Thereafter, the bishop went to the main door, where he expelled the penitents, who had been waiting there all along. In a striking addition to the sixteenth-century rubrics, the bishop was to warn the populace not to mock the penitents or "say such things to them that they might leave their penance or diminish their devotion."[138]

It is surely a sign of the decline of public penance that the solemn penitents of Paris, those who once shocked the whole city, have become cheap figures of fun like adulterers in the stocks. The Maundy Thursday rite in this pontifical went further than fourteenth-century pontificals in providing for popular absolutions. That morning in the cathedral, the bishop of Paris was to say a series of prayers and absolutions for the faithful borrowed from the rite of public penance, and then he repeated the absolutions and benedictions at Saint-Magloire and the cemetery of the Innocents.[139] Although a rubric at the end of the Wednesday rite had reminded the rural deans to return their public penitents to the bishop on Maundy Thursday, there was no explicit mention of them here. Either the morning prayers and absolutions in the cathedral applied to them as well, or the bishop reconciled them after his return to Notre-Dame in the afternoon. The main business of the day was in any case the station-by-station absolutions and benedictions, a series of collective expiations that transformed the day into something much like Rogations. Public penance survived in Paris long after its supposed death, but by the sixteenth century, it was a sideshow.

Contemporary with the development of general absolutions and indulgences for the people in the cathedral was the appearance of a Lenten or Easter omnibus confession by the people in each parish. In a sense, this was a reappearance; we have already noted use of public omnibus confessions before the implementation of *Omnis utriusque*. Like the Ash Wednesday confession in the Romano-Germanic Pontifical, these confessions, said by a parish in unison, enumerated all sorts of sins.[140] And of course the brief, unspecific general confession, the

137. Martène, *De antiquis ecclesiae ritibus libri*, IV.17.2, vol. 3, cols. 143–144; BN latin 957, f. 81v–93r. In the sixteenth-century pontifical it is left unclear who was the target of each absolution. For the first, the bishop raised his hands over the people, and a "benediction of the people" followed; after the sermon, the bishop again "absolved the people."

138. BN latin 957, f. 93r, "ne derideant penitentes vel talia dicant unde retrahantur a penitencia uel eorum devotio minuatur."

139. BN latin 957, f. 95r-v.

140. PRG XCIX.50a, vol. II, pp. 16–17. In the PRG, it is said by the penitents about to

Confiteor before the consecration, had always remained an important moment in the parish confession at Easter. Nicole Lemaître's study of northern French rituals of the fifteenth century and the pre-Tridentine sixteenth century has, however, turned up a large number of parish confessions to be said in French on Ash Wednesday, Maundy Thursday, or Easter Day. These included long omnibus lists of every conceivable crime, from adultery to usury to the neglect of required feasts. Sins against neighbor predominated.[141] Scholastic theologians had argued that these general confessions helped cleanse Christians of venial and forgotten sins, but they could not replace sacramental confession and absolution for mortal sins. Whatever the technicalities, however, the use of indicative absolutions surely tempted parishioners to think that something more was offered.[142] The similarity between these confessions and the cathedral absolutions is clear enough. Like the absolutions, they contributed to the transformation of the season into something more like Rogations, a simultaneous celebration of unity and collective expiation.[143] Like the absolutions, they effectively separated the commission of particular crimes from the general expiation. Everyone confessed and received absolution whether or not he or she was guilty of any of the mortal sins in the list. Unlike public penance, collective expiation had nothing to do with seeing divine justice done on earth.

When did public penance disappear in northern France? It is a difficult question to answer without a great deal more study of fifteenth- and sixteenth-century liturgical books. Leroquais's catalog of pontificals does not indicate any salient decline in the frequency of

---

undergo the public rite; but we know from Caesarius that similar sorts of confessions were said in some parishes. See Chapter 3. Martène, *De antiquis ecclesiae ritibus libri*, I.6.7.18, vol. I, cols. 820–821, has printed a late example in monastic use, from a thirteenth-century missal of Saint-Gatien, Tours: The sinning brother is to confess a long list of crimes, including some highly improbable for someone in a cloister, such as adultery; it may be meant for lay brothers as well as monks. The confession is to be made to one brother, or to the whole community, or to the abbot.

141. Lemaître, "Confession privée et confession publique dans les paroisses du XVIe siècle," pp. 197–198, and "Pratique et signification de la confession communautaire dans les paroisses au XVIe siècle," in *Pratiques de la confession*, esp. p. 145.

142. Cf. Alexander of Hales, *Glossa in quatuor libros sententiarum*, IV. D.16, p. 264; Thomas Aquinas, *Commentum in quatuor libros sententiarum*, IV D.21 q.2 a.1, pp. 856–857; Richard of Middleton, *Super quatuor libros sententiarum*, IV D.21 a.3 q. 1, p. 338; Duns Scotus, *Quaestiones in quartum librum sententiarum* D.17 q. unica, p. 506. Thomas and Richard note that the general confession of forgotten venial sins in secret confession is sacramental; but public liturgical general confession is not. See Lemaître, "Pratique et signification de la confession communautaire," pp. 139–140, 151–153.

143. But it is an exaggeration to suggest, as Lemaître does, "Pratique et signification de la confession communautaire," pp. 147–149, that general confession *replaces* public penance, since we have seen how the expulsion and reconciliation of public penitents is attested into the sixteenth century.

the rites through the sixteenth century. A fifteenth-century ordinal of Evreux revised an earlier text by cutting out the expulsion of penitents and drastically shortening the reconciliation.[144] But we have already seen that there was some sort of public penance in fifteenth-century Rouen and Angers and even in sixteenth-century Paris. Most likely there was a slow but definite decline after 1400 or so, and the latest rites seem to suggest that the public penitents were socially and theologically marginal indeed. In Chapter 8, I look briefly at the survival of quasi-public penances and pilgrimages imposed by city governments and other secular authorities in northern France and Flanders between 1300 and 1600; it may be that these half-religious punishments absorbed some of the cases formerly dealt with by bishops and archbishops.

Only a handful of pontificals composed before 1300 survive from France south of the Loire; those that do typically possess rites of public penance.[145] With the transferral of the papal court to Avignon, however, the majority of dioceses in Provence and in south-central France adopted either the Roman curial pontifical that virtually eliminated public penance or Guillaume Durand's pontifical with an elaborate but suspiciously artificial public penance. At times, some of the surviving southern rites of public penance before and after 1300 look dubious as well, and we may wonder if public penance was ever as strong in the far south as in the north. The imitation of the Roman disuse of public penance may owe something to preconditioning as well as to the arrival of the papal court, since the decline predates the papal residence in Avignon. West-central France, the Poitou and the Limousin, were probably even less welcoming to public penance than Provence. Two late-fourteenth-century pontificals of Luçon said that public penitents were expelled in Paris "and other churches of France," but not in Poitiers, Luçon, and Maillezais (dép. Vendée). Even so, they provided the expulsion and reconciliation, perhaps out of an urge for completeness.[146] Dioceses in the province of Lyon, on the other hand, generally remained loyal to local rites and to public penance.

144. Delamare, *Ordo servicii de l'insigne cathédrale d'Evreux*, pp. xxii, 99.
145. This analysis of rites south of the Loire is based on a review of the southern French pontificals listed in Leroquais's *Les pontificaux manuscrits* as well as the few southern rites in Martène and the inspection of a few manuscript pontificals in the BN. Leroquais lists approximately thirty-five pontificals of the twelfth through fourteenth centuries from what is now France south of the Loire. Of these, twenty-one are fourteenth-century copies of PRC or PGD. There are seven diocesan pontificals composed before 1300; all but one include public penance. And there are seven fourteenth-century diocesan pontificals; only one unambiguously excludes public penance.
146. Leroquais, *Les pontificaux manuscrits*, vol. I, pp. 71, 151.

A few specific examples suffice to show this pattern in practice. Beginning with west-central France, we have already remarked on two twelfth- to early-thirteenth-century monastic books of central France south of the Loire, which were copied for abbeys in Limoges and Aurillac. The ritual-ordinal of Limoges included a short reconciliation of public penitents on Maundy Thursday, but it cited out-of-date fifth-century authorities on penance that overshadowed the rite itself, as if the rite appeared out of respect for the old canons.[147] The ritual of Saint-Gérard of Aurillac included only an *absolutio super penitentes* separate from the Lenten rites.[148] A thirteenth-century episcopal pontifical of Poitiers also apparently omitted public penance.[149] Turning further south, some episcopal pontificals from the twelfth through fourteenth centuries preserved a rite of public penance, but without the experimentation typical of the north. A pontifical of Narbonne contemporary with these had a very conventional Wednesday rite for the expulsion of the penitents. There was still no imposition of ashes on all or absolution in advance of satisfaction.[150] Similar was a fourteenth-century rite from Arles; its Thursday service followed very closely the traditional pattern of the Romano-Germanic Pontifical, from presentation, to *Venite*, to introduction.[151] An early-fourteenth-century rite of Aix-en-Provence made a slight breach with tradition by providing a procession for the people at the beginning of Lent, but it omitted the early absolution, and it spruced up the Thursday service with more obsolescent advice from Popes Innocent I and Vigilius.[152] For a rite of public penance without such a musty air, one must look a little further north. A fourteenth-century pontifical of Lyon, evidently based on a Norman model, prescribed a Wednesday rite with ashes and absolution for the penitents, then ashes and procession for clergy and people, a doubling that we have found to be

147. BN latin 1341, f. 26r-v.

148. BN latin 944, f. 113r–114r.

149. Leroquais, *Les pontificaux manuscrits*, vol. II, pp. 256–261, Poitiers BM 39; but this is not a complete MS. Oddly, a printed missal of Limoges, dated 1483 and republished by Martène, *De antiquis ecclesiae ritibus libri*, IV.17.10, vol. III, cols. 153–154, does provide an Ash Wednesday service of public penance, though without the expulsion. Perhaps Leroquais's pontificals should be compared with ordinals and missals for a more complete study.

150. Martène, *De antiquis ecclesiae ritibus libri*, IV.17.1, vol. III, cols. 140–141. The source of this text remains unidentified.

151. Martène, *De antiquis ecclesiae ritibus libri*, IV.17.3, vol. III, cols. 144–145, and IV.22, vol. III, col. 326. Martimort has identified this as BN latin 1220, a pontifical of Arles from the first half of the fourteenth century. The Thursday rite follows PRG XCIX.224–230 with minimal changes, then selects from the remainder of the PRG prayers and absolutions.

152. BN latin 949, f. 9v–12v, 21r–28v. The Thursday rite includes an interrogation of the penitents' priest, "Is he worthy to be reconciled?" As in PGD, there is no provision for an answer of "no"; see PGD III.2.10, p. 560. Cf. BN n.a.l. 306, a late-twelfth-century pontifical of Rouen, f. 58v–59r, where the distinction is real.

characteristic of northern rites, too.[153] With further study, it may be possible to establish a spectrum from Provence, where public penance ossified or faded; to east-central France, where it survived; to northern and northeastern France, where it both survived and evolved rapidly.

Much as one would expect, rites of public penance from the Rhineland imitated the Romano-Germanic Pontifical more closely than did northern or southern French rites. Yet, as a brief review shows, even these Rhenish rites experienced the same major evolutionary changes as liturgical texts further west. We have already mentioned a late-twelfth-century pontifical of Trier adapted to the use of Paris whose Thursday service was similar in outline and text to the Romano-Germanic Pontifical; the Ash Wednesday service was limited to the blessing of ashes, plus a possible general benediction.[154] A twelfth-century pontifical of Mainz likewise possessed Ash Wednesday and Maundy Thursday rites that were much simplified and shortened versions of their tenth-century predecessor; they were quite independent of Gelasian or later French influence. Yet, already here too the archbishop is to absolve the penitents on Wednesday before their expulsion.[155] Two centuries later, another pontifical of Mainz followed the same general outline as its predecessor for Maundy Thursday, only elaborating the prayers and especially the absolutions. In addition to two standard deprecative formulas, this pontifical borrowed two more absolutions from a rite of extreme unction and added a first-person plural indicative absolution.[156] The experimentation with different types of absolution suggests a dissatisfaction with the traditional forms, which perhaps seemed insufficiently definite and personal. Neither of these manuscripts mentioned rites for the whole people, but fourteenth-century pontificals of Trier and Verdun do, in

153. Martène, *De antiquis ecclesiae ritibus libri*, I.6.7.19, vol. I, cols. 821–823; Martimort identifies this as a pontifical of Downside Abbey. Martène does not print the whole Thursday rite, but as in the PGD, a rubric directs the bishop to inquire which penitents are worthy of reconciliation and which not; we cannot tell whether this was still a real distinction here.

154. BN latin 13315, f. 144r–145r, 149r–155r; the Thursday rite is printed by Martène, *De antiquis ecclesiae ritibus libri*, IV.22, vol. III, cols. 316–319.

155. BN latin 946, f. 126v–127r, 90r–94v. For some reason, the Wednesday rite appears after the Thursday rite, and in a different but contemporary hand. The Thursday reintroduction follows the general outline of the PRG, from presentation to *Venite* to introduction and absolution, and its choice of prayers and textual variants is quite different from that in French rites.

156. BN latin 948, f. 30r–32v, esp. 32r–v; this has been printed by Martène, *De antiquis ecclesiae ritibus libri*, IV.22, vol. III, cols. 335–338. The first of the absolutions that I take to have been adapted from the visitation of the sick refers to the laying on of hands: "deus qui per manus tue imposicione animarum et corporum valitudines effugasti . . . exaudi preces nostras, pro hiis famulis et famulabus tuis morbo criminum hactenus tabescentibus . . . ut infundatur eis spiritus sancti gratia."

addition to the expulsion and reconciliation of public penitents. At Verdun, the bishop blessed the people in one Wednesday rite, and quite possibly absolved them at the same time.[157] At Trier, the liturgist added to the late-twelfth-century model for Maundy Thursday an indulgence for pilgrims and penitents alike.[158] The Trier rite in particular has much in common with rites of several eastern French cities that we have seen, such as Laon and Reims.

The similarity of development in France and the Rhineland is unsurprising. More difficult to interpret is the evolution of public penance in England. We noted in Chapter 4 how certain English statutes referred to the public rite as in need of revival but others continued to treat it as a ready option for the bishop.[159] English liturgical books consistently provide rites of public penance throughout this period.[160] A brief review reveals an evolution rather less well defined than in the northern French or western German rites. We have already noted a twelfth-century pontifical from a diocese in the province of Canterbury that reproduced exactly the same text of public penance found in a contemporary pontifical of Mont-Saint-Michel or Avranches.[161] This was a highly conservative rite, imitating the outline of the Romano-Germanic pontifical's text and choosing the Rhenish rather than the Gelasian form of a key prayer.[162] Some rites later than 1250 or so have absolutions for the people on Wednesday and/or Thursday; some have the Wednesday absolution.[163] But even these

157. BN latin 966 (second half or end of the fourteenth century), f. 22v–28v, 39v–50r, 50v–64v. There are *two* Ash Wednesday rites for the expulsion of penitents, both seemingly in the same hand. The second, f. 39v–50r, is more faithful to the PRG, copying even the opening rubric, PRG XCIX.44, that still expected priests would not reconcile penitents who had not finished their multiyear satisfactions; yet this rite, too, absolved the penitents at once. The first sends the penitents away with candles and *borrea*, like the pontifical of Sens, BN latin 962, and may suggest eastern French influence; this is the one with a general benediction. I cannot explain why there are two.

158. BN latin 950 (first half or middle of the fourteenth century), f. 18r–25v, esp. f. 18v: "nuncietur indulgentia omnibus tam peregrinis quam penitentibus. ipsa ebdomada ecclesiam ipsam visitantibus indulta." Several of the prayers in the reconciliation have been corrected by a later hand to replace *famulos* with *fideles*, and so forth, as if to adapt these for the whole people, not just penitents, for whom *famuli* had become traditional. There is no Ash Wednesday rite in this MS.

159. See Powicke and Cheney, p. 133, 154–155, 235, 370, 409, 616, 721, 1028–1029, for evidence of the survival of public penance, and pp. 899–900, for a complaint in 1281 about its decline.

160. A thirteenth-century pontifical of Saint Andrews, BN latin 1218, lacks the rite, and so do several partial pontificals, but this is no sure proof of the disappearance of public penance in these dioceses.

161. Wilson, *The Pontifical of Magdalen College*, pp. 152–154, 156–159. Cf. BN latin 14852.

162. PRG XCIX.245, "Deus humani generis benignissime conditor," which I have noted as a touchstone of Gelasian influence. Other English rites also prefer the PRG version.

163. The ordinal of the cathedral of Norwich, ca. 1260, provides an absolution for the people on Ash Wednesday: Tolhurst, *The Customary of the Cathedral Priory Church of Norwich*,

still keep very much to the tenth-century outline for the rite of public penance itself, tinkering very little with the time-worn Thursday framework of presentation, *Venite*, and introduction, or even with the selection of prayers. The rites of Sarum and York clung to the old form as well.[164] I have found no English rites that reverse the order on Thursday or eliminate the dramatic goings-on or borrow absolutions and prayers from extreme unction or invent new prayers, all features found in the contemporary French and German liturgies of penance. More study is needed to show whether these rites are moribund or simply more conservative because of a different pattern of the use of public penance in England than in northern France. What can be stated for certain is that England, like northern France, the Rhineland, and southeastern France, did not imitate Rome's swift abandonment of public penance.

The analysis of so many pontificals and rites of Lenten public penance has served to establish something more than the survival of public penance north of the Alps and north of the Loire. The continued references to public penance in synodal statutes, episcopal registers, and chronicles and in pontificals and ordinals conceals a subtler shift in the meaning that penance had for those who watched and those who endured it. We have found that the liturgy of collective penances like Rogations and processions in times of crisis changed relatively little in the later Middle Ages; these penances brought people together to expiate the sins of all under the guidance of the saint. Public penance, by contrast, was more complex from the start. Neither a purely individual nor a collective rite, it brought the many together to pray for the forgiveness of the few and benefit from their expiation. It was originally a communal rite in the sense that it taught the dependence of an individual's salvation on the aid of the community, and the dependence of the community's sanctity on the expiation of the few. Collective processions also celebrated unity, of course, but these tamer rituals did not threaten individuals with exposure or promise divine justice for those who had injured the community.

---

pp. 63–65. The summary of Thursday rites mentions only the reconciliation of the penitents, again a conservative treatment (p. 81). The abbatial pontifical of Evesham, ca. 1300, has what seems to be general absolution on Wednesday and Thursday: Wilson, *Officium Ecclesiasticum Abbatum secundum usum Eveshamensis Monasterii*, cols. 60–67, 71–80. On Thursday, for instance, the rubrics instruct the abbot to "turn to the people and say the absolution in this way," (col. 77), but what follows seems to apply as much or more to the penitents.

164. W. H. Frere, *The Use of Sarum* (Cambridge, 1898), vol. I, pp. 138, 143–144, and vol. II, p. 56, for Lenten public penance in thirteenth-century texts of Sarum; see Bailey, *The Processions of Sarum and the Western Church*, pp. 19–21; and Tyrer, *Historical Survey of Holy Week*, p. 88.

The critical change in the liturgy began relatively early, around 1150, even before the new confessors' manuals or new theology took hold, and was completed quickly, by 1250 or 1275. Further developments merely reinforced the changes initiated by the mid–thirteenth century. Public penance for individuals gradually became a kind of exemplary punishment, a good show to watch, perhaps even amusing, as that late Parisian pontifical suggests, but not so significant for the moral standing of the bystanders who had gathered for it. It might encourage those who watched to avoid such embarrassment by avoiding the sins that incurred it, but it did not teach a lesson about the dependence of their spiritual welfare on the penitence of others. Meanwhile, a separate collective penitential liturgy developed for the ordinary faithful. This liturgy eventually gave Lenten pilgrims to the cathedral their own reward in collective confessions, absolutions, indulgences, and even processions that worked much like the older collective expiations. The public penitents themselves underwent a rite deliberately deprived of much of its drama, a businesslike publication of the crimes, followed by an immediate absolution and a reabsolution at reconciliation. Absolved from the beginning, they were never really expelled from the body of the church, and so never really readmitted; they were just church members paying their debt in public. Why did public penance survive the transformation of its liturgy? Why did it not disappear like the ordeal, another relic of early medieval beliefs about community and the supernatural? We have found one answer in the continued demand to see sinners humiliated, in a lurking distrust of the secret world of the soul. Another answer is that the transformation of its liturgy preserved public penance for a changed society, adapting it to larger towns where the reinforcement of community through the expiation of the few had become implausible. The application of collective and public penances in the cathedral cities of northern France and Flanders is the subject of the next chapter.

CHAPTER EIGHT

Penance in the Cities

While rural priests could exclude parishioners from their churches, most important individual public penances in the thirteenth century took place in the cities. Canon law stated that only bishops or their representatives were to impose solemn public penance for the most serious crimes, and, as we have seen, for the most part the rule was obeyed in practice. We have seen in the registers of Eudes Rigaud and the monastery of Cerisy-le-Forêt some examples of rural public penances in the villages of Normandy, mostly minor humiliations of minor offenders. Here, I turn to more elaborate public penances, frequently performed in the towns not only because they were the bishop's prerogative but because the original quarrel involved city dwellers. And similarly, though collective public penances at Rogations or in times of crisis were no strict monopoly of cathedral towns, only a sizable place with several well-established ecclesiastical foundations could mount the full-scale processions that drew together the whole community in a show of unity and expiation. The study of public penance in northern France is inseparable from the study of community and authority in the cities.

In Chapters 4 and 5, I considered individual and collective public penances and their role in ecclesiastical seasons and church law. There, I asked why such penances survived revisions in theology and how bishops presided over them. Here is the place to focus on the judicial and indeed frankly political uses of public penances, both the Lenten and non-Lenten individual penances, and to a lesser extent, the collective penitential celebrations of Rogations. In previous chapters, I detailed the transformations of the theology and liturgy of public penance; in this one I explain the political and social context of that transformation and suggest reasons for it. Once again, we must note an inconsistency in the evidence about public penance; liturgical sources provide more information on Lenten rites, but the public penances recorded in narrative sources are chiefly of the non-Lenten variety. The consistent direction of the evolution will nonetheless show how a link can be drawn between the transformation of the ritual and the new uses of public penance in the cities. We have seen in the theology and canonical procedure of penance a groping effort to find a middle ground between the private world of the conscience and the public world of the whole city. We have seen in the liturgy of penance a retreat from the dramatic communal scapegoating of early medieval public penance. And here I turn to the increasing political use of public penance in cities lacking any clear public authority and any sense of community. By the end of this chapter, it should be clear how these three metamorphoses are really one.

Penance and Divided Cities

An understanding of the political divisions behind the crimes punished by public penance is the first step toward understanding the politics of penance itself. French towns in the central Middle Ages have not received the same scholarly attention as rural aristocracies and the agrarian economy. A few exceptional works have made this examination of the context of public penance possible,[1] but some of the comments here are inevitably provisional. Within the area under consideration, France north of the Loire and west of the Rhine, I distinguish three major regions: the far north from Artois to Flanders; the Ile-de-France, Picardy, and Champagne; and northwestern France. Each of these shows a different pattern in the use of public penance, reflecting disparities in economic and political development. Uneven development is revealed in uneven population growth. The metropolis of Paris, with around two hundred thousand inhabitants,[2] dominated the central region; but most episcopal sees in

---

1. Chief among these is Pierre Desportes's *Reims et les rémois aux XIIIe et XIVe siècles*; also useful among recent studies are Alain Derville, ed., *Histoire de Saint-Omer* (Lille, 1981), and for a slightly later period, D. M. Nicholas, "Crime and Punishment in Fourteenth-Century Ghent," *Revue belge de philologie et d'histoire* 48 (1970): 289–334, 1141–1176. But the systematic study of economic activity and civic institutions in northern French towns has barely started.

2. The size of Paris has been the object of considerable controversy. Until recently, few historians took seriously the 1328 census of 61,098 hearths, a figure that implies a minimum of 200,000, or Henry of Susa's estimate that Saint-Germain l'Auxerrois had 40,000 parishioners by 1240, implying a total of around 160,000; it seemed difficult to reconcile such figures with the land area available or with the rank-size model of city size. This last hypothe-

this area were no more than a tenth of that size. Reims, an archbishop's see, had perhaps as many as twenty thousand inhabitants at
the height of its expansion around 1270.[3] As we have seen, this region
from the Ile-de-France to Champagne was home to the north-central
family of pontificals, whose rites of penance reveal clearly a transformation in the first half of the thirteenth century. And this north-
central region was also the locale of most of the great political public
penances imposed after urban riots; these penances are the chief
topic of this chapter.

In the west, the largest city was Eudes Rigaud's Rouen, with about
thirty to fifty thousand inhabitants.[4] Tours, the other archepiscopal
see, had perhaps ten thousand or so.[5] In general, the west was poorer
and less urbanized than the Ile-de-France and Champagne, and both
regions were poorer than Flanders.[6] Public penance in the west was
conducted for the most part on a smaller scale. We do not hear of
great urban penances there; typical instead were Eudes Rigaud's punishment of misbehaving noblemen or the monastery of Cerisy-le-
Forêt's disciplining of fornicating villagers. Such penances, discussed
in the Chapter4, are not considered at length here.

By contrast, in Artois and Flanders, there were a large number of
towns with between twenty thousand and sixty thousand inhabitants,

---

sizes a normal relationship between the size of different cities in each region (i.e., population
of a city of a given rank in terms of population should equal the population of the largest city
divided by the rank); this would seem to rule out the first-ranked city being very much more
than twice the size of the second largest; see Hektor Ammann, "Wie gross war die mittelalterliche Stadt?" *Studium generale* 9 (1956): 505. Recent historians of Paris and of cities
have generally dismissed these objections and endorsed the large estimates: Bronislaw Geremek, "Paris la plus grande ville de l'Occident médiéval?" pp. 18–37; Raymond Cazelles, "Le
parisien au temps de Saint Louis," pp. 98–99; Léopold Genicot, "Les grandes villes de
l'Occident en 1300," in *Economies et sociétés au Moyen Age: Mélanges offerts à Edouard Perroy*
(Paris, 1973), pp. 214–215. For the rank-size model, see J. C. Russell, *Medieval Regions and
Their Cities* (Newton Abbot, Devon, 1972), pp. 23–24, 150; Russell estimates the size of very
large cities and thus the size of Paris to have been even *smaller* than the strict model would
predict. For critiques of Russell and the application of the rank-size model, see respectively
David Nicholas, "Structures de peuplement, fonctions urbaines, et formation du capital dans
la Flandre médiévale," *Annales: Economies, sociétés, civilisations* 33 (1978): 524, 527n; and Jan
de Vries, *European Urbanization, 1500–1800* (Cambridge, Mass., 1984), esp. pp. 87–93.

3. Desportes, *Reims et les rémois*, pp. 339–340.

4. For the lower estimate, Philippe Wolff, "Les villes de France au temps de Philippe
Auguste," in Robert-Henri Bautier, ed., *La France de Philippe Auguste: Le temps des mutations*
(Paris, 1982), p. 660; for the larger, see Genicot, "Les grandes villes de l'Occident en 1300,"
p. 216; the latter estimate is based on the *pouillé* of Eudes Rigaud in 1272.

5. For this estimate of the population of Tours, see Genicot, "Les grandes villes de
l'Occident en 1300," p. 207, but Genicot reports that there is no firm basis for it.

6. See Gérard Sivéry, *L'économie du royaume de France au siècle de Saint Louis* (Lille, 1984),
pp. 45–47, for regional differences in development and pp. 223–228 for the midcentury
decline in the fairs of Champagne; cf. also Sivéry, *Saint Louis et son siècle* (Paris, 1983), pp. 164–
165, for the gulf between Flanders and the rest of France north of the Loire, revealed in
claims in the *enquêtes* of Saint Louis.

including Saint-Omer, Ghent, Bruges, Ypres, Arras, and Tournai, only two of which, Arras and Tournai, were episcopal sees.[7] Only in Flanders had recent population growth completely outstripped ecclesiastical organization. Thus, only Flemish towns were relatively free from the domination of lord-bishops that characterized most of northern France, and Flanders alone preserved a precarious independence from royal interference. Not surprisingly, then, there are fewer cases of episcopally imposed public penances in the far north, though the impulse behind such penances survived in secular "penances" imposed by communal authorities or arbiters. These are the subject of the last section of this chapter.

In order to understand public penances, we must appreciate both local variation within this broad region and the consensus that made the rite in one form or another popular everywhere in France north of the Loire. Urban penances in the north-central area from the Ile-de-France east to Reims and north to Flanders characteristically arose from divisions within cities and especially from divisions between bourgeois and clerics or among bourgeois families. I review here the sources of conflict and the reason why those conflicts often could not be settled without appeal to public penance. In fact, the underlying causes for both the conflict and the choice of punishment were the same, and so a brief discussion of the divisions helps explain the popularity of public penance. Northern French cities typically suffered from the lack of any public authority of unambiguous legitimacy. Not surprisingly, they suffered from organized and unorganized violence and, as we shall see, public penance could be a convenient if inadequate solution when a more conventional punishment would have aroused more disputes than it settled.

The efforts of Georges Espinas and Jean Lestocquoy among others have made familiar the domination of several of the larger northern towns by a small number of immensely wealthy merchants and *rentiers*; Jehan Boinebroke in Douai and the Crespinois of Arras have become types of the swaggering financiers who made little secret of their usurious income and none at all of their oppressive treatment of debtors and employees, most often the same unfortunates.[8] What this

---

7. See Genicot, "Les grandes villes de l'Occident en 1300," pp. 207–219; and Derville, *Histoire de Saint-Omer*, p. 29. And Tournai was an exception among episcopal sees in that the bishops were largely excluded by the commune from administration: Gérard Sivéry, *Saint Louis et son siècle* (Paris, 1983), p. 562.

8. Georges Espinas, *Les origines du capitalisme. Vol. 1, Sire Jehan Boinebroke, patricien et drapier douaisien*, Bibliothèque de la Société d'histoire du droit des pays flamands, picards, et wallons, 8 (Lille, 1933); Jean Lestocquoy, *Aux origines de la bourgeoisie: Les villes de Flandre et d'Italie sous le gouvernement des patriciens (XIe–XVe siècles)* (Paris, 1952), and *La vie sociale et économique à Arras du XIIe au XVe siècle* (Arras, 1941), pp. 8–13.

image often obscures, however, is the precariousness of financiers' position even in the far north and the resilience of older families and older institutions, both the rural nobility and, above all, local prelates and cathedral chapters. Except in Flanders, bourgeois communes were limited by the hostility of the French monarchy in the thirteenth century to the establishment and expansion of communal rights.[9] Even in Flanders where royal influence was intermittent, the counts often had some authority over the choice of *jurés* and *échevins*.[10] Thus, everywhere north of the Loire, but especially in the Ile-de-France, Picardy, and Champagne, kings, counts, and clerics curtailed what at first glance might look like the comfortable ascendancy of a bourgeois patriciate; this was the ultimate cause of conflict within the towns and the public penances that were imposed in the settlements.

One of the most important threats to the domination of narrow patriciates in northern French towns was, however, one of the least significant for our study of public penance: the opposition of the urban working classes, culminating in many northern towns in a long series of strikes and riots.[11] Such riots were, however, not typically revenged by public penances, but by summary executions. As we shall see, public penance was a weapon most used against citizens of substance, not against the poor, either by the bishop or by other bourgeois. It was not a weapon in the wars between creditors and borrowers, employers and employees, landlords and tenants, although that war certainly sharpened the patriciate's sense of insecurity and thus their fear of humiliations imposed by the clergy. While rarely suffering public penance themselves, the urban lower classes were often the intended audience for the humiliation of others.

9. For the halt in royal support for communes beginning in the reign of Louis IX, see Charles Petit-Dutaillis, *The French Communes in the Middle Ages*, pp. 51, 79–83. For Philip Augustus's relatively favorable policy toward communes, see Louis Carolus-Barré, "Philippe Auguste et les villes de commune," in Bautier, ed., *La France de Philippe Auguste*, pp. 679, 682, and John W. Baldwin, *The Government of Philip Augustus. Foundations of French Royal Power in the Middle Ages* (Berkeley, Calif. 1986), pp. 62–63. Philip suppressed communes at Laon and Étampes, and confirmed new communes at Tournai, Arras, Amiens, Sens, Caen, and Rouen, as well as in many smaller towns; most of these new confirmations, however, were the result of the expansion of the royal domain in his reign. As Petit-Dutaillis points out, pp. 86–90, the distinction between communes and other *ville franches* grew less important in the course of the thirteenth century with the decreasing legal significance of the oaths of mutual aid and the shift in royal policy away from encouraging narrow patriciates governing the communes. See also Sivéry, *Saint Louis et son siècle*, pp. 559–567: By the mid–thirteenth century, the requirement that many towns present their accounts to the king signaled the end of their financial autonomy.

10. Sivéry, *Saint Louis et son siècle*, p. 562.

11. For the conflicts between *commun* and patriciate, manifested in revolts and *takehans* or armed strikes, see especially Lestocquoy, *La vie sociale et économique à Arras du XIIe au XVe siècle*, pp. 14–16; Sivéry, *L'économie du royaume de France au siècle de Saint Louis* (Lille, 1984), pp. 187–188; and Derville, *Histoire de Saint-Omer*, pp. 56–57.

Usury was perhaps the most important obstacle to the merchants' and financiers' achievement of a social status and respectability in accordance with their wealth. At times, bishops and chapters encouraged their resident and subject bourgeois to skirt the rules against usury because of the payoff they would receive.[12] But accusations of usury were always ready should the necessity arise, and these challenges were difficult to ignore. At Reims, a large profit, accrued when the *échevins* sold a large number of *rentes viagères* on real property to the financiers of Arras, came to naught when Archbishop Henri de Braine complained that the contracts were usurious.[13] (*Rentes viagères* were rents secured by real property but not carrying rights of ownership.) In fact, Henri's objection was that the *échevins* had cut the deal without his authority, but the accusation of usury gave him the chance to turn windfall profits into a sudden loss. Understandably, then, if not quite accurately, a local chronicler at Reims reported that the fear of accusations of usury was the chief cause of the ensuing riots that ended in public penance.[14] Usury may not have been the most important issue, but it could embitter every other quarrel. The provincial council for Reims at Saint-Quentin in 1231 had decreed that prelates should investigate anyone defamed of usury, even if no accuser appeared, and if the clamor was general, they should require canonical purgation, again even if proof was impossible.[15] Since lawyers were known to delay these cases, added the statute, they should be made to take an oath that they believed their case just; if once sworn the lawyer is revealed to have lied, he should be considered under *infamia*, that is, not law-worthy.

Whatever the parties, whatever the political issues, if one could tar one's enemies as usurers, those enemies were liable to be dragged into spiritual court, deprived of legal representation, exposed to the wrath of debtors and the poor, denied the sacraments, and stripped of their inheritance. And those Douasiens who had suffered the depredations of the usurer Jehan Boinebroke openly insisted to his executors after his death that his failure to make restitution ensured his damnation.[16]

12. Lestocquoy, *Les villes de Flandre et d'Italie sous le gouvernement des patriciens (XIe–XVe siècles)* (Paris, 1952), pp. 195, 199–202, remarks on cooperation between canons and merchants and on the ineffectiveness of statutes against usury and Innocent III's efforts to get the bishop to enforce them. Cf. also the accusations traded at Reims about the presence of usurers among the *servientes* of the archbishop and chapter: Ludwig Schmugge, "Ministerialität und Bürgertum in Reims: Untersuchungen zur Geschichte der Stadt im 12. und 13. Jahrhundert," *Francia* 2 (1974): 178–179.

13. Desportes, *Reims et les rémois*, p. 159.

14. *Chronique de Saint-Nicaise*, Varin I:566n.

15. Varin I:551–552.

16. Espinas, *Les origines du capitalisme*, Vol. 1, *Sire Jehan Boinebroke, patricien et drapier douaisien*, pp. 194, 199–204.

Under these circumstances, it is easy to see why merchants would not feel secure, and why public penance could be such a telling weapon for a bishop. The humiliation of public penance played on the merchants' vulnerability to public opinion.

The exclusion of townsmen from the ranks of local cathedral chapters and prestigious abbeys further embittered divisions between the bourgeois and urban ecclesiastical foundations. In the twelfth century, the chapters of northern French towns were often largely staffed by the cadets of local seigneurial families; in the thirteenth, many Italians and, later, southern Frenchmen took their place with the new importance of papal provisions. Even non-Italians usually had to curry papal favor: Studies of several northern French chapters have demonstrated that the papal court controlled about two-thirds of late-thirteenth-century appointments.[17] The local bourgeois rarely managed to curry the necessary favor in the right places; most of the few merchants' sons who secured prebends in thirteenth-century Laon, for example, were promptly accused of simony and suspended, doubtless because they had relied on cruder forms of bribery to take the place of influence and they were resented for it.[18] Further north, in Arras, a few sons of the Cosset, Louchard, and the semi-Jewish Crespin families appear in the rolls of the cathedral chapter and the monastery of Saint-Vaast, although there, too, the rural nobility remained very important.[19] The tide was against local appointments to prestigious ecclesiastical establishments, even in towns like Arras where the political ascendancy of financiers was clear. The bishop or archbishop generally controlled the final one-third of appointments to the chapters, and the merchant families could hardly hope for better luck there. Merchant families in Flemish towns unburdened by archbishops, bishops, and chapters were better able to translate

17. On Laon: Hélène Millet, *Les chanoines du chapitre cathédrale de Laon (1272–1412)*, Collection de l'Ecole française de Rome, 56 (Rome, 1982), esp. pp. 62–78, 151–153; Fernando Picó, "Membership in the Cathedral Chapter of Laon, 1217–1238," *Catholic Historical Review* 61 (1975): 5–29, "Changements dans la composition du chapitre cathédrale de Laon (1155–1318)," *Revue d'histoire ecclésiastique* 71 (1976): 78–91. The two-thirds estimate is from Millet, p. 153. On Amiens, also Soissons and Beauvais: William Mendel Newman, *Le personnel de la cathédrale d'Amiens (1066–1306)* (Paris, 1972), pp. 7–11; L. Genicot, "Aristocratie et dignités ecclésiastiques en Picardie au XIIe et XIIIe siècles," *Revue d'histoire ecclésiastique* 67 (1972): 438–442. On Reims: Desportes, *Reims et les rémois*, p. 300. See also on Saint-Omer, Derville, *Histoire de Saint-Omer*, p. 54, where the papal control of prebends similarly excluded local merchants' sons after 1200 and put an end to merchants' gifts to the foundations.

18. Picó, "Membership in the Cathedral Chapter of Laon, 1217–1238," pp. 21–22.

19. Lestocquoy, *La vie sociale et économique à Arras du XIIe au XVe siècle*, pp. 12–13. The Crespin were nominally Christian in Arras, but members of the family appear in English records as Jewish merchants in London. For the relations between the town and the rural nobility, see Jean-Loup Abbé, "Rayonnement urbain et seigneuries autour d'Arras et de Douai au XIIIe siècle," *Revue du Nord* 65 (1983): 406.

wealth into social standing and to dominate local religious institutions such as hospitals and poorhouses.[20] But in the episcopal cities of the Ile-de-France, Champagne, and Picardy, the bishops ruled.

We may contrast the moral precariousness of the bourgeois of northern France with the confidence of the Italian communes, where the vitality and even political significance of lay religious organizations more than compensated for any exclusion from papal patronage. In northern France, lay orders did not provide a sufficiently prestigious alternative to the cathedral chapters and monastic foundations. The difference between lay and clerical relations in the episcopal towns of northern France and in Italian communes is clearly evident in the relative lack of autonomy of northern French lay religious institutions, particularly confraternities and hospitals. In both regions, there was a general evolution toward greater ecclesiastical control of lay orders and hospitals, but this evolution progressed further faster in France than in the south.[21] The lay penitent orders of southern France and Italy had no success north of the Loire in this period.[22] In general, the role of the mendicant orders in bringing a

20. See Derville, *Histoire de Saint-Omer*, p. 50; the *échevins* of Saint-Omer regulated even processions and burials and the financial administration of parish churches, although the nomination of *curés* remained out of their hands.

21. On the ecclesiastical domination of northern French confraternities in the twelfth and early thirteenth century, see Jean-Marc Bienvenu, "Fondations charitables laïques au XIIe siècle: L'exemple de l'Anjou," in *Etudes sur l'histoire de la pauvreté*, ed. Michel Mollat, Publications de la Sorbonne, série études, 8 (Paris, 1974), 2:566–569; Avril, *Le gouvernement des évêques*, pp. 759–760; and the remarks of R. Foreville, *Latran I, II, III, et Latran IV*, p. 269, on the increasing adoption of the Augustinian rule or the statutes of the Hospitallers by lay fraternities. On a similar trend in southern France in the fourteenth century, see A. Ramière de Fortanier, "La confrérie Notre-Dame de Fanjeaux et son développement au Moyen-Age," in *La religion populaire en Languedoc du XIIIe siècle à la moitié du XIVe siècle*, Cahiers de Fanjeaux, 11, pp. 326, 338. For the evolution in Italy, see Daniela Rando, "'Laicus religiosus' tra strutture civili ed ecclesiastiche: L'ospedale di Ognissanti in Treviso (sec. XIII)," *Studi medievali* ser. 3, 34 (1983): 620–643. Michel Mollat, "Hospitalité et assistance au début du XIIIe siècle," in *Poverty in the Middle Ages*, ed. David Flood, Franziskanische Forschungen, 27 (Werl/Westf., 1975), pp. 38–43, admits the episcopal origin of charitable foundations in northern French cities, but emphasizes a growing lay participation in some cities of the north and in Italy. The communal involvement he describes, however, was mostly limited to municipal intervention to alleviate poverty. It is rarer to see lay *religious* institutions independent of ecclesiastical control.

22. Cf. by contrast the southern French confraternities of *pénitents* and the related Friars of the Sack: Radegunde Amtmann, *Die Bussbruderschaften in Frankreich* (Wiesbaden, 1977), pp. 3–18; Richard Emery, "The Friars of the Sack," *Speculum* 18 (1943): 323–326; and P.-A. Amargier, "Les frères de la pénitence de Jesus-Christ ou du Sac," *Provence historique* 15 (1965): 158–167. For the *battuti* and *penitenti* in Italy and their considerable autonomy, see especially G. G. Meersseman, "Premier auctarium au dossier de l'ordre de la pénitence au XIIIe s.: Le manuel des pénitents de Brescia," *Revue d'histoire ecclésiastique* 62 (1967): 27–29; Ida Magli, *Gli uomini della penitenza* (n.p., 1967), pp. 65–66, 105–109; Giovanni Mantese, "'Fratres et sorores de poenitentia' di S. Francesco in Vicenza dal XIII al XV secolo," in *Miscellanea Gilles Gerard Meersseman*, Italia sacra, 16 (Padua, 1970), 2:707–708; and Mauro Ronzani, "Penitenti e ordini mendicanti a Pisa sino all'inizio del trecento," *Mélanges de l'Ecole française de Rome: Moyen Age–Temps Modernes* 89 (1977): 741.

new urban spirituality to the northern cities has been somewhat exag-gerated.[23] The mendicants were almost entirely shut out from the main Palm Sunday and Rogation processions in cathedral towns. At midcentury there were between one-tenth and one-fifth as many sec-ular religious in the city of Reims alone as mendicants of any order in all of hexagonal France.[24] Of course, many bourgeois favored mendi-cant houses with donations and asked to be buried there. Similarly, the lay Beguines of Flanders and northern France were often daugh-ters of the *échevins*.[25] After all, the merchants were excluded from the more prestigious older institutions. And once again, the Flemish towns represent an exception to this pattern of mendicant weakness; both friars and tertiary houses were more numerous and more signif-icant from Saint-Omer north.[26] Still, we must not overestimate the mendicants' independence or influence, particularly outside the far north. In all the bitter struggles in the thirteenth century between bishop and the bourgeois of Laon, Reims, Cambrai, and Beauvais, there is not a whisper of activity by confraternities or mendicants, whether religious or third-order laymen, as parties in the conflict or as peacemakers.

Political and social divisions in the northern French cities were of-ten defined territorially. We can speak of the "religious geography" of the towns, where collective processions and penances traced invisible but crucial boundaries between different religious authorities and even different social classes. Fundamental were divisions between *cité* and *bourg*; between the older areas of town and the newer, poorer suburbs, and between spheres of influence of different foundations.

23. See André Vauchez, "Conclusion," Mariano D'Alatri, ed., *I frati penitenti di San Francesco nella società del due e trecento: atti del 2° Convegno di studi francescani, Roma, 1976* (Rome, 1977), pp. 374–377, for the contrast between the influence of Franciscanism in the north and in Italy.

24. For the estimate of mendicant strength in 1300 as around ten to fifteen thousand, see Richard W. Emery, *The Friars in Medieval France* (New York, 1962), p. 4; for the estimate of the clerical population in Reims in the late thirteenth century as around two thousand, and the estimate of mendicants as around two to three hundred, see Desportes, *Reims et les rémois*, pp. 331, 338–339. In 1250, the figures would have been more even. Of course, Reims was an ecclesiastical town, and many of those in clerical orders there bore the title as a flag of conve-nience, hoping to escape from various taxes (see on this practice the complaints of Philippe de Beaumanoir, *Coutumes de Beauvaisis*, ed. A. Salmon, Collection de textes pour servir à l'étude et l'enseignement d'histoire [Paris, 1899–1900], 1:166); but the fact remains that in northern French cities a sea of secular clerics surrounded islands of mendicant convents.

25. A strict comparison of donations to ecclesiastical foundations with southern France and Italy is rendered difficult by the absence of a notarial tradition in the north recording and preserving wills. But see Derville, *Histoire de Saint-Omer*, p. 54, on the success of mendi-cants of Saint-Omer revealed in surviving cartularies.

26. Derville, *Histoire de Saint-Omer*, p. 54; and Benjamin de Troeyer, "Beguines et Ter-tiaires en Belgique et aux Pays-Bas aux XIII–XIVe siècles," in D'Alatri, ed., *I frati penitenti*, pp. 134–138.

In Chapter 5, I alluded to the perpetuation of the old split between the bishop's *cité* and abbey's *bourg* in the organization of processions. Collective processions help us map the divisions that were the context for public penance itself. Increasingly significant from the mid–twelfth century on was the split between the growing suburbs outside the old walls and the older center. Mendicant foundations tended to concentrate in the *faubourgs*, outside the informal territories of the established parishes in the city center.[27] The older urban areas had been pretty well carved up into parishes by 1200; newer settlements and rural areas saw an expansion in the number of parishes in line with population growth, but most of them remained under episcopal authority.[28] Besides these small territorial parishes, there were even smaller "personal" ones, gathering the *familia* of a monastery, for instance.[29] In any case, the direction of parishes in most towns still lay in the hands of the older establishments, abbeys as much as chapters and bishops, that continued to appoint and supervise *curés*.[30] Most significant for our study of public penance are the spheres of influence of these foundations, not always well defined geographically, rather than the tiny parishes themselves; these frontiers affected the arrangement of collective religious life and were simultaneously the source of conflicts that ended in public penance.

We can trace these geographical boundaries between spheres of influence in the processions of collective penances. In Chapter 5, we saw how Palm Sunday processions typically expounded the preeminence of the bishop over his flock and not incidentally over other ecclesiastical institutions in the city. Collective expiation could be a difficult thing to arrange, as much a matter for diplomacy as collective peacemaking. Such processions were anything but spontaneous expressions of the communal emotion, and religious houses jealously guarded their rights to participate.[31] Rogations processions were in

27. Jacques Le Goff, "Apostolat mendiant et fait urbain dans la France médiévale: L'implantation des ordres mendiants: Programme-questionnaire pour une enquête," *Annales: Economies, sociétés, civilisations* 23 (1968): 337; see also F. L. Ganshof, *Etude sur le développement des villes entre Loire et Rhin au Moyen-Age* (Paris and Brussels, 1943), p. 50, for the separate secular administration of the suburbs of Ghent and Paris and other towns.

28. Michel Aubrun, *La paroisse en France des origines au XVe siècle* (Paris, 1986), pp. 110; cf. Michel Rouche, *Histoire de Douai* (Dunkirk, 1985), p. 63, for the example of Douai. On episcopal control of parishes, particularly in the countryside, see G. Le Bras, *L'église et le village* (Paris, 1976).

29. See Trenard, *Histoire de Cambrai*, p. 62, and Devailly, "L'encadrement paroissial," p. 389.

30. Trenard, *Histoire de Cambrai*, pp. 62–64. Cf. Desportes, "Les sociétés confraternelles de curés en France du Nord au Bas-Moyen-Age," in *L'encadrement religieux des fidèles au Moyen-Age et jusqu'au Concile de Trente*, pp. 296, 304, on the supervision of parish curates.

31. We may recall the scuffles in Limoges over rights of procession: *Major Chronicon*

principle all-inclusive, "beating the bounds" around the entire city. But whereas processions for the Major and Minor Litanies were in fact more inclusive than the episcopal Palm Sunday processions, they, too, reflected the balance of power among different houses. The sequence and path of processions often marked out the same divisions and hierarchies as rights of jurisdiction and landownership. Most obviously, Rogations processions routinely excluded the new suburbs and the mendicant houses that served them.[32] In effect, the ritual marked not as of old the frontier between city and country, but that between the privileged *cité* and the poorer settlements recently grown up in the outskirts.

In Reims, for example, the canons proceeded on Saint Mark's Day from the cathedral to the northern gate and then to the eastern gate of the *cité*, stopping for stations at a couple of small churches on the way, and then returning. This was anything but a full circuit of even the old central city. The canons avoided any stop at the Franciscans, although there was a house within the *cité* very near their route, and they did not go anywhere near the newly built up areas south and southeast of the old fortifications.[33] Their routes were more inclusive on the three days of Rogations, but they still skirted the new settlements and mendicant houses. On all three days of Rogations, in fact, after stops within the *cité*, the canons ventured outside the bishop's ban to the *bourg* dominated by the Benedictines at Saint-Remi; on the climactic third day they said mass in Saint-Remi itself. At the end of the century, coinciding with the decline in the power of the Benedictines, relations had become sufficiently amicable that a corrector added a stipulation to the rite that the monks of Saint-Remi themselves say mass in the cathedral on the second day.[34] It seems that the pre-

---

Lemovicense, HF 21:774. And in Limoges, too, an impromptu procession to honor Charles of Anjou required extensive negotiations before it could be happily performed: *Major Chronicon Lemovicense*, HF 21:772–773. In Siena, clergy in some processions received tokens from the populace, and so insisted with particular care on their rights to participate: Ronzani, "Aspetti e problemi delle pievi e delle parrocchie cittadine nell'Italia centro-settentrionale," p. 343.

32. Cf. a similar pattern in southern France in the later Middle Ages: Marc Venard, "Itinéraires de processions dans la ville d'Avignon," *Ethnologie française* 7 (1977): 62; Noël Coulet, "Processions, espace urbain, communauté civique," pp. 391–392; Coulet argues that in the early fourteenth century communes began to take control of the processions, a process not evident north of the Loire in the same period. Cf. Ronzani, "Aspetti e problemi delle pievi e delle parrocchie cittadine nell'Italia centro-settentrionale," p. 343, on such processions in Siena.

33. Chevalier, *Sacramentaire . . . de Reims*, p. 142, from a late thirteenth-century ordinal of the cathedral. Information about the topography of Reims has been drawn from Desportes, *Reims et les rémois*, pp. 68, 467.

34. Chevalier, *Sacramentaire . . . de Reims*, pp. 143–146. On the decline in power of Saint-Remi in the late thirteenth century and the early fourteenth century, when fewer bourgeois merchants live within its ban, see Desportes, *Reims et les Rémois*, p. 248.

eminent church would proceed to less eminent churches, whose clergy would receive their visits; thus, Rogations litanies climaxed at Reims with the cathedral canons saying mass in the *bourg*. For the monks to be granted leave to set foot on archepiscopal turf even on the second day suggests an improvement in relations at the end of the century after the conflicts of the middle years.

At Sens, the ordinal of the monks of Saint-Pierre-le-Vif, the Benedictine monastery that dominated the *bourg* there, described a diplomatic dance for the Major Litany. The monks of Saint-Pierre held their relics aloft while the monks of the lesser houses Saint-Remi and Sainte-Colombe passed beneath; the Benedictines of Saint-Pierre then took their place in the procession behind these two houses, while the canons of the cathedral passed under the relics of Saint-Savinien, another major old house, but took up the rear in the procession, the place of honor.[35] This describes a pecking order among the old establishments; the newer mendicant foundations inside and outside the walls did not participate. For Rogations, after two days of processions around other old establishments on the outskirts, the monks of Saint-Pierre joined others at the cathedral, where the canons received their relics and placed them on the main altar; then all the houses together proceeded to Sainte-Colombe for the mass. The public display of relics meant that it was not merely the monks, but the saints themselves, making visits and exchanging civilities. Newer establishments poorer in relics could hardly participate properly. And the liturgy carefully guarded Saint-Pierre-le-Vif's position high on the pecking order without quite conceding their superiority over the canons of cathedral church of Saint-Etienne.[36]

In cities where relations between the chapter and other old houses were cordial, joint processions making many stations in the *cité* and *bourg*, but never the new *faubourgs*, appear in the ordinals. At Chartres, the canons of the cathedral, those of Saint-Jean in the *bourg*, and unspecified others seem to have joined amicably in three days of litanies and making a large number of stations; similar were the busy parades at Laon, ranging over three days to both sides of the hill on which *cité* and *bourg* stood, and down to the valley below.[37] But in other towns, the canons seem more hesitant, less confident of friendship than at Chartres, less imperialist than at Reims; they stayed closer to the walls of the *cité* and even to the neighborhood of their cathedral. At Rouen, the canons' Rogations processions went to Saint-Ouen and Saint-Maclou near the cathedral before going a little further to Saint-Trinité and Saint-Michel.[38] At Amiens, while the canons made a station at the abbey of Saint-Jean, the climactic mass was on the suitably safe ground of Saint-Martin-aux-Jumeaux, an abbey dependent on the chapter.[39]

We know less about the diplomacy behind the newer collective expiations on Ash Wednesday and Maundy Thursday, the episcopal absolutions in outlying parishes that came to rival and eventually overshadow the old individual public penance. Most ordinals and pontificals do not indicate the path that the bishop was to take; at Reims, the archbishop absolved parishioners simply *per congregationes*.[40] Clearly, these peripatetic absolutions typically bypassed both mendicant and monastic foundations, though some of these might have their own services and absolutions for laymen who preferred them to their parish or the cathedral. Where we do know the route, these episcopal absolutions outside the cathedral reveal an effort by bishop and chapter to transform Ash Wednesday and Maundy Thursday into something more like Palm Sunday, a visible demonstration of episcopal authority, if only in nearby churches. There was no question of going into hostile territory with indulgences. At Laon, where Rogations processions took the bishop and canons all over the hill and down to Vaux, the path of absolutions was conservative. On Ash Wednesday they were limited to the Premonstratensians at Saint-Martin, right next to the cathedral, and on Maundy Thursday they traveled to a couple of nearby churches and Saint-Jean in the *bourg*, which was close by and on good terms with the cathedral.[41] Since Lenten absolutions associated with public penance were by their nature episcopal business, it is not surprising that they did not venture so far as the ostensibly inclusive Rogations litanies. One rare case where the bishop went further than usual on Maundy Thursday appears in the sixteenth-century pontifical of Paris; there, the bishop absolved the public at Saint-Magloire and at the cemetery of the Innocents and at Notre-Dame.[42] But by that time in Paris, the bishop's supremacy was well established. In thirteenth-century towns, every procession and every absolution required a balancing act among competing claims.

---

38. Rouen BM 222 (thirteenth-century processional of Rouen), f. 47r–53r.
39. Durand, *Ordinaire de l'église Notre-Dame cathédrale d'Amiens*, pp. 302–307.
40. Chevalier, *Sacramentaire . . . de Reims*, p. 122.
41. Chevalier, *Ordinaires de l'église cathédrale de Laon*, pp. 83, 109.
42. BN latin 957, f.95r–98v.

Such claims often had more practical import than the prestige of a foundation's patron saint. Political and jurisdicational boundaries within cities might not always follow parochial divisions, but they often reflected to some degree the spheres of influence of the cathedral chapter and major abbey, usually the Benedictines of the *bourg*. That is, an abbey might dominate a neighborhood by appointing its *curé*, by administering justice in its streets, and even by claiming the families as its servants or serfs. If the town had a commune, it generally could not claim the entire urban agglomeration for its courts and control, but it had to concede a greater or smaller area and men to the authority of a clerical or sometimes comital foreign body. Even in Tournai, whose bishop had less of a political role than in other cities, the commune had to suffer the existence of a small episcopal quarter that was autonomous from the rest.[43] Similarly, in Ghent, two quarters, Sint-Pietersdorf and Sint-Baafsdorp, fell under the authority of abbeys.[44]

Each narrow quarter of a town might belong to a different authority, each possessed of full rights of civil and criminal jurisdiction, including the right to judge capital cases. The boundaries between commune and bishop and among bishop, chapter, and abbeys were both significant enough and ambiguous enough to have been the occasion for lawsuits and riots. Conflicts over these boundaries turned collective and public penances from a banner of community to a weapon wielded by one side against another. Circumstances varied from one town to another. In Paris, the king dominated, of course, but also important were the bishop and a couple of large abbeys.[45] In Reims, the *échevins* had jurisdiction over only a narrow territory, while the authority of chapter, bishop, and abbey of Saint-Remi were roughly balanced. Even within the territorial ban of the commune at Reims, many escaped the jurisdiction of the *échevins* through their status as clerics, even in lower orders, or as servants of the archbishop or the chapter.[46] In Cambrai, then in the Empire, life was just as complicated. The chapter and several major abbeys had full jurisdiction in

---

43. Sivéry, *Saint Louis et son siècle*, pp. 562–563.

44. Ganshof, *Etude sur le développement des villes entre Loire et Rhin au Moyen-Age*, p. 50; Ganshof also refers to the Bourg Saint-Germain of Paris.

45. Jacques Boussard, *Nouvelle histoire de Paris de la fin du siège du 885–886 à la mort de Philippe Auguste* (Paris, 1976), esp. pp. 289–290; the bishop's territory on the right bank was known as la Culture-l'Evêque extending to Ville l'Evêque, near the present church of the Madeleine. See pp. 309–312, for the embryonic municipal institutions collaborating on occasion with the royal *prévôts* in the absence of *échevins* or commune. See also Cazelles, "Le parisien au temps de Saint Louis," p. 101, on the gradual enfranchisement of serfs in the ecclesiastical seigneuries of the left bank during Saint Louis's reign; but considerable land remained under the jurisdiction of Saint-Germain-des-Prés and other left bank abbeys.

46. Schmugge, "Ministerialität und Bürgertum," p. 179.

their *enclos* and rights of low justice in their *seigneuries*, while the *échevins*, with some supervision by the comital *bailli*, had rights of high and low justice elsewhere. Meanwhile, the bishop's *officialité* had jurisdiction in the quarter within the episcopal ban, as well as in cases involving clerics and so-called spiritual cases. And finally, the court of the *bailli* handled feudal matters.[47]

In the French and Flemish north, as in Lille, Saint-Omer, and Ghent, the *échevins* controlled more, and ecclesiastical foundations less.[48] But in no town did any one authority unambiguously control every quarter. Were men living on a certain street serfs of an abbey or citizens of the commune? Were the merchants of the quarter the bourgeois of the Benedictines or of the bishop? Did the chapter or the count have jurisdiction over the neighborhood?[49] These were the quarrels that divided northern French towns. The more ambiguity, in fact, the greater the likelihood of public penance, as we shall see. It is not surprising in these circumstances that some terms we might expect to be used for the "community" of the city came to be used divisively instead. *Communitas* could mean the poor in opposition to the rich;[50] *civitas* indicated the *cité* as distinct from the *bourg*; *christianitas* could mean all the faithful of the whole diocese; *burgenses*, *cives*, and *poorterie* described only the limited number of residents who were citizens. We may now turn to the public penances that arose from these divisions.

The Uses of Humiliation

The imposition of public penance in the cities depended on a well-established common language of gestures of humiliation. Public penance in the strict sense was by no means the only form of humiliation. Thirteenth-century Frenchmen were familiar with a whole range of humiliating secular punishments, voluntary displays of self-abasement, and informal public penances; together, these established the context for the sacramental rite in the hands of the episcopate. I

---

47. Trenard, *Histoire de Cambrai*, pp. 57–64.

48. Derville, *Histoire de Saint-Omer*, pp. 50–52; Rouche, *Histoire de Douai*, pp. 57–60; Trenard, *Histoire de Lille*, p. 346; for the breadth of echevinal jurisdiction in the far north, see also Grand, "Justice criminelle, procédure, et peines dans les villes aux XIIIe et XIVe siècles," p. 67.

49. For the dispute over serfs, see W. C. Jordan, *From Servitude to Freedom: Manumission in the Sénonais in the Thirteenth Century* (Philadelphia, 1986), pp. 40–44; for the dispute over *burgenses*, see the *Chronique anonyme dite Chronique de Reims*, HF 22:327–328; for rival claims over the quarter, see H. Platelle in Trenard, ed., *Histoire de Lille*, p. 346. The last two conflicts eventually were related to violent episodes punished by public penances.

50. Cf. *Annales Gandenses*, ed. and trans. H. Johnstone (London, 1951), *passim*.

have already remarked how public humiliation was the rule for offenses within many religious communities, including communities of laymen and women, in military orders, in hospitals, and in lay penitential orders.[51] This rule could be extended to other contexts. Statutes of a guild-confraternity of fullers at Saint-Trond in 1237 provide for the practice of fraternal correction among the members, in imitation of purely religious communities. Four fullers were to be chosen to look into the morals of the members ("qui de conversatione, vita et honestate ipsorum sub juramento fideliter inquirent": "who shall faithfully inquire into their conduct, life, and honor under oath"), and anyone accused of dishonesty should be warned three times, then shunned in all matters by all the others.

In a similar vein, Jean de Joinville was struck by the way the Hospitallers administered justice within their order in the Holy Land; his examples reveal how much justice worked not through authoritative decision but through the exchange of gestures of humiliation.[52] Offenders among the Hospitallers would eat on the ground like dogs until forgiven; under the circumstances, the shame of such "penitents" was exposed to outsiders as well as to their brothers. Strictly speaking, such a punishment applied by one layman to another was not a penance, but nobody bothered with such technicalities in the normal course of events. Significant, too, is Joinville's response to the Hospitallers' punishment. The offending knights had chased away some of his knights; but when Joinville saw their humiliation, he begged the Master to allow them to rise, and when the Master refused, Joinville even joined them on the ground, forcing the Master to relent.[53] The story suggests the social code behind humiliation; self-abasement shamed oneself but could also shame one's friend or adversary into agreement, whether grudging or eager. Voluntary humiliation inverted the sense of involuntary humiliation. As John Bossy puts it, ascetic display is in some sense aggressive.[54]

Less familiar, perhaps, than the discipline of lay religious orders and confraternities is the use of gestures of self-abasement in making agreements. Eudes Rigaud's arbitration between feuding families ended in a penitential pilgrimage by a miller whom Eudes believed innocent.[55] But it was not always an arbitrator who decided that a little humiliation would sweeten an otherwise painful compromise. To cut a deal of almost any kind one side might decide to borrow the lan-

51. See Chapter 4, note 50. Cf. Adam, *La vie paroissiale en France au XIVe siècle*, p. 77, for a fourteenth-century confraternity at Nantes with the rule of "fraternal correction."

52. Jean de Joinville, *Histoire de Saint Louis*, XCIX, pp. 212–216.

53. Joinville, *Histoire de Saint Louis*, XCIX, pp. 213–214.

54. Bossy, *Christianity in the West*, p. 5; Bossy cites Nietzsche's *Genealogy of Morals*.

55. Eudes Rigaud, *Regestrum visitationum*, p. 507 (1264). See Chapter 4.

guage of self-abasement to shame the other side into agreement. Geoffroi de Villehardouin explains that, in 1201, when the envoys of the Fourth Crusade needed to coax the Venetians into agreement about the payment for transport, they approached as supplicants on the advice of the doge. The doge had assembled the people in San Marco for a mass to pray for guidance concerning the envoys' requests; meanwhile, the envoys, prepared by the doge's instructions, approached and declared that they would remain on their knees in tears until the people agreed to transport their army. In a great uproar, the people shouted their consent.[56]

In this case, the doge and the envoys conspired to manipulate popular emotion; that such a calculated bargain as the one struck between the doge and the envoys should have been clothed in the trappings of voluntary humiliation suggests the familiarity of this common language. Exchanging gestures of humiliation was a necessary part of compromise, perhaps as necessary to thirteenth-century peacemakers as are expressions of sincerity to twentieth-century diplomats. The thirteenth-century cliché dressed every awkward deal in tears and prostrations. So, too, when the crusaders begged the marquis of Montferrat to assume leadership of the Fourth Crusade, they fell at his feet in tears, "l'enchaïrent as piez mult plorant," only to see the marquis kneel before them in turn to accept their offer.[57]

Diplomatic conventions may seem to be quite a different matter from public penance, but the principles are the same. When after a suit over a parcel of land, the lord of Cargouët came as a suppliant, barefoot, clothed only in his shirt, and with a cord around his neck, to be beaten before the abbot and monks of the victorious abbey of Pontron (diocese of Angers), the abbot's ecclesiastical authority assured that this was a genuine public penance,[58] but the gestures had not changed from those in simple peace settlements. We do not know what sort of settlement the humiliation concealed, whether the lord ostentatiously "lost" but really kept most of the land, whether the

56. Geoffroi de Villehardouin, *La conquête de Constantinople*, ed. E. Faral, Les classiques de l'histoire de France au Moyen Age, 18–19 (Paris, 1961), 1:26–28: "Jofrois de Vilehardoin . . . moustra la parole . . . et lor dist, 'Seignor, li baron de France li plus halt et li plus poesteï nos ont a voz envoiez . . . et nos conmanderent que nos vos enchaïssiens as piez et que nos n'en leveïssiens des que vos ariés otroié que vos ariez pitié de la Terre sainte d'outremer,' Mantenant li .vi. message s'agenoillent a lor piez mult plorant. Et li dux et tuit li autre s'escrierent tuit a une voiz, et tendent lor mains en halt, et distrent: 'Nos l'otrions! Nos l'otrions!' Enki ot si grant bruit et si grant noise que il semble que terre fondist."
57. Geoffroi de Villehardouin, *La conquête de Constantinople*, pp. 42–44.
58. Avril, *Le gouvernement des évêques*, pp. 421–422. Cf. also the case of Geoffrey de Vern, who when defeated after contesting a donation to the priory of Chemillé publicly recognized his fault: Avril, p. 422n.

penance hid an embarrassing compromise, or whether the lord's defeat was indeed total. The gestures of humiliation will appear in all of these circumstances. What is clear, however, is that demonstrations of submission were indispensable to settlement.

The role of "holy men" and of face-saving religious ritual in the settlement of disputes within a community has become a familiar theme in recent historiography. Historians and anthropologists have begun to look at procedures and rituals of decision as means not just of choosing a winner but of reconciling the loser and his friends to their fate.[59] And medieval communities appealed not only to seemingly irrational rituals but to outside arbiters, particularly those with spiritual prestige but free from political responsibilities.[60] At times, penance and especially public penance fit this model of communal peacemaking.[61] We have seen how Eudes Rigaud intervened as neutral arbiter between two families feuding over a killing, and how he found a solution calculated to promote peace rather than justice.[62] But in the thirteenth-century cities, the differences would have been more apparent than the similarities. Public penance was most often imposed precisely by those compromised with political authority, the bishops, or, as we shall see, the king or the Flemish *schepenen*. Flexible as public penance was in its procedure and application, it nevertheless was no option for the itinerant preacher, the mendicant, the "holy man."[63]

An effort to reveal the hidden functionality of seemingly irrational

59. See, for example, Peter Brown, "The Rise and Function of the Holy Man in Late Antiquity," and "Society and the Supernatural: A Medieval Change," in *Society and the Holy in Late Antiquity* (London, 1982); Mary Douglas, *Purity and Danger*, pp. 109–110; and John Bossy, "Postscript," in his *Disputes and Settlements: Law and Human Relations in the West* (Cambridge, 1983), pp. 288–289.

60. See, for example, Brigitte Szabó-Bechstein, "Sul carattere dei legami tra gli ordini mendicanti, la confraternità laica dei penitenti ed il comune di Siena nel duecento," *Mélanges de l'Ecole française de Rome: Moyen Age–Temps Modernes* 89 (1977): 743–747, for a thirteenth-century example of the mediation and diplomatic functions of *penitenti* and mendicants, held in high repute by other Sienese and conveniently exempt from ordinary municipal responsibilities.

61. Bossy, "Postscript," in *Disputes and Settlements*, p. 289, refers to rituals of reconciliation or *amicitia* as "practically indistinguishable" from rituals of penance. This is surely exaggerated, however.

62. Eudes Rigaud, *Regestrum visitationum*, p. 507 (1264).

63. We may note by contrast the Italian cities, where the exclusion of mendicants and lay *penitenti* (including laywomen on occasion) from communal political life allowed them to play a significant part as peacemakers and diplomats, though there, too, they would not have imposed public penances, a rite in any case little used south of the Alps in this period: Szabó-Bechstein, "Sul carattere de legami tra gli ordini mendicanti," pp. 745–747; and Mario Ronzani, "Penitenti e ordini mendicanti a Pisa sino all'inizio del trecento," pp. 734–735. There were no comparable marginal holy men or women in northern French towns with sufficient moral authority to settle differences.

rituals should not conceal the fact that public penance was originally a one-sided punishment that united the community not by reconciling the loser but precisely by dramatizing his humiliation in front of everyone else. It could be adapted on occasion to provide a more equitable as well as a faster settlement than that available through the secular courts, but these were not the typical circumstances. The ritual of public penance evolved away from earlier scapegoating, but even in the early rites there had never been any sign of a balanced peacemaking between equals, no gesture of mediation like the exchange of peace in the mass. And any hint of an emotional reconciliation was effaced in the later rituals of public penance, which tended to rule out any physical contact between bishop and penitent, for instance. It would be naive to think that public penance in the northern French towns resolved conflicts between social equals or on even terms.[64] These towns were not communities, and public penances did not restore peace. Most often they underlined the defeat of one side, and they held up the victims to the contempt and perhaps the laughter of their social inferiors.

If urban public penances were not, for the most part, face-saving rituals for compromise, we must try to understand why they were used in favor of other, more direct, means of inflicting harm on an adversary. Most often, such penances were imposed in circumstances that required a penalty more adaptable than ordinary secular punishments. As was seen in Chapter 4, public penance let the bishop intervene in cases not properly belonging to his spiritual jurisdiction, much less to his seigneurial jurisdiction within a town. It was therefore an attractive option for the punishment of certain types of riots against episcopal rights and property, since public penance, unlike an ordinary secular punishment or even excommunication, was very difficult to challenge. It appears repeatedly as a *deus ex machina*, often after arbitration, in cases where issues of jurisdiction were at the root of the quarrel, and so no normal court could enforce its judgment without engendering further disputes. Public penance also had the advantage of being less extreme than most secular punishments such as mutilation and hanging; it was appropriate when the bishop wished to destroy reputations, not destroy people who might later be useful.

64. Bossy, "Postscript," in *Disputes and Settlements*, p. 293, has called for "a certain naïveté about words like love and friendship," to understand how dispute settlements worked, but as Roberts, "The Study of Dispute: Anthropological Perspectives," in *Disputes and Settlements*, p. 8, has pointed out, functionalist anthropology has all too often naively assumed that the disputes in question are between equals. When unequal men and groups fight, we have cause to doubt that even Christian principles will make their reconciliation evenhanded and their love genuine.

Where the rioters were poor men attacking the rich, public penance was not the response, even where the bishop in an episcopal town could claim the right to make the judgment. Presumably, the poor had no standing in the community that would suffer from mere embarrassment and could offer no threat that might make a bishop back off from extreme measures. Only in rural areas like Cerisy do we find poor men and women doing public penance, and there for very commonplace sins like fornication; such humiliations in front of their fellow villagers had the power to sting the sinners. If the urban poor received public penances for even everyday sins, we do not hear of it. Public penance was similarly not favored in urban cases where the bishop wanted to crush a few obstinate wrongdoers. It was, above all, the punishment of choice for bourgeois, individuals, but especially groups.[65] Once again, however, these large-scale public penances by whole groups, so often imposed after the intervention of arbiters, should not be interpreted as the reconciliation of the entire community through the ritual expiation of a few. In these battles between bourgeois and religious establishments, public penance was only a weapon for one side. We shall find that public penance was often the punishment of choice precisely because it publicized the spiritual authority, indeed the legitimacy, that bourgeois tainted by usury lacked and that bishops and cathedral chapters monopolized.

The nature of urban public penance emerges most strikingly from a number of spectacular public penances that followed violent eruptions of long disputes in several northern cities. A long series of conflicts between the bishop and *échevins* at Cambrai resulted in several public penances. Like the northern French cities, Cambrai, then in the Empire, was split into a number of different bans, and the opportunities for disagreement about boundaries and rights were numerous. The flexibility of public penance permitted a settlement without deciding the fundamental issue of jurisdiction over a case, and so the bishop invoked it a number of times in the thirteenth century. In 1223, the commune made peace with the bishop by sending fifty of their number in groups of ten to do public penance at five cathedrals of the region, where they avowed their fault and received the discipline from the local clergy. This was a real defeat, not part of a concealed compromise, since the bishop soon succeeded in promulgating, with the consent of the chapter, a law prohibiting a commune or sworn association and upholding episcopal rights. The matter did not end there, and conflict continued through the thirteenth

65. Morin, *Commentarius historicus*, V.xxv, p. 322, suggests that public penance in the fourteenth-century survived primarily in rural areas, but there is no evidence for this view.

century, exacerbated by growing economic cleavages. In 1302 and 1305 townsmen rioted to the cries of *"commune, bourgeoisie"*; once suppressed, the riots were punished by elaborate humiliations of the offenders. In 1302, one hundred bourgeois in their shirts met the canons returning from exile and begged forgiveness.[66]

A second example of urban public penance is the case in Lille (discussed in Chapter 4). In some ways, the issue was simpler here than in Cambrai, but it illustrates the same principles. In 1276, a Lillois cleric in minor orders, Adam Blauwet, took refuge in the canons' church from the pursuit of his enemies. The seigneur de Cysoing, the *bailli*, and the provost and sergeants of Cysoing dragged him out and hanged him on the spot. The countess and papal legate intervened, and the *bailli* lost his office and movable goods. He and most of his accomplices were made to cross town dressed only in their shirts to bring the body of the victim back to the cloister for burial. The seigneur de Cysoing escaped the worst indignities of the penance, but every year, dressed in red, he had to follow the procession of Notre-Dame de la Treille, a custom his heirs perpetuated until the end of the sixteenth century.[67] This was one of many conflicts between the town and the canons; the townsmen and the seigneur objected to the privilege of sanctuary, the most extreme and visible form of the jurisdictional tumor that the canons represented. If the canons could threaten the town with interdict, the bourgeois had their own response; in 1283, in a secular counterpart to excommunication, they forbade the inhabitants of the town to attend services at the canons' church.[68]

The public penance of 1276 was typical both in having its origin in a quarrel between townsmen and clerics and in providing an acceptable alternative to strict justice. Ordinary procedure in a secular or ecclesiastical court would have raised issues of jurisdiction, precisely the problem that could not be settled at this point or later; and ordinary procedure would have risked too great a penalty against men of this stature. The point is not that public penances were mere token punishments. In this and other cases, the suffering was real and resented. While public penance appears as part of arbitrated settlements—here we find the intervention of the countess in place of that of the king— it nevertheless underlined the spiritual and moral authority of the canons.

---

66. Trenard, *Histoire de Cambrai*, pp. 54–56.
67. Trenard, *Histoire de Lille*, pp. 178, 345–346. The quarrel arose because the lord of Cysoing or his son was the lover of this minor cleric's wife. See above, Chapter 4.
68. Trenard, *Histoire de Lille*, p. 178.

Guibert de Nogent's autobiography has made famous the twelfth-century conflict between the bishop of Laon and the inhabit;uus who desired a commune.[69] The issue did not die there, and, near the end of the thirteenth century, it was the occasion for our third case of urban public penance. In 1295, two noblemen of Laon got into a fight with a bourgeois of Laon; when they took refuge in the cathedral, a number of bourgeois crying "commune" forced the doors and killed one of the men claiming sanctuary. The canons retired in exile, the bishop laid the city under an interdict, and Philip the Fair pronounced the dissolution of the commune. Taking advantage of Philip's own troubles with Pope Boniface VIII, however, the bourgeois found a compromise: In 1296, the commune was reestablished, and one hundred of their number performed humiliating public processions in penance for the offense against sanctuary.[70] Here is a case where the public penance of the townsmen was part of a real compromise. The communal rights thus reestablished for a generation were limited, and we may recall the continued exclusion of the Laonnais bourgeois from access to the cathedral prebends. The penance told in gestures how distant remained bourgeois hopes of a social status and moral legitimacy to match their economic power.

The Case of Reims

One of the most important and informative episodes of public penances is the sequence of processional humiliations imposed in the aftermath of riots in Reims from 1233 to 1240. This case is worth a closer look not only because it was one of the most prolonged urban conflicts in the century, but because it is one of the best documented.[71] In the 1230s and 1240s, Reims had a population of around twelve thousand, distributed around and between two centers over a mile apart, the old walled *cité* and the Bourg Saint-Remi.[72] The economy of Reims depended on the fairs of Champagne, more on local

69. Guibert de Nogent, *Autobiographie (De vita sua)*, ed. E.-R. Labande, Les classiques de l'histoire de France au Moyen Age (Paris, 1981), esp. Book III.

70. Millet, *Les chanoines du chapitre cathédrale de Laon (1272–1412)*, p. 38. In 1332 the commune was suppressed again.

71. Varin, vol. I, contains most of the relevant documents. Desportes's *Reims et les rémois* is fundamental to the analysis that follows; also important is Schmugge's "Ministerialität und Bürgertum," pp. 152–212.

72. Desportes, *Reims et les rémois*, pp. 49, 56. There had long been significant residential areas with churches in the *suburbium* between the two centers.

trade in this case than on international,[73] and on the presence of an archepiscopal see, which supported a large number of clerics and household servants. In 1218, the townsmen described their position with some exaggeration as "in marchia regni et imperii constituti," surrounded by enemies near and far and even within the walls themselves.[74] It was the last enemies that most occupied the bourgeois of Reims in the thirteenth century. Like other northern French towns, Reims was divided among several competing interests, each of which dominated at least a small territory. Most powerful was the archbishop, and his ban included most of the *cité*;[75] the Benedictine abbey of Saint-Remi controlled the eponymous *bourg*. Also significant was the cathedral chapter, whose canons had a separate small ban in the confines of the *cité*. Their independence from the archbishop is evident in their refusal to accept Archbishop Guillaume aux Blanches-Mains's charter to the *échevins*, the so-called Wilhelmine, on the grounds that the archbishop had made concessions without their consent.[76] Later, Archbishop Joël de Mathefelon would complain that the settlement of 1240 between the townsmen and canons was null because it was completed *sede vacante*, in prejudice to the rights of the archbishop.[77]

The townspeople, referred to as *cives* or *burgenses* in the texts, were not a unified group. The bourgeois of the *cité* were relatively independent; in 1182 they had received from Archbishop Guillaume the right to choose their own *échevins*. The Bourg Saint-Remi had *échevins*, too, but they were selected by the abbot and completely dependent on him.[78] Within both the *cité* and the *bourg* several major families were hereditary *servientes* or sergeants of the archbishop, the chapter, or of the abbey. These were often wealthy men, exempt from the ordinary taxes due from those subject to scabinal jurisdiction. By the 1230s, this privileged group of citizens, and especially the *servientes* of the archbishop, became the target of the jealousy of the other

73. See Desportes, *Reims et les rémois*, p. 104, for the creation of the fairs by Thibaud II in 1125–1152, and pp. 111–112 on Archbishop Guillaume aux Blanches-Mains's new indulgences to promote the fairs in 1176.

74. Varin I:507–508, from a letter of the citizens of Reims to the pope, requesting a confirmation of Milo, the elect of Beauvais, as *custos* of the land and church of Reims.

75. See Schmugge, "Ministerialität und Bürgertum," p. 158, for a map of the bans.

76. Varin I:579; cf. Varin I:533, I:560–562, for two attempts at compromises between the archbishop and chapter in 1224 and 1233 respectively. There was also a fourth ban in Reims, the very small territory of the abbey of Saint-Nicaise in the *bourg*: Desportes, *Reims et les rémois*, pp. 245–248.

77. Varin I:669 (privilege of Innocent IV to the archbishop of Reims, 1245, allowing him to reinstate the excommunication of the citizens of Reims). And in 1252, Innocent wrote the archbishop to remonstrate with him for his treatment of the *mansionarii* and *servientes* of the chapter, whom he had forced to litigate in the archiepiscopal court.

78. Desportes, *Reims et les rémois*, p. 86.

townspeople because of their identification with their masters' inte:
ests.[79]

From the perspective of the archbishop, the canons, and t}
monks, however, the bourgeois were themselves pawns to be foug}
over. In 1254, after the riots and public penances to be detailed here,
the archbishop Thomas de Beaumetz complained bitterly that Louis
IX was usurping archepiscopal rights to the guard of the monastery
of Saint-Remi; the monks preferred the king's protection. Thomas
objected so strenuously because he feared that without his supervision, the abbey would offer better terms for merchants and their
trade in their quarter, and so, as he put it, he would lose his bourgeois
and his city: "Biel signour, que porai-jou dire? Par foi, je serai honnis
se ensi demeure, et arai pierdu ma cité; car tout mi bourgois iront
manoir à Saint-Remi."[80] This was not something to be tolerated, because the taxes merchants paid were a major source of income. The
archbishops of Reims jealously guarded their control over money
changing in the city,[81] while insisting self-righteously that the canons
of the cathedral should not allow any "usurarios manifestos uel pub-
licos" ("open or public usurers") among their servants.[82] As Thomas's
quarrel over the bourgeois in the Bourg Saint-Remi suggests, the
archbishop, canons, and abbey all recognized that they needed to
attract merchants and the wealth they brought with favorable tax
treatment.

It was especially those so-called *servientes* and sergeants whom the
archbishop, canons, and abbey tried to coddle with privileges and
exemptions. This was the elite among the bourgeois, composed of
wealthy merchant families who claimed by inheritance the right to
serve the abbot, the archbishop, or less often, the chapter, sometimes
in specific offices, sometimes without named duties.[83] They escaped
the jurisdiction and taxes of the *échevins*. In the twelfth century, the
bargain may have seemed a workable one. The *servientes* of the arch-

79. Schmugge, "Ministerialität und Bürgertum," pp. 152–212; see esp. 208 on the beginnings of hostility. Cf. Desportes, *Reims et les rémois*, p. 486, on the divisions of Reims into small
quarters.
80. *Chronique anonyme dite Chronique de Reims*, HF 22:327–328.
81. Varin I:394 (the "Wilhelmine," 1182).
82. Varin I:952; and Schmugge, "Ministerialität und Bürgertum," p. 178.
83. Schmugge's "Ministerialität und Bürgertum" is the best guide to these families and
their role; but his argument that these servants were *ministeriales* similar to those in the
Rhineland is only partially persuasive. The term does indeed appear on occasion in twelfth-
century texts; cf. Varin I:439, where the archbishop refers to some of his servants as *ministeriales nostri*. More often the term used is *servientes*, or occasionally *homines* or *franci servientes*.
Schmugge does not address the important question about whether these men were unfree; it
does not seem that they were in the twelfth or thirteenth centuries.

bishop appear early in the lists of the *échevins*, a sign that their preeminence was tolerated by the other bourgeois.[84] But the arrangement started to break down when more men attained the wealth of these few families without being rewarded with the privileges and exemptions of the *servientes*. The archbishop's men disappear from the lists of the *échevins* and instead become early targets for the riots of the other bourgeois in 1233–1236.

The underlying causes of this quarrel should be familiar by now: conflicts over jurisdiction, taxes, the archepiscopal monopoly of money changing, and the threat of accusations of usury.[85] In 1234, Archbishop Henri de Braine threatened to invoke charges of usury against the *échevins* of Reims when, without consulting him, they sold a large number of *rentes viagères* to the financiers of Arras.[86] Henri objected above all because the collective action of the *échevins* was tantamount to communal financial decisions without his authority. As mentioned above, the *Chronique de Saint Nicaise* described the whole battle at Reims as a quarrel over usury.

> In this year, the church of Reims being in great peace and honor, many citizens of the episcopal ban and the chapter ban feared that there would be an inquisition against them concerning usury. A conspiracy was hatched among them and the people were seditiously stirred up against the chapter; by means of injuries and insults made against the canons and their subjects they forced the canons to flee the city in fear of death in early November.[87]

The canons now claimed that the Wilhelmine of 1182 that had established the election of *échevins* was void, since their interests had been neglected.[88] Such a declaration at this juncture inevitably radicalized the townsmen, who now feared the destruction of all their privileges. And coincidentally, the successes of the bourgeois of Beauvais against

---

84. Schmugge, "Ministerialität und Bürgertum," p. 207.
85. Varin I:608–609; cf. Desportes, *Reims et les rémois*, pp. 82–86.
86. Desportes, *Reims et les rémois*, pp. 159–160.
87. Varin I:566n: "Hoc anno [1233] ecclesia remensis existente in multa pace et honore, cives multi de banno episcopi et de banno capituli, timentes ne contra eos fieret inquisitio de usura, conspiratione inter se facta, populo contra capitulum seditiose commoto, per injurias et vituperia canonicis et subditis suis facta, ipsos canonicos metu mortis v. id. novembris de civitate fugere compulerunt."
88. Varin I:533, I:569–570: "Willelmus archiepiscopus sine capituli sui consensu scabinatum pro sue voluntatis arbitrio concessisset, et capitulum ipsum tali concessioni, utpote nimium damnose remense remensi ecclesie, noluit adhibere consensum" (from a letter of Gregory IX to the bishop of Soissons and others, 1235, taking the side of the canons).

their bishop led some at Reims to think Saint Louis might inte:
on their side against ecclesiastical claims to jurisdiction.[89]

The sharpened fears of accusations of usury and the collapse of
liberties, coupled with new hopes of the final establishment of a commune free from ecclesiastical interference, eventually led the bourgeois to violence in 1233 and 1234. On one Sunday, according to
Gregory IX's letter to the bishop of Soissons and others, the citizens
met a procession of the canons solemnizing the death of a monk, and
denouncing them as thieves and traitors, mocked them with howl-
ing.[90] In that incident, we may note how a procession could be the
scene for political violence. The bourgeois of the chapter's ban and
the *servientes* of the chapter living in the archbishop's ban convinced
by threats and blandishments—so says Gregory—the bourgeois of
the archbishop's ban to join them in a sworn association to extract
concessions from the chapter. They harrassed the "poor and few"
who remained in the chapter's service; the merchants of the conspiracy refused to take their goods to the marketplace, and they even
destroyed some stalls. They went so far as to attack the canons themselves, including striking one priest who ventured outside the confines of the cathedral to bring the viaticum to a dying man. The
archbishop had jurisdiction over these men, continues Gregory, but
when he tried to investigate the matter—but not the events themselves, since these were notorious—the *échevins* insisted that no one
should testify at his court. Gregory demanded that Louis IX should
intervene to punish the shameful crimes "fermento corrupta prau-
itatis heretice" ("corrupted by a heretical ferment of depravity").[91]
But Gregory only wanted Louis to execute the judgments determined
by the appropriate ecclesiastical courts. The Council of Meaux in
1235 insisted that the king should not compel the archbishop to re-
spond in a royal court concerning crimes committed by citizens of
Reims, "cum sint justiciabiles sui et fideles" ("since they are his vassals
and answerable in his court").[92] Louis did not intervene at this point,
and hostilities continued unabated in 1234 and 1235; the canons
withdrew from the town and refused settlement, while the townsmen,

---

89. See Desportes, *Reims et les rémois*, p. 159; and Pontal, "Le différend entre Louis IX et
les évêques de Beauvais et ses incidences sur les conciles (1232–1248)," pp. 5–34, for this
quarrel and its influence on events at Reims.

90. Varin I:580: "post ipsos quasi post canes aut lupos fortiter hulularunt, immo quod
turpius in gallico idiomate sonare dicitur, huiaverunt, in grave ipsorum obprobrium, et divine
dedecus majestatis, cujus saltem vexillum debebant humiliter revereri."

91. Varin I:579–581.

92. Varin I:586.

for their part, turned their fury against the archbishop's officers and men, burning a number of their houses and pulling down stones from other buildings, which the rebellious bourgeois had used to fortify their quarters.[93]

The eventual settlement and the public penance that ensued began with Louis's intervention between the archbishop and the bourgeois in 1236. Typically, Louis refused to weigh in on behalf of ecclesiastical authority itself. As we shall see, his well-known coolness to ecclesiastical pretensions and his judicial activism inclined Louis to use public penances imposed under his aegis as a convenient compromise in conflicts between his bishops and his lay subjects or between two lay subjects. Public penances could prevent the concession of extravagant claims of jurisdiction, and besides, this future saint had a taste for punishments that were also moral pronouncements. Louis intervened from January to March 1236 as an arbiter between the parties at Reims, not as the simple executor of the archbishop's judgment, as Gregory might have wished. Louis appointed two arbiters, the abbot of Saint-Denis, and Pierre de Colmieu, *prévôt* of Saint-Omer, to decide on terms. They had the archbishop agree to authorize a tax to buy back the offending *rentes viagères* from the financiers of Arras; the absolution of the bourgeois was to follow "in forma ecclesie." The bourgeois were to pay ten thousand *livres parisis*, and they were to complete a series of processions, with the details left open.[94]

In the meantime, the canons pursued their case at the papal court, much to the displeasure of the bourgeois, who objected that the *échevinage* was a matter for lay courts. It was again arbitration that settled the dispute between the bourgeois and the canons; this time the archbishop intervened. The canons were to request that the Holy See withdraw the excommunications, and the bourgeois were to complete a very elaborate series of public penances, now with the details spelled out. The bourgeois of Reims were first to meet the canons returning from exile near the Porte Mars of the *cité*. In the presence of the archbishop, sixty were to walk barefoot in their shirts and breeches to apologize to the canons according to a written formula, and they were to make reparations. Then, selected bourgeois were to go to churches and men whom they had offended with their actions, each time to make an apology according to a written formula. This procedure of repeated apologies differed a little from the usual forms of public penance, but amounted to the same thing: "Next we order that ten of those who afterwards took themselves and lived on the chapter's land,

---

93. Varin I:618, for the repairs required in the arbitration settlement.
94. Varin I:617–619; Desportes, *Reims et les rémois*, pp. 164–166.

after the prohibition, should make amends to the chapter for this, likewise barefoot, all in breeches and shirts, and say: 'Both we and those for whom we make amends will keep away from chapter lands as long as the archbishop decrees.'"[95] Even these indignities did not satisfy the canons. Twenty of the most guilty bourgeois were to do public penance at every cathedral of the province, and 110 others of the archbishop's ban were to split into groups of ten to do public penance at those cathedrals, too.[96] We have seen how Eudes Rigaud made particularly important offenders go from one cathedral to another in penance, but this remains one of the most elaborate public penances we know of. The canons wanted the humiliation of their enemies publicized from Thérouanne and Tournai to Châlons-sur-Marne and Senlis.

The fundamental issues of jurisdiction and authority remained undecided by the successful arbitration. The archbishop continued to claim that the king had no right to take the case into his court, and he grudgingly accepted the informal arrangment. The canons did not care for either royal or archepiscopal claims, preferring papal protection for their rights. The *échevins* complained that it was a lay matter, and so did not belong in any spiritual court. And the monks of Saint-Remi, originally uninvolved in the quarrel, soon made a point of claiming exemption for their bourgeois from the settlement reached through arbitration.[97] It is hardly surprising, then, that the quarrel flared up again in 1238. Again the bourgeois armed themselves and fortified the city against the archbishop's men, again the archbishop pronounced the interdict, again the canons left town. The process of reconciliation was similar, too. The canons and bourgeois took advantage of the vacancy of the see in 1240 to come to a negotiated settlement. The arbiters, the bishop of Senlis and the archdeacon and *scholasticus* of Reims, decided that the *échevins* should pay one thousand marks surety and all the people should declare their common assent to the terms; all the guilty would be absolved. Then, seventy of the bourgeois, including the *échevins* themselves, should go in groups of six or seven to do public penance in every cathedral of the province, there to be flogged in public by the canons of each cathedral. And before all this, in Reims itself, all seventy were to join the proces-

---

95. Varin I:625: "Item precepimus quod decem ex illis qui postquam se transtulerunt in terram nostram, habitaverunt in terra capituli post prohibitionem ipsius, hoc emendent capitulo, nudis pedibus similiter, in bractis et camisiis conmunibus, et dicant: 'Et nos, et alii pro quibus emendamus, abstinebimus a terra capituli usque ad tempus quod statuerit archiepiscopus.'"

96. Varin I:624–627; Desportes, *Reims et les rémois*, p. 166.

97. Varin I:659.

sions of Notre-Dame on August 15, there to accept another public flogging by the canons.[98] The canons sold peace with the most public of indignities. Interestingly, the archbishop himself did not have the same taste for public penances outside Reims as did the chapter; perhaps he did not think it so necessary to impress other cathedrals with his victories. The quarrels, at any rate, continued a few more years, as new archbishops in 1245 and again in 1250 complained that the canons had settled to the prejudice of archepiscopal interests. But the bourgeois never again rioted and set up barricades against the archbishop and canons in this way; indeed, they never again tried to rival the merchants of Arras with their financial deals. After 1250, Reims became a merely local market town.

The story of the bourgeois of Reims has several lessons for our study of public penance. As so often, the penances were imposed only as the result of arbitrated settlements, which, however, we must not mistake for equitable compromises that reestablished friendship. Public penance survived so long precisely because it escaped all the schemes of classification of the theologians and canonists. In the cities of northern France, the notion of a public authority was particularly problematic. Neither bishops nor canons nor communes nor even the king could claim sovereignty in every quarter, and no one agreed on the frontiers between jurisdictions. Under these circumstances, a means of keeping order that transcended such disputes was an attractive alternative.

It may seem paradoxical that public penance thrived just where public authority was most obscured by the rivalry of conflicting claims. But as we saw in Chapter 7, by the thirteenth century public penance did not draw together an entire community but only sought to single out a few for humiliation and even ridicule. The later rituals of public penance correspond to the political uses of public penance described in this chapter; the rituals presupposed division rather than community. While it is impossible to show that liturgists consciously amended the rite in light of contemporary practice, we can show that rite and practice evolved along similar lines. The bourgeois of Reims were absolved *before* they completed their public penances; and so we find that by 1250 the pontificals routinely placed the absolution before the satisfaction. The later rites de-emphasized the role of the bishop; and so we find thirteenth-century public penances imposed as the outcome of arbitration, often with no indication of what ecclesiastical authority, if any, formally imposed the rite. The later rites

---

98. Varin I:640–642; Desportes, *Reims et les rémois*, pp. 166–167.

divorced the Lenten penitence of the faithful from the public sufferings of the few; and so we find the bourgeois of Reims making public apologies to the canons and their servants outside any specifically religious context. These quasi-public penances in secular contexts appear with increasing frequency in the north of France, and a study of their survival and afterlife concludes this chapter.

Secular Public Penances and Pilgrimages

We have already had cause to remark on public "penances" imposed by secular authorities such as the king or communal *échevins*. Of course many public penances imposed by ecclesiastical authorities had obvious political connotations. The penitential pilgrimage of Guillaume de Nogaret, imposed by Clement V in 1311 as part of a settlement with Philip the Fair, is but one example.[99] In 1209, the count of Toulouse had been reconciled and absolved by the papal legate after he stood barefoot before the door of the church at Saint-Gilles and publicly declared his fault; on Maundy Thursday in 1229, his successor had done homage to the king and had been publicly reconciled to the church.[100] These are quasi-secular penances, perhaps, where the line between political peacemaking and religious reconciliation is difficult to draw. In this section, however, I look at secular public "penances" without even the color of ecclesiastical imposition. We may recall Ralph of Coggeshall's story that Philip Augustus forced a knight who had summarily hanged a *conversus* to do public penance by digging up and reburying the victim in hallowed ground.[101]

Such a borrowing of public penance by secular powers was much more common than one might imagine, and, indeed, there is really no reason to distinguish them as only quasi-penances or bracket the term with quotation marks. Ralph, after all, tells his story about Philip in connection with a similar penance imposed, he says, by the bishop of Chartres; he does not observe a distinction between secular and religious humiliations. The line that a careful theologian or a modern historian might draw between the penance that restores a sinner to grace and mere humiliation that embarrasses him before his fellows does not seem to have struck the kings who imposed such punish-

---

99. Bernard Gui, *E floribus chronicorum . . . necnon e chronico regum francorum*, HF 21:720.
100. Pierre des Vaux de Cernay, *Historia Albigensium*, HF 19:16; Alberic de Trois Fontaines, *Chronicum*, HF 21:599.
101. Ralph of Coggeshall, *Chronicon Anglicanum*, pp. 199–201; see Chapter 4.

ments or the public who watched them. It was the duty of Christian kings and Christian communes no less than bishops to enforce a moral code with laws that exposed criminals to humiliation; even as royal justice might refuse to pursue every excommunicant with the assiduity the bishops might want, it nonetheless provided sanctions for admittedly religious offenses.[102] Louis IX's punishment of blasphemers is well known. Joinville says that Louis once ordered a blaspheming goldsmith in Caesarea to be draped with pigs' intestines and set in the pillory; in Paris, Louis had blasphemers branded on the face.[103]

These are punishments very similar to those applied by the *officialité* of the abbey of Cerisy for malicious gossip, scandalous squabbling between husband and wife, and similar offenses.[104] Often in the *officialité*, as in the secular courts, fines were customary penalties and were replaced by exposure only when the guilty party could not pay.[105] The upper classes received more dignified treatment perhaps, but they did not escape public punishment with a religious tenor. When once a Champenois knight sojourning in Paris cursed God, Louis refused all appeals on his behalf and sent him *outremer* (overseas) in perpetual exile.[106] One can hardly distinguish such an exile from a crusading pilgrimage; once again, Louis borrowed a punishment with religious connotations for an indisputably moral offense. Usury, normally a matter for the bishop's court, could incur secular punishment as well; the council that Louis IX held at Melun in 1230 declared that no usury should be permitted either by the king in his lands or by the barons in theirs.[107] It did not specify the penalties. When on crusade, furthermore, Louis borrowed the penalties Joinville calls customary to the Holy Land, penalties themselves adapted from the discipline of the military orders that readily used humilia-

---

102. Cf. the idealized account Philippe de Beaumanoir, *Coutumes de Beauvaisis*, vol. I, p. 164: "tuit crestien et toutes crestienes sont fil et filles de sainte Eglise et sont tenu a sainte Eglise garder et garantir toutes les fois qu'ele en a mestier et qu'ele se complaint a aus comme a ses enfans." But he notes that penances, among other things, are within the purview of the church. For the frequent difficulties over secular sanctions on excommunicants, see especially Maurice Morel, *L'excommunication et le pouvoir civil en France du droit canonique classique au commencement du XVe siècle* (Paris, 1926), pp. 66–149.

103. Jean de Joinville, *Histoire de Saint Louis*, cxxxviii, pp. 289–290; *Chronique de Primat*, trans. Jean de Vignay, HF 23:66. See also Louis Boutié, *Paris au temps de Saint Louis* (Paris, 1911), pp. 225–226, on fines for blasphemy in the *ordonnance* of 1269; the offender too poor to pay would be put in the stocks "where people customarily assemble," then jailed briefly.

104. Dupont, "Le registre de l'officialité de Cerisy, 1314–1457," p. 312 (1315). and p. 373 (1375). See above, Chapter 4.

105. See, e.g., Dupont, "Le registre de l'officialité de Cerisy, 1314–1457," p. 314), and pp. 381–382 (1330), two cases of fornication where the woman could not pay a fine.

106. *Extraits d'une chronique anonyme intitulée anciennes chroniques de Flandres*, HF 22:345.

107. Albéric de Trois Fontaines, *Chronique*, HF 21:603.

tion as a weapon. Thus, according to Joinville, a knight caught in a brothel was offered the choice of being led around camp on a rope by the prostitute or surrendering his horse and arms; the knight preferred the latter. And when Joinville complained that one of Louis's sergeants had pushed one of his own knights, Louis required the brawling sergeant to make amends to Joinville by appearing in his quarters like a penitent, barefoot in his shirt, and offering a sword to Joinville's knight to cut off his hand should the knight wish. Joinville at last asked his knight to forgive the offense.[108] Here we revisit the principle of reconciliation through self-abasement, particularly apt in the Holy Land, where the disciplinary code of the military orders set the example and where other more direct forms of justice were often impracticable.

The story of Philip Augustus's imposition of public penance on a knight suggests not only the popularity of religious humiliations but also a conscious effort to protect the inviolability of clerical property and persons. The knight's offense was to hang an accused *conversus* instead of first submitting him to the ecclesiastical court for degradation. So it is not surprising to find repeated examples of ecclesiastical and secular cooperation in imposing public penances on offenders in serious crimes against sanctuary. As we have seen, in 1296, Philip the Fair's intervention made possible the settlement ending in the bishop of Laon's imposition of public penance on the bourgeois of Laon who had pursued fugitives into the cathedral in their attempt to establish a commune; here at least Philip was not swayed by the offenders' efforts to exploit his quarrel with Boniface.[109]

The most instructive example of a royally imposed public penance, however, is Saint Louis's negotiation of a suitable punishment for a shoemaker of Paris. The *Vie de Saint Louis* by Queen Marguerite's confessor recounts that Louis typically increased the penalty of wrongdoers who had made peace with their adversaries by agreeing to a fine or to a temporary exile overseas; so it was with this unnamed shoemaker.[110] He and another bourgeois were brought to the Châte-

---

108. Jean de Joinville, *Histoire de Saint Louis*, xcix, p. 214.
109. Millet, *Les chanoines du chapitre cathédrale de Laon (1272–1412)*, pp. 37–38.
110. *Vie de Saint Louis par le confesseur de la reine Marguerite*, HF 20:117–118: "Et quant aucune question estoit aportee devant lui de aucuns maufeteurs, se il avenoit que par aucune achoison il eust conceu aucunes soupeçons contre les malfeteurs, et il avenist que il feissent pès a leur aversaires por somme d'argent, ou porce que il alassent outre mer, si que cil que len disoit qui avoient fet le meffet, fussent ilecques et i demorassent un an ou deux; li benoiez rois meuz de jalousie de justice, pource que les malvès fez fussent restreinz le miex que il pooit, et fussent avecques ce punis, croissoit encore la poine des maufeteurs, ou la somme de largent ou du tens de demorer outre mer, si com il li estoit avis quil fust bien, outre ce que len avoit ordené entre eus."

let, where the shoemaker said that the bourgeois had attacked his home and beaten him, and that in self-defense he had wounded the man, who presently expired in front of the king's men. Since the shoemaker could not prove self-defense, he was held as a homicide, for which reason he had to make peace with the friends of the victim ("pour quoi il convint que il feist pès as amis du mort"). And among other things, it was settled with the consent of the *prévôt* of Paris that the killer should stay overseas for ten years. The case, after all, had not been proved either way by witnesses, and common rumor had it that the dead bourgeois had indeed assaulted the shoemaker. "He [the shoemaker] would be overseas for ten years, by the consent of the *prévôt* of Paris, because . . . the assault was not clearly proved by witnesses and common rumor said that the dead man had made the assault . . . against the shoemaker who was there, and that he has beat him and done him much villainy.[111] It was a relatively mild settlement because of the uncertainty of the circumstances. But, the author explains, since neither royal nor seigneurial *baillis* are accustomed in cases of homicide to approve a treaty of peace without the assent of the king, the matter reached Saint Louis, who added three years to the agreed-upon ten.[112]

The procedure is worth noting carefully, because it will reappear in our study of public penances and pilgrimages imposed in the cities of Flanders and Alsace. In spite of Louis's role in the decision and his vaunted jealousy for strict justice, the penalty is not strictly speaking a royal punishment. Like a great many cases that would come before the king's court, it is the outcome of a treaty of peace between the killer and the "friends" of his victim, very like the settlement that Archbishop Eudes Rigaud drew up between Thomas the miller and the family of his alleged victim Gilbert de Sauqueville.[113] Even on the

111. *Vie de Saint Louis par le confesseur de la reine Marguerite*, HF 20:118: "il [the shoemaker] seroit par dix ans outre mer, par le consentement du prevost de Paris, pour ce . . . que lassaut ne fust pas pleinement prouvé par tesmoinz, non porquant commune renommée disoit que le mort avoit fet lassaut . . . contre le corduanier qui i estoit, et que il lavoit batu et li avoit mout fet de vilainies."

112. *Vie de Saint Louis par le confesseur de la reine Marguerite*, HF 20:118.

113. Eudes Rigaud, *Regestrum visitationum*, p. 507 (1264); for the accusatory criminal procedure typical of thirteenth-century cities, see Grand, "Justice criminelle, procédure, et peines dans les villes aux XIIIe et XIVe siècles," p. 90. See especially John Baldwin, *The Government of Philip Augustus*, pp. 37–44, on the large number of *concordie* (agreements) and *arbritrii* (arbitrations) confirmed by the king's court. He has calculated that for Philip's reign, some 54 percent of the cases in the king's court were agreements, and another 16 percent arbitrations. For arbitrated settlements in Flanders, see R. C. van Caenegem, *Geschiedenis van het Strafrecht in Vlaanderen van de XIe tot de XIVe eeuw*, Verhandelingen van de Koninklijke Vlaamse Academie voor Wetenschappen, Letteren en Schone Kunsten van België, Klasse der Letteren, Verhandeling nr. 19 (Brussels, 1954), pp. 280–307.

streets of Paris in the thirteenth century, justice still means a kin's vengeance. And here, as in Rouen, the facts of the affair were hopelessly ambiguous; so a compromise seemed by far the best solution. But in this case, once the deal is struck, it requires royal approval, and Louis adds to the killer's punishment. In spite of the biographer's praise, one suspects that the shoemaker at least might have preferred Eudes Rigaud's gentler treatment to the intolerant justice of a royal saint. We may note in passing that Louis's biographer has exaggerated the rights of royal intervention; neither seigneurial *baillis* nor Eudes himself seem to have brought peace settlements in homicides before Louis.

The punishment is not explicitly a penitential pilgrimage, only an exile overseas, *outremer*, though it may well have implied the service of the killer in the crusading armies, perhaps even on behalf of the soul of the victim; such stipulations will appear in the punishments imposed by the communes. We can turn once again to the animals of the *Roman de Renart* for confirmation of the popularity of such settlements. When Renart the fox is brought before Noble the lion for his misdeeds, he admits his fault, and offers to go overseas on a crusade in penance as a way of satisfying his victims.

> Or voil venir a repentance.
> El non de seinte penitance
> Voeil la crois prendre por aler,
> La merci Deu, outra la mer.[114]

The lion king, like Louis IX, is a secular authority, and the crimes Renart has committed, such as assaulting Noble's envoy Tibert the cat, are also secular. But Renart offers spiritual penance in atonement, and the offer is accepted.

The use of pilgrimages appears explicitly in grander peace settlements in the wars in early-fourteenth-century Flanders, and these mass pilgrimages are a second link between French royal justice and the Flemish communal pilgrimages of the later Middle Ages.[115] In

114. *Le roman de Renart*, Branche I, ll. 1387–1390, p. 112.
115. The definitive work on imposed pilgrimages in Flanders is J. van Herwaarden's *Opgelegde bedevaarten*, which has replaced Johannes Schmitz, "Sühnewallfahrten im Mittelalter" (Ph.D. diss., Bonn, 1910) as a general overview. A number of more limited studies provide examples of the phenomenon: F. L. Ganshof, "Pèlerinages expiatoires flamands à Saint-Gilles pendant le XIVe siècle," *Annales du Midi* 78 (1966): 391–407; Etienne van Cauwenbergh, *Les pèlerinages expiatoires et judiciaires dans le droit communal de la Belgique au Moyen Age*, Université de Louvain, Recueil de travaux publiés par les membres des conférences d'histoire et de philologie, 48 (Louvain, 1922); Valon, "Les pèlerinages expiatoires et judiciaires de la Belgique aux sanctuaires de la Provence au Moyen-Age," pp. 30–52 and "Les

1305, the treaty of Athis-sur-Orge between Philip the Fair and the Flemish cities stipulated that three thousand men of Bruges should go on pilgrimage, one thousand to Jerusalem; and if any Fleming should offend against the servants and household (*familia*) of the king, that town should be placed under an interdict and the offending Flemings excommunicated. One late-fourteenth-century Flemish chronicle explains the pilgrimages as punishment for the killing of nobles at Courtrai.[116] Like the shoemaker of Paris and the miller of Dieppe, the citizens of Bruges must make pilgrimages to atone for their violent crimes; the chronicler makes no distinction between treaty and criminal law. In any case, after war broke out again, the treaty of Arques in 1326 required that the cities of Bruges and Court-rai send three hundred pilgrims, one hundred each to Santiago, Saint-Gilles, and Rocamadour.[117]

Imposed pilgrimages became a common feature of fourteenth-century peace settlements in Flanders, whether to end a war or to pacify feuding families.[118] Their advantage as a penalty extended beyond the value of getting one party out of the way. A pilgrimage to a saint's shrine gave the punishment a moral authority that it might not otherwise have; pilgrimages were especially popular in cases where the grounds for jurisdiction or the evidence for the decision were weak and its authority needed confirmation. Pilgrimages were appropriate in cases of disputed homicide or treaties where the de-feated cities only reluctantly acknowledged royal suzerainty. But the religious connection could bring very specific political advantages, too. A vow to journey to the threshold of the saints was more difficult to evade than an ordinary exile; as we have seen, Philip insisted that

pèlerinages expiatoires et judiciaires de la Belgique à Roc-Amadour au Moyen Age," pp. 9–37. Also important in this context is D. M. Nicholas, "Crime and Punishment in Fourteenth-Century Ghent," pp. 289–334, 1141–1176. It is worth noting that English has no convention-al term for such pilgrimages, unlike Dutch (*opgelegde bedevaarten*), German (*Sühnewallfahrten*), and French (*pèlerinages expiatoires et judiciaires*). I will most often refer to them as "imposed pilgrimages."

116. *Chronicon Flandriae scriptum ab Adriano de Budt, Corpus Chronicorum Flandriae*, vol. I, p. 311: "in vindictam nobilium occisorum in Curtraco." See van Herwaarden, *Opgelegde bedevaarten*, p. 56; van Cauwenbergh, *Les pèlerinages expiatoires et judiciaires dans le droit commu-nal de la Belgique au Moyen Age*, pp. 85–86; F. L. Ganshof, "Pèlerinages expiatoires flamands à Saint-Gilles pendant le XIVe siècle," p. 405; cf. *Extraits d'une chronique anonyme intitulée An-ciennes chroniques de Flandres*, HF 22:395: "Item lui livreroient jusques à six cens hommes de la ville de Bruges, quy seroient tenus de aler en tels pellegrinages là où le roy les vouldroit envoier, jusques à son rappel."

117. van Herwaarden, *Opgelegde bedevaarten*, p. 57; Valon, "Les pèlerinages expiatoires et judiciaires de la Belgique aux sanctuaires de la Provence au Moyen-Age," p. 43.

118. For later peace treaties, see Ganshof, "Pèlerinages expiatoires flamands à Saint-Gilles pendant le XIVe siècle," pp. 405–406; for royal intervention and arbitrations resulting in pilgrimages, see Herwaarden, *Opgelegde bedevaarten*, pp. 55–56.

truce-breakers should suffer interdict and excommunication. This last stipulation was especially unpopular in Flanders, because, as the author of the *Annales Gandenses* put it, the excommunicated Fleming would not be able to be absolved except by the pope, and the French pope Clement would surely only grant absolution at the king's request.[119] French domination of the Avignonese papacy meant that Philip and his successors could enjoy through these pilgrimages the same kind of monopoly over the mechanism of public penance that we have seen French bishops expoit in the thirteenth century.

The imposition of involuntary pilgrimages in the Flemish communes of the later Middle Ages has been extensively studied by several Continental scholars, while English-language writing on pilgrimage has almost entirely ignored the phenomenon. Here it will be necessary only to outline some of its many forms and to consider why it became such an important weapon against crime in many cities. Communally imposed pilgrimages flourished in the fourteenth and fifteenth centuries in what is now northern France, Belgium, and the southern Netherlands, in towns ranging from Francophone Saint-Omer, Béthune, and Douai through Flemish Bruges and Ghent.[120] They were also common in two regions out of the range of our study: Alsace and Switzerland. In Alsace, public penances in the form of imposed pilgrimages survived into the eighteenth century.[121] It is not surprising that penal pilgrimages were imposed in areas where we know public penance to have survived; but without further work on the early history of public penance in these regions, we cannot pursue Swiss and Alsatian pilgrimage here. In Flanders, the crimes punished by pilgrimages and the procedure followed varied considerably. Communal *échevins* (*schepenen*) in the Flemish towns imposed pilgrimages for moral crimes such as heresy, sorcery, and blasphemy, but more often for offenses against the authority of the commune or prince, such as recourse to outside jurisdiction, slander against the *échevins*, armed assemblies not convoked by the authorities, or even ball games in the marketplace. One of the largest category of offenses, however,

---

119. *Annales Gandenses*, p. 96: "statim ipso facto esset excommunicatus, tali excommunicatione, quod ab ea absolvi non posset, nisi a papa, et nec a papa, nisi ad regis requisitionem et voluntatem."

120. van Herwaarden, *Opgelegde bedevaarten*, pp. 4–5.

121. For Switzerland, see Louis Carlen, "Busswallfahrten der Schweiz," *Schweizerisches Archiv für Volkskunde* 55 (1959): 237–257. Most of these Swiss pilgrimages were imposed in atonement for homicides and took the killer to Einsiedeln, rarely further. For Alsace, see L. Pfleger, "Sühnewallfahrten und öffentliche Kirchenbusse im Elsass im späten Mittelalter und in der Neuzeit," *Archiv für elsässische Kirchengeschichte* 8 (1933): 127–162. Pfleger, p. 127, is one of the few modern historians to recognize that public penance of the conventional sort as well as imposed pilgrimages survived long after its supposed demise.

was acts of violence against other persons, including slander, assault, rape, and house-breaking, but only very rarely theft.[122] For example, a private war among four patrician families in Ghent from 1293/94 to 1306 was partially settled by the arbitration of the count of Flanders, Robert of Béthune, and the *schepenen* of Ghent with a peace agreement requiring fines and pilgrimages to be performed by those guilty of violence. The arbitrators specified pilgrimages to shrines as far as Cyprus, Santiago, Saint-Gilles, and Rocamadour; but not all the pilgrimages were actually performed.[123]

Peacemaking after feuds was often the context for pilgrimages imposed in communes, and as early as the mid–thirteenth century, several Flemish towns had formalized the procedure of arbitration, with appointed communal peacemakers (*paysierders, paysmaekers, vriendelike effeneers, apayseurs,* etc.), drawn chiefly from among the *poorterie* (patrician citizens), landowners, and textile merchants. By the mid-fourteenth century, these arbitrators or the *échevins* commonly would inscribe such peaces in a book of reconciliations, the *zoendincbouc*.[124] From the later fourteenth century, the pilgrimages were often redeemable by the payment of fines, just like the old "tariffed penances," with the money going to the victim or split between him and the commune. The *zoen*, or "atonement," was normally drawn up between kingroups, not individuals, just as Eudes Rigaud typically settled matters between feuding families; and the sanctions involved satisfaction to the injured party, not just penalties demanded by a superior authority.[125] A pilgrimage would obviously serve to distance the parties from each other, and most of the destinations assigned, in Provence, Spain, and the Holy Land, would have required an absence

---

122. Van Cauwenbergh, *Les pèlerinages expiatoires et judiciaires dans le droit communal de la Belgique au Moyen Age*, pp. 34–80. On the absence of theft among the crimes punished by pilgrimage, see especially Nicholas, "Crime and Punishment in Fourteenth-Century Ghent," pp. 289–334, esp. pp. 332–334, who argues that secret crimes against property were considered too serious to be a matter for mere pilgrimage. One might also suggest that violent crimes very frequently were the result of fights, and so the culpability of the survivor might be hard to determine.

123. Ganshof, "Pèlerinages expiatoires flamands à Saint-Gilles pendant le XIVe siècle," pp. 397–398.

124. van Herwaarden, *Opgelegde bedevaarten*, pp. 73–82, 403–405; van Cauwenbergh, *Les pèlerinages expiatoires et judiciaires dans le droit communal de la Belgique au Moyen Âge*, pp. 88–90; Ganshof, "Pèlerinages expiatoires flamands à Saint-Gilles pendant le XIVe siècle," p. 398. For an overview of the use of the *zoen* in Flemish law, see van Caenegem, *Geschiedenis van het strafrecht in Vlaanderen*, pp. 280–307.

125. See van Herwaarden, *Opgelegde bedevaarten*, pp. 11, 51, on the varied treatment of such conciliations in the Flemish cities; some integrated compensation to authority and compensation to the victim, and some specified only one in the surviving records. See also Louis-Théo Maes, "Mittelalterliche Strafwallfahrten nach Santiago de Compostela und Unsere Liebe Frau von Finisterra," in *Festschrift Guido Kisch* (Stuttgart, 1955), p. 103.

of several months at least. Simple exile was sometimes an option, too, although pilgrimage was more common early in the fourteenth century.[126] Besides the obvious pleasure a victim's family could take in seeing the attacker suffer public rebuke, the victim's soul could reap spiritual benefit from the sinner's expiatory visit to the saints; if the guilty party decided to redeem his pilgrimage with money, the reward was more material.[127] Thus, even when the pilgrimage was not in fact imposed by peacemakers arbitrating between families, the procedure before the communal tribunal was frequently accusatory, and the complaint was pursued by the victim's kin instead of the commune. Oaths and compurgation supplemented the testimony of witnesses in the establishment of guilt or innocence.[128]

The procedure for the imposition of pilgrimages in the communes is so close to that followed by Saint Louis in his settlement of a punishment that we may assume a connection; these imposed pilgrimages, therefore, were not a fourteenth-century invention limited to Flanders and Alsace, but they were a phenomenon familiar to many Frenchmen north of the Loire in the thirteenth century. In his account of the laws of the Beauvaisis, Philippe de Beaumanoir discusses the principles of arbitrated settlements at some length. He refers to one case where the arbiters decided that a bourgeois who had killed a horse under a man but had not hurt the man himself should pay three hundred *livres* and make pilgrimages to Boulogne, Santiago, Saint-Gilles, and the Holy Land. Not surprisingly, Beaumanoir thought this punishment excessive, and he used it to illustrate the principle that such "outrageous" arbitrated judgments were void.[129] The procedure Beaumanoir recognizes here is the same as that of fourteenth-century Flemish *zoenen*.

Several historians have emphasized the link between these imposed pilgrimages and penitential pilgrimage, which they identify with nonsolemn public penance in the tripartite scheme.[130] We need not en-

---

126. For an example of exile, see the banishment of the leaders of the *communitas* of Bruges after their violent conflict with the *majores* in 1301, *Annales Gandenses*, p. 15.

127. Cf. Ganshof, "Pèlerinages expiatoires flamands à Saint-Gilles pendant le XIVe siècle," p. 392; van Herwaarden, *Opgelegde bedevaarten*, p. 52; and van Cauwenbergh, *Les pèlerinages expiatoires et judiciaires dans le droit communal de la Belgique au Moyen Age*, pp. 29–33, 101, emphasizes the secular side of reparation, and describes the pilgrimages and other amends required as analogous to the Germanic *wergeld*.

128. See van Cauwenbergh, *Les pèlerinages expiatoires et judiciaires dans le droit communal de la Belgique au Moyen Age*, pp. 95–121.

129. Philippe de Beaumanoir, *Coutumes de Beauvaisis*, vol. II, pp. 168–169.

130. van Herwaarden, *Opgelegde bedevaarten*, pp. 43–47; Ludwig Schmugge, "Die Anfänge des organisierten Pilgerverkehrs im Mittelalter," *Quellen und Forschungen aus italienischen Archiven und Bibliotheken* 64 (1984): 79; Pierre André Sigal, *Les marcheurs de Dieu: Pèlerinages et pèlerins au Moyen Age* (Paris, 1974), p. 19. Van Cauwenbergh, *Les pèlerinages expiatoires et judiciaires dans le droit communal de la Belgique au Moyen Age*, p. 23, suggests that

dorse this faith in the tripartite classification to see the similarity between secular imposed pilgrimages and public penance in its purely religious guise. Indeed, it is pointless to attempt fine distinctions between "genuine" public penance and secular imposed pilgrimages; both drew on similar assumptions about the need to humiliate sinners. When the bishop of Liège, for example, required that one of his subjects make a pilgrimage, this act could be attributed to his secular rights as lord of Liège, to his *officialité* or ecclesiastical court, or to his authority as pastor in the internal forum over all the Christians of his diocese.

Imposed pilgrimage in Flanders is thus the communal form of a punishment much favored by bishops and kings elsewhere north of the Loire. While occasionally historians have wondered why Flanders should have been the chief haven for communally imposed pilgrimages,[131] the answer lies most likely in the near absence of episcopal sees and the ineffectuality of French royal power in this area. In Reims, the king and the archbishop could force an arbitrated settlement with public penance as one of chief requirements; in Paris, Louis IX could revise an arbitrated pilgrimage arranged between a citizen and his victim's kin. In Flanders, *schepenen* and *paisierders* stepped in where no king or bishop could supervise the restoration of public order with a suitable public penance. What we see in Flanders is not the mysterious invention of a new civic punishment or the revival of a moribund penitential pilgrimage known to a few canonists but simply the survival of traditional public penance as it had been practiced in northern France.

Public penance, voluntary and involuntary, secular and religious, imposed and arbitrated, is thus a far more significant and more commonplace feature of northern French and Flemish justice than has hitherto been appreciated. If we understand the term in the broadest sense—and there is every reason why we should—public penance would have been a very familiar event. It could seal a diplomatic compromise, punish an armed insurrection, end a family feud, em-

---

such imposed pilgrimages appear first, in the early thirteenth century, in ecclesiastical principalities, particularly Liège. But that depends on what one defines as an imposed pilgrimage; there are many early-thirteenth-century quasi-secular public penances.

131. See especially van Herwaarden, *Opgelegde bedevaarten*, pp. 12–13, 403–404, who argues that imposed pilgrimages result from a sense of egalitarian bourgeois solidarity in the communes of Flanders, Alsace, and Switzerland. Of course, the strength of the commune is another way of describing the weakness or absence of kings, lords, and bishops. He goes on to argue, pp. 27–28, that imposed pilgrimages declined in late-fourteenth-century and fifteenth-century Flanders as a result of the failure of the idea of a community of the city. But they may also have declined in tandem with the gradual disappearance of other forms of public penance in France.

barrass an adulterer, or avenge the violation of a sanctuary. It is striking how often Frenchmen relied on humiliation both to reconcile and to punish, testimony, no doubt, to that lurking urge to see the secrets of one's enemies exposed and the victory of one's friends publicized. Yet, it is also important to remember that the administration of public penance did not depend on a common agreement about the line between public and private spheres of activity. On the contrary, it thrived on the very ambiguity that would seem to have made such a traditional penalty obsolete, an ambiguity as implicit in urban politics as in contemporary Scholastic theology. In every case, public penance represents a flexible middle ground between two overly stark alternatives. The new liturgy evolving in the pontificals simply accommodated the political and judicial application of public penance in the cities.

CHAPTER NINE

Public Penance
and Communal Religion

This book studies the unintended consequences of a revolution in religious thought and practice in the late twelfth and early thirteenth centuries. Medievalists have long discussed the self-avowed goals of the theologians, popes, and bishops who promoted this transformation, including their efforts to preach introspective contrition to the masses, to reform the mores of the laity and clergy, and to achieve universal participation in the sacramental life of the parish. Some have also recognized the occasional failures of the new theology, and, in particular, the apathy that so often faced the new preachers' moral instruction. They have not talked so much about unplanned directions and unpremeditated results. This was a revolution as surprising to the theologians and bishops who occasionally imagined that they controlled it as to the Christian faithful who were its target.

One of the most important of the unintended consequences was the hardy survival, indeed flourishing, of public penance in the very region that was the heartland of the new theology. Its survival cannot be called a failure of the theologians, since the elimination of public penance was never their stated goal, but its strange life remains surprising and forces us to rethink the nature and purposes of their sacramental reform. In three main sections, I have analyzed in turn the theology and canon law of penance, its liturgy and ritual, and its political applications. All three types of evidence suggest a similar lesson: the adaptability of public penance and the limits of the new teachings.

We have found how the theologians around 1200 shared the most important impulse behind the promulgation of *Omnis utriusque*: the spread of the devotional life of the religious few to ordinary Christians. They enthusiastically embraced its requirement for universal confession. Most endorsed the broadest interpretation, affirming that even those who had committed no sin were bound to confess annually anyway. In the end, however, the spread of private sacramental pen-ance was an awkward obstacle to one crucial purpose of the new theology. In the process of universalizing secret confession, *Omnis utriusque* inevitably made such confession routine. The very success of the effort to spread the devotion of the few to the daily lives of the many threatened that same effort. The theologians had unwittingly debased the currency of conversion. And they had almost as uncon-sciously reconceived both public and private penance as legal courts by defining the two *fora*, interior and exterior. Such legalism brought with it a focus on behavior rather than emotion. In the end, the theologians were the prophets less of *Omnis utriusque* and of private sacramental confession than of the voluntary lay devotions of the later Middle Ages, the books of hours and ascetic self-discipline, and in-deed, the flagellant processions and indulgences.

The theologians had wanted contrition and ended up with a legal-istically applied sacramental penance; so they continued to preach contrition and ended up with the late medieval indulgence trade. Why should their efforts have produced such strange results? The answer lies not merely in the notorious intractability of lay behavior, in the inevitable gap between theory and practice. The causes of the theologians' frustrations lie in the nature of penance itself. First, pen-ance must always comprise exterior performance as well as inner penitence. Some of the most demon-filled pages of the tenth-century pontificals and penitentials contain exhortations for contrition as rig-orous and emotional as anything that the late twelfth century could produce. Conversely, the emotions of penitence were never so secret that they did not result in some sort of outward behavior, if only as proof of the devotion. Penance never became wholly a matter of contrition or wholly a matter of exterior performance. Every medi-eval penance was public in some degree, even secret confession, since the purpose of that confession was undoubtedly self-disclosure, if only to one person or to a very few. So it is hardly surprising that thirteenth-century theologians sometimes still harbored the desire to expose the sufferings of sinners or to use shame as a weapon to bring them back to the fold.

A second principle of medieval penance further explains the gap between theologians' conscious intentions and their unexpected out-come. Penance in the most general sense was obviously about recon-ciliation: the payment of a moral debt, the restoration of social rela-tions, the reinstatement of the excommunicant, the renewal of peace between a sinner and God. Nonsacramental penance as much as sacramental, contrition as much as satisfaction, public as much as private equally promised reconciliation. Penance presupposed the belief that human beings with divine help can patch up ruptures in the social and cosmic orders. The potential for the restoration of the cosmic order to carry over into the restoration of the social order has, to be sure, attracted the interest of social historians. What has attracted less interest is the other face of penance. John Bossy has noted that a principle of retributive compensation underlies the medieval theory of atonement.[1] The implications of this important observation have not been pursued. Divine atonement and human penance worked in a similar way: suffering entails suffering, and violence entails violence. This violence did not imitate the spiraling hatred of the feud, for it was voluntary, passive suffering, rather than active retaliation. Penance inverted the feud instead of suppressing it. Voluntary submission to suffering could be a moral triumph over one's enemies; more often it was a bitter humiliation, voluntary only because the alternatives were still worse. In either case, however, penance reconciled through the defeat of one party. As we saw in Chapter 8, public penance even in peace settlements could conceal an unequal result. The bitterness of submission was the precondition for peace just as surely as, in a Christian world, the first would be last and the last first. This was why medieval Christians found humiliation useful in so many circumstances. The language of Christian humility in penance implied the inversion of hierarchy, not its suppression.

The continued strength of the desire to see sinners humiliated, to make divine justice visible here on earth, should at least cause us to reexamine the labels of interiority and individualism so often applied to twelfth-century religious thought. That public penance thrived well past its supposed demise around 1200 suggests a profound ambivalence in theology and practice alike about the secrecy and emotionalism so often promoted by confessors' guides and wish-fulfilling sermon anecdotes. But in addition, the survival of public penance and the surprisingly public implementation of even private penance force us to reconsider the apparently straightforward distinction in theology and canon law between public and private spheres of action. Further, the practical implementation of rites of private and public penance in northern France shows at every turn the tendentiousness of that distinction. On occasion, the theologians themselves recognized the problem. Their ambivalence about interiority eventually led them

---

1. Bossy, *Christianity in the West*, p. 5.

in their discussion of fraternal correction and of duties to God, neighbor, and the church to formulate a middle ground between the secret world where only God sees us and the public world where the whole church watches. In sum, the mid-thirteenth-century theology of penance suggests the beginnings of a construction of a "private life," a world of obligations to family and neighbors, to customers and employers, to debtors and creditors, quite different from the secret life of the soul praised and shielded by so many twelfth-century writers. Likewise, the liturgy reveals an even more rapid evolution of the ritual of public penance away from the dramatic scapegoating of the early medieval rite. Early-thirteenth-century pontificals already began to provide a Lenten rite of penance for the Christian faithful that allowed a collective observance of contrition without the communal emphasis on purifying the many through the expiation of the few. Here was a halfway option between private confession and the old public penance.

It may seem paradoxical that public penance should thrive just when theologians and even liturgists were struggling to invent a sphere neither purely secret nor purely public; but the contradiction is more apparent than real. One thinks of public penance as an extreme. But in thirteenth-century France, public penance was often used not in extreme but in ambiguous cases, where there was no unchallenged authority, where no one could tell whether the accused was really guilty, where the sin was partly spiritual, partly secular. In any case, the point is not that all public penances are to be identified with this new private life, but that the way public penance survived shows why that new middle ground was necessary and how it came to be formulated. Public penance survived precisely because it was so flexible and adaptable, satisfying both the desire to humiliate sinners—and even sometimes merely apparent sinners—and the need to leave the authority behind the humiliation a little vague. It could shame an adulterer in a village, resolve a feud between two bourgeois families, or proclaim the moral authority of a bishop whose secular supremacy was being doubted. It fell between the exterior and interior *fora*, in a convenient no-man's-land between excommunication and interior emotion. The story of public penance, then, is not really the "decline and fall" that it has seemed to be; it is also the story of a new beginning, the beginning of a redefined private life.

In this light, it is not as surprising as it first seems that public penance should have survived in northern France, precisely where the university masters first developed and preached the new theology of penance. Northern French cities were often dominated by bishops, and that fact doubtless helps explain to some degree the regional popularity of the preeminently episcopal rite of public penance. But the survival of a version of that penance in the independent Flemish towns suggests that it was not the mere presence of episcopal sees but a more deep-seated impulse that favored the rite. The use of gestures of humiliation to settle disputes large and small pervaded northern French and Flemish society. And the new theology of penance, properly understood, did not really imply the abolition of public penance. The theory allowed room for public humiliation, and the reality of divided cities made the flexibility of public penance particularly attractive. More than other towns in Europe, the large, wealthy, and bitterly factious cities of northern France and Flanders were the logical center for the evolution of a middle ground between the secret life of the soul and the indisputably public authority of the king.

Looking Forward: Penance in Early Modern Europe

It has not been possible here to carry the history of penance beyond the end of the thirteenth century. But we may offer several suggestions about the implications of the transformation of medieval penance for the study of early modern religion. We have seen how several recent works on late medieval and early modern religion attempt to trace the transformation of communal forms of religion through comprehensive studies of selected regions. The definition of communal religion remains particularly problematic, however, in most reviews of late medieval religious practice. This study suggests that a distinction must be drawn between communal religion and collective religion, between, that is, an early medieval ritual presupposing an organic view of the social body and the later medieval multiplying of voluntary, individual expiations carried out in groups. In general, the terms "communal" and "social" should only be used with great caution; too often they serve to conceal an assumed functionalist model of ritual and religion. The former term should not be used to describe just any activity of people in groups. The latter term has perhaps by now lost any useful meaning.

Of the many regional surveys of lay religion in the early modern period, A. N. Galpern's detailed investigation of religious practice in sixteenth-century Champagne is one of the most relevant here, since it covers part of the same territory as this study. But his central contention, that the late medieval inheritance was essentially a communal one, which was replaced during the sixteenth century by increasingly individualist forms, is less persuasive. Galpern emphasizes the role of elaborate Corpus Christi processions in the fifteenth and sixteenth centuries, arguing that these served to teach the sovereignty of the king and inculcate community.[2] In the light of my study, however, these processions appear to be not a traditional manifestation of the medieval village community but a relatively new and artificial creation contrived largely for the purpose of royal propaganda. Corpus Christi was a late arrival in France, only widely observed from the second half of the fourteenth century, and like the new episcopal processions on Ash Wednesday and Maundy Thursday, the Corpus Christi processions suggest a calculated attempt to preach episcopal and, in this case also, royal supremacy. For this reason, the supposed late survival of communalism seems less plausible. A comparative study of the paths prescribed for different processions in late medieval ordinals would certainly help clarify the issue. In the absence of communal forms of expiation and punishment, such collective processions are only "communal" in a weaker sense of the word.

Not all historians of the Reformation, however, have taken such an interest in communal forms of religion. Many studies of penance in the late medieval and early modern period have fastened instead on the psychology of sacramental confession, in part on account of Luther's very personal critique of the anxiety that confession could evoke. Steven Ozment argues that the original appeal of the Protestant Reformation to Luther's followers and to Luther himself lay in its promise to overthrow the burden of guilt induced by late medieval penance.[3] Thomas Tentler argues less persuasively that confession as actually practiced generally did not induce the terrified guilt that Luther experienced.[4] Richard Kieckhefer's study of several late medieval saints suggests that some men and women actually preferred the anxiety of frequent confession; not all would have wished, like Luther, to see a release from their self-induced tortures.[5] Historians have applied a psychological description of late medieval religion to related religious practices and to sacramental penance itself. Lucien Febvre directs historians' attention to what he sees as the frenzy of piety on the eve of the Reformation. He calls the Protestants' slogan of justification by faith a "health-giving gift" that soothed the anguish of late medieval men, who had invested ever more in masses and

2. A. N. Galpern, *The Religions of the People in Sixteenth-Century Champagne*, esp. p. 176.
3. Steven Ozment, *The Reformation in the Cities* (New Haven, Conn. 1975), pp. 45–50, 118.
4. Thomas Tentler, *Sin and Confession on the Eve of the Reformation*, pp. 365–366.
5. See Richard Kieckhefer, *Unquiet Souls* (Chicago, 1984), p. 134.

indulgences in the desperate hope of shortening the tortures of purgatory.[6] And Bernd Moeller compares the mass pilgrimages so popular in the fifteenth century to a "psychosis."[7] In this view, a neurotic Europe frantically grasped at anything—masses, indulgences, flagellation—that might assuage the terrors of guilt for this world and the next.[8] Just as the rate of donations to escape purgatory reached a feverish pitch, the Protestant reformers arrived to refresh the patient with the news that Christ alone has already died for our sins. Our works cannot save us, and neglect of them cannot damn us. Annual sacramental confession to priests is not necessary for salvation. The fever subsides—but only until anxiety about predestination replaces anxiety about forgiveness.[9]

The interest in a psychological analysis of late medieval sacramental penance and penitential practices like flagellation, indulgences, and pilgrimages is reasonable, even if the descriptions of psychic torment have sometimes been overdrawn. For one thing, these voluntary lay devotions are one of the most striking of the unintended consequences of that twelfth- and thirteenth-century revolution. But it is especially the Protestant critique of the late medieval system of penance that turns our attention to the psychology of contrition and its effects on religious practice. Luther's acute sense of inadequacy in confession is well known. Surprisingly, perhaps, his early comments on the sacrament of penance in a sermon of 1519 did not criticize the encouragement of scrupulosity in penitents, but simply emphasized that it is the penitent's faith, not the priest's absolution, that makes the sacrament.[10] Luther ultimately sharpened this mild critique; in the *Babylonian Captivity*, he suggested that secret confession to any layman could replace the confession to a priest.[11] Bossy describes Martin Luther as a "utopian traditionalist" who wished to restore the social aspect of penance in his reemphasis of the laying-on of hands in absolution, a gesture borrowed from the early medieval public rite.[12]

6. Lucien Febvre, "The Origins of the French Reformation: A Badly Put Question?" in *A New Kind of History*, ed. and trans. P. Burke (New York, 1973), pp. 60–61, 70, 75–78.

7. Bernd Moeller, "Religious Life in Germany on the Eve of the Reformation," in *Pre-Reformation Germany*, ed. Gerald Strauss (London, 1972), p. 17.

8. See especially Jean Delumeau's *La peur en occident (XIVe–XVIIIe siècles)* (Paris, 1978), and *Le péché et la peur: La culpabilisation en occident (XIIIe–XVIIIe siècles)* (Paris, 1983).

9. See especially W. J. Bouwsma, "Anxiety and the Formation of Early Modern Culture," in *After the Reformation*, ed. B. Malament (Philadelphia, 1980), pp. 215–240, for the argument that the early modern period saw a permanent increase in the level of anxiety.

10. Martin Luther, "Ein Sermon vom Sakrament der Busse," *Studienausgabe*, ed. Hans-Ulrich Delius, (Berlin, 1979–), 1:244–257.

11. Luther, *De captivitate Babylonica, Studienausgabe*, 2:232: "Proinde, ego non dubito eum esse a peccatis suis occultis absolutum, quisque siue sponte confessus, siue corresptus, ueniam petierit et emandauerit, coram quouis pruatim fratre."

12. Bossy, "The Social History of Confession in the Age of the Reformation," pp. 26–27.

But this is to place too much weight on one gesture. Luther also delivered an attack on the system of reservation of sins to bishops or the pope, because, as we found earlier, it brought secret sins into the open.[13] He opposed the use of shame to force sinners to obedience, and so while he did not explicitly discuss public penance itself, it is hard to see how Luther could have tolerated it.

What characterizes both Luther's earlier conservatism and his later, sharper critique, however, is a concern with the psychology of preaching confession and the difficulty of achieving a pure and altruistic faith, untainted by the promise of a heavenly reward in return. The worry about the purity of conscience recalls those late-twelfth- and early-thirteenth-century theologians like Peter Cantor and Robert Courson, who wanted priests to teach parishioners to distinguish worldly attachments from the pure love of God. In this way Luther returned to the psychological precision of the earlier theology. Yet the implications were profoundly different this time.

> Therefore, even if there is something to their teaching that contrition is to be procured by what they call recollection and inspection of sins, nevertheless they teach dangerously and perversely when they do not teach beforehand the beginnings and causes of contrition. . . . Beware, then, of trusting in your contrition or of attributing the remission of sins to your sorrow. God does not consider you according to these things, but according to the faith by which you have believed his threats and promises and which has effected the same kind of grief. Whatever good there may be in penance is owed not to the careful collation of sins but to God's truth and our own faith.[14]

Where Robert and Peter wanted priests to inculcate scrupulosity, Luther wanted to restrain those high-pitched praises of contrition.

Although earlier theologians of the late twelfth century wished to promote contrition and were not afraid at times to use shame and anxiety about salvation to promote it, they would have been surprised by the directions that contrition might take and the criticism it would thus engender. In a perceptive critique of contemporary Anabaptists'

---

13. Luther, *De captivitate Babylonica, Studienausgabe*, 2:231–232.
14. Luther, *De captivitate Babylonica, Studienausgabe*, 2:230: "Quare, et si non nihil docent, qui ex peccatorum suorum ut uocant collectu et conspectu, contritionem parandam docent, periculose tamen et peruerse docent, dum non ante, principia et causas docent contritionis. . . . Caue ergo in contritionem tuam confidas, aut dolori tuo tribuas remissionem peccatorum. Non respicit te propter haec deus, sed propter fidem, qua minis et promissis eius credidisti, quae operata est dolorem eiusmodi. ac per hoc, non diligentiae peccatorum collectrici, sed ueritati dei et fidei nostrae debetur, quicquid boni in poenitentia fuerit."

accounts of the joy of rebaptism, Ulrich Zwingli extended Luther's account of contrition in an analysis of the appeal of late medieval sacramental penance.

> [The Anabaptists] affirmed, however, that God had done something quite new towards them—the very experience which at one time we had in penance. For there, too, we were in great fear and distress before we made our confession, but the moment we had made it we said: "God be praised, I feel a great joy and refreshing." And all that we really felt was a relaxation of the previous tension [*entladung der bychtangst*]. . . . Now those who allow themselves to be rebaptized make much of a similar experience.[15]

Zwingli for one would have understood if not approved the late medieval laymen and women who enjoyed the anxious burden of private confession. He contended that the experience of contrition and release that medieval penitents and contemporary Anabaptists felt was specious, a self-indulgence in subjective emotion. The medieval theologians who promoted tears and contrition certainly recognized the possibility of false penitence, but they did not address this concern of the reformers, that the requirement of a routine self-exposure in confession would always and inevitably produce a hand-wringing, demonstrative anxiety, manifested in repetitive attempts at release through such external actions as pilgrimages and indulgences. In other words, the medieval theologians expressed no serious doubts about the value of self-exposure in confession; in fact, they welcomed the shame of confession. Even the most avid proponents of the secret contrition of the heart in the late twelfth century argued for the necessity of confession. They would have been surprised to see how the combination of private emotion and public shame worked out in practice. They would not have understood the more radical, Protes-

---

15. Ulrich Zwingli, *Von der Taufe, von der Wiedertaufe und von der Kindertaufe*, in *Sämtliche Werke*, 4, Corpus Reformatorum, 91 (Leipzig, 1927), "Und denn sprechend ir, es hab üch got von nüwem etwas gethon; und ist aber nüts anders, denn glych wie uns vor in der bycht beschach. Da hattend wir grosse angst und not, ee und wir bychtetend; und so bald wir gebychtet hattend, sprachend wir: Got sye lob! Mir ist ein besundre fröid worden und erkickung. Die was aber nüts anders weder entladung der bychtangst. Da hett einer ouch mögen reden, er hette ab der bycht oder pfaffenabsolution ein nüwrung in im selbs empfunden, do im die bycht aber einmal ab worden was. . . . Also ist ouch die erwegnus gross by denen, die sich widrumb touffen lassen." The translation is from *Zwingli and Bullinger*, trans. G. W. Bromiley, The Library of Christian Classics, 24:147. Cf. George H. Williams, *The Radical Reformation* (Philadelphia, 1962), pp. 300–301, who accepts this explanation for the popularity of anabaptism, referring to the "experiential void in adult life left by the neglect or programmatic rejection of sacramental penance." He thus inverts the usual account of the wide appeal of Protestantism in Luther's rejection of that anxiety.

tant objection to self-exposure, which was not that it might publicize secret sins, but that the self-dramatizing it implied was an egotistical delusion. The Protestant critique of the psychology of confession is something new, but it is surely the outcome of that earlier revolution.

John Calvin's denunciation of the psychological effects of the preaching of contrition was, if anything, still more caustic than Zwingli's. He complained that the inevitable result of the pressure to produce remorse on cue would be despair or the manufacturing of false sentiment. The greater the insistence on sincerity, the falser the result. "Because if they say that I lie, then let them come forth and show me one person who has not been driven to despair by this sort of doctrine of contrition, or who has not presented to God's judgment a simulation of sorrow in place of true sorrow."[16]

By severing the link between the contrition and the forgiveness of sins, Calvin, like Luther, hoped to free contrition and confession to be purely devout. He shares with other reformers the same concern about the possibilities of self-delusion in private penance. His psychological individualism is wholly alien to that which we found in some theologians on the eve of the Fourth Lateran. Calvin's reaction against the system of private penance did not end in a return to the early medieval practice of communal public penance, however. To be sure, he observed that high medieval theology, codified in Gratian's *Decretum*, had split a system of penance, unified in the ancient church, into public and private reconciliations.[17] And he defended the use of collective processions in times of crisis; even those individuals innocent of the crimes that had brought about the divine punishment should participate, since, he said, no member of a diseased body should boast of his health.[18]

None of this implied a desire to return to communal rather than collective penances, still less a taste for the old scapegoating rites of public penance. In fact, it was especially the collective penances that we may now see were inherited from the later medieval period, the liturgical general confessions and penitential litanies and processions, that survived in the Reformed cult.[19] And neither Calvin nor the

---

16. John Calvin, *Institutiones christianae religionis* (1559), *Opera omnia*, 2, Corpus Reformatorum, 30, ed. G. Baum et al. (Braunschweig, 1864), III.4, col. 458: "Quod si me calumniari aiunt, prodeant sane, et unum aliquem ostendant, qui huiusmodi contritionis doctrina vel non sit ad desperationem adactus, vel simulationem doloris iudicio Dei, pro vero dolore, non opposuerit."

17. Calvin, *Institutiones christianae religionis*, IV.19, cols. 1075–1076.

18. Calvin, *Institutiones christianae religionis*, III.4, col. 465.

19. See R. Bornert, *La réforme protestante du culte à Strasbourg au XVIe siècle (1523–1598)*, Studies in Medieval and Reformation Thought, 28 (Leiden, 1981), esp. pp. 398, 407, 494–495.

other reformers tried to reverse the separation of penance into public and private spheres. In practice, the establishment of consistory courts, the end of regular sacerdotal confession, and the extension of liturgical collective penances actually continued and extended medieval trends to define clear spheres of sin and atonement, in spite of all the reformers' criticism. The Protestant condemnation of the psychology of private sacramental penance was new, and the reformers did not convert it into the reintroduction of the ancient or early medieval system of discipline.

Thus the desire of some Protestant reformers to preserve a measure of public ecclesiastical discipline should not be mistaken for a genuine nostalgia for the old public penance. Their revulsion at the false sentiment of private confession inevitably implied a similar revulsion at the self-dramatization of public penance. As we have observed, every medieval penance, even private sacerdotal confession, was public in some degree, since every penance required that self-exposure which was so humiliating but—as Zwingli pointed out—so pleasurable as well. While Luther was willing to admit that this experience could be useful to a burdened soul, he and the more radical reformers agreed that it did not restore the sinner to grace.

By contrast, medieval public penance, even when transformed in the thirteenth-century liturgy, even when secularized in late medieval cities, never quite lost the link with atonement. Imposed pilgrimages by the Flemish towns were primarily peace offerings to the kin of victims; but those who undertook such pilgrimages had to visit the shrines of the saints to pray for forgiveness of their crime. Continued belief in a connection between appeasing God and self-disclosure was fundamental to the survival of public penance after the communal ritual of scapegoating ceased to make sense. The inverted violence of public penance was far more long-lived than the communal form it took in the early rituals. The elaborate self-display that characterized so many public penances early and late—the processions to thirteen cathedrals, the candles and ashes, even the disinterment of corpses—all these underlined the faith, the utopian dream, that such penances were nevertheless divine punishments and divine redemptions. Though the faith in utopian humiliation underlying late medieval public penance survived far longer than the communal religion that underlay the early medieval version of public penance, in the end it, too, succumbed and was forgotten—at least in the modern historiography of penance. By the time nineteenth- and twentieth-century historians returned to the study of thirteenth-century penance, it was hard for them to believe that this faith had ever existed.

Appendix

I. The two-part Ash Wednesday rite of the
north-central family

*from BN latin 934, f. 63v–65v, printed with some
errors in Martène,* De antiquis ecclesiae ritibus
libri, *I.6.7.16, vol. I, cols. 816–817.*

*Ordo quomodo penitentes in capite .xl. episcopo debent se presentare. In capite
quadragesime omnes penitentes qui publicam suscipiunt aut susceperunt penitentiam ante fores ecclesie se representent episcopo civitatis, sacco induti, nudis pedibus,
uultibus in terram prostratis, reos se esse ipse habitu et uulto proclamantes. Ibi adesse
debent decani, id est archipresbyteri parrochiarum. et presbyteri penitentum qui
eorum conversationem diligenter inspicere debent. et secundum modum culpe penitentem per prefixos gradus iniungant. Post hec in ecclesia eos introducat, et deinde
sermonem faciat et cum omni clero .vii. penitentie psalmos in terram prostratus cum
lacrimis pro eos absolutione decantet. Tunc resurgens ab oratione, iuxta quod
canones iubent manus eis imponat aquam benedictam super eos spargat, cinerem
prius mittat, deinde cilicio capita eorum cooperiat, et cum gemitu et crebris suspiriis
eis denuntiet, quod sicut adam proiectus est de paradiso, ita et ipsi ab ecclesia pro
peccatis abiciuntur. Post hec iubeat ministris, ut extra ianuas ecclesie expellant.
Clerus vero prosequatur eos cum R.* In sudore vultus tui etc. *Quo finito, claudat
eis episcopus ecclesie ianuam et clerus prosequatur, R.* Ecce adam V Cherubin etc.
*Ut uidentes sanctam ecclesiam pro facinoribus suis tremefactam atque commotam,
non paruipendant penitentiam. In sacra autem domini cena rursus ab eorum
decanis, et eorum presbyteris ecclesie liminibus representemur, et in ecclesiam introducatur et sermo fiat. Absolutio penitentium. In primis dicit .vii. psalmos penitentiales, deinde kyrie postea dominicam orationem.* Saluos fac seruos tuos. Mitte eis
auxilium de sancto. Nihil proficiat inimicus in eis. Esto illis Domine turris
fortitudinis. Domine exaudi orationem meam. Dominus uobiscum.

Oratio Exaudi domine preces nostras . . . (= PRG XCIX.57)

Alia Omnipotens sempiterne deus confitentibus . . . (= PRG XCIX.67, plural penitents for singular)

Alia Omnipotens et misericors deus qui peccatorum . . . (= PRG XCIX.237)

Alia Preveniat hos famulos . . . (= PRG XCIX.59, plural for singular)

Alia Adesto domine supplicationibus nostris nec sit . . . (= PRG XCIX.60, plural for singular)

Oratio Domine deus noster qui offensione nostro non vinceris . . .(= PRG XCIX.61, plural for singular)

There are also minor variations from the PRG in the prayers.

II. A comparison of the Maundy Thursday
presentation and introduction in the PRG
and in the Chartres and Senlis branches of
the north-central family

A. *The Maundy Thursday reconciliation in PRG
XCIX.224–229, vol. II, pp. 59–61.*

224. *Tunc egreditur penitens de loco ubi penitentiam gessit, ut gremio presentetur ecclesiae. Sedente autem pontifice pro foribus ecclesiae, penitentibus in atrio ecclesiae eminus cum archidiacono iussum illius prestolantibus, antequam eos offerat, postulat archidiaconus his verbis:*

225C. Adest, o venerabilis pontifex, tempus acceptum, dies propitiationis diuinae et salutis humanae . . .

226C. *Hic ergo dum ad poenitudinis actionem tantis excitatur exemplis, sub conspectu ingemiscentis ecclesiae, venerabilis pontifex protestatur et dicit:* Iniquitates meas ego cognosco, et delictum meum contra me est semper . . .

227C. *Quo ita supplicante et misericordiam dei afflicto corde poscente, dicat archidiaconus:* Redintegra in eo, apostolice pontifex, quicquid diabolo suadente corruptum est . . .

228. *Tunc dicit pontifex antiphonam.* Venite.

Et diaconus ex parte penitentium: Flectamus genua. *Tunc omnes adstantes genua flectunt penitentes. Quo facto, dicit diaconus ex parte pontificis:* Levate. *Similiter agatur secundo, repetente episcopo:* Venite, venite, *subsequente diacono:* Flectamus genua, *ut antea. Et sic ad medium usque atrii pavimentum solotenus veniant. Quando autem tertio domnus episcopus annuntiaverit antiphonam:* Venite, venite, venite, *prosequatur diaconus:* Flectamus genua. *Mox cum diacono penitentes corruant ad pedes episcopi, sicque prostrati iaceant usque domnus episcopus surgens innuat alteri diacono:* Levate, *prosequente clero antiphonam:* Venite, filii, audite me; timorem domini docebo uos, *cum psalmo:* Bene-

dicam dominum in omni tempore, semper laus eius in ore meo, et ...
finem usque ducente.

229. *Quandiu vero psalmus canitur a clero cum antiphona:* Venite filii, *semper manuatim penitentes a plebesanis archidiacono, et ab archidiacono redduntur episcopo, et ab episcopo restituuntur ecclesiae gremio, prostrato omni corpore in terra . . .*

(Prayers and absolutions follow.)

B. *The Chartres branch: the Maundy Thursday rite in BN latin 945 (pontifical of Chartres, second half or end of the twelfth century), f. 129r–130v.*

Reconciliatio penitentium in cena domini. Sedente pontifice pre foribus ecclesie, penitentibus in atrio ecclesie eminus cum archidiacono issum illius prestolantibus dicat pontifex, Venite filii audite me *et diaconus ex parte penitentium:* Flectamus genua. *Tunc omnes stantes genua flectunt penitentes. Quo facto, dicit diaconus ex parte pontificis* Levate. *Similiter agatur secundo, repetente episcopo:* Venite, uenite, *subsequente diacono:* Flectamus genua, *ut antea. Et sic ad medium usque atrii pauimentum solotenus ueniant. Quando autem tertio domnus episcopus annuntiauerit antiphonam:* Venite, uenite, uenite, *prosequatur diaconus:* Flectamus genua. *Mox cum diacono penitentes corruant ad pedes episcopi, sicque prostrati iaceant usque domnus episcopus innuat alteri diacono:* Levate, *prosequente clero antiphonam:* Venite filii, audite me, timorem domine docebo uos *P* Beati immaculati.

Iterum sequitur a. Venite *Postea ab archidiacono dicatur.*

Ad est o uenerabilis pontifex tempus acceptum . . . (= PRG XCIX.225C, with variants) . . . in commune succurrit. Hi ergo dum ad penitudinis actionem tantis excitatur exemplis, sub conspectu ingemiscentis ecclesie, uenerabilis pontifex prostratur et dicit iniquitates meas ego cognosco et delictum meum contra me est semper. Auerte faciem tuam a peccatis meis et omnes iniquitates meas dele. Redde mihi letitiam salutaris tui et spiritu principali confirma me. Cui ita supplicanti et misericordiam dei afflicto corde poscenti redde integram gratiam pontifex quicquid diabolo scindente corruptum est, et orationum tuarum patrocinantibus meritis per diuinae reconciliationis gratiam fac hominem proximum deo, ut qui antea in suis sibi peruersitatibus displicebat nunc iam placere se deo in regione uiuorum deuicto mortis autore gratuletur. (= PRG XCIX.226C– 227C, without breaks or rubrics, with minor variants)

Mox surgat episcopus faciatque omnes penitentes ante se prostrare simulque cum astantibus cantet .vii. psalmos penitentiales. Quibus finitis, sequitur dominica oratio istique uersus Saluos fac . . . (cf. PRG XCIX.229)

Oremus. Adesto domine supplicationibus nostris et me ... (= PRG XCIX.230)

Praesta quesumus domine huius famulis ... (= PRG XCIX.235)

Deus humani generis ... (= PRG XCIX.245, shortened form)

Post hec surgant penitentes et dicit diaconus. Redintegra in eis pontifex quicquid diabolo scindente corruptum est, et orationem tuarum patrocinantibus meritis per diuinae reconciliationis gratiam fac homines proximos deo, ut qui antea in suis peruersitatibus displicebat nunc iam placere se domine in regione uiuorum deuicto mortis autore gratuletur. (= PRG XCIX.227C, with different variants than above)

Et monentur ab episcopo penitentes, ut quod penitendo diluerunt iterando non reuocent et imponat episcopus a. Venite filii audite me *Et clerus cum episcopo, psalmus.* Benedicam dominum in omni *Et uersibus eiusdem psalmi finitis, semper sequatur antiphona, a.* Venite filii *Interim penitentes manuatim ab archidiaconus reddantur episcopo, et episcopus reddat diacono qui ex parte eius est, et ordinatim congregentur sicque restituantur gremio ecclesie.*

(Prayers and an absolution follow.)

C. *The Senlis branch: the Maundy Thursday rite in*
   BN latin 17335 (pontifical of Noyon, second half
   or end of the thirteenth century),
   f. 130v–134v.

Sedente pontifice pre foribus ecclesie penitentibus in atrio ecclesie eminus cum archydyacono iussum illius prestolantibus dicat pontifex a. Venite filii audite me. *Et dyaconus ex parte penitentium dicat.* Flectamus genua. *Tunc omnes stantes flectant penitentes. Quo facto dicat dyaconus ex parte pontificis.* Leuate. *Si similiter agatur secundo repetente et episcopo. a.* Venite filii. *Sequente dyacono.* Flectamus genua *ut supra. Et sic ad medium pauimentum solotenus ueniant. Quando autem tertio domnus episcopus annuntiauerit.* Venite. uenite. uenite. *prosequatur dyaconus.* Flectamus genua. *Mox dum dyacono penitentes corruant ad pedes episcopi, sicque prostrati iaceant usque domnus episcopus innuat alteri diacono.* Leuate. *P   uente clero a.* Venite filii audite me timorem domini docebo uos. *ps.* Beati immaculati. Iterum sequitur *a.* Venite. *Postea ab archdyacono dicatur.*

Adest o uenerabilis pontifex tempus acceptum ... (= PRG XCIX.225C, with variants) ... in commune succurrit. Hi ergo dum ad penitudinis actionem tantis excitatur exemplis, sub conspectu ingemiscentis ecclesie, uenerabilis pontifex, prostratur quique et dicit iniquitates meas ego cognosco et delictum meum contra me est semper. Auerte faciem tuam a peccatis meis et omnes iniquitates meas dele. Redde mihi letitiam salutaris tui et spiritu principali confirma me. Cui ita supplicanti et misericordiam dei afflicto corde poscenti redde integram gratiam pontifex quicquid diabolo scindente corruptum est, et orationum tuarum patrocinantibus meritis per diuinae reconciliationis gratiam fac hominem proximum deo, ut qui antea in suis peruersitatibus displicebat nunc iam placere se deo in regione uiuorum deuicto mortis autore gratuletur. (= PRG XCIX.226C–227C, without breaks or rubrics, with minor variants from PRG, and a few variants from BN latin 945 above)

Tunc introducat eos episcopus in ecclesiam faciatque omnes penitentes ante se prostrare. simulque cum astantibus cantet .vii. psalmos penitentiales. Quibus finis; sequitur dominica oratio istique uersus.

Kyrie eleison. Pater noster. Et ne nos inducas. Saluos fac seruos tuos . . . (cf. PRG XCIX.229)

(Prayers and three absolutions, the last labeled *absolutio,* follow.)

Bibliography

PRIMARY SOURCES

Manuscripts

Abbeville
BM 8 (pontifical of Amiens, beginning or first half 14th c.)

Admont
Stiftsbibliothek 7 (Huguccio, *Summa decretorum*): microfilm in the Hill Monastic Manuscript Library, Saint John's Abbey and University, Collegeville, Minn.

Amiens
BM 195 (pontifical of Corbie, beginning or first half 13th c. and end 13th c. or beginning 14th c.)
BM 196 (pontifical of Amiens, middle 13th c.)

Arras
BM 13 (pontifical of Sens, mid- to late-14th c.)
BM 405 (pontifical of Arras, second half 13th c.)
BM 469 (pontifical of Saint-Vaast, Arras, second half or end 13th c.)
BM 702 (pontifical of Saint-Vaast, Arras, end 13th c. or beginning 14th c.)

Auxerre
BM 53 (pontifical of Auxerre, first half 14th c.)

Bamberg
Staatsbibliothek Can. 17 (*Summa "Permissio quedam"*)
Staatsbibliothek Can. 42 (*Summa Bambergensis*)

Besançon
BM 138 (pontifical of Beauvais, second half or end 13th c.)

Bruges

Stedelijke Openbare Bibliotheek 318 (pontifical of ter Doest, 13th c.)

Brussels

BR 1505–1506 (pontifical of Sint-Pieters, Ghent, 12th c.)
BR II. 1013 (pontifical of Saint-Martin, Tournai, 13th c.)

Cambrai

BM 222 (pontifical of Cambrai, beginning 13th c.)
BM 223 (pontifical of Cambrai, first half 13th c.)

Châlons-sur-Marne

BM 45 (pontifical of Châlons-sur-Marne, second half or end 13th c.)

Douai

BM 649 (*Summa Duacensis*)

Erfurt

Amploniana quart. 117 (*Summa "Reverentia sacrorum canonum"*)

Florence

Bibl. Med. Laur. Libri 82

Laon

BM 224 (pontifical of Laon, beginning or first half 13th c.)
BM 371bis (*Summa "De iure canonico tractaturus"*)

Le Mans

BM 141

London

BL Addit. 38,645 (pontifical of Saint-Sauveur, Anchin, 12th c.)
BL Egerton 931 (pontifical of Sens, 14th c.)

Lyon

BM 570 (17th c. copies of medieval pontificals)

Montpellier

Bibl. de la Faculté de médecine 399 (pontifical of Paris, beginning or first half
    13th c.)

Munich

Staatsbibliothek 16084 (*Summa Monacensis*)

Orléans

BM 144 (pontifical of Chartres, beginning 13th c.)

Paris

Bibl. de l'Arsenal 332 (pontifical of Paris, second half 13th c.)

Bibl. Mazarine 526 (ordinal of Saint Denis, 13th c.)

Bibl. Mazarine 539 (pontifical of Rouen, first half 14th c.)

BN latin 934 (pontifical of Sens, second half 12th c.)

BN latin 944 (pontifical, etc., probably of Saint-Gérard, Aurillac, end 11th c. or beginning 12th c.)

BN latin 945 (pontifical of Chartres, second half or end 12th c.)

BN latin 946 (pontifical of Christian I of Mainz, 1167–1183)

BN latin 948 (pontifical of Mainz, first half or middle 14th c.)

BN latin 949 (pontifical of Aix-en-Provence, beginning 14th c.)

BN latin 950 (pontifical of Trier adapted to usage of Speyer, first half or middle 14th c.)

BN latin 953 (pontifical of Saint-Amand, diocese of Tournai, middle or second half 12th c.)

BN latin 954 (pontifical of Angers, 15th c.)

BN latin 956–957 (pontifical of Paris, beginning 16th c.)

BN latin 962 (pontifical of Sens, middle or second half 14th c.)

BN latin 966 (pontifical of Verdun, second half or end 14th c.)

BN latin 969 (pontifical of Rouen, 15th c.)

BN latin 972 (pontifical of Arras, first half 14th c.)

BN latin 976 (ordinal of Saint-Denis, 13th–14th c.)

BN latin 1206 (ordinal, Sens, late 12th c.)

BN latin 1218 (pontifical of Saint Andrews, 13th c.)

BN latin 1236 (monastic ordinal, 13th c.)

BN latin 1237 (ordinal, diocese of Tours, end 14th c.)

BN latin 1301 (ordinal of Coutances, end 14th c.)

BN latin 1341 (monastic ordinal, diocese of Limoges, end 12th or beginning 13th c.)

BN latin 1591 (synodal statutes of Cambrai, beginning 14th c.)

BN latin 1794 (ordinal of Saint-Jean, Chartres, 12th–13th c.)

BN latin 2593 (Eudes de Cheriton, *Tractatus de paenitentia*, 13th c.)

BN latin 3238F (confessors' manual, second half 13th c.)

BN latin 3258 (Robert Courson, *Summa*, 13th c.)

BN latin 8898 (processional, ritual, etc. of Soissons, second half 12th c.)

BN latin 9970 (ordinal of Saint-Trinité, Fontainebleau, 13th c.)

BN latin 10579 (ordinal of Châlons-sur-Marne, 13th c.)

BN latin 11067 (synodal statutes of Noyon, 13th–14th c.)

BN latin 13315 (pontifical of Trier, adapted to usage of Saint-Germain-des-Prés, Paris, middle 12th c.)

BN latin 13582 (confessors' manuals, 13th c.)

BN latin 14832 (pontifical of Mont-Saint-Michel or Avranches, first half or middle 12th c.)

BN latin 14852

BN latin 14859 (confessors' manual, 13th c.)

BN latin 14891 (confessors' manual, 13th c.)

BN latin 14899 (Pierre de Tarentaise, *Questiones super quartum sententiarum*, 13th c.)
BN latin 14927 (confessors' manual, 13th c.)
BN latin 15162 (confessors' manual, 15th c.)
BN latin 15172 (synodal statutes of Lisieux, beginning 14th c.)
BN latin 15994 (*Summa "Tractaturus Magister"*)
BN latin 16317 (ordinal, Paris, 13th c.)
BN latin 16435 (confessors' manual, end 13th c.)
BN latin 17334 (pontifical of Soissons, second half or end 12th c.)
BN latin 17335 (pontifical of Noyon, second half or end 13th c.)
BN latin 18042 (ritual of Saint-Corneille, Compiègne, 13th c.)
BN latin 18043 (ritual of Saint-Corneille, Compiègne, 13th c.)
BN latin 18044 (ordinal of Saint-Corneille, Compiègne, 13th c.)
BN latin 18045 (ordinal of Saint-Corneille, Compiègne, 13th c.)
BN n.a.l. 232 (Pierre de Roissy, *Manuale de mysteriis ecclesiae*, beginning 13th c.)
BN n.a.l. 306 (pontifical of Rouen, middle 12th c.)
BN n.a.l. 352 (confessors' manuals, second half 13th c.)
BN n.a.l. 1202 (pontifical of Meaux, middle or second half 13th c.)
BN n.a.l. 2358 (pontifical of Saint Corneille, Compiègne, 13th c.)
Bibl. Ste. Geneviève 148 (pontifical of Senlis, middle 14th c.)
Institut de recherche et d'histoire des textes, microfiche, Collection privée, 25
    (pontifical of Senlis, 13th c.)

Reims

BM 330 (ordinal of Reims, 14th–15th c.)
BM 342 (pontifical of Reims, second half or end 12th c.)
BM 343 (pontifical of Reims, beginning 13th c.)
BM 344 (pontifical of Châlons-sur-Marne, beginning 14th c.)

Rome

Bibl. Vat. lat. 1065 (synods of Poitiers)
Bibl. Vat. lat. 1377 (Johannes Teutonicus, Apparatus in Comp. IV; Tancredus
    Bononiensis, Apparatus in Comp. I, II, III, 13th–14th c.)
Bibl. Vat. lat. 9868 (18th c. copies of statutes of Carcassonne)
Bibl. Vat. Pal. lat. 653 (Sicard of Cremona, *Summa decretorum*)
Bibl. Vat. reg. lat. 177 (Joannes de Deo, *Liber poenitentiarius*)

Rouen

BM A27 (pontifical of Saint Germans, Cornwall, 10th c.)
BM 222 (A 551) (processional of Rouen, 13th c.)
BM 370 (A 34) (pontifical of Reims, first half or middle 13th c.)
BM 710 (E 29) (*Summa "Et est sciendum"*)
BM 743 (E 74) (*Summa "Omnis qui iuste iudicat"*)

Saint-Omer

BM 98 (pontifical probably of Saint-Bertin, Saint-Omer, 12th c.)

Sens

BM 7 (processional of Sens, 13th c.)

BM 9 (pontifical of Sens, second half or end 12th c.)
BM 12 (pontifical of Paris adapted to usage of Sens, first half 14th c.)
BM 13 (monastic pontifical, diocese of Rouen, early 14th c.)
BM 20 (ritual of Saint-Remi, Sens, 14th c.)
BM 23 (ordinal, Saint-Pierre-le-Vif, Sens, end 13th c. or beginning 14th c.)
BM 24 (ritual of Saint-Pierre-le-Vif, Sens, 13th c.)
BM 27 (ritual etc., of Sens, 14th c.)

Toulouse

BM 119 (pontifical of Lisieux, first half 14th c.)

Tours

BN n.a.l. 1589
BM 184
BN latin 9430

Troyes

Trésor de la cathédrale, 4 (pontifical of Troyes, second half 12th c.)

Printed Sources

Abelard, Peter. *Ethics*. Ed. and trans. D. E. Luscombe. Oxford, 1971.

Alan of Lille. *Liber poenitentialis*. Ed. J. Longère. Analecta mediaevalia Namurcensia, 17–18. Louvain, 1965.

——. *Summa "Quoniam homines"*. Ed. P. Glorieux. *Archives d'histoire doctrinale et littéraire du Moyen Age* 20 (1953): 113–364.

Albert the Great. *Commentarii in IV sententiarum*. ed. S. C. A. Borgnet. *Opera omnia*, vols. 25–30. Paris, 1894.

——. *De sacramentis*. Ed. A. Ohlmeyer. *Opera omnia*, 26:1–170. Münster, 1958.

Alexander of Hales. *Glossa in quatuor libros sententiarum Petri Lombardi*, 4. Bibliotheca Franciscana Scholastica medii aevi, 15. Quaracchi, 1957.

——. *Quaestiones disputatae "antequam esset frater."* Bibliotheca Franciscana Scholastica medii aevi, 19–21. Quaracchi, 1960.

Andrieu, Michel, ed., *Les ordines romani du haut Moyen-Age*, 5. Spicilegium sacrum Lovaniense, Etudes et documents, 29. Louvain, 1961.

——. *Le pontifical romain au Moyen-Age*. Studi e Testi, 86–88. Vatican City, 1938–1940.

Annales Gandenses. Ed. and trans. H. Johnstone. London, 1951.

Arnauld, Henri. *Statuts du diocèse d'Angers depuis environ l'an 1240 jusqu'en l'an 1679*. Angers, 1680.

ps-Augustine. *De vera et falsa poenitentia*. PL 40:1113–1130.

Beaumanoir, Philippe de. *Coutumes de Beauvaisis*. Ed. A. Salmon. Collection de textes pour servir à l'étude et à l'enseignement de l'histoire. Paris, 1899–1900.

Bernard of Pavia. *Summa decretalium*. Ed. E. A. D. Laspeyres. Regensburg, 1860; repr. Graz, 1956.

Bessin, Guillaume. *Concilia Rotomagensis provinciae*. Rouen, 1717.

Blin, J.-B.-N., ed. *Ordinal de l'abbaye de Saint-Pierre-sur-Dive*. Paris, 1887.

Boeren, P. C. "Les plus anciens statuts du diocèse de Cambrai (XIIIe siècle)."

Revue de droit canonique (Strasbourg) 3 (1953): 1–32, 131–172, 377–415; 4 (1954): 131–158.

Bonaventure. *Commentaria in quatuor libros sententiarum magistri Petri Lombardi. Opera omnia*, 4. Quaracchi, 1889.

Brou, Louis, ed. *The Monastic Ordinale of St. Vedast's Abbey, Arras.* Henry Bradshaw Society, 86–87. Bedford, 1957.

Burchard of Worms. *Decretorum libri viginti.* PL 140:549–1058.

Caesarius of Heisterbach. *Dialogus miraculorum.* Ed. J. Strange. Cologne, 1851.

Calvin, John. *Institutiones Christianae religionis* (1559). *Opera omnia*, 2. Corpus Reformatorum, 30. Ed. G. Baum et al. Braunschweig, 1864.

Chevalier, Ulysse, ed. *Ordinaire et coutumier de l'église cathédrale de Bayeux (XIIIe s.).* Bibliothèque liturgique, 8. Paris, 1902.

———. *Ordinaires de l'église cathédrale de Laon (XIIe et XIIIe s.).* Bibliothèque liturgique, 6. Paris, 1897.

———. *Sacramentaire et martyrologe de l'abbaye de Saint-Remy: Martyrologe, calendrier, ordinaires et prosaire de la métropole de Reims (VIIIe–XIIIe siècles).* Bibliothèque liturgique, 7. Paris, 1900.

Chronicon Flandriae scriptum ab Adriano de Budt, Corpus Chronicorum Flandriae, 1. Bruxellis, 1837–1865.

Conciliorum oecumenicorum decreta. 3d ed. Ed. J. Alberigo et al.. Bologna, 1973.

Crane, T. F., ed. *The Exempla or Illustrative Stories from the Sermones Vulgares of Jacques de Vitry.* London, 1890; repr. New York, 1971.

Delamare, R., ed. *Ordo servicii de l'insigne cathédrale d'Évreux.* Paris, 1925.

Delaporte, Yves, ed. *L'ordinaire chartrain du XIIIe siècle.* Mémoires de la Société Archéologique d'Eure-et-Loir, 18–19. Chartres, 1952–1953.

del Bene, Alphonse. *Codex statutorum synodalium dioecesis aurelianensis.* Orléans, 1674.

Delhaye, Philippe. "Deux textes de Senatus de Worcester sur la pénitence." *Recherches de théologie ancienne et médiévale* 19 (1952): 203–224.

Delisle, Léopold. "Notes sur quelques manuscrits du Musée britannique." *Mémoires de la Société de l'histoire de Paris et de l'Ile de France* 4 (1877): 183–238.

———. "Visites pastorales de maître Henri de Vezelai, archidiacre d'Hiémois en 1267 et 1268." *Bibliothèque de l'Ecole des chartes* 54 (1893): 457–467.

Deshusses, Jean. *Le sacramentaire grégorien.* Spicilegium Friburgense, 16, 24, 28. Fribourg, 1971–1982.

Dickinson, F. H., ed. *Missale ad usum insignis et praeclarae ecclesiae Sarum.* Burntisland, 1861–1883; repr. Farnborough, Hants., 1969.

Du Cange. *Glossarium Mediae et Infimae Latinitatis*, 1 and 2. Niort, Le Favre, 1883–1887.

Dumas, A., ed. *Liber sacramentorum Gellonensis.* Corpus Christianorum Continuatio Mediaevalis, 159–159A. Turnholt, 1981.

Duns Scotus, John. *Quaestiones in quartum librum sententiarum. Opera omnia*, 16–21. Paris, 1894.

Dupont, M. G. "Le registre de l'officialité de Cerisy, 1314–1457." *Mémoires de la Société des antiquitaires de Normandie* 30 (1880): 271–662.

Durand, Georges, ed. *Ordinaires de l'église Notre-Dame cathédrale d'Amiens par Raoul de Rouvroy (1291).* Mémoires de la Société des antiquitaires de Picardie, Documents inédits concernant la province, 22. Amiens and Paris, 1934.

Durand de Saint Pourçain. *In Petri Lombardi Sententias Theologicas Commentariorum libri IIII*. Venice, 1571; repr. Ridgewood, N.J., 1964.

Epistolae saeculi XIII e registis pontificum romanorum. Ed. C. Rodenberg. *Monumenta Germaniae Historica*, 1. Berlin, 1883.

Eudes Rigaud. *Regestrum visitationum*. Ed. T. Bonnin. Rouen, 1852.

Fagniez, Gustave, ed. *Documents relatifs à l'histoire de l'industrie et du commerce en France*, 1. Collection de textes pour servir à l'étude et à l'enseignement de l'histoire, 22. Paris, 1898.

Férotin, Marius. *Le liber ordinum en usage dans l'église wisigothique et mozarabe d'Espagne du cinquième au onzième siècle*. Monumenta Ecclesiae Liturgica, 5. Paris, 1904.

Fransen, Gerard, with Stephan Kuttner, eds. *Summa "Elegantius in iure diuino" seu Coloniensis*. Monumenta Iuris Canonici, ser. A. Corpus Glossatorum, 1. New York, 1969.

Frere, W. H. *The Use of Sarum*. Cambridge, 1898–1901.

Friedberg, E., ed. *Decretalium collectiones*. Corpus Iuris Canonici, 2. Leipzig, 1879.

——. *Quinque compilationes antiquae*. Leipzig, 1882; repr. Graz, 1956.

Gandulf of Bologna. *Sententiarum libri quatuor*. Ed. J. de Walter. Vienna, 1924.

Garcia y Garcia, A. *Constitutiones Concilii quarti Lateranensis una cum Commentariis glossatorum*. Monumenta Iuris Canonici, ser. A. Corpus Glossatorum, 2. Vatican City, 1981.

Gobi, Jean. *Scala celi*. Ulm, 1480.

Goering, Joseph. "The *Summa de penitentia* of Magister Serlo." *Mediaeval Studies* 38 (1976): 1–53.

Goffredus Tranensis (Gottofredo da Trani). *Summa super titulis decretorum*. Lyon, 1519; repr. Aalen, 1968.

Gosse, A. *Histoire de l'abbaye et de l'ancienne congrégation des chanoines réguliers d'Arrouaise*. Lille, 1786.

Gousset, Thomas., ed. *Les actes de la province ecclésiastique de Reims*. Reims, 1842–1844.

Gratian, *Decretum*. Ed. E. Friedberg. *Corpus Iuris Canonici*, 1. Leipzig, 1897.

Guibert de Tournai. *Tractatus de officio episcopi et ecclesiae ceremoniis*. In *Maxima bibliotheca veterum patrum*, ed. M. de la Bigne, 25:401–420. Lyon, 1677.

Guido de Baysio. *Ennarationes super Decreto, autore ipse Rosarium appellari maluit*. Lyon, 1549.

——. *Super sexto Decretalium uberrima commentaria*. Venice, 1547.

Guillaume d'Auvergne. *De sacramento poenitentiae*. In *Opera omnia*. Paris, 1674; repr. Frankfurt am Main, 1963.

Guillaume d'Auxerre. *Summa aurea*. Ed. J. Ribaillier. Spicilegium Bonaventurianum, 16–19. Grottaferrata and Paris, 1980–1986.

Guillaume de Rennes. *Apparatus in summa de casibus Raimundi de Penyafort*: see under Ramón de Peñafort.

Guillaume Durand. *Rationale divinorum officiorum*. Venice, 1577.

Guillaume le Maire. *Liber Guillelmi Majoris*. Ed. C. Port. Collection de documents inédits sur l'histoire de France, Mélanges historiques, 2:187–569. Paris, 1877.

Guy d'Orchelles, "The 'Summa de Officiis Ecclesiae' of Guy d'Orchelles." Ed. V. L. Kennedy. *Mediaeval Studies* 1 (1939): 23–62.

——. *Tractatus de sacramentis.* Ed. D. van den Eynde and O. van den Eynde. Franciscan Institute Publications, Text series, 4. St. Bonaventure, N.Y., 1953.

Hair, Paul, ed. *Before the Bawdy Court.* London, 1972.

Henderson, W. G., ed. *Liber pontificalis Chr. Bainbridge Archiepiscopi Eboracensis.* Surtees Society, 61. London, 1875.

——. *Manuale et processionale ad usum insignis Ecclesiae Eboracensis.* Surtees Society, 63. London, 1875.

Hostiensis (Henry de Segusio). *In I–VI decretalium libros commentaria.* Venice, 1581; repr. Turin, 1965.

——. *Summa aurea.* Venice, 1578; repr. Turin, 1963.

Hugh of Saint Victor. *De sacramentis Christianae fidei.* PL 176:173–618.

Huillard-Bréholles, J.-L.-A. *Historia diplomatica Friderici secundi.* Paris, 1853–.

Innocent IV (Sinibaldo Fieschi). *Commentaria super libros quinque decretalium.* Frankfurt am Main, 1570; repr. Frankfurt am Main, 1968.

Innocent V (Pierre de Tarentaise). *In IV libros sententiarum commentaria.* Toulouse, 1649–1652.

Jean Beleth. *Summa de ecclesiasticis officiis.* Ed. H. Douteil. Corpus Christianorum Continuatio Mediaevalis, 41–41A. Turnholt, 1976.

Jean d'Avranches. *De officiis ecclesiasticis.* Ed. R. Delamare. Paris, 1923.

Jean de Joinville. *Histoire de Saint Louis.* Ed. N. de Wailly. Paris, 1868.

Jean le Moine. *Glossa aurea.* Paris, 1535; repr. Aalen, 1968.

Joannes Andreae. *In quinque decretalium libros novella commentaria.* Venice, 1581; repr. Turin, 1963.

Jocelin of Brakelond. *Cronica.* Ed. and trans. H. E. Butler. London, 1949.

Johannes Teutonicus and Bartolomeus Brixiensis. *Decretum Gratiani nouissime post ceteras omnes impressiones . . . unacumque glossis Joannis Teutonici et Bartholomei Brixiensis.* Venice, 1528.

John of Erfurt. *Die Summa confessorum.* Ed. N. Brieskorn. Frankfurt am Main, 1980.

John of Freiburg. *Summa confessorum.* Augsburg, 1476.

Kennedy, V. L. "Robert Courson on Penance." *Mediaeval Studies* 7 (1945): 290–336.

Lanfranc. *Libellus de celanda confessione.* PL 150:625–632.

Langevin, Raoul. *Consuetudines et statuta ecclesie Baiocensis.* Ed. Ulysse Chevalier. *Ordinaire et coutumier de l'église cathédrale de Bayeux (XIIe s.).* Bibliothèque liturgique, 8. Paris, 1902.

Lecler, A. "Anciens statuts du diocèse de Limoges." *Bulletin de la Société archéologique et historique du Limousin* 40, no. 1 (1892): 122–163.

Lecoy de la Marche, A. *Anecdotes historiques, légendes, et apologues tirés du recueil inédit d'Etienne de Bourbon.* Société de l'histoire de France, publication 58. Paris, 1877.

Legg, John Wickham, ed. *Missale ad usum Ecclesie Westmonasteriensis.* Henry Bradshaw Society, 1, 5, 12. London, 1891–1896.

——. *The Sarum Missal.* Oxford, 1916; repr. 1969.

Liber sacramentorum Gellonensis. Corpus Christianorum Continuatio Mediaevalis, 159. Turnholt, 1981.

Louvet, P. *Histoire et antiquitez du Pais de Beauvaisis.* Beauvais, 1631.

Luther, Martin *Studienausgabe.* Ed. Hans-Ulrich Delius. Berlin, 1979–.

McLaughlin, Terence P., ed. *The Summa Parisiensis on the Decretum Gratiani.* Toronto, 1952.

Mansi, J. D. *Sacrorum conciliorum noua et amplissima collectio.* Venice, 1759–1798; repr. Paris, 1903–1927.

Martène, Edmond. *De antiquis ecclesiae ritibus libri.* Antwerp, 1736–1738; repr. Hildesheim, 1967.

Martène, Edmond, and Ursin Durand. *Thesaurus novus anecdotorum.* Paris, 1717.

——. *Veterum scriptorum et monumentorum historicum, dogmaticorum, moralium, amplissima collectio.* Paris, 1733.

Meersseman, G. G. *Dossier de l'Ordre de la pénitence au XIIIe siècle.* Spicilegium Friburgense, 7. Fribourg, 1961.

Michaud-Quantin, P. "Deux formulaires pour la confession du milieu du XIIIe siècle." *Recherches de théologie ancienne et médiévale* 31 (1964): 43–62.

——. "Un manuel de confession archaïque dans le manuscrit Avranches 136." *Sacris Erudiri* 17 (1966): 5–54.

Mohlberg, C., ed. *Das fränkische Sacramentarium Gelasianum.* 3d ed. Liturgiewissenschaftliche Quellen und Forschungen, 1–2. Münster, 1971.

Mohlberg, L. C., ed. *Liber sacramentorum Romanae Aeclesiae ordinis anni circuli.* Rerum ecclesiasticarum documenta, ser. maior, fontes, 4. Rome, 1960.

Morey, Adrian. *Bartholomew of Exeter: Bishop and Canonist.* Cambridge, 1937.

Ordinarium Canonicorum Regularium S. Laudi Rotomagensis. PL 147:157–192.

Paucapalea. *Summa über das Decretum Gratiani.* Ed. J. F. von Schulte. Giessen, 1890; repr. Aalen, 1965.

Paul of Hungary. *Rationes penitentie.* In *Bibliotheca casinensis seu Codicum manuscriptorum.* Vol. 4, Florilegium casinense, pp. 191–215. Montecassino, 1878–1880.

Pierre de Tarentaise: see under Innocent V.

Peter Cantor. *Summa de sacramentis et animae consiliis,* 2. Ed. J.-A. Dugauquier. Analecta mediaevalia Namurcensia, 7. Louvain, 1957.

——. *Verbum abbreviatum.* PL 205:23–376.

Peter Lombard. *Sententiae in IV libris distinctae.* Spicilegium Bonaventurianum, 4–5. Grottaferrata, 1971–1981.

ps-Peter of Blois. *De poenitentia.* PL 207:1153–1156.

Peter of Poitiers, chancellor of Notre-Dame. *Sententiarum libri quinque.* PL 211:789–1280.

Peter of Poitiers, canon of Saint Victor. *Summa de confessione (Compilatio praesens).* Ed. J. Longère. Corpus Christianorum Continuatio Mediaevalis, 51. Turnholt, 1980.

Pommeraye, François. *Sanctae Rotomagensis Ecclesiae concilia ac synodalia decreta.* Rouen, 1677.

Pontal, Odette, ed. *Les statuts synodaux français du XIIIe siècle,* 1–2. Collection de documents inédits sur l'histoire de France, 9. Paris, 1971–1983.

Powicke, F. M., and C. R. Cheney, eds. *Councils and Synods with Other Documents Relating to the English Church,* 2 (A.D. 1205–1313). Oxford, 1964.

Praepositinus of Cremona. *Tractatus de officiis.* Ed. James A. Corbett. Publications in Mediaeval Studies, 21. Notre Dame, Ind., 1969.

Ralph of Coggeshall. *Chronicon Anglicanum.* Ed. J. Stevenson. Rolls Series. London, 1875.

Ramón de Peñafort. *Summa de poenitentia et matrimonio cum glossis Ioannis de Friburgo* (glosses actually by Guillaume de Rennes). Rome, 1603; repr. Farnborough, 1967.

Recueil des historiens des Gaules et de la France, 18–23. Paris, 1738–1905.

Regino of Prüm. *Libri duo de synodalibus causis et disciplinis ecclesiasticis.* Ed. F. G. A. Wasserschleben. Leipzig. 1840; repr. Graz, 1964.

Richard of Middleton. *Super quatuor libros sententiarum Petri Lombardi quaestiones.* Brixen, 1591; repr. Frankfurt am Main, 1963.

Robert de Sorbon. *De consciencia* and *De tribus dietis.* Ed. F. Chambon. Collection de textes pour servir à l'étude et à l'enseignment de l'histoire. Paris, 1902.

Robert Mannyng of Brunne. *Handlyng Synne.* Ed. Idelle Sullens. Medieval and Renaissance Texts and Studies, 14. Binghamton, N.Y., 1983.

Robert of Flamborough. *Liber poenitentialis.* Ed. J. J. Francis Firth. Pontifical Institute of Mediaeval Studies, Studies and Texts, 18. Toronto, 1971.

Robert Paululus. *De caeremoniis, sacramentis, officiis, et observationibus ecclesiasticis.* PL 177:381–456.

Rolandus. *Die Sentenzen Rolands.* Ed. A. M. Gietl. Freiburg, 1891, repr. Amsterdam, 1969.

———. *Die Summa magistri Rolandi.* Ed. F. Thaner. Innsbruck, 1874.

Rufinus of Bologna. *Summa decretorum.* Ed. H. Singer. Paderborn, 1902; repr. Aalen, 1963.

Sicard of Cremona. *Mitrale seu de officiis ecclesiasticis summa.* PL 213:13–434.

Smet, J.-J. de, ed. *Corpus chronicorum Flandriae,* 1–2. Brussels, 1837–1841.

Stephen of Tournai. *Die Summa über das Decretum Gratiani.* Ed. J. F. von Schulte. Giessen, 1891; repr. Aalen, 1965.

Tailliar, Eugène François Joseph. *Recueil d'actes des XIIe et XIIIe siècles en langue romane wallonne du nord de la France.* Douai, 1849.

Thomas Aquinas. *Commentum in quatuor libros sententiarum magistri Petri Lombardi,* 4. *Opera omnia,* 7.2. Parma, 1858; repr. New York, 1948.

———. *De forma absolutionis paenitentiae sacramentalis ad Magistrum Ordinis. Opera omnia* (Leonine ed.), 40:B–C. Rome, 1968.

———. *Summa contra gentiles,* 4. *Opera omnia* (Leonine ed.), 15. Rome, 1930.

———. *Summa theologiae. Opera Omnia* (Leonine ed.). Rome, 1882.

Thomas de Cantimpré. *Miraculorum et exemplorum memorabilium sui temporis libri duo* (= *Bonum universale de apibus*). Douai, 1605.

Thomas of Chobham. *Summa confessorum.* Ed. F. Broomfield. Analecta mediaevalia Namurcensia, 25. Louvain, 1968.

Thompson, Edward Maude, ed. *Customary of the Benedictine Monasteries of Saint Augustine, Canterbury and Saint Peter, Westminster.* Henry Bradshaw Society, 23, 28. London, 1902–1904.

Tolhurst, J. B. L., ed. *The Customary of the Cathedral Priory Church of Norwich.* Henry Bradshaw Society, 82. London, 1948.

Urtel, H. "Eine altfranzösische Beichte." *Zeitschrift für romanische Philologie* 33 (1909): 571–575.

Varin, Pierre, ed. *Archives administratives de la ville de Reims.* Collection de documents inédits sur l'histoire de France. Paris, 1839.

Vielliard, Jeanne, ed. *Le guide du pèlerin de Saint-Jacques de Campostelle.* 5th ed. Paris, 1978.

Vogel, Cyrille, with Reinhard Elze. *Le pontifical romano-germanique du dixième siècle.* Studi e Testi, I–III, 226, 227, 269. Vatican City, 1963–1972.

Warren, F. E., ed. *The Leofric Missal.* Oxford, 1883.

Weisweiler, Henri. *Maître Simon et son groupe: De sacramentis,* with appendix, *Pierre*

le mangeur: De sacramentis. Ed. Raymond M. Martin. Spicilegium sacrι· ·a-
niense, 17. Louvain, 1937.

Welter, J. T., ed. *Le speculum laicorum.* Thesaurus exemplorum, fasc. ·s,
1914.

———. *La tabula exemplorum secundum ordinem alphabeti.* Thesaurus exeι· ιι,
fasc. 3. Paris and Toulouse, 1926.

William of Middleton. *Quaestiones de sacramentis.* Ed. C. Piana and G. G. ·ι-
otheca Franciscana Scholastica medii aevi, 22–23. Quaracchi, 1961.

Wilmart, A. "Un opuscule sur la confession composé par Guy de Southwι rs
la fin du XIIe siècle." *Recherches de théologie ancienne et médiévale* 7 (1935). ɔɔ7–
352.

Wilson, Henry Austin, ed. *The Benedictional of Archbishop Robert.* Henry Bradshaw
Society, 24. London, 1903.

———. *Officium Ecclesiasticum Abbatum secundum usum Eveshamensis Monasterii.* Henry
Bradshaw Society, 6. London, 1893.

———. *The Pontifical of Magdalen College.* Henry Bradshaw Society, 39. London,
1910.

Woolley, Reginald Maxwell, ed. *The Canterbury Benedictional.* Henry Bradshaw Society, 51. London, 1917.

Wybrands, Aem. W. *Gesta abbatum orti sancte Marie.* Leeuwarden, 1879.

Zwingli, Ulrich. *Von der Taufe, von der Wiedertaufe und von der Kindertaufe.* In *Sämtliche Werke,* 4. Corpus Reformatorum, 91. Leipzig, 1927.

SECONDARY WORKS

Abbé, Jean-Loup. "Rayonnement urbain et seigneuries autour d'Arras et de Douai
au XIIIe siècle." *Revue du Nord* 65 (1983): 400–410.

Adam, Paul. *La vie paroissiale en France au XIVe siècle.* Paris, 1964.

Adnès, Pierre. "Pénitence." In *Dictionnaire de spiritualité,* 12:1, cols. 943–1010.
Paris, 1984.

Amann, E. "Eudes Rigaud." In *Dictionnaire de théologie catholique.* 13b, cols. 2703–
2705. Paris, 1937.

———. "Pénitence–sacrement, I–II." In *Dictionnaire de théologie catholique,* 12a, cols.
748–948. Paris, 1933.

Amargier, P.-A. "Les frères de la pénitence de Jesus-Christ ou du sac." *Provence
historique* 15 (1965): 158–167.

Ammann, Hektor. "Wie gross war die mittelalterliche Stadt?" *Studium generale* 9
(1956): 503–506.

Amtmann, Radegunde. *Die Bussbrüderschaften in Frankreich.* Wiesbaden, 1977.

Anciaux, Paul. *La théologie du sacrement de la pénitence au XIIe siècle.* Louvain, 1949.

Andrieu, Michel. "Le pontifical d'Apamée et autres textes liturgiques communiqués à dom Martène par Jean Deslions." *Revue Bénédictine* 48 (1936): 321–348.

Andrieu-Guitrancourt, Pierre. *L'archevêque Eudes Rigaud et la vie de l'église au XIIIe
siècle.* Paris, 1938.

Ariès, Philippe. *The Hour of Our Death.* Trans. H. Weaver. New York, 1981.

Ariès, Philippe, and Georges Duby, eds. *A History of Private Life,* 1–3. Trans.
A. Goldhammer. Cambridge, Mass., 1987–1989.

Arnould, E. J. *Le manuel des péchés: Etude de la littérature religieuse anglo-normande (XIIIe siècle)*. Paris, 1940.

Aronstam, Robin Ann. "Penitential Pilgrimages to Rome in the Early Middle Ages." *Archivum Historiae Pontificiae* 13 (1975): 65–83.

Artonne, André. "Les statuts synodaux diocésaines français du XIIIe siècle au Concile de Trente." *Revue d'histoire de l'église de France* 36 (1950): 168–181.

Artonne, André, Louis Guizard, and Odette Pontal. *Répertoire des statuts synodaux des diocèses de l'ancienne France du XIIIe à la fin du XVIIIe siècle*. 2d ed. Documents, études, et répertoires publiés par l'Institut de recherche et d'histoire des textes, 8. Paris, 1969.

Aubrun, Michel. *La paroisse en France des origines au XVe siècle*. Paris, 1986.

Aubry, Pierre. *La musique et les musiciens d'église en Normandie au XIIIe siècle d'après le "Journal des visites pastorales" d'Odon Rigaud*. Paris, 1906.

L'aveu: Antiquité et Moyen-Age. Collection de l'Ecole française de Rome, 88. Rome, 1986.

Avril, Joseph. *Le gouvernement des évêques et la vie religieuse dans le diocèse d'Angers (1148–1240)*. Paris, 1984.

———. "Les 'Precepta synodalia' de Roger de Cambrai." *Bulletin of Medieval Canon Law*, n.s. 2 (1972): 7–15.

———. "Remarques sur un aspect de la vie religieuse paroissiale: La pratique de la confession et de la communion du Xe au XIV siècle." In *L'encadrement religieux des fidèles au Moyen-Age et jusqu'au Concile de Trente*. Actes du 109e Congrès national des sociétés savantes, Dijon, 1984, Section d'histoire médiévale et de philologie, 1. Paris, 1985.

Bailey, Terence. *The Processions of Sarum and the Western Church*. Pontifical Institute of Mediaeval Studies, Studies and Texts, 21. Toronto, 1971.

Baldwin, John. *The Government of Philip Augustus: Foundations of French Royal Power in the Middle Ages*. Berkeley, Calif., 1986.

———. *Masters, Princes, and Merchants: The Social Views of Peter the Chanter and His Circle*. Princeton, N.J., 1970.

Banker, James R. *Death in the Community: Memorialization and Confraternities in an Italian Commune in the Late Middle Ages*. Athens, Ga., 1988.

Barber, Malcolm. *The Trial of the Templars*. Cambridge, 1978.

Bautier, Robert-Henri, ed. *La France de Philippe Auguste: Le temps des mutations*. Paris, 1982.

Becker, Marvin B. *Medieval Italy: Constraints and Creativity*. Bloomington, Ind., 1981.

Benrath, Gustav Adolf. "Busse V." In *Theologische Realenzyklopädie*, 7:452–473. Berlin, 1981.

Benton, John F. "Consciousness of Self and Perceptions of Individuality." In *Renaissance and Renewal in the Twelfth Century*, ed. R. L. Benson and G. Constable, pp. 263–295. Cambridge, Mass., 1977.

———. "Individualism and Conformity in Medieval Western Europe." In *Individualism and Conformity in Classical Islam*, ed. A. Banani and S. Vryonis, pp. 145–158. Wiesbaden, 1977.

Bériou, Nicole. "Autour de Latran IV (1215): La naissance de la confession moderne et sa diffusion." In *Pratiques de la confession*, ed. Groupe de la Bussiere. Paris, 1983.

——. "La confession dans les écrits théologiques et pastoreaux du XIIIe siècle: Médication de l'âme ou demande judiciaire." In *L'aveu: Antiquité et Moyen-Age.* Collection de l'Ecole française de Rome, 88. Rome, 1986.

Berlière, U. "Les pèlerinages judiciares au Moyen Age." *Revue Bénédictine* 7 (1890): 520–526.

Berlioz, Jacques. "Les ordalies dans les *exempla* da la confession (XIIIe–XIVe siècles)." In *L'aveu: Antiquité et Moyen-Age.* Collection de l'Ecole française de Rome, 88. Rome, 1986.

——. "'Quand dire c'est faire dire': *Exempla* et confession chez Etienne de Bourbon." In *Faire croire: Modalités de la diffusion et de la réception des messages religieux du XIIe au XVe siècle.* Collection de l'Ecole française de Rome, 51. Rome, 1981.

Berlioz, Jacques, and Colette Ribancourt. "Images de la confession dans la prédication au dèbut du XIVe siècle: L'exemple de l'*Alphabetum Narrationum* d'Arnold de Liège." In *Pratiques de la confession,* ed. Groupe de la Bussiere. Paris, 1983.

Bienvenu, Jean-Marc. "Fondations charitables laïques au XIIe siècle: L'exemple de l'Anjou." In *Etudes sur l'histoire de la pauvreté,* ed. Michel Mollat, 2:563–569. Publications de la Sorbonne, série études, 1.8 Paris, 1974.

Bishop, Edmund. *Liturgica historica.* Oxford, 1918.

Bloch, Marc. *La France sous les derniers Capétiens, 1223–1328.* Paris, 1958.

Bornert, Réné. *La réforme protestante du culte à Strasbourg au XVIe siècle (1523–1598).* Studies in Medieval and Renaissance Thought, 28. Leiden, 1981.

Bossy, John. *Christianity in the West, 1400–1700.* Oxford, 1985.

——. "Holiness and Society." *Past and Present* 75 (1977): 119–137.

——. "The Social History of Confession in the Age of the Reformation." *Transactions of the Royal Historical Society,* 5th ser., 25 (1975): 21–38.

——. "Some Elementary Forms of Durkheim." *Past and Present* 95 (1982): 3–18.

——, ed. *Disputes and Settlements: Law and Human Relations in the West.* Cambridge, 1983.

Boussard, Jacques. *Nouvelle histoire de Paris de la fin du siège de 885–886 à la mort de Philippe Auguste.* Paris, 1976.

Boutié, Louis. *Paris au temps de Saint Louis.* Paris, 1911.

Bouwsma, W. J. "Anxiety and the Formation of Early Modern Culture." In *After the Reformation,* ed. B. Malament, pp. 215–240. Philadelphia, 1980.

Boyle, Leonard. "*Summae confessorum.*" In *Les genres littéraires dans les sources théologiques et philosophiques médiévales.* Publications de l'Institut d'études médiévales, 2e sér., 5:227–237. Louvain, 1982.

——. "The *Summa Confessorum* of John of Freiburg and the Popularization of the Moral Teaching of St. Thomas and Some of his Contemporaries." In *St. Thomas Aquinas, 1274–1974: Commemorative Studies,* 2:245–268. Toronto, 1974.

Braeckmans, Louis. *Confession et communion au Moyen Age et au Concile de Trente.* Gembloux, 1971.

Brooks, Neil C. "Processional Drama and Dramatic Procession in Germany in the Late Middle Ages." *Journal of English and Germanic Philology* 32 (1933): 141–171.

Brown, Peter. "The Rise and Function of the Holy Man in Late Antiquity." In *Society and the Holy in Late Antiquity.* London, 1982.

——. "Society and the Supernatural: A Medieval Change." In *Society and the Holy in Late Antiquity.* London, 1982.

Brown, S. M., and J. F. O'Sullivan, trans. *The Register of Eudes of Rouen*. New York, 1964.

Brückmann, J. "Latin Manuscript Pontificals and Benedictionals in England and Wales." *Traditio* 29 (1973): 391–458.

Brundage, James A. *Law, Sex, and Christian Society in Medieval Europe*. Chicago, 1987.

Bynum, Caroline Walker. *Jesus as Mother: Studies in the Spirituality of the High Middle Ages*. Berkeley, Calif., 1982.

Cabie, R. "Le pontifical de Guillaume Durand l'ancien et les livres liturgiques languedociens." In *Liturgie et musique (IXe–XIVe siècles)*. Cahiers de Fanjeaux, 17. Toulouse, 1982.

Caenegem, R. C. van. *Geschiedenis van het Strafprocesrecht in Vlaanderen van de XIe tot de XIVe eeuw*. Verhandelingen van de Koninklijke Vlaamse Academie voor Wetenschappen, Letteren en Schone Kunsten van België, Klassen der Letteren, Verhandeling nr. 24. Brussels, 1956.

———. *Geschiedenis van het Strafrecht in Vlaanderen van de XIe tot de XIVe eeuw*. Verhandelingen van de Koninklijke Vlaamse Academie voor Wetenschappen, Letteren en Schone Kunsten van België, Klassen der Letteren, Verhandeling nr. 19. Brussels, 1954.

Camporesi, Piero. *La maschera di Bertoldo: G. C. Croce e la letteratura carnevalesca*. Turin, 1976.

Carlen, Louis. "Busswallfahrten der Schweiz." *Schweizerisches Archiv für Volkskunde* 55 (1959): 237–257.

Caro-Baroja, Julio. *Le carnaval*. Trans. S. Sesé-Léger. Paris, 1979; first published Madrid, 1965.

Carolus-Barré, Louis. "Philippe Auguste et les villes de commune." In *La France de Philippe Auguste: Le temps des mutations*, ed. Robert-Henri Bautier. Paris, 1982.

Cattaneo, Enrico. "La partecipazione dei laici alla liturgia." In *I laici nella "Societas christiana" dei secoli XI e XII*. Atti della terza Settimana internazionale di Studio, Passo della Mendola, 1965. Milan, 1968.

Cauwenbergh, Etienne van. *Les pèlerinages expiatoires et judiciaires dans le droit communal de la Belgique au Moyen Age*. Université de Louvain, Recueil de travaux publiés par les membres des conférences d'histoire et de philologie, 48. Louvain, 1922.

Cazelles, Raymond. *Nouvelle histoire de Paris de la fin du règne de Philippe Auguste à la mort de Charles V, 1223–1380*. Paris, 1972.

———. "Le parisien au temps de Saint Louis." In *Septième centenaire de la mort de Saint Louis*. Actes des Colloques de Royaumont et de Paris, 1970. Paris, 1976.

Cazenave, A. "Aveu et contrition: Manuels de confesseurs et interrogatoires d'Inquisition en Languedoc et en Catalogne." In *La piété populaire au Moyen Age*. Actes du 99e Congrès national des sociétés savantes, Bensançon, 1974, Philologie et histoire jusqu'à 1610, 1. Paris, 1977.

Chambers, Edward K. *The Mediaeval Stage*. Oxford, 1903.

Chanteux, H., "Le manuscrit latin 14.832 de la Bibliothèque nationale: Contribution à l'histoire du Pontifical Romano-Germanique." *Bulletin philologique et historique (jusqu'à 1715)* (1955–1956): 485–498.

Chavasse, Antoine. *Le sacrementaire gélasien*. Bibliothèque de théologie, série 4. Histoire de la théologie, 1. Paris-Tournai, 1958.

Chélini, Jean, and Henri Branthomme. *Les chemins de Dieu*. Paris, 1982.

Cheney, C. R. "The Earliest English Diocesan Statutes." *English Historical Review* 75 (1960): 1–29.

——. "Early Norman Monastic Visitations: A Neglected Record." *Journal of Ecclesiastical History* 33 (1982): 412–423.

——. *English Synodalia of the Thirteenth Century*. Oxford, 1941.

——. *Episcopal Visitation of Monasteries in the Thirteenth Century*. Manchester, 1931.

——. "The Numbering of the Lateran Councils of 1179 and 1215." In *Medieval Texts and Studies*. Oxford, 1973.

——. "Some Aspects of Diocesan Legislation during the Thirteenth Century." In *Medieval Texts and Studies*. Oxford, 1973.

——. "Statute-Making in the English Church in the Thirteenth Century." In *Medieval Texts and Studies*. Oxford, 1973.

Chevalier, Bernard. *Les bonnes villes de France du XIVe au XVIe siècle*. Paris, 1982.

Chiffoleau, Jacques. *La comptabilité de l'au-delà. Les hommes, la mort, et la religion dans la région d'Avignon à la fin du Moyen Age*. Collection de l'école française de Rome, 47. Rome, 1980.

Combaluzier, Fernand. "Un pontifical de Mont-Saint-Michel." In *Millénaire monastique du Mont-Saint-Michel*. Paris, 1966–1971.

Coulet, Noël. "Processions, espace urbain, communauté civique." In *Liturgie et musique (XIe–XIVe s.)*. Cahiers de Fanjeaux, 17. Toulouse, 1982.

——. *Les visites pastorales*. Typologie des sources du Moyen Age occidental, 23. Turnholt, 1977.

Le credo, la morale, et l'inquisition. Cahiers de Fanjeaux, 6. Toulouse, 1971.

D'Alatri, Mariano, ed. *I Frati Penitenti di San Francesco nella società del due e trecento*. Atti del 2° Convegno di Studi francescani, Rome, 1976. Rome, 1977.

——. *Il movimento francescano della Penitenza nella società medioevale*. Atti del 3° Convegno di Studi francescani, Padua, 1979. Rome, 1980.

Davis, Natalie Zemon. "From 'Popular Religion' to Religious Cultures." In *Reformation Europe: A Guide to Research*, ed. S. Ozment, pp. 321–341. St. Louis, Mo., 1982.

——. "The Sacred and the Body Social in Sixteenth-Century Lyon." *Past and Present* 90 (1981): 40–70.

——. *Society and Culture in Early Modern France: Eight Essays*. Stanford, Calif., 1975.

Debal, Jacques, ed. *Histoire d'Orléans et de son terroir*, 1. Roanne, 1983.

Delalande, Jean. *Les extraordinaires croisades d'enfants et de pastoureaux au Moyen Age*. Paris, 1962.

Delumeau, Jean. *Le catholicisme entre Luther et Voltaire*. Paris, 1971.

——. *Le péché et la peur: La culpabilisation en occident (XIIIe–XVIIIe siècles)*. Paris, 1983.

——. *La peur en occident (XIVe–XVIIIe siècles)*. Paris, 1978.

Demont, M. A. "Le blé dans les traditions populaires artésiennes." *Revue de folklore français et de folklore colonial* 6 (1935): 31–51.

Derville, Alain, ed. *Histoire de Saint-Omer*. Lille, 1981.

Desportes, Pierre. *Reims et les rémois aux XIIIe et XIVe siècles*. Paris, 1979.

——. "Les sociétés confraternelles de curés en France du nord au Bas-Moyen-Age." In *L'encadrement religieux des fidèles au Moyen-Age et jusqu'au Concile de Trente*. Actes du 109e Congrès national des sociétés savantes, Dijon, 1984, Section d'histoire médiévale et de philologie, 1. Paris, 1985.

Dietterle, Johannes. "Die Summae confessorum." *Zeitschrift für Kirchengeschichte* 24 (1903): 353–374, 520–548; 25 (1904): 248–272; 26 (1905): 59–81, 350–364; 27 (1906): 166–188, 296–310, 431–442; 28 (1907): 401–431.

Dobiache-Rojdestvensky, Olga. *La vie paroissiale en France au XIIIe siècle d'après les actes épiscopaux.* Paris, 1911.

Dornic, François, ed. *Histoire du Mans et du pays manceau.* Toulouse, 1975.

Dossat, Yves. *Eglise et hérésie en France a· XIIIe siècle.* London, 1982.

Douglas, Mary. *Natural Symbols.* Harmondsworth, Middlesex, 1973; first published 1970.

———. *Purity and Danger.* Cambridge, 1983.

Dowden, John. *The Church Year and Kalendar.* Cambridge, 1910.

Dubrulle, Henry. *Cambrai: La fin du Moyen Age (XIIIe–XVI siècle).* Lille, 1904.

Duby, Georges. "Ouverture: Pouvoir privé, pouvoir public." In *Histoire de la vie privée,* ed. Philippe Ariès and Georges Duby. Paris, 1985.

Duby, Georges, ed. *Histoire de la France urbaine.* Vol. 2, *La ville médiévale,* ed. J. Le Goff. Paris, 1980–1985.

Dufournet, Jean, and Andrée Meline, eds. *Le roman de Renart.* Paris, 1985.

Dumont, Louis. *La tarasque.* Paris, 1951.

Dupront, Alphonse. "Pèlerinage et lieux sacrés." In *Méthodologie de l'histoire et des sciences humaines: Mélanges en l'honneur de Fernand Braudel,* 2:189–206. Toulouse, 1973.

———. "La religion populaire dans l'histoire de l'Europe occidentale." *Revue d'histoire de l'église de France* 64 (1978): 185–202.

Durkheim, Emile. *The Elementary Forms of the Religious Life.* Trans. J. W. Swain. New York, 1915.

Dykmans, Marc. *Le pontifical romain révisé au XVe siècle.* Studi e Testi, 311. Vatican City, 1985.

Emery, Richard W. *The Friars in Medieval France.* New York, 1962.

———. "The Friars of the Sack." *Speculum* 18 (1943): 323–334.

———. "A Note on the Friars of the Sack." *Speculum* 35 (1960): 591–595.

L'encadrement religieux des fidèles au Moyen-Age et jusqu'au Concile de Trente. Actes du 109e Congrès national des sociétés savantes, Dijon 1984, Section d'histoire médiévale et de philologie, 1. Paris, 1985.

Esmein, A. *Histoire de la procédure criminelle en France et spécialement de la procédure inquisitoire depuis le XIIIe siècle jusqu'à nos jours.* Paris, 1882.

Espinas, Georges. *Les origines du capitalisme.* Vol. 1, *Sire Jehan Boinebroke, patricien et drapier douaisien.* Bibliothèque de la Société d'histoire du droit des pays flamands, picards, et wallons, 8. Lille, 1933.

———. *Les origines du capitalisme.* Vol. 2, *Sire Jean de France, patricien et rentier douaisien, Sire Jacques le Blond, patricien et drapier douaisien.* Bibliothèque de la Société d'histoire du droit des pays flamands, picards, et wallons, 9. Lille, 1936.

Evans-Pritchard, E. E. *Theories of Primitive Religion.* Oxford, 1965.

Fabre, Daniel. "Le monde du carnaval." *Annales: Economies, sociétés, civilisations* 31 (1976): 389–406.

Faire croire: Modalités de la diffusion et de la réception des messages religieux du XIIe au XVe siècle. Collection de l'Ecole française de Rome, 51. Rome, 1981.

Febvre, Lucien. "The Origins of the French Reformation: A Badly Put Question?" In *A New Kind of History,* ed. and trans. P. Burke. New York, 1973.

Fiala, V. "Die Sündenvergebung und das lateinische Stundengebet." In *Liturgie et rémission des péchés*. Bibliotheca "Ephemerides Liturgicae," Subsidia, 3. Rome, 1975.

Finot, J. "Les répresentations scéniques données à l'occasion de la procession de Lille par les compagnons de la place du Petit-Fret, au XVe siècle." *Bulletin historique et philologique* 16 (1897): 504–520.

Firth, Francis. "More about Robert of Flamborough's Penitential." *Traditio* 17 (1960): 531–532.

——. The 'Poenitentiale' of Robert of Flamborough: An Early Handbook for the Confessor in Its Manuscript Tradition." *Traditio* 16 (1960): 541–556.

Fischer, Ludwig. "Der 'Ordinarius Papae' und der 'Pontificalis Ordinis Liber' des Wilhelm Duranti des Älteren." *Römische Quartalschrift* 38 (1930): 7–21.

Foreville, Raymonde. *Latran I, II, III, et Latran IV*. Paris, 1965.

——. "La réception des conciles généraux dans l'église et la province de Rouen au XIIIe siècle." In *Droit privé et institutions régionales: Etudes historiques offertes à Jean Yver*, pp. 243–253. Paris, 1976.

——. "Les statuts synodaux et le renouveau pastoral du XIIIe siècle dans le Midi de la France." In *Le credo, la morale, et l'inquisition*. Cahiers de Fanjeaux, 6. Toulouse, 1971.

Foucault, Michel. *Discipline and Punish: The Birth of the Prison*. Trans. A. Sheridan. New York, 1977.

Fournier, Paul. *Les officialités au Moyen Age*. Paris, 1880.

Franz, Adolph. *Die kirchlichen Benediktionen im Mittelalter*. Freiburg, 1909.

Frere, Walter Howard. *Studies in Early Roman Liturgy. Vol. 1, The Kalendar*. London, 1930.

Friedmann, Adrien. *Paris: Ses rues, ses paroisses du Moyen Age à la Révolution*. Paris, 1959.

Gabet, Phillippe. "Les dragons processionnels sont-ils ou non bénéfiques?" *Bulletin de la Société de mythologie française* 92 (1974): 16–46.

Gaignebet, Claude, and Marie-Claude Florentin. *Le Carnaval: Essais de mythologie populaire*. Paris, 1974.

Galpern, A. N. *The Religions of the People in Sixteenth-Century Champagne*. Cambridge, Mass., 1976.

Ganshof, F. L. *Etude sur le développement des villes entre Loire et Rhin au Moyen-Age*. Paris and Brussels, 1943.

——. *Etude sur les ministeriales en Flandre et en Lotharingie*. Brussels, 1926.

——. "Pèlerinages expiatoires flamands à Saint-Gilles pendant le XIVe siècle." *Annales du Midi* 78 (1966): 391–407.

Garancini, Gianfranco. "Persona, peccato, penitenza: Studi sulla disciplina penitenziale nell'Alto Medio Evo." *Rivista di storia del diritto italiano* 47 (1974): 19–87.

Geertz, Hildred, and Keith Thomas. "An Anthropology of Religion and Magic, I–II." *Journal of Interdisciplinary History* 6 (1975): 71–109.

Genicot, Léopold. "Aristocratie et dignités ecclésiastiques en Picardie aux XIIe et XIIIe siècles." *Revue d'histoire ecclésiastique* 67 (1972): 436–442.

——. "Les grandes villes de l'Occident en 1300." In *Economies et sociétés au Moyen Age: Mélanges offerts à Edouard Perroy*. Paris, 1973.

Gennep, Arnold van. *Le folklore de la Flandre et du Hainaut français*. Paris, 1935.

——. *Manuel de folklore français contemporain*. Paris, 1947.

——. *The Rites of Passage.* Trans. M. B. Vizedom and G. L. Caffee. Chicago, 1960; first published 1908.

Georges, André. *Le pèlerinage à Campostelle en Belgique et dans le nord de la France.* Académie royale de Belgique, Classe des Beaux-Arts, Mémoires, Coll. in 4°, 2.13. Brussels, 1971.

Geremek, Bronislaw. "Paris la plus grande ville de l'occident médiéval?" *Acta Poloniae Historica* 18 (1968): 18–37.

Gibbs, Marion, and Jane Lang. *Bishops and Reform, 1215–1276.* London, 1934.

Gieben, Servus. "I penitenti di San Francesco nei Paesi Bassi (secoli XIII–XIV)." In *Il movimento francescano della penitenza nella società medioevale,* ed. Moriano D'Alatri. Atti del 3 Convegno di Studi francescani. Rome, 1980.

Girard, René. *La violence et le sacré.* Paris, 1972.

Girard, René, with J.-M. Oughourlian and G. Lefort. *Things Hidden since the Foundation of the World.* Trans. S. Bann and M. Metteer. Stanford, Calif., 1987.

Glorieux, P. "Le Tractatus novus de Poenitentia de Guillaume d'Auvergne." In *Miscellanea Moralia in honorem eximii domini Arthur Janssen,* 2:551–565. Louvain, n.d.

Gluckmann. Max, "Gossip and Scandal." *Current Anthropology* 4 (1963): 307–316.

Goering, Joseph. "The *Summa* of Master Serlo and Thirteenth-Century Penitential Literature." *Mediaeval Studies* 40 (1978): 290–311.

Gougaud, L. "La danse dans les églises." *Revue d'histoire ecclésiastique* 15 (1914): 5–22, 229–245.

——. *Devotional and Ascetic Practices in the Middle Ages.* Trans. G. C. Bateman. London, 1927.

Grand, Roger, "Justice criminelle, procédure, et peines dans les villes aux XIIIe et XIVe siècles." *Bibliothèque de l'Ecole des chartes* 52 (1941): 51–108.

Greyerz, Kaspar von, ed. *Religion and Society in Early Modern Europe, 1500–1800.* London, 1984.

Grinberg, Martine, and Sam Kinser. "Les combats de Carnaval et de Carême: Trajets d'une métaphore." *Annales: Economies, sociétés, civilisations* 38 (1983): 65–98.

Gurevic, A. J. "Au Moyen Age: Conscience individuelle et image de l'au-delà." *Annales: Economies, sociétés, civilisations* 37 (1982): 255–275.

Gy, Pierre-Marie. "Les bases de la pénitence moderne." *La Maison-Dieu* 117 (1974): 63–85.

——. "Les bases de la pénitence moderne." In *L'aveu: Antiquité et Moyen-Age.* Collection de l'Ecole française de Rome, 88. Rome, 1986.

——. "Collectaire, rituel, processionnal." *Revue des sciences philosophiques et théologiques* 44 (1960): 441–469.

——. "Les définitions de la confession après le quatrième concile du Latran." In *L'aveu: Antiquité et Moyen-Age.* Collection de l'Ecole française de Rome, 88. Rome, 1986.

——. "Histoire liturgique du sacrement de pénitence." *La Maison-Dieu* 56 (1958): 5–21.

——. "L'ordinaire de Mende, une oeuvre inédite de Guillaume Durand l'ancien." In *Liturgie et musique (XIe–XIVe s.).* Cahiers de Fanjeaux, 17. Toulouse, 1982.

——. "Le précepte de la confession annuelle (Latran IV, c. 21) et la détection des hérétiques: S. Bonaventure et S. Thomas contre S. Raymond de Peñafort." *Revue des sciences philosophiques et théologiques* 58 (1974): 444–450.

Hanawalt, Barbara. *The Ties That Bound: Peasant Families in Medieval England*. Oxford, 1986.

Hardison, O. B. *Christian Rite and Christian Drama in the Middle Ages*. Baltimore, Md., 1965.

Häring, N. M. "Peter Cantor's View on Ecclesiastical Excommunication and Its Practical Consequences." *Mediaeval Studies* 11 (1949): 100–112.

Haskins, Charles Homer. *The Renaissance of the Twelfth Century*. Cambridge, Mass., 1927.

———. *Studies in Mediaeval Culture*. Oxford, 1929.

Heers, Jacques. *Fêtes des fous et carnavals*. Paris, 1983.

———. *Fêtes, jeux, et joutes dans les sociétés d'occident à la fin du Moyen Age*. Montreal and Paris, 1971.

———. *Le travail au Moyen Age*. Paris, 1965.

Hergemöller, Bernd-Ulrich. "Die hansische Stadtpfarrei um 1300." In *Civitatum communitas: Studien zum europäischen Städtewesen: Festschrift Heinz Stoob*. Städteforschung, Veröffentlichungen des Instituts für vergleichende Städtegeschichte in Münster, Reihe A, Band 21, 1–2, pp. 266–280. Cologne and Vienna, 1984.

Herwaarden, Jan van. *Opgelegde bedevaarten*. Assen, Amsterdam, 1978.

Herz, Martin. *Sacrum Commercium: Eine begriffsgeschichtliche Studie zur Theologie der römischen Liturgiesprache*. Münchener Theologische Studien, 2.15. Munich, 1958.

Hesbert, René-Jean. "Les manuscrits liturgiques de l'église de Rouen." *Bulletin philologique et historique (jusqu'à 1715)* (1955–1956): 441–483.

Hill, Rosalind. "Public Penance: Some Problems of a Thirteenth-Century Bishop." *History* 36 (1951): 213–226.

———. "The Theory and Practice of Excommunication in Medieval England." *History* 42 (1957): 1–11.

Hödl, Ludwig. *Die Geschichte der scholastischen Literatur und der Theologie der Schlüsselgewalt*. Beiträge zur Geschichte der Philosophie und Theologie des Mittelalters, 38.4. Münster, 1960.

Homans, George C. *English Villagers of the Thirteenth Century*. Cambridge, 1941.

Honoré, Léon. *Le secret de la confession*. Bruges, 1924.

Huizing, Peter. "The Earliest Development of Excommunication Latae Sententiae by Gratian and the Earliest Decretists." *Studia Gratiana* 3 (1955): 277–320.

Isambert, François A. "Religion populaire, sociologie, histoire, et folklore." *Archives de sciences sociales des religions* 43 (1977): 161–184.

Jacqueline, B. "Les synodes du diocèse de Coutances avant le Concile de Trente." *Revue historique de droit français et étranger*, 4th ser., 29 (1951): 141–142.

James, Mervyn. "Ritual, Drama, and Social Body in the Late Medieval English Town." *Past and Present* 98 (1983): 3–29.

Jordan, William Chester. *From Servitude to Freedom: Manumission in the Sénonais in the Thirteenth Century*. Philadelphia, 1986.

———. *Louis IX and the Challenge of the Crusade*. Princeton, N.J., 1979.

Jungmann, Josef Andreas. "Bussriten." In *Lexikon für Theologie und Kirche*, 2, cols. 823–826. Freiburg, 1958.

———. "Carena." In *Lexikon für Theologie und Kirche*, 2, col. 940. Freiburg, 1958.

———. *Die lateinischen Bussriten in ihrer Geschichtlichen Entwicklung*. Forschungen zur Geschichte des innerkirchlichen Lebens, 3–4. Innsbruck, 1932.

Kantorowicz, Ernst. *Laudes Regiae*. Berkeley, Calif., 1958.

Kellner, K. A. H. *Heortology: A History of the Christian Festivals from Their Origin to the Present Day*. Trans. from 2d German ed. London, 1908.

Kennedy, V. L. "The Content of Courson's *Summa*." *Mediaeval Studies* 9 (1947): 81–107.

——. "The Handbook of Master Peter Chancellor of Chartres." *Mediaeval Studies* 5 (1943): 1–38.

Kieckhefer, Richard. *Unquiet Souls*. Chicago, 1984.

Krehbiel, Edward B, *The Interdict: Its History and Its Operation*. Washington, D.C., 1909.

Kuttner, Stephan. "Pierre de Roissy and Robert of Flamborough." *Traditio* 2 (1944): 492–499.

——. "Réflexions sur les brocards des glossateurs." In *Mélanges Joseph de Ghellinck*, 2:767–792. Gembloux, 1951.

——. *Repertorium der Kanonistik, 1140–1234*. Studi e Testi, 71. Vatican City, 1937.

I laici nella "Societas christiana" dei secoli XI e XII. Atti della terza Settimana internazionale di Studio, Passo della Mendola, 1965. Milan, 1968.

Landau, Peter. *Die Entstehung des kanonischen Infamiebegriffs von Gratian bis zur Glossa Ordinaria*. Forschungen zur kirchlichen Rechtsgeschichte und zum Kirchenrecht, 5. Cologne, 1966.

Landgraf, Artur. *Dogmengeschichte der Frühscholastik*. Regensburg, 1952–1955.

——. "Grundlagen für ein Verständnis der Busslehre der Früh- und Hochscholastik." *Zeitschrift für katholische Theologie* 51 (1927): 161–194.

Larrabe, José Luis. "Teología de la penitencia y de la confesión segùn S. Buenaventura." *Estudios Franciscanos* 77 (1976): 193–201.

Laude, P. J. *Catalogue méthodique, descriptif, et analytique des manuscrits de la Bibliothèque publique de Bruges*. Bruges, 1859.

Lea, Henry Charles. *A History of Auricular Confession and Indulgences in the Latin Church*. 2 vols. Philadelphia, 1896; repr. New York, 1968.

Le Bras, Gabriel. *L'église et le village*. Paris, 1976.

——. *Institutions eccléstiastiques de la Chrétienté mediévale, Histoire de l'église*, 12. Paris, 1959.

Lecotté, Roger, and Georges Marguet. *La fête du "Bois Hourdy" ou "de la Folie" à Chambly (Oise)*. Publication de la Fédération folklorique d'Ile de France, fasc. 3. Persan, 1947.

Legendre, P. "*De confessis*: Remarques sur le statut de la parole dans la première scolastique." In *L'aveu: Antiquité et Moyen-Age*. Collection de l'Ecole française de Rome, 88. Rome, 1986.

Le Glay, A. *Recherches sur l'église métropolitaine de Cambrai*. Paris, 1825.

Le Goff, Jacques. "Apostolat mendiant et fait urbain dans la France médiévale: L'implantation des ordres mendiants: Programme-questionnaire pour une enquête." *Annales: Economies, sociétés, civilisations* 23 (1968): 335–348.

——. "Ecclesiastical Culture and Folklore in the Middle Ages: Saint Marcellus of Paris and the Dragon." In *Time, Work, and Culture in the Middle Ages*, trans. A. Goldhammer, pp. 159–188. Chicago, 1980.

——. *La naissance du purgatoire*. Paris, 1981.

——. "Ordres mendiants et urbanisation dans la France médiévale: Etat de l'enquête." *Annales: Economies, sociétés, civilisations* 25 (1970): 924–946.

Lemaître, Nicole. "Confession privée et confession publique dans les paroisses du XVIe siècle." *Revue d'histoire de l'église de France* 69, no. 183 (1983): 189–208.

———. "Pratique et signification de la confession communautaire dans les paroisses au XVIe siècle." In *Pratiques de la confession*, ed. Groupe de la Bussiere. Paris, 1983.

Lentzen-Deis, Wolfgang. *Busse als Bekenntnisvollzug*. Freiburger Theologische Studien, 86. Freiburg, 1969.

Leroquais, Victor. *Les pontificaux manuscrits des bibliothèques publiques de France*. Paris, 1937.

Leroy, G. "Note sur le pontifical de Guillaume II de Melun, archevêque de Sens (1346–1378)." *Bulletin historique et philologique* (1896): 557–562.

Lestocquoy, Jean. *Aux origines de la bourgeoisie: Les villes de Flandre et d'Italie sous le gouvernement des patriciens (XIe–XVe siècles)*. Paris, 1952.

———. *La vie religieuse d'une province: Le diocèse d'Arras*. Commission départementale des monuments historiques du Pas-de-Calais, Etudes historiques, 4. Arras, 1949.

———. *La vie sociale et économique à Arras du XIIe au XVe siècle*. Arras, 1941.

———. *Les villes de Flandre et d'Italie sous le gouvernement des patriciens (XIe–XVe siècles)*. Paris, 1952.

Little, Lester K. "Les techniques de la confession et la confession comme technique." In *Faire croire: Modalités de la diffusion et de la réception des messages religieux du XIIe au XVe siècle*. Collection de e'Ecole française de Rome, 51. Rome, 1981.

Liturgie et musique (IXe–XIVe s.). Cahiers de Fanjeaux, 17. Toulouse, 1982.

Liturgie et rémission des péchés. Bibliotheca "Ephemerides Liturgicae," Subsidia, 3. Rome, 1975.

Logan, F. Donald. *Excommunication and the Secular Arm in Medieval England*. Pontifical Institute of Mediaeval Studies, Studies and Texts, 15. Toronto, 1968.

Longère, Jean. "Alain de Lille, Liber Poenitentialis: Les traditions moyennes et courtes." *Archives d'histoire doctrinale et littéraire du Moyen Age* 40 (1965): 169–242.

———. "La prédication et l'instruction des fidèles selon les conciles et les statuts synodaux depuis l'Antiquité tardive jusqu'au XIIIe siècle." In *L'encadrement religieux des fidèles au Moyen-Age et jusqu'au Concile de Trente*. Actes du 109e Congrès national des sociétés savantes, Dijon, 1984, Section d'histoire médiévale et de philologie, 1. Paris, 1985.

———. "Quelques *summa de poenitentia* à la fin du XIIe et au début du XIIIe siècle." In *La piété populaire au Moyen Age*. Actes du 99e Congrès national des sociétés savantes, Besançon, 1974, Philologie et histoire jusqu'à 1610, 1. Paris, 1977.

Lozinski, Grégoire. *La bataille de caresme et de charnage*. Bibliothèque de l'Ecole des hautes études, sciences historiques et philologiques, fasc. 262. Paris, 1933.

Lukes, Steven. *Individualism*. Oxford, 1973.

Lynch, K. F. "The Alleged Fourth Book of Odo Rigaud on the Sentences and Related Documents." *Franciscan Studies* 9 (1949): 87–145.

Maccarrone, M. "'Cura animarum' e 'parochialis sacerdos' nella costituzione del IV concilio lateranense (1215): Applicazioni in Italia nel sec. XIII." In *Pievi e parrochie in Italia nel basso medioevo*. Atti del VI Convegno di Storia della chiesa in Italia, Florence, 1981, Italia Sacra, 35–36, 1. Rome, 1984.

Macfarlane, Alan. "History, Anthropology, and the Study of Communities." *Social History*, no. 5 (May 1977): 631–652.

——. *The Origins of English Individualism: The Family, Property, and Social Transition.* Oxford, 1978.

Maes, Louis-Théo. "Mittelalterliche Strafwallfahrten nach Santiago de Compostela und Unsere Liebe Frau von Finisterra." In *Festschrift Guido Kisch*, pp. 99–118. Stuttgart, 1955.

Magli, Ida. *Gli uomini della penitenza.* N.p., 1967.

Maillet, Germaine. *Religion et traditions populaires aux XIIe et XIIIe siècles.* Travaux du Comité du folklore champenois, 7. Châlons-sur-Marne, 1978.

Mandonnet, Pierre. "La 'Summa de Poenitentia Magistri Pauli presbyteri S. Nicolai' (Magister Paulus de Hungaria O.P. 1220–1221)." In *Aus der Geisteswelt des Mittelalters: Studien und Texte; Martin Grabmann zur Vollendung des 60. Lebensjahres.* Beiträge zur Geschichte der Philosophie und Theologie des Mittelalters, suppl. 3, pp. 525–544. 1935.

Mantese, Giovanni. "'Fratres et sorores de poenitentia' di S. Francesco in Vicenza dal XIII al XV secolo." In *Miscellanea Gilles Gerard Meersseman*, 2:695–714. Italia sacra, 16. Padua, 1970.

Martimort, Aimé-Georges. *La documentation liturgique de Dom Edmond Martène.* Studi e Testi, 279. Vatican City, 1978.

Martin, Hervé. "Confession et contrôle social à la fin du Moyen Age." In *Pratiques de la confession*, ed. Groupe de la Bussiere. Paris, 1983.

Maskell, William. *Monumenta Ritualia Ecclesiae Anglicanae.* London, 1846–1847.

May, Georg. "Bann IV." In *Theologische Realenzyklopädie*, 5:170–182. Berlin, 1980.

Meersseman, G. G. "Les frères précheurs et le mouvement dévot en Flandre au XIIIe s." *Archivum fratrum praedicatorum* 18 (1948): 69–130.

——. "I penitenti nei secoli XI e XII." In *I laici nella "Societas christiana" dei secoli XI e XII.* Atti della terza Settimana internazionale di studio, Passo della Mendola, 1965. Milan, 1968.

——. "Premier auctarium au dossier de l'ordre de la Pénitence au XIIIe s.: Le manuel des pénitents de Brescia." *Revue d'histoire ecclésiastique* 62 (1967): 5–48.

Meersseman, G. G., and E. Adda. "Pénitents ruraux communautaires en Italie au XIIe siècle." *Revue d'histoire ecclésiastique* 49 (1954): 343–390.

Meersseman, G. G., with Gian Piero Pacini. *Ordo fraternitatis: Confraternite e pietà dei laici nel medioevo.* Italia sacra, 24–26. Rome, 1977.

Melleville, Maximilien. *Histoire de la ville de Laon et de ses institutions.* Paris, 1846; repr. Marseille, 1977.

Michaud-Quantin, Pierre. "La conscience individuelle et ses droits chez les moralistes de la fin du Moyen-Age." In *Universalismus und Partikularismus im Mittelalter*, Miscellanea mediaevalia, 5:42–55. Berlin, 1968.

——. "Le 'Liber penitentialis' d'Alain de Lille: Le témoignage des manuscrits belges et français." *Cîteaux* 10 (1959): 93–106.

——. "Les méthodes de la pastorale du XIIIe au XVe siècle." In *Methoden in Wissenschaft und Kunst des Mittelalters*, Miscellanea mediaevalia, 7:76–91. Berlin, 1970.

——. "A propos des premières Summae confessorum: Théologie et droit canonique." *Recherches de théologie ancienne et médiévale* 26 (1959): 264–306.

——. *Sommes de casuistique et manuels de confession au Moyen Age (XII–XVI siècles).* Analecta mediaevalia Namurcensia, 3. Louvain, 1962.

——. "Textes pénitentiels languedociens au XIIIe siècle." In *Le credo, la morale, et l'inquisition.* Cahiers de Fanjeaux, 6. Toulouse, 1971.

Michel, A. "Pénitence—sacrement, III." In *Dictionnaire de théologie catholique,* 12a: cols. 948–1050. Paris, 1933.

Migliorino, Francesco. *Fama e infamia: Problemi della società medievale nel pensiero giuridico nei secoli XII e XIII.* Catania, 1985.

Millénaire monastique du Mont-Saint-Michel. Paris, 1966–1971.

Millet, Hélène. *Les chanoines du chapitre cathédrale de Laon (1272–1412).* Collection de l'Ecole française de Rome, 56. Rome, 1982.

Moeller, Bernd. "Religious Life in Germany on the Eve of the Reformation." In *Pre-Reformation Germany* ed. Gerald Strauss, pp. 13–42. London, 1972.

Mohrmann, Christine. *Liturgical Latin: Its Origins and Character.* London, 1959.

Molin, Jean-Baptiste. "L'oratio communis fidelium' au Moyen-Age en Occident du Xe siècle au XVe siècle." In *Miscellanea liturgica in onore di sua eminenza il cardinale Giacomo Lercaro,* 2:313–468. Rome, 1967.

——. "Un pontifical de Meaux du XIIIe siècle." *Bulletin de la Société d'histoire et de l'art du diocèse de Meaux* 6 (1955): 257–259.

Mollat, Michel. "Hospitalité et assistance au début du XIIIe siècle." In *Poverty in the Middle Ages,* ed. David Flood, pp. 37–51. Franziskanische Forschungen, 27. Werl/Westf., 1975.

Mollat, Michel, and Paul Tombeur. *Les conciles Latran I à Latran IV.* Louvain, 1974.

Moore, Philip S. *The Works of Peter of Poitiers, Master in Theology and Chancellor of Paris (1193–1205).* Publications in Mediaeval Studies, 1. Notre Dame, Ind., 1936.

Morel, Maurice. *L'excommunication et le pouvoir civil en France du droit canonique classique au commencement du XVe siècle.* Paris, 1926.

Morin, Jean. *Commentarius historicus de disciplina in administratione sacramenti poenitentiae tredecim primis seculis in ecclesia occidentali, et hucusque in orientali observata, in decem libros distinctus.* Paris, 1651.

Morris, Colin. "A Consistory Court in the Middle Ages." *Journal of Ecclesiastical History* 14 (1963): 150–159.

——. *The Discovery of the Individual, 1050–1200.* New York, 1972.

Muir, Edward. *Civic Ritual in Renaissance Venice.* Princeton, N.J., 1981.

Munier, Charles. "Discipline pénitentielle et droit pénal ecclésial: Alliances et différenciation." *Concilium* 107 (1975): 23–32.

Murray, Alexander. "Confession as a Historical Source in the Thirteenth Century." In *The Writing of History in the Middle Ages: Essays Presented to Richard William Southern,* ed. R. H. C. Davis and J. M. Wallace-Hadrill, pp. 275–322. Oxford, 1981.

——. "Piety and Impiety in Thirteenth-Century Italy." In *Popular Belief and Practice,* ed. G. J. Cuming and D. Baker, pp. 83–107. Studies in Church History, 8. Cambridge, 1972.

——. "Religion among the Poor in Thirteenth-Century France: The Testimony of Humbert de Romans." *Traditio* 30 (1974): 285–324.

Newman, William M. *Le personnel de la cathédrale d'Amiens (1066–1306).* Paris, 1972.

Nicholas, D. M. "Crime and Punishment in Fourteenth-Century Ghent." *Revue belge de philologie et d'histoire* 48 (1970): 289–334, 1141–1176.

——. "Structures du peuplement, fonctions urbaines, et formation du capital dans la Flandre médiévale." *Annales: Economies, sociétés, civilisations* 33 (1978): 501–527.

——. *Town and Countryside: Social, Economic, and Political Tensions in Fourteenth-Century Flanders.* Bruges, 1971.

Nogent, Guibert de. *Autobiographie (De vita sua).* Ed. E.-R. Labande. Les classiques de l'histoire de France au Moyen Age. Paris, 1981.

Noonan, John. "Who Was Rolandus?" In *Law, Church, and Society: Essays in Honor of Stephan Kuttner,* ed. K. Pennington and R. Somerville, pp. 21–48. Philadelphia, 1977.

Oakley, T. P. "Commutations and Redemptions of Penance in the Penitentials." *Catholic Historical Review* 18 (1932): 341–351.

——. "The Penitentials as Sources for Medieval History." *Speculum* 15 (1940): 210–223.

——. "Some Neglected Aspects in the History of Penance." *Catholic Historical Review* 24 (1938): 293–309.

Oliger, L., ed., *Expositio quattuor magistrorum super regulam fratrum Minorum.* Rome, 1950.

Oursel, Raymond. *Les pèlerins du Moyen Age.* Paris, 1963.

Ozment, Steven. *The Reformation in the Cities.* New Haven, Conn., 1975.

Pascher, Joseph. *Das liturgische Jahr.* Munich, 1963.

Payen, Jean-Charles. "La pénitence dans le contexte culturel des XIIe et XIIIe siècles: Des doctrines contritionnistes aux pénitentiels vernaculaires." *Revue des sciences philosophiques et théologiques* 61 (1977): 399–428.

Payer, Pierre J. "The Humanism of the Penitentials and the Continuity of the Penitential Tradition." *Mediaeval Studies* 46 (1984): 340–354.

Le pèlerinage. Cahiers de Fanjeaux, 15. Toulouse, 1980.

Pérez López, S. L. "El sacramento de la penitencia en las costituciones sinodales de Galicia (1215–1563) y su contexto histórico." *Estudios Mindonienses* 2 (1986): 83–119.

Petit-Dutaillis, Charles. *The French Communes in the Middle Ages.* New York, 1978.

Pettazzoni, R. "La confession des péchés dans l'histoire des religions." In *Mélanges Franz Cumont,* 2:893–901. Annuaire de l'Institut de philologie et d'histoire orientales et slaves, 4. Brussels, 1936.

Pfleger, L. "Sühnewallfahrten und öffentliche Kirchenbusse im Elsass im späten Mittelalter und in der Neuzeit." *Archiv für Elsässische Kirchengeschichte* 8 (1933): 127–162.

Philippeau, H. R. "A propos du Coutumier de Norwich." *Scriptorium* 3 (1949): 295–302.

Phythian-Adams, Charles. "Ceremony and the Citizen: The Communal Year at Coventry, 1450–1550." In *Crisis and Order in English Towns, 1500–1700,* ed. P. Clark and P. Slack, pp. 57–85. London, 1972.

Picó, Fernando. "Changements dans la composition du chapitre cathédrale de Laon (1155–1318)." *Revue d'histoire ecclésiastique* 71 (1976): 78–91.

——. "Membership in the Cathedral Chapter of Laon, 1217–1238." *Catholic Historical Review* 61 (1975): 1–30.

La piété populaire au Moyen Age. Actes du 99e Congrès national des sociétés savantes, Besançon, 1974. Philologie et histoire jusqu'à 1610, 1. Paris, 1977.

Pievi e parrochie in Italia nel basso medioevo (sec. XIII–XV). Atti del VI Convegno di Storia della chiesa in Italia, Florence, 1981. Italia sacra, 35–36. Rome, 1984.

Platelle, H. "La paroisse et son curé jusqu'à la fin du XIIIe siècle. Orientations de la recherche actuelle." In *L'encadrement religieux des fidèles au Moyen-Age et jusqu'au Concile de Trente.* Actes du 109e Congrès national des sociétés savantes, Dijon, 1984, Section d'histoire médiévale et de philologie, 1. Paris, 1985.

——. "Pratiques pénitentielles et mentalités religieuses au Moyen Age: La pénitence des parricides et l'esprit de l'ordalie." *Mélanges de science religieuse* 40 (1983): 129–155.

——. "La vie religieuse à Lille." In *Histoire de Lille*, ed. Louis Trendard, 1:309–418. Lille, n.d.

Pollock, Frederick, and Frederic William Maitland. *The History of English Law before the Time of Edward I.* 2d ed. Cambridge, 1898.

Pompei, Alfonso. "Il movimento penitenziale nei secoli XII–XIII." *Collectanea Franciscana* 43 (1973): 9–40.

Pontal, Odette. "Le différend entre Louis IX et les évêques de Beauvais et ses incidences sur les conciles (1232–1248)." *Bibliothèque de l'Ecole des chartes* 123 (1965): 5–34.

——. "Les plus anciens statuts synodaux d'Angers et leur expansion dans les diocèses de l'ouest de la France." *Revue d'histoire de l'église de France* 46 (1960): 54–67.

——. *Les statuts synodaux.* Typologie des sources du Moyen Age occidental, 11. Turnholt, 1975.

Poque, Suzanne. "Christus Mercator." *Recherches de science religieuse* 48 (1960): 564–577.

Poschmann, Bernhard. *Die abendländische Kirchenbusse im Ausgang des christlichen Altertums.* Münchener Studien zur historischen Theologie, 7. Munich, 1928.

——. *Paenitentia secunda: Die kirchliche Busse im ältesten Christentum bis Cyprian und Origenes.* Theophaneia, 1. Bonn, 1940.

——. *Penance and the Anointing of the Sick.* Trans. F. Courtney. London, 1963.

Pratiques de la confession. Groupe de la Bussière. Paris, 1983.

Radó, Polycarp. *Enchiridion Liturgicum.* Rome, 1961.

Rahner, Karl. "Buss-sakrament." In *Lexikon für Theologie und Kirche*, 2: cols. 826–838. Freiburg, 1958.

Ramière de Fortanier, A. "La confrérie Notre-Dame de Fanjeaux et son développement au Moyen-Age." In *La religion populaire en Languedoc du XIIIe siècle à la moitié du XIVe siècle.* Cahiers de Fanjeaux, 11. Toulouse, 1976.

Rando, Daniela. "'Laicus religiosus' tra strutture civili ed ecclesiastiche: L'ospedale di ognissanti in Treviso (sec. XIII)." *Studi medievali*, ser. 3, 34 (1983): 617–656.

Rei, Dario. "Note sul concetto di 'religione popolare.'" *Lares* 40 (1974): 265–280.

La religion populaire en Languedoc du XIIIe siècle à la moitié du XIVe siècle. Cahiers de Fanjeaux, 11. Toulouse, 1976.

Répertoire des visites pastorales de la France, première série: Anciens diocèses (jusqu'en 1790). Paris, 1977–1985.

Richard, Jean. *Saint Louis.* Paris, 1983.

Rigon, Antonio. "I laici nella chiesa padovana del duecento: Conversi, oblati, penitenti." *Fonti e ricerche di storia ecclesiastica padovana* 11 (1979): 11–81.

Robertson, D. W. "The *Manuel des péchés* and an English Episcopal Decree." *Modern Language Notes* 60 (1945): 439–447.

Rokseth, Yvonne, "Danses cléricales du XIIIe siècle." *Publications de la Faculté des lettres de l'Université de Strasbourg*, fasc. 106. (1947): 93–126.

Ronzani, Mauro. "Aspetti e problemi delle pievi e delle parrochie cittadine nell'Italia centro-settentrionale." In *Pievi e parrochie in Italia nel basso medioevo*. Atti del VI Convegno di Storia della chiesa in Italia, Florence, 1981, Italia Sacra, 35–36, 1. Rome, 1984.

———. "Penitenti e ordini mendicanti a Pisa sino all'inizio del trecento." *Mélanges de l'Ecole française de Rome: Moyen Age–Temps modernes* 89 (1977): 733–741.

Rosa Pereira, Isais da. "Les statuts synodaux d'Eudes de Sully au Portugal." *L'année canonique* 15 (1971): 459–480.

Rosenthal, Joel T. *The Purchase of Paradise: Gift Giving and the Aristocracy, 1307–1485*. London, 1972.

Rothkrug, Lionel. "Popular Religion and Holy Shrines." In *Religion and the People, 800–1700*, ed. J. Obelkevich. Chapel Hill, N.C., 1979.

Rouche, Michel. *Histoire de Douai*. Dunkirk, 1985.

Rubellin, Michel. "Vision de la société chrétienne à travers la confession et la pénitence au IXe siècle." In *Pratiques de la confession*, ed. Groupe de la Bussiere. Paris, 1983.

Rusconi, Roberto. "De la prédication à la confession: Transmission et contrôle de modèles de comportement au XIIIe siècle." In *Faire croire: Modalités de la diffusion et de la réception des messages religieux du XIIe au XVe siècle*. Collection de l'Ecole française de Rome, 51. Rome, 1981.

———. "I francescani e la confessione nel secolo XIII." In *Francescanesimo e vita religiosa dei laici nel '200*, pp. 251–309. Atti dell'VIII Convegno internazionale, Assisi, 1980. Assisi, 1981.

———. "*Ordinate confiteri*: La confessione dei peccati nelle 'summae de casibus' e nei manuali per i confessori (metà XII-inizio XIV secolo)." In *L'aveu: Antiquité et Moyen-Age*. Collection de l'Ecole française de Rome, 88. Rome, 1986.

Russell, J. C., *Medieval Regions and their Cities*. Devon, 1972.

Russo, François. "Pénitence et excommunication: Etude historique sur les rapports entre la théologie et le droit canonique dans le domaine pénitentiel du IXe au XIIIe siècle." *Recherches de science religieuse* 33 (1946): 257–279, 431–461.

Sahlin, Margit. *Etude sur la carole médiévale*. Uppsala, 1940.

Schmitt, Jean-Claude. *The Holy Greyhound*, Trans. M. Thom. Cambridge Studies in Oral and Literate Culture, 6. Cambridge, 1983.

———. "'Jeunes' et danse des chevaux de bois. Le folklore méridional dans la littérature des èxempla' (XIIIe–XIVe siècles)." In *La religion populaire en Languedoc du XIIIe siècle à la moitié du XIVe siècle*. Cahiers de Fanjeaux, 11. Toulouse, 1976.

———. "'Religion populaire' et culture folklorique." *Annales: Economies, sociétés, civilisations* 31 (1976): 941–953.

———. "Les traditions folkloriques dans la culture médiévale." *Archives de sciences sociales des religions* 52 (1981): 5–20.

Schmitz, Johannes. "Sühnewallfahrten im Mittelalter." Ph.D. diss., Bonn, 1910.

Schmugge, Ludwig. "Die Anfänge des organisierten Pilgerverkehrs im Mittelalter." *Quellen und Forschungen aus italienischen Archiven und Bibliotheken* 64 (1984): 1–83.

———. "Ministerialität und Bürgertum in Reims: Untersuchungen zur Geschichte der Stadt im 12. und 13. Jahrhundert." *Francia* 2 (1974): 152–212.

Septième centenaire de la mort de Saint Louis. Actes des Colloques de Royaumont et de Paris, 1970. Paris, 1976.

Shorter, Edward. *The Making of the Modern Family.* New York, 1975.

Sigal, Pierre André. *Les marcheurs de Dieu: Pèlerinages et pèlerins au Moyen Age.* Paris, 1974.

Sirmond, Jacques. *Historia poenitentiae publicae.* Paris, 1651.

Sivéry, Gérard. *L'économie du royaume de France au siècle de Saint Louis.* Lille, 1984.

———. *Saint Louis et son siècle.* Paris, 1983.

Spitzig, Joseph A. *Sacramental Penance in the Twelfth and Thirteenth Centuries.* Washington, D.C., 1947.

Sousa Costa, A. D. de. *Doctrina penitencial do canonista Joao de Deus.* Braga, 1956.

Stone, Lawrence. *The Family, Sex, and Marriage in England, 1500–1800.* Abridged ed. New York, 1979.

Strayer, Joseph R. "The Laicization of French and English Society in the Thirteenth Century." *Speculum* 15 (1940): 76–86.

Szabó-Bechstein, Brigitte. "Sul carattere dei legami tra gli ordini mendicanti, la confraternità laica dei penitenti ed il comune di Siena nel duecento." *Mélanges de l'Ecole française de Rome: Moyen Age–Temps modernes* 89 (1977): 743–747.

Tanon, L. *Histoire des justices des anciennes églises et communautés monastiques de Paris.* Paris, 1883.

Tardif, Adolphe. *La procédure civile et criminelle aux XIIIe et XIVe siècles ou procédure de transition.* Paris, 1885.

Teetaert, A. "Un compendium de théologie pastorale du XIIIe-XIVe siècle." *Revue d'histoire ecclésiastique* 26 (1930): 66–102.

———. "Le 'Liber Poenitentialis' de Pierre de Poitiers." In *Aus der Geisteswelt des Mittelalters: Studien und Texte; Martin Grabmann zur Vollendung des 60. Lebensjahres.* Beiträge zur Geschichte der Philosophie und Theologie des Mittelalters, suppl. 3, pp. 310–331. (1935).

———. "Quelques 'Summae de paenitentia' anonymes dans la Bibliothèque Nationale de Paris." In *Miscellanea Giovanni Mercati,* 2:311–343. Studi e Testi, 122. Vatican City, 1946.

Tentler, Thomas. "Seventeen Authors in Search of Two Religious Cultures." *Catholic Historical Review* 71 (1985): 248–257.

———. *Sin and Confession on the Eve of the Reformation.* Princeton, N.J., 1977.

Thomson, Williell R. *Friars in the Cathedral: The First Franciscan Bishops, 1226–1261.* Toronto, 1975.

Tierney, Brian. "Review of Morris's *Discovery of the Individual.*" *Journal of Ecclesiastical History* 24 (1980): 295–296.

———. "Two Anglo-Norman Summae." *Traditio* 15 (1959): 483–491.

Tönnies, Ferdinand, *Community and Society (Gemeinschaft und Gesellschaft).* Trans. Charles P. Loomis. East Lansing, Mich., 1957; first published 1887.

Toussaert, J. *Le sentiment religieux en Flandre à la fin du Moyen-Age.* Paris, 1963.

Trenard, Louis, ed. *Histoire de Cambrai.* Lille, 1982.

———. *Histoire de Lille.* Lille, n.d.

Trexler, Richard C. *Public Life in Renaissance Florence.* New York, 1980.

Troeltsch, Ernst. *The Social Teaching of the Christian Churches.* Trans. O. Wyon. New York, 1960; first published 1911.

Troeyer, Benjamin de. "Beguines et tertiaires en Belgique et aux Pays-Bas aux XIIIe–XIVe siècles." In *I frati penitenti di San Francesco nella società del due e trecento*. Atti del 20 Convegno di studi francescani, Roma, 1976 Rome, 1977.

Turner, Victor W. *Dramas, Fields, and Metaphors*. Ithaca, N.Y., 1974.

———. *The Ritual Process*. Chicago, 1969.

Turner, Victor W., and Edith Turner. *Image and Pilgrimage in Christian Culture*. New York, 1978.

Tyrer, John Walter. *Historical Survey of Holy Week*. Oxford, 1932.

Ullmann, Walter. *The Individual and Society in the Middle Ages*. Baltimore, Md., 1966.

Valon, Ludovic de. "Les pèlerinages expiatoires et judiciaires de la Belgique à Roc-Amadour au Moyen Age." *Bulletin trimestriel de la Société des études littéraires, scientifiques, et artistiques du Lot* 58 (1937): 9–37.

———. "Les pèlerinages expiatoires et judiciaires de la Belgique aux sanctuaires de la Provence au Moyen-Age." *Provincia: Revue trimestrielle d'histoire et d'archéologie provençales* 15 (1935): 30–52.

Van Engen, John. "The Christian Middle Ages as an Historiographical Problem." *American Historical Review* 91 (1986): 519–552.

Vanneste, Alfred. "La théologie de la pénitence chez quelques maîtres parisiens de la première moitié du XIIIe siècle." *Ephemerides theologicae Lovanienses* 28 (1952): 24–58.

Vauchez, André. "Conclusion." In *I frati penitenti di San Francesco nella società del due e trecento*, ed. Mariano D'Alatri. Atti del 20 Convegno di studi francescani, Roma, 1976. Rome, 1977.

———. *Les laïcs ou Moyen Age*. Paris, 1987.

Vaultier, Roger. *Le folklore pendant la guerre de cent ans d'après les lettres de rémission du trésor des chartes*. Paris, 1965.

Venard, Marc. "Itinéraires de processions dans la ville d'Avignon." *Ethnologie française* 7 (1977): 55–62.

Villehardouin, Geoffroi de. *La conquête de Constantinople*. Ed. E. Faral. Les classiques de l'histoire de France au Moyen Age, 18–19. Paris, 1961.

Villetard, Henri. "La danse ecclésiastique à la Métropole de Sens." *Bulletin de la Société archéologique de Sens* 26 (1911): 105–122.

Vodola, Elisabeth. *Excommunication in the Middle Ages*. Berkeley, Calif., 1986.

Vogel, Cyrille. *Introduction aux sources de l'histoire du culte chrétien au Moyen Age*. Biblioteca degli "Studi medievali" 1. Spoleto, 1966?

———. "Une mutation cultuelle inexpliquée: Le passage de l'eucharistie communautaire à la messe privée." *Revue des sciences religieuses* 54 (1980): 231–250.

———. "Le péché et la pénitence." In *Pastorale du péché*, pp. 147–235. Bibliothèque de théologie, série 2. Théologie Morale, 8. Paris, 1961.

———. *Le pécheur et la pénitence au Moyen Age*. Paris, 1969.

———. "Le pèlerinage pénitentiel." In *Pellegrinaggi e culto dei santi in Europa fino alla crociata*, pp. 37–94. Convegni del Centro di studi sulla spiritualità medievale, 4. Todi, 1963.

———. "Pénitence et excommunication dans l'église ancienne et durant le Haut Moyen Age." *Concilium* 107 (1975): 11–22.

———. "Le pontifical romano-germanique du Xe siècle: Nature, date, et importance du document." *Cahiers de civilisation médiévale* 6 (1963): 27–48.

——. "Les rites de la pénitence publique aux Xe et XIe siècles." In *Mélanges René Crozet*, ed. P. Gallais and Y.-J. Riou, 1:137–144.

——. "Les rituels de la pénitence tarifée." In *Liturgia opera divina e umana: Studi sulla riforma liturgica offerti a S. E. Mons. Annibale Bugnini in occasione del suo 70 compleanno*, ed. P. Jounel et al., pp. 419–427. Bibliotheca "Ephemerides liturgicae," Subsidia, 26. Rome, 1982?

Vovelle, Michel. *Piété baroque et déchristianisation en Provence au XVIIIe siècle*. Paris, 1973.

Vries, Jan de. *European Urbanization, 1500–1800*. Cambridge, Mass., 1984.

Watkins, Oscar D. *A History of Penance*. London, 1920.

Weissmann, Ronald. *Ritual Brotherhood in Renaissance Florence*. New York, 1982.

Wickham, Glynne. *The Medieval Theatre*. 3d ed. Cambridge, 1987.

Williams, George H. *The Radical Reformation*. Philadelphia, 1962.

Winkler, Gabriele. "L'aspect pénitentiel dans les offices du soir en orient et en occident." In *Liturgie et rémission des péchés*. Bibliotheca "Ephemerides Liturgicae," Subsidia, 3. Rome, 1975.

Wolff, Philippe. "Les villes de France au temps de Philippe Auguste." In *La France de Philippe Auguste: Le temps des mutations*, ed. Robert-Henri Bautier. Paris, 1982.

Young, Karl. *The Drama of the Medieval Church*. Oxford, 1933.

Zwingli, Ulrich. *Zwingli and Bullinger: Selected Translations with Introductions and Notes*. Ed. and trans. G. W. Bromiley. Library of Christian Classics, 24. Philadelphia, 1953.

Index

Lightning Source UK Ltd.
Milton Keynes UK
UKHW010036180720
366695UK00013B/195